Muslims and the Gospel

Bridging the Gap

Roland E. Miller

A Reflection on Christian Sharing

Lutheran University Press
Minneapolis, Minnesota

Muslims and the Gospel
Bridging the Gap
Roland E. Miller

Library of Congress Cataloging-in Publication Data

Miller, Roland E.
  Muslims and the Gospel : a reflection on Christian sharing / Roland E. Miller
    p. cm.
  Includes bibliographic references.
  ISBN-13: 978-1-932688-07-8 (alk. paper)
  ISBN-10: 1-932688-07-2 (alk. paper)
    1. Missions to Muslims. 2. Christianity and other religions—Islam. 3.
  Islam—Relations—Christianity. I. Title.

BV2625.M47 2004
266'.088'297—dc22

2004059427

Lutheran University Press, PO Box 390759, Minneapolis, MN 55439
Manufactured in the United States of America

To friends,
Christian and Muslim,
who have shared with me their treasures. . .

Contents

Who are the Muslims?, a factual survey. Relational dilemmas: immensity, mystery, bad historical interactions, misunderstandings. The link between knowing and sharing.

PART 1: THE CONTEXT—PIVOTAL MUSLIM VIEWS

An overwhelming sense of God. Revelation and guidance. Confession. Life as salvation history. Comprehensiveness. The crucial impress of Muhammad. Law and obedience. Community. Equality within limits. Striving and struggle. Success. Sense of perfection. Some reflections.

Caution signals. Human nature: creation and fall. Sin troubles. Sin in the Qur'ān. Accountability and judgment, heaven and hell. Repentance. Muslim thinking about sin: legal, pietist, theological, contemporary streams. Notes for Christian sharing.

Salvation as escape from the Fire. The means to salvation. The will of God. The mercy of God. Faith alone. Faith and works. Intercession. A note on folk Islam. The mystical path. Community membership. The preferred means. Thoughts for sharing.

Muslim admiration of Jesus. The Quranic names of Jesus. The place of Mary. Portraits of Jesus: in the Qur'ān, in traditions, in legends, among scholars and mystics. Modern Muslim perceptions. Ethical and apologetical views. Christian response.

PART 2: BRIDGES FOR THE CROSSING

PART 3: THE TASK—CONNECTING MUSLIMS AND THE MESSAGE

Theology of method. The Word. Practical considerations: purity of means, keeping focused and staying real, accepting diversity. Types of programmatic challenge: contextualization, church-planting, popular Islam, Muslims in the West. The sharing craft. Conversation. Literature. The emotive arts. Electronic media. Methodological medley.

Categories of questioning. Modes of response. The Son of God. The Trinity. The corruption of the scriptures. The crucifixion. Divine forgiveness. Why don't Christians like us? The issue of argumentation. Refutation and controversy. Explanation, and relating it to the core paradigm.

The idea of spiritual transformation. Casual inquirers. Serious inquirers. New believers and the decisive factors. Conversion: the Muslim view, the Christian perspective. The Muslim misunderstanding of baptism, and some proposed approaches.

Dealing with romantic dreams. Reality checks for new and old believers. Preemptive attitudinal adjustments. On being supportive. Loneliness. Insecurity. Economic deprivation. Grounding in the faith. Expectancy. The convert church. The faith journey goes on.

Anticipating the future in the light of the present. Considering the present in the light of the future. The words of the Savior.

Transliteration and Abbreviations

Although this volume is prepared with the general public in view, a limited Arabic transliteration scheme has been utilized, recognizing the general practice in the field. The system used is that of the *Encyclopaedia of Islam* as modified in the usage of *Muslim World,* and further modified by not distinguishing the "h" by a diacritical point below the word. Other arbitrary decisions have been made, related to common English usage. Names of places are unpointed, but names of individuals from the classical period are generally pointed. The writer recognizes that other approaches are equally possible and legitimate.

As for dates, for convenience reasons, the common Western dates are used instead of the Muslim lunar calendar, or a combination of both.

In regard to abbreviations, *EI²* refers to the second edition of the *Encyclopaedia of Islam*, MW to the journal *Muslim World*, and *International Bulletin* to the *International Bulletin of Missionary Research*. In footnotes the second and subsequent appearance of a source is noted by the use of a shortened title and the deletion of publication data. In this and other matters the approach of the companion volume, *Muslim Friends: Their Faith and Feeling* is employed.

Qur'ān quotations are taken from Marmaduke Pickthall's translation and Biblical quotations from the New Revised Version unless otherwise noted.

Preface

This book is about the effort to bridge the gap between Muslims and the gospel, and the Christian sharing required for it. It seeks to introduce that responsibility and task. It is easy to be grateful for the many rich studies that have been made of the topic, and there is no intention of replacing them. In this volume, however, I propose raising to a higher view the critical factor of friendship. The content of Christian witness is the deep friendship of God; the obligation that Christians have toward others, expressed in both word and deed, is born from it; and the approach that controls the exercise of the obligation is that of friends affectionately and anxiously sharing their good things.

It is my conviction, arriving from five decades of personal experience, that it is possible to be a witness to the gospel and a friend of Muslims at the same time, recognizing that some difficulties are inevitable. In truth, I do not see how they can be separated one from the other without losing both. Moreover I believe that this fundamental principle remains true—and indeed becomes even more crucial—in stressful times such as the first decade of this century.

After an opening chapter Part One of the work, comprised of chapters two to six, sets the context for Christian communication. It is an effort to discern and outline the opinion of Muslims on pivotal factors related to their understanding of the gospel. Part Two, including the next four chapters, examines some bridges that span the context and the task, including important learning received from the past. Part Three, chapters eleven to seventeen, deals with the sharing art itself. It takes up the practical effort to connect Muslims with the good news of a gracious God. The conclusion assesses the possibilities of the mission. In full, the study is a companion volume to *Muslim Friends: Their Faith and Feeling* (St. Louis: Concordia Publishing House, 1996), which is a manual on Islam itself.

I am grateful to my wife, Mary Helen, for steady support as well as for editorial assistance; to my family who stood by me in this enterprise; to colleagues and former students who encouraged me to complete this volume, and to a host of Muslim friends whose kindness to a missionary exceeded all expectation and from whom I received much learning. It is possible to pass on some of those treasures, but not the pleasure of the sharing experience itself. That pleasure, in part, is the natural appreciation that arises from any cordial relation. The joy, however, attains a well nigh luminous quality when Muslim friends see Jesus in a new way, and are glad of it. That is a kind of "joy unspeakable" that may be confidently wished for all.

Roland E. Miller
Ottawa, Canada
2005

Some Preliminary Observations on a Challenging Task

The title of this work, "Muslims and the Gospel," announces the challenge and sets the direction of the Christian obligation and task. It suggests that Muslims and the gospel belong together, but also need to be brought together. Something has happened to make that possible. Hence the sub-title references to "bridging" and "sharing." They imply some awareness of the nature of the extraordinary challenge residing in the simple phrase, "Muslims and the gospel."

We may feel confident about our knowledge of the meaning of the gospel—it is the good news of God's grace in Christ Jesus our Lord. We may be somewhat less confident as to the core identity of Muslims, since global events have produced a confusing image. We may be least aware of the dilemmas that history and humanity have created for a true linking of Muslims and the gospel, making it a task that calls for the best of the sharing arts. These dilemmas, on the other hand, have produced one blessing. They highlight the need to recover for our time the Biblical principle of deep friendship. It is the "and" that links "Muslims-Gospel", the substrate that underlines God's mission, the energy of hope.

These preliminary observations are a leading into the primary aspects of our study: context—what do Muslims think about the central themes that relate to the gospel?; bridge—how do we span the gap between the contrasting realities?; and task—what are the means appropriate to the sharing goal, and to the gospel itself?

A. Who Are the Muslims?: A Factual Survey

A Muslim may be a "fact", but before he/she are facts they are persons. Religious facts have to do with people, and that orientation is crucial for our enterprise. Muslims are people in religion. They are human beings with names—Abdullas or

Aminas—just as Christians are Johns and Marys. The relationship among them as people may become deeply personal, and in it they become mutually known.

In December, 2003, a senior gentleman approached me in the front yard of a church building in Malappuram, South India, where I had participated in a worship service. He asked, "Do you remember me?" Seeing my hesitation he said, "I am Abu Bekr. I worked in the post office and saw you often. Don't you remember?" "Of course I do," I replied, as the memories flooded back. "Where is your wife?" he asked. "Alas, she didn't come," I had to answer. (Newspapers had mistakenly reported that she had accompanied me on my journey to Malabar). My Muslim friend was visibly downcast. I repeated, "I'm sorry." He said, "When I was a boy, she saved me." "How was that?" I asked. "When you were living here, I had a festering wound on my foot, and came to her for help. She cleaned it every day and bandaged it, and it healed. I had thought I would lose my foot. I wish she had come. I wanted to say something to her." I responded, "I will tell her," It was now 47 years after the event, but the human relationship remained powerful, bonded in suffering and healing.

At the same time Muslims are not only people who define themselves in terms of their religious conviction. Because religious conviction is intrinsically personal the question "who are the Muslims?" cannot be raised too lightly. It cannot be assumed that the answer is simple. An easy answer may appear possible because Islam is relatively straightforward in its teachings, as many scholars attest. From another perspective, however, the answer is not as simple as it may appear. Because there are millions of Muslims in the world, who are living in many different geographical and cultural contexts, and who are enjoying varying traditions and differing outlooks on life, the question "who are the Muslims" is about as difficult to deal with on a descriptive level as the question "who are the Christians." More importantly, the assumption of an easy answer may conceal the fact that genuine knowing—in the sense of understanding—becomes possible only through a personal relationship.

Recognizing these difficulties perhaps the easiest way to answer the question "who are the Muslims?" is to say that Muslims are people who follow the religion of Islam. This is not avoiding the issue because of the significance of the two words "Muslim" and "Islam." They are intimately connected, for both the adjective and the noun stem from the same verbal root, *salama*, which in turn has three important meanings: to be safe and secure, to surrender, and to be at peace. Thus Muslims (the believers), who follow Islam (the religion), hold that by surrendering to and obeying God they have security and peace in life. To put the matter succinctly, the word *muslim* means "one who surrenders to God," and the word *islām* signifies "the surrendering." A passage of the Qur'ān that expresses the idea is 4:125, which declares:1 "Who can be better in religion than one who submits his whole self to God, does good and follows the way of Abraham, the true in faith? For God did take Abraham for a friend." It may therefore be suggested that a Muslim is a human being with a God-ward direction, and with the faith that God has a mercy-direction toward humans.

This conviction is simply expressed in the Muslim form of the everyday greeting. Non-Muslims have come to know it in the term "Salaam!" The full phrase in Muslim usage is *as-salām aleikum*, salaam to you!, and in its shorter form *salām aleik*. The word *salām* comes from the same root as *muslīm* and *islām*. Although usually translated "peace be with you!", the greeting really means: "I wish you the peace that comes from surrendering to God." There is a comparative phrase in the Jewish greeting, *shalom aleichem*, which fundamentally signifies "I wish you every good thing in the world." For the Muslim believer those good things can only come from God before whom we may confidently surrender ourselves. This conviction about the divine-human relation will hold great interest for Christians who know that they are advised to "submit yourselves to God" (James 4:7), and who believe that God befriended Abraham and the whole world through Jesus the Messiah in self-surrendering love.

When and how did Islam arise? Muslims believe that the religious attitude we have been discussing—surrendering to God—is the original religion of humanity that started with the creation of Adam. It is the natural birthright of every human being. It needs nourishing, however, because human hearts are frail. The people of the world need constant reminding and guidance. God mercifully provides it, and that provision produced historic Islam. The latter began in Mecca in Arabia, in a.d. 610, when the prophet Muhammad (570-632) received what Muslims regard as the first of many revelations. Gathered as the Qur'ān Muslims regard those revelations as God's ultimate message to humanity, and Muhammad as its final messenger. After early difficulties Islam became established as the religion of most of Arabia before Muhammad died. Within fifteen years thereafter Arab Muslims had overcome much of the Middle East, and within a century they had reached Tours in southern France. Today Islam is a worldwide community of faith. It stands out as numerically the second largest religion of the world. About 20.1% of the global population or about 1.3 billion people are Muslims. There are at least 42 Muslim majority nations, and Muslims are represented in virtually every country of the world. The global dispersion of Islam in the six decades after World War II means that it is now present in areas where previously there were few Muslims. Religiously, politically, economically and socially Islam has again become a major global force, a position it strongly held from the eighth to the sixteenth centuries.

What then do Muslims believe, at a basic level? In briefest form Muslims themselves describe Islam as "the religion of one God." They point to the beloved first chapter of the Qur'ān as the best summary of their faith:

Praise be to Allah, Lord of the Worlds,
    The Beneficent, the Merciful,
    Owner of the Day of Judgment;
    Thee (alone) we worship;
    Thee (alone) we ask for help;
    Show us the straight path,
    The path of those whom Thou hast favored,
    Not the path of those who earn thine anger,
    Nor of those who go astray.

This chapter is called "the Opening" (*al-Fātiha*) and "the Essence of the Qur'ān." It is omnipresent in Muslim devotion and life, and points to the chief elements in Muslim faith and practice.

Those elements are further defined by five basic beliefs and five common practices. Together they make up the straight path. The five beliefs are:

1 Faith in God
2 Belief in angels
3 Acceptance of prophets
4 Acceptance of sacred books
5 Acknowledgment of the Day of Judgment

The five common practices are:

1 The confession of faith
2 The five-fold prayer
3 The yearly month of fasting
4 Almsgiving
5 The pilgrimage to Mecca

The rhythm of daily religious life in Islam takes place in the context of faith in God, acceptance of the Qur'ān as God's guidance, the following of Muhammad's example, and a seeking "to prohibit the evil and commend the good." The rhythm is reinforced by community consensus and by a variety of social laws and festivals. Within that context Muslims find their frame of reference for pious living, and from it they consider the prospect of the final Hour, as the final judgment is named. It is that awesome and dreaded Day when all mankind shall be shown their deeds in the presence of the Almighty. "And whoso doeth good an atom's weight will see it then. And whoso doeth ill an atom's weight will see it then" (99:7-8)!

In addition to the basic beliefs and practices of Islam we need to survey the major spiritual themes that run through Muslim thought and life, but before that it is necessary to examine some serious dilemmas that condition the sharing art.

B. What are the Dilemmas?

There are four particularly daunting aspects of Christian sharing with Muslims. They are: the immensity of Islam, the mystery of Islam, the history of bad relations between Christians and Muslim, and mutual misunderstandings.

1. The Immensity of Islam

We have noted the vast number of Muslims in the world. Is it possible to convey the good news of God's salvation to so many people? Where, and with whom is the sharing to be done? Numerical size, however, is only one aspect of the immensity. The hugeness of Islam also relates to its history, its civilization, and its theology.

Historic Islam has completed almost fourteen centuries of existence according to the western Gregorian calendar. The Muslim calendar is based on the movement of the moon, a slightly shorter year, and dates from 622 A.D. when Muhammad emigrated from Mecca to Medina (the hijra). Thus in 2005 A.D. Muslims entered their year 1426 A.H. It is impossible to summarize such a long and far-flung development in brief form. Their early period is best known by Muslims themselves and is taught—with an emphasis on biography—in the vast network of Muslim religious schools (madrasas). The memories of those stirring early events linger and remain a constant and vibrant factor in Muslim consciousness. What obligation does a Christian friend have to know this history in view of the fact that it has molded Muslims? Common sense indicates that there is an obligation but the task is daunting.

The size of Islam also involves its extensive civilization. It is helpful to examine a coffee-table art-book on Islamic civilization and its achievements. The latter include a broad range of intellectual and artistic accomplishments. From the magnificent arabesque frescos of the Alhambra in Granada, Spain, to the monumental Dome of the Rock in Jerusalem; from the majestic Taj Mahal, seemingly floating in the air at Agra, India, to the intriguing pagoda mosque in Sian, China, Muslim architectural achievement overwhelms. The civilization story only begins there, however. In the "Golden Age" of Islam—the ninth to the thirteenth Christian centuries—Muslim scholars excelled in mathematics and astronomy, geography and medicine, literature and philosophy. Its artistic writing, calligraphy, has never been surpassed. Its poetry, especially the poetry of love produced by Sufi mystics, continues to move readers today. How can a Christian sharer appreciate what is beautiful to a Muslim friend, what gives her or him pride, and what moves that person's soul? The task is challenging.

The size of Islam also involves its large corpus of theology. Muslim scholars in the course of Islamic history have examined almost every possible theological question and have recorded their views in hundreds of texts. It is instructive for Christian observers to see how these fundamental issues have been considered without the informing element of the Christian understanding of Christ. Theologians like al-Ghazali (d. 1111), who is called "the Teacher of Islam," continue to influence Muslims today. Modern Muslim thinkers from Iqbal to Shariati, from Mawdudi to Qutb, have poured out treatises on various religious topics. But theology is only one element in the production that includes the huge body of Islamic law, the theories of Muslim philosophers, and the reflections of the mystical writers. How can one discover what has filtered down to a Muslim friend from this range of intellectual investigation, and what is finally true for him or her?

The size of Islam is daunting, but the dilemma of numbers can be addressed by shifting from Islam as a system to Muslims as people, and by devolving the mass into those with whom a personal relation is possible. The cultural immensity can become pleasurable learning by heading the canoe between the shores of over-perplexity and over-simplification, controlled by the paddle of appreciation.

2. The Apparent Mystery of Islam

This daunting factor is more apparent than real. The problem is not with Islam but with ourselves. It is normal to view what is external to our own experience as mysterious. It appears strange and incomprehensible, even dangerous and threatening. While this is ordinary feeling, for Christians intent on sharing the gospel the attitude needs correction. Such correction is itself an act of friendship, but above all it is important for the sake of the gospel and its intelligible communication. That is not difficult for as we have already seen from the discussion in Section A, Islam is possibly the least mysterious of the world's major religions.

Muslims believe that God created the world and appointed human beings as His servants. Human nature, however, is naturally weak, so people repeatedly choose to go astray from God's path and command. In response to that straying God mercifully sends prophets, again and again, to remind and to warn humans, and to bring them back to the way of piety, but the moral rise and fall of men and women goes on continually. So, as we have noted, God sends a final messenger and a final message. In its book form, the Qur'ān, that revelation represents God's ultimate gift to people. The essential content of divine truth and human piety has now been set plainly before men and women. The Qur'ān itself says, "Now it is sufficient for you." The rest is up to human beings. Those who conform to the instruction have a hope for a good verdict on the Day of Judgment, while those who are disobedient will suffer in the Fire. This, in a nutshell, is Islam. God is a mystery, in Muslim thinking, but Islam is not. In fact, Muslims speak proudly of its essential simplicity.

The dilemma of mystery is readily addressed with intentional learning.

3. The Dilemma of Bad Relationships

The story of bad relationships between Christians and Muslims is a story of fault on all sides. What happened?

When Muslim military forces burst out of the Arabian peninsula in the seventh Christian century, they entered the Christian world. The first encounter was with Syria. Syria was Semitic in spirit but was imbued with Graeco-Roman culture, and had been Christianized. It had become a battlefield between Christian Orthodox armies from Constantinople (Byzantium, Istanbul) and Persian armies from the East. These were the two great powers of the age, and they had virtually exhausted themselves in their mutual struggle. Moreover they had left Syria itself in a weakened condition. When Muslim armies entered, it turned out that they captured Damascus (625) and Jerusalem (638) with surprising ease. Ctesiphon, the capital of Iraq, fell about the same time (637), and so did Alexandria in Egypt (640). From there Muslim forces went on to North Africa, taking Christian Carthage (705) and Spain (711). Fallen were the great centers of Christian tradition and culture! Although the invaders were generally lenient in their administration, the military conquest by the Muslim armies set a relational tone.

Christian armies fought back in a similar vein, and the mutual struggle swirled around the Mediterranean basin for the next 450 years. While some Christians like Peter the Venerable and Francis of Assisi argued that this was not the Christian way, the majority mood was a militant one, and it culminated when a politically astute pope, Urban II (d. 1099), initiated the First Crusade. On November 27, 1095, he mounted a platform outside Clermont in southern France and issued an urgent challenge. He called on Christians to cease killing each other in western Europe and instead to participate in a righteous war, an armed "crusade" to recover the holy places in Palestine for Christendom. The audience responded with enthusiasm: "God wills it!", and the sad development was launched.

For the sake of duty, for the remission of sins, for an opportunity for martyrdom, booty and conquest—with mixed motivations the crude force of crusaders, led by knights, scorched its way via Constantinople and on July 15, 1099, the crusaders scaled the walls of Jerusalem. There they massacred a large number of inhabitants, both Muslims and Jews.[2] One of the Christian leaders, Raymond of Aguileres, recorded that on visiting the Temple area he had to walk through blood up to his knees. Is it surprising then that the word "crusade" evokes such negative emotions in Muslim hearts? Stephen Runciman states: "It was this bloodthirsty proof of Christian fanaticism that recreated the fanaticism of Islam."[3] The series of Crusades, one of which was directed against the Orthodox Christians of the East, continued up to 1271. It was then that the small, tenuous crusader kingdom in Palestine ended, when Muslims overcame its capital at Acre and in retaliation slaughtered the Christian inhabitants.

The Christian crusading mentality, however, continued to color the interreligious relations throughout the medieval period, finding another of its expressions in the Inquisition, which operated in various forms between 1231 and 1834. The mentality took a modern form in the "economic crusades," that is, the European imperial expansion, when most of the Muslim countries of the world became colonies of western nations. Muslim regard this development as a form of Christian imperialism. It was not until the close of World War II that many Islamic societies obtained their political and economic freedom. The history of bad relationships reached its modern peak with the Palestine issue. The creation of Israel in 1948 was carried out with the laudable intent of providing a homeland for Jews, but it also dispossessed a vast number of Palestinians, some Christians but the bulk Muslims. The fallout from that decision has not yet ended, as the ongoing resentment of those affected arouses liberation efforts.

Sparked by the Palestine issue and fueled by various internal Muslim grievances, extremist movements developed in the Muslim community and surfaced at the beginning of the new century, some of them developing anti-Christian attitudes that further distorted relations at the beginning of the new millennium. The uneasiness produced was greatly compounded by the Muslim terrorist destruction of buildings in New York City on September 11, 2001, and other attacks elsewhere. These events did not usher in a changed world, as some commentators suggested, but rather it continued and intensified what had become an age-old pattern.

Ensuing events, including warfare, have made it clear that both Christians and Muslims are called to deep reflection in regard to the spiritual resources that need to be drawn upon and the practical agendas that need to be set in order to develop a new and wholesome pattern of relationships. Since history reveals shared faults, the primary lesson for dealing with the dilemma of bad relationships is the ability to say: "I'm sorry" and "please forgive us." Certainly the sharing art depends on the cultivation of that attitude.

4. Mutual Misunderstandings

This is the final daunting dilemma that we will consider. It has to do with both ideological and psychological factors. By ideological misunderstanding we mean the incorrect apprehension of the other's teaching. Psychological misunderstanding refers to the emotional bias that interferes with communication.

Muslim ideological misunderstanding is severe, and will be the subject of larger treatment in subsequent chapters. There are four major misunderstandings that Muslim harbor in regard to Christian teaching. The first is that Christians worship three distinct deities that some Muslims consider to be Father, Mother and Son, and thereby Christians have regressed into polytheism. For Muslims the act of associating someone with God is the greatest sin (*shirk*). The second misunderstanding is that Christians have fallen into idolatry by worshiping a human being as divine. They have elevated a noble person and an important prophet, Jesus, into the stature of God, and then have compounded the problem by calling him the Son of God, thereby ascribing human parenthood to God. The third misunderstanding is that Jesus did not die on the cross; rather, in the Muslim view, God saved the Messiah from that brutal fate and took him directly to heaven. The fourth misunderstand is that the Christian scriptures have been corrupted in their present form and are unreliable.

Christian misunderstanding runs to the psychological dimension. The emotional bias of Christians in relation to Muslims has two primary sources. The first is media sensationalism and misrepresentation. Muslims, with considerable justification, complain bitterly in regard to the caricatures of Islam and the stereotyping of Muslims that are an almost everyday event. This is still the case despite recent improvement. Whatever the cause, the phenomenon has produced bias among non-Muslims, and anger and defensiveness on the part of Muslims. There is a second source of the problem. That is the mindless violence of terrorists operating in the name of Islam. This factual reality produces the negative conclusion that all Muslims are inherently violent and dangerous. It is an unfortunate fact that ordinary Christians have often been unable to distinguish between the aberrant behavior of some Muslims and the conduct of the mass of average Muslims, even though they have learned to make that distinction about themselves. The tendency of Muslim leaders to remain publicly silent, reserving their criticism of extremists to private admonition, has not been helpful in alleviating the negative feelings.

Taken together these misunderstandings represent formidable difficulties, but they are amenable to improvement. In regard to the Muslim ideological misunderstandings it must be remembered that their origin is in the post-Christian status of Islam. Islam includes Christian elements in its purview, but understands them differently than Christians do. To convey the Christian interpretation of those elements requires knowledge of the issues and a large quotient of patient effort. In sum, *it means that the sharing art involves correction as well as proclamation.*

In regard to the Christian emotional bias, Christians are called upon to engage in corrective ministry also towards themselves. They must redirect themselves from the sterile paths of complaint and judgmentalism to the possibilities revealed in the embracive love of Jesus and his resolve to alter the human situation. It is this compassion that moves the followers of Jesus from facts and dilemmas to sharing.

C. Knowing and Sharing: The Link

Are knowing and sharing distinct ideas? Certainly they have different connotations, and certainly for the sake of academic study they can and must be distinguished. Even in such contexts, however, it will be recognized that they are intimately linked, for knowing facilitates sharing and sharing deepens knowing.

When we turn to the Christian perspective, the conjunction and interrelation of knowing and sharing become evident. Both are based on one underlying principle, and both draw their motivation from a common source. Let us name it the principle of deep friendship that St. Paul identifies as "the mind of Christ" (Philippians 2:2). Founded thereon, the combination of knowing and sharing result in genuine communication. We may draw a simple equation to illustrate the point:

$$\frac{\text{knowing and sharing}}{\text{deep friendship}} = \text{communication}$$

Deep friendship lies under and informs both knowing and sharing. It is their common source and link. In Chapter 7 we will examine its theological base in greater detail. Here we will simply point out the significance that it has for both the functions of knowing and sharing.

In terms of the knowing task the principle teaches Christians not to think of Muslims in the mass, nor as objects, but rather as individuals whom one can know with the knowledge of a friend. The question then no longer the rather grand inquiry "who are the Muslims?", but rather "who is a Muslim?" Immediately there is a sense of relief. A Muslim is not in the first place the representative or a system or a history, but rather he or she is an individual whom one can get to know, and with whom one can have a relation. To that kind of engagement Muslims themselves are open. While past relations with Christians have produced some caution, often suspicion and even animosity, on the whole they have welcomed friendly overtures. It is a demonstrable and noteworthy fact that a Christian and a Muslim can draw very closely together. Whenever and wherever such an experience takes place, real knowing occurs. The faith of the friend becomes transparent. The Christian partner is able to answer the question "who is a Muslim?" in a discerning way, almost from within.

What applies to knowing applies equally to sharing. That too depends heavily on individual relationships in which people actually see others as friends and communicate intelligibly within that ambience. This can be said to be the most important missing factor in the history of Christian sharing with Muslims. The basic meaning of the English word share is "to distribute to others." Distributing involves real seeing. With friendship vision we see the essential humanity of Muslims. They are men, women and children who have the same spectrum of realities and conditions that Christians have, who face a similar set of problems and needs, who participate in the same hopes and fears. We find that there is within us that which enables us to laugh together and to cry together, in deep mutual awareness

Our common humanity makes the sharing possible, desirable and useful.[4] Deep friendship makes it inevitable, fascinating and effective. And the gospel not only has "free course" but also the demonstration of its power.

In sum, the bridge that connects knowing and sharing, over which Muslims and the gospel can travel and meet, is the friendship of God revealed in Jesus Christ and now embodied and expressed in the attitudes and deeds of those who "follow in his train."

With these beginning thoughts in mind we turn to selected aspects of the knowing task, looking at the key principles of Islam and how they shape and mold the lives of Muslims.

Part 1

The Context: Pivotal Muslim Views

Whenever and wherever the seed of the gospel is sown, it falls on occupied soil. In the case of Muslims there are some decisive elements that provide the context for its communication and reception. These include the guiding Islamic principles that inform thoughts and attitudes. They also embrace the Muslim viewpoints in regard to sin and salvation, and Muslim opinion about the person of Jesus the Messiah, and of his Christian followers. In Part 1 we consider these pivotal notions and offer some suggestions on how Christians may communicate the gospel.

2

Key Principles for Understanding Islam

"What a Muslim Would Want a Christian to Understand." A Christian group once asked the writer to address that vital topic. I answered that it would be useful to first identify who the intended person is, since there is a great variety among Muslims. I then suggested that there are probably three things that most Muslims would like a Christian friend to realize:

—what he or she believes;
—how he or she feels; and
—what problems he or she faces.

This chapter deals with the first of these aspects of the Muslim desire, i.e. The hope that Islam might be correctly understood.

A traditional Muslim tends to define faith in terms of the list of beliefs and practices that have already been cited. Many classical scholars did so, stating that Islam is a combination of faith (*imān*) and practice (*dīn*). Faith includes belief in God, angels, prophets, books and day of judgment, with predestination sometimes added. Practice involves confession, prayer, fasting, almsgiving, pilgrimage, and some include struggling for God's will. This listing is standard and important, but it is also in a sense stereotypical because Islamic piety includes much more. In what follows we will examine the foundations of the Islamic world view rather than the ritual requirements, and we suggest that there are twelve key principles for understanding Islam and Muslims. In making the suggestion we recognize that there will be differences of opinion about what belongs or does not belong in such a summary.[1]

Key Principle One: Islam Is Marked by an Overwhelming Sense of God

At the root of every description of Muslims is their overwhelming sense of God. The fact is the central reality of Islam. Muslim believers are God-conscious in thought and God-directed in action. This reality is reflected by the Muslim language of praise and in the symbolism of prayer.

Muslims cherish hundreds of names for God, but the 99 most important ones are called "the Beautiful Names of God." They all bow, however, before another name, the name "Allah." This term is derived from the word *al-ilāh* that simply means The Deity, the August and Awesome One, the only being in, divine category. The sacred name of Allah is the first word whispered into a newborn baby's ear by the Muslim midwife, and it is the one word recited when a funeral procession makes its way to the cemetery. Between these terminal points the frequent repetition of the sacred name in everyday life announces that God the Almighty Lord is its Ruler and Sustainer.

Four oft-repeated pious phrases express the Muslim awareness of God and reverence for God:

Allāhu akbar!—"God is greater!

This is the most formal expression of God's greatness. Not God is great. There are, after all, many things that are great. Not God is greatest, as though God is at the end of a series of great things. Rather, God is greater, beyond imagination and comparison, greater than the greatest.

Al-hamdu lilāhi!—"Praise be to God!"

This is the everyday word of praise. It is the phrase that is spoken when a person has been granted a new child, or when someone wins first prize in an examination, or when a job is found.

Subhana 'llāhi!—"Glory be to God!"

This exclamation is used often in the Qur'ān and in the Muslim prayers. It signifies that their is no deficiency in God, Who is the Perfect, the Pure and Transcendent One.

In shā' Allāh!—"If God wills!"

All things fall under God's rule. If God wills, I shall finish reading to the end of this sentence, and not otherwise. God's will is supreme and decisive, in life and death.

In addition to being pious expressions of faith these phrases serve as reminders. They remind the Muslim believer that God is the Reality (al-Haqq) the chief fact in human life. The acceptance of the fact is demonstrated in a physical way by the Muslim liturgical prayer. Almost everyone will have seen Muslims at prayer. As they touch down their foreheads—five times a day—they demonstrate the primary religious attitude in Islam, surrender to the Almighty God. *Surrender*

The mind too must be surrendered, as well as spirit and body, and that includes humility in relation to the nature of God. Muslims are somewhat hesitant to discuss the characteristics of God. God is to be worshiped and served, not explored and analyzed. In Muslim perspective the human mind cannot comprehend the divine mystery. Moreover, the use of human language about God tends to humanize or to limit the Divine Being. It is for this reason that the theologian al-Ghazālī (d. 1111) advised: "Meditate upon Allah's creation, and do not meditate upon the Being of Allah."[2]

Nevertheless, from the Muslim point of view, there are some basic things that God has made known and that God's creatures should recognize and confess. They include these three fundamental affirmations:

God is one.—There is no one beside God. God has no partners, is single and incomparable.

God is Almighty.—There is nothing that God cannot do, and there is nothing outside of His[3] authority.

God is the Lord.—God creates the world, rules it and will judge it. His will and command are final.

What about the many characteristics that appear to be inherent in the ninety-nine beautiful names of God? Scholars are generally of the opinion that they describe what God does rather than what God is. But one quality holds particular significance for Muslims today: the mercy of God. Two titles for God, the All-Merciful and the All-Compassionate, appear with repetitive force in the Qur'ān, together with their verbal root (rahima) as many as 400 times. Contemporary Muslims struck by this emphatic testimony have in effect made the mercy of God a fourth basic affirmation.

God is Merciful.—God the Merciful One (Rahmān) show a mercy (Rahīm) to His creatures through his providential care and His moral guidance.

What then is the relation of Allah to human beings? Muslims find this an easier matter discuss. The primary relationship is that defined by the word Master and its companion servant. God is al-Malik, the Absolute Ruler, the Owner of the universe, the Sovereign Lord. One who surrenders to "the Master of all greatness" becomes His willing and obedient servant ('abd). As Master God directs human beings, and as servants humans obey God's direction. In obeying God they accept the vocation of piety (taqwa). Piety is a religious attitude combining the fear of God and applied obedience. Towards God it involves gratitude and faith, penitence and trust, remembrance and worship. Towards fellow humans it implies generosity and righteous conduct. Thus Islam holds forth the Lordship of God, and in response to it our surrender, servant obedience, and piety in human affairs. Therein lies the essence of Islam.

In short Muslim faith in God is grounded upon solemn respect. Respect may seem too light a word to use, but it describes the reality. Muslims are not ostentatious about the matter, and do not parade their faith. For them it is something as natural as breathing. God is there. I must believe in Him and follow Him. In that sense Muslims are God-conscious people, and drawing on the symbol of the prayer we may say that Islam is a forehead touching the ground before God world view. For Muslims the Qur'ān declares why it must be so.

God
There is no god but He
The Living, the Everlasting.
Slumber seizes Him not, neither sleep!
To Him belongs
All that is in the heavens and the earth.
Who is there that shall intercede with Him
Save by His leave?
He knows what lies before them
And what is after them,
And they comprehend not anything of His knowledge
Save such as He wills
His throne comprises the heaven and the earth;
The preserving of them oppresses Him not;
He is the All-high, the All-glorious! (2:255)

Key Principle Two: Islam Is a Religion of Revelation

The second key principle of Islam is that God makes known His will to mankind. The Master tells the servants what they need to know. Islam is therefore a religion of revealed guidance (hidāyat).

Why would God, so majestic, so beyond and remote, condescend to us in this way? In the first place, in Muslim view, it is our status as creatures that makes it necessary for God to "send down" the revelation of His will. It is impossible for mere human beings to apprehend the wishes of the August Ruler, and if there is to be any knowledge about God, it is God Himself Who must provide it. God does make available this knowledge, revealing what we need to know about God and about God's will for our lives. God does this not simply out of a desire to give information, but because by His creation God has established a relationship with His people. He is their *Merciful Master.* If the Lord and Master does not give direction to His servants, how will they know what to do? God does not make transparent the inner nature of the Divine Mystery, but rather reveals His desire and command.

It is not only creatureliness, however, that makes revelation necessary. It is also the fact of human moral frailty that requires it. Muslims believe that human beings are not only physically limited but morally weak. They are "prone to evil" and continually wander from God's straight path. Therefore they need to be "straightened out" as to what God wants, to be reminded, to be redirected. Unfortunately the human tendency to sinfulness is a persistent one. This means that God has to straighten out human beings again and again. That is why revelation is not a one-time thing. Islam holds to a theory of repeated revelation that has a final culminating point.

The reason that God is willing to engage in such a revelatory process is the Divine Mercy. God's mercy extends beyond His providential care over our physical needs and takes in our need for spiritual guidance. Through whom does God give the revelation? The answer is through a long series of prophets and sacred books. Muslims may argue about the exact number of prophets and books, but they agree that ultimately every society receives some revelation of God's will. No one can say, "I didn't know." The 28 known prophets are all associated with Jewish, Christian and Muslim history. They include familiar names such as Adam, Noah, Abraham, Ishmael, Moses, David, Jesus and others. The periodic revelations are required by human stubborness. God sends a prophet and a scripture to give the message of God's unity and to clarify the nature of godly living. For a while people listen, but then they turn away. Again God sends a messenger, and once more the dismal pattern is repeated. Finally, as Muslims believe, God determined to end the confusion by sending one last prophet, Muhammad, and through Him one final revelation, the Qur'ān. The Qur'ān is not only God's final Word, but it is His ultimate gift to humanity. It is therefore the most precious Muslim possession.

There are three other extant scriptures that the Qur'ān commends. They are the Tawrāt (Torah) revealed through Moses; the Zabūr (Psalms) sent down through David; and the Injīl (Evangel or Gospel) revealed through Jesus. The Qur'ān, however, sums up and clarifies all other previous teaching. About the size of the New Testament it has 114 chapters (sūras) and 6226 verses (āyas). The chapters are arranged according to their length rather than chronologically. Their original and still preferred language is Arabic, the language of Muhammad. Muslims believe that the Qur'ān, which means "recital," is in every part the Word of God, inerrant, timeless and inviolable. Because of its miraculous and sacred quality it is usually memorized and recited rather than studied and discussed. It is the music of Islam, chanted in mosque and home; it is the art of Islam, written in beautiful calligraphy; but above all it is the source of spiritual knowledge, the primary rule of faith and life. It is given many names, the most simple one being The Book (the kitāb). By the believer it is always carried reverently, and in the home it holds the most honored place. With it God's guidance is complete, and through it Muslims believe that God's mercy has fully addressed the human problem.

Key Principle Three: Islam Is a Confessional Religion

We use the word "confessional" in the sense of having a confession of faith and making it a requirement for believers. Muslims maintain this position and possess such a confession. They hold that believers should openly acknowledge their faith. Since God has revealed His will, humanity is faced with a decision, the choice either to accept the guidance or to reject it. There can be no middle ground. Moreover the acceptance should be articulated and the commitment publicly declared. The words used to do that constitute the Muslim confession of faith. They are simple and straightforward, and every Muslim knows them: "There is no god but God, and Muhammad is the messenger of God." In the Arabic form that is normally utilized, the words are: lā ilāha illa lāh, wa muhammadu rasūl lāhi.

The confession is called the shahāda, which means "the witnessing," or the kalima, which signifies "the confessing word." A full declaration of the confession is preceded by the phrase "I bear witness that. . ." or "I testify that. . ." The first of the two parts reflects the Quranic passage 27:26 which declares: "Allah, there is not god save Him." The second part is a response to such passages as 48:29 that says: "Muhammad is the messenger of Allah." One who utters the words of the confessing formula with faith is a Muslim. The words must be expressed willingly, from the heart, and ideally should result in faithful action. The essence of the confession, however, is its declaration and the mental assent that accompanies it. God alone is Lord and Muhammad is His apostle!

Islam knows of longer confessions and creeds but does not give them practical importance. None are prescribed. Implicit in this attitude is the Muslim dislike for expressing the inexpressible, the Muslim preference for regulating behavior rather than refining doctrine, but above all the Muslim love of simplicity. It may be noted at this point that Muslims find trouble in following the creedal formulations of basic Christianity, and the extended confessions of some denominations are quite beyond them. They regard the statements as unnecessarily complicated and find relief in the apparent simplicity of the *shahāda*. On this point Islam has remained firm—nothing more than the "*lā ilāha illa lāh. . .*" is required as a formal statement of belief, whether by an uneducated person or a religious scholar, whether by an individual or by a group. This approach has resulted in a combination of core allegiance and a broad diversity of opinion beyond that core.

Key Principle Four: Islam Is a Religion of Salvation History

By salvation history we mean that a person's life in this world has results for the life beyond. Islam is therefore a religion of fateful history, of consequential history. In saying this there are three implications. We are saying that from the Muslim point of view the world belongs to God, is under God, and has divine purpose. Secondly we are saying that my own life should be conducted in the awareness of the divine rule. And thirdly we are saying that human history will come to a final conclusion that will decide the fate of every human being, my own included. In elaborating this principle we shall consider each of these three factors.

In Muslim perspective this world in a real sense belongs to God. God created it in the first place. The story of creation is told in several places in the Qur'ān. It states that God created the world out of nothing, in six days, including both angels and human beings. The divine intention is expressed in phrases like "that they may worship me" and "that they may be thankful." God "owns" the world, and is therefore interested in what happens to it.

God is also continuously involved in the world. Earthly history is divine history as well as human history. God is involved in it in several ways. God preserves the world, with providential care. Again and again the Qur'ān affirms: "Who can deny the bounty of the Lord?" From cattle to camels, from rain clouds to palm-trees it extols the mercy of God in creation. But that is not all. God as we have seen also guides the world, giving directions to His creatures. They are not left to walk aimlessly on the earth. Even that is not the ultimate truth about God's involvement. The ultimate truth is that God rules the world. God's powerful will is involved in the course of earthly events. It is supreme in human affairs. God punishes as He wills, and forgives as He wills. "He is the Powerful, the Wise."

The Almighty God Who creates and rules is also at the close of history. At a time know only to Him God will bring history to a conclusion. The conclusion will be the great Day of Judgment when all things will be exposed and decided. The Muslim mystics used to say that this world is a bridge to the next. Classical Islamic thought declares that God is at the beginning of the bridge, is the Lord of our passage over it, and is waiting at the and when God's final purpose will be known.

The second factor depends on the first. The fact of God's presence in history means that my life in this world should be deliberately conducted in the awareness of God, and should be a preparation for the final Judgment. The length of my life is the time I have to get ready for that day, and I will have no more than that amount. I must take the right decisions and do the appropriate things that will secure my deliverance from punishment and escape from the pains of Hell-Fire, and assure an open door to the delights of Paradise. How to escape is a matter of deep concern because the Judgment Day is a fearful reality. It is called the Hour of Doom, and is described very graphically in the Qur'ān. One of the most terrifying pictures is that of a scale. Our evil deeds will be placed on one side, and the good on the other. The great scale will measure the result accurately. "Whoso doeth an atom's weight of good will see it then, and Whoso doeth and atom's weight of evil will see it then" (99:7-8). The following words remind the believer of the penalty of a negative result: "The Calamity! What is the Calamity? Ah, what will convey unto thee what the Calamity is! . . . Raging Fire" (101:1). There are many different opinions among Muslims about the spiritual methodology that will lead to deliverance. The uncertainties account for the fact that many Muslims prefer not to think too much about the matter, but rather go about their daily life as well as they can and leave the final issue to God. "The (absolute) command on that day is Allah's" (82:19).

On the other hand, pious Muslims know and believe that this fact does not diminish human responsibility. They give attention to the faith and practice of Islam. Controlling their apprehension about the final Hour is the constant hope that God "the Forgiving One," God "the Very Forgiving One," and God "the Relenting One," as God is named in the Qur'ān, will overlook their weaknesses and sins. All Muslims hope that in the end they will hear these words:

But Ah!, thou soul at peace! Return unto
thy Lord, content in His good pleasure!
Enter thou among my bondmen! Enter thou
My garden (89:27-30).

Key Principle Five: Islam Is a Comprehensive Religion

Islam maintains the principle that religion has to do with all of life. It is therefore comprehensive in nature. It has an inclusive quality, is holistic in its concerns, and is sweeping in its application.

Muslims have a word that incorporates this principle. It is *tawhīd* or "unity." Like "surrender" and "obedience" and "guidance" it is an all-important term. God is one, it declares, and therefore the life of this world should be a unified life under God. The first verse of the Qur'ān calls God "the Lord of the Worlds." If this is so, all the plural realities within the universe are under God. This applies to us humans. If God exists, and if the God Who exists is Lord, then He must also be the Lord of our personal worlds. One cannot, as it were, take one day of the week and assign it to God, the other days belonging to us humans. Similarly one cannot take one area of human behavior, i.e. the cultic area of religious ritual, and assign it to God, leaving the worlds of culture and social life, economics and politics, to exclusive human rule. Life is truly interconnected, but the interconnection is not only horizontal but vertical. God is Lord of the worlds.

Thus Islam does away with the distinction between the sacred and the secular. More accurately, it never existed for Islam. Muslims do not understand the distinction and cannot approve it. They do distinguish between devotional practices and the conduct of daily life. Thus prayer and fasting, alms-giving and pilgrimage, may be described as "the religious practices of Islam." They have been specifically commanded, and their regular observance, we have noted, gives a spiritual rhythm to Muslim life. But "religion" itself cannot be narrowed down so that other areas of life appear to be apart form God and God's will. Everything we do, think and say in a unified life under God has a sacred quality.

Another significant Islamic term expresses the human application of this theory. It is *khalifa*, or "vice-regency." The term comes form the creation account in the Qur'ān. God tells the angels: "I am about to place a viceroy (*khalifa*) in the earth." The angels object. Looking ahead they correctly see how humans will do harm in the world. But God says, "Surely I know that which ye know not" (2:30). "Vice-regent" means a deputy of another, i.e. one who governs and administers on behalf of a superior. We are therefore commissioned to take care of the world on behalf of God Who is its true Ruler and Sovereign. As vice-regents we are God's representatives on earth, and the stewards of His creation.

Theory and practice frequently collide. Islamic history shows the difficulty of applying the principle of comprehensiveness in the everyday affairs of life. The problem is not merely one of understanding the limits of human freedom or the intention of God in new situations. It also has to do with both the sinful human desire to be lords and the sheer human inability to put the holistic theory into practice. At the level of human moral incapacity the angels were right when they prophesied that men and women "will do harm therein, and will shed blood." The problem, however, is not only one of sinful human pride, but also one of human incapacity. Modern life is extremely complex, and it is not always clear how to express the principle of divine rule in concrete human matters. Just as those who attempt to divide the sacred and the secular have problems of application, so also those who regard all of life as directly ruled by God have problems in interpretation. Albert Einstein once said: "I want to know God's thoughts . . . The rest are details." Muslims believe that they know God's thought in regard to the principle of comprehensiveness, but they are not agreed about the details. Some believe that the spirit of Islam should inform the various spheres of life, while others hold that the specific rules of Islamic tradition should control all areas of life.

Nevertheless, Muslims agree that the factor of human inability should not annul the divine principle. A relevant Quranic passage states that the reason God appointed human beings as viceroys was "that he may try you" (6:166). In a world that is increasingly deconstructed, Muslims are "tried with" the challenge of leading a unified life under God. For many this means discovering new and creative ways by which the principle of wholeness may be joined with the principles of freedom, human rights, and natural development. For their inspiration Muslims tend to look back to the earliest period of Islam, especially the forty years 622-661, from the time of Muhammad's entry into Medina to the death of his fourth successor, 'Alī, as really the only period when this key principle was truly expressed in human life. The common Muslim prayer in applying this principle is: "Show us the straight path . . . not (the path) of those who earn thine anger" (1:6).

Key Principle Six: Islam Is Characterized by the Overwhelming Impress of the Personality of Muhammad

It has been well said that to understand Islam is to know Muhammad whom Muslims revere as God's final prophet. The Qur'ān reveals Islam, and Muhammad defines it. His footprints are everywhere on the sands of the Muslim story. We used the adjective "overwhelming" to describe the Muslim sense of God. We must use it a second time now to describe the deep impact of Muhammad on the faith and feeling of Muslims everywhere.

The reverence that Muslims have for Muhammad must be understood as respect not worship. There are two great sins in Islam. Unbelief (*kufr*) is one. The other is idolatry (*shirk*), i.e. associating a partner with God. Sainthood in Islam is a very controversial subject simply because Muslims all over the world cherish their saints. Yet every Muslim also knows that a distinction must be preserved between the divine and the human. It is *shirk* to give too much reverence to a human being, including even Muhammad. His shrine in Medina was destroyed in 1804 by some Arab Muslims who believed that the attitude of respect toward Muhammad had exceeded its limits. Muhammad is only a man. At the same time the Muslim heart cries out: what a man! This feeling was captured by the confession of Islam where Muhammad's name is placed next to the name of Allah. Can any human rise higher than that?

Muhammad (570-632) is the historical founder of Islam. Muslims believe that *islām* began with Adam, and the successive prophets simply renewed the faith. What we call today the religion of Islam, however, began with Muhammad. He received his first revelation in the year 610 in the city of Mecca, his Arabian home. For twelve years he preached his message under persecution and with few visible results. In 622, a date that marks the first year of the Islamic lunar calendar, he and his followers emigrated to Medina. During the subsequent decade with a great outburst of creative energy he established and consolidated a Muslim state. There he also received the remainder of his revelations. These were gathered together in the Qur'ān after his death.

Even within such a brief description the two reasons why Muhammad is accorded such veneration become visible. The first is that he is believed to be the messenger of God, certainly in line with the great prophets of the past, but not only that. He is God's *final* messenger, and so the Qur'ān describes him as "the seal of the prophets" (33:40). It is true that he is only a human being, but in Muslim opinion it must mean something that God chose this man as the channel for His final word to humanity. ~~With Muhammad's death prophecy has ceased because it is no longer required.~~

The second reason for the reverence is that Muhammad is regarded as the pattern of what it means to be Muslim in daily life. In Muslim view his character is unblemished. The Qur'ān says of him: "Verily in the messenger of Allah ye have a good example for him who looketh unto Allah and the Last Day" (33:21). ~~Muslims happily accept him as their supreme example and strive to model their lives after him.~~ That is why they want to know everything about Muhammad, whatever he said and did. The stories of his sayings, his actions, his family life, his personal habits have been vigorously collected. They are called the ~~Hadīth~~, a term that means communication or tale, but is frequently translated as "tradition." Hadīth constitute a supplementary source of Muslim faith and life, and have almost as much authority as the Qur'ān itself. The stories in sum contain the custom, *sunna*, of the Prophet. ~~If you want to know what it means to be an authentic human being, then consider the *sunna* of Muhammad as it appears in the Qur'ān and Hadīth, and you will not go wrong.~~

There is no mystery in the psychology of Muslim respect for Muhammad. If you believe that someone has set you on a good path and given you a clear direction for your life, would you not honor him? Muslims honor Muhammad with an every-increasing fervor and conviction. He is the best man who ever lived, as the poet laureate said over his grave. He is assigned great titles. One list of honorifics starts with Ahmad, the most praiseworthy, and two hundred names later ends with Sāhib al-Faraj, the source of consolation.[4] His birthday is celebrated, his exploits are sung, and when his name Muhammad is mentioned the words "may God bless him!" spring to Muslim lips. Some Muslims even hope for his advocacy and intercession of the Day of Judgment for he is God's special friend. At his death the poet expressed what became the universal and continuing conviction of the entire Muslim family when he said:[5]

> I say, and none can find fault with me,
>> But one lost to all sense—
>> I shall never cease to praise him. . .

~~Key Principle Seven: Islam Is a Religion of Law~~

God commands and servants obey. God guides and true believers follow. There can be little surprise that Islam is a religion of law. Fazlur Rahman calls this "the most central concept of Islam."[6] ~~In the Muslim view God regulates life through a series of laws that give order to our existence.~~ This divinely prescribed ordering is called the sharī'a. It is an all-inclusive code of behavior. Although the words "Allah," "Muhammad," and "Qur'ān," rank unquestionably as the most important words in the Islamic vocabulary, the term sharī'a comes close to them in significance. Next to the Qur'ān itself it is the most precious of all Muslim possessions. It became the unifying factor in Muslim life and the mould of Islamic culture, and its modern application is a deeply emotional issue for Muslims, whom Ismail Faruqi defines as "the world-fellowship of the law."

In its root meaning the word sharīʿa means "a clear road to a watering-place." It is found only once in the Qurʾān, but that passage convey the sense of its religious significance: "And now we have set thee…on a clear road of (Our) commandment" (45:18). Through His commandment God designates the straight path for His people. We have noted that the Islamic view is that God reveals His will, and that His will has to do with all of life. We must now add that God's will is made known in specific commands. The idea of law in Islam is that it includes both principle and regulation, but the sharīʿa concentrated on the latter. Of course behind every regulation is a principle, and the Qurʾān is full of principles. In certain key matters, however, God is not content, as it were, to provide only a principle and then leave it to humans to work out its application by trial and error. As a wise master will not ordinarily leave his servants in doubt about the specifics of what he wants, so also the Lord of the worlds does not leave some important things to chance. In such crucial matters God also provides the application. Out of this master-servant theory was born the religious law of Islam, and the concept of regulation soon came to dominate Muslim religious thinking. It has been estimated that only three percent of the Quranic verses actually deal directly with legislation, but the whole Qurʾān itself came to be regarded as a book of laws, an opinion that is now being challenged by Muslims seeking to understand the Qurʾān afresh.

The formulation of Muslim law and its application to daily living required a practical science. Other religions may emphasize doctrine, but their law-conscious-ness moved Muslims to emphasize practice. The science of law took precedence over theology, and in medieval Muslim times was greatly elaborated. Once embarked on the road of regulation its sources needed to be expanded. Life is complicated, and the Qurʾān itself covered only some of the requirements. When the Qurʾān did not speak directly to an issue, Muslims looked to the Hadīth of the Prophet Muham-mad. As the true example of the surrendered life, his precedent could safely be cited for legal requirements. In situations where neither the Qurʾān nor the Hadīth seemed to proved an answer, Muslims used the idea of analogy and the common sense consensus of believers to find an appropriate regulation.

On the basis of these sources the Muslim legal scholars studied the principles and regulations of the law, classified human actions, codified the needed penal-ties, and create an administrative framework and a working operational system. Eventually a huge corpus of law was built up and passed on to Muslims today. It is found in various sharīʿa handbooks, but essentially its power rests in the religious habits of everyday Muslims.

The law of Islam brings down to earth for Muslims the principle of compre-hensiveness, the idea that all of life is to be ordered under God's governance. As a result there is ritual law, family law, business and property law, state and inter-national law, judicial law, and social law. Not every human action is defined, but no area of human life is omitted form its purview. Among these categories of law the most important for Muslims today are the ritual (religious) law and the family law. The ritual law governs the devotional practices of Muslims. The family law controls such matters as marriage, dowry and divorce; parentage and guardian-ship; family maintenance and inheritance; bequests, donations and endowments.

Many Muslims also hold that the sharī'a should be the state law where Muslims are a majority. Even where Muslims are a minority and the formal implementation of the shari'a is impossible, they contend for the right to observe at least the ritual and family laws of their faith.

The sharī'a is perhaps the hottest subject in Islam today. Muslims love to discuss it. They also feel the need to do so for the main body of the sharī'a came into existence in the early days of Islam, and was more or less finalized by the end of its third century. Since then the modern world has brought in a host of new situations and complexities. Is the ancient heritage of the law adequate for conditions today? Can it be changed according to need? Can it be updated or supplemented? Can its role in contemporary society be revisited? There is intense debate about these questions, and strong differences of opinion in regard to the appropriate answers. Those who argue for change feel that the traditional shari'a has become rigid and chokes the dynamism of Islam. Those who argue against change maintain that the law has a divine quality and is therefore untouchable. There is no debate, however, about the law principle itself, or the idea that Muslims as individuals and families should live by the law. In Muslim thinking, to live that way is to implement the Divine Will.

Key Principle Eight: Islam Is a Religion of Community

To say that Islam is a religion of community is to say that its members have a sense of being part of a distinctive family. That feeling is not unusual in groups. In Islam, however, the sense is so highly developed that it constitutes a powerful reality and an emotional force. Involved in the concept are the ideas of being one in faith, of being chosen, of being exclusive, of having brotherly concern, of being blessed, of being sacred and inviolable. The outsider sees the divisions in Islam. The insider feels the unity.

The word for community is umma. The term is used broadly in the Qur'ān. In its view there were valid communities of faith before Islam, and some exist today in less valid forms. In practice, however, the word is used to denote the body of Muslim believers who share the faith of Islam and who strive to keep their duty to God in a unified way. The word umma literally means mother. It points to the special relationship that the confession of faith creates. The lā ilāha illa lāh. . . bond of faith is so strong that this has an almost mystical quality. The community mothers the believer in a family of faith. There is not only a bond in faith, but a bond of sacred duty. The family of Muslims is appointed to realize, to demonstrate, to make visible the will of God at work in human society. The umma is to be organized around that task. The ideas of a family unity in faith and task come together in this well-known passage of the Qur'ān (3:103):

> And hold fast, all of you together, to the cable of God, and do not separate. And remember Allah's favour unto you: how you were enemies and He made friendship between your hearts, so that you became brothers by His grace. . . . And there may spring from you an umma who invite to goodness and enjoin right conduct and forbid indecency. . . . You are the best community that hath been raised up for mankind.

Within the Muslim community human relations are to be governed by the spirit of mutual concern. In the sermon he gave on his last pilgrimage to Mecca the Prophet Muhammad is reported to have said: "Know that every Muslim is a Muslim's brother, and that the Muslims are brethren."[8] Hadīth record many practical examples of what Muhammad intended by that utterance, theologians elaborated on the implications, and jurists turned them into legal requirements. Al-Ghazālī sums it up:[9]

> The duties of a Muslim to a fellow-Muslim are that you say Peace be unto you!, if you encounter him, and respond if he gives you an indication, that you bless him if he sneezes, visit him if he is ill, and attend his funeral if he dies. They are to honor his oath, if he swears something to you, to advise him when he seeks advice, and take care of his interest when he is absent, to want for him what you want for yourself.

A legally required expression of this concern is the zakāt, the alms-giving that is one of the basic practices of the faith. It is charity intended for fellow Muslims only.

In the light of this principle of communal brotherhood what is to be said about the divisions that exist in the Muslim community, the wars between Muslim nations, and the antagonism between Muslim individuals and groups? The image of Northern Alliance Muslims and Taliban Muslims killing each other in Afghanistan only crystallized a long-standing reality. The major division in Islam is between Sunnīs and Shīʿas. The Sunnīs are self-designated as "the people of the Prophet's custom and community." They constitute the overwhelming majority, perhaps 80-85 percent of the global Muslim population. The minority Shīʿas, about 10-12 percent, differ profoundly with Sunnīs over the issue of community leadership. While Sunnīs hold that leadership is based on moral merit. Shīʿas maintain that it is handed down form the Prophet's family. Beyond this divergence there are other smaller groups such as the Ismaʿīlīs, a Shīʿa subdivision, and various movements and orders influenced by Sufi mystics. In modern times there have been other group developments including reform and liberation movements. At cultural levels tribal and racial affiliations continue to affect the umma ideal. In political affairs Islamic history is in part a long saga of disharmony, contention and open warfare.

Well-intentioned Muslims know that there have been and are today a host of theological, sociological and political disagreements among Muslims. They deplore them, but point out that the Qur'ān predicted that very development. They believe that the breakdown of human behavior does not lessen the validity of the theory. The theory is that Muslims are fundamentally held together by a common commitment and task. They may disagree internally, at times violently, but will come together and stick together in the face of a common foe. They are counseled to pray for the forgiveness of each other's sins, and to help one another:

> And the believers, men and women, are protecting friends one of another; they enjoin the right and forbid the wrong, and they establish worship and they pay the poor-due, and they obey Allah and His messenger. As for these, Allah will have mercy on them (9:72).

For their pattern the believers should look to what Muhammad did at Medina. There he created a new community that transcended tribal and personal divisions, and he himself provided a model for its life in his lenient treatment of former enemies. That achievement remains the constant ideal toward which Muslims are challenged to strive.

Despite everything, then, the community of Islam has a sacred quality for its members. It is derived from the sense of being chosen, the possession of God's final revelation, the replicable model of Muhammad's life, the noble example of early Muslims, a comprehensive code of law for righteous living, and the promises of God's blessing. The relationship of the *umma* with other religious communities is set in that context. This important question, together with the issue of leaving the *umma*, will be taken up in subsequent chapters. Muslims are to maintain a proper relation with other religious communities, but should always remain aware of their distinctive role and function to be a "central *umma*" in the world (2:134).

Key Principle Nine: Islam Is a Religion That Affirms Personal Equality within Limits

Islam may be called a religion of individual equality, but it is more accurate to say that it pursues equality as a goal. This satisfies the fact that at practical levels there are many inequalities among Muslims. Poor Muslims are obviously not equal to the rich. Kings and saints have high authority. Religious leaders seek to assert their power. Arab-blooded people maintain a certain status, and members of the Prophet's family receive special respect. Muslim women are struggling for their rights that they believe are being ignored. Despite these distinctions in principle Islam espouses equality within defined freedoms, and that espousal has been strong enough to produce a major impact on the life of Muslims.

We have noted that Islam is comprehensive, the law is prescriptive, and community feeling is strong. Do these overarching principles mean that the individual is lost to view? That conclusion would fail to discern the special blending of community and individual emphases in Islam. The principle of individual equality stands at the same level as other key principles, and conditions them. Thus, although Islam has to do with all life, it is the individual believer who determines what this means. Although the law is prescriptive, it also declares that major areas of life area a matter of personal discretion. Although community opinion is important, Muslims also maintain that no one person can lord it over others.

We will divide our treatment of the principle of equality into two areas. The first has to do with the bodily realm and the affairs of this life. In this area the principle of freedom is restrained. The second has to do with the spiritual realm where unrestrained equality is affirmed.

Muslims believe that in the realm of human life and human relations equality is an equilibrium of two characteristics given by God in creation: the aspect of freedom and the aspect of obligation. In a sense equality is the coinage of God minted in His creative act, but the coin has two sides. On the one hand human beings are created free and equal. That does not mean they are the same. The

Qur'ān says that if God had chosen to do so He could have made everyone identical. But He chose not to do so. Everyone is not the same. People are born with different personalities and abilities, and within differing situations. But they are free to develop their lives in their own way, slaves to God alone. This is one side of the coin. The other side is obligation. Personal freedom is not unlimited because every individual right is accompanied by an obligation. In developing his or her personal life an individual must remember the rights of God, the rights of other human beings, and the rights of creation itself. In short, the essence of the Muslim view of equality is individual freedom controlled by moral obligation to others. Muslims are to work out the implications of this balanced approach in economic, social and political spheres.

We take an illustration from the economic area. Individuals have the freedom to develop their own abilities, interests and life styles, but they are obliged to help the unfortunate. I have the right to make money, but I do not have the right to forget the poor. The Qur'ān speaks very harshly against greed, and commends generosity just as highly. Muhammad's life was a simple one, and he showed great hospitality to others. Muslims are therefore called upon to climb up from selfishness. "Ah, what will convey unto thee what the Ascent is!—(It is) to free a slave, and to feed in the day of hunger an orphan near of kin, or some poor wretch in misery. . ." (90:12-16).

We draw another example for the social realm. In recent years Muslims have come to western countries in large numbers. When there seem to be enough potential members, they establish mosques. It is quite common for Muslims of one nationality to attend one particular mosque, and it is their freedom to do so. Yet it is also their obligation to resist racism of any kind. Islam does not "see color," and racial distinctions are seldom visible, though not wholly absent. This was a major factor in the decision of a large number of black American Christians to accept Islam. The movement accelerated after 1964 when Malcolm X made the pilgrimage to Mecca where he experienced Islamic equality first-hand. It affected him profoundly. He cried out: "The brotherhood! The people of all races, colors, from all over the world, together as one! It has proved to me the power of the one God."[10]

In the social realm, however, specific restrictions on personal freedom are added to the general restraint of moral obligation. These restrictions govern especially family relationships, and are based on the idea of divine "orders of creation." On that basis certain governing patterns determine relations between husbands and wives, parents and children, as the Qur'ān spells out. In addition, the principle of equal rights is modified in matters related to wills, bequests, and witnesses in court. Muslim tradition has often extended the restrictions to other areas such as dress. Since the bulk of these regulations have to do with the status of women, some Muslims today view the limitations as time- or culture-bound, and believe that the basic principles of the Qur'ān itself require that they be given fresh interpretation.

We move to the spiritual realm where the principle of equality is unlimited. Every human being is individually created by God, personally responsible to God, and with equal access to God in prayer. It is the pilgrimage at Mecca that best symbolizes the principle of spiritual equality. The crowds surge around the central shrine together, as it were circling together around God. Then they face inward and without distinction at the same time and in the same way they bow before God in solemn surrender. The event is a foreshadowing of what will take place on the Judgment Day. There every man and woman will individually face the throne of God. The only distinction that God will recognize then is that of faith and works.

The principle of spiritual equality defines the Islamic theory of religious authority. The Qur'ān knows of no authority but that of God and that which God delegated to the Prophet Muhammad, and in the Sunnī view Muhammad in turn instituted no line of succession. If there is to be any competition among you, the Prophet said, let it be in piety! Thus Islam is egalitarian, with no priestly theory. No other person may stand between the individual and God. No one may dictate what a Muslim believes beyond the *shahāda* itself. You can be a Sunnī teacher, a Sufi mystic or a Shī'a scholar. You can go to Mecca, or if you prefer take a pilgrimage to a saint's tomb. You can join any religious movement you please. You can be a conservative or a liberal or a moderate of any combination. You are free to choose, and even the most autocratic of Islamic movements or states that attempt to impose a single vision on their citizens must fail in the end, simply because the stream of the equality principle runs deeply and powerfully.

In fact, as is well-known, Islam does have clergy ('ulamā'). Someone must lead the prayers, and on Fridays preach the sermon. Islam has religious scholars, often clergy. Someone must interpret the Qur'ān, and administer religious law. Quite paradoxically, the management of these functions has in the end produced a powerful clergy. This in turn has impacted on the realm of intellectual freedom. Muslim clerics give high place to the concept of imitation (*taqlīd*), the idea that the tradition of Islam should be faithfully observed and handed on. From the point of view of the orthodox clergy new thought or innovation (*bid'a*) was considered un-Islamic, and this stifled the free intellectual movement that marked early Islam. Nevertheless the principle of intellectual equality and freedom was never formally superseded, and in modern times it has come alive again.

The revival has been led by Muslim laity who desire reform, improvement and healthy change. They have reinvigorated the basic idea of the spiritual and intellectual equality of all believers. Utilizing what is called the right of private interpretation (*ijtihād*), they have breathed fresh air into Islam. In some cases, however, the revival has led to demagogic movements, bypassing the respect for community consensus maintained by orthodox clergy. For Muslims the search for equilibrium between the demands of freedom and obligation makes equality a pursuit as well as a principle.

Key Principle Ten: Islam Is a Religion of Striving and Struggle

And strive for Allah with the endeavor which is His right... He hath named you Muslims... that ye may be witnesses among mankind (22:78)

Strive...endeavor....witness. The words point to the fact that Muslims have a task in the world. They are to be for God and against evil. They are to be committed and determined in that mission, aggressive in opposing wrong, and enthusiastic for God's work. They are in a sense to migrate from the world of misdoing to the world of God's standards. The entire process is called jihād. The word stems from the root jahada which means to strive or to struggle. Recognizing the high importance of this function, some Muslims added it as the sixth pillar of Islamic behavior.

The principle of striving is divided into two elements: the effort to improve personal behavior, which is called the greater Jihād, and the struggle against public corruption, which is designated as the lesser jihād. The following illustration pictures the two sides of each:

Negative		Positive
1. Struggling against personal evil [the greater jihād]	and	1. living piously (taqwā)
2. Struggling against public evil [the lesser jihād]	and	2. building the umma (islāh) and promoting Islam (da'wa)

We turn first to the struggle against personal evil. Under the pressure of current events more attention has been given to public evil, but Islam is clear that the first thing to take care of is personal conduct. Every muslīm, i.e. everyone who formally surrenders to God must also become a mu'min, i.e. a faithful servant of God. Every born Muslim, in other words, must through his or her actions become a genuine one. This means viewing religion as something more than ritual behavior. The process begins with remembering the goodness of God and being grateful for His mercies. This inspires a believer to engage in moral and ethical struggle. The believer strives to overcome the negative tendencies in his/her makeup, and to resist the temptations of the world and the whispering of the devil. The Prophet Muhammad himself called this "the greater jihād."

The goal of the greater jihād is pious living in conformity with the divine will. That goal is summed up in the two words: taqwā (piety), and birr (righteousness). There are of course other closely connected terms such as justice, grace, kindness, affection, generosity and modesty, all commended by Islam. A Muslim is called upon to try to realize them in life. The law of Islam provides the framework for the struggle, but behind it is God's call to ethical obedience. The Qur'ān puts forth the challenge to believers to rise above mere ritual behavior to a God-fearing life in memorable words: (2:177)

> It is not righteousness that ye turn your faces to the East and the West, but righteous is he that believeth in Allah and the Last Day, and the angels and the Scriptures, and giveth his wealth for love of Him, to kinfolk and to orphans and the needy and the wayfarer, and to those who ask, and to set slaves free, and observeth worship and payeth the poor-due. And to those who keep their treaty when they make one, and the patient in tribulation and adversity and time of stress. Such are they who are sincere. Such are the God-fearing!

There is, however, also a public struggle against evil as well as a private one. We have noted that the whole of life should be submitted to God. That is an ideal not readily attained, and failure can be expected. But when corruption and oppression appear violently and systemically in high places, they must be opposed. This is called "the lesser jihād." How is this striving to be carried out? The *umma* is to be a witnessing community. With all the spiritual resources at its command, it is to speak out and work against evil. It is when evil is entrenched and threatening, particularly when it does violence against the religion of Islam, that the possible use of warfare must be admitted in defense of the faith. Classical Muslims viewed violence against fellow Muslims who are corrupt leaders as a last resort. The consensus developed that if such rulers allow Muslims to pray their oppressive behavior can be tolerated. In other words, Muslims can live under unjust governments without engaging in revolution. If non-Muslim enemies from the outside threaten Islamic faith the lesser jihād is a necessary action.

The admission of the possible use of violence to overcome public evil introduced the potential for the aggressive employment or even the perversion of the principle of the lesser jihād. In early Islam it was used, for example, as an argument for seizing the territories of non-Muslims. As time passed it became common thought to divide the world into two entities, the "house of Islam" and the "house of war." In other words, aggressive and militant action must be taken to change non-Muslim territory into an area that functions under Islamic law. That theory has now been set aside. In modern times Muslims have sought and found in the Qurʾān and in Islamic tradition more positive ground for healthy interreligious and international relations, including people of the book theory, the constitution of Mecca and consultative parliamentary theory.

Not only did the concept of the lesser jihād become subject to aggressive interpretations, but it also suffered from actual perversion. The perversion occurred in both the past and the present. In the past the abuse took place as part of the personal search for power that has been an ever-present factor in human history. Ruthless Muslim tyrants used the concept to foster their own drive for prestige and wealth; calling for holy war they heaped up the skulls of those who opposed their aspirations. In modern days the abuse of the concept is familiar through the actions of extremists and terrorists. In the name of jihād they seek support for a variety of personal agendas and attempt to justify mindless violence. The perversion became clear in such horrendous actions as the assassination of Anwar Sadat in Egypt in 1981 and in the destruction of the World Trade Center in New York in 2001.

Perhaps aware of the weakness of human nature Muslim legal scholars surrounded the application of the lesser jihād with a variety of conditions to assure that the warfare was indeed just and holy. Only the acknowledged leader of the united community of Islam could call for such an action. That right could not be assumed and exercised by any Muslim individual or group at will. The implementation of the just war must bring no harm to women and children, must abjure the destruction of nature, must avoid aggression against other protected religious communities, and above all must abstain form unnecessary cruelty. Substantially, they said, this kind of jihād must conform with the positive principles of Islam including piety and righteous behavior. It was in that light that a Muslim observer suggested that the real problem of Osama bin Laden was that he had failed to engage in the greater jihād, spiritual self-discipline. He and others like him ignore what the favored father of the Muslim revival, Ibn Taimiyya (d. 1328) declared: "God does not love evil."[11] Contemporary Muslims who are engaged in their review of the definition of evil and the methodology of struggle against it, are taking this idea as their basic clue.

The lesser jihād has its positive side for Muslims in the struggle for the uplift of the community and the faith. This takes the form of striving for internal reform (islāh) and external growth (da'wa). All over the world dedicated Muslims are contending for a reformed and revitalized Muslim community. The term islāh implies general welfare. Thus the reform activities are broad—schools, hospitals, job training programs, the uplift of women, and the modernization of clergy formation. Islam is being set forth as a progressive movement, supportive of modern developments, peaceful and interested in the well-being of others. For many the heart of the reform is a purified, lively and unified body of believers, and it is the duty of every believer to give some time, talent and financial support to the activity of encouraging fellow Muslims to deepen their spiritual commitments.

The call must also reach non-Muslims. The principle of striving has now also taken the form of a developing missionary movement. Islam has always commended the activity of witness. That explains why one-fifth of the world is Muslim, a remarkable increase for the tiny struggling community in Mecca. But that witness was basically the informal witness of life. Islam grew through travelers, business people, the influence of mystics, and intermarriage. Currently, however, individuals, societies and governments have begun to institutionalize the activity of mission through formal organizations and structures. The process is called da'wa, a summoning. In part it is a response to the Quranic emphasis on warning men and women. But in part it is also a response to the mission activities of others. As they strive and struggle for the good name and development of Islam Muslims hope "that men of understanding may take heed" (14:52).

Key Principle Eleven: Islam Is a Religion of Success

Striving. . .struggle. . .and success. Muslims believe that true religion and success go together. When the muezzin gives the call to prayer, the fifth phrase in his formula is "Come to success!" The word may be translated as prosperity or safety or happiness, or even salvation. Islam has a principle of success, and Muslims today a psychology of success. But how is success defined?

Until modern times Muslims tended to think of religious success in terms of the world to come. In this opinion they reflected the early preaching of the Prophet Muhammad. The vindication of Islam would become manifest in the last days. It is then that evil-doers will be consigned to the Fire and the faithful will receive their just reward, a better place. "Those will prosper who purify themselves. . . Nay (behold) ye prefer the life of this world. But the hereafter is better and more enduring" (87:16-17; Yusuf Ali).

Muslims certainly agree that Heaven is the better place, but their attention has shifted to success in this world. The topic of the next world has become somewhat marginal in conversation and writing. While still deeply imbedded in the Muslim consciousness, it is in the background. With this development the idea of success has changed. "Come to prosperity" is a promise related to life in this world as well as to a farther hope. Jamāl al-Dīn al-Afghanī (d. 1897), a father of the modern Muslim revival, made the point clear.

Let me repeat for you, reader, one more time, that unlike other religions Islam is concerned not only with the life to come. Islam is more: it is concerned with believers' interests in the world here below and with allowing them to realize success in this life as well as peace in the next life. It seeks "good fortune in two worlds."[12]

Many Muslims hold that his interpretation is in the spirit of the Qur'ān. It states in regard to those who fear God: "For them are good things in the life of this world, and in the future too" (10:65; Palmer). It further declares: "Successful indeed are the believers who are humble in their prayers..." (23:11). The translation by Yusuf Ali makes the point very clear: "The believers must (eventually) win through." In common Muslim perspective the prospect of success in this world is also logical for two reasons. The first is that Islam is under God, and therefore must be successful. The second is that Islam is pragmatically well geared to human capacities and requirements, and therefore it can be successful.

Historical developments have something to do with this conviction. From the close of the Islamic Golden Age in the 1200's, to March 1938 when oil well #1 gushed out in Saudi Arabia, the heartlands of Islam were in a kind of limbo. For centuries the cry had been: "Where is God?" The discovery of black wealth signaled that God was smiling on the *umma* again. Not only economic factors were improving. Success included the political liberation of Muslim nations after World War II. It was revealed by the numerical increase of Islam. And it was celebrated in the accomplishments of individual Muslims, from boxing champions to Nobel Prize winners. While suffering and sorrow continue to affect Muslims in many parts of the world, the increasing well-being warms the hearts of believers with the thought that the glories of the Muslim past will be repeated.

That Islam and Muslims will be successful finds it visible form and proof in the experience of the Prophet Muhammad and the early Muslims. They were a weak and unpretentious group. Harassed and mistreated, they were compelled to observe the humiliation of their leader and forced to flee. The change from gloom to prosperity for the first Muslims came after the hijra, the emigration from Mecca to Medina. The change was dramatic and brought far-reaching results. There in Medina the religion of Islam was established, a state was formed, Muslims overcame their enemies, and individuals became prosperous. By the time of the death of the Prophet Arabia was Muslim, and in the next century it became a world religion. Looking back Muslims believe that what happened then can happen again, and is happening now. "Lo! Is it not Allah's party who are the successful?" (58:22).

The principle of anticipated success carries over into the lives of individual Muslims as well as to the community as a whole. Personal success, however, is very strongly linked with the spiritual dimension—fearing God, striving for the good, keeping duty. The best provision is to be God-fearing, for God is "the best of providers." Success rests on the condition that we remember God, for then God will remember us. When God saved the family of Lot, God said: "We reward him who giveth thanks" (54:34). Remember your blessings! Remember your blessings! The refrain runs through the Qur'ān, and is backed up by the recitation of God's providential care.

> Unto Him belongeth whatsoever is in the heavens and the earth, and religion is His forever. Will ye then fear any other than Allah? And whatever comfort [blessing] ye enjoy, it is from Allah! (16:52-53).

The Qur'ān notes how material and social blessings cause people to forget God. Perceptive Muslims today can see how success produces selfishness and materialism. They are calling Muslims back to the spiritual bases of success, the idea that the blessings of this world must be hallowed by gratitude to God, and by the spirit of 'ibādat, service to God. They fear that the seduction of the golden calf (20:90ff.) is being repeated as it has been in the Christian world. Muslims are being warned about the danger of allowing the prosperity of life, real or hoped for, to distract them from the life of God. "Allah is not unaware of what you do. . .(Consigned to doom) are those who obey the life of the world at the price of the Hereafter. Their punishment will not be lightened, neither will they have support" (82:86). With that warning the wheel of reality turns. The Day of Judgment indeed will be the final revealer of true success.

Key Principle Twelve: A Mystical Sense of the Perfection of Islam

Our final principle needs only a brief statement. Muslims share a deep sense of the perfection of Islam. The feeling is a mixture of faith, emotion and mystique. Within heart and mind Muslims harbor a quiet feeling of pride, the conviction that Islam is the best religion and the umma is the best of communities. Though others may make a similar claim, they are confident that Islam in incomparable. They are satisfied with God and His religion.

What about the obvious problems of Islam that have been there from the beginning? It is clear that what is common to all humans is also common to Muslims. The forces of evil are constantly invasive, and there are some who have done great wrong in the past, and are doing so in the present also. In the face of this empirical imperfection, how can there be such confidence? Muslims deal with this sober reality in three ways. Some choose to ignore it. Some romanticize the facts. The bulk of Muslims today, however, are honest and realistic. They recognize the weakness of Muslims, but have a response. They say, "Yes, we Muslims are bad, but Islam is good." Again and again that statement is reiterated. For Muslim believers Islam is beautiful and has the grace of perfection. Muslims may misbehave, but their misbehavior cannot annul its excellence. Does not the Word of God, the Qur'ān say: "Surely true religion with God is Islam?" (3:19).

There are various factors that contribute to building up Muslim pride and satisfaction. One is the sense of the finality of Islam. The last and greatest of God's mercies it is therefore implicitly matchless. An important ingredient is the cultivated tradition and habits of Islam, centered in mosque and madrasa, worship and education, which gives order to life and produces serenity. The mutual encouragement of those who maintain that Islam is the most practical religion for life in this world has its own psychological effect. A factor that thrills is the rehearsal of the exploits of the saints and heroes of Islam. But perhaps the crucial element is the focused Muslim practice of recalling to mind the goodness of God, manifested in the giving of rain that produces the beauty of the earth or in the giving of the family joys that make our existence joyful. God's mercy is revealed in the way He has remembered His people. Islam is good. *Al-hamdu lilah!*

In the end, however, the mystical sense of the perfection of Islam is a matter of faith that is not susceptible to analysis or explanation. In faith Muslims feel that way about their *dīn*, their religion. Their emotion was summed up long ago by one of the great saints of Islam, Hasan al-Basrī, who said: "Am I not a Muslim? My face is ever turned toward God!"

A Preliminary Christian Reflection

A Christian, and certainly Christians interested in sharing the gospel, will view the principles of Islam with interest. They will note the overlaps and parallels as well as the contrasts with Christian thought, as well as sense the interrelatedness and dynamism of the world view that they represent. In dealing with them the Christian will have at least four choices, not mutually exclusive. One can ignore the principles. One can debate them. One can learn from them. One can take them into account in the task of sharing the gospel.

We may quickly lay aside the first option of ignoring what is before us. Someone may argue that what Muslims believe does not matter because in the communication of the gospel we are sharing something new. However, if what Muslim friends care about does not concern Christians, the reverse will ordinarily be the case, and that gospel message will not matter to Muslims. It will tend to be viewed as something irrelevant, as a curiosity, or even as a form of enmity. The second and third possibilities need careful consideration, and there will be a variety of opinion about them. The fourth option—the importance of taking the principles into imaginative account in the task of sharing—will draw little disagreement.

An imaginative account-taking will first of all be self-critical and self-challenging. The treatment that we have given above to the principles of Islam has been necessarily bare and skeletal. They need expansion. Moreover Muslims themselves might state things differently, adding or subtracting, correcting or re-phrasing, improving the material from their point of view. We are challenged to a deeper ·understanding. A logical path for that is to engage with Muslim friends in dialogical converse.

A second aspect of imaginative account-taking will be felt immediately. It is the need for a deeper understanding of the Christian faith. Christians may not wish to follow the path of stating principles. They are more accustomed to thinking of a Person from whom principles flow, rather than thinking of principles per se. The Master said, "Follow me," not "frame a philosophy." Nevertheless there are in fact key Christian ideas that need to be explored in the light of Muslim affirmations, and Muslims will want to know some of them.

The third element in imaginative account-taking follows on the first two. It is certainly the most important and challenging one for Christians sharing, and that is to develop the capacity to integrate ideas in such a way that Muslims can relate to them, so that Muslims can grasp the meaning of Christ and the gospel within their own context. That task is demanding because it implies that ideas be inter-related in a way that is fair to both, in a way that is loyal to the Christian conviction and task, and in a way that is productive for the movement of the Spirit. While there is much truth in the common saying that to share the gospel is a simple act, and while that truth applies to Muslims also, the element of simplicity can be overstated. We must minimally examine ourselves as to how well Christians have taken the gospel into the Muslim thought world where alone it becomes sensible to Muslim believers.

This approach, it appears, was St. Paul's, reflected by his famous message to the Greek thinkers at Athens. What he did there was only one example of the incarnational aspect of his witness. The apostle who said, "Woe unto me if I preach not the gospel" was also remarkably adept at really conveying it. Conveyance is taking something to its intended place. "Woe unto me if I convey not the gospel!" The key principles of Islam help to show us where the gospel must go.

There is a caution to be borne in mind as we strive to take some of the pivotal Muslim emphases into our consideration. It is simply that Islam and its teachings belong to Muslims, and constitute their sacred treasure. In dealing with what Muslims believe and do, a Christian therefore walks into someone else's sacred space. Kenneth Cragg entitled one of his well-known volumes *Sandals at the Mosque*.[13] The title reminds us of the custom of taking off our shoes when we enter someone else's home or sanctuary. We put tags saying "Handle With Care! Fragile!" on material things. In matters of the spirit we can hardly be less concerned. The discussion of the principles of others must be a principled one. The caution underlines the necessity of sharing as friends, for it is only when ideas travel across the bridge of friendship that they are conveyed to the other and given their due.

With these thoughts as our background let us move to a more thorough examination of the Muslim view of sin and salvation.

Endnotes

1 I am indebted to Edwin E. Calverly for the phrase "key principles for understanding Islam;" cf. his *Islam. An Introduction* (Cairo: American University, 1958), pp. 19–21. Calverly argued in favor or four key ideas, the most important being "totalitarian." I prefer a wider range of principles.

2 *Ibid.*, p. 62; quoted from Jawāhir al-Qur'ān (Cairo, 1329), p. 29.

3 In Part One of this study, which deals with Muslim views, I will follow the Islamic practice of referring to the divine being with a masculine pronoun.

4 Sheikh al-Jerrahi al-Halvēli, *The Most Beautiful Names* (Putney, Vt.: Threshold Books, 1985), pp. 143–63.

5 Hassan b. Thabit, in A. Guillaume, tr., *The Life of Muhammad. A Translation of Ibn Ishāq's Sirāt Rasūl Allāh* (Lahore: Oxford University Press, 1967) p. 798.

6 Fazlur Rahman, *Islam* (New York: Doubleday & Co., Inc,. 1968), p. 75.

7 Isamil Faruqi, *Tawhīd* (Plainfield, Ind.: International Federation of Islamic Students, 1983), p. 143.

8 Guillaume, *Muhammad*, p. 651.

9 John A. Williams, tr., *Themes of Islamic Civilization* (Los Angeles: University of California Press, 1971), pp. 16f.; quoted from Al-Ghazālī's *Ihyā*.

10 *The Autobiography of Malcolm X. As Told to Alex Haley* (New York: Ballantine Books, 1964), p. 338.

11 "Commanding the Good and Forbidding the Evil," quoted in Kenneth Cragg and Marston Speight, *Islam from Within* (Belmont, Calif.: Wadsworth Pub. Co., 1980), p. 114.

12 Al-Afghanī, "Islamic Solidarity," *Political and Social Writings of Sayyid Jamāl al-Dīn al-Afghanī*, tr. and ed. by Nikki R. Keddie, in J. Donohue and J. L. Esposito, eds., *Islam in Transition* (New York: Oxford University Press, 1982), p. 23.

13 Kenneth Cragg, *Sandals at the Mosque* (London: SCM Press, 1953); Cragg says: "....The fine art of knowledge is the fine art of wise inquiry" (p. 27).

The Muslim View of Sin

In the Christian view the gospel has to do with the crucial issues of sin and salvation. Yet we look in vain for those topics among the key Islamic principles. They lurk in the background, but are not lifted up. Thus the "and" in the title "Muslims and the Gospel" becomes all-important. Its significance is that the connection must be made.

In reality, there is a great common denominator in the world, named sin. Whatever the opinion about its cause or cure, no one can deny its factuality, both universal and destructive. Muslims recognize it. In the next two chapters we will therefore deal with the Islamic concepts of sin and salvation in their particular form. We will note the variations that determine the core content of Christian sharing, but we begin with the commonality. The problem is expressed by the prayer of a North African saint name Sheikh Idris al-Sansui (d. 1859). In distress over his sinfulness he uttered the following plea to Almighty God:[1]

> Allahumma, it is from Thee that I seek help, so help me. ... O Succourer of those who seek help [I am] the anxious one at Thy door. O Thou who dost uncover the grief of all the grief-stricken, I am the one who has rebelled against Thee. O Thou who dost seek those who seek forgiveness, [I am] the one who stands constantly at Thy door. O Thou who dost forgive sinners, [I am] the one who is submissive at Thy door. O Most Merciful of those who show mercy, [I am] the guilty one at Thy door. O Lord of mankind, [I am] the evil-doer at Thy door, the unhappy one, the humble one at Thy door. Have mercy upon me, O my Lord. ... O my God, security, security on the Day when a call will come from the midst of the Throne; "Where are the rebellious? Where are the sinful? Where are those who went astray? Let them come to the reckoning. ...!

Allahumma! I am thy wicked, sinful servant. Save me from the Fire. ...
O Most Merciful of those who show mercy! O best of helpers! O most
wonderful of forgivers! Allah alone is my sufficiency.

Not all Muslims will express such profound sensitivity to their spiritual condition. Some Muslim believers would rather not dwell on the problem because it
seems insoluble. They are aware of the reality but do not want to be disturbed by
it. Others are really not interested in the subject at all, and give it scant attention.
Pious Muslims, however, have no trouble in relating to the petitions of Sheikh
Ahmed. His vivid words reflect their own understanding of the Qur'ān that is full
of references to sins and their punishment.

In this chapter we will discuss the Muslim view of human nature beginning with
creation, which is the controlling factor in the doctrine; the Qur'ānic treatment of
sins; the need for accountability in view of the judgment, and contrition; as well as
later Muslim reflections on sin ranging from the legal stream to current thought.
We close with some notes on Christian sharing. But first we point to three caution
flags that Christians must be aware of as they approach these topics.

A. Observing the Caution Signals

Despite the commonality of the problems of sin and salvation Christians must
resist the natural temptation to interpret Muslim views through the Christian lens.
There are three specific caution flags to be raised. The first is that the theology of
sin and salvation is not a first-order topic for Muslims today. The second is that
the words "sin" and "salvation" have distinct Islamic connotations. The third has
to do with the broad diversity of Muslim opinion in regard to these topics, and the
fact that the ideas themselves are evolving and taking new shape.

The First Caution

The idea that sin and salvation are not number one topics may come as a shock
to a Christian. Nevertheless it is true that Muslims are not engaged with these
issues as intensely as Christians are. If a Muslim were writing an article entitled
"Muslim Sharing with a Christian Friend," the author would not take sin and salvation as the lead subjects. What a Muslim might mention first would be the Reality
of God; God's unity and authority; Muhammad as God's final messenger and our
example; and the importance of surrendering to God and obeying the commands
laid down in the Qur'ān and the law. These core themes are summed up in the
word 'ibādat, the worship and service of God. The writer would talk about 'ibādat.
Sin and salvation are related subjects, but they do not constitute the focus of the
Muslim concern.

What we have stated is the "the great tradition" of Islam. There are circles of
thought in Islam where sin and salvation are more prominent. Muslim saints such
as Sheikh Ahmed often express a deep consciousness of the tragedy of sin. Muslim
mystics express their longing to draw near to God, a form of salvation thinking.
Shī'a Muslims in their devotions frequently refer to the saving intercession of
their fallen and hallowed hero Husain, the grandson of Mohammad. The average
everyday Muslim, however, is not preoccupied with the issues of sin and salvation.

The majority of orthodox religious scholars reflect this phenomenon, paying some attention to sin but little to salvation. Modernist thinkers do not greatly differ. Thus, for example, when Fazlur Rahman listed his Qur'anic thought chain, he selected the following key terms: "Creation—preservation—guidance—judgment, all as manifestations of mercy."[2] Sin and salvation are conspicuous by their absence. As we indicated in the first chapter on key principles in Islam human history is consequential, but the consequences are not taken up under the paradigm of sin and salvation.

On the other hand these issues do constitute the central focus for Christians. Christian sharing with Muslims therefore involves bridging the focus gap. That need takes us to the second caution.

The Second Caution

This caution has to do with the meaning of terms and the connection of ideas. As to terms, the content of the Islamic words for sin and salvation is molded and colored by the larger context of Muslim thought. Sin is an unlawful action and not a condition, and salvation in Islam is escape from the consequences of bad actions and not the altering of a condition. As to connection, the relation of the two terms sin and salvation is not the same in Islam as it is in the Christian faith. For Muslims they are not so closely linked because both the human problem and its solution are viewed differently. As we shall see, the potential for sin is an aspect of God's creation and is regarded as a necessary tool in the workshop of humanity's moral development. Salvation for most Muslims—although change is affecting the view—has to do with a future escape to Paradise to be determined on the Day of Judgment. The connection between sin and salvation is there, but it has a quite different nature.

The Third Caution

The third caution is that there are many differing ideas current in Islam about these topics. There is no official teaching on sin and salvation, and they are regarded as "open" subjects. A Christian sharing with a Muslim friend cannot assume that the friend represents some mandatory view. Rather one needs to find out what the friend believes. There are general patterns that are constant, but the individual quality of Muslim faith must be given full weight. What an orthodox Muslim theologian in the al-Azhar seminary in Cairo, Egypt, or a mystically inclined Muslim in Java, or a marxist Muslim in Bengal, or a liberation fighter in Palestine, or a modernized intellectual in France, or a Mawdudi-influenced student in the U.S.A. believe about salvation may vary dramatically. Moreover Muslim views are in a state of flux. The various intellectual movements permeating Islam affect sin and salvation thinking. For some Muslims the topic of sin has moved from the level of legal regulation to a deeper ethical level. The subjects of injustice in society and half-heartedness in personal piety are entering into sin discussion. Similarly the use of the term salvation is becoming more common, especially in connection with this-worldly improvements. Under the circumstances a dialogical approach to Christian sharing is unavoidable.

The key factor in the Muslim view of sin is the understanding of human nature, and we turn to that issue first.

B. The Muslim View of Human Nature

1. The Starting-Point

Four elements involved in a discussion of sin are God's character and will, the created nature of human beings, the directives and warnings of sacred scripture, and the actual behavior of people. Our emphasis will fall on the second element that provides the basis from which Muslims view the issue.

God is involved for the Muslim, but not in the way that the Christian expects. A Christian might start the discussion of sin with the nature of God. What is God's own character like, and what therefore does God expect of us humans? In the Christian view holiness and love are primary characteristics in God, and therefore God also expects human beings to be holy and loving. "Ye shall be holy, for I the Lord your God am holy" (Lev 19:2). "God is love, and he that dwells in love dwells in God, and God in him (1 Jn 4:16).

Muslims, however, do not begin with God's character but God's command. As we have seen they prefer not to expound on God's nature, which is regarded as a mystery. That discussion is deemed inappropriate. What is important is God's will, and this in turn means God's commands to His servants. It is God's command that determines what is good and sinful, and God is free to command whatever God desires. This point of view explains the debate among Muslim thinkers over the question of whether things become right because God orders them, or whether God orders them because they are right. The majority of scholars agreed that things become good and evil because God commands or forbids them. They took this position in order "to protect" God's absolute sovereignty. No principle, even though it seems right to human beings, can be declared incumbent on God. That would place something, some human conception, above God. To say that God is so and so is to imply that God is not the opposite; but that won't do because it would limit God's authority, and reduce God's power and freedom. Be satisfied with God's command, which of course was identified with the revelation of the Qur'ān, and later with various interpretations of scholars.

While this was the majority view in Islamic history there was always a minority that protested it on the grounds that it makes God's will arbitrary and does not accurately reflect the Qur'ān. They argued that God in fact is moral, and therefore commands only just and moral things. Quite a number of Muslims today prefer that view and are now speaking of the nature of God. Fazlur Rahman, for example, declares that ultimate reality "is conceived in Islam as merciful justice."[3] A startling personal experience reinforces the point. It came in a public dialogue with a Canadian Muslim scholar in Minnesota in 1991. The latter (Professor Badawi) displayed in outline the Muslim understanding of God and the relation of God to humans, with the help of an overhead slide. The first two characteristics the learned scholar assigned to Allah were holiness and love! While this world of thought is still the exception rather than the rule, it reveals that the Muslim understanding of sin is taking on new dimensions that have great significance for Christian sharing.

For Muslims, however, it is not the question of what God is like, but rather it is God's creation of human nature, and what God requires of humans, that constitutes the heart of the discussion. The question is—how are we formed, with what intention, and with what capacity? Two simple points need to be made to summarize the Muslim consensus on the answers:

> By God's creation a person has a double endowment, a tendency to good and a tendency to evil; this being the case,

> Human nature today is exactly what God always intended it to be.

We will therefore turn to the Islamic tradition of the creation of humanity as the appropriate beginning point for the Muslim teaching concerning human nature.

2. The Creation of Human Beings

The idea that God is Creator is a central motif in Islamic thought. "He is God, the Creator, the Maker, the Fashioner" (59:24; Palmer). It is God who brought the world and humanity into existence, and He is therefore rightly named "the Lord of the Worlds." The Qur'anic account of the creation of the universe and humanity resembles the Biblical account, with significant variations.

According to the Qur'ān God created the world out of nothing, doing it with His powerful and commanding Word: "BE!" He created the heavens and the earth in six days (there is no seventh day), assigning seven levels to each. In correct proportion, quantity and term God added the various elements of nature. The Creator made all things good that He created, and therefore "all that is in the heavens and the earth glorifieth Allah" (64:1).

Then God turned His attention to the creation of humanity. He first made man, Adam, and later his mate from a common soul. He made the human form of material substances including earth and water. The Qur'ān emphasizes the "clayness" of humanity—potter's clay, clinging clay, black mud, as if to stress the humbleness of human origins. Yet despite the fact that humans are only mortal clay God bestows great dignity on His creatures by endowing them with a spiritual constitution. The final act of creation came, the Qur'ān says, when God "breathed into him of His Spirit" (32:9).

What moved God to create humanity is hidden in the mystery of God's will. There is no mystery, however, in what God expects from humans. People are to fear God, to praise and worship Him; to have faith, to remember God, to give Him thanks; and, not least, to serve God. The final phrase points to the essential factor in creaturehood. "I have not created jinn and mankind except to serve me" (51:56; Arberry). There is no suggestion that humans were to have fellowship with God. Nor are they intended to be immortal. the Qur'ān declares: "We have appointed immortality for no mortal before thee. ... Every soul must taste of death" (21:34–35).

In the creation account Muslims perceive the two essential elements of human nature—earthiness and spirituality. There is in human beings an inclination to lowliness on the one hand, and to godliness on the other. Earth pulls down, spirit lifts up. The story of human development is the tale of the working out of this in-built, created tension. It is the critical factor in the Muslim doctrine of sin. Ali Shariati (d. 1977), a prominent Iranian thinker, has vividly portrayed this inherent conflict. Man, he says, is a "choice," a struggle, a constant becoming. "He is an infinite migration within himself from clay to God."[4] Elsewhere he pictures the inevitable ongoing struggle of a human being as a conflict between Cain and Abel. This is God's endowment to every human being. What gives human beings "the best stature" (95:4) making them a little "higher" than angels, is the reality of moral struggle.

The spiritual side of human nature, the inclination to good, is pointed to in a number of ways in Islamic thinking. The fact that God reminds people of His commands through prophets and revelation is an indicator of human responsibility and the capacity to respond. Also in the act of creation a human being is given the vocation to be God's deputy (khalifa) on earth. To go along with that assignment every person is given an inner fitra, a "direction" toward God, a natural desire and ability to surrender to God and do God's will. The Qur'an says: "Set thy face steadfastly towards the religion as a hanif [one who turns from polytheism to one God, ed.], according to the fitra whereon God has constituted man" (30:29). Although the word conscience is not used in the Qur'ān it is implied in the fitra. Vocation and conscience! Direction and capacity! Al-Ghazali referred to this bright side of men and women as "the angelic heart" (qalb) of the human. The angelic heart is the source of a person's positive religion, every individual by creation and birth being a natural Abel, able to surrender to God.

There is the other side of human nature, however, the dark side. It is also very much a part of an individual's created nature. Human beings are constituted with frailty as well as nobility, with weakness as well as strength, with the capacity and potential for sinfulness as well as for piety. In Muslim opinion this created tension was necessary to ensure human responsibility and the ability to grow morally. Therefore the contradictory extremes of human nature are "not so much a 'problem' to be resolved by theological thought, as tensions to be 'lived with' if man is to be truly 'religious,'" i.e., a servant of God. It is the 'God-given' framework for human action."[5] What must be added to this clear statement is that in the Muslim perspective within this framework God mercifully cooperates with people by giving them guidance and by forgiving behavioral lapses.

Thus what Islam teaches is original human frailty going back to God's act of creation, not original sin going back to Adam's failure. The Qur'ān, in describing this original frailty, declares that humans were created with a "hastiness" of spirit and with the tendency to pray for evil things as much as for the good (17:11). They were formed with an inborn impatience that makes them fitful and niggardly (70:19). In fact, as Joseph (Yusuf) said to Pharaoh: "Lo! the soul enjoins to evil" (12:53). As a consequence humans are created "in trouble," i.e., destined for struggle (90:4). This might appear to be unkind on the part of God if it were not for the fact that God measures His commands against natural human capacities. The divine commands are strict enough to challenge human moral abilities, but they are not beyond attainment. The Qur'ān declares: "Allah would make the burden light for you, for man was created weak" (4:28).

The bipolar created nature of human beings sets the stage for moral struggle. Most Muslims tend to take an optimistic view of that process. It is assumed that given the right conditions, and in the light of the fact that the divine commands are geared to human ability, the good that a person can do will outweigh the evil. Others like Mohammed Fadhel Jamali, however, objectively analyze the spiritual dilemma that is implicit in this situation, without diluting its difficulty. Jamali (b. 1903), a distinguished Iraqi statesman and twice the prime minister of his nation, who signed the Charter of the United Nations on its behalf, lost favor when a revolution overthrew the monarch in 1958, and he was condemned to death by a military tribunal. Freed as the result of intense international pressure he became Professor of Philosophy of Education at the University of Tunis. Jamali wrote a series of spiritual letters to his son while in prison. One of them provides a balanced statement of the moral tension involved in the Islamic concept of human nature. He declares:

> Allah, glory to Him, with His wisdom, kindly gave to man mind and guidance on the one hand, and, on the other side inflicted man with the devil who tempts him and deceives him and leads him to disobedience and sin. And Allah ... warned man of the wiles of the devil and laid on him the responsibility for protecting himself from those evils. Allah also ... inflicted the human soul with many defects and put on man's shoulders the responsibility for making up for them. ... But men did not take this trust seriously, and, by his injustice and ignorance, he did not honor his trust. The struggle within self, then, between the forces of good and the forces of evil continues, and blessed is he in whose soul the mercy of Allah and His guidance dominate.[6]

The story of Adam's fall indicates the severity of the moral tension within human beings.

3. The Fall of Adam and His Wife

The story of Adam's fall is found in four places in the Qur'ān.[7] The following is summary of its narrative that also involves a fallen angel, Iblis (= Satan).

According to the Qur'anic account the angels objected to God's plan to create a human being. They predicted that people will only do harm on earth. God told them, "Surely I know what you do not," and went ahead with the creation plan. The crucial moment came when God commanded the angels "to prostrate before Adam." All obeyed except one name Iblis (*diabolos*, devil). Pride was the reason, but Ibis argued that it was not right to ask him to bow before a mortal made of mud. "I am better than he is. You created me of fire." His pride was equivalent to unbelief so God said, "Get out! You are cursed." Iblis asked for a reprieve until the Day of Resurrection. God granted the request, but then Ibis declared war against humanity to get even for what he claimed was God's responsibility. He promised that he would disguise himself and pervert humanity. "I shall lurk in ambush. I shall come upon them from every side. Most of them will not be thankful to You." God ended the matter by banishing Iblis. "Surely I will fill hell with all of you." To

Adam God said that he and his wife were to live in the Garden where they could enjoy all of its fruits except one tree, "lest ye become wrong-doers."

In Muslim interpretation it was probable that Adam would fall at some time as every human will because of natural frailty. Adam's fall, however, was hastened by the temptation of Satan. Satan approached Adam and his wife pretending to be a sincere advisor. He whispered, "Don't you realize you are naked?" Then he openly went on the attack. "God does not want you to approach that tree because eating its fruit will make you angelic and immortal, and will give you great power." Adam forgot what God had told him, and together he and his wife gave in to the temptation. One result of their disobedience was that they discovered their nakedness and tried to cover it. God called to them: "Did I not warn you that Satan is your enemy?" Adam then admitted that they had committed an error, describing it as one against themselves. They confessed: "Our Lord! We have wronged ourselves. If thou forgive us not and have not mercy on us, surely we are of the lost!" (7:23). There is no suggestion in the narrative that God was wounded by their action, but the life of the first humans was decisively affected. Adam and his wife lost their happy state and were ordered out of the Garden as their punishment. While they could live on the earth and enjoy its provisions, a shadow had descended over their future: "One of you a foe to the other" was the prediction.

Nevertheless God the Relenting and the Merciful did not let the matter rest there. God intervened with a "saving" promise. Its nature is crucial for our topic:

> We said: Go down, all of you, from hence; but verily there cometh unto you from Me a guidance; and whoso followeth My guidance there shall no fear come upon them, neither shall they grieve. But they who disbelieve, and deny Our revelations such are rightful owners of the Fire (2:38-39).

The good news following Adam's fall was the promise of divine guidance to come. As for clothing—let people remember, God says, that the best clothing is the garment of a God-fearing attitude. "The raiment of restraint from evil, that is the best" (7:26). Thus at the beginning of human history Islam received its shape as the religion of divine guidance and the pious human response.

It should be noted that the sin of Adam and his wife, whom later Islamic tradition calls Eve, was their own. It had negative results for them—exile from the Garden. It did not, however, imply a break in the human relationship with God. It did not result in death which is part of the natural human lot. And its effect was not passed on to anyone else, except as a bad example. Their error remained their own, but it serves as a warning to later generations. It reminds people that the call to be obedient to God involves moral struggle, and the certainty of some failure. But that leads us to the fact of sin.

C. The Troubling Fact of Sin

I. The Movement from Weakness to Sins

How does the weakness of human nature get translated into sin? Bauru Kateregga, a Kenyan Muslim, argues that is not actually inevitable. It is possible to avoid sinning. He says: "Sin is acquirable, but not innate, and therefore if man rightly uses those special qualities which he has been endowed with, he can easily avoid sin. Sin is not inevitable because man is not sinful."[8] Despite this optimism everyone sins. According to the Islamic analysis what are the chief factors?

In the Qur'anic analysis of Adam's sin there is a suggestion of a rebellious spirit in humanity. "And Adam rebelliously disobeyed his Lord, so went astray" (20:21). The Qur'ān also warns that whosoever "rebelliously disobeys Allah and His messenger" (72:23) will be punished. Nevertheless, it is not rebellion but forgetfulness that holds the field in the Qur'ān. It pictures human beings as constantly forgetting God, His mercy and will. This is astonishing considering the fact that God's signs are everywhere. Yet even in the Garden, with all its natural testimony to God's power and providence, Adam forgot. "Verily We have made a covenant of old with Adam, but He forgot, and We found no constancy in him" (20:115). Adam is considered to be a prophet in Islam. If he suffered from inconstancy, it is not surprising that it is a constant factor in the human condition. Because of it God has to go on reminding people through prophets and revelations, and then people remember again, at least for a while. The emphasis on forgetfulness is a factor in the distinction frequently made between prideful rebellion that produces great sins, and inadvertent mistakes or light sins that are easily forgiven. The sinner is exhorted by the Qur'ān to pray: "Condemn us not if we forget or miss the mark" (2:286).

The second aspect in the movement from weakness to sins is the activity of Satan. We have seen Satan's role in Adam's fall. He continues the same whispering and beguiling of humans down to the present day. The Qur'ān therefore explicitly exhorts believers to seek God's aid in withstanding the wily foe. The last chapter of the Qur'ān is given over to this warning:

> Say: I seek refuge in the Lord of mankind,
> The King of mankind,
> The God of mankind,
> From the evil of the sneaking whisperer,
> Who whispers in the hearts of mankind ... (114:1–5).

You should seek help now. On the last Day when it becomes evident that Satan has led many astray, it will be too late. God will remind sinners of his warnings and say, "O ye in sin, get ye apart this day!" (36:59–62). Some secularized Muslims may think of Satan only in terms of the "forces of evil." In folk Islam Satan means active and often evil spirits that must be exorcized. For the majority in the middle Satan is a personal being who encourages evil and distresses humanity. For pilgrims at Mecca they are reminded of him in a powerful ritual moment at Mina where they pelt three ancient pillars with small stones declaring: "In the Name of the Almighty I do this, and in the hatred of the devil and his shame." At that moment Satan becomes very real.

2. The Qurʾān Names and Condemns Sins

Al-Jīlānī (d. 1166), one of the most well-known Muslim saints, prayed to God "that Thou wilt forgive this urgent soul, this anxious heart which cannot bear the heat of Thy sun; how then will it bear the heat of Thy Fire."[9] What helped produce this prayer was *al-Jīlānī's* spiritual awareness that came from his reading of the Qur'ān.

The Qur'ān takes sin very seriously indeed. No matter that the natural constitution of a man or woman makes their sinning unavoidable. That does not lessen the evil of those actions or soften their consequences. There are as many as 43 separate terms for evil and sin in the scripture, and in no uncertain language it condemns persistent sinners. Pride and corruption; wickedness and impiety; lust and pollution; weakness, immoderation, and disease; slipping and erring; rebelliousness and concealment; deceit and hypocrisy—like a waterfall cascading down the verbal expressions for sin overflow the reader of the Qur'ān.

We will cite seven words that bear much of the weight of the teaching, recognizing that they overlap in meaning. They are: evil, darkness, wrong-doing, error, offence, disobedience, and transgression. The two foundational terms are evil and darkness, which are used 475 times.

a. *Evil (sā'a)*: The word abounds throughout the Qur'ān in several forms. Although Satan is involved with *sā'a*, it refers especially to the evil that humans do. Shame, vileness, and malice join the base meaning of iniquity. God is the only hope for its resolution, for on the Resurrection Day the load of sinners will be heavy. "Ah!, *sā'a* is that which they bear" (16:25).

b. *Darkness (zulm)*: This is the most frequently used term. Darkness produces ignorance, and that becomes deliberate wrong-doing. The concept is strongly related to corporate evil, the failure of nations and peoples to acknowledge the Almighty and turn to Him. In its various forms it carries with it the ideas of overstepping bounds, of acting unjustly and oppressively. "Their habitation is the Fire, and helpless the abode of the *zulm*-doers" (3:151).

The following five terms are more specific, and are used 160 times in the Qur'ān:

c. *Wrong (dhanb)*: The word is commonly used for a single act of transgression. It expresses all forms of unbelief, and the wrong actions that proceed from them. This includes the non-acceptance of God's signs. Unbelievers are exhorted to seek pardon for their lack of faith: "Our Lord! Lo! We believe. So forgive us our *dhanb*" (3:16).

d. *Error (khatī'a)*: The term has the connotation of deliberate sin, and is frequently used in theological writing in that sense. Intentional sin has the effect of creating an atmosphere, a condition. The Qur'ān advises: "Nay, whosoever has done evil his (*khatī'a*) surrounds him; such are the rightful owners of the Fire" (2:81). At its root the word has the idea of stumbling and missing the mark.

e. *Offence (ithm)*: The wide-ranging word implies a wrong attitude toward others, and the injustices that emerge from it. But it also applies to the transgression of ordinances of all kinds. God commands: "Forsake the outwardness of *ithm* and the inwardness thereof. Lo! those who garner *ithm* will be awarded that which they have earned" (6:121).

f. *Disobedience (fasaqa)*: As an active verb it refers to breaking or neglecting God's command, quitting the right way, participating in unrighteousness. It can be summed up as acting in ungodly ways, or simply disobedience. It is the "original" sin for the fallen angel, Iblis, who broke the command *(fasaqa)* of His Lord" (18:50).

g. *Transgression (junāh)*: *Junāh*, meaning fault or blame, has a narrow scope. It applies to the breaking of social and ceremonial laws, and especially those related to marriage. It is frequently couched in the negative form "there is no fault if ..." In an issue related to adopted sons the Qur'ān says: "And there is no *junāh* for you in the mistakes that you make unintentionally, but what your hearts purpose. Allah is Forgiving, Merciful" (33:5).

The abundance of general terms for evil and sin is enlightening, pointing to their gravity. Apart from them specific transgressions are also named and condemned in the Qur'ān. They include the great sins of polytheism and unbelief, and their companions hypocrisy and arrogance. There are five sins for which specific punishments are prescribed: murder, adultery, theft, treason, and forbidden drink. Other transgressions include usury, mistreating orphans, and disrespect toward parents. Sin also embraces a broad array of ethical failures that are mentioned in the Qur'ān—pride and corruption; extravagance and niggardliness; lying and slander; envy, cheating, and wastefulness; quarreling and treachery. All actions contrary to justice, kindness, affection, and generosity are likewise considered to be sinful. Muslims believe that we are held accountable for this entire range of evil.

3. Accountability and Repentance

The Muslim sense of accountability is sparked by the knowledge that God is observant and the expectation that God will judge. A common, reminding phrase is: "God is the observer of all that you do." Every Muslim knows that the accounts of his or her behavior are being meticulously kept by the recording angels. The account books will be opened and on that basis God will make the judgment, but as He wills. It is possible to push the whole matter into the back recesses of the mind and, as we will see in Islamic development, there has been a progressive weakening of the Qur'anic emphasis on sin. Nevertheless, the ominous fact of God's observation and judgment is inescapable. "Everything will perish save His countenance; His is the command and unto Him will ye be brought back" (12:28).

In the preceding chapter we have already touched on the extraordinarily fearsome reality of the Judgment. The divine punishment for sins is already under way in this life, but that process is a hidden one. There is nothing hidden about the main events of the Judgment Day. The procedures are graphically described in the Qur'ān and vividly elaborated in the Traditions. From the initial questioning in the grave by God's angels to the final decision of the Almighty step by step the events are laid out. Hence, sinners, alert! You cannot avoid giving account and no excuse will be accepted! Despite your natural and innate weakness, and despite the temptations of Satan, the responsibility will come home to you! Appeals to helpers will not avail. On that day "no laden one shall bear another's load, and man has only that for which he taketh effort" (53:38–39). For the ordinary sinful human being the prospect is a forbidding one. "Say, Lord!, if I should disobey my Lord, I fear the doom of a tremendous day" (39:13).

In Islamic understanding there is an appropriate spiritual response to this dangerous situation. Sinful human beings are called to repentance (*tawba*). The word implies "turning toward someone." The sinner is to turn toward God in contrition and God then turns toward the sinner. The Qur'ān places great stress on *tawba*, referring to it 86 times in various ways. This passage illustrates the frequent exhortations: "O ye who believe! Turn unto Allah with sincere repentance" (66:8). Repentance goes together with surrendering. In a discussion of kindness to parents, an individual who attained maturity declares: "Lo! I have turned unto Thee repentant and lo! I am of those who surrender [unto Thee]" (46:15).

The repentance of a sinner should be accompanied by confession. It is in that connection that the phrase "I have wronged myself" comes into play. It reflects what Adam said after his first transgression. Constance Padwick notes the prevalent use of the phrase in the prayer manuals of Islam. The common use goes back not only to Adam but also to the words that the Prophet Muhammad is said to have customarily used when he stood up for prayers:[10]

> Thou art my Lord, I Thy servant.
> I have wronged myself, and I confess my sin.
> Forgive me then all my sins, for there is
> None that forgiveth sins but Thee.

The repentance should also be accompanied by the determination to improve one's life and behavior. "Whosoever repenteth and doeth good, verily he repenteth toward God with true repentance" (25:71). Al-Jerrahi al-Halveti says: "One has to dig out all the roots. The repentance acceptable to Allah is the effort of inner cleaning, trying to eliminate the cause of sins.[11]

Muslim mystics in particular have responded to this Qur'anic emphasis, which receives less attention in orthodox writings. *Al-Sūsī* defined repentance in this way:

> Repentance is the return of everything that knowledge condemns toward what knowledge praises.

Abul-Hasan al-Nūrī described it as:

> Turning away from everything except God most high.

Ruwayn ibn Ahmad stated it in the form on an aphorism with simple force:

> It is repentance from repentance.[12]

Al-Ghazālī spoke often and eloquently of contrition. He said:

> Contrition results from the realisation that sin intervenes between the sinner and the Beloved; it is the grief of the heart when it becomes aware of the absence of the Beloved.[13]

God on His part is *al-Tawwāb*, a name that is translated both as "The Guide to Repentance" and "The Accepter of Repentance." Through signs and warnings God makes people aware of their condition and then mercifully responds to the repentant sinner. God is "the Forgiver of sin, the Accepter of repentance. ... Unto Him is the journeying" (40:3). The history of God's dealing with humanity is overwritten with the words: "Then God turned toward them." God's relenting attitude is the divine response to our attitude of penitence. The Qur'ān summarizes it with these words: "And lo! verily I am forgiving toward him who repenteth and believeth and doeth good, and afterward worketh aright" (20:82).

In sum, in Islam repentance takes a central position between sin and salvation. Five times a day, as part of every normal prayer cycle, a Muslim confesses personal sins and prays: "Absolve me!" M. A. Quassem ties together the themes in the following way:[14]

> Islamic teaching is that sin stands between man and God no doubt, but he is not dead in it, so no new birth of the spirit is needed; he must, however, repent; his repentance is not salvation, but only a means to it. Salvation is safety from the punishment of sin after death.

Later Muslim thinking took the discussion of sin in a variety of directions, the general trend being to soften the human engagement with "the exceeding sinfulness of sin."

D. Muslim Thinking about the Fact of Sin

We will deal with four streams of thought that brought their influence to bear on Muslim reflection on the fact of sin. They were the streams of legal thinking, the pious ascetics, the predestinarian and ethical theologians, and modern this-worldly thinkers.

1. The Legal Stream
Islam- religion of law

This stream of influence dominates practical thinking on the subject. Islam as we have seen is a religion of law. The development of the shari'a defined the discussion of sin(s) as well as positive behavior. It was not the interplay of weakness and responsibility within human nature that occupied the attention of the jurists, but rather the questions of what is permitted (halāl) and what is forbidden (harām). They believed that they had a solid foundation for their approach in the concept of the divine command and in specific Qur'anic passages such as 7:157—" He will enjoin on them that which is right and forbid them that which is wrong. He will make lawful for them all good things and prohibit for them only the foul." The legists developed great interest in classifying human actions, and they put together a schematic set of categories to cover the entire field of behavior: forbidden, reprehensible, neutral, recommended, and obligatory. Only forbidden actions are sins, although reprehensible behavior may become sinful.

It did not take long for sins also to be categorized. The idea appeared to have a basis in the Qur'ān which says: "Those who avoid great sins and shameful deeds, only (falling into) small faults—verily Thy Lord is ample in forgiveness" (53:22). People began to make lists of the greater and lesser sins. There was little argument about the worst ones. They are associating another being with God, and thankless unbelief. Apart from this agreement, however, there was a wide variation in opinion as to what fell under great sins and light sins respectfully, and there were many differing lists.

The legal scholars assumed that all human beings are sinners, pointing to the passage of the Qur'ān that says: "If God were to punish men for their wrong-doing, He would not leave upon the earth a single breast" (16:23). The issue of prophets and saints soon arose. Jesus had always been deemed to be a special case in that regard, but he did not remain an isolated example. In the course of time all the prophets and saints received a special status. It is true that many prophets in the Qur'ān, including Muhammad, pray for the forgiveness of their sins, but Muslim emotion was not happy with the thought that they might be sinful like ordinary people. As a result Islam developed a theory of sinlessness in regard to prophets and saints. They may have committed minor human faults, but their prayers for forgiveness were not so much for themselves but for others as an example. This was considered to be especially true in the case of Muhammad who is the perfect exemplar for human behavior.

The dominance of legal thinking in Islam had a lasting effect on the Muslim understanding of sin. The emphasis on individual actions turned the discussion in the direction of sins rather than sin. The stress on regulation and classification put the issue into a formalistic mode, and Muslim ethics (akhlāq) took a back seat. Because the legal theory included the idea that wrong actions could be made up by right ones, it opened the way for the development of a commercial approach to piety. Finally, the limitation of sins to evil deeds bypassed the essential linkage between thought and action. The overall impact of regarding sins as basically the non-observance of regulations, many of which were human interpretations, opened the door to two major problems for Muslims. The first was the manipulation of the definition of a sin. But is it really sinful to educate girls in schools? Does the Qur'ān say so? The second was the growth of superficial attitudes. Is a sin only external disobedience, or is there something deeper involved? There were some Muslims, the pious ascetics, who were not content to stay on the surface of the issue.

[margin note: Surface-just based on actions]

2. The Pietist Stream

Islam has always had a steady stream of pietistic thinkers who emphasize moral duty and take a strong stand on unrighteous conduct. The pietists began in early Islam with a group of earnest Muslims who loved to hear and recite the Word of God, and who were intent on sincere and careful obedience to God's commands. There were several shades of difference among them. The majority were simply ethical Muslims who have their counterpart today. Some were ascetics wanting to withdraw from the world. Others were moved to separate themselves from those whom they regarded as erring Muslims, and to form their own exclusive groups. At their fringe were the extremists who held that greatly sinning Muslims should be harassed and even killed. The latter too has a modern ring. But here we are concerned with the mainstream pious Muslims who took seriously both duty and sin. Hasan al-Basrī (d. 728) is their prime representative.

Caliph 'Umar ibn 'Abdul-'Azīz, at the beginning of his rule wrote to this pious saint, asking him what constituted a just imam (leader). Hasan replied in strong language, setting forth the ethic of the Qur'ān. Such a just leader is "the prop of every leaner, the straightener of every deviator, the reform of all corrupt, the strength of all weak, the justice of all oppressed, the refuge of all who are pitied ... the guardian of the orphan, and the treasury of the poor, fostering the little ones, and providing for the old ones ... away from wickedness and immorality." [15] The issue of who is ultimately responsible for evil and sin had arisen very early in Islam. On that point Hasan al-Basrī took an unwavering position which has now won the day:

> Oppression and wrong are not from the decrees of God; rather, His decree is His command to do good, justice and kindness, and to give to relatives ... God would not openly prohibit people from something and then destine them to do it secretly. If that were so, He would not have said in the Qur'ān 41:40 "Do what you wish!"[16]

3. The Theological Stream

Although the idea of predestination to good and evil that for ten centuries was the ruling theory in Islam has now been quietly shelved in Muslim thinking, its impact on the concept of sin is a lingering one. The theological tension that produced the original doctrine came from the Qur'ān which speaks of both divine and human responsibility. Muslim theologians felt constrained to take a position in the matter. They had learned logic at the feet of Aristotle after his works were translated into Syriac and Arabic. As they read the passages in the Qur'ān that emphasize God's absolute sovereignty, God's powerful will and God's eternal decree, their logic took over. To them the issue was clear. What is God's relation to evil and sin? There can be only one answer. After all, God is the only Creator. Since sin and evil exist, God must have created them. They found support for the idea in such passages of the Qur'ān as 53:43—"It is He Who granteth laughter and tears. It is He Who granteth death and life." Does not the Qur'ān challenge believers to say: "I seek refuge in the Lord of the Daybreak from the evil of that which He created" (113:1–2)? There are many similar passages. While it seemed conclusive to the predestinarians that God is ultimately responsible for the existence of evil and sins, they did not like the implications. Therefore they attempted to qualify their conclusion with the fine-tuned argumentation that God is responsible in that He creates the ability to do sin and the sin itself as an act, but He is not pleased with the sinful performance of humans. The following quotation illustrates their effort to preserve God's goodness alongside God's creative role:

> Allah is the creator of all the actions of His creatures whether of Unbelief or Belief, of obedience or of disobedience ... [The vile in those actions] is not by His good pleasure.[17]

The jurists had tended to reduce sin to the breaking of regulations. The predestinarians moved it into the arena of God's will. Led by their dean Al-Ashʿarī (d. 935) their view became the orthodox one, and some even added predestination to the required beliefs of Islam, making it number six on the list. The net effect of the development was to further reduce the element of human responsibility for sin.

There are many concrete examples of evildoers who were glad for the opportunity to blame God for their choices and deeds.

We turn to the ethical theologians who were a counter-balance to the predestinarians. Like the early Muslim pietists they too had a deep ethical concern, but by the time they came along Islamic thought had become stratified. It required their great intellectual acumen reforming vigor, and above all their personal spirituality to bring the issues of good and evil back into the center of Muslim thinking. Al-Ghazālī and Ibn Taimiyya are the two prime representatives of this movement towards moral religion.

Al-Ghazālī wrote his major work, the *Ihyā'*, as a guide for the purification of the heart and for pious conduct. His personal spiritual crisis and journey are told in his Confessions, which is a landmark in Muslim ethical/mystical literature. His sense of unworthiness and sin drove him to distraction, and the search for answers carried him mentally into all the major areas of Islamic thought and physically around the Muslim world. In the end he recovered his faith and set himself to the task of refocusing Islam. He declared that "the basic idea of religion is to eschew evil." [18] To do so hard spiritual effort is needed on the part of every sincere believer. The mirror of our lives, he says, is stained with rust and impurities of this world, and it must be cleansed and polished so that we reflect the Divine Reality. Moreover, we must engage in a constant spiritual struggle with the Evil One. He concluded that the problem can be dealt with by a process of spiritual discipline and the praise of God, but it must be tended to urgently in the light of what lies ahead for every human being. "Man's chief business in this world is to prepare for the next."[19]

In the Ihyā' Al-Ghazālī invites Muslims to advance on the path of God, beginning with the knowledge that God is a loving God who wants to have intercourse with His creatures. God, whom Al-Ghazālī called Friend, will assist us in our ethical struggles. With these emphases, and especially by moving the discussion of good and evil into a consideration of the condition of the human heart, Al-Ghazālī makes his signal contribution to the Islamic spiritual tradition.

Taqī ad-Dīn ibn Taimiyya (d. 1328) of Damascus was an influential scholar from the Hanbali school of thought and was as different as can be imagined from Al-Ghazālī. Whereas the latter tended to concentrate on the issue of personal piety, Ibn Taimiyya wanted to get things straight for the Muslim community. This involved him in fierce controversy with fellow Muslims who did not share his wide-ranging reformist views, and he was no stranger to jails. Whereas Al-Ghazālī drew much of his inspiration from the mystical Sufi idea of nearness to God, Ibn Taimiyya looked rigorously to the Qur'ān for his direction. What held the two together was their common commitment to the overcoming of evil.

Ibn Taimiyya came to the conclusion that Muslims were losing the clear and simple affirmations of the Qur'ān. He called for a return to the Word of God and literal adherence to its principles and prescriptions. Such adherence includes accepting the human responsibility for sin. Against the logic that would make God the author of evil Ibn Taimiyya argued that the opposite is true. God commands righteousness, and commends its doers. Not only is it sinful to do what is forbidden, but the omission of duty is also a culpable error. Underlying the sharīʿa is the Qurʾanic ideal of justice (*ʿadl*): "Justice is the principle regulating everything."[20] That principle in turn is interpreted by the Qurʾanic call "to enjoin what is right and forbid what is wrong" (30:104). This passage was crucial for Ibn Taimiyya. There are some things hidden in the mystery of God, but we know our responsibility. Who is the dead person among the living, he asks? He is the one who does not know the good and does not forbid the evil. Moreover the duties that arise from this basic command are to be done from the heart. "If they are not performed from the heart, then he who does them is not a believer."[21] Through sincere devotion to God's command its intention can be fulfilled "to promote general welfare and to eliminate evil."[22] With these emphases Ibn Taimiyya became the fount of many Islamic revivalist and reform movements. His aggressive and judgmental style also made him the forerunner of contemporary fundamentalist groups that are openly critical of Muslim moral standards.

The legal stream, pietism, fatalism, and ethical theology, each in their own way influenced common Muslim thinking about sin, but it is optimism about the human capacity to build society that has come to dominate the modern mood, and we turn finally to that development.

4. The Contemporary Stream

Two factors have decisively affected current Muslim thinking about sin. The first is the retreat from end-time thinking. The second is the advance in hopeful thinking about Muslim progress. We have noted both of these important factors earlier, but must now relate them to the doctrine of sin.

Because early Muslims were oriented toward the end-time the issues of personal sin and salvation were immediate and relevant. The Judgment Day did not come, however, and some of the edge was taken off the issue. Muslims today continue to be aware of its reality, but the awareness is not always deeply personal or at a highly existential level. The moral implication of this development has moved a Shīʿa scholar to give this warning: " To forget or lack faith in the Day of Judgment is the essential root of every evil act and sin."[23] Be that as it may it is the second factor that is the key one for the contemporary interpretation, and that is the change from sin consciousness to progress consciousness. *Sin consciousness to progress consciousness*

This change has become a paradigm shift, as the spirit of optimism runs through Islam. It is an aspect of the developing emphasis on success in this world. The Islamic view of human nature provided a basis for arguing that human beings have the innate potential to overcome deficiencies and evils of various kinds. Revivalists concerned about the stagnation of Muslim society built on that hopeful motif. It gave to believers an Islamic base for the idea of human progress that marks our age, and provided an answer to the energy and advance of other societies. We can overcome. We have the potential to do so. Let us wake up! The shift in attitude is tangible. What is driving Muslims today is a combination of faith in divine guidance, confidence in the unlimited human capacity for achievement, and a conviction of the virtually inevitable success of the believing community. As optimistic philosophies of dynamism, social responsibility, and positive change take center stage, the doctrine of personal sin is correspondingly lowered in importance. Sin is considered especially in relation to social and psychological evils. It is injustice. It is a crime against the welfare and image of the umma. It is unfaithfulness to the Islamic dream. It is defeatism and passivity.

Sir Muhammad Iqbal (d. 1938), the poet-philosopher of Pakistan and arguably the greatest revivalist thinker of the past Islamic century, set out to overcome that pessimism and replace it with a new and dynamic "doctrine of man." He symbolizes the Muslim confidence in human powers. As with all reformers he read the Qur'ān through a different lens than that used by the thinkers of the past. His rallying-cry was 13:11a: "Lo! Allah changeth not the condition of a folk until they (first) change that which is their hearts." He interpreted this to mean that God wants us to change and has given us the ability to do so. He called on fellow Muslims to take up the challenge: "Re-chisel then thine ancient frame, and create a new thing!" In the process we will become the co-creators of the world with God. In Islamic terms that was a daring idea indeed, but Iqbal cried: "Dost thou want life? Then live dangerously!"[24] Thus Iqbal sought to destroy the apathy that came from both traditional predestinarian theory and Sufi escapism from the world.

As part of his thought Iqbal reinterpreted the fall of Adam. Rather than being a disaster it was necessary for human growth. He argued that you cannot progress unless you experience failure. Adam accepted the challenge to act, and he fell, but it was an upward and not a downward fall. It was a perilous developmental stage that he accepted as the price of realizing his selfhood. The purpose of the fall, he declared, is "to indicate man's rise ... to the conscious possession of a free self, capable of doubt and disobedience. The fall does not mean any moral depravity, it is man's waking ... a throb of personal causality in one's own being."[25] In words reminiscent of Algernon Swinburne's "Glory be to man!" Iqbal insists that humans have the capacity to rise. This is the real Islam.

When attracted by the forces around him, man has the power to shape and direct them; when thwarted by them he has the capacity to build a much vaster world in the depths of his own inner being, wherein he discovers sources of infinite joy and inspiration. Hard is his lot and frail his being, like a rose-leaf, yet no form of reality is so powerful, so inspiring, and so beautiful as the spirit of man! Thus in his inmost being man, as conceived by the Qur'ān, is a creative activity, an ascending spirit who in his onward march, rises from one state of being to another![26]

The effort to realize these latent capacities is pleasing to God and reflects His intention. "Burn with our fire all that is not God. ... His image I will mould of mine own clay."[27]

With less poetic passion but with equal firmness Muslim optimists today identify rational power as that positive element in the human makeup that can overcome the innate negative tendencies. Starting from original innocence it can lead humanity onward and upward despite some failure. C. N. Ahmed Moulavi, a leader of the Muslim reform in Kerala, India, sums up the position: "Man is by birth innocent and pure. He has extraordinary abilities. The aim of Islam is to point out

to man his potentialities and to develop them steadily."[28] Ismail Faruqi spells out
the idea, not hesitating to draw on the concept of the image of God. That image is
the human soul. The lower aspect of the soul has to do with senses and desire, but
the higher aspect is mind and rationality. It is the latter that "constitutes man's
essential humanity."[29] With this "God-like" faculty men and women can know God,
and they can do God's will. Ali Shariati, as we have seen, shared the optimism.
While a human being has a dualistic and contradictory nature and the self is "the
stage for a battle between two forces," the struggle results in "a continuous evolution towards perfection."[30] Stated less grandly Charles le Gai Eaton suggests that
people are both "this and that." The positive pole of a person is the vocation of
vice-regent, the negative aspect is the individual's "slave character." The resolution of the struggle is moral effort. "The ambiguities in the Islamic context and in
the human situation as such are therefore resolved in the effort that the children
of Adam, made from dust, exert in the direction of the vice-regal idea and in the
Divine Help that is offered in response to this effort."[31] Eaton, a former Christian,
adds: "We have here a sharp contrast to the Christian view, which posits a primordial corruption of the innermost core of the human creature. For Islam this core
remains sound and cannot be otherwise. The command inherent in this message
is: "Be what in truth you are!"[32]

In the light of this idealistic urge to elevate human possibilities, and despite
the evidence of human failure, the issue of human sinfulness receives less and less
attention. Fazlur Rahman recognizes that the Qur'ān condemns pride and self-
righteousness, but affirms that it equally condemns the hopelessness and despair
that lessen moral energy. The latter arise from the basic weakness of man which
he reduces to "pettiness" and "narrowness of mind."[33] They can be overcome.

> On the whole, despite the sad accounts of the human record in the
> Qur'ān its attitude is quite optimistic with regard to the sequel of human
> endeavor. It also advocates a healthy moral sense rather than the attitude
> of self-torment and moral frenzy represented, for example, by the teach-
> ings of St. Paul and many Sufis. ... Given a merciful and just God, and the
> solidarity of character called taqwā, human well-being is provided for.[34]

Shabbir Akhtar accepts the positive analysis of human possibilities but is less
sanguine regarding their outcome. He says: "The divinely implanted religious
seed—providing the knowledge of Allah's radical uniqueness and of human accountability to the divine—acts as a heavenly counterpoise to man's natural way-
wardness."[35] His realism, however, takes over in his conclusion: "Only the Last Day
will witness a decisive resolution of a permanently ambiguous destiny, vacillating
between good and evil."[36]

There has been more discussion of sin among radical fundamentalist Muslims,
who are critical of modernist attitudes and who channel their own approach
through their desire to establish a pure Muslim community. While they also espouse
the merits of dynamic action, they believe that it should be carried out in the interests of developing a theocratic society governed by the Qur'ān and the sharīʿa.
Their understanding of sin is connected with the utopian vision put forward by a

charismatic leader. It is the controlled rationality and opinion of the founder that determines what is sinful and how sins are to be treated. The treatment usually includes judgmental criticism of erring Muslims, separation from them, and even violent action against them. In this radical perspective the primary sin of a human being is rejection of the pure Islamic vision, and sins are breaking the laws of the ideal community which are presented in modern dress and defined as supremely rational and pragmatic. Moderate fundamentalists, on the other hand, avoid the group mentality of the radicals, and can scarcely be distinguished from ordinary pious Muslims. They are simply contending for a faithful form of Islamic obedience in the threatening context of modernity, and their understanding of sin is formed by the injunctions of the Qur'ān.

The two leading representatives of radical fundamentalism are Abul Ala Mawdudi (d. 1979), a South Asian journalist-theologian, and Sayyid Qutb (d. 1966), an Egyptian educator-revivalist. Both were prolific writers, including extensive Qur'ān commentaries, and their works are widely read and very influential. Mawdudi traces the interest of modernist Muslims in developing new laws to a rebellious attitude toward God. "All of these are acts of rebellion: false claims to sovereignty and recognition of those claims both amount to manifest rebellion, and those who are guilty of these offenses are bound to be punished."[37] What is needed is not the creation of something new but the revival and re-introduction of genuine Islam. Mawdudi believed that all of society must be brought under the rule of God in a totalitarian system that would not recognize a false distinction between sacred and secular and that would be governed according to the traditional sharīʿa. He founded a party called the Jamaat-i-Islam that would reflect this ideology and would bring into existence such an Islamic state in Pakistan. He believed that the vision would triumph through political action, that corruption could be overcome, and that the true Muslim community could be rebuilt. For that to succeed there must be committed Muslims who believe in purity, discipline, and personal devotion, and Mawdudi dedicated his life to winning them. He declared: "What we need is a group of people—a leadership—which is determined to establish Islam, come what may."[38]

"Come what may" is a phrase that could be applied to Sayyid Qutb who read Mawdudi. Qutb argues that God alone possesses sovereignty and the right to ordain a path for mankind. A true Muslim community understands what that path is and is "the real guarantor for its fulfillment." When a believing group visibly applies God's way, "that will disperse the clouds of ignorance from human nature."[39] As in the early days of Islam it will be possible once again for Muslims to assume leadership and bring humanity "out of darkness into light through the Law of God and under the banner of Islam."[40] The development of such a pure theocratic community must involve the rejection of so-called progressive elements drawn from the West. "This vision is of such comprehensiveness and breadth, of precision and depth, of authenticity and integratedness that it rejects every foreign element."[41] Sayyid Qutb also came to the conclusion that revolutionary force rather than political action may be needed to liberate Muslims and to institute the righteous society. What stands in opposition to the triumph of truth is the Party of Satan, and that must be defeated, "come what may." Sayyid Qutb has in mind a blueprint of the kingdom of God on earth. Sin is opposition to this vision. Ironically, in Utopian visions it is the sin of *shirk* that lies at the door.

We have seen that the Muslim view of sin has been molded by a variety of influences. Their general effect has been to lower the level of sin discussion in Islam, and even to insulate against a lively consciousness of its peril as proclaimed by the Qur'ān. In the case of many sensitive Muslims the awareness of sin's power and its unresolved dilemmas remains a reality. Many other Muslims are represented by Abdul Khader, a friend with whom the writer once had a teashop discussion. Together we carefully considered various Qur'anic words regarding the heinousness of sin and its just reward. After an hour we concluded that the human situation had within it an element of desperation and hopelessness. I directed a question to him: "Does this give you a sense of despair?" Abdul Khader replied, "Yes, I am in despair." But he spoke the words with a smile on his face. This was not really something that he was worrying about.

E. Some Notes for Christian Sharing

1. A realistic appraisal of sin and its consequences is basic to the Christian understanding of Christ. The subject is therefore pivotal for Christian sharing with Muslims.

2. Since there are many Muslim sources that point to the gravity of the human condition, particularly the Qur'ān itself, and since both conscience and common sense testify to it, Muslims are quite ready to discuss the topic. Some Muslims believe that Christians tend to be over-preoccupied with the issue. Christian sharers will seek to demonstrate that it is God's own preoccupation.

3. Realism must be a goal in sin discussion. Romanticism about the human condition flies against experience and history. This, as the scriptures declare, is a radical problem and such a problem requires radical treatment.

4. God created human beings good. "And indeed it was very good" (Gen 1:31). Sin distorts and spoils God's good creation. It is an aberration and quite unnatural in terms of God's intention. That is why human beings need "a new creation."

5. Sin entails disobedience to God's commands and is the transgression of God's law, but these, as Al-Ghazālī pointed out, have to do with the condition of the human heart that produces them. Jesus the Messiah said: "It is from within the human heart that evil intentions come: fornication, murder, adultery, avarice, weakness, deceit, licentiousness, envy, slander, pride, folly. All these evil things come from within, and they defile a person" (Mk 7:21–22). Therefore David prayed: "Create in me a clean heart, O God, and put in me a new and right spirit" (Ps 51:10).

6. Human beings were created for fellowship with God as well as for the service of God. Since God is holy and apart from evil, sin separated humans from God and disrupted that intended relation. Adam's fall and exile from the Garden was a personal event with corporate implications. All humanity has left the beautiful garden of fellowship with God. "Sin came into the world through one man, and

death through sin, and so death spread to all because all have sinned. ..." (Rom 5:12). Only God can re-create the Garden condition.

7. The promise of God after Adam's fall included the assurance of a Savior. We must thank God for that, for the abysmal human record reveals that education does not overcome evil. God in mercy shows another way of dealing with it. God saves as well as guides. That is the welcome promise of Jesus the Messiah, Teacher, and Savior.

8. We have sinned against God as well as wronging ourselves—rebelling, spoiling, separating. It is not a light problem. In fact, what humans have done is a horrendous irreverence and blasphemy. Through Jesus the Messiah we learn how God chooses to deal with the problem. It is a wonder. "He himself bore our sins in his body on the tree that we might die to sin and live to righteousness. By his wounds you have been healed" (1 Pet 2:24; RSV).

9. The goal of human behavior is truly to prohibit the evil and to commend the good. It is easier to work toward that goal when we know that God is our Friend who forgives us, accepts us, and empowers us to do what sometimes seems impossible.

10. Christians and Muslims have good reasons for working together to combat evil, to establish justice, and to build the human family.

We turn next to the Muslim understanding of salvation. As we leave the topic of sin the saintly prayer goes with us. "Allahumma ... so help me, help me!" What is the help that is offered?

Endnotes

1. Arthur Jeffrey, ed. Islam, *Muhammad and His Religion* (New York: Liberal Arts Press, 1958), p. 234; quoting the Sheikh's *Jumlat Awrat munifa* (Stambul, 1923).

2. Fazlur Rahman, *Major Themes of the Qur'ān* (Minneapolis: Bibliotheca Islamic, 1980), p. 9.

3. *Ibid.*, p. 29. Cf. Ziaul Hasan Farugi, "The Concept of Holiness in Islam," *Isalamochristiana*, Vol. II, 1995, p. 15.

4. Ali Shariati, *On the Sociology of Islam*, tr. by H. Algar (Berkeley: Mizan Press, 1979), pp. 88, 91–96. For the basic moral dilemma see also Toshiko Izutsu, *Ethico-Religious Concepts in the Qur'ān* (Montreal: McGill University Press, 1962), pp. 105–116.

5. Rahman, *Major Themes*, p. 27.

6. Mohammed Fadhel Jamali, *Letters on Islam* (London: World of Islam Festival Trust, 1978), p. 73.

7. Qur'ān 2:29:29–39; 7:11–26; 15:26–40; and 20:15–24.

8. B. D. Kateregga and D. W. Shenk, *Islam and Christianity. A Muslim and Christian in Dialogue* (Grand Rapids: Wm. B. Eerdman's Publishing Co., 1990), p. 18.

9. Padwick, *Devotions*, p. 283.

10. *Ibid.*, p. 192.

11. Al-Jerrahi al-Halvēti, *Most Beautiful Names,* p. 103.

12. Michael A. Sells, tr. *Early Islamic Mysticism* (New York: Paulist Press, 1966), p. 199.

13. Margaret Smith, *Al-Ghazali, the Mystic,* (Lahore: Hijra, 1983; repr. of 1944 ed.), p. 153.

14. Muhammad Abul Quassem, *Salvation of the Soul and Islamic Devotion* (London: Kegan Paul International, 1983), p. 28.

15. Williams, *Themes*, pp. 70f.; quoting from *Ibn 'Abd Rabbihi.*

16. A Rippen and J. Knappert, eds., *Textual Sources for the Study of Islam* (Chicago: University of Chicago Press, 1986), p. 117.

17. Earl E. Elder, tr. *A Commentary on the Creed of Islam. Sa'd al-Dīn al-Taftazānī on the Creed of Najm al-Dīn al-Nasafī* (New York: Columbia University Press, 1950), pp. 80, 87.

18. *The Book of Knowledge*, tr. by Nabih Faris (Lahore: Sh. Muhammad Ashraf, 1974), p. 205.

19. *The Alchemy of Happiness*, tr. by Claud Field (London: The Octagon Press, 1980), p. 65.

20. Cragg and Speight, eds., *Islam from Within*, p. 117.

21. *Ibid.*, p. 115.

22. *Ibid.*, p. 114.

23. A.S.M. Tabataba'i, *Shi'ite Islam*, tr. by S.H. Nasr (Albany: SUNY, 1975) p. 166.

24. Muhamman Sadiq, *A History of Urdu Literature* (London: Oxford University Press, 1964), p. 363.

25. Muhammad Iqbal, *The Reconstruction of Religious Thought in Islam* (Lahore: Sh. Muhammad Ashraf, 1962), p. 85.

26. *Ibid.,* p. 12.

27. Muhammad Iqbal, *Secrets of the Self*, tr. by R. A. Nicholson (Delhi: Arnold Heinemann, 1978), pp. 109, 112.

28. C. N. Ahmed Moulavi, *Religion of Islam* (Calicut: Azad's Book Stall, 1979), p. 20.

29. Faruqi, *Tawhīd*, p. 83.

30. Ali Shariati, *Sociology of Islam*, p. 92.

31. Charles Le gai Eaton, "Man," in Sayyed H. Nasr, ed., *Islamic Spirituality* (New York: Crossroad, 1987), p. 375.

32. *Ibid.*, p. 367.

33. Rahman, *Major Themes*, p. 25.

34. *Ibid.*, p. 30.

35. Shabbir Akhtar, *A Faith for All Seasons* (Chicago: Ivan R. Dee, 1990), p. 143.

36. *Ibid.*, p. 147.

37. Abul Ala Mawdudi, *The Road to Peace and Salvation* (Lahore: Islamic Publications Ltd., 1966; original lecture 1940), p. 16.

38. C. J. Adams, "Mawdudi and the Islamic State," in John Esposito, ed., *Voices of Resurgent Islam* (New York: Oxford, 1983), p. 131.

39. Sayyid Qutb, *The Religion of Islam* (Kuwait: International Federation of Student Organizations, n.d.), p. 99.

40. *Ibid.*, p. 50.

41. Yvonne Y. Haddad, "Sayyid Qutb: Idealogue of Muslim Revival," in Esposito, ed., *Voices*, p. 76.

4

The Muslim View of Salvation

The Muslim view of salvation is a concentration on the theme of escape and deliverance. In the first section of our chapter we will consider that theme and the debate in regard to the term salvation. The major portion of the chapter will be given over to the questions: How shall I escape? What is the path to deliverance? We will examine seven answers to that important question. While Muslims generally agree on the focus of deliverance, there is no consensus as to the means, and that remains an open and unresolved question.

A. Salvation Is Escape from the Fire

There is some disagreement over the appropriateness of using the word "salvation" in the Muslim context. Although contemporary Muslims are utilizing the term more frequently, that is a relatively recent development. As we move from the topic of sin to salvation, in fact we cannot help but notice a difference in the intensity of interest and the level of treatment. There are not many Muslim writings on the subject of salvation, and Muslim conversation does not flow around the issue.[1] At first glance, then, our title for this chapter may not appear to be very Islamic. But there is a kind of paradox here. That conclusion is applicable, only in regard to language use or if we were thinking of the Christian frame of reference. While the specific term "salvation" is not used very much, many of the issues that it represents are not only present in Islam but are also deeply felt by those who are moved to reflect on them.

With respect to language use it may be helpful to remember that the absence of a particular term does not necessarily imply the absence of the underlying idea. For example, the Malayalam language of Southwest India does not have a traditional word for saying "thanks!" From its absence it would be quite incorrect to conclude that Malayalis lack a concept of gratitude. The idea incorporated in "thank you" is ordinarily communicated by the expression of the face or by a bodily movement.[2]

Is the absence of the term salvation in Islam the result of a similar pattern? While that possibility must be considered, it cannot be the decisive factor because the Qur'ān actually makes frequent use of the verbs "to deliver" and "to save." On that basis A. K. Brohi, a modern Pakistani scholar, does not hesitate to assert that man "is called by the Qur'ān to seek his salvation."[3]

A second, weightier factor affects Muslim use of the word salvation, and that is its long association with Christian teaching. With that usage in mind some Muslims argue that the very idea of salvation is not present in Islam. Ismail al-Faruqi, for example, states that "Islam has no soteriology." Maintaining that "man stands in no predicament from which he is to be saved," he argues that salvation is therefore "an improper religious concept which has no equivalent term in Islamic vocabulary."[4] Faruqi prefers the term "felicity" to convey the Muslim sense of the concept. Nevertheless, although it is quite clear that Islam does not embrace the assumptions of the Christian doctrine, from within Islamic thought and devotion there rise the basic spiritual concerns that lie at the heart of the term salvation as it is widely understood. The following two petitions are taken from a prayer that is recited by the pilgrims visiting the sacred cemetery where Muhammad is buried in the city of Medina:[5]

> May Allah's friendliness accompany your loneliness!. . . Cause us to enter Paradise in safety, O Thou most merciful of those who show mercy, Amen.

Thus, while the use of the specific term salvation may be occasional, there is no dearth of salvation thinking in Islam.

Islamic salvation thinking is connected with two major Muslim concerns. It is the Qur'anic use of the verbs "to deliver" and "to save" that establish the two meanings. The primary one has to do with the next life, with escape from the perils of Hell to the pleasures of Paradise. M. A. Quassem makes the point: " Even though the fundamental idea in salvation is safety from the punishment in Hell, this safety alone is not salvation; for salvation needs to be conjoined with Paradise."[6] The second concern is for the improvement of life in this world, an idea that is gaining in importance among contemporary Muslims. The Qur'ān, however, underscores the eschatological dimension of salvation thinking in Islam. It declares: "And Allah summoneth to the Abode of Peace, and leadeth whom He will in the straight path." The Abode of Peace signifies Paradise. Its attainment must be humanity's first priority. The Qur'ān beckons people to consider this invitation (89:27–30; Yusuf Ali):

> O thou soul!
> In (complete)rest and satisfaction!
> Come back thou
> To thy Lord!—
> Well pleased (thyself)
> And well pleasing
> Unto Him!

Enter thou, then
Among My Devotees,—
Yes, enter thou
My Heaven!

What stands in the way of realizing this goal is the reality that sins are punished. God penalizes sinners, and the "raging Fire" is His instrument to do that. Therefore salvation, in the Muslim view, is escape from that doom. This is borne out by the Qur'anic term *najat*, which is the word that roughly corresponds with "salvation." It is used only once but in a highly significant way. "O my people, how is it that I bid you to salvation (*najat*), but you bid me to Fire (40:44)? Paradise and Hell are contrasted. Salvation is escape from the latter to the former.

The root *najā'* is utilized 66 times in other linguistic forms in the Qur'ān, mostly to describe how God delivered people from bad situations, especially Noah and Lot. The promise is: "Then shall we save our messengers and the believers in like manner (as of old). It is incumbent upon us to save believers" (11:104). Referring to the dangers of the sea the Qur'ān says: "Allah delivereth you ... from all afflictions" (6:64). Viewing these promises Muslims might well argue that God's deliverance has to do with this world as well as the next. Yet undoubtedly in the perspective of the Qur'ān that is a secondary prospect. The satisfactions of this world are illusory, and we must give priority to our liberation from all that the future "Calamity" entails:

> Whoso is removed from the Fire and is made to enter Paradise, he indeed is triumphant. The life of this world is but comfort of illusion (3:185).

Najā' returns to its primary point of reference in this passage:

> God shall rescue (*najā'*) those who fear Him into their place of safety (39:62; Palmer).

Rescue and safety!—that is salvation. It was in the face of the impending doom that Sheikh Idrisi raised his poignant cry: "Security! Security!" But on what basis does God rescue humans" How will the individual escape Hell and attain Paradise? What are the means to salvation in Islam? We turn next to that crucial question.

B. The Means to Salvation

We may speak of seven means to salvation in Islam. They are: the divine will; divine mercy; faith; faith and works; intercession; the mystical way; and community membership.

With this listing three questions come to mind immediately, and each requires an answer:

Question One: Are these distinct ways?

An Answer: There is a close interplay among some of these seven categories, but they may be distinguished; there is value in seeing them in their particularity before examining their interrelation.

Question Two: Why is there not a single means?

An Answer: The Qur'ān has a variety of emphases, as do the *Hadīth*. It is a series of messages, not a systematic treatise. Muslims select from these emphases according to their training and preference. The community has not tried to resolve the matter by establishing a normative doctrine, although some individuals and groups have insisted that their viewpoint is the correct one.

Question Three: Are Muslims troubled by the diversity of means?

An Answer: Most Muslims are not visibly disturbed. They regard the uncertainty as something to be lived with. God will clarify things in the end. Some individuals are troubled when they reflect on their personal situation.

We turn first to the belief that our salvation depends on the will of God.

I. Salvation by the Will of God

Who is ultimately responsible for my salvation? The basic Muslim answer is God. The way to salvation is from above, not from below. We have referred above to the fact that Islam is marked by an overwhelming sense of God. To recognize that God is responsible for our salvation is simply to express this primary principle. Is he not "the Lord of the Worlds?" As the great names declare God is the ultimate decision-maker. God is the "Owner of All," the "Creator of Good," the "Creator of Evil," and the "Compeller." His will is supreme. God decides who will be saved and who will be damned. Not only do the names of God testify to salvation by the will of God, but there is ample support for this view in both the Qur'ān and the Hadīth.

The Qur'ān, however, has a double stream of thought in regard to responsibility for salvation. On one side it emphasizes the primacy of the divine role, and on the other it asserts human responsibility. Muslims who hold that God pre-determines our salvation choose the first of these emphases. As noted earlier, the Qur'ān firmly teaches that God is the sole Creator, and the fashioner of all things. It declares: "We have created everything by measure" (54:49). The literal meaning of the world "measure" is "decree." On this basis, as well as considering other passages, Muslim theologians developed the concept of God's eternal decree. God has determined all things in advance and has written them down in the eternal book of His decrees. This includes human actions. Thus my salvation and damnation are decided by God before my birth, and my personal history is merely the working out of God's decree. The famous saying that expresses this teaching is the following: "The pens are lifted up and the pages are dry."

The scriptural passages that support this understanding can be piled up. "Allah sendeth whom He will astray, and guideth whom He will. He is the Mighty, the Wise" (14:4). God's will is irresistible. "He whom Allah leadeth, he indeed is led aright, while he whom Allah sendeth astray—they are the losers. Already We have urged unto hell many of the jinn and mankind" (7:177f.). The Almighty could have created humanity in one pattern, but this was not the divine pleasure. We read the stern words: "Verily I shall fill hell with jinn and mankind altogether" (11:119). A doubt may arise as to the intention of these firm passages. Do they really mean what they appear to say? For, as soon as the Qur'ān declares that we are dependent on God's prevenient will, in the next breath it affirms our responsibility for what happens. In addition, there are other independent passages which indicate that God sends people astray as a punishment for rejecting God's message or acting rebelliously. Because of that misbehavior the Lord wills that they should not hear the message and be saved. In the theological discussions that took place in regard to this issue the Traditions become an important factor. The Hadīth came down firmly in support of the idea of God's decree, even though they revealed awareness of the tensions involved.

A typical Hadīth reports that the Prophet Muhammad told this story. After God created Adam God stroked his back with His right hand and brought forth Adam's descendants. God declared: "I have created these for Paradise, and they will perform the acts of the people of Paradise." Then God brought forth another set of Adam's descendants, saying: "I have created these for the Fire and they will perform the deeds of the people of the Fire." With natural logic someone asked the Prophet: "Of what use will deeds of any kind be?" The Prophet answered: "When Allah creates a servant for Paradise, He bids him perform the actions of the people of Paradise, and thereby causes him to enter Paradise. And when Allah creates a slave for the Fire, He bids him perform the actions of the People of the Fire, and thereby causes him to enter the Fire."[7]

In the classical period of Islam Muslim thinkers made predestination to heaven and hell the orthodox position. That position was crystallized in the writings of al-Ashʿarī (d. 935) and al-Māturīdī (d. 944), the founders of orthodoxy. Nothing could be clearer than the words of al-Nasafi (d. 1142), a member of al-Māturīdī's school of thought. The Egyptian scholar put it this way in a popular catechism that received many later commentaries:[8]

> Allah is the Creator of all the actions of his creatures, whether of Unbelief, or of Belief, of obedience or of disobedience. And they are all of them by His will and desire, by His judgment, by His ruling, and by His decreeing. His creatures have actions of choice for which they are rewarded and punished. And the good in these is by the good pleasure of Allah, and the vile is not by His good pleasure.

Al-Nasafi recognizes the conundrum that the predestinarian position produces, but he lets it stand as an insoluble problem. God is the Author of both salvation and damnation.

The emphasis on the controlling will of Allah powerfully influences Islam but many modern Muslims regard its outcome in predestinarian theory as a complete misinterpretation of the Qur'ān. Their position is well represented by Daud Rahbar. In a lengthy and penetrating study of the critical passages he came to the conclusion that the Mighty Allah of the Qur'ān cannot be portrayed as a capricious deity. Rather, he suggests, "the central theme, in the light of which the character of the Qur'anic doctrine of Allah is to be determined, is God's strict justice."[9] While many modern Muslims take a similar view, the impact of the traditional approach has not vanished. It is reflected in the frequent use of the pious phrase, "if God wills" (*in sha Allah!*). The ejaculation is used habitually but not carelessly. As a Muslim you will probably not say, "I will catch the next bus, if God wills." You will, likely say on parting with a close friend: "I'll see you again, if God wills." It is especially in the ultimate matters of life, death, and eternity that the spirit of *inshallah* comes into play. We may sense it in a recent poem that was written as a memorial to an early-departed friend:[10]

Inshallah
"—which is to say 'God willing,' more or less:
a phrase that rose routinely to her lips
whenever plans were hatched or hopes expressed,
the way we knock on wood, yet fervently,
as if to wax too confident might be
to kill the very thing she wanted most.
It used to pique and trouble me somehow,
this cautionary tic of hers, but now
I understood why she was skeptical
of what Allah in His caprice allows,
because that she should live He did not will
or, more terribly, He did that she should not."
[In memoriam, Mirel Sayinsoy, 1967–1999]

Muslims who reflect this level of thought hope the Final Day will reveal that the decree of the Divine Will has been favorable to them. Consistent with their view, however, they will not be inclined to say, "I am saved," but rather to say, "I am saved, if God wills."

Thoughts for Christian Sharing

a. Like Muslims Christians have struggled with the issue of the relation of God's will to human salvation, and there have been differing opinions on the proper understanding of the Christian scriptures.

b. Christians believe that salvation comes from God who "desires that everyone be saved and come to the knowledge of the truth" (1 Tim 2:4). God's will is a saving will. That is evident from the fact that God acts graciously and decisively to deliver us from our insoluble problems. He does so through Jesus the Messiah who bore our sins and is therefore called "the savior of all" (1 Tim 4:10). And God does so through the Divine Spirit working in our hearts and lives. In all this it is God who is the Savior, and the salvation God provides is deliverance from the power of sin, death, and the devil. For this reason grateful humans will say: All glory be to God alone!"

c. God works in human beings not by the raw power of compulsion, but rather by the power of attraction. Divine love wins without compelling. God is responsible for our salvation as the Lover-Inviter-Attracter who draws people to Himself, but it is we humans who come to the feast.

d. A person who has experienced the love of God in Jesus Christ has the assurance of salvation and can confidently say: "I am saved." The visible fact of God's suffering love for me, an unworthy sinner, testifies that God has willed it.

e. To his or her friends a Christian will say: "God has saved you." What you must do is to believe it and come to the feast.

2. Salvation by the Mercy of God

The second standpoint from which a Muslim may view the doctrine of salvation is that of the mercy of God. I will be saved because God will be merciful to me and will forgive me.

The position is reflected by a pious phrase often referred to as the bismilla. It is a short form of a longer phrase: *bismillahi rahmani rahimi*. The bismilla may be translated in a number of ways:

"In the Name of God, the Merciful, the Compassionate"
"In the Name of God, the Beneficent, the Merciful"
"In the Name of God, Most Gracious, Most Merciful"

The phrase appears at the beginning of every chapter of the Qur'ān except one. Muslims regularly use the phrase for special occasions. For example, when a Muslim delivers a public speech, he will frequently begin it with a recitation of the bismilla. Its words are believed to hallow and sanctify what is to follow. The bismilla reminds believers that the One who overshadows their life is the Rahmān (the Merciful) and Rahīm (the Mercifier).

The two titles belong to the "Beautiful Names" of God that have been mentioned previously. Those names provide concentration points for Muslim devotions. To assist in the process of meditation Islam accepted the use of the rosary—one type having 99 beads, the other 33. When a devotee fingers the beads, he or she remembers the glorious and the terrible names of God, each in turn. The starting-point in the act of remembrance are the names Rahmān and Rahīm, and the end is reached with the title Sabūr, the Patient One. The process reminds the pious believer that God begins with showing mercy to us and ends with patience toward our frailties and deficiencies. The believer may also remember the verse that is said to be written on the base of the Throne of God: "Verily, My Mercy overcomes My Wrath!" The phrase expresses the hope of Muslims who look to the mercy of God as the answer to the question: "How shall I escape the Fire?"

This portrayal of the Divine Being differs from that of an Awesome and Majestic Master who from the remoteness of the Beyond gives commands to His servants and arbitrarily disposes of their destinies with an inscrutable and irresistible will. In this perspective God is pictured as One who is tender and inclined to show favor to His people. This divine inclination towards humanity is expressed not only by the term mercy, but also by the triad grace-love-favor, all of which are represented in the Qur'ān. Accordingly Mohammad Hashim Kamali states:[11]

> Man's creation was an expression of Divine love. This is manifested, as the Qur'ān confirms, in God's direct involvement in the creation of man.

... Direct involvement also signifies intimacy and closeness, a feature of God-man relationship, which did not cease with the first act of creation, but continues to be expressed and unfolded as a reality of the religious experience of the believers.

In the Qur'ān the love of God is pictured as affection for the loyal servant. The Prophet is commanded to say: "If ye love Allah, follow me: Allah will love you and forgive you your sins. Allah is Forgiving, Merciful" (3:29). God loves the kind, the patient, those who trust, who do good, the pious, and the clean. He does not love the unjust, the arrogant, the unbelieving traitor, those who exult, the evil-doers, the miserly, the corrupt, the transgressors, the extravagant, and the unbelievers. "Lo! Allah loveth not one who is treacherous and sinful" (4:103). The terms grace and favor are used more frequently than love. The grace of God usually refers to the superabundance of created blessings that God has given to humans, while the favor of God is frequently applied to God's final gift of Paradise. Yet despite the references to love, grace, and favor, the term mercy stands out as "the lord of the words" in the Qur'ān. Used nearly 300 times it is an expansive and embracive concept that contains promised "treasures" for humanity (17:100). The angels who bear up the Throne of God hymn the praise of the Almighty for divine mercy. "Our Lord! Thou comprehendest all things in mercy and knowledge. Therefore forgive those who repent and follow thy way. Ward off from them the punishment of hell" (40:7). To Moses who pleads for forgiveness for the errant people of Israel God declares: "My mercy embraces all things" (7:156).

Traditional Muslim theologians who had decided that God's will is the determining factor in human salvation had to deal with this emphasis on mercy. They did so in a way that blunted its potential impact. They made it a function of God's will rather than a prime characteristic of God's being. In their view divine mercy belongs to the realm of God's discretionary actions, and not to the character of God's nature. In taking this approach the theologians were not being simply arbitrary. The Qur'ān does affirm: "Say: Unto whom belongeth whatsoever is in the heavens and the earth? Say: to Allah. He hath prescribed [ed. emphasis] for Himself mercy that He may bring you all together to a Day whereof there is no doubt" (6:12). The idea is repeated later in the same chapter. "Peace be unto you! Your Lord hath prescribed for Himself mercy that whoso doeth evil and repented afterward thereof and doeth right (for him) lo! Allah is Forgiving, Merciful" (6:54). On this basis the Qur'ān declares: "God chooseth for His mercy who He will" (2:105). It asks: "Who is he who can preserve you from Allah if He intendeth harm for you, or intendeth mercy for you?" (33:17). The idea is brought to a summary conclusion in the following words: "He punished whom He will, and showeth mercy unto whom He will" (29:21). In the light of these and other passages many Muslim theologians interpreted the mercy of God as a policy decision that God makes from time to time, and therefore did not include it in the list of God's eternal qualities and essential attributes. Some even said: "It is not incumbent upon God to do that which is best for His creature." They did not want a theory of mercy that would limit God's authority and will.

An almost dramatic change is taking place in Islamic thought. Without exactly saying so, contemporary Muslims are adopting the position that the traditional theological view was a misunderstanding, and they are taking a different direction. That direction is a new emphasis on the mercy of God as central to God's being and character. The Muslim appreciation of God's power is being conditioned by a more deliberate recognition of God's mercy, and its implication for life in this world as well as for the assurance of Paradise. Hammudah Abdulati, for example, states:

> The mercy of God gives us hope and peace, courage and confidence. It enables us to remedy our griefs and sorrows, to overcome our difficulties and obtain success and happiness. Indeed, the mercy of God relieves the distressed, cheers the afflicted, consoles the sick, strengthens the desperate, and comforts the needy.[12]

In this connection other Qur'anic words and ideas associated with mercy are being cited, including providence, deliverance, guidance, and forgiveness. All of them are related to an expanding theory of salvation. In regard to the first two, it is pointed out that God's providential care and deliverance, illustrated by a series of saving acts, reveal the greatness of the Divine Mercy. The Qur'ān lists those saving acts: delivering God's people from their enemies, the sending of messengers, the provision of revealed books, and the promise of Paradise. These are all described as "a mercy from Us." When human beings see this overflow of generosity, they are impelled to give God praise: "Thou art the most merciful of the merciful!" "Thou are the best of the merciful ones!" The Qur'ān makes a qualification, however. Although it sometimes refers to the Divine Mercy as if it were independent of human behavior, more usually it is presented as the divine response to human attitudes and actions. It is repeatedly stressed that the expression of God's mercy depends on or follows upon our loyalty to God's commands.

The other two terms that are associated with divine mercy are guidance and forgiveness. There is a Qur'anic refrain that describes God's revelations as "a guidance and a mercy" for human beings. We have dealt above with the theme of guidance. The problem comes from our unwillingness or inability to follow God's guidance. That universal failure introduces the issue of forgiveness. It is clear for many Muslims that any hope for escape from the Fire rests on the possibility of divine forgiveness. But what constitutes forgiveness in Islam?

In essence, the forgiveness of God is the decision to overlook a punishment that is deserved. While the ideas of repentance and the need to improve are present in the concept, its central thought is that God may take a merciful decision to remit a penalty that is due. Since the basic punishment for sinful behavior is Hellfire, forgiveness really means enabling a sinner to escape the terrors of that situation and to enter unharmed into Paradise. God, if He chooses, has the power and the authority to be lenient toward sinners in this way. Nothing more is needed than the divine decision. Moreover, Muslims at this level believe that God is in fact so inclined. In the Qur'ān God is called the "Very Forgiving One" and the "Most Forgiving One." He is named as the "Pardoner" and the "Clement One." And the scripture has a plethora of references to God's inclination to forgive. What is needed then is for the individual to pray for a favorable decision, that God will mercifully exercise forgiveness in his or her case.

The Qur'ān frequently urges such prayer: "Our Lord! ... Pardon us, absolve us, and have mercy on us" (2:286). So also Noah prayed to God, thereby establishing a pattern for all penitent sinners: "Unless Thou forgive me and have mercy on me I shall be among the lost" (11:47). The principle is stressed in the teaching of children. An elementary madrasa catechism asks:[13]

Q: Who can forgive sins?

A: Allah and Allah alone can forgive sin.

Q: What should you do so Allah may forgive sins?

A: In order that my sins be forgiven I must pray to Allah with all my heart, and atoning for my evil deeds resolve never to do any such misdeeds again.

And five times daily in the ritual prayers Muslims call upon the Lord to have mercy upon them and to forgive their sins:[14]

O Lord! Forgive us and our parents and ancestors, and our leaders and all the believers who preceded us. O Lord! Absolve all our sins and those we may fall (into) in the future: those open sins and those concealed and all that You know but we may not be aware of. O Lord! Grant us good things in this near life and good things in the life to come, and protect us from the punishment of the Fire!

There remains one insistent question: Will God forgive me? God promises us pardon, a generous provision and a mighty wage, and I have done my best to behave as a true Muslim. I have repented of my failures and prayed for forgiveness. But when my books are opened on the Last Day, what will happen? I see Paradise on the other side of the narrow pathway, as narrow as the edge of a sword, a pathway that separates hell and heaven. Will I be able to walk across that narrow way? The Hadīth are filled with worries about the answer to such questions. An example involves 'Ā'isha, the wife of the Prophet Muhammad. It is reported that she heard God's messenger say these words in the course of his prayer: "God, grant me a light reckoning." She asked him, "Prophet of God, what is a light reckoning?" He replied to her, "That one's book should be examined and that God should forgive him. He who is severely taken to account that day, 'Ā'isha, will perish."[15] Other Traditions report how God at the last moment, and quite unexpectedly, may receive into Paradise someone who appeared not to deserve it, and put into Hellfire someone else who seemed not to merit it. It is this uncertainty that accounts in part for the fervency of Muslim prayers for forgiveness.

We turn for a moment to the celebration of Dhu'l-Hajj, the major festival in Islam. It is pilgrimage time. Nearly two million Muslims have gathered at the Ka'ba, the central shrine of Islam at Mecca. As part of the ceremony they circle around the Ka'ba seven times. During each circuit they utter a prayer for forgiveness. While the pilgrimage to Mecca holds a huge communal significance for the Muslim family, the prayers at the shrine are very personal. The prayer for the seventh circuit, for example, reads as follows:[16]

O God, I ask of Thee
Perfect Faith and true conviction,
And Thy boundless bounty,
And a God-fearing heart,
And a tongue praising Thy Name,
And lawful joys,
And lasting repentance,
And repentance before death,
And tranquillity in death,
And forgiveness and mercy after death,
And Pardon on the Day of Reckoning,
And that I be rewarded with Paradise,
And salvation from the Fire,
By Thy Mercy, O Glorious, O Oft-Forgiving!

The reiteration of such prayers points to the fact that some Muslims live in "hope of Allah's mercy" (2:218) and believe that the mercy of God is the first means of salvation in Islam.

Thoughts for Christian Sharing

a. Many Christians believe that God's merciful forgiveness is the central theme of the Christian faith. Their hearts resonate sympathetically with phrases like "the Compassionate and the Merciful."

b. Christians believe that compassion and mercy belong to the very nature of God. Rather than doing merciful things from time to time God always seeks to do that which is best for God's creatures. The "incumbency" is from God's heart. God is love, and is gracious to humans because of the inner compulsion of the divine nature. God's will is a will of love, and God's power is the instrument of God's love.

c. In the Christian view the divine mercy is expressed in providence, deliverance, guidance, redemption, and forgiveness. Redemption is the link between guidance and forgiveness. God's loving and saving action in Jesus Christ provides that redemption.

d. The forgiveness of sins is God's affair, for we have sinned against the Holy One. If God does not forgive us, our situation is hopeless.

e. As the Lord of all God can choose to set aside the penalties or to change the human condition that produces sin. God chose to do the latter, entered the path of suffering love, assumed our penalties on our behalf, and restored us to the status of God's children in a new creation. The action is quite extraordinary and totally unexpected. Who is worthy of such care? These words express the feelings of those who experience God's forgiveness: "O the depth of the riches and wisdom and knowledge of God!" (Rom 11:33).

f. How God chooses to forgive is a matter that belongs to the divine will and choice. Because God's love and wisdom are far greater than our imagination or understanding God may act in ways beyond our limited comprehension. It is God's decision to save us through His saving work in Jesus Christ, and no one can deny God the right to love and to act and to forgive as He pleases.

g. In the Christian view the forgiveness of sins begins now, is the power that rescues us from the condition and influence of sin in this life, and is the means to a sure deliverance in the life to come. "Thanks be to God who gives us the victory through our Lord Jesus Christ!" (1 Cor 15:57).

3. Salvation by Faith Alone

The third strand in the Islamic teaching is salvation by faith alone. With this emphasis we enter the area of human responsibility for salvation. I will escape the Fire because I believe. The "alone" in the phrase "salvation by faith alone" is significant. In the next section we will consider the category of salvation by faith and works. The idea that an individual might be saved by works alone has never been countenanced in Islam, but the issue of faith alone versus faith and works has been hotly debated.

The natural Muslim stress on faith is well expressed by Mohammed Fadhel Jamali who had been imprisoned. He wrote about his awe of death, but declared that he also had another feeling, namely "that of comfort and inner peace." He identified the first factor in that feeling. He said that it is "a deep faith in Allah, the Sublime, and confidence that He will prevail over everything." He adds: "I felt that the blessing of faith and spiritual peace which goes with it is the most precious treasure in this life."[17] Jamali clearly felt "saved" by his faith, and in this respect he is a representative believer. The element of trust comes close to the root meaning of the Arabic word for faith, imān. The term means a turning to, a trusting, a feeling secure. In noun forms it adds the ideas of sincerity and loyalty. To many that seems clear enough. We must trust God for our security, and in the meantime lead pious lives. The level of our obedience determines whether we are good or bad Muslims, but our failures do not make us non-Muslims. Faith establishes our relation with God, and it is faith that ensures our salvation. Yet faith as trust gradually became agreement to a set of beliefs. For that development we must go to the Muslim thinkers.

With their strong emphasis on the divine role in human affairs the classical Muslim scholars gravitated to the idea of salvation by faith alone.[18] Yet they did not regard the concept of faith as a simple one. Apart from the basic problem of the place of good works, there were other questions involved, and they examined the issue from several angles. What is faith? Heart, mind, and behavior are involved. What is its primary constituting factor? Is it the loving conviction of the heart, the feeling that God is a merciful Lord? Is it intellectual agreement about truths of religion, implying some level of knowledge and formal confession? Or is it a spiritual attitude that leads the believer to achieve a recognizable standard of religious performance? Each of these emphases found some support. The interplay of knowing, believing and confessing became a particular point of contention. Confessing did not appear to be enough to establish faith since hypocrites can confess. Knowing was also not the final answer because unbelievers can know the facts. So the scholars fixed on believing, either with the mind or heart, as the core idea. With their thrust to logical conclusions they were moved to ask, in which of these—mind or heart—is faith grounded? Those who made believing an aspect of the mind emphasized assent as the critical factor—that is, I agree that Allah is God and Muhammad is God's apostle. Those who made it an aspect of the heart took faith to be an inner conviction that involves the whole person.

What came to be the orthodox Islamic position emphasized intellectual assent as the key factor in faith. The dawning Muslim position had been a holistic one, as this early creedal statement indicates: "Faith consists in confessing with the tongue, believing in the mind, and knowing with the heart."[19] When it came to identifying a true believer, however, this was not specific enough because the human heart is impenetrable. Its condition will always be a mystery. For that reason Islamic law stayed away from regulating inner attitudes, and it legislates only what can be seen, human actions. So also in the realm of theological belief Muslim thinkers decided to identify faith with what could be measured—agreement with a set of beliefs, such agreement becoming verifiable by confession. Although this did not happen overnight the element of intellectual assent gradually took over as the central feature of faith. The theologian al-Nasafī (d. 1142) represents that development. He said: "Belief is assent to that which he [Muhammad] brought from Allah, and confession of it." A commentator, al-Taftāzānī (d. 1388), added: "Belief, linguistically is assent, that is to say, acknowledging the judgment of a narrator, accepting it, and considering it to be veracious."[20] Almost as a concession the latter admitted that assent also has something to do with the heart because the Qur'ān says: "He hath written faith upon their hearts" (58:22).

Once intellectual agreement was anointed as the critical element in saving faith, it became relatively easy to define the content of that agreement. To what must I assent to be a saved Muslim believer? The *shahāda* or *kalima* was the answer. The term *shahāda* means the witnessing, while *kalima* implies the witnessing word. Both have reference to the common Muslim confession: "I testify that there is no deity but Allah, and that Muhammad is the messenger of Allah." A Hadīth declares that the Prophet Muhammad said.[21]

> I bear testimony to the fact that there is no god but Allah, and I am His messenger. The bondsman who would meet Allah without entertaining any doubt about these (two fundamentals) would enter heaven.

While the confession refers only to God and the last prophet, it was assumed that the other basic beliefs were included: angels, prophets, books, and day of judgment. The Qur'ān after all had declared: "The messenger believeth that which hath been revealed unto him from his Lord, and (so do) the believers. Each one believes in Allah, and His angels, and His scriptures, and His messengers" (2:285). To this list of beliefs the Traditions eventually added faith in God's eternal decrees. A Hadīth sums up the whole matter in this way. The angel Gabriel came to the Prophet in disguise and asked: "Inform me about faith." The holy Prophet replies: "That you affirm your faith in Allah, in His angels, in His Books, in His Apostles, in the Day of Judgment, and you affirm your faith in the Divine Decree to good and evil."[22]

Al-Ghazālī, who attacked formalistic religion, was the leader among those who maintained that faith must be the agreement of the heart. By agreement of the heart he simply meant that it is love for God that is the central idea in faith, not the acceptance of doctrines. Declaring that love is the highest of all topics he said:[23]

> Human perfection resides in this, that the love of God should conquer a man's heart and possess it wholly, and even if it does not possess it wholly, it should predominate in the heart over the love of all other things. Nevertheless, rightly to be understood, the love of God is so difficult a matter that one sect of theologians altogether denied that man can love a Being Who is not of his own species, and they have defined the love of God as consisting merely in obedience. Those who hold such views do not know what real religion is.

Most mainstream Muslims will whole-heartedly agree with the great "Teacher of Islam" that love for God must be an element if faith, but they also tend to exercise restraint in saying so. They recognize what the Qur'ān says, that "those of the Faith are overflowing in their love for God" (2:165; Yusuf Ali). Yet they will not ordinarily express their faith in these terms. No observer should understand this restraint as anything other than the expression of piety. Orthodox Muslims love God, but they do not as the Sufis do, frequently say so. Some know that even Al-Ghazālī himself said: "If you are asked, do you love Allah?, be silent; for if you say 'no', you become an unbeliever; if you say 'yes', your saying is not the description of those who love."[24]

Just as Al-Ghazālī and the Sufis strove to bring the loving conviction of the heart into the meaning of faith, so Muslims today are bringing forward the factor of performance. What is the proof of one's agreement if it is not the integrity of one's life? Faith implies commitment that issues in action. The actions that verify commitment are generally taken to be involvement in the ritual requirements of Islam, especially prayer. When a convert to Islamic faith is received by the community, the essential requirements are usually an honest recitation of the shahāda, the acceptance of circumcision, and at least a rudimentary knowledge of the prayer cycle. The requirements recognize a minimal level of performance, but it is regarded as a beginning only. As we shall see in the next section many Muslims today are attempting to reinforce the basic Islamic religious attitude itself—as a believer I should fear God, love God, remember God, trust God, surrender my life to God, and be obedient to God. They believe that this is what God expects from people of faith. God will respond to such faith with the boon of Paradise. "Whatever you have been given is but a passing comfort for the life of the world, and that which Allah hath is better and more lasting for those who believe and put their trust in the Lord" (42:34).

Whatever the precise definition of faith may be all Muslims agree that it is God who awakens it in the human psyche. The Qur'ān says: "Allah endeareth the faith to you" (49:7). This recognition keeps God at the centre, and is an essential element in salvation by faith alone. It is the kernel of faith that God creates within us, and not our inconsistent performance, that will avail for us on the Day of Doom, and for that gift believers should be grateful. Miss Cigdem Bilginer, a Turkish Muslim, spoke of her inner discontent with her life and her search for faith. "Then I saw that God gives the opportunity to acquire faith. It is up to me to choose to want it; and also, once I want it, to work for it." She said:[25]

> I need faith—where I am bound to fail—for myself, for others, and for my nation. All ideologies take faith, and all revolutions take a lot of faith. But some rely on men and do not demand everything. The faith I speak of asks for everything and depends on God.

That dependence on God is the essential element in the Muslim understanding of saving faith. "O ye who believe! fear God and believe in His apostle. He will give you two portions of His mercy and will make for you a light to walk in, and will forgive you; for God is forgiving, compassionate" (57:28; Palmer).

Thoughts for Christian Sharing

a. In the Christian view the essence of faith is trust. It is not agreement with an idea or a statement but a personal relationship of trust between God and the believer.

b. It is God's love for us that calls forth our trust. God reveals His own faithfulness by reaching down in saving love to help human beings. True faith will recognize the incredible grace of God. Even demons know God and believe. Faith becomes saving faith when it lays hold of the saving God. It declares: "God is my refuge and strength, whom shall I fear?"

c. Salvation is by faith alone because human beings are lost in bondage to sin, death, and the devil. Only God can save, and God needs no helpers. God does so through Christ the Savior and we accept God's gift by faith. Faith links our inability with God's ability.

d. Christians believe that to be saved by faith and to be "justified" by faith mean essentially the same thing; that is, God for Christ's sake graciously accepts us, forgives our sins, and declares us righteous (justifies us). God does so on the basis of His work, not ours.

e. Faith overflows in gratitude and is fruitful in love. It is guarded by the Spirit of God who created it and sustains it. A Christian prayer is: "Lord, I believe, help thou my unbelief."

4. Salvation by Faith and Works

A large percentage of Muslims, perhaps a majority, will contend that salvation is by means of faith and works. This is the fourth position from which a believer may view the question. A believer must act, as well as believe and confess. Faith and works cannot be divided. The actions authenticate the confession. The emphasis in this means is on works, assuming faith. I am saved by what I do. There is a little Qur'anic phrase that illustrates the tension between this view and that of faith alone. The frequently-used phrase is "believe and do right." "Aha," the faith alone people say, "the 'and' separates, and gives precedence to faith!" "Aha," the faith and works people say, "the 'and' connects the two and requires both!"

The fact that many Muslims regard the combination of faith and works as the prime means to salvation cannot come as a surprise. The concepts of surrender and obedience, the development of laws to control behavior, the ritual practices of the religion, and the portrayal of the last judgment as a weighing of recorded works all contribute to this opinion. To many it seems that the very essence of Islam is to accept God's guidance and do it. Three sub-principles undergird this concept. The first is that humans have the natural ability to do good. The second is that they have the free will to do it. And the third is that they have received a God-given call to live lives of piety (*taqwā*) and righteousness (*birr*). The evidence seems overwhelming to many. Salvation must be by works, with faith understood.

The Qur'ān and Hadīth can be easily quoted in support of salvation by works because of their commands to observe religious duty and their warnings against evil-doing. In the very passage of the Qur'ān that outlines the content of faith the obligation to deeds is powerfully stated:

> Righteous is one who believes in God, and the last day, and the angels and the books and the prophets, and who gives wealth for love of Him to kindred and orphans and the poor and the son of the road and beggars and those in captivity, and who is steadfast in prayer and gives alms, and those who trust in their covenant when they make a covenant, and the patient in poverty and distress and in time of salvation (2:177).

The Qur'ān repeatedly asserts that the combination of faith and works is what counts. "Those who misbelieve, theirs will be an awful doom, and those who believe and do good works, theirs will be forgiveness and a great reward" (35:7). It offers good news for those who have faith and are faithful. "And give glad tidings (O Muhammad) unto those who believe and do good works, that theirs are gardens underneath which rivers flow" (2:25). It does not hesitate to use the term "reward." In the midst of a description of Paradise the Qur'ān says: "Lo! this is a reward for you. Your endeavor (upon earth) hath found acceptance" (7:22).

The theory of salvation by works, in fact, is based on the concept of reward. Works become merits that are credited to one's spiritual account, thus overcoming the effect of sins. Muslims have recognized that the idea can easily lead to a commercial and self-serving approach, and they have struggled to offset it. Is there a deeper spiritual motivation that sanctifies the idea of compensation? The jurists believed that they found it in the concept of intention, mystics in the idea of love, and theologians in the principle of the fear and worship of God. The jurists stated that the intention (*niyya*) behind a work must be right for it to be a good work. A saying developed that intention is even more important than the work itself! The concept of intention was applied to the ritual practices to preserve their spiritual purposes. The mystics looked to the love of God as the element that would liberate Muslim behavior from self-centered utilitarianism. They were moved by the declaration of the Qur'ān that brightness and joy await those who "feed with food the needy wretch, the orphan, and the prisoner, for love of Him (saying): We feed you for the sake of Allah only. We wish no reward or thanks from you. We fear from our Lord a day of frowning and fate" (76:8ff.).

No one has ever expressed the principles of pure intention and disinterested love more eloquently than Rabīʿa, the woman mystic from Barra (d. 801). Someone asked her why she loved God, at the same time confessing that it was the seven degrees of hell that influenced him, while another person said that it was the rare delights of heaven that motivated him. Rabīʿa rejoined: "He is a bad servant who worships God from fear and terror or from the desire or reward—but there are many of these." [26] They pressed her harder on why she worshiped God. She replied: "The Neighbour first, and then the House." By "Neighbour" she meant God. That saying is no more famed in Islam than the following words: "O God! if I worship Thee in hope of Paradise, exclude me from Paradise, but if I worship Thee for Thine own sake, withhold not Thine everlasting Beauty!"[27]

There are "Rabi'as" today who express the same approach. The first mosque in Canada, and the second in North America, is located in Edmonton, Alberta. It was built by Lebanese Muslim immigrants in 1938, who received help from Jewish and Christian friends. The tiny 30 x 50 feet red-brick structure was named the Al-Rashid Mosque. In recent years the historic building was not much used, having been supplanted by five other modern mosques. Urban development that had forced one re-location required that the mosque be torn down to make space for a hospital parking lot. A group of Muslim women whose families had worshiped in the building were saddened and resolved to take remedial action. They persuaded the City Council to allow them to move the structure to the city's Heritage Center. Then they raised the money needed for the move. Brick by brick the little mosque was transported to the new site and re-assembled. It is now used at special festival times. It was clear that action of these women was not done to draw attention to themselves or to seek reward, but it was rather a simple act of dedication and love. As such it belongs to the "best" good works that are extolled in Islam and that will be taken account of on the Day of Judgment.[28]

Many theologians, and certainly contemporary fundamentalist theologians, take the fear of God as the true motivation for our works. The same word taqwā means both fear and piety. From this perspective it is the Godwardness" of the believer and not the simple desire for salvation that moves a Muslim to surrender life and to become obedient to the divine commands. One modern Shīʿa theologian, Ayautallah Mutahhari, views works done in this spirit as a form of worship. Whether ritual ceremonies or ethical actions "Islamic tauhid accepts no other motive than God." He argues that one must do both one's own work for God's sake and the people's work for God's sake. It is true that "the road to God passes among people," but the goal is always God. To work for oneself is simply egoism, and for people alone idolatry, but to do one's own and the people's work for God is the worship of God. Worship is both the love of God and the love of God's command.[29]

The principles of pure motivation are recognized in Islam. Nevertheless the utilitarian aspect of salvation by works has undoubted force for the average Muslim who believes that he or she will be judged on that basis. The elements of reward, atoning for sin, and gaining the merit that will avail for a favorable decision on the Last Day all run together in common thinking. The believer knows that the accounts are being kept, that they will be brought forward, and that decisions will be made on their basis. "Whoso doeth good works and is a believer, there will be no rejection of his effort. Lo! We record (it) for him" (21:94). The merit principle is stated forthrightly in several passages, especially those related to the giving of alms. In many parts of the Muslim world the poor and handicapped wait in lines outside a mosque or in the market, murmuring "Allah, Allah!" as they extend their hands. Few Muslims will fail to help at least one begging person. That assistance has value. "If ye publish your almsgiving, it is well, but if ye hide it and give it to the poor, it will be better for you and will atone for some of your ill-deeds" (2:271). The Qur'ān asks: "O ye who believe! Shall I show you a commerce that will save you from a powerful doom?" It then gives the answer: "Ye should believe in Allah and His messenger, and should strive for the cause of Allah with your wealth and your lives. ... He will forgive your sins and bring you into gardens (61:111f.).

What then are the works that are considered essential for those who approach salvation on this level? On the one hand there are the ritual practices of Islam that provide the basic framework of a believer's daily life. As the concept of faith was spelled out in terms of several specific beliefs, so that of religious behavior (dīn) was defined as a combination of the following activities: confession of faith, prayer, fasting, alms-giving, and the pilgrimage. Some authorities added the element of struggling for God. In everyday Islam it is these practices that are regarded as the core good works which Muslims must carry on in the service of God ('ibādat).

On the other hand, there are the ethical actions that are clearly commanded and that are modeled in the life of the Prophet Muhammad. There was always in Islam, and there is today, a constant pietist trend that calls Muslims back to the moral concern. We have noted that trend in our discussion of sin. The ascetics and ethical theologians maintained it. They have their modern counterparts in the reformers who contend that being a Muslim must mean something beyond ceremonial obedience, and that is true ethical behavior. There were rationalist Muslims in Islamic history, called the Mu'tazilites, who maintained the same principle. In the "Golden Age" of Islam they argued powerfully that morality and justice represent the essence of Islam. They too have their counterparts today in modernist movements that regard social progress and moral behavior as two sides of one religious coin. What about ordinary citizens? Sincere Muslims are responsive to these calls to piety, but they do not deal with them in isolation. They relate them to the existential awareness that all behavior—ethical or ritual—has to do with one's eternal destiny. Good works are more than noble deeds and contributions to the standards and image of the community. They are actions that affect my future. Who can possibly forget the great scale, the Mizan, and the weighing that lies ahead? The One Who is named "The Reckoner," will be in charge. "We shall set up scales of justice for the day of Judgment, so that not a soul will be dealt with unjustly in the least. ... And enough are We to take account" (21:47). With the fervency called forth by this awareness Muslims pray: "Lead us in the straight path, not the path of those who go astray."

We must note one work, however, that automatically qualifies a Muslim believer for immediate entry into Paradise. That work is martyrdom, struggling and dying for the faith. The word for martyr, shahīd, means "witness" and has a double meaning. It may refer to one who gives evidence in court, or it may apply to one who witnesses unto death on the battlefield. It is the latter meaning that is being considered here. After urging his followers to fight for God the Prophet Muhammad says in the Qur'ān: "And repute not those slain on God's path to be dead. Nay alive are they with their Lord, richly sustained" (3:164). This and other passages are amply supported by the Hadīth. The Traditions report that a martyr has six privileges with God: his sins are pardoned when the first drop of blood falls; he is shown his seat in Paradise; he is safe from the punishment of the grave and the terror of the Judgment; a crown of dignity is placed on his head; he is married to seventy dark-eyed virgins; and he makes intercession for seventy of his relatives. The shahīd idea has been raised at various times in Muslim history in the interest of particular causes, not all of which have been Islamically valid, including the activity of terrorists. The true shahīd, however, is paid immense respect and honor.

That raises a doubt that perplexes Muslims. The theory of salvation by works struggles with uncertainty. No one except martyrs to the faith will bypass the judgment. The doubt arises whether one's good works will or will not suffice to overcome one's sins. On the Day of Resurrection "every soul will pay in full what it hath earned, and they will not be wronged" (3:161). For most people who are aware of their shortcomings the prospect of a fair judgment is not good news. Have I earned enough? Will my credits exceed my debits? Will the scales balance in my favor or not? The basic inconclusiveness gave rise to two developments: the grading of sins and the idea of a purgatory. We have already noted the factor of grading sins. Building on the distinction between great sins and light sins the thought developed that God will mercifully overlook slight mistakes and credit the believer's overall intention. This still left unsettled the issue of greatly sinning Muslims, but the notion that there will be a kind of purgatory developed to take care of that problem. Somewhere, perhaps at the top level of hell, erring Muslims will be punished for a time, but will be eventually admitted into Paradise.

In the end Muslim believers at this level must set aside the disturbing question of how many works are needed for salvation. Since it is impossible to answer they are not inclined to speculate about it, anymore than they are inclined to be judgmental about their neighbor's prospects. Influenced by their own conscience and the Qur'anic call to obedience they regard the regular performance of the prescribed duties of Islam—that is, a "respectable" amount of prayer, fasting and almsgiving—combined with a decent life, to be cumulatively sufficient to obtain the desired result of Paradise. The Qur'ān declares: "They shall have, before their Lord, all that they wish for ... for God is Oft-Forgiving, Most Ready to appreciate (service)" (42:22f.; Yusuf Ali).

Thoughts for Christian Sharing:

a. In the Christian understanding good works have crucial importance, but they cannot cancel sin. God who is holy asks us to be holy, and God does not bargain. Our right deeds do not undo our wrongs in God's sight.

b. Only God has the authority to cancel the guilt of sin. The miracle of divine love is that what we could not do for ourselves, God does for us. We cannot escape the consequences of our sin by our own goodness. It is God's goodness that makes it possible. God's work of salvation is "the best work."

c. Jesus the Messiah taught that the final judgment will be based on works. This is not a "weighing" to find out whether an individual has done enough works to make up for his or her sins. He, "the ransom for many," has already taken care of that ultimate human problem. The judgment rather reveals whether humans have taken God's gifts seriously.

d. In the Christian view faith is a relationship of thankful love, and good works are the inevitable outflow. Christians do good works not in order to be saved, but because they have been saved and are grateful. By faith we become children of a holy, loving, and saving God. By works we reflect what we have become—through holy, loving, and saving actions.

e. True piety is not formalistic or self-centered. Its pattern is the servant-love of Jesus. But a genuine believer also knows that he or she is God's unworthy servant, and prays for the purifying and uplifting power of God's Spirit in daily life.

f. Christians and Muslims need to examine together what are the works of God, and where they agree they need to cooperate in doing them, for the health of the world.

5. Salvation by Intercession

Will the divine decree favor me? Will God's mercy reach me? Will my faith be accepted? Will my good works overcome the effect of my sins? Doubts about the answers to questions such as these helped to produce the fifth means of salvation in Islam—salvation by intercession. The idea is that one of the prophets or saints, possible Muhammad or his grandson Husain, will intercede on one's behalf on the Last Day. It is an idea that developed very early after the death of the Prophet. I will escape from the Fire because someone will step in and plead for me.

Differing from the other means that we have considered to this point, salvation by intercession has only a slight basis in the Qur'ān. The Qur'ān suggests the possibility, but only if God gives permission. "Allah! there is no god save Him, the Alive, the Eternal. ... Who is he that intercedeth with Him save by His leave? (2:255). One passage (40:7), however, says that the angels implore forgiveness for the believers, and another (43:86) hints that those "who witnessed to the truth," that is, God's prophets, will do so. In general the Qur'ān takes another approach. The individual believer is wholly responsible for his actions, and has a lifetime to work out the responsibility. Don't look for help when it is too late, it advises, and certainly don't expect it if you are an unbeliever. "Then guard yourselves against a day when one soul shall not avail another," says the Qur'ān, "nor shall intercession be accepted for her, nor shall compensation be taken from her, nor shall anyone be helped (from outside)" (2:48; Yusuf Ali). Furthermore, on the Judgment Day nobody can help anyone else. "No bearer of burdens can bear the burden of another" (6:164; Yusuf Ali). All sovereignty, and every decision, on that Day will be God's.

Despite these cautions the idea of intercession became a major stream of thought in Islam. It met a need, the sense that a sinful human being requires help.

We may speculate about another factor. As we have seen Islam holds to a very strong emphasis on God's overwhelming majesty. The Lord is beyond human comprehension, the Incomparable One. That August One is far above and beyond possible human contact. Will our petitions for help ascend to the Lord of the Worlds? The human limitations are serious indeed, but that applies to ordinary people like us. What about the extraordinary individuals, the prophets and the saints? They are certainly nearer to God. They may be the witnesses to whom God will listen, and surely they would be moved to plead for us. From this complex of human need and emotion the idea arose that there will be some form of intercession in the Hour of Doom, and that idea is now firmly entrenched in Muslim consciousness.

Once the possibility of intercession was admitted it was inevitable that the Prophet Muhammad would be regarded as the primary mediator. Like an advocate he will speak for his fellow Muslim believers. Traditional Islam teaches that at a critical moment in his career, when Muhammad was undergoing severe persecution, he was taken to heaven in a miraculous journey that led from Mecca to Jerusalem, then from Jerusalem to the presence of God where he received divine instruction. If this is the case, then surely the Lord will also heed his intercession! Does not the Qur'ān say that God will raise him "to a laudable station" (17:79)? The Hadīth took up the idea and carried it forward with extensive elaboration. An oft-recited Tradition tells how distressed believers will seek help on the day of Resurrection. They come for aid to the various prophets—Adam, Noah, Abraham, Moses, Jesus—but all excuse themselves, one by one. Then they turn to Muhammad who is granted leave to enter God's presence. God informs the Prophet that he may speak freely and hopefully. Then Muhammad cries out: "O Lord, my people, my people!" As he goes on imploring: "Save, O my Lord, save!", the people miraculously pass by into Paradise until only those are left behind for whom eternal punishment is appropriate.[30] The high place of Muhammad in this means to salvation is summed up by an Indian Muslim poet, Mir Muhammad Taki Mir (d. 1810) who wrote: "Why do you worry, O Mir, thinking of your black book? The person of the Seal of the Prophets is the guarantee for your salvation."[31] A contemporary Muslim expresses the feeling in these words. Sheikh al-Halveti explains the significance of Muhammad's title "Sayyid" and then says of the one that he calls "the Prince of Life:"

> Can you think of the awe and dread of that day whose judge is Allah, and the grandeur and majesty of the one who is master of all men [Muhammad; ed.] on that day? On the day, when all men are raised, when a thousand feet will stand on one foot, when men are trembling with fear, immersed in their own sweat, brains boiling in their skulls, all hoping for each others' aid—mothers, fathers, priests, popes, saints, even all the prophets thinking of their own salvation, and unable to help. The Beloved of Allah, the Master of the Day of Last Judgment, will be the only one to turn to for help.[32]

Both the scope of the help and the privilege of interceding widened out in the course of Islamic history. The scope broadened to include the practical needs of this life, the privilege widened to include all the Prophets and the family and companions of Muhammad. Eventually the saints too found a place in the rank of intercessors. Their shrines dot the Islamic world, and at every shrine devotees plead that they may intercede with God in their behalf. As the story of intercession unfolded, not even pious believers were excluded from the possibility. Their intercession is expressed in two ways—by the prayer for forgiveness for past believers, which are uttered as part of the five-fold daily *salāt*, and by the funeral prayers that they recite at the grave side. There they pray:[33]

> O Allah! pardon our living and our dead ... !
> O Allah! make him our fore-runner, and
> make him a reward and a treasure, and
> make him for us a pleader, and
> accept his pleading!

A Hadīth says that the wife of the Prophet, 'Ā'isha, reported Muhammad as saying: "If a company of Muslims to the number of a hundred pray over a dead person, all of them interceding for him, their intercession for him will be accepted."[34] While the idea of intercession spread out like the delta of a river, there is no doubt that among Sunnī Muslims its primary focus is on the Judgment scene, its primary issue is deliverance from the Fire, and the primary intercessor is the Prophet of Islam.

In the Shī'a section of Islam intercession is strongly associated with the family of the Prophet Muhammad. It is his son-in-law, 'Alī, the martyred grandson Husain, and the eleven successor-leaders (imāms) who are the intercessors par excellence. Shī'as believe that when Husain and 72 family members were massacred in the battle of Kerbela (680), only fifty years after the death of the Prophet himself, in an action led by a general of the Caliph Yazid, he died for the sins of Islam. As a Shī'a historian puts it: " He himself laid down his life at the altar of Truth and for the sake of humanity."[35] Thus an element of voluntary and redemptive sacrifice enters the Islamic scene. It is vividly expressed in the commemorative festivals of the Shī'as and in their prayers. Although Muhammad and 'Alī continue as the major intercessors, for Shī'as it is Husain who has become both the pattern for self-giving struggle against evil in this world, and a prime mediator on the Day of Judgement. Without the mediation of 'Alī, the Imāms, and Husain, it will be impossible for humans to avoid the due punishment for their sinful deeds. A Shī'a tradition records that the Prophet Muhammad said to 'Alī:[36]

> There are three things that I swear to be true. The first is that you and your descendants are mediators for mankind. ... The second is that you are to present to God those who may enter Paradise. ... The third is that you are the absolute mediators, for those who will go to Hell will only be those who do not recognize you and whom you do not recognize.

Connecting with intercession the salvation thinking of Islam has also included the expectation of a deliverer to come. The expectation arose with the internal struggles of early Muslims, but very quickly became associated with eschatological events. One of those happenings will be the coming of the Mahdi, "the guided one," a descendant of the Prophet, whose advent will immediately precede the descent of Jesus the Messiah. A charismatic and militant deliverer, the Mahdi will unite the divided Muslim community, end its sufferings, fill the earth with equity, and exerting power over all Muslim lands for seven years will prepare the world for the next stage in the end-time. It is noteworthy that all the references to this personage are from the Hadīth.

The Mahdi tradition found a special home in the Shī'a community. It holds that its tenth leader, Imam Mahdi (b. 868), is alive and in hiding, and will return again. This passage drawn from a shrine prayer in Iraq, illustrates the longing for the advent of the Mahdi, "the Door of Approach to God," together with the hope for his intercession:[37]

> I bear witness that thou art the established truth, that there can be no mistake or doubt, and that God's promise of thy coming is sure. But I am dismayed at thy tarrying so long, and do not have the patience to wait for a distant time. It is not surprising that some have denied thee. I am waiting, however, for the day of thy coming. Thou art an intercessor who will not be questioned, and a master who will not be taken away. God has kept thee for the assistance of the Faith, a protection for believers, and a punishment for infidels and heretics. ... O my leader, if I should die before thy coming, grant me thy intercession and that of thy pure fathers. ... I bear witness that it is by thy favour that our actions will be approved, our works made pure, and our merits multiplied. Whosoever comes to thy friendship and acknowledges thee as the Imam, surely his works will be accepted, his word believed, his good deeds made many, and his sins blotted out.

We will only summarize the ramifications of the Mahdi idea. As centuries passed it began to be applied to political salvation in this world. That reflected the Muslim longing for a vital and victorious Muslim community that would initiate God's kingdom on earth. The desire for such a conclusion was often joined with a thirst for personal power, and hence from the twelfth century forward Mahdi pretenders arose in various parts of the Muslim world, who initiated revolutions and established political states. It is that longing that has come down to modern times, rather than the emphasis on the end-time. Many Muslims today look for deliverers in the here and now who will courageously struggle to overcome evil and to reform the Muslim community. One Shi'a poet puts it this way:[38]

> Thrones are usurped, gold stolen,
> But not the thorny Crown,
> That always rests on the brow of a rare Jesus.

The Mahdi idea is adapted by the revivalist, Abul A'la Mawdudi, who says: "if the expectation that Islam will dominate the world of thought, culture, and politics is genuine, then the coming of a Great Leader is also certain."[39] It is that constant search for charismatic heroes of the faith that gives opportunity to the self-appointed and extremist "mahdis" of our time.

The carry-over of the idea of intercession from the area of final salvation to the problems of this life has its reflection in a form of Islam that some non-Muslims call "folk Islam." We will briefly consider this varied phenomenon in the context of this discussion.

Intercession and Folk Islam

What has often been called "folk" Islam is a form of popular Islam. It is debatable how firm a line can be drawn between "official" Islam and "popular" Islam. In the first place no one has the authority to declare an official Islam. Secondly, popular Islam is a collective term for a broad variety of phenomena. Thirdly, the two streams have steadily merged in the development of mainstream Islam. With some caution then we may use the term "folk" Islam to refer to the "Islams" of particular folk who maintain a close bond with local non-Muslim cultures. Such cultures are often characterized by the beliefs and practices of primal religions, and as Islam is grafted on to it the daily life of Muslims take on syncretic forms.

Within such Muslim sub-cultures the need for intercession is deeply felt, because of their emphasis on unseen and often inimical powers that must be dealt with effectively. The idea of salvation is broadened to include security from these nearby physical and spiritual enemies that threaten our lives and safety. At one end of the spectrum of needs are physical ones, often related to the life cycle and health issues, and at the other end are apparent forms of demonic influence in the mental and spiritual realms. These all are considered to be interconnected and interactive, within a holistic understanding of life. The overcoming of these dangerous or malevolent powers involves not only the use of intercession but also forms of magic. Human beings who are believed to have authority over such influences are sought out. But who, from the Muslim point of view, are those who possess such power?

Muslims at this level often turn to those who possess what is called *baraka*. This is considered to be a divinely-given supernatural force or saving power that is capable of producing blessings and that enables its possessors to do miraculous works (*karāmāt*). These individuals are not only the saints of old, but they include also their descendants who continue to possess at least a fragment of their founding personality's grace and authority. But the grace of *baraka* may well be possessed by others as well. Such saint-heirs and power-dispensers generally seek to work within the frame of reference of traditional Islam, although they are often the objects of strong criticism from reformers who are seeking to eliminate what they regard as superstitious and un-Islamic practices.

Some practitioners of spiritual power, however, are less orthodox and go to the very edge of Muslim tolerance, or beyond it in their approach. These certainly include the purveyors of various forms of witchcraft. Their focus is on overcoming Satan the Whisperer and the influence of evil jinn or spirits, which represent a common Muslim concern. Their methods, however, are uncommon, thinly disguised forms of magic. This is the world of amulets and charms, incantations and oaths, divination and fortune-telling, the evil eye and black magic, dreams and trance, exorcism and outright miracles. It is a world in which escape from the Fire of the future retreats before the pressing need to deal with the fires of everyday life. In many ways, some bewildering, Muslims in different parts of the world are attempting to deal with those fires.

It may well be argued that the world view of folk Islam presents a distinct concept of salvation and an explicit methodology for attaining it. Such a sharp division would obscure the truth that some aspects of folk Islam have their source in Muslim tradition, while others invade and inform all the various approaches that have been considered. Bill Musk summarizes this basic point:[40]

> The folk-Islamic model of the universe is vastly different from that which supports the assumptions and behavioural activities of the official faith. The result should be a clash. The surprising truth is that ... official and popular expressions of Islam tend to live easily with one another. Indeed, both views may operate in veiled partnership within any one single Muslim.

Khadija is a member of a traditional Muslim family, and was a helper in a Christian nursery school. She used to listen to the stories of Jesus that were told to the children, and was fascinated with the personality of 'Īsā Masīh and his power to help her escape from the Fire. She had a desire to follow him openly, but her position did not allow her to do so. The tensions played heavily on her tender nature, and she suffered a mental breakdown. In her delirium she constantly repeated the name "Jesus." To her kindhearted family this development appeared to be the sign of demonic influence, and they called in Muslim exorcists. The magicians utilized a broad range of magic to drive out the evil spirits, but they were not able to do so. At the urgent request of the family Khadija was then taken many miles to a Christian hospital where she received shock therapy, and eventually recovered. Many Islamic worlds met in Khadija and her family, searcher and searchers for saving power.

Thoughts for Christian Sharing:

a. Christians believe that we human beings dare not appear before God the Judge in the garments of sin. They hold that the problem is so serious that it requires more than human pleading to overcome it. It needs the deep intercession that only God can provide.

b. In the Christian view intercession does belong wholly to God and therefore must come from God. The good news is that it has come indeed. God sends from Himself His Word and Spirit, Jesus the Messiah, to be our intercessory Friend. As the Gospel declares, "There is one God; there is also one mediator between God and humankind, Christ Jesus, himself human, who gave himself a ransom for all" (1 Tim 2:5). There is no need to look for another.

c. It is true that no burdened soul shall bear another's burdens. The sinless son of Mary bore the sins of many, atoned for them, and because he is alive "he is able for all time to save those who approach God through him, since he always lives to make intercession for them" (Heb 7:25).

d. To those who fear the demonic powers comes this consolation: God is stronger than Satan, and Jesus cast out the demons.

6. Salvation by the Mystical Path

The sixth means of salvation in Islam is salvation by the mystical path that leads to the goal of union with God. It is the Sufi way. Al-Junayd (d. 910), a Sufi thinker, said: "Sufism is that God should make thee die away from thyself and live in him."[41] In this approach I will be saved by becoming one with God.

The perspective of mysticism differs dramatically from what we have considered thus far. The difference is not only one of means, but in the definition of salvation itself. The goal of union with God is different than escape from Hellfire to Paradise. In the view of some Muslims one of the joys of Paradise will be the vision of God. That is not the same, however, as uniting with God. The means to achieve that goal are also unorthodox. Sufi Muslims do not deny the need for traditional religion, but they regard it as only the starting-point in the journey of faith. The Sufi path goes on from there. Utilizing various techniques of spiritual methodology, and passing through a series of stages and states the mystic not only experiences a deeper knowledge of God, but enjoys a sense of ecstatic illumination that is described as a condition of oneness with God.

How different from the forehead-touching-the-ground world view of traditional Islam! No wonder that orthodox Muslims looked askance at the rise of mysticism in their midst. There was pressure, however, that forced its development. One was the need for and desire for nearness to God. Orthodox Islam lays stress on the distance between the Creator and the creaturely, between the Master and His servants. That distinction is the central motif of Islam, and it captures an essential element in the Qur'ān. But there was another idea in the Qur'ān that some Muslims preferred. God says that He is closer to us than our jugular vein (50:16). Did God not say: "Wheresoever you turn, there is God's face" (2:115)? Did He not also speak of "a people whom He loves and who love him" (5:54)? This Qur'anic testimony to God's nearness and love merged with the need and desire of the human spirit for a relation with God. Muslim mysticism rose from that basic human thirst. A Tradition came along to underline the theological principle. God says: "I was a hidden treasure and wanted to be known, therefore I created the world"[42] Once again, it was Muhammad who became the practical example. He certainly was aware of God in his life, and he personally experienced a mysterious ascent to the divine (mi'rāj) that is an allegory for his followers. Mysticism arose, but not overnight.

The Sufi mystics began as pious ascetics who were critical of the corruption and formalism that was beginning to characterize Muslim behavior. They banded together into groups that practiced dhikr, the concentrated recital of the Qur'ān and God's names. Gradually Sufis took this pious protest into a quite different direction. The fear-based desire to serve God purely became the love-based desire to draw near to God's being. They also developed specific steps to enable that process to take place under the direction of a leader who knew the way. Sufi groups gathered around such leaders and their descendants, creating religious orders that spread across the Muslim world. Since the leaders were also recognized as saints, the multiplication of their shrines followed in the wake of Sufism. Could anyone have predicted such a development?

Orthodox Muslims sensed a basic conflict with their view of Islam, and were deeply troubled. They believed that there is a fundamental difference between surrendering to God and the divine will, and drawing near to God in a mystical union. Their fears were confirmed for them when some mystics began to describe that relation not as union but as unity. Abū Bistāmī (d. 874), called Bayezid, even said: "*Subbhāni*—Praise be to Me, how great is My Majesty!"[43] Orthodox Muslims could not help but believe that by obliterating the distinction between God and creatures, and by elevating humans to this stature, Sufis were committing the sin of *shirk*, associating a partner with God. The problem was bad enough when it was confined to a relatively few members of religious orders and convents, but when aspects of mysticism began to influence the rank and file of Muslim believers, it became a threat to the safety of traditional religion and to the authority of its guardians. It is impossible to predict what would have happened if Al-Ghazālī (d. 1111) had not appeared on the scene.

Al-Ghazālī had rediscovered his faith as a result of his Sufi experience. Building on that experience and his immense standing as "the Teacher of Islam," he managed to combine orthodoxy and Sufism into one system of thought despite the uneasiness of that marriage. In effect he put together the orthodox practice of behavioral religion with the heart religion of the mystics by arguing that behavior shrivels without its heart meaning, and true heart religion on the other hand confirms orthodox practice. Through experiential religion believers will come to know that the real meaning of faith is the friendship and love of God. The closing words of Al-Ghazālī's famous Confessions summarize this "orthodox mysticism" that reflected his own personal experience:[44]

> I pray to God the Omnipotent to place us in the ranks of His chosen, among the number of those whom He directs in the path of safety, in whom He inspires fervour lest they forget Him; whom He cleanses from all defilement, that nothing may remain in them except Himself; yea, whom He indwells completely, that they may adore none beside Him.

The Sufis produced much of the great religious poetry of Islam. The poetry expressed rejection of everything that separates believers from the thought of God, especially material attractions, even religion itself. It spoke of a longing for Reality, the Reality of God. Exoteric religious practices have value as preparation and means, but it is the esoteric inner knowledge of God (*ma'rifa*) that matters. Mir Daud of Delhi (d. 1785) expressed this dominant note in the Sufi song of salvation: "O God, since Thou has given an eye, show us Reality, for the object of the eye is seeing; and since Thou hast opened the door for seeking, open also the gate of arriving, for the goal of searching is reaching, and an eye which is not honored by the vision of the Unity is like a squinting eye."[45] The celebrated Rūmī said that when a mystic does finally arrive and sees, he becomes silent. "When it comes to love, I have to be silent. To describe Love, intellect is like an ass in the morass, the Pen breaks when it is to describe love."[46] Rabī'a, whom we quoted earlier, does not hesitate to describe that ecstasy:[47]

O my Joy and my Desire and my Refuge,
My Friend and my Sustainer and my Goal,
Thou art my Intimate, and longing for Thee sustains me. ...
Thy love is now my desire and my bliss,
And has been revealed to the eye of my heart that was athirst,
I have none beside Thee, Who dost make the desert bloom,
Thou art my joy and firmly established within me,
If Thou art satisfied with me, then
O Desire of my heart, my happiness has appeared.

Muhammad al-Niffarī (d. 961) summarizes the Sufi experience. Looking at the world and at one's personal life brings dismay. "I saw Fear holding sway over Hope." Our knowledge and actions leave us helpless. "And I saw the Fire." But when God and His mercy become unveiled for us, the Fire dies down. "And He said to me, 'I am thy Friend,' and I was established."[48]

What are the means by which the mystic "arrives" and "sees" the Friend? The techniques of the Sufis are complex, and differ in various orders and regions. They may be summarized, however, as a combination of unquestioned obedience to the leader and a disciplined adherence to the meditative practices of the path (tariqa) being followed. The remembrance of God, dhikr, is central however to all Sufi ritual. In conservative orders it is a silent ritual, but in extreme orders it may be accompanied by rhythmic bodily motions, music, sound, and even hypnosis. By utilizing the prescribed discipline the devotee passes through a set of spiritual "stages." These are a series of ascending virtues beginning with abstinence and repentance, and ending with reliance upon God. It is noteworthy that reliance upon God, which is the end-point of orthodox spirituality, is only the starting-point in a second series of "states." The states include nearness to God, fear, hope, intimacy, contemplation, certainty, knowledge (gnosis), and love. Finally the journey is over. The mystic arrives at fanā', the final state, which is union with God. In defining this ultimate experience Sufis tend to part ways. Conservative believers view it as a joining of two selves, the divine and human, both retaining their identity in a mutual bond of love. Left-wing Sufis regard the experience as an absorption and finally an annihilation of the human self in God, wherein as Ibn 'Arabī (d. 1240) put it "everything is He."

Some Sufi ideas and practices have penetrated into general Islamic spirituality, but they are under attack in the Muslim world today. In their later years Sufi orders degenerated into superstitious forms and harbored immoral practices. Surveying the latter R. A. Nicholson, the sympathetic chronicler of Islamic mysticism, said: "Let us acknowledge that the transports of spiritual intoxication are not always sublime, and that human nature has a trick of avenging itself on those who would cast it off."[49] For their escapism, superstition and immorality modern Muslim reformers have rigorously denounced the Sufis, so that this means of salvation has restricted application today. What the Sufis gave to Islam, however, was a rich heritage of warmth and passion, the spirit of contemplation, and the idea that salvation must involve at its core a drawing near to a loving God. Among individuals the Sufi search goes on, expressed poignantly in the words of Kabir:

"All speak of God, but to me this doubt arises, how can they sit down with God whom they do not know?"[50]

Thoughts for Christian Sharing:

a. The desire for nearness to God is a fundamental human longing that God has put in human hearts. David said: "My soul thirsts for the living God" (Ps 42:2).

b. It is essential to know that God also intensely desires to have a relationship of love with human beings. Even though we are unworthy sinners, God loves us. As God says in Hosea the Prophet (11:3-8): "I taught you how to walk, took you in my arms, bent down and fed you. How can I give you up?"

c. Through Jesus the Messiah God our loving Friend creates the basis for a new relationship. God does that by drawing very near to us humans, and by wiping out the separation that sin created. It is not necessary for us to do what is impossible, to ascend to the divine. God has come into our midst to bridge the gap and to restore the possibility of human fellowship with God. "My compassion grows warm and tender. I will not execute my fierce anger ... for I am God and no mortal, the Holy One in your midst" (Hos 11:9).

d. Edna Hong wrote a book on sin and grace with the challenging title, *The Downward Ascent.*[51] We need to descend to an awareness of the cause of our separation from God, and then to rise with Christ to newness of life.

e. Our newness of life is formed and nurtured by God's Spirit. God who at creation breathed His Spirit into humans continues to enliven us with that gift, so that our life is "hidden with Christ in God" (Col 3:3). To live in One God Father Son and Spirit is Paradise on earth.

f. The true mark of our nearness to God is our nearness to suffering humanity. As the characteristic of God is to reach out to us and save us, so the characteristic of one who lives in God is to reach out to other human beings in their troubles.

7. Salvation by Membership in the Muslim Community

The last means to salvation in Islam is by membership in the Muslim community. The theory is based on the conviction that the *umma* is sacred and that God will bless its members and rescue them from the Fire. Many believers are content with this level of confidence. I will be saved because I am a Muslim.

On the surface of it this approach is similar to salvation by faith. The two means are closely connected in that faith is what makes one a member of the saved community. Salvation by faith, however, points God-ward, while salvation by membership in a human community has a different focus. It is that focus which we will consider in this final source of hope for Muslims.

In our discussion of the key principles of Islam we noted the great stress on community feeling. The community of Muslims is regarded as sacred because God has chosen it, has endowed it with guidance, and has given it a special role in the world. It is also blessed because it has received God's protection and promises, in the Muslim view. To some this simply implies that membership in such a community is what will count in the end. Surely God will not eternally punish someone who is a member of his *umma*! Community membership becomes a kind of password into heavenly joys. Those who have this opinion do not reject the other means of salvation, but there is an uncertainty in them. There is no uncertainty about my membership in the *umma*. It is concrete, visible. I am a Muslim. "My face is ever turned toward God." The undeniable fact of my being a Muslim is what will carry me safely through what lies ahead. In a Tradition Ibn 'Umar reported God's messenger as saying: "God's hand is over the community, and he who is separate from it will separate in hell."[52]

The Qur'ān upholds the privileged status of the Muslim family and its special destiny. It is "the best community" ever brought forth" (3:110). It is the community that is guided in truth, and that acts with equity" (7:180). Allah is "the patron" of those who believe (47:10). Therefore membership in the God-blessed community will bring recompense and prosperity to come. "Whosoever keepeth his covenant with Allah, on him will He bestow immense reward" (48:10). The reward is Gardens of Eternity, bracelets of gold and pearls, silken garments, a home that will last, "with no toil, nor sense of weariness" (35:33ff.). Believers are reminded that if God were to punish people according to their deserts there would not be a single creature left, "but God has in His sight all His servants" (35:15).

Yet Muslims who uphold the idea of salvation by membership in the community of faith must contend with three intractable problems:

(1) The problem raised by divisions within Islam. Which is the "true" community in which I must be a member?

(2) The problems of lukewarm adherence and nominalism. Are there no criteria for salvation?

(3) The problem of greatly sinning Muslims. Is there a justice issue?

We will briefly examine the three problems and the response that some have given.

With the first problem Muslims have to face the fact that within the collectivity of Muslims there are actually distinct communities. Sunnī Muslims, the large majority, simply assume that they properly represent the *umma*. Shī'as and Ismaʿīlīs on the other hand see themselves as the true believers, and some even make membership in their group mandatory for salvation. An Ismaʿīli creedal statement from the 1200s illustrates the exclusive approach:

(Religion) and faith are to be found only in Shī'ism (along with true) following the Sunna of the Prophet. ... The Prophet predicted the splitting up of the Islamic community into seventy-three sects after his death; of these only one is that which brings salvation. It is the one which follows the Prophet and his descendants, who are the Ark of Noah, giving religious salvation ... Walaya or support for Ali and love for him and his cause, is the greatest religious virtue in Islam.[53]

The divisions are not merely historical but continue with great vehemence today. Ordinary Muslims do not like to think about them, tend to downplay them as a non-problem, and deplore them when they take visible form.

The problems of lukewarm adherence and nominalism raise the question of who qualifies as a Muslim. Lukewarmness and nominalism differ. Lukewarmness is halfheartedness, nominalism is indifference. Lukewarm Muslims regard themselves as in every respect members of the community, and would be offended if anyone suggested that they were in danger of losing salvation. Their approach is typified by a discussion the writer once had with a Cairo taxi-driver named Ali. There was a long delay at one road junction, not an unusual event in that crowded city's traffic, and this produced ample time for a good discussion. In response to a question Ali answered: "Now I am only a fifty-percent Muslim. When I get old like my father I will be a hundred-percent Muslim." He clearly did not think that his attitude would in any way prejudice his eternal destiny. Concerned members of the Muslim community deal with lukewarm adherence as a challenge to persuasion and revival, rather than to judgment.

The situation differs with nominalism. It refers to secularized Muslims who have no interest in religious practice. Many are contributing citizens of society and upstanding in their private lives, but they seldom pray and never darken the door of a mosque. Moreover, some among them are publicly critical of popular religion and its leaders as being backward and corrupt. In recent years the extreme example were Marxist Muslims who opposed traditional religion and interpreted true Islam to mean social progress. Yet nominal believers retain the name Muslim, and presumably the ultimate hope that community membership offers. Sincere Muslims face this difficulty from different perspectives. One is to make a distinction between born Muslims and religious believers (mu'minīn), a distinction not new in Islamic history. You may be born as a Muslim, but you must become a faithful believer. Another approach, that of "Islamists," is to levy withering criticism at nominal Muslims. These approaches run counter to the "live and let live" instinct of the wider community, and the feeling that the final outcome of such individuals must be left in God's hands.

The third problem of greatly-sinning Muslims is more straightforward. A person confesses, prays, fasts, and gives alms, but leads a very bad life. On the one hand, the individual regards himself as a Muslim, but on the other hand, the crimes are serious. Is Yazid saved by his community membership even though he was responsible for the destruction of the Prophet's family? What a thought! Yet greatly-sinning Muslims bear the name of the faith, and it is unbecoming in the mind of many that such a member of the umma be punished eternally alongside unbelievers. In the section on faith we pointed out one resolution of the dilemma. Without specific Qur'anic sanction the idea developed that unworthy Muslims could enter Paradise after a period of purgative punishment in Hell. Their faces will be black as coal, but at some point they will be taken to the river at the gates of Paradise where they will be cleansed and will be admitted to its pleasures. In the end, their being Muslim will save them.

Behind these various "solutions" lies the conviction, often expressed in the Hadīth, that no Muslim can call a fellow Muslim an unbeliever for any reason. Although it is often violated, this tradition remains strong. As a member of the community a Muslim has a hope for salvation. This does not mean that God the Watcher is not observing His community's doings, or is tolerant of evil done by Muslims. The evil will be punished, but in this world. A Hadīth declares: "The Prophet said—may God bless him and give him peace!—'This Community of mine has been given a great mercy. It will not be punished in the next world, but in this world its punishments will be rebellions, and earthquakes and slayings."[54]

J. W. Sweetman summarizes the approach of salvation through community membership in these illuminating words that bring this section to a close:[55]

> Thus in Islam salvation is by identification with a community. ... Primarily the institution of the community of Islam, enshrining within it the practice of the Prophet, possessed of the authoritative code of God in the Qur'ān, presenting a concrete and external unity, composed of members rejoicing in a special divine election, the interim stage of the theocracy, never to be superseded, endowed with inerrancy despite apparent differences, is the first means of salvation and all that follows must be within this framework.

Thoughts for Christian Sharing:

a.   In the Christian perspective the blessed community is the company of forgiven sinners who live gratefully for God.

b.   Salvation in the Christian faith does not come through identification with a human community but with God's forgiving love and redemption. It is not a person's "Christianity" that saves him or her. The One who saves is the One who says: "Come unto me all you who labor and are heavy-laden, and I will give you rest." (Mt 11:28).

c.   The family of those who are restored to God's fellowship in Christ is blessed and sacred. It is blessed because God the Father has made "not-people" the children of God. It is sacred because it is the steward of the good news of salvation.

d.   The marks of a true Christian community are the marks of Christ who said, "Follow me." The community of the redeemed is to be a community of love. But Christians are at the same time saints and sinners, and Christ's people often fail to demonstrate his marks. The church is therefore always under the judgment of God, and must also listen patiently to the criticisms of Muslim friends. Christians are called to repent of their sins, seek the help of God's Spirit to become what they are in Christ, and to strive "to declare the mighty acts of Him who has called us out of darkness into his marvelous light" (1 Pet 2:9).

C. Conclusion: The Preferred Means

According to the individual preference a person may look at the problem of escape from the Fire in several ways. We have categorized the means of salvation in this way in order to make transparent the various elements that run through Islamic tradition. The categories will not always be distinct in the minds of ordinary Muslims, however, and many will not be interested in responding to the question: which means do you prefer?

Other Muslims will discuss the issue, but tentatively since it is not a standard topic of inquiry in Islam. Among them will be those who express their preference in a combined form. Some may give precedence to a combination of faith and membership in the community. Others may contend for faith and works, combined with the mercy of God. Still others may consider the matter from the perspective of God's will and saintly intercession. Several of the means we have outlined may merge in the formation of any individual's salvation thinking. In Islam the preferred means is a matter of personal intuition and choice.

Whatever the approach that may be chosen the Muslim believer must live with an element of uncertainty regarding his or her ultimate fate. M. A. Quassem puts the matter this way:[56]

> It will be seen that salvation in the Qur'ānic sense is attainable only in the life to come, and that the decision on it will also be made in that life; it is impossible, then, to say anything categorically concerning the ultimate fate of an individual believer, even though some indication of it can be found. Salvation in the Hereafter is a continuous process, beginning from the life immediately after death and culminating in the life in Paradise; in this process it is a receiving, not a becoming; it is the receiving of the fruit of faith and action performed in this life.

In expanding on the phrase "some indication of it can be found" the writer adds: "If an individual finds the path of good easy to follow, this indicates he will be among the saved. If, however, when he intends to do something good, he faces obstacles and averts it, this is a clear indication that he will be among the damned."[57]

The need to operate with inferences points to the uncertainty in this picture. It is a reminder of the one consistent theme in the Islamic picture of salvation—the final decision belongs to God and that decision is hidden in God's will, to be revealed on the last Day. Until then, the Qur'ān advises that believers should persevere in their duty, "in order that you may succeed" (3:200; Pickthall). Another translation puts it in this way: "Perhaps you may prosper" (Palmer).[58] Whether explicit or implicit, there is a "perhaps" in the situation. It brings forth the Qur'ānic prayer to God: "Give us Salvation from the Penalty of the Fire" (3:191; Yusuf Ali). It also produced the following Hadīth, narrated by Munammad b. Fadl: "The Prophet ... said: 'For a true believer the distress and anxiety of dying are equivalent to that from three hundred sword strokes."[59] The uncertainty carries over to the feelings of Muslim believers, great and small. The majority block out the apparent problem, do not fret about it, and go on with life. As one Muslim puts it, "The rest is in other hands."[60] Others take their consolation in one of the means to salvation that we have discussed. A lesser number are troubled, wondering, and some have a sense of despair.

Al-Hajjāj ibn Yūsuf (d. 741) was a cruel and violent leader who cried out, "Would that God ... when He puts us in this world, had made us independent of the next and delivered us from anxiety about what will save us from the punishment!"[61] With good reason this individual should have been anxious about his future, for when he died Muslims wept for joy over the tyrant's demise. Yet also pious Muslims share the anxiety. An early Muslim ascetic said, "The thought of death leaves the believer no joy, his knowledge of God's laws leaves him no friend."[62] Another believer lay dying and said to the friends who visited him. "I have no hope though I have fasted eighty Ramadan."[63] The frankness echoes a pessimistic phrase common in Muslim literature: "My fear overcame my hope."[64] A modern Muslim *ghazal* (two-line poetic form) catches the mood:[65]

> Restless heart has lost its way in the city of grief,
> Careful when you go in search, it is dark indeed.

It may be fairly said that the Islamic view of salvation produces an emotional mix, an oscillation between confidence and concern, between fear and hope.

Summary Reflection:

In Islam salvation, conceived negatively, refers to escape from the punishment of sin, the terrors of Hell-Fire. In the Christian faith salvation, conceived negatively, refers to deliverance from the bondage of sin and its effects—the power of evil, death, and hell. In Islam salvation, conceived positively, refers to the felicity provided by God in Paradise, pleasures that begin after the Day of Judgment. In the Christian faith salvation, conceived positively, refers to the abundant life in restored fellowship with God, beginning now and continuing eternally. In Islam salvation is pursued through a variety of means, behind which lie God's final and unknown decision. In the Christian faith salvation rests on God's known decision to save humanity through Jesus Christ, and its means is faith in the Savior. Muslims and Christians both think of heaven as "the abode of peace and rest," and both have discussed the idea of the vision of God as the ultimate joy of heaven.

We next turn to the Muslim view of Jesus the Messiah.

Endnotes

1. For a Muslim view of salvation cf. Muhammad Abul Quassem, *Salvation of the Soul and Islamic Devotions, op. cit.* A. Yusuf Ali in his *Commentary on The Holy Qur'ān*, pp. 1464–1470, deals with salvation under the aspect of "The Muslim Heaven." Helmut Gätje, *The Qur'ān and its Exegesis,* tr. and ed. by A. T. Welch (Berkeley: University of California Press, 1976), pp. 92–129 on "Salvation History," compiles materials of Muslim exegetes on the history of God's guidance. Non-Muslim treatments include Frederick M. Denny, "The Problem of Salvation in the Qur'ān: Key Terms and Concepts," in A. H Grau, ed. *In Quest of an Islamic Humanism: Arabic and Islamic Studies in Memory of al-Nowaihi* (Cairo: The American University of Cairo Press, 1984), pp. 196–210. James Robson, "Aspects of the Qur'anic doctrine of salvation," and Annemarie Schimmel, "A 'sincere Muhammadan's' way to salvation" are found in Eric Sharpe and John Hinnells, eds. *Man and his salvation* (Manchester: Rowan & Littlefield Publishers, 1973), pp. 205–242. W. Montgomery Watt deals with "The Muslim Yearning for a Saviour: Aspects of Early Abbasid Shī'ism," in S. G. Brandon, ed. *The Saviour God* (Westport, Ct.: Greenwood Press Publishers, 1963),

pp. 171–190). Roland E. Miller, "The Muslim Doctrine of Salvation," *The Bulletin* (Hyderabad: Henry Martyn Institute of Islamic Studies), July-September, 1960, pp. 33–55; October-December, 1960, pp. 10–27, includes Christian reflection in his study; cf. also the reprint in the same journal, Vol. V, January-December, 1982, pp. 152–196. A similar but older work is W. R. W. Gardner, *The Qur'anic Doctrine of Salvation* (Madras: Christian Literature Society of India, 1914). The best encyclopaedic treatment of the twin themes is J. S. Reid on "Sin (Muslim)," and Edward Sell on "Salvation (Muslim)" in *The Encyclopaedia of Religion and Ethics*, Vol. X, pp. 567–570; 148f. For a study and full bibliography on eschatological events, including the Fire and the Garden, cf. Jane I. Smith and Yvonne Y. Haddad, *Understanding of Death and Resurrection* (Albany: State University of New York Press, 1981).

2. Under the pressure of modern culture a word for "thanks!" was artificially manufactured by using terms for benefit (upakārum) and appreciation (nandi).

3. A. K. Brohi, "The Spiritual Significance of the Qur'ān," in Nasr, ed. *Islamic Spirituality,* p. 15.

4. Faruqi, *Tawhīd*, p. 83.

5. Jeffery, ed. *Islam*, p. 234; quoting Muhammad al-Hawari's *Al-Kawhab al-Murdiy,* (Cairo, 1927), p. 28.

6. Quassem, *Salvation of the Soul,* p. 28.

7. *Mishkat al-Masabih,* ed. by James Robson (Lahore, Sh. Muhammad Ashraf, 1962), Vol. 1, p. 27.

8. Elder, *Commentary,* p. 80.

9. Daud Rahbar, *God of Justice* (Leiden: E. J. Brill, 1960), p. 25.

10. Ben Downing, *The Atlantic Monthly,* Vol. 285, No. 3, March 2000, p. 62.

11. Mohammed Hashim Kamali, *The Dignity of Man,* The Islamic Perspective (Selangor: Ilmiah Publishers, 1999), p. 22.

12. Hammudah Abdalati, *Islam in Focus* (Aligarh: Crescent Publishing Co,. 1973), pp. 5f.

13. Siddiqqi, *Elementary Teachings,* p. 22.

14. Muhammad Rauf, Islam, *Creed and Worship* (Washington: The Islamic Center, 1975), p. 63; from the Malikite rite.

15. *Mishkat,* III, p. 1177.

16. Ahmad Kamal, *The Sacred Journey* (New York: Duell, Sloan & Price, 1961), p. 47.

17. Jamali, *Letters,* pp. viif.

18. Louis Gardet, "Imān," *EI²*, III, p. 172; Gardet makes the strong statement that "all the scholars state that faith ensures salvation."

19. Wāsiyat Abu Haīfa, tr. by A. J. Wensinck, in Wensinck, *Muslim Creed* (London: Frank Cass & Co., Ltd., 1965), p. 125.

20. Elder, *Commentary,* p. 126.

21. Imam Muslim, *Saḥīḥ Muslim,* tr. by Abdul Hamid Siddiqqi (Beirut: Dar al Arabiya, 1971), I, p. 19.

22. *Ibid.* p. 2.

23. Al-Ghazzali, *Alchemy of Happiness,* p. 105.

24. *Iḥya,* IX, pp. 621ff., quoted in Elder, *Commentary,* p. 125.

25. Charis Waddy, *The Muslim Mind* (London: Longman, 1976), p. 127.

26. Margaret E. Smith, *Rabī'a the Mystic and Her Fellow-Saints in Islam* (Cambridge: Cambridge University Press, 1984; first ed. 1928), p. 100.

27. Quoted in A. J. Arberry, *Sufism* (George Allen & Unwin Ltd., 1950), pp. 42f.

28. Stephanie Nolen, "Little House on the Prairie," *The Globe & Mail,* Monday, March 20, 2000, p. R5.

29. Ayatulla M. Mutahhari, *Fundamentals of Islamic Thought* (Berkeley: Mizan Press, 1985), p. 114. Similarly, the Sunnī theologian, Abul Kalam Azad, declares: "The Qur'anic assertion was that salvation was the result of devotion to God and righteous living," in Tarjumān, I, p. 180.

30. *Saḥiḥ Muslim,* I, pp. 129–133.

31. Annemarie Schimmel, "Shafā'a, *EI²,* IX, p. 179.

32. Halveti, *Most Beautiful Names,* p. 149.

33. Siddiqqi, *Elementary Teachings,* pp. 56f.

34. *Mishkat,* I, p. 349.

35. Syed Husain M. Jafri, "Twelve-Imam Shi'ism," in Nasr, ed. *Islamic Spirituality,* p. 170. In Moojan Momen, *An Introduction to Shī'i Islam* (New Haven: Yale University Press, 1985), p. 32, the same scholar says that it should not be difficult to have regard for Husain's sacrifice for those who appreciate "above all the great sacrifice of Jesus Christ for the redemption of the world."

36. Majlisi, *Hayatu'l-Kulub,* IV, 1, 7, quoted in Dwight M. Donaldson, *Shī'ite Religion* (London: Luzac & Co., 1933), p. 344.

37. Donaldson, *Shī'ite Religion,* pp. 247f.

38. A. K. Esmail, "The Conqueror of Kerbela," Muharram, Compiled and published by Yousuf N. Lalljee (Bombay, 1975), p. 15.

39. Williams, ed. *Themes,* p. 250; quoting Mawdudi's *A Short History of the Revivalist Movement in Islam* (Lahore, 1963), pp. 40f.

40. Bill Musk, *The Unseen Face of Islam* (Pasadena: MARC, 1989), p. 224.

41. Martin Lings, *What Is Sufism?* (Berkeley: University of California Press, 1977), p. 108.

42. Annemarie Schimmel, *As Through a Veil,* (New York: Columbia, 1982), p. 328.

43. Schimmel, *Mystical Dimensions,* p. 49.

44. *The Confessions of Al-Ghazzali,* tr. by Claud Field (Lahore: Sh. Muhammad Ashraf, 1978), p. 69.

45. Schimmel, "Sincere Muhammadan," Sharpe and Hinnells, eds. *Salvation,* p. 234.

46. Schimmel, *As Through a Veil,* p. 101.

47. Smith, *Rabīa,* p. 28.

48. Arberry, *Sufism,* pp. 64f.

49. Reynold A. Nicholson, *The Mystics of Islam* (New York: Schocken Books, 1975), p. 67.

50. G. H. Westcott, *Kabir and the Kabir Panth* (Cawnpore: Christ Church Mission Press, 1907), p. 69.

51. Edna Hong, *The Downward Ascent* (Minneapolis: Augsburg Press, 1979).

52. *Mishkat,* I, pp. 45f.

53. Williams, ed. *Themes,* p. 41; quoting W. Ivanow, *A Creed of the Fātimīds,* 1936, pp. 50ff.

54. *Ibid.* p. 10.

55. J. W. Sweetman, *Islam and Christian Theology, Part One,* Vol. II, (London: Lutterworth Press, 1947), pp. 210f.

56. Quassem, *Salvation of the Soul,* p. 28.

57. *Ibid.*

58. The issue is the translation of la'alla, which is either "perhaps" or "so that." Translators differ. Cf. Robson, "Doctrine of Salvation" in Brandon, ed., *Man and His Salvation,* p. 210.

59. Arthur Jeffery, *A Reader on Islam* ('S-Gravenhage: Mouton & Co., 1962), p. 199.

60. Eaton, "Man," in Nasr, ed. *Islamic Spirituality*, p. 375.

61. A. S. Tritton, *Muslim Theology* (London: Luzac & Co., 1947), p. 10; quoting Jahiz 14, 3.5.

62. *Ibid.;* quoting b. Sa'd, 6,114.

63. *Ibid.;* quoting b. Sa'd, 6,121.

64. For examples see Eric Schroeder, *Muhammad's People* (Portland, Maine: The Bond Wheelright Co., 1955). Schroeder quotes a dervish who said: "All religious hope is the product of despair" (p. 713).

65. R. S. Firaq (d. 1982), quoted in K. C. Chanda, tr. and ed., *Masterpieces of Urdu Ghazal* (New Delhi: Sterling, 1992), p. 302.

5

The Muslim View of Jesus

In considering the Muslim view of Jesus we must reckon with the following points:

—Islam is a post-Christian religion, and unlike other major religious traditions its adherents have some knowledge of Jesus.[1]

—The Muslim teaching is drawn from Muslim sources, including the Qur'ān and Tradition. It is not drawn from Christian sources.

—There are significant differences in the Muslim and Christian pictures of Jesus.

—Muslims generally do not know the Biblical account of Jesus, nor the Christian interpretation of his life and meaning.

—The orthodox Muslim view of Jesus is marked by respect and admiration.

We will begin our examination with the Muslim esteem for Jesus the Messiah, leading into a discussion of the names of Jesus in Islam. We will then turn to the life and career of Jesus as presented in the Qur'ān. This includes his childhood in which Mary has a prominent place, his life as a mature prophet, and his death. Following that we look at the elaborated picture in Tradition, in legend, in classical and mystical writings, and in modern perceptions. We conclude with some preliminary thoughts on Christian sharing, reserving the full discussion for later chapters.

A. Muslim Admiration for Jesus

Ordinary Muslims have nothing but respect for Jesus, and they are very interested in him and his life.[2] They commonly refer to him as Jesus the Prophet ('Īsā Nabī) or Jesus the Messiah ('Īsā Masīḥ). The following poem by an Arab Muslim,

Ahmad Shawqi (1868–1932) is one example of that admiration:[3]

> Kindness, chivalry, guidance and humility were born
> The day Jesus was born.
> His coming brightened the world,
> His light illuminated it.
> Like the light of dawn flowing through the universe
> So did the sign of Jesus flow.
> He filled the world with light,
> Making the earth shine with brightness.
> No threat, no tyranny, no revenge, no swords, no raids,
> No bloodshed did he use in his call to the new faith.
> A king he lived on earth,
> But wearying of his state,
> He substituted heaven for it.
> To his faith men were attracted,
> Humble, submissive and weak before him.
> Their submission was followed by the submission
> Of kings, common folk and sages.
> His faith found roots on every land,
> And anchors on every shore.

The modern poem accurately reflects the respect for Jesus that is evident throughout the history of Muslim culture. The Qur'ān itself has many important references to Jesus as we shall see, and the same is true of the Traditions. Hasan al-Basrī, whom we have quoted, admired Jesus as an example of ascetic devotion. The mystics esteemed him as a primary source of inspirations, Al-Hallāj (d. 922) taking him as the example of one in whom God dwells. Al-Ghazālī, the definitive Muslim theologian, regularly quoted the sayings of Jesus. Muslims today continue to pay honor to Jesus. They regard him as the premier example of self-denial, the teacher of humility, the possessor of spiritual power, and a pattern of nearness to God. While the New Testament teachings on the Sonship of Jesus and his functions as Savior and Redeemer are not part of the Muslim view, there is steady appreciation of his purity and his ethical principles. It is especially the picture of Jesus in the Qur'ān that creates a compelling image of Jesus for Muslims and moves them to their veneration. The outlines of that portrait are provided by the names that are assigned to him there.

B. The Quranic Names of Jesus

"Name" is an important concept in Islam. A name conveys knowledge about a truth, and its possession gives one power. God taught Adam the names of things, and thereby gave humanity greater knowledge than the angels possessed (2:29–31). The "Beautiful Names" of God that are cherished by Muslims tell something about God, but their repetition also brings spiritual blessing. So also the names of Jesus in the Qur'ān reveal who he is, in relation to his origin, status, character, and functions. They appear in fifteen chapters of the Qur'ān, in 93 verses, often in some combination with each other. We will examine fifteen names, the large number testifying to the formidable Qur'anic witness of Jesus. We begin with the three names that are most commonly used in personal identifications: 'Īsā, Son of Mary, and Messiah.

1. 'Īsā (25 times): This name is an Arabic form of the word "Jesus." It may be a derivative of the Syriac Yeshū'. Another Syriac form, Yasū', is used in the Arabic translation of the New Testament. The Hebrew background of the name is Yeshua, which translated means "God saves." In the New Testament the angel commands Mary to name her son Jesus (Greek: *Yesous*) because "he shall save his people from their sins"(Mt 1:21). The Qur'ān makes no reference to this theological meaning, and Muslims are generally not aware of it.

2. Son of Mary (33 times): The frequent use of this name contrasts with the New Testament where it is found only once (Mk 6:3). Jesus is often called 'Īsā ibn Maryam, Jesus the Son of Mary. In Arab culture a son (ibn) is usually known as the son of his father, although there are some instances of the opposite usage. Why does the maternal reference take place in the case of Jesus? Some Muslim commentators suggest that it is to emphasize the special origin of Jesus in that he was born of a virgin. The Qur'ān speaks frequently and highly of Mary but does not mention Joseph. The frequent use of Son of Mary may also be a preferred contrast to the Christian use of Son of God. Parrinder suggests that from Islam the use of Son of Mary possibly spread into some early Christian documents, but it is really found only in church liturgies.[4]

3. Messiah (10 times): In the Qur'ān the title Masīh is mostly used in combination with Son of Mary. The Qur'anic use gives no hint of the intrinsic meaning of the term; thus the significance of "anointed one" in the sense of appointed savior, which belongs to the Old Testament root, is not Islamic. Muslim scholars have rather looked for the understanding of the term in other roots that have such diverse meanings as the wandering one, the pilgrim-mystic, the honored one, the one with a supernatural touch who healed the sick, and others. The most common understanding is that of a figure of spiritual renunciation. Muslims frequently quote a Tradition attributed to Jesus which says: "This world is a bridge. Do not spend time on it."

We turn next to two names of Jesus in the Qur'ān that describe his function.

4. Prophet (8 times): The Muslim term for prophet is nabī, and Jesus is therefore often called 'Īsā Nabī. It is probably the most commonly used Muslim phrase for Jesus. In the Qur'ān the name of Jesus appears in various lists of the recognized prophets. In fact, Jesus and Abraham are the only two names that appear in all the lists. The idea of Jesus' prophethood does not differ from others. A prophet is someone who receives a revelation of God's Word and delivers it to his society. There is equality and continuity among the prophets. A typical passage of the Qur'ān says: "Say (O Muslims): We believe in Allah and that which is revealed unto Abraham and Ishmael and Isaac and Jacob and the tribes, and that which Moses and Jesus received. ... We make no distinction between any of them: (2:136).

5. Messenger (10 times): The Islamic term is rasūl, which literally has the same meaning as apostle. Jesus is one of the messengers of God. In this category distinc-

tion is admissible. A key passage states: "Of those messengers, some of whom we have caused to excel others, and of whom there are some unto whom Allah spake, while some of them He exalted (above others) in degree, and we gave Jesus, son of Mary, clear proofs of Allah's sovereignty, and We supported him with the Holy Spirit (2:253). In Islamic interpretation the Holy Spirit is the angel Gabriel. The passage in ascending scale points to the high excellence of Jesus, the prophet-messenger. In the view of some Muslims, the distinction between the two is that a prophet speaks the Word of God given to him, while in the case of a *rasūl* a written scripture may also be transmitted.

We next examine four names that relate to the status of Jesus.

6. Servant (3 times): The Muslim term for servant is *'abd,* and it points to what is regarded as the true role of a human being in relation to God. A creaturely human being is to be the servant of the Almighty. That also is the role of Jesus, with the difference that he fulfilled it to perfection. The Qur'ān says: "The Messiah will never scorn to be an *'abd* unto Allah" (4:173). While he was still in the cradle Jesus spoke, saying: "Lo! I am the *'abd* of Allah. He hath given me the Scripture and hath appointed me as Prophet" (19:30). In connection with his status as a servant Jesus also fulfils his vocation to be a model for his people: "He is nothing but an *'abd* on whom We [God] bestowed favour, and We made him a pattern for the children of Israel" (43:59). Thus Jesus is a surrendering and obedient human being. Muhammad Pickthall states that *'abd* signifies slave of God, and it is a "proud distinction with the Muslims, bondage to Allah implying liberation from all human servitudes."[5]

7. Sign (3 times): The term is *āya,* which has the double meaning of a sign to be observed and a revelatory communication. It is a synonym for a verse of the Qur'ān, the implication being that every Qur'anic word is both a revelation and a miraculous sign. This significant term is applied to Jesus. He is both a sign of God's mercy and a communication from God. In two of the verses where the title appears Jesus and his mother are linked together, appointed "to be signs unto all human beings." The angel Gabriel appeared to Mary announcing that she would have a son. She was troubled and wondered how this would be possible. Then the angel said to her: "Thus says thy Lord, It is easy for Me! and We will make him an *āya* unto man and a mercy from Us" (19:21).

8. Mercy (once): The word for mercy that appears in the verse quoted above is *rahma.* It is linguistically connected with the two words used for God at the head of the Qur'ān chapters: Rahmān and Rahīm. Jesus is a mercy from God the Merciful. He brings a revealing and wondrous communication from God as God's *āya,* and in so doing represents "a mercy from Us." The next name incorporates both ideas.

9. Word (twice): The Arabic term is *kalimat.* It is applied to Jesus only in the Qur'ān, and it takes the Qur'anic recognition of Jesus to a high point. In the first of the two passages involved the Qur'ān says (3:45):

> And (remember) when the angels said: "O Mary! Lo! Allah giveth thee glad tidings of a word from Him, whose name is the Messiah, Jesus, son of Mary, illustrious in the world and one of those brought near (unto Allah).

The second passage (4:171) says that God's Word was "bestowed" on Mary. Perplexed Muslim commentators have rendered various opinions regarding the meaning of this title. Their suggestions include that Jesus is created by the Word of God, that he is prophesied about in previous scriptures, that he speaks on behalf of God, or that he is in his own person a message to humanity.[6]

10. Spirit (once): The word for spirit is *ruh*. The Islamic teaching about the concept of spirit is undefined. The Qur'ān speaks in a general way of the spirit of humans. In relation to God it refers to God's Spirit without further details. God breathed His Spirit into humans at the creation, but in a special way the Almighty breathed into Mary "of Our Spirit." Jesus, the son of Mary, is called a Spirit from Him" (4:171).

The following names of Jesus refer to his character and work.

11. The One Near to God (once): The angels said to Mary (3:45) that Jesus will be "one of those brought near to God." Muslim interpreters relate this announcement to events after the ascension of Jesus, and his high place in Paradise. Muslim mystics, however, see nearness to God as a characteristic of Jesus' spiritual life in this world, and an incentive for them to attain the same felicity.

12. Illustrious in the World (once): The same passage speaks of Jesus' eminence in this world. Most Muslim commentators believe that this praise has reference to his prophetic office.

13. The Blessed One (once): The common Arabic term *mubarak* is applied to Jesus. The Qur'ān says: "(Allah) ... hath made me blessed wheresoever I may be and hath enjoined upon me prayers and alms-giving so long as I remain alive. And hath made me dutiful toward her who bore me, and hath not made me arrogant, unblest. Peace on me the day I was born, and the day I die, and the day I shall be raised alive" (19:31–33). The blessing of Jesus is related to the pious quality of his life including prayer, generosity, a proper and humble attitude toward his mother, and the power (*baraka*) to do good. The blessing includes the promise of peace through life, death, and resurrection.

14. Example (twice): The word *mathal* means example, likeness, parable. The Qur'ān says that Jesus is only a servant whom God has blessed, and in that sense his likeness to God is similar to that of Adam. Nevertheless, "he is of the righteous" (3:46), an eminence that includes all the great prophets (6:85), and he is a model for the children of Israel. In the title "Example" there is a hint of a parable to be read.

15. Witness (twice): The underlying term for Witness is *shahīd*. Jesus declares (5:117) that as long as he was in this world he was a witness among the people to whom he was sent, and he will continue that function on the final day. The Qur'ān therefore further states: "And on the Day of Resurrection he will be a witness against them" (4:159), and all mankind will believe in him.

The list of Qur'anic Names for Jesus is like a roll-call of greatness, and it goes a long way in explaining the interest that Muslims have in him and in his story. We turn next to that connected narrative.

C. Portraits of the Messiah

Muslims do not lay claim to a developed biography of Jesus the Messiah. The Qur'anic story itself is brief. It concentrates on Jesus' birth and childhood, having few details on either his adult ministry or his last days. It gives attention to his status and relation to God. "Jesus in Islam" represents a wider view, including apocryphal material and legendary tales, particularly in relation to his descent from heaven. There is enough information to stimulate a desire among Muslims to know more about the one who receives such great honor and bears such unusual names. As they consider the Muslim portrayal of Jesus Christians who are accustomed to the fuller accounts of the Gospels and are aware of the riches of Jesus' teaching will have the feeling of listening to a tape with important sections omitted and will have a desire to share their treasures with their friends.

1. The Story of Jesus in the Qur'ān

a. Birth and Childhood

The story begins with the family of Mary. She is called Maryam, and her father's name is 'Imrān. (In the Old Testament the father of Moses, Aaron, and Miriam is Amram.) 'Imrān's wife became pregnant, and she promised that she would dedicate her child to God when it was born. When the child turned out to be a girl, she wondered how to proceed. After naming her Maryam she asked God to protect her from Satan. God did watch over Maryam, giving Zechariah the responsibility of taking care of her. Whenever Zechariah came into the child's room he found food and water there, and Maryam would say: "It is from God."

Zechariah now had another unusual experience related to his own family. His great sorrow had been the fact that he did not have a son, and he used to cry to God for help. I am old and grey-haired. What will happen to my wife when I am gone? You have always answered by prayers. "O give from Thy presence a Successor!" One day an angel came to him while he was at prayer and gave him the surprising news that he would have a son. The child would become a dignified and righteous man who would proclaim the Word of God. He was to name him Yahyā (John). Doubt, however, overtook the old man and he could not accept the news. God addressed him: Did I not create you? Cannot I give you a son? When Zechariah insisted on having a sign, God said that he would not be able speak for three nights. Then John was born, "a grace from God." He had a love for scripture, and possessed purity and good judgment, wisdom, and compassion. He was pious and obedient to his parents. Thus Zechariah, who is included in the list of the prophets, became blessed.

The story now turns back to Maryam, whom we shall call Mary. Angels had informed her that God had chosen and dedicated her "above the women of the world" for a special function. They encouraged her to be devout and prayerful. In fact, the privilege of conveying that message was so great that there had been a tussle among the angels as to who would have the honor. Mary had secluded herself in a place with an eastern exposure. Now God sent another angelic spirit to her who assumed the likeness of a fine-looking man. Mary was startled and ill at ease over such an unusual entry. If you are a pious man, you will have mercy, she said. The angel calmed her fears. I am here only as a messenger of God to let you know that you will have a faultless son. This is good news, the angel (Jibra'īl = Gabriel) declared, for the child will be a Word from God and a Mercy from God. He will speak to his people from the cradle itself. Mary was troubled, and she objected. How could this be when she had never had relations with a man? The angel announced that the creative power of God would be at work in the event. When God decides a matter, "He only says BE!, and it is."

The angel went on to describe the mission of Jesus the Messiah. God would teach the child the Book and Wisdom, the Torah and the Gospel. As a prophet he would then come to the people of Israel with marvelous signs. He would make a bird out of clay, blow on it and make it live. He would heal the blind from their birth, as well as the lepers, and would raise the dead. All this he would do "with God's permission." He would bring various instructions: to fear God and to worship Him; to confirm the previous Law, but relaxing it somewhat; and to advise people what to eat and to store up. In summary, he would call people to the right path, saying: "Follow me, for God is my Lord."

As promised God spoke the creative Word. After she conceived Mary went into retreat, perhaps to hide her unexplainable pregnancy from her family and friends. The pangs of childbirth drove her to the trunk of a palm-tree. In acute distress she cried out, "Would that I had died and become a thing of nothing and forgotten!" Then a voice came "from below her," urging her not to grieve. The Lord was sending a stream of refreshing water. Moreover, if she would shake the palm-tree, ripe dates would fall. She was to eat, drink, and be consoled. Should anyone chance by, she was to tell them that she had taken a vow and could not speak. There Jesus was delivered. She carried the baby to her family who were stunned and challenged her, "O sister of Aaron, thy father was not wicked, and thy mother was not a harlot!" She asked them to talk to the child. They replied, How is that possible? Then Jesus spoke up and uttered words we have already considered above: "I am the servant of Allah. He hath given me the scripture, and appointed me a prophet". The story of Mary and child end at this point.

b. The Mature Prophet

The vocation and task of Jesus the Messiah was to communicate a prophetic message and to validate it with signs. The assignment is summed up in the Qur'ān in these words (5:46):

> And We caused Jesus, son of Mary, to follow in their footsteps [the previous prophets], confirming that which was (revealed) before him. And we bestowed on him the Gospel wherein is guidance and a light, confirming that which was (revealed) before it in the Torah.

Jesus is regarded as having received a sacred scripture (Injīl =Gospel) in the same way as Moses received the Torah. His mission is to communicate a message common to all the prophets, the call to fear one God alone and to do His will.

As he carried out his work Jesus encountered opposition. He came with "clear proofs" and with the gift of wisdom to make plain God's truth. Very simply he said: "Lo! Allah, He is my Lord and your Lord. So worship Him. This is the right path" (43:64). But there were factions among those who listened to him. Some said that Jesus' signs were only magic. Others tried to harm him. When Jesus became aware of their disbelief, he cried out: "Who will be my helpers in the cause of God?" At that time God inspired the disciples to come forward who said, We will. We believe in God. We have surrendered to God. We will be God's helpers. God also gave a comforting promise: "O Jesus! Lo! I am gathering thee and causing thee to ascend unto Me, and am cleansing thee of those who disbelieve, and am setting those who follow thee above those who disbelieve until the Day of Resurrection" (3:55).

There is little additional material in the Qur'ān in regard to the teaching of Jesus. Somewhat in passing it refers to the topic of a heavenly feast, which may be an allusion to the Lord's Supper. The disciples asked whether God could send down "a table spread with food from heaven." They wanted to eat of such a table and be satisfied. Moreover, it would confirm Jesus' vocation. Jesus therefore prayed for it to happen, and God responded: "Lo! I send it down for you. And whoso disbelieveth of you afterward, him surely will I punish" (5:115).

Jesus also prophesies about a messenger coming after him. The Qur'ān says: "And when Jesus son of Mary said: O children of Israel! Lo! I am the messenger of Allah unto you, confirming that which was (revealed) before me in the Torah, and bringing good tidings of a messenger who cometh after me, whose name is the Praised One" (61:6). In the New Testament Jesus promises the coming of the Holy Spirit, the Spirit of Truth, who will come after him to guide God's people. Muslims, however, generally view this passage as the prophecy of the coming of Muhammad, since the short form of Muhammad, namely Ahmad, means "the Praised One."[7]

c. The Status of Jesus

The high status that the Qur'ān gives to Jesus the Messiah is the status of a noble human being, to whom God chose to give a special birth as to Adam: "Lo! the likeness of Jesus with Allah is as the likeness of Adam. He created him of dust, then He said unto him: BE!, and he is" (3:59). He eats and sleeps like the other prophets, and is in every sense a human being. "The Messiah, son of Mary, was no other than a messenger, messengers (the like of whom) had passed away before him. And his mother was a saintly woman. And they both used to eat (earthly) food" (5:75). The Qur'ān reports the notion that Jesus was elevated to the stature of God and vigorously opposes it. "They indeed have disbelieved who say, Lo! Allah is the Messiah, son of Mary." The Sovereign of the heavens and the earth is distinct from and in control of Mary, Jesus, and all creatures. "Who then can do aught against Allah if He had willed to destroy the Messiah, son of Mary, and his mother and everyone on earth?" (5:17).

In that connection the Qur'ān also opposes another mistaken idea, namely, that God has sexual relations with creatures. This is certainly in the first instance an attack on current popular ideas in Arab religious culture related to the world of spirits (jinn). Those who falsely impute that God intermarries with spirits and produces sons and daughters, who are then given some sort of divine status, are wrong and blasphemous. "The Originator of the heavens and the earth! How can He have a child when there is for Him no consort?" (6:102). The very idea that God would act the way spirits do in their world is an atrocious lie. "And we believe that He—exalted by the glory of our Lord!—hath taken neither wife nor son!" (72:2). The discussion of the phrase "Son of God" is set within that context. Why should God need a son, the Qur'ān asks, when He owns the universe? "They say: Allah hath taken (unto Him) a son—glorified be He! He hath no needs! His is all that is in the heavens and the earth. Ye have no warrant for this" (10:69). God would not add a son from the outside and thereby initiate plurality and competition within His own being. "Allah hath not chosen any son, nor is there any God along with Him" (23:91). The very thought causes nature itself to shudder. The heavens tear apart, the earth splits asunder, and the mountains fall in ruins "that ye ascribe unto the Beneficent a son!"

The criticism of the idea of son of God in the sense described above leads also to a rejection of the concept of Trinity. The latter is viewed as an extension of the same basic error, i.e. adding to God. "The Messiah, Jesus son of Mary was only a messenger of Allah, and His word which He conveyed unto Mary, and a spirit from Him. So believe in Allah and say not "Three"—Cease! (It is) better for you!—Allah is only one God. Far is it removed from His transcendent majesty that he should have a son" (4:171). Jesus himself confirms that view, denying that he had campaigned to have himself and his mother included in a divine triad. "And when Allah saith: O Jesus son of Mary! Didst thou say unto mankind: Take me and my mother for gods beside Allah?, he saith: Be glorified! It was not mine to utter that to which I had no right. ... I spake unto them only that which thou commandest me (saying): Worship Allah, my Lord and your Lord!" (5:116).

The latter words in Muslim view demonstrate that Jesus is content with the proper role given to him as a human messenger. The Qur'ān states that like the angels, "The Messiah will never scorn to be a servant unto Allah" (4:172). The Qur'ān regards it as inconceivable that a prophet would first accept his vocation to call people to surrender to God alone, and then turn about and say: "Be servants of me instead of Allah." Rather he would proclaim: "Be ye faithful servants of the Lord" (3:79). Jesus does say, "Keep your duty to Allah, and obey me," but he immediately adds: "Lo! Allah is my Lord and your Lord, so worship Him. That is the straight path" (3:50–51).

In short, the Qur'ān portrays Jesus as one who speaks against idolatry and rejects the idea that a human being—even himself—can be raised to the level of the divine. Man cannot become God.

d. The Death of Jesus

The story of Jesus in the Qur'ān ends with reference to his death. There is a great variety of opinion among Muslim commentators in regard to those references. All, however, agree that Jesus did not die on the cross. Many Muslims today believe that Jesus was put on the cross in an effort to slay him, but the attempt was unsuccessful, and he was taken to heaven bodily without dying. Of the three critical

Qur'ān passages two say Jesus will die, the third says, but not by crucifixion:

—Jesus had announced from the cradle that he would die and be raised up. We have quoted the passage above: "Peace be on me the day I was born, and the day I die, and the day I shall be raised alive" (19:33).

—Later God addressed these words to Jesus: "O Jesus! Lo! I am gathering thee and causing thee to ascend to me. ... " (3:155). The word for "gathering thee" is commonly used for "cause to die."

—The two passages above that witness to the death, raising and ascension of Jesus must be taken together with the only verse that deals directly with the crucifixion. The Jews are criticized "because of their saying: We slew the Messiah, Jesus son of Mary, Allah's messenger—They slew him not nor crucified him, but it appeared so to them ... they slew him not for certain. But Allah took him up unto Himself. ... And there is not one of the People of the Scriptures but will believe in him before his death" (4:157–159).

—In another passage Jesus speaks to God, apparently in heaven: "I was a witness to them while I dwelt among them, and when Thou tookest me Thou wast the watcher over them" (5:117).

Muslim interpreters have tried in different ways to put these passages together. In the process they have not looked to the Biblical account as a possible answer to the dilemmas. Two main theories have evolved. A minority view suggests that Jesus was crucified but was saved from death in some way, died at a later time and place while still on earth, and then ascended spiritually to God while His body awaits the final resurrection. The majority opinion significantly differs. According to its view Jesus was put on the cross but was saved by a miraculous intervention—someone was made to look like him and then substituted for him. Then he ascended bodily to heaven where he is with God today. Before the end of the world he will return to earth again as a sign of the Judgment to come, and only after that will he himself die. He will rise again as part of the general resurrection of all humanity. Yusuf Ali, the Qur'ān translator, comments on the uncertainties of these opinions:

> The end of the life of Jesus on earth is as much involved in mystery as his birth and indeed the greater part of his private life, except the three main years of his ministry. ... The Qur'anic teaching is that Christ was not crucified or killed by the Jews, notwithstanding certain apparent circumstances which produced that illusion in the minds of some of his enemies. ...[8]

B. D. Kateregga sums up the orthodox opinion regarding the implication of this single mysterious passage, 4:157ff., in these words: "According to the true belief of Islam, it would seem most inappropriate for the Messiah to die through a shameful crucifixion. God, who is just, would not permit the righteous Messiah to suffer in that manner. Muslims believe that Allah saved the Messiah from the ignominy of crucifixion much as Allah also saved the Seal of the Prophets from ignominy following the Hijra."[9]

The elaborations of the story of Jesus by the Traditions, in legends, by scholars, and by mystics takes us to the popular picture of Jesus in Islam.

2. Jesus in the Traditions

a. The HADĪTH Picture

Although the Traditions concentrate on the events of the last days, there are some references to his birth and career, and some of his sayings are quoted. They reveal the influence of the Christian environment on early Muslims.

Tradition expands on the family tree of Jesus the Messiah. The mother of Maryam is Hanna, and she was the sister of Elizabeth, Zechariah's wife. Joseph is mentioned only casually. The annunciation of Jesus took place near a well and cave where Mary had gone with her pitcher to get water. Gabriel appeared as a young man with a shining face. After the conversation with Mary Gabriel blew his breath into the folds of her outer garment which she had laid aside, and this caused her pregnancy. Another version suggests that the spirit of Jesus entered Mary through her mouth.

Tradition introduces the story of the wise men, the flight into Egypt, Jesus settling in Nazareth, the temptation in the desert, the calling of the disciples, Jesus walking on water, the raising of Lazarus and the cleansing of the Temple. The primary image of Jesus in the Hadīth is that of a self-denying saint, but his joyful demeanor is also contrasted favorably with that of John the Baptist. Although his teachings are only lightly touched on, various aphorisms are reported that later became part of Islamic folklore. They include phrases about the salt, about throwing pearls before swine, about the difficulty the rich have in entering heaven, and the saying: "Judge not, that ye be not judged." The details of the crucifixion of Jesus are expanded. It is here that we have the source of the idea that someone was substituted for Jesus, such as Simon of Cyrene or Judas Iscariot. The substitute was miraculously made to resemble Jesus, thus confusing his enemies. There are various accounts of what happened to Jesus after he descended from the cross, but all the Traditions agree that he is in heaven now and will come again. Wearing two reddish-dyed garments he will descend at Damascus, kill the Dajjāl ("Deceiver"), slay the swine and break the crosses, turn all people to Islam, and establish peace and justice. He will make the pilgrimage to Mecca. After forty years he will die and be buried at Medina in the space left vacant near the graves of Muhammad, Abu Bekr, and 'Umar. After the Resurrection Jesus will become a witness at the Last Judgment against all those who regarded him and his mother as equal to God, and he will perform acts of intercession on behalf of true believers.

b. HADĪTH Illustrations

The sinlessness of Jesus

God messenger said: "Satan touches every son of Adam on the day when his mother gives birth to him with the exception of Mary and her son."[10]

God's messenger said: "All the descendants of Adam have their sides pierced by the devil with two of his fingers at birth, except the son of Mary."[11]

The appearance of Jesus

God's messenger said: "Last night I found myself in a vision at the Ka'ba and saw a ruddy man like the most good-looking man of that type that you can see with the most beautiful lock of hair you can see. He had combed it out, and it was dripping with water. He was leaning on the shoulders of two men and going round the House. When I asked who he was, I was told that he was the Messiah the son of Mary."[12]

'Ali's opinion about Jesus

'Ali [son-in-law of Muhammad] told that God's messenger said to him, "You have a resemblance to Jesus whom the Jews hated so much that they slandered his mother, and whom the Christians loved so much that they placed him in a position not rightly his."[13]

Muhammad's relation with Jesus

God's messenger said: "I am close to Jesus, son of Mary, among the whole of mankind in this worldly life." They said, "How is it?" Thereupon he said: "Prophets are brothers in faith, having different mothers. Their religion, however, is one, and there is no apostle between us [i.e. in the period between them, ed.]."[14]

The descent of Jesus

God's messenger said: "By him in whose hand my soul is, the son of Mary will soon descend among you as a just judge. He will break crosses, kill swine and abolish jizya [the tax on Jews and Christians, ed.]. ... Spite, mutual hatred and jealousy of one another will certainly depart."[15]

God's messenger said: "The dajjal will come forth. ... Then God will send Jesus son of Mary, looking like 'Urwa b. Mas'ūd, who will search for him and destroy him. He will remain among mankind for seven years during which period no two people will be at enmity with one another."[16]

The status of Jesus

God said: "If anyone testifies that there is no god but God alone, who has no partner, that Muhammad is His servant and messenger, that Jesus is God's servant and messenger, the son of His handmaid, His Word which He cast into Mary and a spirit from Him, and that paradise and hell are real, God will cause him to enter Paradise no matter what he has done."[17]

3. Legendary Materials

For our purposes it will not be necessary to go beyond noting the existence of this type of material. It has already become evident that legendary matter crept into the Hadīth, although Muslim scholars succeeded in eliminating much of it. It was perhaps inevitable that the story-telling culture of the region would produce many strange tales about Jesus. Some of them, including stories that first appeared in Christian apocalyptic writings, also surfaced in Muslim literature. With few exceptions Muslims today pay scant heed to these legends.

The more sober of the reports follow the pattern of representing Jesus as an ascetic wanderer. He was without home or property, walked barefoot, and had food only for the day. He is reported to have said words like these:[18]

> My seasoning is hunger, my undergarment is from God, my outergarment is wool, my fire in winter is the rays of the sun, my lamp is the moon, my riding-beast is my feet, and my food and fruit are what the earth brings forth. At night I have nothing, and in the morning I have nothing, yet no one on earth is richer than I.

Jesus was pleased to be known as "the poor one." He is reputed to have said: "One of the worst things about wealth is that one will disobey (God) to become rich, while he will not disobey him to become poor." He advised: "Seek a great amount of that which fire cannot consume."[19]

4. Scholars and Mystics

Scholastic theology in Islam is called *kalām*. Qur'anic exegesis is *tafsīr*. Jurisprudence is *fiqh*. In classical times Muslim scholars freely ranged over these three disciplines. Their task was to stabilize and give form to Muslim religious thinking. In that connection they dealt with Jesus in relation to their interpretive tasks, but not in a focused way. Muslim mysticism in *tasawwuf*. The mystics, in contrast to the theologians, saw Jesus as their own because of his emphases on love and nearness to God, and their writings are full of references to him. It is not surprising that the mystical theologian, Al-Ghazālī, who combines all the disciplines, was most interested in Jesus.

The scholarly respect for Jesus is everywhere evident. "Peace be upon him" routinely follows the mention of his name. An early creed, *Al-Fiqh al-Akbar*, declares that not to view Jesus as an apostle is equivalent to infidelity.[20] In a thirteenth century doctrinal statement Muhammad al-Fādali grades the prophets (a practice frowned upon) in terms of their excellency, listing Muhammad, Ibrāhīm, Mūsa, 'Īsā, and Nūh in that order.[21] It was through the work of the scholars that the orthodox view of Jesus was confirmed. Jesus is the sinless prophet of God whose mission was to the Jews, whose sanctity is a model, who ascended to heaven without death, and who will come again as a precursor of the final Judgment. Notable scholars that dealt with him include al-Muhāsabī (d. 837), an ethicist whose awareness of Jesus, according to Kenneth Cragg, "is nowhere surpassed in the Muslim story";[22] al-Tabarī (d. 923), the prolific historian, who had some knowledge of the New Testament; al-Zamaksharī (d. 1141), a Qur'ān commentator and philologist in the rational Mu'tazilite stream; and al-Baidāwī (d. 1282), a judge, theologian and exegete, whose commentary became a standard Sunnī text.

The scholars were honest and sober in their work, but they used materials without discrimination from Hadīth, legendary history and the views of other scholars. This led them to such comments as the following one that al-Baidāwī makes in regard to the crucifixion passage in the Qur'ān (4:157). After reporting that God had turned some people into swine because they were insulting Jesus and his mother, he adds: "Then God informed Jesus that He would raise him to heaven, so Jesus said to his disciples, 'Who among you will agree to take a form similar to mine and die (in my place) and be crucified and then go (straight) to Paradise?' A man among them offered himself, so God changed him into a form to look like Jesus, and he was killed and crucified."[23]

The scholars also discussed what they mistakenly regarded as the Chrsitian view of the relation of Jesus with God. In a comment on 4:171 al-Zamaksharī asserts that according to the evidence of the Qur'ān Christians maintain that God, Jesus, and Mary are three gods, and that Jesus is the child of God by Mary. However, he says, the words "to him belongs all that is in the heavens and the earth" show the impossibility of such a position. He declares: "Here is set forth why God is free from what was ascribed to him (by the Christians). If everything that is in the heavens and the earth is God's possession, how then can one of His possessions be a part of Him, when one can properly speak of a part only according to bodies, while God is exalted above the properties (sifat) of corporeality and inconstant attributes."[24]

We turn from the scholars to the mystics. It is Al-Ghazālī who is our bridge, one who was acquainted with sources external to the Qur'ān and who regularly quotes Jesus. He too was attracted by Jesus' self-renunciation. It underlined his own teaching that one must be detached from this world and wholly concerned with God. He quoted what he regarded as one of Jesus' sayings: "He who seeks this world is like one who drinks salt water, the more he drinks the more his thirst increases until it kills him."[25] He loved the phrase, "Consider the birds of the air ...: That was not all he appreciated. He was especially taken with the condemnation of self-righteous teachers, the teaching of the Beatitudes, Jesus' call to the piety of love, and his exhortation to trust in God. Al-Ghazālī believed that Jesus was filled with the spirit of God, although he also held that Christians had erred by confusing the person of Jesus with the Light of God that was shining in him.

It was natural for Sufi mystics to pick up on the idea of self-denial that they had incorporated into the Sufi path. On the Last Day God will command a herald to cry, "Where are the ascetics of this world? Let them come to the wedding feast of the ascetic Jesus, son of Mary!"[26] But Jesus was also viewed by Sufis as "the pure lover of God."[27] Jalāluddīn Rūmī (d. 1273) is the noted poet of passionate love for God. Such a lover is ever-thirsting for God like a sand-dune, and sleep runs away from him until the goal of union with God is achieved and God's love is experienced. In Rūmī's view Jesus manifested that kind of love, and therefore he extols him: "Die before his beauty!"[28] Jesus expressed that love by healing the unfortunate. Rūmī says:

From all sides the people ever thronged
Many blind and lame, halt and afflicted.
To the door of 'Īsā at dawn,
That with his breath he might heal their elements.

Yet Jesus turned the attention away from himself. He asked People to acknowledge the mercy and beneficence of God and, as it were, to go up to the highest heavens and grasp His skirt. It is God who is the true Friend who "will bring peace out of perturbation, and when thou art afflicted will keep His promise."[29]

Ibn 'Arabi (d. 1240) took the Sufi veneration of Jesus to a final stage. He was a Spanish Muslim mystic who received the titles "animator of religion" and "the greatest master." A philosophically-minded mystical thinker he was never in favor with orthodox teachers—despite his 300 books—because he emphasized the nearness of the divine Reality to the human heart. God in a sense is incarnate in humans, and man in a sense identifies with God. He considered twelve prophets who he felt demonstrated his thesis. Among them Jesus is the prime example of the truth that God manifests Himself in a way that is appropriate to the recipient. He was created in a special way, attached to Mary, to Gabriel, and to the Spirit of God. This unusual constitution is why people may view him from different aspects.

> Certain considering him by virtue of his terrestrial form affirmed that he was the son of Mary; others, envisaging in him the apparently human form, attach him to Gabriel; and still others, because the resurrection [i.e. raising, ed.] of the dead emanated from him, attached him to God by the Spirit, saying of him that he was the Spirit of God, meaning that it was he who communicated life to whomever received his breath. Thus—each in turn—one sees in him either God, or the Angel, or human nature; so that he is for each spectator whatever the spectator imposes on himself. He is the Word of God, he is the Spirit of God, and he is the servant (that is to say the creature) of God.[30]

In summary, Muslims of the past delivered their portrait of Jesus to the present with deep respect and a sense of mystery:

—The Qur'ān with its limited biographical sketch initiates Muslim esteem for Jesus the Messiah, assigns him a panoply of intriguing names, places him in the ranks of the great prophets, and takes a position against both the deification of man and the plurification of God.

—The Hadīth continues the reverence, but focuses on Jesus as an end-time figure, a development strengthened by legendary material.

—The scholars define the position of Jesus as a model of sanctity, but are visibly perplexed about the meaning of some of the Qur'anic references.

—The mystics take a high view of Jesus as the prime example of loving nearness to God.

What do modern believers add to the Muslim portrayal of Jesus?

D. Modern Muslim Perceptions of Jesus

Muslims today, arguably, are paying somewhat less attention to Jesus the Messiah than in earlier days. The same honor is given, but not the same intensity of interest. Two factors come into play. In the first place contemporary Muslims are showing less interest in eschatological matters and, as we have seen, the traditional picture of Jesus became end-time oriented. The second factor is the Muslim concentration on the figure of the Prophet Muhammad, which tends to reduce the discussion of other prophets, Jesus included. It is Muhammad, the "perfect man," who is the authentic pattern for our time. Nevertheless, a lively awareness of Jesus and his significance remains a central factor in Muslim mentality. We may note four ways of thinking among Muslims today in regard to Jesus the Messiah. The traditional approach, along the lines that we have outlined above, is common among ordinary people. The second approach stresses the ethical example of Jesus and represents the main thrust of modern Muslims. Thirdly, we cite an apologetic tendency related to Christian claims that marks Muslims in Western contexts. Fourthly, we will briefly note an exploratory approach that seeks to penetrate into the spiritual meaning of Jesus for Muslims.

1. The Ethical View

Many modern Muslims lack interest in the legendary material related to Jesus and other prophets. The increase of modern education has brought with it a critical attitude toward such stories. Muslim reform movements opposing superstitious beliefs and practices encourage the attitude. Hence Muslims are now much more interested in the picture of Jesus in the Qur'ān itself, a picture that is viewed through the lens of moral rationality. The miraculous elements are given less attention in favor of emphasizing the role of Jesus as an ethical guide and advocate of human justice. In the same way the idea of Jesus as an ascetic wanderer is set aside in favor of the vision of Jesus as the socially involved change-maker. Jesus was an ordinary human being who struggled against the forces of evil, becoming a global example of self-sacrifice on behalf of justice and truth. He was not only the lover of God, but the lover of suffering and oppressed human beings. He gave himself away to improve their condition, in the process bringing new life to and revolutionizing traditional religion.

The contemporary view of Jesus as an advocate of justice and as a trustworthy ethical guide is well represented by Abul Kalum Azad (d. 1958), an Indian Muslim Qur'anic scholar and freedom fighter. Independent India's first Minister of Education Azad starts his discussion of Jesus from the premise that the true prophets of God have a fundamentally identical message. "Even like the other prophets Christ did not come to set aside the teachings of the prophets who went before him. He came to confirm them, since the basis of religion was but one and the same in every age and among every people."[31] He explains what this means. It is clear "that everyone of the prophets invited mankind to but one task—devotion to God and righteous living."[32] The particular service of Jesus was to provide the needed exposition of ethical principles. He stressed the importance of the inner life, as against mere externality, and tried to revive the forgotten but eternal message of humanity and love."[33] The Qur'ān on its part is especially interested in the practical applications of spiritual principles, but there is a congruence between its emphasis and that of Jesus: "For Christ it was sufficient to lay stress on ethics and purity of heart, since the Mosaic law was available. ... But the Koran had to explain at the same time ethics and regulations. Therefore it chose such a mode of expression in which precepts and regulations were explained in clear practical and precise wordings instead of metaphors and similes (as Jesus did)."[34]

Ismail Faruqi follows the same approach. He says that Jesus emphasized the ethic of inner attention over against externalized religion and in opposition to the kind of law enthusiasm that ignores its spirit. Jesus favored moral action, but his own effort was oriented "toward the internal, radical self-transformation of the person." That involved defining moral good as the human will under the direction of the love of God. That was his essential contribution, the "single-minded determination to cleanse and purify the spring of all action—the will."[35]

Other Muslims do not agree that Jesus was primarily engaged at the level of the inner life. He was, certainly, a model of spiritual thinking, but he also attempted to put his ethical principles into action. Ghulam Ahmad Parwez, a Pakistani exegetical scholar, suggests that it was the disciples of Jesus who invented sayings like "love your enemies" to protect themselves from danger. Jesus himself was an involved liberator. It was his mission "on the one hand to free the Israelites from slavery and from the domination of the Romans, and on the other side to found society on ethical principles which former prophets too had come to build up."[36] A symbolic moment typifies the mood of those who perceive Jesus as one who struggled to bring people to the promised land of political freedom. It came in 1995 when in a Christmas Eve speech on Bethlehem Square Yasser Arafat (d. 2004) spoke of the Messiah as "Jesus the revolutionary."

2. The Apologetic Tendency

We turn to the gently apologetic approach of some conservative Muslims living in majority Christian societies. They are not so much interested in reinterpreting the Qur'ān as in responding to Christian teaching. The approach is illuminated by Fadel Abdullah, an immigrant American Muslim, who affirms that Muslim awareness of Jesus is "deep and durable." Down to the present day "there is a rich mine of veneration in celebration of Isa." He takes issue, however, with Christian claims. "The most cherished aspect of the Jesus story in Islam is related to the quality of his birth," but this event does not imply a theory of incarnation. In fact, the Qur'anic statement that Jesus is "near to God" implies a negation of the possibility of identifying himself with God. Similarly he addresses Muslim disagreement with the Christian creedal phrase, "the only-begotten Son." He states that "for Muslims Jesus will always remain a great Prophet and Leader, but not a Savior or Divine in the Christian sense of these words." The specific mission of Jesus was to the Jewish people, involving liberation "from the triumph of legalism." He suggests that Muslim scholars "see the ethics of the Gospel ... valid equally for Muslims as for Christians, and in no way time-bound or superseded."[37]

The stream of Muslim apologetic related to Christian views runs in a separate channel with the Ahmadiyya Movement. Non-Muslims, particularly in the West, have been confused and have caused confusion by failing to distinguish the Ahmadiyyas from orthodox believers who regard them as heretics. They do so because Ahmadiyyas consider the founder of their movement, Mirza Ghulam Ahmad (d.

1908) to be a prophet. This position contradicts the Muslim view that Muhammad is "the seal of the prophets," i.e. the final prophet of Islam. Now headquartered in Pakistan the Ahmadiyyas are strongly missionary in their outlook. In that connection they have developed a negative apologetic against Christianity that even includes criticism of the behavior of Jesus. He erred, for example, in dealing with women of ill-repute and in his use of wine. Ahmadiyyas therefore teach that Jesus was not sinless. Moreover they have a strange theory of his death, taken from a fictional source. Jesus was taken down from the cross while still alive, recovered, and traveled to Kashmir in India, where he preached to the supposed ten lost tribes of Israel. There he died at the age of 120 and was buried on Khan Yar Street in Srinagar. An additional area where Ahmadiyyas differ from orthodoxy is that they interpret *jihād* as a strictly non-violent effort of peaceful nurture and communication. Although ordinary Muslims do not accept specific theories of the group, its widely-distributed polemical literature has had some impact on the Muslim consideration of Jesus.

3. The Exploratory Desire

Some Muslim scholars of our time are attempting to explore new dimensions of the traditional picture of Jesus. Muhammad Kamil Husain of Egypt is notable in that regard. He concentrates on the issue of collective evil and the murdering of the conscience that make the event of the crucifixion "the supreme tragedy of humanity." Thus he is interested in the ethical implication of the cross rather than the effort to resolve various details of the event. How Jesus escaped from the situation is for him not the crucial issue. He says:[38]

> The idea of a substitute for Christ is a very crude way of explaining the Qur'anic text. ... No cultured Muslim believes in this nowadays. The text is taken to mean that the Jews thought they had killed Christ, but God raised him unto Him in a way that we can leave unexplained among the several mysteries which we have taken granted for faith alone.

What matters most is the spiritual implication of that dark Friday "that was unlike any other day." He declares:[39]

> That day's deeds are a revelation of all that drives men into sin. No evil ever happened that does not originate in the will of men to slay their conscience and extinguish the light, while they take their guidance from elsewhere. ...

The events of that day do not simply belong to the annals of the early centuries. They are disasters renewed daily in the life of every individual. Men to the end of time will be contemporaries of that memorable day, perpetually in danger of the same sin and wrongdoing into which the inhabitants of Jerusalem then fell. The same darkness will be theirs until they are resolute not to transgress the bounds of the conscience.

We conclude with the remark of another Egyptian scholar, Fathi 'Uthman (b. 1928). Concerning the crucifixion he says: "The teaching regarding the crucifixion does not involve merely events that may have happened in a certain way or in another way. Much more, it has to do with a derived result. What we mean by that is the thinking about deliverance."[40]

Thoughts for Christian Sharing

1. Muslims love Jesus, and are usually happy to know more about him.

2. The Names of Jesus in Islam do not include the title "Savior."

3. The Qur'ān rejects false teachings about Jesus that Christians also reject—idolatry, i.e. raising a human to the level of God, and polytheism, i.e. associating a partner with God.

4. By the phrase "Son of God" Muslims do not understand the same thing that Christians understand.

5. At least some of the misunderstandings of Muslims regarding Christology have to do with Christian heresies current at the time of the Prophet.

6. The Qur'ān is not a biography of Jesus. Thus the major portion of Jesus' words and works are not recorded there. The Qur'ān warmly commends to Muslim readers the Injīl where they are recorded.

7. For Jesus himself the ethical impulse and his "nearness" to God are one indivisible whole. He said: "I seek not to do my own will but the will of him who sent me" (Jn 5:30).

8. The clear communication of the Christian understanding of Christ is the central theme for Christian sharing with Muslim friends.

9. A Christian who shares the Gospel will bear in mind the context of the Muslim friend, but at the same time will speak from his or her own experience of God's power to save, and his or her own "thinking about deliverance." The darkness has been overcome.

We turn next to the Muslim view of Christianity and Christians. The plural "views" would be more accurate. In this area too there are a multitude of opinions, with individual perceptions and relationships varying from "official" positions.

Endnotes

1. Scholars such as Kenneth Cragg, Michel Hayek, Neil Robinson, James Robson, and Samuel Zwemer have written on Jesus in the Qur'ān and Jesus in Islam. A full bibliography may be found in G. C. Anawati, "'Īsā," E2², IV, pp. 81ff. Cf. also Don Wismer, *The Islamic Jesus: An Annotated Bibliography of Sources in English and French* (New York: Garland Publishing Co., 1977). For material on the names of Jesus I am particularly indebted to Geoffrey Parrinder, *Jesus in the Qur'ān* (London: Faber & Faber, 1965). The following may also be consulted: Kenneth Cragg, *Jesus and the Muslim* (London: George Allen & Unwin, 1985); Jane D. McAuliffe, *Qur'anic Christians* (Cambridge: Cambridge University Press, 1991); Olaf H. Schumann, *Der Christus der Muslime* (Gütersloh: Gütersloher Verlaugshaus Gerd Mohn, 1975); and various

articles in *Muslim World*. Ernest Hahn, *Jesus in Islam: A Christian View* (Toronto: Fellowship of Faith, n.d.), provides a short overview of the Qur'anic descriptions and a Christian response. Standard collections of Hadīth are *Mishkat al-Masabih*, 4 vols., tr. and annotated by James Robson (Lahore: Sh. Muhammad Ashraf, 1963–1964) and *Sahīh Muslim*, 4 vols., tr. and annotated by A. H. Siddiqi (Beirut: Dar al Arabia, 1971). For a moderate Muslim approach cf. M. Kamal Hussein, *City of Wrong*, tr. by Kenneth Cragg (Amsterdam, 1958); while Muhammad 'Ata ur-Rahim, *Jesus, A Prophet of Islam* (New Delhi: Adam Books, 1983), is an example of a polemical work.

2. Later in the chapter we deal with the Ahmadiyya Movement, a heterodox group rejected by orthodox Muslims that has made some criticism of Jesus.

3. Quoted by Fadel Ibrahim Abdallah in a speech at the Lutheran School of Theology, Chicago, June 7, 1990, from Shawqi's *Great Events of the Nile Valley;* Shawqi was an Egyptian poet and dramatist.

4. Parrinder, *Jesus,* p. 27.

5. Pickthall, *The Meaning of the Glorious Koran,* p. 351.

6. G. C. Anawati, *op. cit.,* p. 83.

7. E. H. Palmer, *The Koran,* p. 482, sums up the issue related to this verse: "The allusion is to the promise of the Paraclete in John 16:7, the Muslims declaring that the word has been substituted in the Greek ... which word means the same as Ahmed." The New Testament word is *parákletos;* it is alleged that it should be *paraklutos,* "praised one."

8. Yusuf Ali, *The Holy Qur'ān,* p. 230.

9. Kateregga and Shenk, *Islam and Chrsitianity,* pp. 141ff.

10. *Sahīh Muslim,* IV, p. 1261.

11. *Mishkat,* III, p. 1225.

12. *Ibid.,* III, p. 1151.

13. *Mishkat,* IV, p. 1342.

14. *Ibid.,* p. 1261.

15. *Ibid.,* III, p. 1159.

16. *Ibid.,* pp. 1163f.

17. *Ibid.,* I, p. 11.

18. James Robson, "Muhammadan Teaching about Jesus," *MW*, Vol. XXIX, No. 1, January, 1939, p. 46, quoting his *Christ in Islam,* pp. 67f.

19. *Ibid.,* p. 47.

20. A. J. Wensinck, *The Muslim Creed* (London: Frank Cass & Co., Ltd., 1965), p. 104.

21. D. M. MacDonald, *Development of Muslim Theology, Jurisprudence, and Constitutional Theory* (Lahore: Premier Book House, 1964), p. 362.

22. Cragg, *Jesus*, p. 50.

23. Helmut Gätje, *The Qur'ān and Its Exegesis. Selected Texts*, tr. by A. T. Welch (Berkeley: University of California Press, 1976), p. 128.

24. *Ibid.*, pp. 126f.

25. Margaret Smith, *Al-Ghazali the Mystic* (Lahore: Hijra International Publishers, 1983), p. 78; for a convenient selection of al-Ghazali's quotations cf. Cragg, *Jesus*, pp. 47–49.

26. *Abu Nu'ayam al-Ifsahānī, Hilayat al-awliya*, Cairo, 1932, Vol. 6:310, in Tor Andrae, *In the Garden of Myrtles*, tr. by B. Sharpe (Albany: SUNY, 1987), p. 28.

27. Annemarie Schimmel, *Mystical Dimensions*, p. 34.

28. *Dīwān-i-kabir*, 214:12918, in Schimmel, *As Through a Veil*, p. 121.

29. E. H. Whinfield, tr. and abridged, *Teachings of Rumi, the Masnavi* (New York: E. P. Dutton & Co., Inc., 1975), pp. 116–118.

30. Muhyi-d-Din Ibn 'Arabi, *The Wisdom of the Prophets (Fusus al-Hikam)*, tr. by Titus Burckhardt and A. Culme-Seymour (Aldsworth, U.K.: Beshara Publications), 1975, p. 73.

31. Abul Kalam Azad, *The Tarjuman al-Qur'ān* (Bombay: Asia Publishing House, Vol I in 1962, Vol. 2 in 1967), tr. by Syed Abdul Latif, Vol. 2. p. 154.

32. *Ibid.*, I, p. 169.

33. *Ibid.*, pp. 176ff.

34. *Ibid.*, pp. 109ff.

35. Ismail Faruqi, *Tawhīd*, p. 85.

36. J. S. Baljon, *Modern Muslim Koran Interpretation* (Leiden: E. J. Brill, 1961), p. 169.

37. Fadel Ibrahim Abdallah, *op. cit.*

38. Quoted from *City of Wrong* in Cragg, Jesus, p. 175.

39. *Ibid.*, pp. 3f.

40. Quoted in Schumann, *Der Christus*, p. 144; tr. by R. E. Miller.

Muslim Opinion of Christians and Christianity

Things were not going well for Muhammad and his followers in Mecca. It was the year 615, about five years after he had received his call. Muhammad had gone out into the hot roads of Mecca preaching about God and the Judgment, about generosity and justice. His own people had severe doubts. What has happened to Muhammad? Has our family man and business leader lost his senses? Soon their wonder turned to anger. Muhammad's preaching was offending their loyalties to their deities and was affecting their income from the Ka'ba shrine where the images were housed. Soon the persecution began. Muhammad himself was protected by his uncle Abū Tālib, but his followers were vulnerable. They were mostly from the poor classes, and they had no guardians. They began to visibly wilt under the fierce oppression. At last Muhammad suggested that they emigrate to Abyssinia (Ethiopia), across the Red Sea. He had heard that a Christian king presided there, who would not tolerate injustice.[1]

The decision was taken. About 83 men, 16 women, plus children, followed Muhammad's advice and migrated to Abyssinia. They were allowed to stay there in safety under the protection of the Negus or ruler (Najishi). A poet among them wrote joyfully:

O rider, take a message from me ...
To everyone of God's protected servants,
Mistreated and hard tried in Mecca's vale,
Namely, that we have found God's country spacious,
Giving security from humiliation, shame ...[2]

The Meccan enemies could not leave well enough alone. They sent two emissaries to persuade the Abyssinians to send back the refugees. The Meccan messengers brought leather gifts to bribe the ruler's generals and gain their support. The king was enraged by this underhanded attempt and called for a hearing into the matter. "No people who have sought my protection, settled in my country, and chosen me rather than others shall be betrayed, until I summon them. ..." Surrounded by bishops and books he invited the Muslims to make their case. Ja'far, son of Abū Tālib, told the story of how through the apostle [i.e. Muhammad] they had left the life of idolatry and immorality, and how they had been attacked for these convictions. They also read to the king a passage from Sura 19 of the Qur'ān dealing with Mary, the mother of Jesus. Upon hearing the words the king decided in the Muslim favor. The next day the Meccan emissaries, however, renewed and increased their attacks, suggesting that the Muslims were teaching a "dreadful thing" about Jesus, namely, that he is a creature. When the hearing was re-opened Ja'far replied to the charge: "We say about him that which our prophet brought saying, he is the slave of God, and his apostle, and his spirit, and his word which he cast into Mary the blessed virgin." When the Negus heard this response, he took a stick from the ground and declared that "his own understanding of Jesus, son of Mary, did not exceed what they had said by the length of the twig." Thereafter, the Muslims reported, "We lived with him in the best of security."[3] The migrants eventually returned to Arabia in two batches, except for the few who had died. The latter included Ubaydullah b. Jahsh who had become a Christian (627); the Prophet Muhammad later married his wife.

From the Muslim point of view this stirring event represents perhaps the highest moment in Christian-Muslim relations. The story is very familiar to Muslims who with gratitude rehearse how in the hour of their need it was Christians who received and protected them. The rock of memory has not broken under the impact of animosities that have developed in later generations. Christians who receive Muslims as good neighbors, or as immigrants or refugees, are repeating a friendly moment in history that moves the Muslim heart.

This early expression of Christian friendship is not an isolated example. At personal levels Muslims have often had the experience of pleasant relations with Christians. Similarly, Christians have known Muslim friendship. On the other hand, there has also been a conscious reserve on both sides that has sometime become dislike and even hostility. In this chapter we are restricting ourselves to the Muslim opinion. Muslim reserve in regard to Christians is grounded in the Islamic belief that Christians have allowed errors to creep into their faith—whether deliberately or inadvertently. This feeling is aggravated by a history of conflict between Christian and Muslim empires. In modern times the suspicion that Christian-majority states have sometimes been unjust toward Muslims in their policies has further exacerbated the relationship. Thus there is an ambivalence in the Muslim attitude toward Christians—a tension between the favorable and the critical. This ambivalence emerged quite soon and may be illustrated by two Hadīth related to greeting Christians. The two Traditions stand side by side, and yet they differ significantly. The first is outrightly positive:

Anas reported God's messenger saying, "When the people of the Book salute you, say, 'The same to you.'"

The second Tradition, however, has a sharper edge:

Abu Huraira reported God's messenger as saying, "Do not salute Jews and Christians before they salute you, and when you meet one of them on the road, force him to go to the narrowest part of it."[4]

Historically Muslims have always had the choice of which approach to adopt, the gentler or the sharper one. When the relations with Christians have not been strained to the breaking point by political and social factors, Muslims have routinely related to them in normal and friendly patterns, and that also applies to the matter of salutations. While a Muslim friend will not ordinarily give non-Muslims the household greeting *salām aleikum*, "peace be with you," when a Christian friend takes leave to utilize the salutation Muslims are ready to respond, *wa aleikum salām*, "and to you, peace!"

In the Muslim view there is a considerable distinction in approach in regard to Christianity and Christians. Individual opinions may vary about Christians, but the estimate of Christianity is sharply defined. the Qur'ān itself knows about Christians, noting both positive and negative elements, but it does not employ the term Christianity. As Islam moved outward from the confines of Arabia and became itself more sharply formed its adherents met the established religion of Christianity. It was not a neutral encounter. Arab Islamic forces were engaged in a military and social expansion into the existing Christian and Persian worlds. Furthermore Islam, which had come into existence six centuries after the founding of the Christian movement, was dealing with familiar and established theological materials of Christianity. As the newcomers Muslims were in the position of having to develop a formal position on Christianity as a religion. Muslim religious scholars ultimately decided on a theory of decline, that is, in its original form Christianity had been a true religion, but in its practical expression it had gone astray. This decision about the religion, however, still left open the relationship with individual Christians, based on the positive elements in the Qur'anic assessment and on living Muslim experience. On a day to day basis amiable relations were possible. The ambivalence comes down to the present, as we must now spell out.

Muslims continue to make the practical distinction between Christians and Christianity. In ordinary converse with Christians they enjoy personal friendships and maintain cordial family relations. They may criticize the behavior of some Christians, but they know that Christians differ in their personal standards as Muslims do. At the same time, however, they often express deep disagreement with formal Christian positions and even condemn them in their public discourse and literature. The apparent contradiction stems from the double reality—Muslims believe that they enjoy a special relationship with Christianity, but they also maintain that Islam is distinct from it and corrects it. In short, the Muslim view of both Christians and Christianity is at the same time a commending one and a censuring one. While this results in a relational schizophrenia that perplexes Christians who do not know its reasons, the ambiguity also creates a virtually endless possibility for positive interaction.

With this introduction we now move forward into the various considerations of our chapter. First examined is the theory that underlies the Islamic view of other religions, and the special position of the "people of the book" among them. In the next section we take up the Muslim attitude toward the Jews and Judaism that connects directly with the approach to Christians. We then consider the specific Qur'anic attitude toward Christians, which defines the issue for Muslims ideally. In the following section, however, we turn to the formal legal theory that was later developed, referred to as the dhimma theory, which moves beyond the Qur'ān. As examples of the application of juristic theory we take up the delicate areas of conversion and inter-marriage. The chapter concludes with a reflection on some of the emotional problems that Muslims have with Christians.

A. Islam and Other Religions

The Muslim view of Christianity is set in the wider context of the Islamic understanding of other religions. That opinion is theoretically controlled by the principle that God guides all human beings. God's guidance (hidāyat) comes through the human conscience and reason, through the signs of creation, but especially through the sending of prophets and the giving of revealed books. Muslims believe that the basic message of God's prophets is always the same, although laws may vary for different cultures. The common message is that God is one Lord, and human beings should surrender to the Almighty and obey God's commands.

Why then are there different religions? The reason, in Muslim opinion, is that humans respond in different ways to the common message. There are the true surrenderers, the Muslims. Then there are those who have elements of the truth but have fallen into error, "the people of the book." Finally, there are those who have gone totally astray from a combination of human weakness and Satanic influence. These are covered by the term polytheist.[5] We look first at the category of polytheist.

1. The Strictures against Polytheism

In Muslim opinion obstinate unbelief reaches its lowest point in the evils of polytheism and idolatry. These fundamental sins are covered by the term *shirk*, associating a partner with God. When this sin occurs, God's terrible wrath is aroused, and that displeasure is communicated through the prophets. Moses said to the children of Israel who were desirous of having a god like the people around them: "Shall I seek for you a god other than Allah when He hath formed you above (all) creatures" (7:40)? And when they persisted and made a golden calf in his absence, Moses prophesied on his return: "Terror and humiliation will come upon them" (7:152)! Such kinds of polytheism and nature worship dominated Arabian religion at the time of Muhammad. The Qur'ān commands that stern action be taken against the idolaters, especially those in the peninsula who were actively opposing Islam. Unless there is a specific treaty, which then must be observed, or unless the idolaters repent, they fall under the stringent sanction of the divine sentence: "But when the sacred months have passed, slay the idolaters wherever ye find them. ..." (9:5). Is that command to kill idolaters still valid today?

Most Muslims today believe that there is another important Qur'anic principle that controls the severity of such passages as the one just quoted. That principle is enshrined in a well-known verse of the Qur'ān: "Let there be no compulsion in religion." (2:256). The passage goes on to point out two things. The first relates to those who use their powers to distinguish truth from error, who reject false deities and believe in God. They are blessed and have grasped "a firm handhold" that will never break. The second has to do with those who misbelieve. They are "fellows of the Fire." God will take care of the matter. Their punishment will come from God on the Day of Judgment, and Muslims must await that divine decision. True believers must be governed by the principle: "Let there be no compulsion in religion." Many Muslims today regard this clear direction as the defining word for relations between Islam and other religions. The harsh passages are intended for and restricted to the active opponents and oppressors of the religion of Islam. They were especially required in the adversarial situation that the early Muslims faced in Arabia, but they are not to be taken as a universal principle of action and are not ordinarily applicable elsewhere. With that understanding Islam adopted a practical principle of tolerance toward non-threatening polytheists in areas that they controlled. Thus, for example, the Muslim rulers of India freely allowed Hindus to practice their faith despite its polytheistic approach. At the same time it must be recognized that some Muslim interpreters, especially in the period of classical Islam, argued that the "no compulsion" verse was abrogated by later passages calling for militant struggle against idolatry.[6] In their opinion, the strictures against polytheists have eternal validity. Although this opinion is not frequently heard today, from time to time extremists take this view, as the Taliban in Afghanistan did when they destroyed the nation's ancient Buddhist images.

We see that there is a range of views regarding the punishment of the sins of polytheism and idolatry, but there is no difference of opinion regarding their disapproval. Muslims today recognize that the implications of idolatry are far-reaching. True believers themselves must be on their guard against the new and modern forms of idolatry that are everywhere pervasive, including the most obvious ones of money, power, and sex. These may be more dangerous than the gods and goddesses of old. We leave this point, however, and move next to the special relation Islam maintains with the religions that accept one God and possess revealed scriptures. The category, in Muslim thought, is called "people of the book."

2. The Special Position of the People of the Book

The phrase "people of the book" (ahl al-kitāb) applies especially but not exclusively to Jews and Christians. Each of them is believed to have a monotheistic base and to have received a genuine revelation. The Jews have been blessed with two such scriptures: the tawrāt, i.e. the Torah, revealed through Moses, and the zabūr, i.e. the Psalms, revealed through David. The Christians have received another scripture, the Injīl, i.e. the Evangel or Gospel, revealed through Jesus. The Qur'ān speaks with the highest respect of these sacred books that preceded the Qur'ān. They too come from God. The Qur'ān says: " He revealed the Torah and the Gospel aforetime for a guidance to mankind" (3:3f.). Another passage declares: "Lo! We inspire thee as We inspired Noah and the prophets before him, as we inspired Abraham and Ishmael and Isaac and Jacob and the tribes, and Jesus and Job and Jonah, and Aaron and Solomon, and as we imparted unto David the Psalms ... messengers of good cheer and warning, in order that mankind might have no argument against Allah after the messengers" (4:163–165). In this light the Qur'ān declares approvingly that monasteries, churches and synagogues are all places "wherein the name of Allah is often mentioned" (22:40).

The people of the book have the promise of divine blessings and care along with Muslim believers. The Qur'ān says: "Lo! those who believe ... and those who are Jews and Christians and Sabaeans—whoever believeth in Allah and the Last Day and doeth right—surely their reward is with their Lord, and there shall no fear come upon them, neither shall they grieve" (2:62). Here the Sabaeans are added to the ranks of the people of the book. They are an unknown group who have been identified with a wide range of religious movements.[7] The final destiny of the members of all the peoples of the book are in God's hands. "Lo! those who believe (this revelation) and those who are Jews and Sabaeans and the Christians, and the Magians and idolaters—Lo! Allah will decide between them on the Day of Resurrection" (22:17).

It is the inclusion of the Magians, another unknown group, and even the idolaters in this Qur'anic listing that enabled some Muslim interpreters to extend the people of the book principle to other faiths. Yusuf Ali, for example, comments on the passages quoted above: "I think that ... the term [i.e. people of the book] can be extended by analogy to the followers of Zoroaster, the Vedas, Buddha, Confucius and other Teachers of the moral law."[8] He states: "The addition of Polytheists—those who join gods with God—may seem a little surprising. But the argument is that all forms of faith that are sincere ... are matters in which men cannot interfere. Our duty is to be tolerant within the limits of tolerance—i.e. so long as there is no oppression, injustice and persecution."[9] Although many Muslims would disagree with this interpretation, in a *de facto* way the broadening of the people of the book principle has actually come into effect. What the Qur'ān stated, in the context of Medina: "Unto you your religion, and unto me my religion" (109:6), has become the functional principle, and it represents the modern response to a literal interpretation of "slay the idolaters."

The transfer of the Prophet Muhammad from Mecca to Medina in 622 brought the issue into focus. In Medina there were four categories of religious people: idolaters, *hanīfs* or monotheists, Jews, and Muslim believers. In addition Muhammad had to deal with the hypocrites who hovered between the categories. To handle the pluralist situation the Prophet established the *mu'ahada*, a covenant or treaty. One Muslim scholar describes it as "the first written constitution in the world."[10] The covenant gave full equity, including religious toleration, to the citizens of Medina, reserving administrative authority to the Prophet. The Jews who made up a large proportion of the city's population were regarded as a recognized religious community (*umma*) along with the Muslim believers, or as the covenant reads—"for the Jews being their religion, and for the Muslims their religion."[11] This agreement has crucial contemporary significance. It provides a fully validated and workable pattern for Muslims in organizing relations with others in modern pluralist societies. It was the basis on which the authorities of *al-Azhar*, the premier Muslim theological institution in Cairo, published a statement (1979) in support of the Egyptian-Israeli peace treaty. The Mu'ahada takes us to the Muslim relationship with the Jews.

B. Islamic Interaction with the Jews and Judaism

The Qur'ān also refers to the Jews as the children of Israel. Their history is part and parcel of Islamic history. From the creation of Adam to the advent of the Prophet Yahya (John the Baptist), Jewish events and personalities sprinkle the pages of the Qur'ān. We have previously noted the story of creation and the fall of humans. In addition to them such events as the following are recorded in the Qur'ān: the exile in Egypt, the exodus through the Red Sea, the wandering in the wilderness of Sinai, the division of the Jews into the twelve tribes, and their entry into the promised land. The children of Israel are regarded as God's chosen people who are the fortunate recipients of divine providence, the gift of the law, and the promise of Paradise. The following Jewish prophets are recognized in the Qur'ān:

Adam (Adām)	Aaron (Harun)
Noah (Nūh)	David (Dāwūd)
Abraham (Ibrahīm)	Solomon (Sulaimān)
Lot (Lūt)	Enoch (Idrīs)
Ishmael (Ismā'īl)	Job (Ayūb)
Isaac (Īshaq)	Jonah (Yūnus)
Jacob (Ya'kūb)	Elijah (Ilyās)
Joseph (Yūsuf)	Elisha (al-Yasa')
Moses (Mūsa)	Ezra ('Uzair)

The identification of Enoch with Idris and Ezra with 'Uzair is tentative, but assuming its correctness eighteen Old Testament prophets receive respectful mention in the Qur'ān, and their stories taken together make up a significant proportion of its content. The information about each has both similarities and differences from the Old Testament accounts. Abraham has a major position as "the Friend of God." Moses is mentioned over a hundred times in the Meccan chapters alone, while the entire twelfth chapter of the Qur'ān is dedicated to the story of Joseph.

Jewish religious customs were also attractive to the early Muslims who were looking for new patterns of worship and piety. Because of the extensive Jewish population these customs were quite visible to the first Muslim believers. It was natural for them to draw on the practices of those whose prophets they revered. Although indigenous Arab culture provided the bulk of the Islamic rites, the Jewish impact was a tangible one. As an example, the Jewish Day of Atonement, Yom Kippur, was initially accepted by Muhammad and was observed on the tenth day (*ashura*) of the month of Muharram. Later it was replaced by the fast of Ramadan, and the Ashura became a voluntary fast in Sunnī Islam, while for *Shī'a* Muslims it became the day or remembrance of the saint-martyr Husain. This hospitality to Jewish tradition was an early phase in the life of the Prophet. It reflected his expectation that the Jews would accept him as a divinely commissioned prophet, in continuity with the great prophets of the past.

That expectation was not fulfilled. The Jews were disinterested and outrightly dismissed Muhammad's prophetic claims. The Qur'ān charts the subsequent alienation that took place, and it also expresses regret over the general behavior of the Jews. Severe criticism is levied against them as a rebellious people. They persecute the prophets. They break God's law. They do not only disobey their own scriptures, but they actually pervert its meaning. They are divided into various factions. Above all, returning to the basic disappointment, they fail to respond positively to Muhammad's preaching and collaborate with his enemies. It is true that some are loyal servants of God, but that is not true of the majority. The Qur'ān censures them and declares: "And if the people of the scripture had believed it had been better for them. Some of them are believers, but most of them are evil-livers" (3:110). The denunciation is strong in this passage: "Thou wilt find the most vehement of mankind in hostility to those who believe, (to be) the Jews and the idolaters ..." (5:82a). This change in the Muslim-Jewish situation required the clarification of the relation of Islam to the people of the book. It came in the theory that Islam corrects and supercedes the foregoing revelations.

The Qur'ān repeatedly makes the accusation that the Jews have intentionally altered their scriptures. The alteration took three forms: distorting its meaning, suppressing certain portions, and deliberately mis-copying the text itself. The following passage describes the first error of distortion:

> And lo! there is a party of them who distort the Scripture with their tongues, that ye may think that what they say is from the Scripture. And they say: It is from Allah, when it is not from Allah; and they speak the lie concerning Allah knowingly (3:78; cf. 4:46, 2:59).

The charge of concealment is expressed in these words:

> Those who hide the proofs and guidance which We revealed after We had made it clear in the Scripture, such are the accursed of Allah (2:159; cf. 2:174, 2:146, 3:71).

The following passage combines the accusation of distortion and concealment:

> They change words from their context, and forget a part whereof they were admonished (5:14: cf. 5:41).

The most serious charge was that of tampering with the written text itself, either by altering existing words or by interpolating new elements:

> Woe unto those who write the Scripture with their hands, and then say, "This is from Allah," that they may purchase a small gain thereby (2:79).

As we shall see later Muslim religious scholars chose to interpret the charge of scriptural corruption as applicable to Christians as well, although the text does not convey that meaning.

The steady deterioration in the relation with the Jews was marked by three other critical developments. The first was a new Qur'anic emphasis on the role of Abraham. Abraham is the father of monotheism and represents the primordial *islām* that pre-dates and informs the Jewish tradition. Through Moses God revealed the specific laws by which the Jews must live, but it was through Abraham that God established the fundamental principle of devotion to One God. The second development had to do with the direction of the prayer (*qibla*). At first the Prophet and his followers had prayed in the direction of Jerusalem, the Holy City, thus identifying with Judaism. But at Medina the command came to change the practice. "And now verily We shall make thee turn (in prayer) toward a qiblah which is dear to thee. So turn thy face henceforth toward the Inviolable Place of Worship" (2:144). From that moment Muslims began to pray in the direction of the Ka'ba, the ancient Arab shrine in Mecca.

The final symbol of the deterioration between Muslims and the children of Israel came in the militant action that was taken against the Jews of Medina who were caught in the conflict between the Muslims of Medina and their foes in Mecca. Muhammad and his followers believed that the Jews had taken the side of the Meccans when the latter threatened Medina militarily, and they took punitive action against them. Of the three Jewish tribes resident in Medina two were exiled, and the male members of the third tribe were executed as the result of the verdict of an arbitrator named Sa'd ibn Mu'adh. The noted Muslim biographer of the Prophet, Muhammad Haykal, reports that Muhammad agreed with the action, saying: "God is pleased with your decision."[13] The outcome reflected the roughness of the times but also the paradoxical relation between Islam and Judaism that has continued throughout history to the present day. Thus Muslims continue to be aware of their special relationship with the children of Israel as people of the book, even as the expression of that recognition is diminished amidst the turmoil of the sad political and social events of our own harsh age.[14]

C. The QUR'ĀN and Christians: The Ambiguity of Commendation and Censure

Muslims use the terms "Christian" and "Christianity" in ordinary conversation, but the Qur'anic word for Christians is *nasrāni* (pl. *nasārā*). The usage reminds us of the fact that by some the first followers of Jesus of Nazareth were called "Nazarenes" (Acts 24:5), probably before they received the name "Christian" in Antioch (Acts 11:26). Some Muslim authorities derive the meaning of the same *Nasrāni* from a quite different root that means "help," recalling what Jesus says in the Qur'ān: "Who will be my helpers (*ansār*) for God?" (61:14) In some later Muslim writings Christians are also called *masīhīyūn*, i.e. "adherents of the Messiah."

The amount of descriptive material about Christians in the Qur'ān is very limited, as is the material in Hadīth and other early sources. There is sufficient reference, however, to enable us to characterize the attitude as a combination of commendation and censure. Commendation is at the root because Christians are followers of Jesus the Messiah, and through him they have been blessed with a valid scriptural revelation. They are therefore people of the book, and their religion is a legitimate pre-Islamic *din*. Nevertheless, the Qur'ān also makes some quite serious charges against Christians, leaving Muslims the task of sorting out the ambiguity. Some Muslims do so by concluding that it must be the original Christianity that is being praised, while present-day Christians have to a degree lost their moorings.

I. The Commendation

The Qur'anic commendation of Christians parallels that of the Jews, but is marked by passages of great warmth. Christians like Jews have faith in God, believe in the Last Day, and are committed to morality. These attributes, together with the possession of a revealed scripture, were regarded as the basic criteria for people of the book. The Qur'ān therefore includes Christians in the lists of those who will be rewarded for their works, and who may look forward to Paradise without fear (2:62; 5:69). This is not a blanket approval of all Christians, for the Qur'ān recognizes the behavioral difference that exists among the followers of the Messiah. Some do not follow their scripture, and are obstinate and rebellious. The Qur'ān advises: "If they had observed the Torah and the Gospel, and that which was revealed unto them from their Lord, they would surely have been nourished from above them and from beneath their feet. Among them are people who are moderate, but many of them are of evil conduct" (5:66). Yusuf Ali translates "moderate" as "on the right course." The promise of happiness for those on the right course is clear, and cannot be set aside.

Nevertheless, some commentators do effectively set aside that meaning by re-interpreting the Islamic theory of the history of revelation. Muslims ordinarily think of the process of divine revelation as the periodic repetition of universal truths. Some scholars, however, have added the idea of progressive "salvific stages."[15] That is, the Jews were to follow the Torah and the practice of Moses until Jesus came. Then they were to observe the Evangel and the practice of Jesus. Thereafter, both Jews and Christians are to accept the Qur'ān and the practice of Muhammad, God's final prophet. If they do not do so, they will suffer in the Fire. That is the implication of the passage 3:85 that says: "Should anyone desire a religion other than Islam it will be accepted, and in the Hereafter he will be among the lost."

This "solution" leaves many modern Muslims uncomfortable. They believe that these scholars have missed the point, namely, the idea of essential Islam. The Sunnī scholar, Fazlur Rahman, declares: "In both these verses [2:62; 5:69], the vast majority of Muslim commentators exercise themselves fruitlessly to avoid having to admit the obvious meaning: that those—from any section of humankind—who believe in God and the Last Day and do good deeds are saved."[16] And Allama S. H. Tabataba'i, a contemporary *Shī'a* scholar, declares that names and titles will not matter at the Gate of Bliss. "The only important thing is belief in God and the Last Day and doing good."[17]

An all-important Qur'anic passage that underscores the commendation of Christians is 5:82:

> And thou wilt find the nearest of them in affection to those who believe (to be) those who say: "Lo! We are Christians." That is because there are

among them priests and monks, and because they are not proud. When they listen to that which hath been revealed unto the messenger, thou seest their eyes overflow with tears because of their recognition of the Truth. They say: "Our Lord, We believe. Inscribe us among the witnesses."

This strong commendation also produces a mixed reaction among Muslim exegetes. Some blunt its meaning by narrowing its scope. They do so by analyzing the occasion for the revelation of the passage. It came about when a group of twenty Christians, either from Abyssinia or Najran in Yemen, arrived at Mecca to carry on a conversation with Muhammad. In the opinion of these commentators the words refer only to that specific group rather than to the generality of Christians. But other scholars yield to the obvious warmth of this passage. Ibn Kathīr (d. 1373), a Syrian, suggests that Christians as a whole have friendship in their hearts, "since kindness and compassion are part of the religion of the Messiah."[18] He says that the Qur'ān proves this when it declares (57:21):

> We caused Jesus, son of Mary, to follow, and gave him the Gospel, and placed compassion and mercy in the hearts of those who follow him.

Their Gospel, says Ibn Kathīr, moves Christians to turn the other cheek against provocation, and to act with equity. Badru Katerega Kashanī (d. 1580), a Persian who follows the same approach, sums up the Christian attitude as "the nearness of friendship" (*qurb-i-muwaddat*).[19] Christians, he says, have soft and tender hearts, and are open to truth. Even though some Christians have injured Muslims, and even though their doctrines are repugnant, their educated people ["priests"] and their pious worshipers ["monks"] faithfully lead the community in its commitment to friendship.

2. The Censure

On the other side of the commendation is the strong criticism of Christians that is also in the Qur'ān. It censures various aspects of Christian failure, and since then classical and contemporary Muslims have added other complaints. The Qur'anic critique covers three main areas: the Christian spirit of exclusivity that involves the rejection of the Prophet; a serious of doctrinal errors; and the monetary rapaciousness of some Christians.

The critique of exclusiveness is directed at both Christians and Jews. They make the delusory claim that no one enters Paradise but them (2:113, 120). They are invited to bring proof for this untenable position (2:111). It is ironic that they dispute among themselves as though they have no scriptures, but at the same time they will not be pleased until others follow their creed. Muslims however follow the foundational religion of Abraham who was neither Jew nor Christian, but rather the righteous one who surrendered to God alone (2:135; 3:167). Surely it cannot be said that Abraham, Isaac, and Jacob were Jews or Christians (2:140)! Both Jews and Christians claim a privileged status as the sons of God, but it is clear that God punishes them for their sins also. They would be better off to remember that they are mortals of His creating. God forgives whom He wills and punishes whom He wills (5:18).

The Christian attitude toward Muhammad is the focus of this critique. Directly or indirectly, in one way or another, the Qur'ān repeats the charge that the people of the book fail to accept Muhammad as a prophet. This is also a key disappointment of Muslims today. They observe that while they accept the prophets and books of the Jews and Christians, the latter will not acknowledge the Prophet Muhammad and the Qur'ān. That refusal is said to be at the background of this passage: "And with those who say, "Lo! 'We are Christians,' We made a covenant, but they forgot a part of that whereof they were admonished. Therefore we have stirred up enmity and hatred among them till the Day of Resurrection when Allah will inform them of their handiwork" (5:14).

The second facet of the Qur'anic critique of Christians has to do with the alleged doctrinal errors of Christians, which are vividly set forth. Christianity has gone astray from the straight path of monotheism, for some reason ignoring its original revelation. The basis for this charge is the doctrine of the Trinity that is interpreted as a form of tritheism and is condemned as *shirk*. The incarnation of the eternal Word is interpreted as the elevation of a human being to the rank of God, and is reproved as sacrilegious. The concept of divine-sonship is understood to be a reference to a divine-human marriage, an abhorrent thought that is denounced as blasphemy. "The Jews say Ezra is a son of Allah; and the Christians say the Messiah is a son of Allah. ... they imitate a saying of those who disbelieved of old. Allah (Himself) fighteth against them. How perverse they are" (9:30)! Because of their misleading errors Muslims must be watchful in their relationships with Christians, as well as Jews, "O ye who believe! Take not the Jews and the Christian for your friends and protectors. They are but the friends and protectors to each other. And he amongst you that turns to them (for friendship) is of them" (5:54; Yusuf Ali).

The final criticism of Christians has to do with the greediness of some of its clergy. Economic oppression, including usury, was an early target of Muhammad's preaching. Meccans, Jews, and Christians were all involved in the accusation, although the most severe criticism was reserved for the Meccan profiteers. The Qur'ān says: " Many of the (Jewish) rabbis and the Christian monks devour the wealth of mankind wantonly and debar (men) from the way of Allah. ... Unto them give tidings (O Muhammad) of a painful doom. ..." (9:34).

A century after the death of the Prophet Islam entered into the classical age of its history. It was a period that was marked by great political rivalries among Muslim and Christian states. It spawned a new set of indictments against Christians. Since warfare does not make friends, the accusations of cruelty and injustice could be anticipated. More unexpected was the charge of scriptural corruption that the Qur'ān had raised against the Jews. It was now extended to Christians—surprisingly so, since there is no Qur'anic word that accuses Christians of tampering with the sacred text. There is a complaint that some Christians are forgetful and also conceal meanings. "O people of the Scripture! Now hath our messenger come unto you, expounding much of that which ye used to hide in the Scripture. ..." (5:15). That complaint is repeated (2:62), but Christians are not accused of corrupting the sacred text. We must look elsewhere for the reason for extending that charge to

The Muslim Opinion of Christians and Christianity ■ 139

include Christians. It stems from the desire of Muslim scholars to resolve perceived differences in the teachings of the revealed scriptures.

The Qur'ān, as we have seen, commends the previous scriptures, recognizes them as divinely inspired, and appeals to their authority. Among them the Injīl or Gospel is given an honored place and is considered to be the true revelation of the Word of God. As Muslim scholars became more aware of the content of the New Testament, however, they discovered apparent contradictions with Qur'anic material. For example, the New Testament teaching is built on the crucifixion of Jesus, but a passage in the Qur'ān takes issue with the historicity of that event. The New Testament cherishes the phrase "Son of God," but the Qur'ān regards it as a serious error. As the Muslim scholars considered the problems two points of view emerged, both of which are current today. The first opinion is that the present scriptures of the Jews and Christians are authentic documents, and only require the correct explanation and exegesis. An example is Deut 18:15 which reads: "The Lord your God will raise up for you a prophet like me from among you, from your brethren—him you shall heed." Many Muslims interpret this passage as a prediction of the coming of the Prophet Muhammad.

The second opinion is a critical one. It holds that the Tawrāt, the Zabūr, and Injīl, i.e. the books of the Bible, have all been somehow altered. The Qur'ān commends them, but in this view what is commended is the original version of the texts. The existing version has been deliberately amended by some process to include incorrect teaching. As damaged goods these scriptures cannot be trusted and should not be used as an authority for believers. Although this opinion is distant from the strong affirmations of the Qur'ān, it nevertheless has become increasingly popular and appears frequently in Muslim apologetic writings.

In passing we will note a third opinion that will be considered later in this volume—that is, the attitude of many ordinary Muslims who simply esteem the scriptures of the people of the book, without attempting to solve the intricacies of variation in content. Moved by the commendation of the Qur'ān many such believers take an interest in reading them.

What we have sketched above indicates that the Qur'anic attitude toward Christians is a double-sided one, as it is in the case of the Jews. Muslims retain the privilege of emphasizing either one or the other in their personal relations and decisions. This creates a flexible situation, and at grassroots levels it has opened the way for routinely cordial relationships. These normal patterns have often deepened into warm regard and deeply meaningful personal relationships. The near legendary Muslim grace of hospitality has further served to promote this outcome.

The relationship of Muslims with Christians, however, is affected by another level of influence, namely the formal stipulations of Muslim classical law. This introduced a structured frame of reference and a stylized approach that is still applicable in some Islamic states. We turn next to that topic which is known as the dhimma system.

C. Legal Relations with the People of the Book

By "Islamic state," in this context, we mean a Muslim majority nation that has institutionalized the sharīʿa as the law of a country. There are Muslim majority nations, such as Turkey with its secular constitution, that have no established religion. There are others that have their own freely adopted system such as Indonesia with its panchsila ("five principles") approach. It ignores the *dhimma* laws. Still others, from Libya to Malaysia, go their own way, with unique styles and systems. A limited number of nations such as Saudi Arabia and Iran fully and formally subscribe to the classical regulatory code as the way for defining interfaith relations today. The fact that this approach varies so fundamentally from the modern principle that is based on equality, human rights, and freedom of choice does not mean that the *dhimma* laws can be treated as an anachronism. There are two reasons why they cannot be consigned to the historical dustbin. The first is that some Muslims regard them as a still useful way of sorting out the statutory rights of members of different faiths. The second reason is that their memory remains alive simply because the regulations are imbedded in the sharīʿa that all Muslims revere.

But what is the *dhimma*? The term signifies a pact, an agreement, an obligation. It suggests that Christian minorities, along with other people of the book, are in a contractual relation with the Muslim majority and with Muslim authorities. In addition to being *ahl al-kitāb*, people of the book, they are also *ahl al-dhimma*, people of the covenant. The covenant implies the acceptance of Muslim domination in return for receiving certain rights. One scholar aptly describes the arrangement as "the status of tolerated subordination."[20] In practice, the extent of the rights and the type of subordination varied from period to period.

It is the idea of law that drove the development of the *dhimma* concept and its discriminatory rules. As a religion of law there is in Islam an inherent pressure toward definition and regulation. Muslim jurists do not appreciate ambiguity, and the Qur'anic commendation-censure motifs in regard to the people of the book needed to be clarified. So in medieval times they went hard at the task of systematizing the legal position of Christians in Islamic societies. They believed that this was not only required in principle, but also because of the administrative needs of Muslim empires and states. The heritage of their work comes down to the present, and it is this legal perspective that accounts for many of the difficulties facing Christians today in some Muslim societies. Thus when Pakistan passed the Enforcement of the Shariah Act in 1991, declaring itself in that sense an Islamic republic, it continued "the progressive erosion of the status of minorities" that had begun with dhimmization of laws under General Zia and the passage of the notorious Blasphemy Laws in 1986, placing Christians in a situation that from their perspective was difficult and even "devastating."[21]

Although the ideological root of the *dhimma* is in the concept of law, its historical origin is in the religious situation that prevailed in Arabia at the time of the Prophet. He had established a basic model with the constitution of Medina (*mu'ahada*). When the relationship of the Jews hardened, however, calling forth another response, Muslim-Christian relations were also affected. A Qur'anic passage calls for vigorous action: "Fight against such of them who have been given the Scripture as believe not in Allah nor the Last Day, and forbid not that which Allah hath forbidden by His messenger, and follow not the religion of the truth, until they pay the tribute [*jizya*], readily being brought low" (9:29). The passage indicates that after Muslim forces have achieved military dominance, the relationship with the people of the book is to be a regulatory one, marked by the payment of tribute. Was the severity of the command—so different from the spirit of the *mu'ahada*—the result of the particular exigencies of that time? Was it therefore a time-bound arrangement, rather than a permanent model? Some Muslims think so. Mohammed Arkoun, a contemporary philosopher, emphasizes the importance of remembering the context of this passage, and he says: "Only a calm, objective and open brand of history can illuminate declarations such as this."[22]

Muslim jurists, however, took another view and developed a full theory of legal relationships on the basis of this Qur'anic passage. In effect, they followed the dominance/regulatory motif rather than the covenant/equality model. Various incidents in Muhammad's life were drawn upon by the scholars to provide the content for the legal theory that emerged. For example, very late in his career the Prophet's army captured the Jewish-populated oasis of Khaybar in northern Arabia. The subsequent treaty granted the Jews security, provided for their religious freedom, and gave them the right to keep and to cultivate the land. In return the Jews would be obligated to submit to Muslim political rule and to pay a substantial land tax. In a similar way the Prophet made a treaty with the Christians of Najran, a city to the south in Yemen. The pact was struck with a Christian delegation that had come to Medina for religious discussions in the year 630. While these discussions ended inconclusively, the treaty became another model. The acceptance of Muslim political authority was again the key element. The Christians also agreed to an annual assessment of 2000 garments, to give up usury, to provide hospitality for Muslim emissaries, and to give additional support in wartime. In return the Prophet guaranteed security for life and religion.

> No bishop or monk shall be displaced from his parish, and no priest shall be forced to abandon his priestly life. No hardships or humiliation shall be imposed on them, nor shall their land be occupied by [our] army. Those who seek justice shall have it: there will be no oppression or oppressed.[23]

Later, through a messenger whom Muhammad sent to Yemen, the Prophet declared in a similar statement:[24]

> A Jew or a Christian who becomes a sincere Muslim of his own accord and obeys the religion of Islam is a believer with the same rights and obligations. If one of them holds fast to his religion, he is not to be turned from it. Every adult, male or female, bond or free, must pay a golden dinar or its equivalent in clothes. He who performs this has the guarantee of God and His apostle.

It is clear that the Prophet Muhammad employed a variety of models, according to the situation, in his dealing with the people of the book. This pragmatic, contextual approach provides the base for modern Muslims to introduce new arrangements in accord with modern democratic institutions. Many Muslims, however, are still interested in transferring the classical model, more or less intact, to contemporary societies. Let us see how that model developed from the variable approach of the early Muslims into a pattern of rigorous regulation.

A major factor in the development was the statistical change in Muslim populations after the death of the Prophet. As time passed the majority of people in Muslim lands changed their status by becoming Muslims. That was not the case in the beginning. Muslim armies made amazingly rapid and astonishingly successful advances into the regions bordering Arabia that were inhabited mainly by Christians, Jews, and Zoroastrians. At first the new Muslim rulers were relatively few in number, mainly warriors who kept to their military camps. At the same time as consolidating territory they had the task of administrating large numbers of non-Muslims, with the help of existing systems. The principle of mutual contract seemed to Muslims to be appropriate for the situation. They bound themselves to provide security and religious liberty to the people, who in turn agreed to accept Islamic rule and to pay the special *jizya* tax. In Muslim interpretation the levy of the tax was offset by the fact that those who paid it were not subject to military duty. In this way the people of the book became known as *dhimmis*. Christians had to accept the situation. At first it did not cause them severe disadvantage. Apart from the subordinate status and the required tribute Christians were generally free to conduct their own affairs. In any event, in these areas that were torn by a century-long conflict between the super-powers of Byzantium and Persia and where there was severe oppression, people were accustomed to the need to accommodate themselves to the ways of foreign rulers. In fact, Christians and Jews played important roles in the administration of the Muslims, who seemed relatively benign and friendly. Two factors materially changed the situation—the new population ratios and the Muslim defensiveness after the Crusades and the Mongol invasions.

Gradually people in the conquered lands chose Islam as their religion. Very seldom was this due to compulsion. The old story that Muslims forcibly converted Christians to Islam is only occasionally factual. The reasons for Christians changing their faith were quite diverse. They ranged from a desire to avoid taxation to a hope for employment and economic advantage. A Muslim named Abul 'Ala may have been reporting accurately when he said: "The Christian accepts Islam not out of conviction but from greed. He seeks power or fears the judge or wishes to marry."[25] Ibn Kammūna, a thirteenth century Jewish philosopher, wrote similar words about the motive of Jews converting to Islam: "He is moved by fear or ambition, he is liable to a heavy tax, or wishes to escape from humiliation, or is taken prisoner, falls in love with a Muslim woman, or some other motives like these."[26] Laurence Browne in tracing the eclipse of Christianity in Asia attributes this development not to utilitarian instincts but to a fundamental failure of the Christian spirit. He states:[27]

> The history that we have tried to unfold ... shows that Islam was not forced upon the Christians of Asia at the point of the sword, at any rate, until the days of bitter persecution under the Mongols. Nor, on the other

hand, was Islam spread among Christians by preaching. ... The thing that turned Christians to Islam was, as we have seen, the common acceptance by Muslim and Christian alike of the error that the favour of God is shown by worldly success. ... The people who called themselves Christians had accepted the false idea of the supremacy of worldly might—an idea closely akin to what in our own day we call secularism—in other words, the denial of the supremacy of the spirit.

Be that as it may, Christians became definite minorities where once they had been the majority, and the *dhimma* regulations became gradually more stringent, although Adam Mez's comment must be heeded: "The necessity ... to live side by side created an atmosphere of toleration absolutely unknown in Medieval Europe."[28]

Change in religious population was only one factor that affected the application of the *dhimma* theory. Perhaps more important were the political struggles between Christian and Muslim rulers. The bitterness associated with those conflicts produced a negative atmosphere and hardened Muslin attitudes toward Christians. That is evident in the elaboration and stiffening of the *dhimma* laws. Many new discriminatory requirements were added that had not been present earlier, but were now incorporated into the legal code. The *dhimma* idea became a kind of submission-humiliation principle. The right to construct worship buildings, the height of houses, the forms of transportation, employment opportunities, identifying dress codes, and even the practice of some religious ceremonies were regulated for *dhimmis*. As one ninth century imperial document put it:[29]

> You will be subject to the authority of Islam and to no contrary authority. You will not refuse to carry out any obligation which we think fit to impose upon you by virtue of this authority. ... You may not display crosses in Muslim cities. ... Nor build churches or meeting places for your prayers. ... Nor proclaim your polytheistic beliefs on the subject of Jesus, son of Miriam, or any other to a Muslim. You shall wear the girdle [a yellow sash called a *zunnar*] over all your garments. ... Every free male of sound mind among you shall have to pay a poll tax [jizya] of one dinar, in gold coin, at the beginning of each year.

The famed Muslim historian *Al-Tabari* states that Caliph Mutawakkil (d. 869) also commanded that wooden images of devils be affixed to the house doors of *dhimmis* to distinguish them from Muslim homes.[30] These were the extremes, but they indicate the trend in the Muslim view of Christianity. Needless to say, Christian minorities adopted various defensive attitudes and techniques in the interest of survival.[31]

We return to the present day and the question: Do Muslims regard the *dhimma* regulations, in whatever form, as applicable in our time? The answer is buried in the larger question of whether the shari'a can be adapted to the new circumstances of the modern world. There are various points of view on this heated issue, as we have already observed.[32] In regard to the *dhimma* laws we may note three trends in the search for appropriate models. Strictly fundamentalist Muslim states will not agree that the rules inherited from the past can be altered at all, except in narrow points of application. A second more moderate but less precise opinion looks for middle ground. The old legal principles must be respected, but they can somehow be adapted in terms of specific regulations, or some regulations can be ignored, or the old and the new can be maintained side by side in some integrated form. The third approach affirms that the *dhimma* laws are outdated. They were intended for a certain time and situation, and are no longer valid today. The prophetic vision and pattern must now be freshly applied to contemporary conditions. In that process the Prophet's principle of contextuality is more important than the imitation of the past.

It is particularly in areas where Muslims themselves are in a minority position that we find a new Islamic consensus on human rights under formation, including religious rights. So, for example, in India Muslims are contending that the principle of equality that is embedded in a secular state is Islamically valid and at the same time is the best hope for Muslims within a majority Hindu environment. Syed Shihabuddin, an Indian Muslim leader, declares:[33]

> Those who love India, must love all its people. Those who nurse the hope of reuniting the Sub-continent some day, must respect all religions. Those who wish to promote unity and integration must not only tolerate but must be prepared to embrace our diversities. Only those who believe in the ultimate equality of citizens are humanists. Only those who believe in the equality of Man are humanists.

This is a stirring appeal to Indian Muslims to identify with the secular principle and to see Muslim values in the ideas of humanism. It is not yet clear how the logic of this position will be extended and to what extent the Muslim attitude of the future will reflect this kind of view.

D. Laws Related to Muslims Who Become Christians and to Muslims Who Inter-Marry with Christians

Two emotional areas in the Muslim attitude toward Christians and Christianity are conversion and intermarriage. We will briefly examine these subjects as illustrations of the legal regulatory system that both expressed the Muslim attitude and powerfully influenced its development.

I. The Islamic Law of Apostasy

The law of apostasy expresses the legal attitude of Muslims toward Christian believers from Islamic background. The larger issue of conversion, and the special needs of converts from Islam, will be taken up in Chapter 17 of our study. Even a cursory examination of the traditional law of apostasy, however, reveals that there is a different attitude toward Muslims who have chosen to become Christians as compared with that displayed toward born Christians. The relation with born Christians is governed by people of the book theory, but a much harsher regulation called "the law of apostasy" governs the issue of religious change (*irtidād*). The law of apostasy is also a construct of medieval Islam, and it is undergoing review by Muslims today, not only because it appears to be socially outdated, but also because the Qur'ān itself points in a different direction.[34]

Muslims generally disapprove of a member of their community joining another religion. They can tolerate the espousal of new ideas, and will even blink at an individual's liking for the ideas of another religion, but they disfavor the formal adoption of another religious affiliation. Such an action is deemed wrong and punishable. Some Muslims prefer to leave the issue of punishment up to God, but others follow the legal tradition of the law of apostasy. This law in not limited to a few mild sanctions. Rather, it decrees that "one who turns back" (*murtādd*) is considered deserving of the death penalty. A related law of the *dhimma*, as we have seen, prohibited people of the book from inviting Muslims to their faith. But what is the position of the Qur'ān?

The Qur'ān condemns apostasy but clearly associates its punishment with the end-time, the Day of Judgment. At the root of the Qur'anic condemnation lies the concept of blasphemy. It is blasphemy that a person who has once known the truth of God should commit the sacrilege of repudiating it. God will penalize such behavior at the appropriate time and in His own way. The key passages are these:

> Whoso disbelieveth in Allah after his belief—save him who is forced thereto and whose heart is still content with Faith—but whoso findeth ease in disbelief: on them is wrath from Allah. Theirs will be an awful doom. ... Assuredly in the Hereafter they are the losers (116:106, 109).

The previous works of such individuals will not be any use to them.

> And whoso becometh a renegade and dieth in his disbelief, such are they whose works are fallen both in the world and in the Hereafter. Such are the rightful owners of the Fire, and they will abide therein (2:117).

In these words the Qur'ān establishes that the punishment of a Muslim who changes religious faith is God's business at the end of time. It belongs to the Hereafter.

The legal law of apostasy, however, made the punishment mankind's business in the present time. How did this reversal take place? It occurred when another concept entered the scene that affected the understanding, aggravated by new political conditions. The concept was the idea of the sanctity and inviolability of the umma. How dare anyone as it were belittle the sacred community by leaving it! Merging with this strong notion was the factor of treason that arose in the Muslim empire. Where religious membership and citizenship are virtually identified, conversion bears the opprobium of treasonable activity, and this accounts for the frequent use of the term renegade for converts. Treason will always be considered a severe crime. The context of the Islamic empire, then, was also the context for the development of a sterner view toward religious change. Religious jurists took the lead in forging a new interpretation, namely, that converts to Christianity or any other faith, should be punished in this life, and utilizing Hadīth for their authority they introduced the idea of the death penalty. If the apostate is an adult of sound mind and not under compulsion, he should be executed. A woman should be either imprisoned or executed. There was disagreement over the question of whether or not such individuals should be given the opportunity to repent—one opinion was that there should be three such opportunities—but there was no disagreement over the punishment. The method of execution varied, but torture was banned. Civil consequences were taken for granted. The convert's right of property ownership was suspended, inheritance was cancelled, the individual's marriage contract became void, normal family relationships were annulled, and the convert could not be buried in a Muslim cemetery.

These draconian regulations were the product of a rough age. In some Muslim societies local cultures never embraced them. In others the law was recognized but was not implemented. In still others it was set aside. In some areas of the Muslim world, however, this legal tradition remains firmly in place. Even where official national laws may prevent the implementation of the death penalty, "law of apostasy atmosphere" pervades and social sanctions remain the norm. In such areas individual Muslims are keenly aware of the implications if they are considering the adoption of another faith. The situation is currently in the process of change. Many educated Muslims today are taking the approach that the law of apostasy is inappropriate for the modern age and gives Islam a bad name. Islam must return to the instruction of the Qur'ān and leave the judgment to God. There is another practical factor influencing change. Since believers of other religions have the freedom to choose Islam as their faith, and many are doing so, the reverse must be considered. The Qur'anic principles of reciprocity, moderation and religious tolerance are being cited against perpetuating the law of apostasy. In this way Islamic communal consensus is moving against the medieval tradition, but the process of change is incomplete, and in some areas it is barely perceptible.

On the other side of the coin Muslim societies welcome converts from the people of the book. In welcoming converts the procedures of the shari'a are observed. The essential factor in the conversion is the confession of faith: "There is no deity except Allah, and Muhammad is the messenger of Allah." The observance of circumcision and a rudimentary ability to perform the five-fold prayer are other requirements. In the last half of the twentieth century a significant number of western Christians opted for Islam as their religion. This was mainly the result of factors other than organized Muslim mission activity. Muslim da'wa or mission was largely an informal effort of individuals, and only in recent times have organized forms of Islamic mission developed. Moreover, there is some disagreement over the basic question of whether or not mission work should be carried on among the people of the book who are recognized religious traditions. Nevertheless, da'wa has now become commonplace in contemporary Islam. The activity is based on a Qur'anic command: "Call unto the way of thy Lord with wisdom and fair exhortation, and reason with them in the better way. ..." (16:25). Kerbala states: "Both Muslims and Christians strive to proclaim 'good news' to the world, as commanded by God and exemplified by their respective Prophets."[35] Ismail al-Faruqi declares the da'wa is to be addressed to both the Muslim and the non-Muslim, "to the Muslim to press forward to actualization, and to the non-Muslim to join the ranks of those who make the pursuit of God's pattern supreme."[36] On this basis some contemporary

Muslims now intentionally issue the call to Islam also to members of the people of the book. This development will undoubtedly have some reciprocal influence on the continuation of the law of apostasy, for many Muslims are aware that their own mission depends in part on a balanced attitude toward the mission of others.

Legal relations with Christians are specific in the matter of intermarriage. We turn to that subject which is directly legislated by the Qur'ān.

2. Muslim Intermarriage with Christians

What follows is not a discussion of the major topic of marriage in Islam, but only the question of Muslim intermarriage with Christians. Such intermarriage is allowed but is limited to the marriage of a Muslim male to a Christian female. The permission flows from the special relation of Muslims with the people of the book, while the restriction stems from the Muslim view of husband-wife relations.

The Qur'ān forbids the marriage of Muslims, whether male or female, with those who are outside the people of the book relationship. It commands: "Wed not idolatresses till they believe; for lo! a believing bondwoman [slave] is better than an idolatress, though she please you; and give not your daughters in marriage to idolaters till they believe, for lo! a believing slave is better than an idolater though he please you" (2:221; cf. 60:10). However, the case is different with a Christian or Jewish woman. "This day are (all) good things made lawful for you. The food of those who have received the Scripture is lawful for you, and your food is lawful for them. And so are the virtuous women of the believers and the virtuous women of those who have received the Scripture before you ... when you give them their marriage portions and live with them in honour, not in fornication, nor taking them as secret concubines" (5:5). It is noteworthy that the Prophet Muhammad had a Christian wife, a Coptic maiden presented to him by Egyptian authorities. After she bore him a son, Ibrahīm, who died in infancy, Mariya was freed and raised from the status of slave to wife.

The Qur'ān does not in so many words reject the marriage of a Christian man with a Muslim woman, but because it allows only the opposite that rejection is assumed. The sharīʿa therefore does not approve of such unions, although they occasionally take place. The limitation is defended on several counts. Hammudah Abdalati, for example, makes the case with the following justifications of the prohibition. A Christian husband, he says, would not recognize the validity of the Muslim woman's faith, while a Muslim man does accept the right of a Christian woman to practice her faith. Another justification relates to the Muslim understanding that by the natural order the wife will be obedient to her husband. In doing so, however, the Muslim wife of a Christian mate would run into conflict with the prohibition that forbids a Muslim believer to subject one's conscience to a non-Muslim. He also suggests that the inherent tension between a Christian husband and a Muslim wife would lead either to the tragic breaking of the marriage union, or to the shameful apostasy of the wife. Abdalati concludes his belabored argument with these words:[37]

To protect their women from exposure to uncertainty, to avoid the risk of degradation or disgrace, to honor their religion by placing it outside the category of the "exchangeable" in mate selection, and to save their "honor" from being at the mercy of those who are not "trustworthy"—these were probably the major reasons for the prohibition of intermarriage between Muslim women and non-Muslim men.

The Muslim legal tradition, however, follows the Qur'ān in recognizing the validity of the marriage of a Muslim man to a Christian (or Jewish) woman. From a patriarchal point of view it is assumed that the offspring from such a marriage would follow the religion of their father. Although this type of marriage is allowed, it is not encouraged. The jurists do not consider it to be advisable, and when it does take place it is anticipated that the Christian wife will eventually accept the religion of her Muslim spouse.

Although the formal Islamic legal position on intermarriage is very clear, there is considerable variety in actual practice in various Muslim societies. This is particularly true where the local indigenous culture remains more powerful than the formal legal tradition. In such societies marriage outside one's own religious community (exogamy), without limitations and without social sanctions, is common. This is the situation from Africa to Southeast Asia. Moreover the movement of people in the world, combined with the effect of cultural globalization, has meant an increase in Christian-Muslim marriages in western societies. In the majority of cases, however, the religious affiliation of the children becomes an inevitable and disturbing question. The difficulty of handling the problem in any other way often results in a superficial "religion in general" compromise, with the children of the union ending up religiously unaffiliated. As the practice of intermarriage with Christians increases Muslim jurists will be called upon to consider new applications of the wisdom of the great legal scholar Abū Hanīfa (d. 767), who utilized his concept of preference (*istihsān*) to advise the discretionary approval of "what seems best."

E. Some Current Muslim Problems with Christians

The following excerpt from an impassioned letter to the editor by a Muslim, Nazira Tareen, summarizes some of the standard Muslim critiques of Christians, most of which focus on events gone by. In response to a critical article that deals with Islamist terrorism and Muslim militants she writes, with evident sincerity:[38]

Would the author say that he doesn't fault Christianity for Christians kidnapping slaves from Africa and selling them in the United States (and drowning many in the oceans); building up colonial empires around the world and enslaving and killing innocent people during the Inquisition, Crusades and the Holocaust; instituting apartheid; killing off aboriginals; fighting incessant wars, including two world wars; developing nuclear and thermonuclear weapons and dropping atomic bombs on civilian cities; and selling billions of dollars worth of arms to kill and main ...

The indictment is severe, based on general fact, and constitutes a challenge to self-righteousness, even though it follows the simplistic approach of assigning corporate responsibility. Not all Christians can be blamed for the Holocaust, and not all Muslims can be blamed for the World Trade Center. What makes the path represented by the letter a rather futile one, however, is not because every Christian sin of the past can in some way be matched by a Muslim sin, but because it belongs to the past. Critics on that path tend to wander through history looking for the weaknesses of others, and raising an accusing voice when they find them. The psychology of rehearsing past evils deters from dealing with the hard issues of the present.

Muslims seeking understanding avoid this approach but point to some real current difficulties that occupy their minds, and Christians need to be aware of what they are. The felt problems fall into three categories—problems related to fair communication, dilemmas in connection with the condition of Muslim minorities, and larger issues belonging to the economic and political realms.

The problems in the area of fair communication are the most immediately abrasive ones. Muslims are distressed over the caricatures of Islam and the stereotyping of Muslim behavior that frequently characterizes the media treatment of these subjects. The misrepresentation may sometimes result from ignorance rather than from Islamophobic malice, but the effect is the same. In particular Muslims long for more knowledgeable and better balanced treatment of such "hot" topics as violence, women, and fundamentalism. In that connection Muslims are sometimes critical of aspects of communication involved in Christian mission activity. On the whole they recognize the obligation that Christians have to share the Gospel with Muslims along with others, but they have a rightful quarrel with one-sided portrayals of their faith and with methodologies that are insensitive, lack respect, and utilize questionable inducements to achieve their goals.

The second category of felt problems has to do with Muslim life in Christian cultures. Many Muslims have voluntarily chosen residence in secular western nations, or have come as refugees. The influx has altered the religious population patterns of such countries. Secular nations in the West at their root have deeply Christianized cultures, although not everyone is conscious of the fact. Muslims feel the subtle realities of the situation and often wonder how to cope with them. Shall they, for example, allow their children to participate in Christmas programs at public schools in violation of their principles, or shall they withdraw them causing their children separation and disappointment? Or, in another instance, how can they obtain the admission of the two chief Muslim religious festivals, 'Īd al-Adhā and 'Īd al-Fitr, into the calendars of national holidays? Similar questions abound at the practical level. The issues obviously involve Muslim behavior as well as Christian. At what points must Muslims themselves modify their tradition to accommodate their new life, and at what point should Muslims expect equal treatment? Muslims are attempting to work through these questions, and they appreciate Christian awareness of the struggles that the process involves for them. There is another level of Muslim concern that has to do with the breakdown of family values in society. Muslims fear the impact of drugs, alcohol, and sexual exploitation on the consciousness and habits of their children. They recognize that faithful Christians also have the same concerns, and they wonder how the people of the book can work together in addressing such basic moral problems.

The larger issues related to political and economic affairs are also viewed by Muslims as religious concerns because of the Islamic principle of the wholeness of life under God's beneficent rule. Muslims assume that other people of the book have the same concept. As a result many still identify the "West" as "Christian," and any western activity as Christian or Jewish activity. The combination of elements produces frequent misunderstanding. The latter is not confined to Muslims for even western scholars use phrases such as the "the clash of civilizations."[39] In the economic realm the pattern of globalization that is sweeping the world is taken by some Muslims to equate a new form of Christian imperialism, intended to keep Islam at a disadvantage. It is believed that Muslim destiny is thereby falling or has fallen into the partial control of western (= Christian) business conglomerates. In the same way, Muslims care deeply about the political decisions that affect their lives and future. To many it seems that at formal political levels Christians are not very sympathetic to Muslim concerns even though individual Christians may have friendly attitudes. Nothing focuses these impressions more than the issue of Palestine. Muslims feel that the people of the book have joined hands against them, although many Palestinians are Christians. It is difficult for non-Muslims to fully appreciate the effect of this unhealed wound on Muslim emotion. Those Christians who show their understanding of these larger issues, not necessarily agreeing on their substance but recognizing the need for fairness, are deeply appreciated by Muslims.

F. Some Thoughts for Christian Sharing

1. The Muslim attitude toward Christians and Christianity is not like an empty slate. Muslims have a point of view before they ever meet Christians. What is written on the slate affects their interest in hearing and considering the gospel. Christian communicators need to erase some old things and write new things.

2. Those who share Christian ideas with Muslims must distinguish between following Christ and adhering to a religion called Christianity. Their primary task is to communicate Christ's invitation to follow him.

3. As a religion Christianity is associated with the evils done by some of its members, even though they are only nominally members. The need to ask forgiveness is plain. Two Christian principles are relevant: do unto others what you want others to do; and, to whom much is given much is required.

4. Friends respond to actual feelings, even when these seem to be ill-founded or even hypocritical. Christian communicators with Muslims will resist the impulse to "get mad." At the same time they will also firmly oppose a merely selective or inaccurate use of facts, and as friends can do, will speak the truth in love.

5. Human rights, religious freedom, and true reciprocity are legitimate themes for Christian-Muslim dialogue. Considering the frequent predicament of individual Muslims who wish to follow Jesus the Messiah, they become urgent themes.

6. From the side of Christian theology Christians have a relationship with Muslims deeper than "people of the book." It is "the nearness of friendship" brought into being by Jesus. By it Christians are called to be responsive to Muslim felt needs and problems, with whatever creativity and energy God gives them.

Endnotes

1. Frumentius had brought the gospel to Aksum in northern Ethiopia in the period 300–350 A.D., and was appointed a bishop by Athanasius. Soon thereafter a Christian king established Christianity as the state religion. By the 500s Aksum had become Monophysite in theological leaning.

2. Ibn Ishaq, *The Life of Muhammad*, tr. by A. Guillaume, p. 148. The description of the migration is taken from this source.

3. *Ibid.*, pp. 151–153.

4. Mishkat, III, p. 970.

5. On the basis of certain Qur'anic passages some Muslim scholars believe that the pluralist situation is part of God's mysterious overall plan but this idea has not been fully developed by theologians.

6. The theory of abrogation (*naskh*), espoused by some Muslim interpreters, holds that about twenty Qur'anic passages have been superceded by subsequent revelations. Cf. J. Burton, "Naskh," *EI²*, VII, pp. 1009–1012.

7. Some authorities identify the Sabaeans with the pre-Islamic monotheists in Arabia, otherwise known as the *hanīfs*; others with Zoroastrians or gnostic groups in northern Persia.

8. Yusuf Ali, *Holy Qur'ān*, fn. 76, p. 33.

9. *Ibid.*, fn. 2788, p. 854.

10. This is the title of M. Hamidullah's work on the subject (Lahore: Sh. Muhammad Ashraf, 1941).

11. *Ibid.*, p. 34.

12. For a summary of the Qur'anic accounts, see Miller, *Muslim Friends*, pp. 176–178.

13. Muhammad Haykal, *Life of Muhammad* (Plainfield, Ind.: North America Trust Publications, 1976), pp. 313f.

14. A. I. Katsh, *Judaism in Islam* (New York, 1962), traces the impact of the Jews on early Islam. For the subsequent period cf. S. D. Gotein, *Jews and Arabs. Their Contacts through the Ages* (New York: Schocken Books, 1974) and Bernard Lewis, *The Jews of Islam* (Princeton: Princeton University Press, 1984).

15. Jane McAuliffe, *Qur'anic Christians*, p. 117.

16. Rahman, *Major Themes*, p. 166.

17. S. H. Tabataba'i, al-Mizan 6:67, quoted in McAuliffe, *Qur'anic Christians,* p. 121.

18. McAuliffe, *Qur'anic Christians,* p. 225; quoting *Tafsir al-Qur'ān al-'azim,* 2:86.

19. *Ibid.,* p. 226; quoting *Minhaj al-sādiqīn* 3:291.

20. Bernard Lewis, ed., *Islam* (New York: Harper, 1974), II, p.217.

21. Cf. Charles Amjad-Ali, "Political and Social Conditions in Pakistan," in R. E Miller and H. Mwakabana, eds., *Christian-Muslim Dialogue. Theological and Practical Issues* (Geneva: Lutheran World Federation, 1998), pp. 327–347; in this brilliant analysis the former Chairman of Pakistan's Human Rights Commission speaks of the ideological framework "in which there is no place for pluralism of belief and existence" (p. 331).

22. Mohammed Arkoun, *Rethinking Islam,* tr. and ed. by R. D. Lee (Oxford: Westview Press, 1994), p. 72.

23. Quoted in M. Khadduri, *War and Peace* (Baltimore: Johns Hopkins Press, 1955), p. 179.

24. Ibn Ishaq, *Life of Muhammad,* p. 647f.

25. Adam Mez, *The Renaissance of Islam,* tr. by S. Khuda Baksh and D. S. Margoliouth (London: Luzac & Co., 1937), p. 33; quoting Abul 'Ala (#8449/1057. *Luzumiyyat,* Bombay ed. 250).

26. Lewis, *Jews of Islam,* p. 95; quoting Moshe Perlmann, ed., *Sa'd b. Mansura Ibn Kummūna's Examination of the Inquiries into the Three Faiths* (Berkeley, 1967), p. 102.

27. Laurence E. Browne, *The Eclipse of Christianity in Asia. From the Time of Muhammad till the Fourteenth Century* (New York: Howard Fertig, 1967), p. 183f.

28. Mez, *Renaissance,* p. 32.

29. Bernard Lewis, ed., *Islam,* II, p 221.

30. Lewis, *Jews of Islam,* p. 49.

31. Cf. the magisterial summary of this complex issue by Claud Cahen, "Dhimma," *EI²,* II, pp. 227–231.

32. See Miller, *Muslim Friends,* pp. 282–289.

33. Syed Shahabuddin, editorial, *Muslim India,* Vol. XI, No. 129, September 1993, p. 387.

34. The normal pattern of legal change in Islam may be noted. It does not occur by formally altering the regulations of the traditional *sharī'a,* but rather by holding then in abeyance or re-interpreting them. It is interesting to compare this with Christian legal change. The shari'a laws on apostasy and inheritance were virtually duplicated by similar laws against Muslims in Christian Byzantium. The same applied to Jews. Bernard Lewis reports that "a Christian could marry a Jewish woman, but a Jew could not marry a Christian woman, under pain of death" (*Jews of Islam,* p. 27). Norman Daniel observes that a Muslim in Christian lands had to wear distinctive clothing and observe various restrictions. He notes: "The protec-

tion of Muslims in Christendom approximated temporarily to that of tributary Christians in Islam, except that the ultimate aim was their conversion" (*Islam and the West*, p. 116). The difference in the Christian and Muslim religion-legal development is that the Christian laws faded away while Muslims must still contend with the medieval regulations. An Egyptian Muslim scholar, Abdullah Amed al-Na'im, therefore advocates using the abrogation technique to change such regulations as the dhimma laws. He proposes: " Some of the verses of the Qur'ān which were not deemed to be legally binding in the past are to be legally enacted into law today, with the necessary consequence that some of the hitherto-enacted versions are to be rendered unbinding in the legal sense" ("Religious Freedom in Egypt: Under the Shadow of the Islamic Dhimma System," in Leonard Swidler, ed., *Muslims in Dialogue. The Evolution of a Dialogue* [Lewiston: The Edwin Ellen Press, 1992], p. 511). Mahmoud Ayoub, a U.S.-based Muslim scholar simply takes the view that there is no real basis for the *riddah* (apostasy) law in either the Qur'ān or Hadīth. (Cf. his "Religious Freedom and the Law of Apostasy in Islam," in *Islamochristiana*, No. 20, 1994, pp. 75–91.

35. Kateregga and Shenk, *Islam and Christianity*, p. 171.

36. Isma'il R. Faruqi, "On the Nature of Islamic *Da'wah*," in *Christian Mission and Islamic Da'wa: Proceedings of the Chambessey Dialogue Consultation* (London: The Islamic Foundation, 1976), p. 35, quoted in Larry Poston, *Islamic Da'wah in the West* (New York: Oxford University Press, 1992) p.6.

37. Hammudah Abdalati, *The Family Structure in Islam*, pp. 137–145.

38. *Ottawa Citizen*, June 23, 2002, p. A15; in response to a critical article by George Jonas.

39. The phrase "clash of civilizations" was popularized by Samuel P. Huntington, *The Clash of Civilizations and the Re-Making of World Order* (New York: Simon & Schuster, 1996), but was used earlier by Bernard Lewis, "The Roots of Modern Rage ...", *Atlantic Monthly*, September 1990, p. 60. Huntington's identification of the West and Christianity is virtually complete, e.g.: "Some Westerners ... have agreed that the West does not have problems with Islam but only with violent Islamist extremists. Fourteen hundred years of history demonstrate otherwise. The relations between Islam and Christianity, both Orthodox and Western, have often been stormy" (p. 209). In that light Muslims may be pardoned for making the same error. Huntington sees the relation between the two in terms of "conflict," "quasi-war," and "threat" whose causes "flow from the nature of the two religions and the civilizations based on them" (p. 210). The sweeping analysis is based on partial data, and cannot stand. For a more balanced view by an Islamic scholar cf. John L. Esposito, *The Islamic Threat* (New York: Oxford University Press, 1995); Esposito wisely advises: "Islam and most Islamic movements are not necessarily anti-Western, anti-American, or anti-democratic. ... Our challenge is to better understand the history and realities of the Muslim world ..." (pp. 252f.).

Part Two

Bridges for the Crossing

When we reflect on the Muslim views and opinions as we have done in our first six chapters, and then consider the task of connecting Muslims with the gospel, what comes to mind is a Biblical passage that says, in another context: "A great chasm is fixed, so that those who might want to pass from here to you cannot do so, and no one can cross from there to us" (Luke 16:26). Is it possible to cross over to the Muslim thought world and into the Muslim heart? Fortunately there are bridges over the chasm—the bridge of deep friendship, the bridge of restitution, and the bridge of inspirational learning from the past. In Part Two we consider how they help us to join context and task.

The Bridge of Deep Friendship: Crossing the Why

We have already stated our intention to raise to a higher view the critical factor of friendship in the Christian engagement with Muslims. It is not only a fundamental idea for our time but for all times, hinted at in human affection but grounded in the divine pattern. It is our first bridge over the river Why. Why cross over from awareness to engagement, and how? Deep friendship is the answer to both, and it represents the essential paradigm for Christian sharing with Muslims today.

In foregoing chapters we have described the context for Christian communication. Muslims have a structure of principles, a viewpoint on sin and salvation, and a set of opinions in regard to Jesus and his followers. All these condition the way they react to the gospel. This makes sharing with Muslims a unique task with special factors. We may think of it as art as well as task. Ramon Lull (d. 1315), whose name will be forever linking with this sharing challenge, authored an immense work entitled *Ars Magnus*, "The Great Art," an attempt to encompass all human knowledge. We will borrow the title and apply it to the task of Christian communication with Muslims that preoccupied him throughout his adult life. That activity is a great art, not because of its difficulty, but because of its importance, fascination, and requirements. The first and basic requirement is to set foot on the bridge of deep friendship.

It is hard to overstate the significance of the Christian engagement with Muslims. Modernity tends to lack priorities. At its heart is information, and the information overload that marks our age leads to an equalization process. Each item of information has a little space symbolized by the thirty-second TV clip, and in endlessly wearying succession our attention is equally demanded by each new item. Priorities disappear in a sea of sameness. Everything is important, and nothing is very important. An advertisement for a TV channel includes three featured items on its list of new programs: "Extreme Weather Week," "Jesus: The

Complete Story," and a "Returning Series on the Wilderness."[1] Jesus must take his place between weather and champions of the wild. Modernity lacks priorities.

Calling the Christian engagement with Muslims an *ars magnus* defies the trend to level and homogenize reality. If any activity deserves the adjective "great," this may be one. It looms as the irreducible Mount Everest for the missional concern of the Christian church. As the followers of Jesus consider the vastness of Islam, the uncomfortable nature of past Christian-Muslim relations, and the long neglect of this spiritual obligation, many recognize the need to underscore the Islamic reality as a priority consideration for the church in the twenty-first century. Neither Christians nor Muslims are content to let Jesus be only an item between the weather hour and an adventure series! For both communities He stands tall above the leveled multiplicity as the Word of God. The desire and need for Christians to share with their Muslim friends and neighbors what this means for them is a matter of high precedence. Assuming such priority, what is the beginning point for action?

Certainly, someone might say, there is a need for creative freshness. No art can be great without drawing from that well. As we move forward into the second part of this volume, we will note the need for the new, a fresh blending of crucial elements—learning from the great communicators of the past, digging again into theological and spiritual resources and drawing forth new treasures, recognizing and taking up the intellectual and emotional challenges hidden in the garments of habit, dealing with hard praxis issues and the human emotions involved as individuals make their way closer to Christ, lifting up the engagement from paths of acrimony to heights of amity, and allowing the Spirit of God to lead us into truth and to make all things new. The art of Christian sharing becomes great, however, only when it draws on the inspiration of God whose mercy has a special quality of greatness and who takes us beyond merely human awareness to the truth of deep friendship. We begin our reflection on what this implies with a reminder about the desire of God.

A. The Desire of God

Christians must shoulder their responsibility to Muslims—accept it, deal with it, and discharge it. They do so, however, not for reasons of strategy, guilt, or even affection. They will do so because they have an obligation to the Lord of the worlds that has not been well met. It is a simple fact that in the Christian understanding God wants Muslims to know the fulness of the divine compassion for the universe and for them, desires them to know about the feast of salvation that has been readied for them, and wants them present at the banquet. "God desires that everyone be saved and come to the knowledge of the truth" (1 Tim 2:4).

It is God's desire that determines our task and defines its arts. Our sketch of the key Islamic principles noted a series of powerful ideas, but also revealed what is not there—the good news of the salvific grace of God in Christ Jesus our Lord. Our review of the Muslim ideas of sin and salvation underlines the significance of St. Paul's sure and faithful saying: "Christ Jesus came into the world to save sinners, of whom I am chief" (1 Tim 1:15). Muslims, as we saw, have some information about Jesus, but it is very limited in scope and content. Unknown is the major portion of

His words and works that reveal his principle of self-giving and suffering love. The Muslim understanding of Christians frequently fails to capture their essence—that they are the people of hope who live by the forgiveness of their sins. Muslim understanding of Christianity screened by a history of antagonism and misconception also falters in its ability to grasp its core message—that God saves humanity, gives it a new view of life, and empowers people to follow the path of love. God's desire involves an imperative that His people address these problems, and do so with energy and intelligence. The church may have failed its responsibility in the past, but there is neither merit nor good health in dwelling upon that failure. Rather, the need for the moment is to be up and doing. The church is called to respond in a new way with old words ... deus vult! ... may God's desire become our will.

The saving will of God and God's desire for humanity's well-being, however, is the expression of deep friendship. We therefore take the position that the Christian approach to Muslims in our time must be founded on that principle. We use the expression deep friendship to distinguish it from merely casual usage. The phrase covers both aspects of friendship to which Christians may aspire in their relationships with Muslims—that which is considered noble in human converse and that which represents the mind of God. It is the latter that is definitive. In the final analysis the controlling pattern for a follower of Jesus in relating to Muslims is not that which is provided by various models of human behavior, as appealing as they may be, but rather it is the example of God's love for humanity. Human and divine friendship united and imaged in Jesus the Messiah constitute deep friendship. Without this principle brought naturally and effectively into the engagement with Muslims, the task and art of Christian sharing will be only a noisy gong and a clanging cymbal. But what does it mean to be a friend to someone in this sense?

B. Human Friendship: The Forming Idea

We draw our idea of friendship first of all from human experience. Friendship is the most friendly of words. It represents one of the most precious elements in human life, and is one of the most powerful forces in the world. It unites people. It builds bridges over valleys of separation, and brings about mutual understanding. It is light amidst the gloom of hatred. It causes people to forgive and to forget. It makes one person respect another. It is the salt that gives taste to our lives. It warms us and gives us happy times. Proverbs in every language extol it. An old saying puts it this way: "Two friends are like a pair of hands, one of which washes the other." Samuel Johnson wrote this verse on the theme:[2]

Friendship, peculiar boon of Heaven
The noble mind's delight and pride
To men and angels only given,
To all the lower world denied.

The Bible affirms the value of human friendship, but with a double perspective. Sometimes the word "friend" is actually used as an illustration of human frailty in contrast to the faithfulness of God. Thus the prophet Micah declares: "Put no trust in a friend. ... But as for me, I will look to the Lord" (7:5–7). More frequently, however, human friendship is put forward as a noble virtue, and in this sense it is found in the Book of Proverbs. Proverbs 18:4 declares: "Some friends play at friendship, but a true friend sticks closer than one's nearest kin." A true friend can speak openly without fear of being misunderstood. "Well meant are the wounds a friend inflicts, but profuse are the kisses of an enemy" (Prov 27:6). One verse powerfully sums up the profound meaning of friendship, in the simplest of language: "A friend loves at all times" (Prov. 17:17). Perhaps Solomon (Suleiman Nabi), the writer of the Proverbs, was thinking of the relationship between his father, David, and Jonathan, who was the son of King Saul, the king of Israel. Saul hated young David whom he considered to be a rival, but his son Jonathan loved David in spite of that, "loved him as he loved his own life" (1 Sam. 20:17). The relationship was a profound demonstration of human friendship at its highest.

Human friendship of this quality belongs in the paradigm for Christian-Muslim relations today, including the activity of Christian sharing. A certain kind of single-masted, sea-going sailing ship was customarily built in the town of Friendship, Maine, U.S.A. Designed with a forward tilt, it is meant for fishing and lobstering along the North Atlantic coast. This type of vessel was named "Friendship," after its origin.[3] That is also a good design for the Christian ship of friendship, tilted forward in hope and anticipation, to set sail on Muslim waters.

In everyday use the term friendship involves about as many shades of meaning as the number of relationships, but we may recognize four common categories. At one extreme the word friend is used very lightly, and means nothing more than casual acquaintance. When you lose your way and ask a stranger for directions, the person may say, "My friend, you're really lost!" Or, as you enter a barbershop, the barber may say, "Sit in that chair, my friend," even though he/she does not know you. The second category is somewhat nearer. It could be represented by the familiar relationship you have with your fellow office workers, or with the neighbors in your village. You know them, like them, call them friends, but they are not particularly close to you. The third category refers to a more select group of individuals whom you have known over the years, with whom you may attend reunions, whom you can depend on in case of need, and whom you love to visit. Finally there is the fourth category, an extension of the third, and that is the category of "best friend"—the one or two people who seem closer to you even than brother or sister, with whom you are deeply bonded, and with whom parting is such sweet sorrow.

Christians may have relationships with Muslims at any of these levels. The first category of casual acquaintance, however, is only a preliminary one. It may be argued that Christians and Muslims have for too long been merely casual with each other. To the extent that the relationships move forward across the categories to that extent the lives of both are enriched and real communication enabled. But is that possible? Some say no! Absolutely not! This ship can't sail. And certainly, it is held, a friendship relation will not be possible if you are interested in communicating religious values. Suppose the Christian overcomes his/her hangups or fears. That still leaves the Muslim with the stereotypical frame that we have discussed in the previous chapter. Can these attitudes be overcome? Can the relationship move to the third or even to the fourth category? No, say some. However, those who discount the possibility need to remember both the basic humanity and humanness of Muslims.

Certainly it is possible for a Muslim. We have repeatedly differentiated between formal positions and individual initiatives. The ambiguities we have noted leave Muslims plenty of choice at personal levels. Their choices are not uninfluenced by the fact that friendship is a primary value in Islam. Al-Ghazālī tells the story of the Prophet Muhammad welcoming an old woman (probably not a Muslim) who used to visit their home in the days of Khadīja, his first wife. Muhammad welcomed the aged woman and said, "Honoring true friendship is part of religion."[4] The writer vividly remembers two Muslim teachers, Mr. C. Muhammad and Mr. V. Abu Bekr. The former was a neighbor, the latter his companion. Very soon after taking up residence in their community the two Muslim "masters" came for a visit, at their initiative. There was an immediate sense of mutuality. Mr. Muhammad proposed, "May we come occasionally for tea and discussion?" "Of course!" They came, usually once a month, for the next twenty-two years. When we left their town permanently, they stopped our car by standing in the middle of the street. Mr. Muhammad reached through the window and placed a banana in my lap, and Mr. Abu Bekr gave my wife an orange. It was their way of saying, "We had a good friendship,"[5] My Muslim friends broke through my frame of reference and dispelled my myths. Readers are advised that friendship with Muslims is as possible as it is durable, as affectionate as it is surprising, "the peculiar boon of Heaven."

Nevertheless, when all is said and done, despite its frequent beauty human friendship has its limitations. It bears the stamp of human frailty. It is emotional and changeable, and often lacks staying power. There is no more poignant phrase in all of literature than the words that the dying Emperor spoke in Shakespeare's *Julius Caesar*: "Et tu, Brute?" "You too, Brutus?", he asked. Human friendship rarely fails in such dramatic fashion, but it is also rarely pure. It is often self-directed. Am I being friendly with someone because I enjoy it, or because my needs are being met? When the I has too big a place in it, the friendship easily gives way to jealousy. Three friends of Job (Aiyub) came from a distance to weep for him in his ill-health, but wound up accusing him and blaming him for his suffering. The Bible pictures the Lord as disgusted over such friendship. The Lord ask Job to pray for them to save them from the due punishment for their self-serving attitudes (Job 42:9–10).

With this in mind two figures who stand at the apex of Muslim spiritual reflection, Al-Ghazālī and Jalāluddīn Rūmī, point out that it is the vertical relation not the horizontal one that gives friendship its true meaning. The ultimate defining factor is not the relation of human to human, but human to God. Their approach differs, however. Al-Ghazālī emphasizes our friendship for God, whereas Rūmī approaches the idea of God as our Friend.

Al-Ghazālī spoke strongly on the subject of love for God. He too thought of God as his friend, coveted intercourse with God, and even described death as "going to see a friend."[6] But he stressed the human side of the equation. As he considered the Satanic influences that seem so easily to disrupt human to human relations, he said: "Lasting affection is that which is for the sake of God. That which has some other object passes away with the passing of that object."[7] The phrase "for the sake of God" was central for this influential theologian.

Rūmī, the premier mystical poet of Islam, echoed the same sentiment. Good friends pass on and go to heaven above, while bad friends go below. But God who transcends the worlds of above and below invites humans to remember Him, so Rūmī advises: "Grasp His skirt." God is the One

Who will abide with thee in the house and abroad,
When thou lackest house and home.
He will bring forth peace out of perturbations,
And when thou art affected will keep His promise.[8]

But Rūmī strives to penetrate more deeply into the divine dimension of friendship. Is it possible that the Friend's love for His friends is the final truth? Rūmī said, "Love is the astrolabe of God's mysteries."[9] But "the Friend is absent" and "you cannot see Him outside His work," that is, except in His creation. Therefore the poet advises, "Go into that workshop and see Him face to face."[10]

So we must turn from the shadowed picture of human friendship and learn from God what true friendship is. But in addition to creation God has another workshop called salvation. It is there that we discover how deep God's friendship for humanity is, and at the same time we have revealed for us the power and direction for the Christian relation with Muslims. We find that truth opened up for us in the New Testament.

C. Divine Friendship: The Defining Truth

In the New Testament friendship and *agapé*, self-giving love, are virtually inseparable. When Jesus calls his disciples "my friends," he is therefore pointing to an extraordinary reality. God, who is love, is at the same time God our Friend. The wonder of this defining truth shakes all who contemplate it—the Lord of the Universe loves people and regards them as friends. An even greater wonder, if possible, is what that deep friendship moves God to do. The following New Testament passages are stunning in their implication, and go a long way in construing the Christian attitude toward life and toward others.

a. In the first passage we learn that God is friendship itself. God is not friendly occasionally when feeling like it, or when we deserve it. God's face is always turned towards us in love.

We have known and believed the love that God has for us. God is love, and those who abide in love abide in God, and God abides in them (I Jn 4:15–16).

b. We learn that God's friendship is shared with those who do not deserve it. God does not evaluate how nice we are before becoming our friend.

God proves his love for us in that while we were still sinners Christ died for us (Rom 5:8).

c. We learn that God's friendship is self-forgetting and self-giving. As we see in the life of Jesus the Word, God puts others ahead of self and ahead of personal considerations.

> And the Word became flesh and lived among us (Jn 1:14).

> For you know the generous act of our Lord Jesus Christ, that though he was rich, yet for your sakes he became poor, so that by his poverty you might become rich (2 Cor 8:9).

d. We learn that God's friendship is the kind that holds nothing back. Through the prophets and through Jesus the Savior God reveals what humans could never have conceived of, God's readiness to suffer for friends.

> This is my commandment that you love one another as I have love you. No one has greater love than this, to lay down one's life for one's friends (Jn 15:12–13).

This is the New Testament outline of the pattern for human friendship—the love of God that we learn about and receive through Jesus the Messiah. God calls us to this model of self-giving and suffering love. We may wonder, even object—is it not too high a pattern of behavior for us? In a way it is, but we are called to it.

—We are called to it by our knowledge. Jesus said: "I do not call you servants any longer because the servant does not know that the master is doing; but I have called you my friends because I have made known to you everything that I have heard from my Father" (Jn 15:15).

—We are called to it by Christ's command. "You are my friends, if you do what I command you" (Jn 15:14).

—We are called to it by the spirit of gratitude. "Beloved, since God loved us so much, we also ought to love one another" (1 Jn 4:11).

—And we are called to it by the gift of the Holy Spirit who brings divine possibility into the realm of human weakness. "The Advocate, the Holy Spirit, whom the Father will send in my name, will teach you everything and will remind you of all that I said to you" (Jn 14:26).

The distinction between divine and human friendship is especially striking in the way it deals with rejection. Human friendship breaks down when reciprocity ends. Divine friendship goes on. This truth overcomes the tension between desire and possibility.

A Christian seeking friendship with Muslims may logically and realistically ask: "But what can I do if a Muslim does not want to be my friend? He/she is not interested. He/she has bad memories from our miserable past, is suspicious and does not trust me. He/she does not appreciate my desire to witness to Christ. He/she has been told not to accept Christians as friends. Friendship goes two ways. What can I do it I am regarded as an enemy?" The answer to the last question is probably very little if we are operating on the human level of *quid pro quo*, "one thing in return for another," but in the divine pattern friendship keeps on going even though it is not reciprocated. Love "bears all things, believes all things, hopes all things, endures all things" (1 Cor 13:7). Rejection cannot stop its flow. When Judas came to betray his master in the Garden of Gethsemane, Jesus still called him friend. "Friend, do what you have to do" (Mt 26:50). When rejection took him to the cross, he prayed for those who put him there: "Father, forgive them for they know not what they are doing" (Lk 23:34). A Roman soldier, startled by what he saw and heard, was moved to make a famous confession. Deep friendship of this kind startles and transforms, breaks down barriers and opens eyes to the vision of the saving God.

To the end of his brief but productive life Martin Luther King believed and kept on saying that love is the most durable power in the world. In his perspective the radical friendship taught by Jesus Christ reaches out to the other, is willing to be one-way, puts the welfare of the other ahead of one's own, and is ready to sacrifice oneself for the other. Such love may alter a situation, or on the other hand it may also lead to undeserved suffering. Or it may do both, as we see in King's life. I remember being present when he spoke these eloquent words:[11]

> To our most bitter opponents we say: Do to us what you will, and we shall continue to love you. ... But be assured that we will wear you down by our capacity to suffer. ... We shall so appeal to your heart and conscience that we shall win you in the process, and our victory will be a double victory.

He also said on another occasion: "My personal trials have also taught me the value of unmerited suffering. As my sufferings mounted I soon realized that there were two ways in which I could respond to my situation—either to react with bitterness or seek to transform suffering into a creative force."[12] The radical friendship of Jesus Christ has a persistent quality. Its image is that of Jesus seeking entry at our heart's door: "Listen I am standing at the door and knocking ..." (Rev 3:20). Knocking, too, is a Christian vocation. It is deep friendship's creative force.

In setting forth the necessity and possibility of friendship with Muslims we must add the proviso that the friendship be perceived as genuine. Muslims, as all humans do, have ESP when it comes to friendship. They know who means it and who doesn't. Friendship often has wonderful results, but friendship in the divine pattern should not be confused with ecclesiastical utilitarianism. As Christians we do not become friends with people in order to produce a certain result. We do so because we are friends, because that is what we have become in Christ. For that reason phrases like "friendship evangelism" that have surfaced in recent years, although undoubtedly well intended, seem singularly out of place. The reasons are clear. In the first place there is no other kind of evangelism than that which is based on love. Secondly, the phrase seems to consider friendship a methodology that can be assumed or discarded at will. Friendship is not a method but a way of looking at people. In the third place, the possible assumption that friendship more or less automatically leads to demonstrable "success" is distant from the reality that it may end in a cross. The friendship of God arouses the enmity of the world, and love for the needy and oppressed often does likewise. Those who look at people in this way stand in the greatest danger, as Jesus demonstrated and as history teaches.

We turn to Abraham for the lesson that the traveling companion of deep friendship is not technique but faith. In the Bible Abraham is twice named "the Friend of God" (2 Chr 20:17; Is 41:8). So also the Qur'ān says: "So Allah chose Abraham for friend" (4:125. Accordingly Muslims refer to Ibrahīm as *khalil-ullāh*, the Friend of God. The Bible explains why Abraham is paid this great honor: "The scripture was fulfilled which says, Abraham believed God and it was reckoned to him as righteousness—and he was called the friend of God" (James 2:23). Abraham gladly and faithfully surrendered to God and accepted God's friendship. That faith in God's promises was the power of his life. But as the apostle James points out, his was a faith active in love that enabled him to do extraordinary things, even to the offering up of his son. He was a man of unusual generosity, even pleading that God would spare the wicked cities of Sodom and Gomorrah. Certainly he wanted to save his relatives, Lot and family, but also whoever were righteous among the people there. He was far from being perfect, but in God's companionship he, traveled in faith and thought of others. In a sense, then the theology of friendship means becoming Abrahams, spiritual pilgrims on a new journey of faith that crosses the bridge to human hearts. For the friends of God the Friend are the friends of all whom God befriends.

Conclusion

We conclude with the observation that deep friendship is nothing other than self-giving love applied to real life relationships. It is human friendship embraced in and lifted up to the love of God, and then returned to the world in the Christ-pattern. It is both attitude and activity. Borne up on the wings of love friendship soars, but always returns to earth, to the place of human endeavor. If sharīʿa obedience can be said to define Islamic praxis, deep friendship does so for the Christian. It not only defines the spirit of a follower of Jesus the Messiah, but it takes her/him to where he went.

Without further elaboration we will underline two applications of the principle to the engagement with Muslims. First, deep friendship is the chasm-crossing principle. It can span the gap that exists between Christians and Muslims. Moreover it is a bridge strong enough to bear the often unsettling and essentially unpredictable activity of Christian communication. Secondly, it is the empowering principle because it is the divine paradigm, and finally it alone can inspire and creatively uplift otherwise inadequate humans to follow his self-giving path. Harold Moulton sums it up when he says: "Of all the missionary journeys the Incarnation was the first, the costliest and the most effective. God has never asked men to do what He himself has not done before them."[13] God's deep friendship is the core principle for contemporary sharing with Muslims.

It is true that Christians have seldom lived up to this high vision, which is always a personal goal that lies ahead, as well as an empowering faith and spirit. Hence St. Paul said: "Not that I have already ... reached the goal, but I press on to make it my own because Christ Jesus has made me his own" (Ph 3:12). Were it not for the promise of God's forgiveness and the Master's voice saying, "Rise up and walk!", Christians would be continually redefining friendship back and down to the natural and comfortable level of human likes and dislikes. But the Word is clear: "Put away from you all bitterness and wrath and anger and wrangling and slander, together with all malice, and be kind to one another, tenderhearted, forgiving one another as God in Christ has forgiven you. Therefore be imitators of God as beloved children, and live in love, as Christ loved us and gave himself up for us, a fragrant offering and sacrifice to God" (Eph 4:31–5:1). In that light a prayer of Samuel H. Miller is appropriate as a final thought for our reflection on deep friendship, and as a proper beginning point for the journey ahead:[14]

> Forgive us, O God, for the pretentiousness with which we have built vast but empty ideals, and restore to us such humility and honesty that we may do thy will in the plain circumstances of life.

From this point we move to the second span that leads from context to action, the bridge of restitution.

Endnotes

1. Cover, *Discovery*, September-December, 2001.

2. Samuel Johnson, "Friendship, an Ode," *The Pocketbook of Quotations*, ed. by Henry Davidoff (New York: Pocketbook, Inc., 1951), p. 107.

3. *The Random House Unabridged Dictionary*, 1967, p. 569.

4. Al-Ghazālī, *On the Duties of Brotherhood*, tr. by Muhtar Holland (Woodstock, New York: The Overlook Press, 1976), p. 72.

5. In *Muslim Friends,* pp. 13f., I share a response that I gave to an unexpected question put forward by some Muslim acquaintances: "When did you become our friend?"

6. Al-Ghazālī, *Alchemy of Happiness*, pp. 121f.

7. *Duties of Brotherhood, op. cit.*, p. 72.

8. *Teachings of Rumi, the Musnavi*, tr. and abridged by E. H. Whinfield, p. 118.

9. *Ibid.*, p. 5. Christians may be excused for thinking of God's seeking love in Jesus Christ when they read Rūmī's allusive couplet: "Not only the thirsty seek the water, but the water seeks the thirsty as well." Cf. Schimmel, *Mystical Dimensions of Islam*, p. 392.

10. *Teachings of Rumi, op. cit.*, p. 70f.

11. Martin Luther King, speech delivered in Hartford, Connecticut, 1956; from the writer's notes.

12. Martin Luther King, *Strength to Love* (London: Collins, 1969), p. 154.

13. Harold K. Moulton, *The Mission of the Church—Studies in Missionary Words the New Testament*, (London: Epworth Press, 1959), p. 4.

14. Samuel H. Miller, *Prayers for Daily Use*, (New York: Harper & Bros., 1957), p. 53.

Making Up for the Past: The Bridge of Restitution

There is second bridge that enables the crossing of Christian to Muslim, and to it we give the name restitution. To set foot on it means resolving to make amends for the past through a clear and faithful presentation of the gospel in the present. But why is restitution needed? This chapter attempts to deal with that question. We have stated that an over-preoccupation with the past is a form of self-indulgence and is not helpful. Knowing what happened, however, is not only useful for identifying the agendas of Christian sharing today, it encourages the effort to implement them. The story is not a pretty one, and when Christians become aware of it, the term restitution does not seem out of place. The bridge of deep friendship takes us to the bridge of amends.

There is not a Muslim in the world who would come close to saying that Islam is the unnecessary religion. Muslims love their faith too much to think along those lines. Yet even Muslims will argue that Muhammad and the Qur'ān became necessary largely because men and women did not heed the previous prophets and revelations. There is a sense of the unnecessary within that historical judgment. There is also, however, a truth of another kind in the birth of Islam.

That is the truth about a tragedy, a tragedy of failed communication. It was a crucial moment not only in the history of the Middle East, but also for the history of the world. Dramatic events were about to take place. At that time and place, however, God's remedy for human sin was badly obscured and widely unvoiced. This failure was almost complete for the inner region of the Peninsula. There the good news of the grace of God in Christ Jesus was not laid out, opened up and made visible. What was in the air was something else, the need for a recovery of monotheism, and for Muslims the basis for that renewal came through the giving of the Qur'ān. Hardly anyone there could have heard, let alone understood, the significance of the word that Jesus had spoken from the cross: " It is finished." The problem is well illustrated by the figure of Zechariah. He was known, but his announcement was not—that the tender mercy of our God and the dayspring from on high had already dawned "to give knowledge of salvation to his people by the forgiveness of their sins" (Lu. 1:77). The city of Mecca was not really far from Alexandria and Antioch, the centres of the Christian movement, but the gospel had not reached there except in confused hints. Neither Christians nor Muslims have fully confronted the implications of that tragedy.

This chapter concentrates on two issues: the extent of the gospel in Arabia at the time of Muhammand, and the nature of the doctrinal struggles that preoccupied and agitated the church at the time of the advent of Islam. The story is disheartening, but also clarifying. It illuminates the source of Muslim problems in understanding the gospel, and also accounts for the rather standardized forms of Christian response that developed. Above all, it urges forward the consideration of possible amends. The chapter therefore concludes by asking, given these facts what are the agendas for the present.

A. The Gospel in Muhammad's Arabia

Although the thought is not a pleasant one, Christians must face the fact that there was a breakdown and a botching of the Christian witness right at the beginning of Islam.

No fair-minded person will deny that Muhammad the Meccan merchant and social leader, who spent quality time thinking and meditating in a cave on Mt. Hira in the midst of a culture of polytheism and nature worship, was a sincere seeker after God. As time passed he reached out to the people of the book in that regard. He respected both Jews and Christians, considered their teaching to be from God, and wanted to know as much as he could from those he so honored. Despite his attitude of readiness the results were unhappy. The impressions he received were both fragmentary and distorted. There is little mystery in what happened. His knowledge could not be complete because none of the New Testament documents were available to him in Arabic, either to be read by him or to be read to him. Secondly, his knowledge was unclear because Christians, who themselves were at odds over certain issues, presented a confused picture. These inadequacies materially affected the history of the world and the lives of many individuals.

We must first remember the basic fact that written copies of the New Testament were not available in Arabia at the time of Muhammad. Oral communication dominated its culture. Only after the revelation of the Qur'ān and its appearance as a complete book around 650 did Arabic emerge as a powerful literary language. There was therefore no urgency on the part of Christians to put God's Word into the dialect. It was only after it became a dominating language of the Middle East that they felt the necessity of providing translations.[1] J. W. Sweetman describes the situation at Muhammad's time in the following poignant words:[2]

> The Arabic language as a written language had yet to come into being.
> Its first letters were to be derived from the Syriac, and the first great book

was the Qur'ān which Muhammad brought. ... The characteristic name by which both Jews and Christians were known among the Arabs was "the people of the book" which meant the people of the Bible. Yet that by which they were famous [the Bible] was kept as a hidden treasure, hoarded and not cast abroad like seed to bring forth fruit. Here is the tragedy of the Church at the time of the rise of Islam. All truth demanded that, when Muhammad's spirit was stirred with the needs of his people and when he was groping after Him who could save and unify, he should have had in his hands the true Jewish and Christian Scriptures.

Alas! he did not have them in his hands, and the repercussions are still with us.

It may be objected that it is precisely in oral cultures that the importance of written words should not be overstated. The Arabs—it is clear—could not read the story of Jesus, but could they not hear it? As the New Testament says: "Faith comes from what is heard, and what is heard from the word of Christ (Rom 10:17). For the Arabs to hear the word of Christ two things would have been required—message bearers and a clear narrative. Both were missing in Arabia. The Christian presence in what is called inner Arabia, the territory that includes Mecca and Medina, was limited to a few individuals, and there were no Christian settlements. Nor for that matter were they well represented in the entire peninsula. On the northern border the Ghassanid tribe was partially Christianized. On the eastern border Nestorian Christians were present at Hira where the Lakhimids lived. In the south, which is Yemen today, there were Christian communities at Najran and Sana'a. Westward across the Red Sea, as we have seen, a Christian king held sway over Abyssinia. Eastern orthodox Christianity was not visibly present although there were monasteries on the caravan route to Syria. There appear to have been a scattering of Christian heretical sects in the general area who taught various confusing ideas. But there is no evidence of mission-minded Christians in the homelands of Muhammad in his day. Inner Arabia never had the equivalent of a Frumentius who came to Abyssinia.

It is difficult to assess what information might have been derived from these few scattered Christians but it must have been minimal and superficial. There is a Muslim tradition that Waraqah ibn Nawfal, a cousin of Muhammad's wife Khadīja, was an Arab monotheist (hanīf) who later "attached himself to Christianity and studied its scriptures until he thoroughly mastered them."[3] If the record is true, those scriptures could only have been portions of the Hebrew Bible. The story is told that Waraqah informed Muhammad that the Prophet had been visited by the same angel that had come to Moses, and also that Jesus had predicted Muhammad's coming. But Muhammad Haykal, the Muslim biographer of Muhammad, believes that Muhammad's first knowledge of Christians resulted from a caravan trip to Syria that he took as a youth in company with his uncle. According to Muslim Tradition on that trip a Christian monk named Buhīra found "the seal of prophecy" on his back and predicted a great future for Muhammad. But in Haykal's opinion Muhammad's major source of information came through listening to the tales that Christians told in the Meccan and other marketplaces.[4] In regard to these itinerant

Christians Maxime Rodinson surmises: " It was unfortunate that they knew very little about their own religion. They were for the most part poor folk. ... They had no organized community, no priests or churches. They belonged to different sects, each convinced that the rest were heretics. They were certainly none too well up in theology. Their religion was the popular faith of simple people."[5]

With these gleanings Muhammad developed his information base in regard to the Christian faith. It was a very limited one. He and his followers were the interested but essentially uniformed observers of a distant religious scene. This failure of the Christian church to sound a clear trumpet in inner Arabia was a missed moment of such gravity that it takes on the character of an "originating sin."[6]The unhappy tale does not end here, however. To the problem of inadequate information must be added the additional factors of confused and distorted information. The Qur'ān reflects the problems, but they met Muslims full force as they proceeded to the borders of the Arabian peninsula and beyond.

B. Christian Doctrinal Controversies around Arabia

The confused and distorted information filtered down from the serious Christological discussions of the period. These important debates often degenerated into severe disputes and divisions, and a variety of cults spun off to add to the disarray.

The basic Christian concern behind these events was a laudable one. Christians of that age were trying to penetrate as far as humanly possible into the mystery of the Messiah's personality as God and man. In such a demanding process differences of opinion could be anticipated. They were not really the problem. The problem came about when those differences crystallized into parties that divided one from the other, leaving a trail of acrimonious contention and even violence. Muslims were naturally perplexed by the disagreements, and initially found it very difficult to follow the Greek subtleties of the Christian theological discussion. In the end, they could not remain apart from them because the theological debates became connected with political alignments and military conflicts.

To understand the issues which formed Muslim opinion we must turn to those debates. The Christian faith that Jesus is both true God and true man produced two conceptual problems:

How are we to understand the unity of God?

How are we to understand the personality of Jesus?

The church had dealt with the first question at an earlier period, but we must begin with the unity of God because of its primary significance for both Christians and Muslims.

Christians faithfully and fervently hold to the unity of God. For Christians there is only one God and one Lord. As the Old Testament of the Bible declares: "Hear, O Israel, the Lord our God is one Lord" (Deut 6:4), and as the New Testament affirms: "There is no god but One" (1 Cor 8:4), so Christians believe and confess. But what is the nature of God's unity? In the light of the incarnation of God's Word in

Jesus Christ and the sending of God's Spirit it was clear that God's unity is more profound than human mathematics can express. Just as God transcends humanity, so the oneness of God transcends the simple number one.[7] The early Christians discussed the issue from different perspectives. The major question, however, was how God's Word and God's Spirit related to God's being, for God always has Word and Spirit. To deal with the issue, and at the same time to ensure peace and harmony, the Christian Emperor Constantine (d. 337) convened a Council in 325 A.D. at Nicea, near Constantinople (= Byzantium and = Istanbul), the new capital of the Roman Empire. The Council agreed on the doctrine that the One God is manifested as Father, Son, and Holy Spirit, i.e., the doctrine of the Trinity. Of the Word of God, Jesus, the Nicene Creed says: "God of God, Light of Light, Very God of Very God."

That left the second conceptual problem—the nature of the personality of Jesus. This was the major issue at the time that Islam arose. The question was: how can we understand and express the combination of the divine and human elements of Jesus? There seemed to be three choices. Either these two facets of Christ's being are sharply divided, or they are fused into one, or they are separate but interactive. There is certainly a deep mystery here. Just as the human mind cannot fully penetrate into the hiddenness of God's being, but must depend on God's self-revelation, so also it cannot fully penetrate the unfathomable mystery of God's working in Christ. The primary response to God's self-revelation is faith not rational understanding. Nevertheless, faith-filled Christian believers also sought understanding, striving to grasp to some degree and to put into acceptable language the deep implications of Jesus' personality. It seemed important to try to do this because it affected the truth of salvation. But Christians of the time could not agree. One group called the Nestorian Christians took the approach that the divine and human in Jesus are sharply divided. Another group called the Monophysites were of the opinion that the two were fused into one. The third opinion became the orthodox view. It maintained that the two natures in Jesus were distinct but interactive.

The debates over this question did not go on in the same atmosphere as the discussions in regard to God's unity. They were occurring at a time when political and personal rivalries had become very common in the church. As J. N. D. Kelly states: " At no place in the evolution of the church's theology have the fundamental issues been so mixed up with ... the clash of politics and personalities."[8] The disagreements led to bitter recrimination and quarreling. This is the situation that prevailed in the church at the time of the Prophet Muhammad. Not only did it divide and weaken the church but it produced confusion for those who were not Christians. Because both the Nestorians and the Monophysites were influential in Muslim areas and because their opinions affected Muslim understanding, we will briefly outline their view.

The Nestorians were named after Nestorius (d. 451), a bishop of Constantinople who emphasized the humanity of Jesus. He argued that we cannot lose sight of the fact that Jesus was truly human without also losing the truth that he is fully our brother and representative. Only as a truly human being could he really suffer for us, and only as fully human could he be our ethical example. Therefore he strongly held that the divine and human elements in Jesus must be maintained in their distinction and not confused. They are related to each other by association and not by fusion. The humanity is not swallowed up in the divinity. They are joined in Jesus but not altered. The joining is a correspondence of will and not a union of the two natures in which one is lost to sight. In this light Nestorius felt that Christians should not use such language as "mother of God." Mary was the mother of a human child, and beyond that language must be more discreet. By emphasizing the true and full humanity of Jesus the Messiah, Nestorius was striving to uphold an important truth, but his critics complained that he had fallen into the danger of having two Christs instead of one.

After the Nestorian views were condemned at the Council of Ephesus (431) his followers became a separate and persecuted church. Many were compelled to move eastward to what is now Iraq, and adjoining Arabia. This area was under the rule of the Persian Emperor who chose to welcome the Nestorians. As the great rival of the orthodox Christian Emperor at Constantinople he was certainly happy to see Christians divided, but he also appreciated the Nestorian capacity to build up educational and medical centers. They were also the most mission-minded of Christians and took their gospel to the Lahimid tribes of eastern Arabia where their emphasis on the human Jesus was known. We can only speculate to what extent it may have become a factor in the Arab understanding of Christ.

We turn to the Monophysites, a movement that dominated Christian views in Ethiopia, Egypt, and Syria. The term "monophysite" means "one nature," which indicates the point of view. The most notable representative of this position was Bishop Cyril (d. 444) of Alexandria in Egypt. In sharp contrast to the Nestorians the Monophysites emphasized the divine aspect of the personality of Jesus. They did so for two reasons. The first was because it seemed to them to be the crucial aspect for the understanding of Jesus as Savior and Lord. Certainly he is a true human being, but it is because he is God manifest in the flesh that Jesus is able to bring about our redemption. The second reason was their concern for the unity of Jesus' personality, and in that connection the oneness of God. Jesus is not bi-personal. He is the incarnation of the One God. His divine nature has absorbed the human spirit into itself, "without losing what is its own." Jesus is the Eternal Word who has for our sakes chosen to be "enfleshed," but he is One Christ and One Lord, and his nature is therefore one and divine.

The critics of the Monophysites felt that their opinion was also a one-sided one. They had veered too far in the other direction from Nestorians, and they too were condemned, this time at the Council of Chalcedon (451). This had more serious results than the castigation of the Nestorians because Alexandria had far-reaching influence and many Christians supported the Monophysite view. Their list included most of the Christians contiguous to the Arabian peninsula—the Syrian Jacobite Christians, the Copts of Egypt, the Ethiopians, the Armenians, and the partially Christianized Ghassanid tribes of northern Arabia. The ensuing struggle became very bitter and left its marks on the perceptions of Christianity in that region. Although we do not have sufficient information to trace the exact passage of these controversies and their possible impact on inner Arabia, the information that did reach the area must have appeared confusing indeed, and the Christian rivalries no less perplexing. It would have taken persistent seekers indeed to work their way through the confusion to a clear picture of the Christian message of hope, namely that "in Christ God was reconciling the world to himself" (2 Cor 5:18a).

We come to the third movement of thought that occupied the center between the Nestorians and the Monophysites. We may call it the orthodox opinion that became the accepted view of Latin and Greek Christians. The leaders of this central stream believed that if the experience of Jesus as both true God and true man is to be fully reflected, then equal weight must be given to both the divine and the human nature in stating the mystery of Jesus' personality. To seek this middle ground and to clarify the matter the Christian Emperor Marcian called a special council to meet at Chalcedon, across the Bosporus Strait from Constantinople, in the year 451. Over 500 bishops attended the largest of all the ecumenical councils. They examined the testimony of scripture, in particular the words of Jesus, and the tradition of the church, and arrived at an agreed formula which was stated with extreme care in meticulous language. They affirmed that Jesus is "perfect in deity and perfect in humanity." With respect to his humanity he is like all of us human beings except that he is without sin. With regard to his deity he is "of one substance with the Father," and was born of Mary for us and for our salvation. The Council seemed to bow to the Monophysites by referring to Mary as "the mother of God," but at the same time appeared also to respond to the Nestorians in their presentation of the two natures. Jesus, they declared, is

> One and the same Christ, Son, Lord, only begotten, acknowledged in two natures, without confusion and without change, without division, without separation; the distinction of the natures being by no means taken away because of the union, but rather the property of each nature being preserved, and concurring in one person. ...[9]

It was a compromise, but soundly based on the faith of the church, and a noble effort to find the middle ground. Only so far could anyone dare to penetrate the mystery declared in John 1:14: "And the Word became flesh and lived among us, and we have seen his glory ..."

The Chaldeconian wording did not satisfy everyone, certainly not the Monophysites, who felt that their opinions had not received adequate recognition. The ultimate problem, however, was not at that level, for differences of opinion could be expected. The problem came in the way that the decision was administrated—it was imposed on those who disagreed with it, utilizing the full scale of imperial power, with insensitivity, persecuting zeal, and even cruelty. The unity of Christians was important for the Eastern Roman Emperor at Constantinople. He faced the Persians in a great struggle that surged across the Middle East, not to mention the invasion of the barbarians against western Rome. To maintain a unified Christian front emperors had gotten into the practice of imposing orthodox views as they developed, and this process accompanied the implementation of Chalcedon's findings in the next two centuries. They did not consider this out of place. As K. S. Latourette notes:[10] "The Byzantine Empire ... to a large extent controlled the Church and made it an organ of the state." The approach alienated Christians of other persuasions, however, particularly in the long and active reign of Justinian I (d. 565).

The following account illustrates how this aggressive policy affected the situation in Arabia. Justinian had appointed Harīth ibn Jabala (d. 579), a Christian Ghassanid chief, as governor of the northern Arabs, even though he had Monophysite views and demanded a Monophysite bishop. The appointment was part of a larger strategic policy. Not only were the Ghassanids a defense line against the Persians, but the Byzantines also employed some of them as mercenaries in their military forces, while the Persians used Lakhimid Arabs of Nestorian persuasion. Thus the two sides played off Christian divisions for political purposes on the borders of Arabia. When Harīth died, his son Mundhir succeeded him and forthrightly proclaimed himself as the defender of Monophysite Arabs. He pleaded with the orthodox rulers to show charity toward the Christian Arabs, but received only anathemas for his pains. Granted a safe conduct to present his case at Constantinople by Emperor Maurice (d. 602), he was betrayed, taken in chains to the capital, and from there exiled to Sicily. His furious son Nuʿmān raged against the Byzantine Christians, but he too was captured and taken to Sicily. All this transpired as a few miles to the south Muhammad was growing up in the city of Mecca. Alfred Guillaume succinctly states the result: "Thus the Greeks prepared the way for their own downfall."[11]

Matters approached a climax when Heraclius (575–641), the contemporary of Muhammad, became the Emperor of Eastern Rome, which he ruled from 610 to 641. The Persian Emperor, Chosroe II, had captured Jerusalem in 614 and carried off what was believed to be Christ's cross. In 622, that same date as the *hijra* of Muhammad from Mecca to Medina, the stalwart Heraclius defeated the Persians and restored the cross to the Church of the Holy Sepulcher in Jerusalem. These were dangerous times, and he needed full support from the majority Christians in the area. He therefore tried to placate the Monophysites with another theological compromise,[12] but it was too late for such gestures. The Christians of the region were alienated and angry, and it is not surprising that they often welcomed Muslim invaders into their territories and cities, regarding them as liberators from Byzantine oppression. The weakened nature of the church not only facilitated Persian conquests, but when the time came for the Arab Muslims to sweep into Palestine, there was surprisingly little resistance, and Heraculius and his forces were defeated at the vital battle of Yarmuk (636), a tributary that meets the Jordan River near Lake Tiberius, by a smaller Muslim army. Eventually the Emperor lost Syria, Egypt, and Mesopotamia, as well as Palestine itself.

Muhammad the Prophet died in 632. By the close of his career the efforts of Christians to clarify the mysteries of God's oneness and Christ's personality—in the light of God's great and universal act of redemption—were winding down. Clarity was attained, but its message reached inner Arabia only in bits and pieces. Like an incomplete jigsaw puzzle it left no clear picture of Jesus, and his words and works. It is true that there are other factors that made for a weak Christian witness in addition to doctrinal controversies. There were moral weaknesses in the church, including corruption at court levels and easy-going morality at popular levels. The knowledge of Christian truth among ordinary Christians was often superficial, while clerics were abstruse. The monasteries with which Arab travelers were familiar were a strength, but they did not engage in a clarifying oral witness. The final difficulty was the widespread development of heretical cults, which added distortion to confusion. It was in some of those distorted forms that the message finally reached Muhammad's Arabia.

The cults, not all of which were Christian, were part of the immediate context of early Islam. Their history is obscure, and the full story awaits further scholarly efforts. We are aware of one early stream of thought evidenced in the Ebionites and Elkasites, and represented by Paul of Samosata (fourth century) who basically taught that Jesus was only a human being. The Samosatan said that Jesus was a man of great moral excellence, and it was for that reason that he was graciously chosen for the indwelling of the Logos, the Word of God. As an honor he was adopted as "Son of God." We also know of groups who followed the persistent Gnostic and Docetic streams, who argued that Jesus was not really crucified. The Eternal Spirit in Jesus withdrew and evaded the suffering and death. There were other groups who elevated the Virgin Mary to the level of deity and worshiped her. Apocalyptic cults dealing with the end-time were common. Even some of the non-Christian "prophets," such as Mani in Persia and Maslama in Arabia, may have used Christian materials. Our study of the Muslim view of Jesus revealed the presence of several of these points in the Qur'ān and in Muslim tradition. The tracks of the cults are visible on the canvas of the religious scene that was the matrix of Islam.

Muslims today are generally quite unaware of the Christian context in which the development of Islam took place. If they were to consider these facts, however, they would be inclined to look at them from a different perspective than the purely historical one. What might be their thinking? We venture to suggest the following possibilities:

—To the extent that a Muslim might consider voicing an opinion on the early Christian controversies about the person of Jesus, he/she would be likely to say that they result from the primary mistake of elevating a human being to the level of God.[13]

—Muslims generally believe that everything they need to know about Jesus the Messiah is available in the Qur'ān. It provides an accurate and sufficient picture. There is no sense of Muslim regret that Muhammad and the early Muslims did not receive more and better information about Jesus.

—While many Muslims believe that the study of the historical background of Islam and the "occasions" for the revelations of God's Word is interesting, these cannot be considered to be vital matters because the Qur'ān is the eternal book descended from heaven by direct inspiration. It is not the product of a human being or human influences, and the misunderstandings of that cultural period do not affect it.

—Muslims would tend to point out what they consider to be the simplicity of Islam and its doctrine of God in contrast to the complexity of Christian teachings.

—For Christian friends of Muslims, however, who wish to share with them the love of God in Christ, the implications of the context that we have descried above are compelling. Muhammad and his followers did not—and could not—know the gospel as Christians know it. Islam is therefore certainly not a Christian heresy as some early Christian interpreters mistakenly took it to be. It was not a movement away from truths that were once received and grasped. Those truths must have been seldom received, and less frequently grasped. The missional interest of the Greek orthodox church after Justinian was toward the north where the pagan Slavs, Avars, and Bulgars challenged, and its undoubted theological acumen and energy was not directed to the task of clarifying Christian ideas for the new Islamic believers in One God in the Arabian peninsula.

The full spiritual consequences of that neglect, and the negative elements that accompanied it, may never be known. What is apparent and known is an undeniable responsibility to convey the good news to Muslim friends today, and to do so with clarity. To the weight of God's desire is added the burden of making up for the past. The span of deep friendship leads forward to the span of restitution. In their combination they take us to the engagement with Muslims. The church in the twenty-first century may not be better prepared for this engagement than the church in the seventh century, but it has the advantage of hindsight. What can we do now to make amends for such an "originating sin"? What agendas need to be identified and set for today?

C. Agendas for the Present

Making amends involves setting appropriate agendas. There will be a wide range of opinion among Christians as to what they might be. We have taken for granted some measure of agreement on the primary task—that the gospel must now be shared, crisply and cleanly, taking the measure of the misconceptions stemming from a bad start. Even that point, however, may produce a question. How can God's message of deep friendship be seen for what it is if its bearers are not visualized as friends? How is that visualization to occur? As we shall see in the next chapter the peculiar circumstances that we described above dictated the nature of Christian-Muslim interaction, turning it in the direction of mutual criticism and rejection, leaving little room for a normal development. To break that pattern means wise agenda-setting. There is no need, however, for Christian sharers today to be naive or supercilious. The old agendas, on which so much time and energy was expended, will not go away, and they will always be relevant in individual encounter. By new agendas we mean the freshness that the attitudes of deep friendship can give to any situation and any consideration. It is High Time for that. We will draw on ancient wisdom for a reflection.

In the Old Testament of the Bible, between Proverbs and the Song of Solomon, is the Book of Ecclesiastes, a word that indicates the Preacher or Teacher of the assembly. In Hebrew the word is *koheleth*. We do not know his name so we shall call him "Koheleth." He knew about futility. He taught that in the past there are disappointments and the future is uncertain but we can deal with the present. With wisdom he declared: "For everything there is a season, and a time for every matter under heaven" (3:1). He went on to offer ideas that can be applied directly to the Christian engagement with Muslims today. Let us examine those ideas and try to make the application to our season in the light of our need to bridge gaps. Koheleth said there is

—A time to be born and a time to die

A new thing needs to be born, and that is a communication of the gospel in a way that relates dynamically to the key principles that Muslims hold dear (see Chapter 2), thereby opening the meaning of Christ in new ways.

—A time to kill and a time to heal

It is time to slay the demons of animosity. The time of healing is upon us. Christians need to reach out with a genuine "I'm sorry," and to follow the Healer in word and deed.

—A time to break up and a time to build up

There is a need to leapfrog over aspects of the heritage, breaking past them, and in forms of togetherness to build new relationships and new worlds.

—A time to weep and a time to laugh

It is okay for Christians and Muslims to enjoy each other in the simple pleasures of mutual association and companionship.

—A time to mourn and a time to dance

It is okay for Christians and Muslims to explore together what it means to praise and serve God in the practical affairs of life.

—A time to throw away stones and a time to gather stones

It is okay for Christians and Muslims to take seriously what their scriptures say about friendship, and to use the past to reconstruct rather than to deconstruct the present.

—A time to embrace and a time to refrain from embracing

We do not embrace our disagreements about truth, but we do embrace each other, and in embracing each other we deal with our disagreements.

—A time to seek and a time to love

Now, while it is day, Christians are called upon to lose themselves and to become seekers and finders of Muslims, in the spirit of Jesus the Messiah and Savior who used those verbs.

—A time to keep and a time to throw away

What Christians have to throw away are dislike and ire, disappointment and feelings of helplessness, and keep positive.

—A time to tear and a time to sew

The fabric of new communication will be woven by a host of individual Christians, each tearing up some of their past, and each wherever they are and in their own way quietly and faithfully adding their own thread to the new design of hope.

—A time to keep silence and a time to speak

Is this a time for reticence or a time for communication? The issue must be faced. But why not, in God's Name, roll up the carpet of neglect and share the best gift Christians have to give anyone: "Here is the Lamb of God who takes away the sin of the world!" (Jn 1:29).

—A time to love and a time to hate

Let us roll up the carpet of rancor and find new ways of demonstrating to Muslims what Christians believe and confess: "And now faith, hope and love abide, these three; and the greatest of these is love" (1Cor 13:13).

—A time for war and a time for peace

The New Agenda says no to religious war. Let us roll up the carpet of conflict, and say to each other: *salaam aleikum* and "the God of peace will be with you" (Ph 3:9).

With new time and fresh agenda thoughts in mind, we now go on to examine what we can learn from those who have gone before, the pioneers in witness. The bridge of restitution leads to the bridge of learning.

Endnotes

1. R. A. Nicholson, *A Literary History of the Arabs* (Cambridge: Cambridge University Press, 1969), pp. xxiif., takes the view that Arabic literary composition began in pre-Islamic times; however, he also recognizes that the *qasida* (ballad poetry of that period was orally transmitted, "very few" among the pre-Islamic Arabs were able to read or write, and the Qur'ān was the first Arab book. In *The Arab Christian* (Louisville: Westminster Press, 1991), p. 46, Kenneth Cragg suggests that "Arabic was only slowly moving from an oral to a scripted speech in the two centuries preceding Islam." George Hourani, *A History of the Arab Peoples* (Cambridge, Massachusetts: Harvard University Press, 1991), p. 27, notes that in the new Ummayad capital of Damascus, "from the 690s the language of Administration was altered to Arabic." The translation of the New Testament into Arabic probably took longer until the time when Arabicization had taken wider hold and created the need. F. C. Burkitt, "Arabic Versions," in James Hastings, ed., *Dictionary of the Bible* (Edinburgh: T. T. Clark, 1900), Vol. I, p. 136, states that the oldest Arabic manuscript of the Gospels, found at the Convent of Mar Saba in Jerusalem, is a translation of the Syriac Vulgate

(Tischendorf, ar/vat) and is to be dated no earlier than the eighth century A.D. Sir Frederick Kenyon, *Our Bible and the Ancient Manuscripts* (New York: Harper & Bros., 1938), p. 170, says of the Arabic versions: "None are earlier than the seventh century, perhaps none so early ..." There are no known translations directly from the Greek before the ninth century A.D. Peninsular Arabs at Muhammad's time, even if they had been literate, could not have read the Gospels in their language.

2. J. W. Sweetman, *The Bible and Islam* (London: The British & Foreign Bible Society, n.d.), p. 10.

3. Ibn Ishaq, *Muhammad*, tr. by Guillaume, p. 107.

4. Muhammad Haykal, *The life of Muhammad*, p. 55. Tor Andrae, *Mohammed, the Man and His Faith*, tr. by T. Mendel (London: George Allen & Unwin Ltd., 1936), quotes a Tradition that Muhammad heard a Christian preacher named Qass ibn Sa'ida, from Hira via Najran, proclaiming a message in the Ukaz marketplace.

5. Maxime Rodinson, *Mohammed*, tr. by Anne Carter (London: Penguin, 1961), pp. 60f.

6. I credit Professor Terence Freitag of Luther Seminary, St. Paul, MN, U.S.A., with this phrase, used orally in another context.

7. Cf. *infra*, chapter 16, where Muslim questions about the Trinity are taken up.

8. J. N. D. Kelly, *Early Christian Doctrines* (London: Adam & Charles Black, 1958), p. 310.

9. A. C. McGiffert, *A History of Christian Thought* (New York: Charles Scriber's Sons, 1932), Vol. I, p. 285. For a full and clear exposition of the Chalcedon story, cf. Jaroslav Pelikan, *The Emergence of the Catholic Tradition* (100–600) (Chicago: The University of Chicago Press, 1971), pp. 263–266, *et passim*; Pelikan describes the formula as an "armistice" and an "agreement to disagree," but recognizes its great importance.

10. K. S. Latourette, *A History of the Expansion of Christianity, Vol. II: The Thousand Years of Uncertainty* (Grand Rapids: Zondervan, 1966), pp. 224f.

11. Alfred Guillaume, *Islam* (Baltimore: Penguin, 1964), pp. 16–18. For a still valuable study of Christianity in the Arab regions see Richard Bell, *The Origin of Islam in the Christian Environment* (London: Macmillan, 1926). Cf. also J. Spencer Trimingham, *Christianity among the Arabs in Pre-Islamic* (London: Longman, 1979). Jane McAuliffe's complete bibliography in *Qur'anic Christians, op. cit.,* is a goldmine of information.

12. To appeal to the Monophysites the idea was also put forward that Jesus has one will (monothelitism), Heraclius making it a formal proposal in 638. Weary of fine-tuning, the church was not interested, and remained with the classical belief that Jesus has both a divine and human will.

13. For a Muslim opinion cf. Ahmad von Denffer, *Christians in the Qur'an and Sunna. An Assessment From The Sources to Help Define Our Relationship* (Leicester: The Islamic Foundation, 1979).

Bridges of Learning: John of Damascus to Martin Luther

There are two reasons for looking at the past as we reflect on the task of Christian sharing with Muslims. The first is that we can learn from it, and the learning becomes another bridge to the crossing. The second is that Muslims are not in a good mood to forget it. The two reasons are connected.

There is learning available from the past—both negative and positive—that illuminates and facilitates the communication of the present. To access the learning we need to adopt two attitudes—we do not disdain, and we do not glamorize. First, we do not disdain. We strive to overcome any tendency in us to believe and act as though we were the first people who ever thought about sharing the gospel with Muslims! History teaches us otherwise and disperses such a fog of self-delusion. To re-invent wheels is not only costly, but foolish and self-indulgent. In the second place, we do not glamorize. Not all the past efforts to engage with Muslims are perfect demonstrations of grace and wisdom, providing replicable models for the present. In fact some of the approaches are out of date, while others are simply wrong. In short, we can draw double learning from the engagement story, things that we can still consider as valid and useful, and things that we must avoid in our current understandings of the task.

The positive learning gets less attention than it ought. When Christians and Muslims look at the history of relationships, the first sense is that of a bad scene, a history of discordance. Yet the past is not all a record of antagonistic societies in bitter contention, not all the stories of self-interested individuals unable to rise above the crudeness of their times. It is more than an unhappy tale of abrasive relationships. There have always been Christians reaching out to Muslims in the spirit of the Messiah, and there have always been Muslims cordial to Christians in the spirit of the people of the book. It is the purpose of this chapter to draw forth some of those positive experiences and to listen to some of the great voices from the past as they speak to us today.

At the same time, as we have already seen there is enough and more of negative learning to go around. This leads to the second factor urging us to consider the past—the simple fact that for Muslims much of it remains a bad, living memory. What is remembered is the sufferings of Muslims at the hands of others. It is been well said that all Islamic historiography is biography. It is not so much interested in cause and effect relationships as it is in the experience of the members of the community. That experience is rehearsed in story and song, the past events continuing to inform contemporary emotion. The significance of this phenomenon for our study is the fact that included in those Muslim memories are negative ones related to undeniable demonstrations of Christian enmity.

The writer recalls a conversation with a casual Muslim friend in a south Indian village. We observed custom, and shared information about our families. We discussed the weather and current politics. After about an hour my new friend put out the question that he really wanted to ask. The question was: "Why did you do that to us in the Crusades?" The question seem irrelevant, and I was completely taken aback. For me the Crusades were in the distant past, truly sad, but we have passed that stage and moved on. Moreover the Crusades took place in a context far removed from our coconut-leaves thatched café in a village remote from the Mediterranean world. For my friend, however, this was living reality, not transcended by time or space. "Why did you do that to us in the Crusades?" I finally blurted out, "I didn't do it," but then added, "I'm sorry it happened."[1]

The lesson was clear enough. Christians who want to share the Gospel with Muslims today must look squarely at the substance of Christian failure yesterday. A Christian may legitimately ask, what about Muslims and their failures? Muslims must obviously carry on a similar process of reality checks. There is a tendency among some to romanticize their own past. Everything Muslims did was good, everything Christians did was bad. Muslims with historical integrity recognize that this is incorrect, and they will conduct their own self-analysis. What we are discussing in this volume, however, is Christian sharing, and Christian sharing with Muslims must go on in the honest awareness of the past and with a determination to learn from it. There has, in fact, been exploitation and cruelty perpetrated against Muslims by Christians. The historical record of hatred and calumny cannot be denied. "Why did you do that to us?" is therefore a question not as out of place as it seems. In response we can point out that the actions of the people involved were not in line with the teachings of the Master whose Name they bore. We may suggest that many of them were nominal or deluded Christians at best. We can deny any personal complicity. In the end, however, as members of the family of faith we must repent for Christian shame in relation to Muslims of the past, and we must pray for clean hearts and right spirits, for the Lord's forgiveness, and for better things to come. Negative learning thus becomes a way of "overcoming evil with good" (Rom 12:21).

With these thoughts in mind we turn to our survey of Christian communication with Muslims. Christianity and Islam have been in contact with each other from the time of Muhammad to the present, a long span of fourteen centuries. This chapter considers the first nine of those centuries, which we may broadly describe as the first or early period of the Christian engagement with Muslims, from John of Damascus to Martin Luther. It is possible to consider only the highlights of this saga, dividing it into three sections. In the initial part we look at the first Christians who engaged in depth with Muslims and their thought, the two most prominent being John of Damascus and Theodore Abu Qurra. The second section deals with a time period that is dominated by the crusading mentality, and yet out of that darkness three lights shine into the present: Peter the Venerable, Francis of Assisi, and Ramon Lull. Our last section leads up to the Reformation, giving special attention to John Wycliffe and Martin Luther. While we recognize that the engagement of these individuals is set within the cultural and political context of their times, it will not be possible to elaborate on that background.

A. The Opening Phase of the Engagement: 640–1095

When Islam expanded into settled Christian communities, Christians had to deal with a new religio-political force. They were not sure who the Muslims were, and could not have guessed the long-term implications of their arrival on the scene. Attitudes varies among different Christians. To the orthodox Byzantine Christians dependent on the rule of the church-state of Constantinople (Byzantium) Muslims were an enemy encroaching on their territory. Syrian Christians who resented the imperialism of Byzantium at first viewed Muslims as their allies in their liberation struggle. Arab Christians, who had the closest proximity with Muslims and an ethnic relationship, had mixed emotions. The differences in attitude run through the Christian-Muslim encounter. From whatever perspective there may have been, the engagement was fully on after Damascus fell to the Muslims in 635, Jerusalem in 638, and Alexandria in 642.

To many Christians of the day Islam looked like a new kind of Christian heresy rather than a new and different religion. Could it be a new form of Arianism (a heresy that denied the full deity of Jesus)? They wondered about it, and were primarily thinking about defense and correction rather than mission. The gospel was spreading especially on the borders of the Christian world, but mission was not associated with the heartlands where the Muslims had now arrived. Moreover Christian theology at the time did not show any concentration on the doctrine of salvation, but rather Christological issues dominated the scene. For several reasons then Christian sharing of the gospel with Muslims appears to have been somewhat rare, and we know of it mainly through the reports of colloquies and in the dialogical writings of Muslims. An additional factor developed when Muslim power consolidated—Muslim rulers forbade Christians to invite Muslims to the Christian faith, and in turn because it affected their tax base they were not generally interested in Christians becoming Muslims.

As Muslims entered the Christian world, therefore, the tendency of Christians was to deal with them either apologetically or polemically.[2] From the outset this affected the style of the engagement. Most Christians of the day would not be likely to interpret their task as one of "Christian sharing with Muslim friends." After all, Muslims had just invaded Christian territory. It may have been in large part an Arab ethnic explosion, but the religious factor was present. It may also be noted that the Greek-based Christian culture of the area was a sophisticated one, and Christians must have felt little compatibility, socially or linguistically, with the rough and ready warriors from inner Arabia. Perhaps some friendships developed at grassroots levels; yet even in later years after a common culture had to some extent come about, friendly communication was inhibited by the style of interaction that had emerged. Taking Islam as a Christian heresy meant dealing with Muslims in more or less the same way that one would contend with heretics, i.e. by using argumentation based on a common authority and by the frequent application of anathemas. Norman Daniel states the problem: "This technique of argument set the tradition. ... It was really the application to Muslims of the technique used among Christians themselves; it had established heresy and orthodoxy with the finest of definitions, but it was too alien from Islam to fulfil this new function effectively."[3]

These factors account for the largely disputatious rather than evangelistic interaction with Muslims that continued for nearly a millennium. Quite often the thoughts expressed and language used were wounding in nature. In part that was customary. Christians had unfortunately become used to throwing hard diatribes at each other in connection with their own doctrinal struggles; and after all, if Muslims are heretics, as they thought, should they not be castigated? Fortunately the insults were not always visible to Muslims because Christians were writing *about* them in languages (Syriac and Greek) that few Muslims could follow, and not *to* them. If the comments had become better known, they would certainly have angered Muslims and aroused them to retaliation. The starkness of this history is relieved by the efforts of those thoughtful Christians who sought to reach out to Muslims in a gentler way, and it is from the latter that we draw our positive learning. We turn to the earliest known example of the colloquies where attempts at irenic dialogue were made.

Early tradition reports that such a colloquy took place between John, the Syrian Orthodox patriarch of Antioch, and a Muslim general named 'Amr.[4] The Muslim general had summoned the colloquy somewhere in Syria for an exchange of views, and many Christians assembled with John for the occasion. Undoubtedly there was considerable trepidation as they faced the conqueror. The discussion that took place, somewhere between 639 and 644, centered on the Old Testament prophecies, the deity of Jesus, and the idea of law. The Muslim leader, 'Amr, not surprisingly wanted to know what the Christian law is and whether it is found in the Injīl (the Gospel). Another Syriac tradition[5] reports that the Muslim governor also wanted John to make an Arabic translation of the Bible; however, he requested that it omit any reference to Christ's divinity, baptism, and cross. The implied assumption is that thereby Christians could and would be more likely to recognize the equivalence of Muslim teaching. John declined to tamper with the scripture, so the Muslim leader agreed, "Write as you please."[6] Patriarch John later sent a letter to the churches regarding this momentous occasion, seeking prayers for God's blessing on the matter.[6]

Learning:

1. Muslim questions about the Christian faith arise natually from Muslim convictions and perspectives. It is the task of Christian sharers to create intelligible bridges to that perspective.

2. A Christian sharer has the duty to explain, from the Christian point of view, what is the difference between law and gospel.

3. Islam does not meet the criteria of a Christian heresy, and Muslims rightly reject that opinion.

I. John of Damascus (675–749)

In the early period of Christian-Muslim relations the figure of John of Damascus looms high. John was a great Eastern Church father and theologian who was close to Muslims in a number of ways. His grandfather Mansur negotiated with Khalīd ibn Walīd, the Muslim general who was attacking Damascus. Preferring the Arab newcomers over the harsh Byzantine Christian overlords, Mansur is reported to have opened the eastern gate of the city to Khālid in 635. John's father, Sergius Ibn Mansur, was a leading administrator in the caliphate of ʿAbd al-Malik (d. 705) who built the Dome of the Rock at Jerusalem. In the early years of their rule the Muslims were naturally dependent on the existing Christian administrative infrastructure, and many Christians held high positions in their service. Among them was John. He himself had studied Arabic as a youth, and became a senior financial officer and counselor in the Ummayad court at Damascus. He had knowledge of Islam and understanding of Muslims. In fact, his affinity was so pronounced that he was labeled as "Saracen-minded" by some Christians.

In 725 John resigned from the court in favor of the contemplative life at St. Sabas Monastery near Jerusalem. There he wrote in Greek his famous works on the Christian faith, concentrating on Christology.[7] One of his works is his *Fount of Knowledge*. Its second part, "Concerning the Heresies," contains a chapter on the so-called Muslim heresy. A somewhat similar apologetic writing is his *Disputation Between a Muslim and a Christian*. In these essays John takes up many of the topics that concerned early theologians in their dialogue with Muslims including: monotheism; the Unity and the Trinity; the two natures of Christ; the freedom of the will; the source of evil; the prophethood of Muhammad; the Qurʾān as revelation; Paradise; and questions about the virtue of various Muslim practices. The agenda points to John's intimacy with Muslims whom he calls Ishmaelites, or sometimes Hagarenes or Saracens. The fact that sympathy is not coupled with knowledge is indicated by the first phrase in the "Heresies," which describes Islam as "the deceptive superstition of the Ishmaelites." It must be noted that John wrote in the elevated style of Greek thought that only a few Muslims of his time could possibly have understood.

Two things stand out in "Concerning the Heresies" that have direct relevance to communication with Muslims today. The first is that John of Damascus utilizes the unity of God as the starting-point for his discussions. The second is that he pays special attention to the ideas of Word and Spirit in relation to the being of God. His reflections on these points constitute a basic and still-valid contribution to the field. In regard to the unity of God John clearly considers it to be the beginning point of contact with Muslim thinking, and he affirms the Christian commitment to that principle, saying:[8]

> We believe in one God, one principle, without beginning, uncreated, unbegotten, incorporeal, unchanging, unaffected, inalterable, invisible, source of goodness and justice, light intellectual and inaccessible ... maker of all things, visible and invisible.

He insists that for Christians too the unity of God is a primary theme: "We know one God, and Him in the properties of fatherhood and sonship and procession only."[9]

The latter statement takes us to John's second emphasis, namely, his explanation of the Trinitarian understanding of the Unity, based on the concepts of Word and Spirit. He apprehends the common Muslim accusation that Christians are "associators" because of their use of the term "son," but he argues aggressively that Muslims could be similarly charged with being "mutilators" since they leave Word and Spirit out of the being of God. He says:[10]

> The Word and Spirit are inseparable from that in which they have been by nature. Therefore, if His Word is in God, it is obvious that He is God. But if He is outside God, then according to you (Muslims) God is without reason and without Spirit. ... And you treat Him like wood, or a stone, or some irrational being.

In John's interpretation the term "son" must be understood against the background of Word and Spirit in God and issuing from God.

John carries forward these thoughts in his second work dealing with Islam, the Disputation. In it he adds the critical point that we must carefully distinguish between the Word of God, Jesus, and the words of God as scriptural revelations. He also takes up a topic considered important by the eastern theologians, namely, the freedom of the human will. The topic is a controversial issue in Muslim thought.

Learning:

1. The accurate knowledge of Islam by Christians represents both a form of respect and a key to communication with Muslims.

2. The Unity of God is an affirmation of the Christian faith as well as a bridging theme for Muslims.

3. The concepts of Word and Spirit are pathways to an understanding of God's self-revelation, and they illuminate the implications of "Son."

4. Christological and Trinitarian discussion need to move from head to heart, and their linkage with the theme of salvation is crucial.

Head to Heart

2. Theodore Abu Qurra (740–825)

Theodore Abu Qurra was a recognized leader among Arab Christian theologians writing in Arabic. The latter were naturally aware of their Islamic context, but by the time they began writing in the eighth century their situation had changed. Not only had Muslims increased greatly in number by that time, but they had also begun to absorb Greek learning and were advancing into a new era in Islamic history. It was called "the Golden Age" of Islam, and no one symbolized it more that Caliph Ma'mūn (d. 833) who fostered rational thought in Islam. Abu Qurra once debated before him with a Muslim scholar. The Arab Christian apologists were interested in convincing inquisitive Muslims of the merits of Christian ideas, including such hotly debated issues as the crucifixion of Christ. Their own cultural roots facilitated their access and communication with Muslims.

Abu Qurra also had spent time at the St. Sabas Monastery in Jerusalem and he regarded himself as a disciple of John of Damascus. One scholar suggests that he reproduced some of John's own arguments, but "with more asperity."[11] Abu Qurra became the Melikite bishop of Harran; a town now in southeastern Turkey, Harran was then a major stopping-point on a caravan road and a religious center of considerable importance. The views represented there included Muslim, Jewish, Christian, and a syncretistic Harranian religion, a kind of Neoplatonic polytheism that emphasized star worship. Abu Qurra ministered in that context, particularly engaging with Muslim opinions. His works included: *On the Necessity of Redemption, On the Possibility of Incarnation,* and *On the Divinity of the Son.* Not only did he deal with these core issues in communication with Muslims, but to the agenda dealt with by John of Damascus he also added such topics as miracles, prophecy, and Christ's fulfilling of the law.

The debate before Caliph Ma'mūn took place in the imperial capital of Baghdad around 820. As John of Damascus had done before him, Abu Qurra also utilized the Qur'anic phrases "a Word from Him" and "a Spirit from Him" to underline the divinity of the Messiah. In response the Muslim participant cited John 20:17, "my Lord and my God," to point to Jesus' declaration of his essential humanity, and then went on to ask whether God still had Word and Spirit while Jesus was on earth. Abu Qurra replied that you cannot define God locally. The Muslim then suggested to Abu Qurra that he worships a piece of wood, i.e. the cross, whereupon Abu Qurra replied that the Muslim worships a stone, i.e., by kissing the sacred stone imbedded in the corner of the Ka'ba in Mecca.[12] The latter exchange indicates that there was as much arguing going on as discussing in what was an essentially inconclusive debate.

In his apologetic Abu Qurra placed great emphasis on miracles. One of the points he dealt with was the Muslim argument that was made from the apparent parallelism of Moses, Jesus, and Muhammad; that is, all three believed, all three taught, and all three brought moral advancement to their communities. This evidence should move Christians to accept Muhammad as a prophet. Abu Qurra in responding to this argument took the position that the reason for accepting Moses and Jesus rests not only on the fact that they believed, taught, and guided people, but also because they did miracles. Muhammad, on the other hand, did none, and therefore he cannot be so accepted. As the history of Muslim thought shows, Muslims soon took care of this apparent difficulty from their point of view, for Islamic tradition became filled with the stories of wondrous deeds performed by the Prophet Muhammad who in the Qur'ān had disavowed any miracle except that of the Qur'ān itself.

Finally, Abu Qurra attempted to deepen the discussion of the crucifixion, moving the debate from event to meaning. Mark Swanson points to three themes that Arab Christian apologists addressed to illustrate the necessity of the crucifixion: the Son's "cunning" victory over Satan, Christ's control over death, and Christ's resolution of the just claims of the law against sinful humans.[13] Abu Qurra developed the latter concept, undoubtedly well aware that the subject of the law is dear to Muslim hearts. He argued that because God revealed His law, God also demands obedience to it and punishes disobedience. The punishment is inevitable and just, for if God simply forgave without punishment, the law would be "frivolity." Through the pains of Christ, however, the punishment was borne for us, and that satisfies the demand and curse of the law. Abu Qurra declares:

> He purchased us human beings from the curse of the Law by his pains and crucifixion and death. What he endured of that became the settlement of what had been incumbent upon every one who believed in him. In him is sufficiency to settle this for all of us because he is an eternal son, better than all of us without compare.[14]

Learning:

1. The miracles of Jesus are primarily acts of love, not demonstrations of power. They are therefore most helpfully presented in the context of God's powerful love for humanity, rather than as proof of divinity.

2. Christians need to steadily reflect on the central implication of the atonement and resurrection of the self-giving Messiah, and how to communicate that meaning in an appealing and effective way to Muslim friends today.

3. Timothy I (d. 823) and the Translators

Our search for learning from the past takes us next to a representative of the Nestorian Christians. The Nestorians had been vigorously persecuted by Byzantine Christians, and as a result had sought and received refuge in Persia. After Islam came to Persia they continued to receive the protection of Muslim authorities. In 755 the headquarters of the Nestorian leader, called the Catholicos, was moved to Baghdad. That city was the seat of the Abbasid Caliph and the administrative hub of the Muslim Empire. This context illuminates the diplomatic approach of Timothy I, who assumed the mantle of Catholicos around the year 780. He had obtained the position in a somewhat unscrupulous fashion, but once in place he went energetically to work, including the appointing of bishops from Yemen to Turkey. He also engaged in cordial theological conversations with his Muslim neighbors. The most notable occasion was a dialogue with Caliph Madhi (d. 785), the transcript of which became his Apology.

The dialogue with Caliph Madhi took place in 782 and covered a broad range of topics. The report of what took place gives the impression that the questions and answers may have been prepared in advance. To the Caliph's plain and simple questions Timothy gives fairly elaborate replies based on a combination of reason and scripture. He uses a number of analogies from nature in the course of his argumentation, but he depends most strongly on reasoning drawn from Old Testament prophecy. When he is asked why he does not accept Muhammad, Timothy replies that if he knew of any prophetic foretelling of Muhammad he would not hesitate to accept him, but "I never saw a verse in a Gospel or the Prophets or elsewhere bearing witness to Muhammad or his works or his name."[15]

Islamic tradition soon take care of the argument from prophecy just as it did with the argument from miracles. The passages Deuteronomy 18:18 and Isaiah 21:7 were used in the debate. The former passage refers to "another prophet like you" whom God will raise up. This was taken to be a prediction of Muhammad. The passage from Isaiah speaks of riders on donkeys (i.e. Jesus) and on camels (i.e. Muhammad) entering Jerusalem. Al-Tabarī worked through the Syriac Old Testament to discover all the uses of the root for "praise" because the meaning of the name Muhammad is "the praised one." Thus he found the Old Testament to be full of prophecies of Muhammad. As an example, he points to Psalm 48:1, and interprets it in the following way: "And David said in the forty-eighth Psalm: 'Great is our Lord, and He is greatly mahmud [the Arabic root for praise is hamada, ed], and in the city of our God and in His mountain there is a Holy One and a Muhammad; and the joy hath come to the whole earth."[16]

We return to Timothy. Although denying that the coming of the Prophet has been foretold, the Catholicos is unusually complimentary toward Muhammad and even eulogizes him. Muhammad contended for the unity of God, taught about His Word and Spirit, opposed idolatry, and promoted morality. That is why God bestowed the power of a kingdom upon him. "Muhammad deserves the praise of all the Arabs, and that because his manner of life was in the way of the prophets and the lovers of God, and Muhammad taught concerning that." Timothy asserts that the Prophet also "turned the children of his people away from wickedness and led them to integrity and virtue, so he also walked in the way of the prophets." Like Moses who slew the worshipers of the golden calf, Muhammad too fought for the sake of God with the sword as well as the word.[17] In response to this praise the Caliph in effect declared: "Then you should accept him."

Perhaps the most moving aspect of Timothy's testimony was his reference to Christ's resurrection and its significance:

> If he had delivered himself from the Jews, then he would not have been crucified. If he had not been crucified, neither would he have died. If he had not died, neither would be have risen to everlasting life. And if he had not risen to everlasting life, then people would have remained without a sign of, or arguments for [the reality of] everlasting life. ... So that this expectation of everlasting life and of the world to come be firmly impressed upon the people, therefore, it was fitting that Jesus Christ rise from the dead; and so that he rise from the dead it was fitting and right

that he first die; and so that he die it was right first that this death—as also his resurrection—be witnessed by all.[18]

Whatever we may think of Timothy's approach the Nestorian experience points to the place of warmhearted, neighborly relations among Christians and Muslims as arguably the greatest single resource for sharing in friendship. Within such a relationship the mission-minded Nestorians reached out to others. While their most notable ventures were to China and India, they undoubtedly remembered their immediate neighbors. The further in distance from the Mediterranean world and its heritage of antagonism the greater the opportunity there was for developing such basic human relations. In the southwest India region of Malabar, now known as Kerala, an unusual example of such a situation was to be found. There one of the most peaceful inter-religious situations in the world existed where Christians and Muslims, both coming in the earliest days of their respective histories, mingled harmoniously with Hindus, providing a basis for communication that continues to exist today. The Nestorians were participants with other Syrian Christians of St. Thomas in that experience.[19]

Learning:

1. Good Christian sharing with Muslims will always be mentally and emotionally "from within," even if there is physical distance.

2. Forthrightness and generosity are commendable virtues in Christian communication with Muslim friends.

3. Argumentation as an approach must reckon with the fact that every argument produces a counter-argument, and every proof a contrary proof.

4. The commendation of Muhammad for legitimate achievements deserves consideration by those who claim to be friends of Muslims.

The modality of Christian presence, also enabled another aspect of the engagement with Muslims to take place, namely the service of Christian scholarship represented by the brilliant translators of Greek thinkers into Arabic and Syriac. The best known of these was Hunayn ibn Ishaq (d. 872), a scholar of Arab descent and a member of the Syrian Nestorian church. Caliph Ma'mūn had welcomed this physician-linguist and his composite mind to the celebrated institute at Baghdad that he had established, "The House of Wisdom." There Hunayn produced his numerous works at the same time as he served as chief physician to the court. His translations of Hippocrates and Galen opened the door for the development of Islamic medicine, and he added other translations of several philosophers, astronomers, and mathematicians. The journey of Greek thought into Islam, and from Islam into Western thought is the saga of an astonishing intellectual movement from which the whole world benefited. The translators made it possible. To that remarkable achievement Hunayn added his own reflection on Islam. He established what for him were the four criteria of revealed religion: miracles, consistency, proofs, and ethical worth, and then he applied them to Christianity and Islam. He maintained that the Christian faith meets these criteria but Islam does not.

The second great translator was a Syrian Jacobite Christian, Yahya ibn ʿĀdī (d. 974) of Takrit (Iraq), who translated many works of Aristotle. Utilizing Aristotelian logic he took the view that Christian dogma, including the Trinity, is reasonable. The three persons of the Trinity represent the substantial attributes of existence (Father), wisdom (Son) and life (Spirit). All the other attributes of God such as seeing, hearing, mercy, righteousness, and so on, are only characteristics related to creatures. In addition he utilized other analogies including the common ones such as sun, sunlight and warmth, and uncommon ones drawn from Neoplatonism such as potential intellect, active intellect, and passive intellect, to help clarify the doctrine of the Trinity.

The translators brought a philosophical stream into Christian communication with Muslims that joined the theological and apologetic currents. It provided freshness and new themes for the discourse. What was common to all was the rational impulse—to somehow prove Christian truth and with that the superiority of the Christian faith. This tendency to a cool intellectualism often gave way to warmth and simplicity at the level of personal piety. This is certainly so in the case of Hunayn ibn Ishaq and Yahya ibn ʿAdi. The latter wrote:[20]

> The Gospel ... bids us bear humiliation and leave off seeking honor and to prefer poverty, and to be patient in unbearable fatigue, and to leave the concessions of the law and its restrictions, and to command [people] to be brave in bearing sufferings, and to leave off seeking pleasures, and to leave off being afflicted by fears.

Whether it was the strain of their vulnerable position or their heavy workload, the fatigue of the scholarly task undoubtedly weighed on these pioneers, as it has on all those who have followed their trail.

Learning:

1. Objective scholarship is a form of Christian service that Muslims appreciate.

2. Our interest in proving the truth must bow before the fact that the Divine Truth of self-giving love is really supra-logical.

4. The Apology of Al-Kindī

We have considered elements of positive learning that come to us from some early apologetic figures. It was the polemical stream of "communication," however, that increasingly dominated the field of Christian-Muslim interaction. We turn to the *Apology of Al-Kindī* as a notable example of this development.

The Apology is both a dialogical defense of the Christian faith, and a refutation of Islam. There is uncertainty in regard to the author. Al-Bīrūnī gives him the name ʿAbd al-Masīh al-Kindī.[21] It has been suggested that he was a Nestorian Christian who served as a senior official at the court of al-Maʾmūn, who ruled 813–833. Other scholars, however, place al-Kindī in the early part of the tenth century. It is not clear whether the dialogue on which the Apology is based was real or manufactured. The alleged Muslim participant, one Al-Hashimi, mildly censures Christian teaching and invites al-Kindī to join Islam; but he also says that if al-Kindī does not wish to do so, he should feel free and fearless in putting forward his case, arguing with whatever words he pleases.

Al-Kindī walks through this open door and presents a withering critique of Islam. In the course of his treatment he takes up the concepts of Unity and Trinity; Muhammad's claim to prophethood; his martial expeditions; the assassinations he is said to have ordered; the Muslim military failure at Uhud; Muhammad's wives and their internal disputes. The work is generally accurate in presenting historical events and scriptural quotations, but the material is set in a controversial mode. The intention is to prove that Islam is false and unworthy. Al-Kindī repeats the argument that there are no prophecies or miracles that support Muhammad's claims. The Qur'ān also brings no new truth. Its ceremonial commands call for outward purity only. The pilgrimage to Mecca and its rites are idolatrous. In closing al-Kindī briefly describes the Christian faith and, quite illogically, appeals to the Qur'ān for its proof. He concludes the polemic by calling on his Muslim friend to follow Christ.

A remarkable characteristic of many polemicists was their ability to compartmentalize hostility toward Muslims and awareness of the loving spirit of Jesus. So also al-Kindī says of Jesus:[22] "He urged them ... to desire earnestly works of piety, and to abstain from iniquity, and to love to confer benefits on everyone, and to abstain from taking vengeance for wrong, and to forgive them, and to do good to everyone. And he taught them that this would bring them near to God." The apparent contradiction continued in later centuries and is best illustrated from the career of St. Bernard of Clairvaux (d. 1153). He proclaimed his support for the Second Crusade, advocating "the necessary" killing of pagans, at the same time as he wrote his beautiful hymns extolling the love of Jesus, "that neither tongue nor pen can show." *Hypocrisy — hostility toward / love of Christ*

Al-Kindī seemed to be aware of the mission of the church, for with regret he reported that "the monks today are not missionaries." He undoubtedly viewed his own writing as a communication of the gospel. Yet it had another spirit than that of the gospel. That such a provocative exposition could survive at all is a marvel and calls for explanation. It may have had to do with the sad fact that this type of communication was becoming the norm. It may be attributed to the reality that it was an age of low literacy, and perhaps few Muslims actually read it. Yet the survival of the *Apology* was certainly also a tribute to the Muslim age of toleration that Caliph Ma'mūn so notably represented. The work endured beyond its period. It was translated into Latin as part of the Toledo Collection a century later, and through translations into English (Sir William Muir, 1882), Persian and Urdu, its influence entered the modern era.

Learning:

Whether conscious or unconscious, hurtful approaches serve to alienate rather than attract, and squander the possible merit of argumentation. There is no Muslim today who would not be offended by the tone and language of the *Apology*.

B. Amidst Darkness Lamps Are Lit: 1095–1320

The first four centuries of Christian-Muslim engagement ended in the severe deterioration of relationships, and mutual bitterness prevailed. The Eastern Roman Empire was hemmed in by the military advance of Islam led by the Seljuk Turks. Christian anger took many forms, among them increasing invective against Muhammad. An example is Nicetas, a Byzantine scholar who around 880 was commissioned by the Emperor to write a treatise on Islam. In his work (*the Antrotope*) he attacked Muhammad as "an ignorant and shameless liar, a false prophet, a tempter, son of Satan, devoid of any divine and human wisdom."[23] The Qur'ān is only a pack of lies and fables. Muslim polemics reacted in the same vein. The most vehement representative was in the West in Cordoba, Spain. There the brilliant and tempestuous revivalist, Ibn Hazm (d. 1064), produced the perhaps most devastating critique of the Bible ever written by a Muslim. The subtitle to the first volume of his *Al-Fisal* makes clear his intention: "Concerning the manifest contradictions and clear falsehood in the book which the Jews call the Torah and in the rest of their books and in the four gospels."[24] Christian negativism was producing a bountiful harvest.

The worst was still to come when the leader of the western church, accepting holy war as appropriate methodology, launched the Crusades in 1095. It is an infamous date that introduces a gloomy time. We will not dwell on the details of the events, which we have referred to in earlier chapters, but will restrict ourselves to their effect. The purpose of the Crusades was not to convert Muslims but rather to gain control of the sacred sites in Jerusalem, to give aid to the Eastern Roman emperor and to blunt the advance of Islam, but in the course of their 300 years of history they were also from time to time directed against other enemies including fellow Christians. For the Muslims the Crusades were at first a minor disruption on the western extremity of their vast empire, but in the end their cumulative effect was large indeed. They disrupted Christian-Muslim communication and poisoned the well of human relationships like no other event. J. W. Sweetman puts the matter in wider perspective: "Here is the tragic predicament inevitably experienced when men are ranged in hostile camps, dangerously wrapped in the mystery of alien ideas and practices. It is hardly unexpected ... that opposition of force to force should become normal procedure."[25] K. S. Latourette sums up the new "normal procedure" as he discusses events in Spain and Portugal. Along with some toleration, and persuasion by teaching and preaching, there were "wars, crusades, crusading orders, compulsory baptism, and exile."[26] In 1232 the Inquisition was established to root out Christian heresy, but the atmosphere of cruel compulsion also embraced Jews and Muslims in its dreary grasp.

Adding to the trauma was the general ignorance of Islam in the West. With the Crusades the leadership of the Christian encounter with Muslims passed from east to west, but the western Christians could not compare with the eastern knowledge of Muslim faith and practice. Moreover, the antagonistic relations precluded the possibility of easily bridging the gap. In the main, the entire Christian engagement with Muslims had entered its Dark Ages. What must thrill us, however, is that there were still great figures whose light shone in the darkness and from whom we can continue to learn today. In our present time when both psychological and physical militancy exist, producing new forms of darkness, it is well to learn from medieval times how some determined individuals filled with the Spirit of Christ can light lamps and brighten the scene. We turn, then, to three of these remarkable persons: Peter the Venerable, Francis of Assisi, and Ramon Lull.

1. Peter the Venerable (1092–1156)

It has been said that the actions of Pierre de Montboissier, better known as Peter the Venerable, represent "a momentous event in the intellectual history of Western Europe."[27] Certainly he represents a milestone in Christian sharing with Muslims. This is so for two reasons—he stated that the primary responsibility of Christians toward Muslims is to preach the gospel, and he declared that this must be done with peaceful methods. In the context of his time these simple affirmations constituted a momentous break-through indeed.

At Peter's time two movements were developing among Christians that gave some light in the gloomy scene that we have sketched above. The first of these was a revival of the missionary movement under Pope Gregory VII (d. 1085), who was interested in Muslims. The second was a movement to revive the spiritual life of the church, especially the monastic orders. These two movements met together in the person of Peter the Venerable, resulting in a dramatic witness to the fundamental character of Christian sharing with Muslims. The witness came when it was desperately needed. There was no clear vision in Europe in regard to Muslims. R. W. Southern suggests that there were three views that were current. The first of these he describes as "Biblical and unhelpful," i.e. the tendency to look at Muhammad as the Anti-Christ and the harbinger of the last time: the second was "imaginative and untruthful," i.e. the practice of viewing Islam through spectacles of romantic fantasy; and the third was "philosophical and (at least for a short time) extravagantly optimistic," i.e. the thought that with the advent of the Mongols Islam was on the point of dissolution.[28] The obvious fourth attitude, perhaps too plain for Southern to state, was the spiteful and militant, i.e. regarding Muslims as the enemy. What Peter the Venerable did was to point to the New Testament way of looking at people, and then apply it to Muslims.

Peter the Venerable's spiritual father was St. Benedict (d. 547) who was the greatest single influence in western monasticism. His famous "Rule" guided the activities of many monasteries, one of the greatest of which was the Abbey at Cluny in east central France. Peter was chosen to be its abbot in 1122, at the tender age of twenty-eight. Combining spiritual-mindedness with strong scholarly instincts, energy with initiative, and strength in personnel management he had dedicated himself to the reform of monasticism. A journey to Spain in 1142, however, served to enlarge his vision. Profoundly peace-loving, he did not like what he saw. He came to the conclusion that European Christianity was not being true to the mind of Christ in its relation to Muslims. Not only was there a problem of ignorance, but the approach itself was wrong.

When Pope Urbanus II called for the First Crusade the response of Christians present was to cry "God wills it!" Peter wrote to the King of France, Louis VII, that "God does not will cold-blooded murder or outright slaughter."[29] The abbot argued that Christ took away the sword from St. Peter. "The church does not have the sword of a king, but the staff of a shepherd," he declared. The sword that the church now has is the sword of the Spirit and that is wielded through the preaching of the gospel. That gospel must be shared with Muslims who have a place in God's salvation. It is not the extermination of Muslims, but it is their conversion to which Christians should aspire. The term "enmity" may be used for an unaccepting attitude towards God's salvation—and in that sense Muslims are enemies of the cross of Christ—but enmity ceases when rejection ends. Moreover, enmity is not an appropriate descriptive for the relation between Christians and Muslim people. This was the stirring statement of his own intention toward Muslims:

> "I attack you, not as some of us often do by arms, but by words; not by force, but by reason; not in hatred, but in love. I love you; loving you, I write to you; writing to you, I invite you to salvation."[30]

He defined the love as that attitude which God bears toward perishing humanity: "He loved them before he was loved by them."[31] Thus the Magna Charta for Christian sharing with Muslims became visible again in the words of the abbot of Cluny.

Peter the Venerable applied his approach in an unique project. He held that the position of Islam on certain matters must be refuted, but in order to do that it must also be accurately known and understood. He accepted as his personal task the challenge to provide comprehensive and accurate information about Islam, using original sources. On his trip to Spain he saw the scholarly work that was going on at Toledo in the translating of Islamic scientific and philosophic materials from Arabic into Latin. Why not do the same for Muslim religious materials? Committed to that inspiration he gathered together a group of five accomplished translators led by Peter of Toledo, whose idea it might have been in the first place. One of the five scholars was Robert of Ketton, an English priest, mathematician, and astronomer who was in Spain at the time. Another was a Muslim named Muhammad whose undoubted task it was to verify the accuracy of the Arabic translation. Peter had to defend the ground-breaking effort at the highest levels, appealing to the precedents of the church fathers, but the project was a success. It resulted in what is known as the Toledo Collection which contains the following works: a chronicle of Islamic historical traditions; a kind of *mawlūd* (birth story) that traces the movement of the Divine Light from Adam to Muhammad; an imaginary dialogue in which the Muslim participant submits a hundred questions to four Jews and wins the conversion of the Jewish leader; the *Apology* of al-Kindī; and most importantly, the Qur'ān itself, the work being completed in 1143 A.D./538 A.H.

The translation of the Qur'ān was indeed a milestone. Primarily executed by Robert of Ketton, with the assistance of Herman of Dalmatia, it represents the first translation into a European language, and perhaps the first full translation anywhere. Both Peter the Venerable and Robert made biting comments about what they regarded as base aspects of the Qur'ān, but they stuck to the principle that it must be known. We need to reckon with the courage and determination of this trail-blazing group. Robert wrote of the problem they faced with the hatred of Christian priests who even opposed the conversion of Muslims. "They say in the presence of all, either by ignorance or negligence, that His beautiful portion of the human race [Muslims, ed] should hear nothing of His nuptials ... ignorant that His redemption has been accomplished."[32]

Peter the Venerable's purpose in his extraordinary translation project, namely to provide good information as a basis for ministry, was ahead of his times, but in other respects he was also within his context. He still regarded Islam as a Christian heresy and called it "the error of errors." He believed that its arguments must therefore be formally countered and hoped that someone else, perhaps Bernard of Clairvaux, the "virtual pope" of his age, would undertake the task, but the latter declined. When no one else came forward, Peter finally engaged in the apologetic task himself, writing two works, "Summary of Muslim Heresies" and "Refutation of Muslim Heresies." They were traditionally controversial in content, and Peter pointed to the fault in Muhammad's character and claims. Nor did Peter formally denounce the Crusades. Nevertheless, his spirit was different, and his lamp continues to glow. Because he wrote in Latin, the direct influence of his works was probably limited, but his attitude must have moved people to a fresh consideration of what needed to be done. What he had advised Peter Abelard reflected his own heart: "Set thyself to know only Jesus Christ, Jesus the Crucified."[33] The Qur'ān translation itself, however, gathered dust in European libraries until 400 years later when Martin Luther ordered its publication.

Learning:

1. The study of Islam, and its accurate knowledge, is an essential basis for effective Christian communication.

2. The spirit of Christ demands of its representatives that they "depart from evil, and do good; seek peace and pursue it" (Ps 34:14).

3. Peter's manifesto of love is the only possible basis for Christian communication with Muslims today.

2. Francis of Assisi (1182–1226)

The general outline of the remarkable life of St. Francis of Assisi is common knowledge. What is not so well known is his deep concern that the gospel be shared with Muslims.

A series of events changed the life of the wealthy and exuberant youth, Francesco de Bernardone, who had been set for a career as a knight in Italy. The key event was the discovery of the harsh reality of poverty and the contradictions in Christian behavior toward the poor. But behind all the factors was his personal vision of Christ and his hearing the Lord's call: "Repair my house ..." He turned his back on the wealth of his bewildered father and took a vow to follow Christ. For him this meant begging for food for the day, working selflessly for the poor and the suffering, loving all of God's creatures, and caring for nature as the mirror of God. Francis sought to develop these principles not only by his own personal action but also through a governing "Rule" for all those who chose to follow him, whom he called "Brothers" (friars). His self-denying commitment greatly moved the general public and deeply influenced the church.

St. Francis soon turned his attention to Muslims. He felt that he would not be a friend of Christ if he did not cherish all those for whom Christ died, and the awareness that this included Muslims began to preoccupy him. He lived in the midst of the Crusades, but sensed their incongruities. Fr. Bassetti-Sani puts it this way: "Continual meditation on the Passion of Christ made St. Francis understand that God brought about the salvation of man through annihilation and affliction ... and not through violence and the deployment of material power."[34] Francis perceived a bond between Christians and Muslims, a bond related not only to creation but to the salvific action of Jesus the Savior. He saw Muslims as "alienated brothers who had to be led to their Father's house through kindness and goodness. Jesus treated men with love and saved them by giving Himself on the Cross. The church, which is His mystical Body, cannot pursue another way; she must treat Muslims with charity and understanding, and save them by prayer and suffering."[35]

The personal implications of his theory did not escape St. Francis. Three times in his busy life he attempted to go to the Muslim world in search of direct personal contact with Muslims. His first plan to visit the Holy Land was thwarted by a shipwreck. Then, when he became ill in Spain he was frustrated in his intention to go to Morocco and had to return. He had hoped to meet Muslims who had been exiled from Spain and had fled to Morocco. Finally his third attempt succeeded. It came in 1219 at the time of the Fifth Crusade, a particularly misguided enterprise. The brother of Saladin, al-'Ādil, ruled the Ayyubid kingdom from Damascus and his son, Sultan Malik al-Kamal governed Egypt. Both had been conciliatory toward Christians, and Malik at-Kamal had even welcomed 3000 Italian traders to his territory. In spite of that the Fifth Crusade was directed against Egypt, and the Crusaders besieged Damietta at the mouth of the Nile River. St. Francis took a ship and in July, 1219, he appeared in the Crusader camp from where with great dismay he observed the unfolding battle. He sought permission from the Crusade commander, Cardinal Pelagius, to try to cross the firing-line and reach the Sultan on a peace mission. Perhaps happy to see him go, Pelagius sent Francis forward under the protection of a white flag, and he went to the Sultan's camp. The startled Muslim leader graciously received the daring Christian figure from nowhere, and he listened to him with respect as the saint spoke not only of ending the fighting but also on spiritual issues.[36]

Two valid observations by Kenneth Latourette and Norman Daniel respectively, clarify this extraordinary event:

> A frank, humble and courageous affirmation of the Christian faith without any offence to the Muslim conscience, is respectfully heard in the Muslim circle.[37]

> Muslims have always been liable to revere the sanctity of individual Christians.[38]

The meeting of saint and sultan was inconclusive. St. Francis made an offer to witness to the truth by undergoing a trial by fire. The sultan politely declined but was moved to declare his respect for Francis' faith and sent him back with an honorary escort. Two months later the sultan made an offer to relinquish Jerusalem and Galilee in exchange for retaining control of Egypt, an offer that the Crusaders for some reason declined. On his part St. Francis now returned to Italy via Palestine.

To his followers St. Francis suggested that the engagement with Muslims would involve two phases. In the first phase the message will be transmitted by the practice of Christian virtues, including the ethic of "reparation in suffering,"[39] for which there must be spiritual preparation. In the second phase that will come when God permits the task of proclamation may be undertaken, for which there must be intellectual preparation. Accordingly the Rule of St. Francis declared to the Friars: "Spiritually they can behave among other people in two ways. One way is not to make disputes and controversies, but to be subject to every human creature for God's sake, and to witness that they are Christians. The other way is, when they see that God pleases, to preach the Word of God ..."[40]

Bassetti-Sani sums up St. Francis' significance for Christian sharing with Muslims in these words: "Thanks to him the expression 'brothers and friends' is found in the church, an expression to which Muslims have the right."[41] It is the prayers of St. Francis, however, that best express his spiritual approach, as we see from the following expression: "Praised be my Lord for all those who pardon one another for His love's sake, and who endure weakness and tribulation; blessed are they who peaceably shall endure, for Thou, O most Highest, shalt give them a crown."[42]

Learning:

1. Christian sharers do not wait but go to the other, even when the going seems absurd or impossible.

2. Where there is hatred, Christians sow love, and where there is war, they sow peace.

3. The chronological relation of deed and word in Christian witness is an unfinished discussion, and considering the variety in the Spirit that marked the ministry of Jesus, it can never be arbitrarily framed.

3. Ramon Lull (1235–1315)

The third lamplighter was Ramon Lull. Like the "Phantasticus" that he was called he towered over his century. Only Thomas Aquinas, who was less directly involved with Muslims, rivaled him. Ramon Lull was not as pacific as Peter the Venerable and not as self-renouncing as Francis of Assisi, but he was unsurpassed in his intellectual power and his missionary dedication. He wrote about 150 works that touched on many branches of human knowledge and which defy easy classification. What interests us here, however, is his concern for Muslims.

Lull's early career was centered in Majorca, a large Spanish island in the Mediterranean, about a hundred miles from Barcelona. He was tutor to Prince James of Aragon, his lifelong friend and supporter, but his occupation was really that of a courtier. He lived a loose life of fun and frolic. One day at the age of thirty as he was writing a poem to a lady friend he saw a vision of Christ hanging in agony on the cross but looking at Ramon. The vision would not leave him, reappearing four times. He concluded that the Lord was asking him to change his life and enter his service. St. Francis had been dead only eleven years but there was already a festival in his memory. Ramon decided to attend it. He heard the message of self-denial and his conversion was total. The general public were astonished and wondered about his mental condition, but he persevered, eventually becoming a lay Franciscan. Ramon decided to try to do three things for his Master: to prepare apologetic literature, to establish missionary colleges, and to die as a martyr. He was overwhelmed by his lack of preparation to fulfil these commitments and concluded that he must first master other languages. For seven years he studied Latin and Arabic. While doing so, he also began his writing that continued throughout his long and tumultuous career.

Ramon's personality was a mix of rationality and love, common sense and idealism. He was quite convinced of the power of reason and the value of argumentation in support of faith. In fact he believed that all human knowledge could be rationally mastered and interpreted, and in that process the truth of the Christian faith would emerge visible and undeniable. He was passionate but objective in presenting the position of others, displaying fairness and kindness. The other side of Lull was the lover. His rationality was fired by love, and he wrote: "Love is engendered in thought and nourished in patience."[43] Both a practicing mystic and a poet of love, he produced many moving expressions of the loving relation between God the Beloved and the believing Lover. In the end he became known both as "the Apostle of Reason" and "the Fool of Love." Both rationality and love became the mediums by which Lull channeled his energetic efforts to reach Muslims with the gospel.

The variformed works of Ramon Lull include the *Book of Contemplation*, an encyclopedic compilation of theology, philosophy and prayer, and the *Tree of Service*, a similar study on the scientific thought of the age. It was his *Ars Magna*, however, that represented Lull's supreme intellectual effort. In it he tried to pull together and to rationalize all human knowledge, with the help of numbers and diagrams. In connection with his missionary purpose Lull wrote three imaginary dialogues with members of other faiths. The *Blanquerna*, whose core section is "The Book of the Lover and the Beloved," represents the peak of his writing on the principle of love. In the pattern of mystical poetry he concentrates on the relation between the Lord and the devotee, but with Muslims never far from his mind he takes the implication farther—the devotee's love will be an outreaching one. Like Peter the Venerable and St. Francis of Assisi he recognizes the true center of the Christian concern for Muslims. Some phrases from the *Blanquerna* reveal his mind.

Lull finds the source of love in God whose mercy and pity are "essentially in His will:"

> They asked the Lover where his love first began. He answered: "It began in the glories of my Beloved, and from that beginning I was led to love my neighbour even as myself and to cease to love deception and falsehood." Say, Fool of Love! If thy Beloved no longer cared for thee, what

wouldst thou do? "I should love him still," he replied, "else must I die; seeing that to cease to love is death, and love is life."[44]

Lull grieved for those who through ignorance do not know the love of God in Christ:

> And if Thou, Beloved, hast so greatly honoured Thy Lover, through none of his merits ... wherefore honourest Thou not so many ignorant men who knowingly have been less guilty of dishonouring the Name, Jesus Christ, than has this Thy Lover?[45]

Lull understood that love drives a lover out to fill others with love:

> The Beloved said to His Lover: "Thou shalt praise and defend me in those places where men most fear to praise me." The Lover answered: "Provide me then with love." The Beloved answered: "For love of these I became incarnate, and endured the pains of death."[46]

Lull believed that love for others means lightening one's load:

> The Lover had to make long journeys over roads that were rough and hard, and the time came when he should set out, carrying the heavy burden that Love makes lovers to bear. So the Lover unburdened his soul of the cares and pleasures of this world, that his body might bear the weight with more ease, and his soul's journey along those roads in company with its Beloved.[47]

And it means a fearless acceptance of the implication of dying love:

> They asked the Lover: "Wherein is love the greater, in the Lover that lives or in the Lover that dies?" He answered, "In the Lover that dies." And wherefore? "Because in one that lives for love it may yet be greater, but in one that dies for love it can be no greater."[48]

To promote his concern for Muslims the persistent Lull again and again traversed the Majorca-Montpelier-Paris-Rome ambit, experiencing many rebuffs and some final recognition. In 1311 the Council of Vienne agreed to establish five schools of language and literature to prepare men for mission work—to be located at Rome, Bologna, Paris, Oxford, and Salamanica—with chairs in Hebrew, Chaldaic, and Arabic. He was often disappointed, however, in his visits to popes. Those visitations also revealed the inconsistencies in Lull's own position, for he failed to clearly distinguish between the merits of proclamation and the advisability of the Crusades. He even petitioned the pope to assign ten percent of the church's income to missionary work and to the support of crusades until the Holy Land was conquered, and he formulated a war plan of his own. His ambivalence, however, and perhaps his true feelings came to the surface in the following comment:[49]

> Many knights I see going to the Holy Land to conquer it by force of arms. But looking at the result of it, all give up before they fulfil their desire. It seems to me, therefore, O Lord, that the Holy Land will never be conquered except by love and prayer, and the shedding of tears as well as blood. Let the knights go forth adorned with the sign of the Cross and

filled with the grace of the Holy Spirit, and preach the truth concerning Thy passion.

While he was in Paris Lull also debated with the supporters of the theories of the Muslim philosopher Ibn Rushd (Averroes) whose ideas had penetrated the Christian intellectual world. This was another of his lifelong causes, but always in the background of Ramon's mind was the intention of going to the Muslims personally, "That I may do honour among them to our Lord God."[50]

In 1285 Ramon Lull attempted to make his first African mission journey. At Genoa he was immobilized by unanticipated anxieties and fears, and he deliberately missed the boat. Rising from his psychosomatic illness, however, he caught a later vessel and sailed to Tunis. There he debated with learned Muslim scholars. He was to find that his natural polemical style was not well suited to evangelism, but perhaps it was his desire for martyrdom that drove him to his tactless provocation. As the result he was maltreated and ejected from the city. In his *Blanquerna* he had anticipated the possibility of suffering and said: "And if Thou does help sinners to lead just lives, help Thy Lover that he may sacrifice his will to Thy praise, and his body for a testimony of love in the path of martyrdom." [51] After subsequent mission trips to Aragon in Spain and to Cyprus he set out on a second trip to North Africa. This time he went to Bugia, a hundred miles east of Algiers. According to one report he spoke words like these in the middle of the market: "The law of the Christians is holy and true, and the sect of the Moors is false and wrong, and this I am prepared to prove."[52] It was only the grace of the qādī, a Muslim judge, that preserved him from the result of his temerity. Nevertheless, he was imprisoned for six months and then placed on a ship to Pisa. The ship was wrecked, but he escaped as one of only a few survivors.

Wisely Lull now drew up his will, making provision for his two children, and carefully assigning his many published works. In August 1314, about eighty years old, he returned to Tunis. Politically it was a favorable time, and he was able to engage in peaceful preaching tours, even dedicating a new volume to the muftī of Tunis. One tradition holds that at that point something drove him back to Bugia where he was stoned to death in the marketplace, but others suggest that he returned to Majorca. In any event he returned, or was returned to his beloved island where he was buried in 1316. He had once, and truly, written: "Love is an ocean, its waves are troubled by the winds; it has no port or shore. The lover perished in the ocean, and with him perished his torments, and the work of his fulfilment began."[53]

Learning:

1. Christian sharing with Muslims requires the honoring of the mind as well as the purifying of the heart.

2. Love that bears all things and hopes all things is the *Ars Magna* of the Christian engagement with Muslims.

3. Courageous boldness must be a managed asset in Christian communication with Muslims.

4. Within every Christian sharer there are contradictions that need to be resolved with penitence and prayer. Unexamined love has its own dangers.

The cumulative impact of such innovative figures as Peter the Venerable, Francis of Assisi, and Ramon Lull cannot be accurately assessed. Their loving concern for Muslims remained a minor tone that did not replace the discordance of the age. Minor tones can be heard, however. Here and there Christians were thinking in fresh terms about the church's responsibility toward Muslims. They were typified by Raymund of Penaforte in the west and William of Tripoli in the east. Both were Dominicans who were active in Lull's day. A contemporary of St. Francis, Domingo de Guzman of Castile, Spain—better known as St. Dominic—had established a begging Order of Friars in 1216, which became known later as the Dominicans. An intelligent, low-key, and scholarly priest St. Dominic emphasized the importance of education in the moral reform of the church and in preparation for missionary proclamation. Along with the Franciscans the Dominicans too gave their attention to communication with Muslims. Raymund and William represented that concern.

A professor turned missionary Raymund of Penaforte insisted that the gospel must be commended to Muslims in their own language, with knowledge of their faith, and in a kindly way. He set up schools for the study of Arabic in such places as Tunis to back up his vision. William of Tripoli, also a Dominican priest, was located at Acre in Palestine. He wrote a remarkably factual account of Islam for his archdeacon, "Concerning the State of Muslims," in 1273. He personally sensed a restlessness among Muslims and the beginning of critical attitudes. Perhaps he was more imaginative than realistic. Who can say that he was totally wrong, however, in the face of the fact that Islam had just experienced its greatest catastrophe when the Mongols destroyed Baghdad, in a massacre that took over 100,000 Muslim lives[54] and subdued the Abbasid Empire. William said: "Though their beliefs are wrapped up in many lies and decorated with fictions, yet it now manifestly appears that they are near to the Christian faith and not far from the path of salvation."[55] He prepared an effective "Story of Mary and Jesus," collating and using only passages from the Qur'ān. Its written version was in Latin, but he must have used the material in communication with Muslims for his stated purpose was "to show Muslims that their beliefs were really or nearly Christian."[56] He felt that Muslims were on the way to Christ, and claimed to have baptized over a thousand Muslims himself, "by the action of God."

These were the exceptions, however. The major tone continued to be a medley of ignorance, misconceptions, prejudice, and bitter attitudes, with the defamation of Muhammad on the increase. Not all the polemical writers were ignorant and took the low road. Among them was Ricoldo of Montecruce whose influence was far-reaching, continuing into later centuries, and we look at him as the example of an informed polemist.

4. Ricoldo de Montecruce (1243–1320)

Ricoldo was a scholarly Dominican missionary among the Mongols, whom he called Tartars, in what was left of Baghdad. He took interest in Muslims, however, and wrote three treatises on the subject, probably in Arabic. His principal work, *The Confutation of the Qur'ān,* was apparently a compendium for the use of missionaries, but he also seems to be addressing Muslims directly. The work exerted major influence on the Christian world.

Ricoldo was a polemist in the sense that his primary purpose is to disprove and confute Islam. He took the approach that it is easier to prove Islam false than Christianity true. In that light he carefully refutes every Qur'anic statement that seems to be in opposition to the Christian position, using "rational" arguments to do so. In the process he used classic materials that had become the bread and butter of critics in dealing with Muslim objections to Christian teaching. But Ricoldo was a knowledgeable polemist. He knew the Qur'ān and had some acquaintance with Muslim traditions and legends. He was competent in their presentation and in his argumentation, even though controversial in style. More significantly, his writing shows the marks of someone who had personal contact with Muslims themselves.

Neither knowledge nor contact automatically produce fairness or gentleness. We have noted the problem of contradiction in theory and practice related to Muslims. Ricoldo understood and explicitly stated that the gospel inculcates "friendship and perfect charity, and sharing with others,"[57] and he witnesses to Christ's teaching "love your enemies." Yet he did not hesitate to go on the attack, impugning motives and using opprobrious epithets, and the points he made were often as silly as they were one-sided. Part of Ricoldo's problem was that he was making use of earlier polemical writings as sources, apparently whatever he could lay his hand on, making no distinction in materials and using them indiscriminately. He was much kindlier when he was reporting his own actual observations. On the basis of what he has seen he praises Muslims for their reverence for the name of God, the prophets and the holy places; their inclination to study; their devotion in prayer; their piety toward the poor; their sobriety; their hospitality; and "their harmony and love for each other."[58]

Whatever the sources of the *Confutation* the themes of the work illustrate the fact that not much had changed in the agenda of communication with Muslims. In the first two chapters Ricoldo describes the chief errors of "the law of the Saracens." Chapters 3–5 demonstrate that neither the Old Testament nor the New Testament support it, while chapter six argues that the Qur'ān does not agree with them in style or content and is self-contradictory. The Qur'ān is not confirmed by any miracle (ch. 7), is not in accordance with reason (ch. 8), and it contains outright falsehoods (ch. 9). The violence of the Qur'ān is attacked (ch. 10), as is its disorderliness (ch. 11), and its injustice (ch. 12). The Qur'anic teaching is viewed as distorted in a number of ways, and its author is dishonest (chs. 13, 14). In the three concluding chapters Ricoldo finally turns to the Christian faith. Chapters 15–16 seek to demonstrate the superiority of Christ and the gospel, while chapter 17 takes up the objection that the law of Christ is unnatural and too difficult. Ricoldo argues that the law of the Qur'ān is more difficult because of the sanctions it imposes, while the gospel as the holy law of God from God is easier to obey in this world than the Qur'ān.[59] J. W. Sweetman's restrained critique of Ricoldo is that "attack and defence are more permanently displayed than appeal or persuasion," but he adds the perceptive point that "one would be justified in asking whether it is not in the choice of the subject for his book that he is most to be criticized."[60]

Learning:

1. Rational exposition, which has a place and role, becomes Christian communication when it reflects the love of Christ in content, language, and spirit.

2. Winning debates is distant from the task of sharing the good news of God's salvation.

3. The repetition of old and well-rehearsed arguments is less helpful than the development of new and living relationships.

C. The Period from Wycliffe to Luther: 1320–1544

Significant events were taking place in general culture and major changes were under way in both Christianity and Islam that would alter the shape of Christian communication with Muslims. These included the development of the Renaissance and the Reformation. It is not our place here to deal with these events and changes as they deserve, and we will restrict ourselves to one comment—there is a time warp in the comparative development of Christianity and Islam which comes down to the present. Christian change in the direction of a more evangelical concern for Muslims was accompanied by a growing intellectual stratification in Islam and a gradual closing off to outside influences. Nevertheless the pre-Reformation period is marked by a dawning awareness of some convergence between Christians and Muslims, and a need for new approaches and relationships. We shall consider John Wycliffe, Nicholas of Cusa and Martin Luther as our representatives for these two centuries. John Wycliffe underscores the truth that the engagement with Muslims must have a moral base. Nicholas of Cusa, seeks a new way of thinking about Islam that starts from the principle of peace. Martin Luther, amidst great complexities, calls the church to a more knowledgeable awareness of Muslims.

1. John Wycliffe (1330–1384)

John Wycliffe touched the issue of Islam tangentially but importantly. An Oxford theologian he was a pre-Reformation reformer who arranged for the first full English translation of the Bible. His emphasis that many take for granted today appeared revolutionary at the time, and he was strongly condemned by the Council of Constance. After his death his writings were burnt and his body desecrated. It was the moral condition of Christianity that especially concerned and preoccupied Wycliffe. He was disturbed and disgusted by the condition of the church, and he sought to reform its clergy and to restore the authority of scripture. In the last six years of his life he began to think about Islam in connection with his critique of Christian conditions.

Wycliffe's approach opposed a position that almost everyone until then had taken for granted, namely that Christianity and Islam were totally different. A behavior-conscious person he saw a convergence between the two at the level of practical reality. In both religions the same problems were visible: pride, cupidity, desire for power, lust for material things, violence, and overconfidence in human reason. In effect, he turned against Christians their own criticisms of Muslims, and spoke of "we western Mohammedans." That analysis led to his fundamental thesis that you have to cure Christianity before you can cure Islam.

Wycliffe argued that it was the failures and vices of Christians that produced Islam in the first place. Islam is primarily a moral heresy rather than a doctrinal one, and the spirit of misbehavior is within Christians and Muslims alike. Christians and Muslims both need and are eligible for the salvation that comes only from the renewal of God through Christ. Muslims, however, will not be able to see it until they observe its power in a reformed and moral church. "This anti-religion [Islam, ed.] will grow until the church returns to the poverty of Jesus Christ and to its original state."[61] Thus the reform of the church must be the primary task of Christians, and concern for Muslims follows on that.

The church was undoubtedly full of corruption in Wycliffe's day, and it would furthter deteriorate in the next century. In particular Wycliffe was distressed by the heartless treatment of the poor. The conclusion he came to, however, in relation to Islam, raises a fundamental question: how sanctified must the church be before Christians share the gospel? Wycliffe's contention that the deficiencies of Christianity are responsible for Muslim reluctance to consider the Christian faith and that therefore those deficiencies must be given priority attention, strikes a contemporary chord. Christians who are in contact with Muslims will readily agree that the failure of Christ's followers to live up to his precepts dilutes and often vitiates the force of his message. The fact certainly enables well—intentioned Muslims to advise Christians "to clean up their own act" before venturing farther. And at another level that Wycliffe could not have anticipated, his idea resonates with an aspect of the modern relativist mood, namely, that Christians should attend to their own backyard and apart from mutual conversation and cooperation should basically leave people of other faiths alone.

Wycliffe's contention that the sins of the church hinder the witness of the church has great force. They distract the church. They suggest that the church lacks spiritual power. They give the church a negative witness. Despite these facts the crucial point dare not be overlooked—that we live by the forgiveness of sins, and in that power and joy strain toward the pattern of God's life. The only hope that Christians and Muslims commonly have is the forgiveness of God that God graciously makes available to the world in Jesus Christ and that God grants freely to penitent sinners who come in faith. The message of the church is God's salvation and not its own worthiness, even as it struggles to become more worthy in the sight of God. "All this is done by God, who through Christ changes us from enemies into his friends, and gave us the task of making others his friends also" (2 Cor 5:18; Good News Bible).

Learning:

1. Christian sharers will judge themselves with the same criteria as they apply to others, and will get accustomed to using the word "we" in discussions with Muslims.

2. The task of sharing with Muslims does not have its origin in the ethical standards of Jesus' followers, but rather in the work and word of Jesus.

2. Nicholas of Cusa (1401–1464)

Nicholas of Cusa said that a learned man is one who knows he is ignorant. This is a strong statement from one of the most learned individuals of his age. A philosopher and theologian; mathematician, experimental scientist, and physician; influenced by both Neoplatonism and humanism, this German thinker was the Renaissance personified. Yet he found time to be a cardinal, a church statesman, and an advocate of peaceful relations with Muslims. Nicholas was an irenic man, interested in reconciling people. He was not unaffected by the controversial writers of the past, but he followed his own path. As Nicholas was doing his work Constantinople had come under the attack of the Ottoman Muslims, but before it was captured he had completed his startling work, *De Pace Fidei*, a call to religious peace. When Mehmed II took the city in 1453 and renamed it Istanbul, the great Byzantine Empire came to a formal end. It was after that traumatic event that Nicolas wrote his sterner *Cibratio al-Corani*, "The Sieving of the Qur'ān," which reflected Ricoldo de Montecruce's content and approach.

The *De Pace Fidei*, "Concerning the Peace of Faith," is essentially a call to religious unity based on the hope that the correct explanation of Christian teaching would lead to an comprehensive orthodox faith. Thus he opened his work with the prayer: "As Thou art one, may there be one religion and one cult of worship."[62] In doing so Nicholas may have been naive about the power of good explanation, but he had not fallen prey to syncretism. He believed firmly in the truth of the Christian faith, but felt just as strongly that it must be presented to others in a relevant manner. In developing the explanations one must take careful account of the difficulties other religious people have with the Christian faith. The *De Pace Fidei* is an imagined discussion involving a Hindu, a Muslim, a Chaldaean, a Jew, and a Christian. Nicholas knows the differences among them but he wants to emphasize their commonalities in order to lay the foundations for peace. He also held the view that since we are justified by faith in God's promises as Abraham was, we can go a long way in accommodating different rites and ceremonies. The goals of Nicholas were unmistakable: in the short run "peace in our time," and in the long run oneness in Christ.

In moving toward these goals Nicholas had a double-sided approach. On the one hand he knew and believed that intellectual interpretations of difficult truths must be attempted. On the other hand he was also sure that some truths are beyond explanation and can only be experienced. This paradox common to all discussion about the mysteries of God is well illustrated by his treatment of the Trinity. Nicholas takes the view that the Trinity is implicit in the Unity, and the task of the

Christian evangelist is to make it explicit by thoughtful exposition. He himself proceeds along that line, utilizing various familiar analogies from nature and human life. We can see the mathematician at work here as he moves outwardly from the concept of Unity. Undoubtedly some of the great philosopher-mathematicians of Islam would have enjoyed conversing with Nicholas about a subject dear to them. Yet in his own heart of hearts Nicholas believed that the mystical experience of God is more important than discursive explanations about God. God is ineffable, beyond human analogies, and a mystery pointed to in the Name revealed to Moses in the burning bush. Jaroslav Pelikan states that he "spoke of God as transcending all concepts, and the Trinity as transcending all numbers."[63]

Nicholas' second work, the *Cibratio al-Corani*, is more specific to Muslims. The work is a compendium of information on the Christian-Muslim controversy intended for the Pope and his advisors. Although he himself uses Robert of Ketton's translation of the Qur'ān, much of the material is a repetition of Ricoldo de Montecruce's *Confutatio al-Corani* and is therefore more polemical in nature. Nevertheless Nicholas continues to look for points of agreement on which some reconciliation can be based. His treatment of the crucifixion is an example. The Qur'ān, he says, is correct when it claims that the Jews did not crucify Jesus, for it was the Romans who slew him. The Muslim view that such a death would show a divine lack of care for the Messiah is the result of a misunderstanding. The cross actually demonstrates God's triumph—victory for Christ himself in his exaltation and glorification, victory for Christians in their justification and new life, and victory for all humans in the resurrection. J. W. Sweetman suggests that the approach of Nicholas "to seek to win opponents by reconciling affirmations ... in the end must be the method which best commends itself to the Christian evangelist."[64] During his career the Cusan also took up John of Segovia's idea to conduct a great study conference on Islam, a plan that anticipates modern developments, but he was not able to achieve that goal.

Learning:

1. The seeking and finding of commonalities both recognizes reality and provides a basis for friendly communication.

2. The idea that God is greater than our thoughts is important for Christian sharing with Muslims.

3. The search for peace among religious people requires the constant and careful attention of the followers of Jesus.

3. Martin Luther (1483–1546)

Martin Luther may never have met a Muslim personally, but amidst an undiscerning and unmindful church he stood tall, and his strong message still resounds: "Pay heed, and see the Muslims."

Luther's criticism of Islam and Muslims—whom he called "Turks"—is better known than his positive contributions. That criticism is related to his religious and political context. On the religious side he was contending for the recovery of the gospel and its centrality in the life of the church. The papacy and the Turk each in their own way held to the contrary theory of salvation through human merit. Luther often lumped them together, the papacy representing the soul of the anti-Christ, and the Turk its body. On the political side Luther's career was set in the context of the Ottoman invasion of eastern and southern Europe. The Turk was a military foe and Luther was operating in war conditions. In addition to these contextual realities it must be added that Luther was not immune to the continuing influence of the medieval attitudes that were predominantly negative toward Muslims. Finally there was also very limited time and opportunity for Luther to become closely acquainted with Islam.

Against this background it is not surprising that Luther's response to Islam and Muslims is a mixed one. His writings on the subject reveal a considerable knowledge but an incomplete one, and his attitude moves between vehement condemnation and generous concern. What is thoroughly surprising, however, is the extent of that knowledge and the spaciousness of his attitude toward Muslims as people, showing awareness of their spiritual dimensions and needs. C. Umhau Wolf provides a useful summary of Luther's approach:[65]

> Luther's attitude toward Islam was partly characteristic of the unfair polemic atmosphere of the age, but partly in advance of his age with regard to self-judgment and the urging of tolerance. Luther had firsthand knowledge of the Koran, but only a secondhand and inadequate knowledge of other aspects of Islamic and Turkish culture.

In what follows we will examine Luther's positive contributions toward the Christian engagement with Muslims, but before doing so we will consider the dramatic historical context of those contributions.

In the sixteenth century western Europe was locked in a major power struggle between two Catholic rulers whose bitter rivalry lasted 27 years. The first of these was King Francis I of France (d. 1547), a humanist ruler who had some sympathy for the Reformation. The second was the rising star of the Habsburg family, Charles V (d. 1558), before whom Luther appeared at Worms. Charles was ruler of Spain and Emperor of the Holy Roman Empire. There was a third power hovering nearby, however, perhaps the most formidable of the three. He was Suleiman the Magnificent (d. 1566), who controlled a far-flung empire centered at Istanbul, as the Caliph and Sultan of the Ottoman Muslims. The struggle between Charles and Francis brought Suleiman actively into European politics. In 1525 Charles defeated Francis at Pavia in Italy, and imprisoned him for months. Francis conceived a plan. Through an emissary in Istanbul he sent a message to the Muslim leader, basically saying: "Come over and help us." Suleiman was only too happy to oblige. It was an opportunity for him to keep Europe divided, to impede Charles and his ambitions, and to increase his own power and domain. Francis I, in turn, benefitted by obtaining a loyal ally and by receiving special trade concessions called "capitulations."

Up to Suleiman's time Islamic forces had moved into the Balkans only as far as Belgrade, but he now invaded Hungary. Suleiman's forces received a welcome as they captured Budapest in 1526, taking it from the control of the hated Habsburg. Thereafter he twice besieged Vienna (1529; 1532). The city was only about 450 miles from Luther's own residence at Wittenberg, and the first siege was taking place at exactly the same moment as the Marburg Colloquy where the leading reform theologians had gathered. Islam was now becoming an existential reality. The siege was lifted as Luther was traveling from Marburg to Wittenberg, and he rejoiced at the "miracle." It was in this period that he wrote his treatise *On War against the Turk* (1528), and his *Sermon against the Turk* (1529). In these writings he called upon the Emperor to vigorously defend the territory against Suleiman, and appealed to the German people to resist the incursion. He interpreted this activity, however, as an affair of the state and he opposed religious war. Neither then nor later did Luther know how well-disposed Suleiman was toward the Reformation.

Suleiman supported the Protestant movement as part of his overall strategy, but he also had a religious reason for doing so. He regarded it as much closer to Islamic monotheism than the Catholic approach. Suleiman's actions reflected his conviction. In 1533 he gave the large sum of 100,000 gold pieces to Francis to help him form an alliance with German Protestant princes. In 1552 he himself sent a letter to the German princes inviting them to cooperate with himself and Francis against the Emperor and Pope. In the same period he also protected the Calvinists in Hungary and Transylvania, encouraging them to propagate their ideas, and later did the same in Holland. He engaged in treaty discussions with Elizabeth I of England along the same line, granting also the English trade concessions. Without much doubt Suleiman's military and diplomatic initiatives in Europe served to distract and to weaken Catholic opposition to the Reformation. They were in the long run "an important factor in the consolidation of the forces of the Reformation, and their final recognition."[66] In the short run, however, the presence of the Ottomans created a very heated context for the Christian encounter with Islam, and that fact makes Luther's contribution all the more unexpected.

Luther was not aware of all the political complexities that were engulfing Europe, but he was certainly aware of Muslims. He did not ignore Muslims. He looked at them, saw them, and responded. We will deal with four main strands in that response: tolerance toward Muslims and their rights; respect for their commendable qualities and conduct; a knowledgeable opposition to their errors; and the hope for their conversion to the gospel.

Luther's idea of tolerance toward Muslims was combined with a sense of God's judgment upon Christians. Already early in his career he urged tolerance toward the Muslims. "Let the Turk believe and live as he will, just as one lets the papacy and other false Christians live."[67] Related to this view is a specific theological interpretation that Luther entertained. The Turks are not to be hated but rather to be regarded as God's punishment on faithless and erring Christians. In that sense they are "the plague of God" and represent a divine call to repentance. He declared: "To make war against the Turk is nothing else than to strive against God who is punishing our sins by means of the Turk."[68] He later modified his position to approve of fighting in defense of the people.

Luther did not hesitate to commend the fine qualities and good behavior of the Turks. In modern perspective the principle of seeking and seeing good in others does not seem particularly noteworthy, but in the Reformer's day it represented a radical change from the general medieval tradition in regard to Muslims. Luther stated: "Those who only censure and condemn the base and absurd characteristics of the enemy, but remain silent about matters that are honest and worthy of praise, do more harm than good to their cause."[69] Did Luther obtain his information from hearsay, or perhaps from the reading of Ricoldo of Montecruce, or other sources? We do not know, but Luther is glad to know that many traits and customs of the Turks are of high quality, often exceeding Christian behavior in their standard. He warmly asserts: "It is said that the Turks are among themselves faithful and friendly, and careful to tell the truth. I believe and I think that they probably have more fine virtues than that."[70] Luther takes note of and praises the modesty and simplicity of Muslims, and their sincere devotion to fasting, prayers, and assemblies. He also appreciates the noble aspects of Suleiman's temporal rule in comparison with the shameful behavior of some Christian rulers.

Luther's primary criticism of Muslim teaching had to do with the issue of "works righteousness." He uses the discussion of Muslim behavioral standards to remind Christians that the gospel is something else than human achievements. He also hopes that Muslims too will grasp the truth that "the Christian religion is by far something other than good customs and good works."[71] Although he frequently chides the Turks for other theological errors and for wrong practices, there is no doubt that it is the way of salvation that is the watershed issue for Luther. Either humanity is saved by God's action through Christ, or by human action. Luther is sure that it is the former and thus his criticism of both the Turks and the Pope on this issue are virtually the same, and equally outspoken. In his engagement with Islamic thought Luther is turning around the medieval "comparison of values" approach to the essential core of the gospel.

This brings us to the third and perhaps most startling strand in Luther's positive contribution to the task of Christian sharing with Muslims. He was deeply concerned about the pervasive lack of genuine knowledge about Islam and Muslims. In his view the misunderstanding of Muslims and others about the central truth of the gospel is the result of the activity of Satan. Christians must engage in spiritual warfare to overcome the misleading of the devil. To do that knowledge is crucial. You must know what the Turks hold if you are going to refute their errors and bring them to faith. Luther does not appreciate the failure of Christian scholarship in this regard. He says:[72] "To be sure, it has—and often—disquieted me, and still does, that neither our great lords nor our scholars have been at any pains to give us any certain knowledge about the life of the Turks in the two classes, spiritual and temporal." He himself went after information, knew a lot, and wanted others to know.

Three of Luther's writings stand out in his effort to overcome ignorance about Islam. The first was his thoughtful foreword to a treatise entitled *Tract on the Religion and Customs of the Turk* (1530). This booklet was probably written by Georg von Mühlbach, who for twenty years had been a prisoner of the Turks and became a priest in 1498 after his release.[73] The second was his friendly introduction to the German translation of Ricoldo's *Confutatio al-Koran* (1542), a work that we have discussed above. The third was the "Preface" prepared by himself and Philip Melanchton, to the Swiss publication of the Qur'ān (1543). The production of this corpus of Islam-related materials amidst the pressures of the Reformation movement and the tensions of war is nothing short of remarkable. Of quite special interest is the publication of the first European version of the Qur'ān.

It may be recalled that Robert of Ketton's rendering of the Qur'ān into Latin was the jewel in the crown of Peter the Venerable's great translation project in 1141, but the manuscript had lain around in European libraries, virtually ignored. The situation would change now, bringing Luther into action. In Basel, Switzerland, an editor named Thomas Bibliander (d. 1564) and a well-known printer named Oporinus resolved that the time had come to publish Ketton's manuscript. For his pains Bibliander was clapped into prison by the City Council of Basel, and the Qur'ān copies were confiscated and banned. Luther was agitated when the news reached him, and he vigorously upbraided the citizens of Basel. The City Council relented and Thomas issued another edition. This time Luther himself, together with Melanchton, provided the Preface. Luther supported this venture for apologetic reasons. He believed that "once the book of Muhammad has been made public and thoroughly examined in all its parts, all pious persons will more easily comprehend the insanity and wiles of the devil, and will more easily be able to refute them."[74] Whatever the motive, Luther had delivered a stunning signal to the Christian world of his time, and one that still reverberates today.

We move to the final element in Luther's contribution. Although his criticisms of Muslim belief and practice were often couched in language that by today's standard would be considered quite offensive, through the frequent denunciations there appears a genuine desire to reach Muslims personally and to touch them at spiritual levels. His writings are sprinkled with prayers not only for Christian penitence but also for the conversion of Muslims. He knows the obstacles but believes that God may employ extraordinary ways of working through Christians who for some reason are present in Muslim contexts. "So now too God perhaps; will call some to the Turks from their darkness through the Christian captives who have been instructed."[75] Or perhaps, he thought, the very reading of the Qur'ān will help to strengthen oppressed and uninstructed Christians living in Muslim's lands. For "if indeed we do not convert the Turks, let us remain strong in our faith."[76]

Learning:

1. Christians have a vocation to take Islam and Muslims seriously, and to increase in tolerance, appreciation, knowledge, and prayerful concern.

2. Christians must strive to understand Islam theologically, i.e. in terms of the gospel as well as descriptively, and must reckon with the centrality of the gospel in the task of Christian sharing.

3. The period up to and including Luther's age involved the use of hurting language; our modern age involves hurting images. Neither is appropriate in the task of Christian sharing with Muslim friends.

4. Christians engaged with Muslims will benefit from reflecting on Luther's word: "Where man's power departs, God's power enters in."

For the continuation of our learning from the past we turn next to the "later" period that is associated with the modern missionary movement. It covers the span from the post-Reformation era to the present.

Endnotes

1. The current trend of Christians to reduce the use of the word "crusade in Christian programming comes none too soon. What the word jihād does to Christians the word crusade does to Muslims. Language too needs occasional cleansing.

2. The term "apologetics" refers to the reasoned defense of the faith, and the term "polemics" to controversial disputation; the line between the two is easily blurred but needs to be maintained.

3. Norman Daniel, *Islam and the West* (Edinburgh: University Press, 1969), p. 4.

4. Harry G. Dorman, *Toward Understanding Islam* (New York: Columbia University Press, 1948), p. 13, suggests that he was ʿAmr ibn al-ʿĀs, the conqueror of Syria and Egypt; other sources point to ʿAmr ibn Saʿd or ʿUmayr ibn Saʿd, a Muslim governor of Emesa.

5. I am grateful to Mark Swanson for advice in regard to early mss. I have also utilized his translation of M. F. Nau's, "Un Colloque du Patriarche Jean," *Journal Asiatique*, XI, v. 225–279, p. 15.

6. Dorman, *Islam*. p. 13.

7. A. C. McGiffert, *A History of Christian Thought*, Vol. I (New York: Scribners, 1932), pp. 321ff., expresses the view that "the orthodox faith of the eastern church at John's time included no definite doctrine of Christ's saving work. The doctrine of his person had so absorbed the attention of theologians as almost to crowd out all interest in anything else. ... The connection between Christ's person and saving work, which had meant so much to Paul and Irenaeus and Athanasius, was altogether lost sight of by John."

8. Daniel J. Sahas, *John of Damascus on Islam* (London: E. J. Brill, 1978), p. 75.

9. *Ibid.*, p. 76.

10. *Ibid.*, p. 83.

11. Kenneth Cragg, *The Arab Christian* (Louisville: Westminster Press, 1991), p. 80.

12. Dorman, *Islam*, pp. 14ff.

13. Mark Swanson, *Folly to the Hunafāʾ, The Cross of Christ in Arabic Christian-Muslim Controversy in the Eighth and Ninth Centuries A.D.* (Cairo: Pontificium Institutum Studiorum Arabicorum et Islamologiae, 1995), pp. 12f.

14. *Ibid.*, p. 87.

15. Lawrence E. Browne, *The Eclipse of Christianity in Asia*, (New York: Howard Fertig, 1967) p. 116, quoting from Fr. Cheiko's Arabic rescension in *Trois Traits anciens de polemique*, p. 12; Browne, "The Patriarch and Al-Mahdi," MW, Vol. XXI, No. 1 (January 1931), pp. 38–45, argues that the Arabic not the Syriac is the original form of Timothy's Apology. M. Swanson in his dissertation abstracted in *Christian-Muslim Controversy, op. cit.*, suggests that while the debate took place in oral Arabic, Timothy's report was in Syriac which was then translated into Arabic.

16. Browne, *Eclipse*, p. 118, quoting al-Tabarī.

17. *Ibid.*, pp. 112f., quoting Cheiko.

18. Swanson, *Christian-Muslim Controversy*, p. 46.

19. After 1498, Vasco da Gama and the Portuguese disrupted the co-existence, as they imported division and exported pepper; cf. Roland E. Miller, "The Dynamics of Religious Co-existence in Kerala: Muslims, Christians and Hindus," in Y. Y. Haddad and W. Z Haddad, eds., *Christian-Muslim Encounters* (Gainesville: University Press of Florida, 1995), pp. 263–284.

20. Browne, *Eclipse*. p. 68, quoting Cheiko.

21. G. Troupere, "al-Kindī, 'Abd al-Masīh," EI², V, p. 120; this Al-Kindi should not be confused with the Muslim philosopher, Ya'kub ibn Ishaq al-Kindi.

22. Browne, *Eclipse*, p. 65.

23. *Ibid.*, p. 112; cf. Daniel, *Islam*, p. 5.

24. *Al Fisal*, Vol. I, pp. 116 sqq., in J. W. Sweetman, *Isalm and Christianity Theology*, Part II, Vol. I, p. 179.

25. *Ibid.*, p. 60.

26. K. S. Latourette, *A History of the Expansion of Christianity*, Vol. 2, p. 31.

27. James Kritzeck, *Peter the Venerable and Islam* (Princeton: Princeton University Press, 1964), p.14.

28. R. W. Southern, *Western Views of Islam* (Cambridge: Harvard University Press, 1962), p. 67.

29. Kritzeck, *Venerable*, p. 21.

30. Tr. and quoted by Southern, *Western Views*, p. 39.

31. Sweetman, *Islam*, p. 79.

32. Kritzeck, *Venerable*, p. 64, quoting Robert's preface to his Qur'ān tr.

33. Sweetman, *Islam*, p. 72.

34. Fr. G. Bassetti-Sani, "Muhammad and St. Francis," MW, Vol. XLVI, No. 4 (October 1956), p. 346.

35. *Ibid.*

36. Steven Runciman, *A History of the Crusades*, Vol. III (Cambridge: Cambridge University Press, 1987), p. 160. For the influence of this experience on Francis' instruction to his followers (Ch. 16, Earlier Rule) to go "among the Saracens and other nonbelievers," cf. J. Hoeberichts, *Francis and Islam* (Quincy: Quincy University, 1997).

37. K. S. Latourette, *A History of Christianity*, Vol. I (New York: Harper & Row, 1975), p. 432.

38. Daniel, *Islam*, p. 117.

39. Bassetti-Sani, "St. Francis," p. 353.

40. Daniel, *Isalm*, p. 117.

41. Bassetti-Sani, "St. Francis," p. 353.

42. Quoted in John Baillie, *A Diary of Readings* (London: Oxford University Press, 1955), p. 27.

43. *Blanquerna*, tr. from the Catalan by E. Alison Peers (London: Jarrolds, 1926), #224, p. 445.

44. *Ibid.*, #61/62, p. 420.

45. *Ibid.*, #321, p. 461.

46. *Ibid.*, #135, p. 431.

47. *Ibid.*, #346, p. 465.

48. *Ibid.*, #361, p. 467.

49. *Book of Contemplation*, p. 112, in Sweetman, *Islam*, p. 113; cf. pp. 96–115 for Lull's apologetic. See Eric de Bruyn, "Ramon Lull's Methods of Engagement with Muslims, with Special Reference to his Art," M. A. Thesis, 1999, Luther Seminary, St. Paul, MN, USA, for a current bibliography on Lull.

50. E. Alison Peers, *Fool of Love* (London: SCM Press Ltd., 1946), p. 67; I have drawn freely from this summary of the author's *Ramon Lull, A Biography* (London: S.P.C.K., 1929).

51. *Blanquerna*, Peers, #223, p. 461.

52. Peers, *Fool of Love*, p. 86.

53. *Blanquerna*, Peers, #235, p. 447.

54. A. A. Duri, "Baghdad," *EI²*, p. 904; Will Durant, *The Age of Faith* (New York: Simon & Schuster, 1950), p. 340, follows Muslim sources and puts the figure between 800,000 and two million.

55. Southern, *Western Views*, p. 62.

56. Daniel, *Islam*, p. 237.

57. Sweetman, *Islam*, p. 157.

58. Daniel, *Islam*, p. 196.

59. Sweetman, *Islam*, pp. 115–159, provides an extended summary of this work.

60. *Ibid.*, p. 159.

61. Southern, *Western Views*, p. 80, quoting Wycliffe's Dialogues.

62. Sweetman, *Islam*, p. 171.

63. Jaroslav Pelikan, *The Christian Tradition*, Vol. IV (Chicago: University of Chicago Press, 1984), p. 67.

64. Sweetman, *Islam*, p. 160.

65. C. Umhau Wolf, "Luther and Mohammedanism," *MW*, Vol. XXXI, No. 2 (April 1941), pp. 176f.

66. P. M. Holt, A. K. S. Lambton, and Bernard Lewis, *The Cambridge History of Islam. The Central Lands from Pre-Islamic Times to the First World War* (Cambridge: Cambridge University Press, 1970), p. 329; the quotation refers to the 1521–1555 period. *CHI* is our primary source for these events.

67. Wolf, "Luther," p. 163; quoting *On War against the Turks*.

68. *Ibid.*, p. 162; quoting *In Defense of the Articles of Dr. Martin Luther*.

69. Sara Henrich and James L. Boyce, tr. and ed., "Martin Luther—Translations of Two Prefaces on Islam," *Word & World, Special Edition on Islam*, Vol. XVI, No. 2 (Spring 1996), "Preface to Tract," p. 258. This work provides a basic resource for Luther and Islam, together with Wolf, *op. cit.*, pp. 161–177, and Gottfried Simon, "Luther's Attitude toward Islam," *MW*, Vol. XXI, Nov. 3 (1921), pp. 257–162. Luther's Works remain the primary source. Cf. American Edition, 1955ff.

70. Wolf, "Luther," p. 174; quoting *On War against the Turks*.

71. Henrich and Boyce, "Preface to Tract," *Word & World*, p. 259.

72. Wolf, "Luther," pp. 161f.; quoting *On War against the Turks*.

73. Henrich and Boyce, "Martin Luther," *Word & World*, note 20, p. 258.

74. *Ibid.*, "Preface to Qur'ān," p. 263.

75. *Ibid.*

76. Quoted by Simon, "Luther's Attitude," *op. cit.*, p. 261. Luther was connected with Islam in another way in 1529; commissioned by Johannes Cochlaeus, Hans Brosamer created a critical Catholic woodcut of Luther with seven heads, one of which was wearing a turban (!); reproduction in *Frankfurter Zeitung*, English ed., October 31, 2001, p. 8.

10

More Bridges of Learning: Henry Martyn to the Unnamed Servant

Our pursuit of learning from the past takes us now to the later period of the Christian engagement with Muslims, from post-Reformation times to modern days. We continue the search by considering selected individuals whose service took place in this tumultuous period of rapid change. Henry Martyn was born in 1781, and during the two centuries since then the world saw revolutionary development, and the church experienced dynamic change. The Muslim world too was caught up in events, and in its own way suffered the strains of the developments and built on the new possibilities.

The Reformation was a definitive movement in civilization as well as in the history of the Christian faith. It led into developments that directly influenced the Christian engagement with Muslims, including the Enlightenment in western thought, the Industrial Revolution that concentrated power, and the colonial expansion of the West. These were accompanied by such churchly developments as the rise of the modern mission era, followed by a surge of awareness of ecumenical and national church realities. After World War II a series of paradoxes have evolved bringing new configurations in global society. Economic globalization and political internationalism contend with the rise of culture-based nations and ethnic self-expression. On the one hand there are strong movements to human solidarity, marked by the acceptance of common human rights. On the other hand, individuals and local traditions demand affirmation and mutual respect. The religious development has its own paradoxes. The late twentieth century re-emergence of a confident Islam came at a time when the western church was weakened by secularization and uncertainty, and the statistical center of gravity of the global church had shifted nearer to the heartlands of Islam. The movement of peoples and the upsurge of information technology added to the bewildering context of what some called a post-modern age.

Christian communication with Muslims took place within these complexities, but did not itself experience change in the same radical sense. As we seek learning from the past we cannot identify watershed moments that decisively altered what had gone on before—either the birth of a sudden conviction in the church or a memorable turn to a new direction. As we saw in the early period Peter the Venerable signaled to the church in a militant age—"not by force of arms but by works of love"—but not many were attentive. Martin Luther urged the church to take Islam seriously, but that call is still to be fully heeded. It is therefore wiser to think of the development of Christian communication with Muslims as a series of shifts. The shifts become more visible and cumulatively more significant in the later period that we will be discussing in this chapter. What are those shifts? In summary, we can identify at least the following elements:

—In connection with the expanding activity of the church there was more missional contact with Muslims, although the church as a whole remained relatively remote from the engagement.

—There were a set of pioneers who were determined that the gospel reach Muslims, and their determination became an inspiring force for others.

—There was a partial movement away from the controversial style of approach to a relational mode in witness.

—Dialogue emerged as a prominent function in Christian-Muslim relations.

—There was a recurring need to deal with the negative influence of religious extremism, and for Christians to live and work within the contexts created by it.

The list of those who led the way in sharing with Muslims in the later period cannot be fully compiled, for it must include individuals from every corner of the world, many of whom are hardly known. Only on the last day will God reveal their names and their works. It is perilous therefore to attempt to identify representative figures. We will limit ourselves to the consideration of a few selected individuals who illustrate facets of change in approach, and from whom obvious learning may be drawn.

The chapter has four sections. It first provides a brief sketch of the relatively barren period between Luther and Martyn, about 250 years. The second section deals with six well-known and impressive missionary figures whose names are familiar in the story of the church's outreach to Muslims. Following that in the third section we examine a typical example of less well-known missioners who constitute the majority of those involved in intentional engagement with Muslims. In the final section we turn to "the admirable anonymous," a term we use to describe the unnamed and "ordinary" laity and pastors of the church in the world who are "extraordinary" in their everyday relations with Muslims and in their sincere witness in word and deed. It is in the empowerment of this category of Christian sharers that the future of the enterprise is held.

A. The Interim from Luther to Martyn

In the eastern area of the church there was a continuity of experience in Christian-Muslim relations, and there was no perceptible change of views in this interim period of two and one half centuries. A hope for something better was often expressed, but the attitude of Orthodox Christians at formal levels was at best a cautious one. The sad events of the past could not be easily forgotten, and tensions continued. In our contemporary times the power of negative memory was starkly underlined in the Balkan events of the first years of the twenty-first century, involving Serbs, Croats, and Bosnians. The same phenomenon marked Christian relations with Muslims in the east and near east, and the changes in the western church barely affected its course. As Pelikan indicates,[1] into the 1700s polemists still pointed to the Muslim methodology of conquest as the sign of Islam's inherent falseness, but when necessity or opportunity arose Christian militance was unabashed. In the decade after 1743 Queen Elizabeth of Russia (d. 1761) levied severe sanctions on the Muslims of Tatarstan, partly in reprisal for a revolt. Out of 536 mosques in the district of Kazan 418 were destroyed, and conversions ran into the several thousands.[2] The forcible Christianization reflected an ongoing attitude remote from a friendship-based missional outreach. The shift in approach would have to come from elsewhere. Would it be from Protestantism?

The fact stands, however, that for several decades after Luther there was no significant Protestant follow-up to his pioneering interest in Islam and Muslims. It was a follower of John Hus who is the first known Protestant witness.[3] Vaclev Bodovec z Budova (d. 1621) was a Bohemian nobleman and diplomat in the service of the Habsburg Emperor Rudolf II. In his diplomatic capacity he was at the court of Sultan 'Abd al-Hamīd I in Istanbul from 1577–1581, where he also engaged in personal evangelism and prepared an apologetic work. This learned and devoted Christian who was in contact with many religious leaders of his day was unfortunately martyred by other Christians (!) in the rigorous persecution of Bohemian Protestants. Vaclev was an exception. It was not until Pietism brought its warmth and vigor to the church a full century later that the idea of mission became prominent. Even then, it was still a struggle, and the first Protestant missionaries, Bartholomew Ziegenbalg and Henry Plutschau, depended on the good will of King Frederick IV of Denmark for entry into India in 1706. Fifty years later the mission concern finally began to embrace Muslims. John Henry Callenburg (d. 1760), a Pietist professor at Halle in Germany, became interested in communication with Muslims. He studied Arabic, Persian, and Turkish, translating part of the New Testament into Arabic, as well as Thomas a Kempis' *Imitation of Christ* and Luther's *Small Catechism*.[4] It was the Moravians in the little village of Herrnhut in Saxony who adopted a world view and were apparently the first Protestants to actually send out an assigned missionary to work among Muslims. He was Frederick Hocker, who served in Egypt 1752–1769. The action took place more than two centuries after Luther's death.

In the period between the Reformation and modern times it was the Jesuits who were more intent on undertaking mission work related to Muslims.[5] The most prominent moment in their effort came about in India, as the result of the interest of the Mughul Emperor of India, Akbar the Great (d. 1605). The Emperor was an astonishing personality, playing a major role in both Islamic and Indian history. He was personally a seeker after enlightenment, and he encouraged a rapprochement between Muslims and Hindus. He even set up his own short-lived syncretic religious movement that he named *dīn-ilāhi* ("the religion of God"). In this light it is not a total surprise that Akbar invited the Jesuits at Goa, in 1579, to send missionary representatives to his presence. Between 1580 and 1605 three such visitations were made by the Jesuits. Their centerpiece was the conduct of debates in the court, which followed a predictable style and were inconclusive. Akbar, however, also allowed the Jesuits the freedom to preach publicly, issued an order permitting his subjects to accept the Christian faith, and even extended financial assistance to the missionaries. He himself remained aloof from the Christian invitation, and in its visible results the Jesuit effort was limited to some converts from the lower classes. Emperor Jehangir (d. 1627), Akbar the Great's successor, was also favorably inclined toward discussions with Christians, but after his death this initiative became a casualty of the Mughul-Portuguese wars and the papal displeasure with the Jesuits.[6]

A stronger wave of concern for Muslims was needed than that represented by these noble but sporadic expressions. That came with what Kenneth Scott Lattourette has called "the Great Century" of mission. An aspect of its dawning was the awareness that there had been no substantial, ongoing engagement with Muslims for literally hundreds of years. A series of groundbreaking individuals began to turn their attention to Muslims and to reach out to them in a new way. We turn next to that development.

B. Six Inspired and Inspiring Figures

We will deal briefly with the following six well-known and impressive figures: Henry Martyn, Charles de Foucald, Samuel Zwemer, Lilias Trotter, Constance Padwick, and L. Bevan Jones. At the conclusion of each we will suggest a three-word phrase that attempts to gather up the genius of the individual and an element that should inspire those who "follow in their train." These individuals are exemplary, and others among the rich host of dedicated interpreters of the gospel could be chosen with equal justification.[7]

I. Henry Martyn (1781–1812)

"Weak in body, gifted in mind, strong in spirit"[8] are words that aptly describe the personal qualities of Henry Martyn. Others might prefer the frequently applied functional description: "The pioneer Protestant missionary to Muslims." Constance Padwick chose the phrase "Confessor of the Faith" as the subtitle of her study of Martyn.[9] The descriptions meet together like streams each carrying some of the truth about this dedicated young Englishman whose life continues to be a reminder to Christians of an unfulfilled obligation. As his primary biographer,

George Smith, puts it: "Henry Martyn is first of all a spiritual force," and "his death became a summons."[10]

The phrase "weak in body" refers to the fact that Henry Martyn suffered from tuberculosis as a child, and the disease eventually killed him at the early age of 31. "Gifted in mind" points to his brilliant and prizewinning academic career, especially in languages, at Cambridge University. The ability enabled him to achieve a great deal in a short time with a high scholarly standard. "Strong in spirit" relates to a profound religious experience that drove him to offer himself for missionary service in India. His sister Sally, who had contact with Wesleyan teaching, and his Cambridge evangelical mentor, Charles Simeon, were powerful influences in that development. His university colleagues were shocked at the idea that someone of Martyn's potential would want to be a missionary, and they attempted to dissuade him. His love for Lydia Grenfell whom he hoped to marry also held him back. Nevertheless he persevered, choosing the role of chaplain in the British East India Company, a position that provided enough income to help him support his sister.

After a long sea journey Martyn landed in Calcutta in 1806 where he was met by the famed William Carey, and the two took "sweet counsel" together. On arrival Martyn spoke the words for which he later became well-known: "Now let me burn out for God." He worked at Patna and Cawnpore—preaching, establishing a school, and doing literary work. His initial interest had been in Hindus, but his heart soon inclined toward Muslims. In terms of approach, he had one foot in the controversial style of the past although he recognized its limitations, and the other foot in an emphasis on personal relations. He was derisively named "the black clergyman" by his colonial peers because he moved so freely and intimately with Indians.

Martyn loved literary work with a special intensity, and he was skilled at it. His mind became preoccupied with the plan to translate the New Testament into Urdu and to improve its Persian and Arabic translations. With the help of Nathaniel Sabat, a Muslim convert, he completed the Urdu translation in 1810. His illness had now advanced, however, and he wondered how he could attain his goals. His next priority was the translation of the Persian New Testament and Psalms, and he felt that for that purpose a visit to Persia would be helpful, and its climate might be beneficial. At the back of his mind dwelt the desire to somehow reach home again so that he might marry his Lydia. Traveling via Arabia he spent a year in Persia where he did the work of an evangelist, participated in debates, wrote his scholarly Controversial Tracts, and by 1812 completed his New Testament translation that was later published in St. Petersburg and Calcutta. A dying man he now turned his face to the arduous 1300-mile long overland journey from Tabriz to London, but he was overcome and expired on the way.

Those who worked with Henry Martyn were much taken with his engaging personality and commented on the special symmetry of his qualities. An India colleague (D. Corrie) said of him: "A more perfect character I have never met with," while another (T. Thomason) wrote: "He shines in all the dignity of love."[11] He enjoyed music and poetry, playing, and laughing with children. On his journey home he noticed nature's display of magnificence, moon and nightingale, water tortoises, and gardens. His spiritual dimension was central to his personality. "True happiness," he had said, "does not consist in the glorifying of self ... but in conformity with God."[12] Martyn's own journals reveal his faith and dedication, as well as his unusual courage. On the one hand, he was very sin-conscious, wondering whether God allowed his illness to keep him from becoming overconfident. On the other hand, he had an almost mystical sense of nearness to God. This is clear from the poignant passages of his last painful journey. He placed his trust in God: "Yet my soul rests in him who is the anchor of my soul, sure and steadfast, which though not seen keeps me fast."[13] He longed to be with Christ. Ten days before his death he wrote: "I sat in the orchard and thought with sweet comfort and peace, of my God; in solitude—my company, my friend and comforter. O! when shall time give place to eternity!"[14]

In his engagement with Muslims two of Henry Martyn's characteristics stand out, his Christ-centeredness and his boldness. Two learned men who met him on his travels in Persia asked him: "What are the principles of your religion?" With faith and acumen he replied, "They are all centered in Jesus; not in his precepts, but in himself." [15] It was clear that Martyn was not going to compare laws with laws but rather he was intent on elevating Christ. His boldness is evident in the dramatic events of June 12, 1812, when he left Shiraz for Isfahan, hoping to present his translation of the New Testament to the Shah himself. Instead he was brought into the camp of the Wazir (chief minister) and was confronted with a clamorous verbal attack. When the Wazir advised him to recite the *shahāda* (Muslim confession) in order to save himself, Martyn gave his testimony in these words: "There is no god but God, and Jesus is the Son of God." The agitated listeners cried: "He (God) is neither born nor begets!" Martyn records that they rose up "as if they would have torn me to pieces." It may be that his reputation as a man of God helped to save him from harm. Miraculously he was able to wrap up his translations in a towel and withdraw from the attackers. He says:[16]

> Thus I walked away alone to my tent to pass the rest of the day in heat and dirt. What have I done, thought I, to meet all this scorn? Nothing, I trust, but bearing testimony to Jesus. I thought over these things in prayer, and my troubled heart found the peace which Christ hath promised his disciple.

His personal focus and deeply earnest desire that Muslims experience the joy of salvation in Christ helped to sustain him. Muhammad Rahim was a young Persian mulla who came to Martyn as he was leaving Shiraz to tell him that he had been convinced by Martyn's witness. To him Martyn gave a copy of his Persian New Testament, inscribing on the flyleaf the words: "There is joy in heaven over one sinner that repenteth."[17]

On his homeward journey Henry Martyn was helped by Armenian Christians as he made his way over the often dangerous roads. The latter also provided him with a guide named Hasan. A furious horseman the guide took his sick companion on a merciless pace across Anatolia. Exhausted and virtually alone he died at Tokat, Turkey, October 16, 1812, where he was buried by local Armenian faithful. Later, standing before his portrait painted at Cambridge his mentor, Charles Simeon, declared to his students what in his opinion the image conveyed: "Be serious, be in earnest; don't trifle, don't trifle!"[18]

Learning: selfless, courageous commitment

2. Charles de Foucauld (1858–1916)

1) selfless
2) commitment

Like Henry Martyn, Charles de Foucauld was a bridge figure. In his case he had one foot in the colonial tradition and the other in the spirit of identifying servanthood.

The need to intentionally engage with Muslims in North Africa had been led by Cardinal Charles Lavigerie (d. 1892) who had established the order of White Fathers (so named for their dress) to carry out the task. Lavigerie viewed the effort through the lens of a colonial ideal—as a combined work of civilizing and Christianizing. It was Charles de Foucauld who became the symbol of a new way that was really the old way of Francis of Assisi, the path of servant love taught by Jesus the Master.

No one would have guessed that de Foucauld would become such a symbol. The Vicomte Foucald was an aristocrat, very much inclined to riotous living, and a religious skeptic. His first life change occurred when he became an army officer in Algeria where he displayed much bravery. The second development came when he left the army and, disguised as a Jewish rabbi, became a pioneering explorer in Morocco. It was his third change, however, that was the most dramatic. As Henry Martyn did, so also de Foucauld had a profound religious experience and became a convinced Christian believer. On a visit to Nazareth he decided to enlist as a monk, joined the Trappists, and took ordination as a priest. He committed himself to a life of penitence, prayer, and adoration—the spiritual practices that he considered basic for ministry among Muslims. After three years in Palestine, in 1901 he returned to the Sahara. At his first interior base, Beni Abbes, he undertook a five-year period of service to the poor and sick, and then commenced an arduous journey across the searing sands to the foothills of the Hoggar mountains in the deep south of Algeria. There he made his solitary home among the Tuareg people. The Tuaregs were a Berber-speaking nomadic tribe who had been Islamicized in the fifteenth century but continued many of their indigenous customs. In de Foucald's time they were noted for their fierce pillaging. As far as is known the people had not been touched by the gospel since early Christian days.[19] There at Tamanrasset Charles de Foucald set up his mission station, a very small and narrow building that he divided into two parts, a tiny chapel and equally tiny living quarters. He called it "Fraternity," and from this simple base became "the friend of everybody."[20]

Above de Foucald's table were inscribed two mottos: "To live this day as though I were to be martyred before the evening comes," and "to be all things to all men that I might win all men for Jesus."[21] As his primary service he chose to address elemental human needs, although he also translated the Gospels, prepared a dialectical dictionary, and collected local proverbs. His attitude was marked by a combination of naturalness and brotherhood. Here was no grand "strategy" but only the artless simplicity of joyful and helpful faith in the context of shared living.

A French doctor who later joined him inquired of de Foucauld: "How do I reach the Tuaregs?" Fr. Charles replied:[22]

> You must not be shocked by anything. Be human, merciful and always happy. You must laugh all the time, even when they say the most commonplace things. As you see, I am always laughing; and showing my bad teeth. People come closer to one another when they laugh, they understand one another better.

Two people had come to the Christian faith before he died, a freed slave named 'Abd Jesu and a blind woman, Maria. He had once written: "I am no apostle. I am not a sower—all I do is break up the ground a little; others will come and sow, and others again will reap."[23] Caught up in a Tuareg rebellion that was a product of World War I politics, de Foucauld was dragged out of his hut, bound, and shot to death. His life reflected the hope that he had once expressed in his diary: "My desire is to do my upmost for the salvation of the people of this land, and that in utter forgetfulness of myself."[24]

Learning: incarnational servant love *Servant love*

Apostle to Islam 3. Samuel M. Zwemer (1867–1952)

One of Samuel Zwemer's favorite words was boldness, and he engaged Muslims with knowledge, directness, and courage. The very boldness seemed to be appreciated, and he had many Muslim friends. He traveled everywhere, challenging Christian believers and linking Christian workers, serving as a kind of personal Internet on behalf of the apostolic mission in the Muslim world. Moreover, with an energetic zeal expressed both in writing and in platform rhetoric he excited young people, especially youth in North America, with his powerful call to missionary service."[25] John A. MacKay said of him: "Not since the days of Ramon Lull ... has any Christian missionary taken more truly to his heart the whole Muslim world, in the complexity of its spiritual problem and the range of its geographical discussion."[26] It is in that light that his biographer designated him "Apostle to Islam."[27] In farewell remarks a longtime colleague, Edwin Calverley, used phrases such as the following to describe Zwemer: "valiant evangelist," "pioneer and leader," "strong faith," "zeal and devotion," "mentally alert," and "tremendous energy."[28] Stubbornness and impetuosity may also be included in the attributes that marked his strenuous efforts. These were leavened by a strong sense of humor.[29]

Samuel Zwemer was an active Christian from his youth in Michigan, USA. As a college student he was moved by Robert Wilder, founder of the Student Volunteer Movement, to which he later dedicated personal service. His early interest in missions matured during his studies at a Reformed Church seminary in New Brunswick, New Jersey, where he also developed a taste for conservative theology, Biblical studies, and medicine. Along with his close friend, James Cantine, he was inspired by a teacher, John Lansing, and chose Arabia as his field of interest. When their church could not afford to support their initiatives, the two determined pioneers set out on their own in the direction of the Near East.

After language study and a two-year period in Basra Zwemer settled in Bahrein. In 1896 in Baghdad he married an Australian nurse, Amy Wilkes, and together they made up a formidable team. The difficult climate (two daughters died) and religious opposition each in their own way wore them down, but they consoled themselves with the thought: "The harvest is the end of the world, and the reapers are the angels."[30] Zwemer's penchant for travel was not easy on his family, but in this he would not be denied. He equally loved conversation with Muslims and distributing tracts, many of which he wrote himself. An indefatigable and creative evangelist he was one of the main contributors to the establishment of the Arabian Mission on the Gulf. His ministry took another direction, however, when in 1905 he accepted the joint position of Field Secretary for the Reformed Board of Foreign Missions and Traveling Secretary for the Student Volunteer Movement.

This appointment ushered in Zwemer's lifelong recruiting and organizing ministries. He was involved with the first general conference of Protestant missionaries among Muslims, held in Cairo in 1906, and he played a leading role in the seminal World Mission Conference at Edinburgh in 1910. He was also the engine behind the second general conference of missionaries at Lucknow in 1911. At Cairo a quarterly magazine had been proposed as a forum for information and ideas, and Edinburgh had endorsed the suggestion. Thus in 1911 the influential journal, *Moslem World*, was born. This mission-oriented journal that Zwemer edited for 36 years became an important vehicle for both scholarly and inspirational writings. In 1912 Zwemer moved to Cairo which became the hub of his many activities including frequent networking journeys to North Africa, Iran, India, and Indonesia as well as within Europe and America. The purpose of the visitations was encouraging missionaries and workers, gathering information, lecturing on Islam, arousing churches to an interest in Muslims, and exciting youth to become involved in the missional task. Late in the 1920s Zwemer assumed the Chair of History of Religion and Christian Missions at Princeton Theological Seminary where he was known for his lively teaching, retiring in 1939. To the end of his life he passionately and persistently called upon Christians to remember Muslims, and his infectious and visionary faith influenced not only his direct hearers, but generations to come.

Samuel Zwemer's voluminous writings were not the least of his contributions. They numbered fifty books and many articles and pamphlets. He had an acquisitive as well as an inventive mind, and did firsthand research. He was himself widely read, and he quoted extensively from other sources in his writings. His interests were as much on popular Islam as they were in classical thought. As to the latter he particularly appreciated Al-Ghazālī, using his "Ninety-Nine Beautiful Names of God" to teach missionaries. He also wrote on such subjects as Qur'ān translations, the Hadīth Qudsi, Mecca and Medina, the Muslim clergy and pulpit, the qibla, the "unlettered" Prophet, Adam, Hagar, the Muslim calendar, Muslim catechisms, and the law of apostasy. He had a special interest, however, in non-traditional Muslim customs and reported on saints, sacrifice, animism, the rosary, initiation ceremonies, and other topics. While his scholarship was relatively objective, his overall purpose was clearly evangelistic. He wanted to direct Muslims to Jesus. In an editorial he once asked, "What is the one aim of missions? He answered it with pointed and pointing words of John the Baptist: "Behold the Lamb of God that takes away the sins of the world!" These were the closing words in the *Ars Magna* of Ramon Lull with whom Zwemer felt a close affinity.[31]

This basic unwavering conviction is consistent through the methodological progression of Zwemer's thought. His earlier writings and speeches were indeed "flaming," but later they became more measured. His nature was to be forthright, and he had great agility in dealing with hard questions. He also believed that the attitude of the pioneers who prepared controversial literature has often been misrepresented by critics. These pioneers "wet their pages with their tears and agonized in love for souls." But he agreed with the Literature for Muslims Committee in India that in 1935 issued the following significant decision:[32]

> In view of the undesirability of circulating literature which contains attacks on the Muslim prophet, Muhammad, it was voted to ... consider the immediate suspension of the sale of such literature; also the C.L.M.C. adopts as a guiding principle for the future, that it will not recommend grants for the publication of any book or tract which falls in this category. ... The delightful positiveness of the Gospel and the attractiveness of the Lord Jesus Christ provide ample material upon which to work, without unduly pursuing lines of negative criticism.

Samuel Zwemer himself declared: "I am convinced that the nearest way to the Muslim heart is the way of love, the way of the cross."[33] It is not methodology, but the path of the cross and trust in God's promise that matters. With that conviction he combined a confidence in prayer that he referred to as a taking hold of God. He declared: "By claiming such exceeding great and precious promises we become partakers of the Divine Nature in a love that will not let go. ... Our spiritual dynamic is in direct proportion to our fearless, unflinching faith that God is able to perform what He has promised and that He will."[34]

In a comment added to a review of J. Christy Wilson's biography of Zwemer, Kenneth Cragg puts forward the fundamental question that arises from the stirring career of this mission leader: [35]

> How shall we discharge in our time the basic convictions which made him what he was? Clearly in many particulars the days are new and different. But the convictions remain. Zwemer lived and died for the twin belief that Christ must somehow be mediated to Islam and that Islam constitutes a supreme call to Christian devotion, patience and resolve in that glorious obligation. ... Where is the succession and how should it be fulfilled through loyalty and under change? An apostle to Islam is at rest: the apostolate remains.

Learning: bold visionary faith

4. l. Lilias Trotter (1853–1928)

At the time that the writer was serving as a Literature Secretary for the National Christian Council in India we looked about for literary materials that excelled in terms of their sensitive understanding of Muslim culture and emotion. It was no contest. The story parables of Lilias Trotter stood out in a special way, and their transfer from Algeria to India was made with little cultural dissonance, a tribute to her deep awareness of fundamental Muslim categories. In her remarkable forty-year career in Algeria Isabella Lilias Trotter had a near-mystical rapport with Muslims. Along with that she had an inner strength that many attributed to her joy in the Lord. It sustained her and encouraged her amidst the special difficulties that were inevitable for single women in her chosen milieu. The fact that she was there at all was the first in a series of "miracles."

During her upperclass English childhood Lilias Trotter developed a personal and loving relationship with God that was "fed by a hidden life of prayer, for which time had been snatched when most of the family supposed her to be making doll clothes."[36] Inspired by the evangelists Moody and Hankey, at a young age she undertook a ministry among prostitutes on the streets of London. This reflected her practical desire to be up and doing, but there were two other major factors in her personality. She had great artistic gifts and was taught by the famed John Ruskin who wanted her to take up the career of an artist. The other aspect was a reflective spirit that issued in deep spiritual insights and a life of prayer. At times the combination of practical-artistic-reflective within her caused turbulence in her emotions, but they all found an outlet and a kind of synthesis in her life of service among Muslims in North Africa. The educated and comfortably situated Lilias responded to a call to service in that field, issued by a mission society spokesman. She ignored the problem of frailty in health that affected her throughout her life, even ignoring the fact that mission societies themselves for health reasons declined her offer to serve. "He is calling me," she decided, and in that conviction chose lifelong ministry in Algeria over a career as an artist.

Trotter's enthusiasm also deeply affected two other women, Blanche Haworth and Katie Stuart, and together the three women formed the Algiers Mission Band. Although technically ill-prepared, with faith and optimism they arrived in Algiers in 1888, and after many trials and years of effort they succeeded in establishing fifteen mission stations. Lilias Trotter is best known for her literary ministry, and she utilized her artistic talent in illustrating her own works, but even more significant was the personal impact she had on the populace. People called her Lili, regarded her as their friend, and welcomed her into their midst as "she passed up and down the wide lands of Algeria and Tunisia, a figure of intrepid courage and "a pure flame of love."[37] Constance Padwick, who journeyed with her, writes: "Her eye would kindle at the sight of a map or camping outfit, and she had the born traveler's sense of direction and of the salient points of any route or landscape."[38] But the map was more than a challenge to adventure. She called it her "manual of intercession,"[39] and she was steady in lifting up prayers on behalf of the people she met.

Trotter's impact was felt by the Sufi mystics who seemed to recognize in her a kindred spirit, and she was invited to their convents (zawiyas) for spiritual discussions. While she responded to this unusual opportunity there is no doubt that her deepest concern was for Muslim women. She loved them and desired for them the experience of the Samaritan woman whose life was changed when she met Jesus.

Trotter struggled in her spirit with the issue of "small returns," recognizing that it was not until they reached death's door that some women could utter words like "Jesus has all my heart." These struggles were the womb that produced her beautiful statements of spiritual confidence that continue to be uplifting today.

Lilias Trotter brought much to the Christian engagement with Muslims—the element of selfless determination; the lifting up of the role of Christian women in mission service; an almost agonized concern for converts who frequently did not survive their persecution; a stream of thoughtful interpretations of the missional task; and a body of literature for outreach to Muslims. But amidst the abundance of contributions two things stand out—her closeness to God and her spirit of hope. Trotter believed that communication with Muslims in the first place requires a personal living in the presence of God, and the seeking of God's will. To place God's glory first in life is for her the key, the empowering principle. She stated: "One is beginning to see that a sight of what will make for His glory in anything is all that one needs. Once one sees that, one can make straight for it, as it were, in His Name, across the heads of probabilities and possibilities, in the most absolute simplicity."[40] This, in turn, means to be aware that Christ's strength becomes visible in and through our weakness. She declared:[41]

> I am seeing more and more that we begin to learn what it is to walk by faith, when we learn to spread out all that is against us, all our physical weakness, loss of mental power, spiritual inability, all that is against us inwardly and outwardly, as sails to the wind, and expect these things to be vehicles for the power of Christ to rest upon us.

Along with that emphasis, and flowing from it, was Trotter's hope. She could very well be described as "the Lady of Hope." The roses will bloom in the desert, she affirmed. One must believe that God will respond to prayer and will pour water on the dry ground. Her following well-known comment is germane:[42]

> We engaged in Muslim work, live in a land of blighted promises—that is a fact that those who love its people best cannot deny; and the deadly heartsickness of hope deferred makes even the most optimistic among us almost despair of seeing abiding fruitage to the work. ... But we hear the sound of water ... distant it may be, and only discerned in a God-given stillness. But once we have heard it and know what it means, a new courage takes possession of us; life can never be the same again.

Her interpretation of the miraculous is interesting and helpful. "Difficulty," she said, "is the very atmosphere of miracle. It is miracle in its first stage. If it is to be a great miracle, the condition is not difficulty but impossibility."[43] The great miracles too will come, but we must await God's time.

> I am full of hope that when God delays in fulfilling our little thoughts, it is to leave Himself room to work out His great ones. And more and more as time goes on I feel that the longer He waits the more we can expect. ... It has been dawning on me more and more that God ... is certainly here and now doing a far greater work than He can as yet let appear on the surface.[44]

Therfore one can in confidence say: "There is a sense of dawn all around. I do not know that outsiders will recognize it; it needs eyes accustomed to the darkness to recognize the first streaks of the dawn."[45]

Like a soft glow Lilias Trotter's words shed a light of their own on the task of Christian sharing with Muslims.

Learning: stalwart prayerful hope

5. Constance E. Padwick (1886–1968)

Constance Padwick and Christian literature are virtually synonymous, but much more needs to be said. Padwick combined scholarship and love, and she wrote about Muslims and for Muslims with a deep sensitivity that reflects a life-long engagement with Muslim friends. Imagine a bustling figure haunting the marketplaces and the bookshops of the Middle Eastern world, seeking prayer manuals and devotional materials. She was driven to understand Sufi spirituality, and the materials that she gathered became the basis for her magnum opus, *Muslim Devotions*, which is far and away the best work ever to appear on that subject, an achievement representing nearly forty years of effort.[46] That, however, was only the most visible of the many accomplishments of this missionary who served as a "Prime Link" for those who loved Muslims.

Constance Padwick grew up in the English countryside, and developed there her love for flowers that later resulted in the production of a flower index for the Royal Historical Society. In addition to studying Greek and pedagogy she became active in the Student Christian Movement, and served as an editor in the Youth Department of the Church Missionary Society. Padwick also suffered from health problems, but she was determined to become a missionary herself. Inspired by W. H. Temple Gairdner of Cairo she studied Arabic at the University of London and then served under the Church Missionary Society in Egypt and Palestine for almost thirty years, and for nearly another decade in the Sudan and Istanbul.

Living in Cairo Padwick became Editorial Secretary for the Central Committee for Christian Literature for Muslims, and while in Jerusalem she was Secretary for Literature of the Near East Christian Council. From these locations she traveled widely from Fez to Lahore, and conducted extensive correspondence with missionaries involved in communication with Muslims, and with scholars such as Louis Massignon. Hardworking and patient, affectionate and modest, she became the hub of a network of concern. When the turbulent political conditions of 1947 compelled Padwick to leave Jerusalem she went to Kordofan in the Sudan and for three years worked at preparing textbooks for Christian schools. Becoming ever more frail in health she moved to Istanbul, and finally in 1957 returned to England. It was only after she left that people fully realized the unique role that she had filled. Yet the core of her strength was not in her quiet ability but in her spiritual orientation. Padwick combined realism with spirituality, piety with a sense of poetry, and she deeply appreciated Gairdner's statement: "The Spirit of Jesus is the only asset of the church."[47]

Constance Padwick's wide-ranging literary productions included specific materials for Muslim readers, biographies about missionaries among Muslims, and scholarly writings on the subject of Islam itself. She brought two great qualities to the writing task. The first was a sense of urgency. Writing in 1946 she expressed a thought that is still relevant today: "Our Muslim world is being flooded with literature that speaks in every name but Christ's."[48] The second quality was a sense of relevancy drawn from her intimate walk with Muslims. In regard to her specific materials for Muslim readers they were of two kinds. She saw to the production of evangelistic works such as *A Book of Instruction for Catechumens—the Gift of the Lord Jesus Christ* (1932), which she co-edited with Gairdner, a work for Muslim inquirers. But she also produced literature of a broader type. She had carefully observed the reading desires and habits of Muslim youth, and recognized the importance of providing general materials that would assist them to deal with the stress and strain of modern living. Thus she viewed Christian literature as a medium for helping people both spiritually and socially. Her special love for biography is noteworthy, and she prepared warmhearted studies of such mission stalwarts as Henry Martyn, Lilias Trotter, and Temple Gairdner.

Constance Padwick's scholarly writings on Islam reflected both her deep respect for people and her awareness of the importance of genuine knowledge. For her, the scholarly study of Islam was a form of service, and it was one that she conducted with high standards, dedicated research, and true objectivity. Underlying her effort, and giving it reality and life, was the deep sensitivity to Muslim emotion that we have already noted. Reflecting her own bent, it was the realm of Muslim spirituality that especially attracted her. She was sure that Christians must understand it better, and her lifelong effort was to make that possible. "All that she wrote," says her colleague Kenneth Cragg, "she wrote out of a profound, and missionary commitment to Christ as Christians receive Him. Yet she attained a patient kinship with Muslim norms and themes, and made their world her own."[49] Padwick believed that there was a continuity of spirit that united Muslim people, scholars, saints, and common folk. She did not therefore neglect the classical scholars of Islam. An example of her capacity for meticulous scholarship is her brief study of the sources of the New Testament quotations that are cited by Al-Ghazālī.[50] But it is her tracing out of popular Muslim spirituality that was her special contribution. In bringing to light the story "The Nebi ʿĪsā and the Skull," a simple tale that narrates a conversation that Jesus had with a condemned sinner, she wrote what might be a statement of her general purpose: "I thought it worth translation, that it might be shared by others who care for the common folk and their stories."[51] To that task she brought her "powers of mind." "openness," "courtesy," "sympathy," "imagination," and "sustained and patient effort," all attributes suggested by Kenneth Cragg.[52]

As we reflect on Constance Padwick's life of inspiring others, as she had once herself been inspired, what she wrote about Gairdner might be said of her own influence: "Wafts of its beauty were felt in many lands."[53]

Learning: informed sensitive communication

6. Lewis Bevan Jones (1880–1960) Old to New

With L. Bevan Jones the approach to Muslims moves steadily forward in its transition from "old" to "new." Some regard him as the last of a great set of pioneers.[54] We may equally well consider his articulation of cordiality and friendship, set within a devoted evangelistic concern, as ably representing a new form of engagement. A longtime Baptist missionary in India and first principal of the Henry Martyn Institute of Islamic Studies his ideas were forged in a lifetime of grassroots relations with Muslims and ring with contemporary relevance.

Born in Agra, India, the son of missionaries, Bevan Jones took up Semitics at Cardiff and London Universities, and after arriving back in India in 1907 he studied Bengali and Urdu, the two leading Indian Muslim languages. In 1914 he received an assignment to give special attention to Muslim peoples, and studied Arabic in Egypt and London. He became a lecturer and literature worker in Dhaka (now Bangladesh), and married Violet Stanford, a nurse, in 1915. Later the two would collaborate on a well-known study, *Woman in Islam* (1941). When the Henry Martyn Institute was formed in 1930 in continuation of the worldwide desire to form Islamic Study centers that began with the Cairo conference of missionaries in 1906, L. Bevan Jones moved to Lahore to assume its charge, and he continued in that role until 1941. His pastoral instincts took over at that point, and he served congregations in Delhi (1941–1944) and in England (1944–1947). He chaired the Fellowship of Faith, a prayer ministry, from 1950–1959, but he also continued his effective writing to the end of his life.[55]

The accounts of L. Bevan Jones' discussions with Muslims reveal two important points. The first is that he was centered on the task of contextually communicating to Muslims the Christian understanding of Christ. It was that focus that informed his strong personal commitment to the study of Islam and the training of students in the knowledge of Islam and its literature. A careful scholar in his own right he advised his students to acquaint themselves well with the Qur'ān, its commentaries, the Traditions, the development of Muslim theology, and not least of all with current Muslim events in the daily press. He respected the good, and rejoiced in "whatever evidence we find of the presence of God's Spirit in Islam, in every witness it makes to His Being and majesty."[56] He believed, however, that the scholarly concern does not replace "our primary obligation," that is "the presentation to them of Christ as the only Savior from sin ..." That is the supreme issue, "bringing the Muslim face to face with the Living Christ, in the confident assurance that He has the will and power to draw such to Himself." This confidence will accrue to the Christian sharer not from competence in Islamic, or even in Biblical Studies, but rather "it must be grounded in his personal experience of Christ's Grace and Power in his own life. A missioner goes to a Muslim in his sin, as himself a sinner, saved by Grace."[57]

The second point that emerges is Bevan Jones' spirit of friendship. That is illustrated by the title that he chose for his biography of Jesus, *Best Friend* (1926), prepared for Muslim readers. That spirit was expressed in several ways. Jones deplored the continuation of the controversial tradition that he felt had outlived whatever value it may once have had, and that had produced more negative than positive results. He asks, "Is it not possible to approach the task in another spirit?"[58] He found the answer to his question in the direction of 2 Corinthians 5:20—"We beseech you on behalf of Christ, be reconciled to God." A Christian sharer beseeches Muslim friends. He pleaded that Muslims be looked upon in the ordinary way as people rather than as the representatives of a religious system. In that perspective he entitled his well-known introduction to Islam *People of the Mosque* (1932). The still useful work, prepared in the context of India and for the use of the average Indian evangelist, contains his remarkable chapter, "A Candid Enquiry into Our Methods." Jones argues that we must see Islam through Muslim eyes, expressing Islamic realities in a manner that is accurate, sympathetic, penetrates inner meanings, and sets forth Islamic ideas in such a way that Muslims will recognize their faith. He struggled to bring about better understanding, and this was the purpose of his work, *Christianity Explained to Muslims* (1938), a thorough examination of the chief issues at stake. He wanted to deal with the root causes of Muslim prejudices, and to that end he felt the need to bring Christian theology into a creative relation with Islam. He said, "We should rethink—if necessary, restate—our Christian beliefs so as to remove all possible causes of misunderstanding and offence." As to the offence of Christ himself, "that is something which only the grace of God can remove.[59]

L. Bevan Jones was firm in his view that Christ-likeness and prayer are essential elements in communicating the Christian understanding of Christ. He put it very simply: "We must give ourselves." The task is so formidable that "it demands of us our utmost and our best."[60] He himself prayed: "God, give to us all a love that persists in the service of the Gospel, that is never discouraged." [61] His insights came from a combination of long-term contact with Muslims, a learning approach, and a down-to-earth attitude. Ian Douglas, a successor at the Henry Martyn Institute, summed it up well: "He never lost the point of view of a practical evangelist."[62] A colleague, Bishop John Subhan, a former Muslim himself, pointed to his strengths in these phrases: "magnetic personality," "evangelistic zeal," "good friend to all," "at home with every type and class of Muslim."[63] A Muslim with whom he had once debated, Maulvi Muhammad Yakub Khan, rendered this generous tribute after his death:[64]

> Christian missionary societies have sent us some very fine specimens of Christianity, but Rev. Bevan Jones was a jewel among them. Personally, if there was one man who made me respect Christianity in a real sense, in the sense of love and charity of heart—it was Bevan Jones. They could send no better ambassador to the Muslim peoples. May Bevan Jones' soul rest in peace in the living presence of God whose name he glorified in his life.

Learning: Knowledgeable friendship-based witness

C. Drawing On the Lesser-Known

We turn to a relatively unmined field of resource and inspiration. This is the large body of Christian witnesses who have been active in the last half of the twentieth century, but who are lesser known than prominent figures such as those we have considered in the preceding section. We have chosen Henry and

Mary Esther Otten to exemplify the learning that can be drawn from this significant group, recognizing that many others of equal stature might represent "the partly-known."[65]

1. Henry J. Otten (1924–1985)

Henry Otten was inspired by an energetic Lutheran missionary named Henry Nau, and by others, to consider the vocation of Christian sharing with Muslims. An American who completed his divinity studies at Concordia Seminary, St. Louis, Missouri, USA, he attended the Kennedy School of Missions in Hartford, Connecticut, where he undertook pre-field training. There he met his future wife, Mary Esther Briggs. The Ottens originally hoped to serve among the Kurds in Iran who had been designated as an area of Lutheran concern by the 1910 World Missionary Conference at Edinburgh, but entry visas were not available. Instead the Ottens chose service among the Mappila Muslims of Kerala State in South India. There in Malabar from 1950 forward they carried on lifelong careers of service that were prominently marked by a spirit of pious servanthood. In a remarkable blending of talent and personality Henry Otten appeared as both a professional evangelist and a natural healer, while Mary Esther Otten was a professional healer and a natural evangelist. Their joining in a unitive ministry was enhanced by the shared characteristics of devotion and prayer.

Henry Otten's special contribution was to combine loving word and loving deed. He grew to understand that these were two sides of the coin of Christian presence. The communication of the Word was important to him. He once wrote that the "main purpose for being in India" was for "commending the Gospel to the Muslims of this country."[66] He understood that the work of commending the gospel to India Muslims is primarily the obligation of Christians in India. Yet he also believed that "whatsoever we can do to help the church now should theoretically help them in that great task."[67] To that goal Otten committed himself personally, and he tirelessly addressed the twin tasks of direct evangelism and preparing others for witness to a resistant community. There was a simplicity in him that did not disdain humble tasks, a patience in his efforts that overcame disappointment, and a steadiness of hope and confidence in God. On returning from a typically demanding outreach program early in his career, he wrote: "Such interest is more than we expected when we entered the work among Moslems, and though the fruits of this work are as yet invisible, we go back to Wandoor [Otten's mission station] happy for the opportunity to witness to Christ and confident that God will let His church reap the harvest in His own time."[68] He was deeply moved when some individuals chose to follow Christ, and he greatly enjoyed teaching in camps for inquirers and new believers.

While Henry Otten never turned aside from his evangelistic calling, he joined to it a life of sacrificial healing. Moved by the poverty, sickness, and suffering that he saw around him he became an advocate of the healing ministry. It was especially his loving attitude that Muslims and Hindus deeply appreciated. Working closely together with his wife, he succeeded in establishing a medical mission center, Karunalaya Hospital (= "Abode of Mercy") that became a byword in Malabar for genuine care. Much of his own time was spent in conveying medical staff to the homes of the helpless, engaging in prayer while the health professionals labored. Not only did he initiate and administer therapeutic healing programs, but he also strove to overcome some of the problems that produced and resulted in health crises. The fact that his tenderhearted concern was taken advantage of at times did not lessen his commitment to helping people.

Typical of this missionary age Otten was not able to confine his sphere of service to a single task or location, but he also engaged in a set of wide-ranging trans-India ecclesiastical activities. He traveled hither and yon, assisting his own and other church structures in different ways, in a pattern so exhausting that it finally led to his demise. Well-trained in Islamic Studies he had a scholarly bent—though short of time to exercise it—his chief publication being the *Ahmadiyya Doctrine of God* (1983). For many years he was involved with the work of the Henry Martyn Institute of Islamic Studies as a lecturer and as an Associate Director. He attended national and international conferences, illuminating many issues with his honestly stated and penetrating insights. On furloughs in his homeland he communicated the Christian concern for Muslims to wide audiences. What commended him to listeners, apart from the fascination of his grassroots reporting, was the sincerity and commitment that shone through his presentations.

While Henry Otten's many contributions to the people of his community may easily be quantified, it was their quality that was distinctive. With his undoubted practical skills he combined a servant-like approach that he learned from Christ. His *qibla* was toward Christ. The people could see it, were moved by it, and the word "saintly" was not infrequently used to describe him. His close relation with his Lord was reflected functionally not only in his social ministry, but also in the focus of his witness. He put Christ at the center of his communication with Muslims and Hindus, taking to heart the Pauline testimony "we preach Christ and him crucified." He was not really interested in argumentation about the relative merits of this or that—he wanted Muslims to see Jesus. He said, "Jesus is the embodiment of that [saving; ed.] Gospel, and there is more power in that life than in arguments about books."[69] Within that theological frame he communicated Christian ideas to Muslims with clarity and depth. That applied also to such thorny questions as the crucifixion. He declared: "The Cross is God's way of dealing with the greatest problem of the world on realistic terms. ... It defines majesty and power in ways that go beyond the ideas of brute force and power. ... It is the demonstration of the strength of His love, a love that seeks to save."[70]

The people among whom Henry Otten worked knew that he was their special friend. That awareness explains the unusual phenomenon that the town of Wandoor literally shut down on the occasion of his funeral, and many thousands of Muslims and Hindus attended the service at which he was laid to rest, beside the little chapel that he had so happily constructed. The one who knew him best, his wife Mary Esther, said:[71] "All were bearing witness to his gentle ways and his love in action for all he met." The words accurately describe the man and his contribution.

2. Mary Esther Otten (1924–1993)

For forty-three years and through periods of great personal difficulty Mary Esther Otten kept alight her flame of love for Malabar. Stemming from an American Methodist background and with and advanced degree in bacteriology from Columbia University in New York, Mary Esther had prepared well for service as a medical missionary in India. She was dedicated to the healing mission, but was equally interested in the verbal sharing of the gospel. For her these were two sides of the same coin. In her passionate desire to help Muslims in their physical needs and to point them to the Savior she felt a special burden for Muslim women, and helped by her great linguistic fluency she moved among them freely. With these activities she combined the task of bringing up a family of four children, one of whom (James Martyn) died on the field.

Mary Esther loved the vocation of missionary, and brought to it a flow of excitement combined with an acute and honest mind. She was well-informed in regard to mission theology and practice. She also understood that societal conditions had changed in India since Independence in 1947, but she believed that God's call and the basic task of mission was unchangeable. She wrote in 1972:[72]

> Rapid social change, restlessness, conflict between capital and labor, cross-currents of various political philosophies and rising expectations all form the background for mission work in India today. The days when a missionary was often regarded as a dispenser of bounties from a more progressive part of the world are quickly disappearing. Why are we here? What can we do? The world may regard us as excess baggage, but we know that the Gospel is the power of God unto salvation.

A pragmatist to the core, Mary Esther Otten knew that in fact there was still work to be done. Friend, servant-healer, Bible student and teacher, and a woman of faith are some of the phrases appropriate to her description. In her early years in Malabar she concentrated on the task of building up the medical work at Karunalaya Hospital, Wandoor, especially its laboratory facilities. The service was marked by twin concerns for high professional standards and commitment to the individual person. She was as demanding of herself as others, and was vocal in expressing her opinions when these concerns seemed to be slighted, yet she maintained a strong collegial relationship with her co-workers. In later life when her body was crippled by the ravages of rheumatoid arthritis she turned to literature work as her contribution. At an earlier stage she had maintained a lending library of Christian literature from her home, but she now directed her attention to the actual production of witnessing literature, specializing in Bible Correspondence Course lessons, booklets, and tracts. In one year (1985) she was chiefly responsible for producing 150,000 booklets, and her home was "cluttered" with printed materials. Well aware of the interactive requirements of production and distribution, she worked at both. Just before her death she completed a dream by putting into Malayalam the classic and stirring testimony of Dr. Said of Iran.

In addition to her commitment to the service of people and love for evangelism the spirit of Mary Esther Otten was marked by a strong devotion to the Bible and a fervent powerful faith that transcended the final limitations of her wheelchair. She was an adept student of the scriptures, and the devotions that she conducted with her husband Henry were marked by both depth and piety. She would rarely discuss with others her ailments or numerous operations, but continually turned the conversation to the work she loved. She spent many hours with inquirers and new believers who sensed the depth of her Christian commitment and were warmed and comforted by it. Mary Esther's personal vision was dominated by the principle of hope. She believed that in due time and under God's blessing some Muslims would grasp as their own the Biblical understanding of Christ, and in that confidence she was steady to the end in reaching out to her many Muslim friends.

In a 1989 letter from India that challenged Christians Mary Esther Otten referred to what she called "the heart of our work," that is "the daily contact with individuals who will judge the reliability of the Gospel and be drawn to the Savior by what they see and hear from us. ... I would like to encourage you to find out what Muslims believe and learn how to befriend them and join hands with us."[73] When contrary to medical advice she returned to India late in her life, she simply said: "There is much to be done, and laborers are few."[74] It is a word that remains true today.

Learning: devout and loving word-deed service

D. The Admirable Anonymous

The list of witnesses in the eleventh chapter of Hebrews in the Bible includes many well-known names from Abel to Abraham, and some lesser-known figures from Rahab to Barak. The comment made in regard to Abel applies to them all: "Through his faith he is still speaking" (Heb 11:4). Similarly the well-known and partly-known witnesses among Muslims—those whom we have discussed above, and many others—speak to us from the past, and the learning that we receive from them is impressive.

It may well be argued that the genius of such eminent individuals cannot be duplicated, and while that may be true, it can be allowed to inspire us. And, with God's help, the learning that we receive is certainly something that we can with God's help seek to emulate. We will take further account of some of the aspects of this learning when we deal with the profile of an evangel-sharer today.

Our opportunity to learn from the past, however, is not fully seized unless we recognize and take account of one other category of Christ's servants whom we shall designate as "the admirable anonymous." The people in this category are the pastors and church members in every land who with quietness and dignity represent the Master before Muslims in such a way that they see him. They are the unnamed servants, and with some exceptions are personally unknown to us. Admittedly we cannot directly learn from those we do not know. Yet in another sense without knowing them they speak to us, and intuitively we learn from them. In fact, their very anonymity teaches us. We recognize that quiet faithfulness must be at the heart of authentic contemporary engagement with Muslims, and we are grateful for that learning. It comes to us from every part of the world.

The Christian church is global and Islam is global. These two facts have existed for some time, but particularly Christians in the West have become more consciously aware of the global realities than they once were. The worldwide nature of Islam is being realized by the movement of Muslim peoples into Western Europe and the Americas. The worldwide nature of the church has become strikingly apparent in our time. In 1900 only 17 percent of the Christian population resided in Africa, Asia, and Latin America, but the proportion is now over 60 percent. It is significant that at the same time Africa and Asia make up 97 percent of the global Muslim population. Thus the statistically compelling meeting-ground for Christians and Muslims is in Africa and Asia, and in fact it is there that the anonymous Christian witnesses have been at work, sharing with Muslims their daily lives, their friendship and their faith in a vast complex of ways and with much experienced blessing.

As a symbol of this anonymous host I have chosen an Indonesian acquaintance from the Solo region of Java in Indonesia. A pastor interested in evangelization he had made his goal the establishment of two dozen congregations in his area, a Muslim region. When I visited him I found my new friend somewhat downcast. When asked the reason he replied that despite a decade of effort he had been unable to reach his goal. He had only succeeded in establishing sixteen (!) groups of new believers. I dutifully commiserated with him but inwardly wondered at the spiritual power of the "simple" worker. The experience was a reminder of the fundamental truth that the Christian engagement with Muslims is divine before it is human. The prophetic word rings with truth: "Not by might, nor by power, but by my Spirit," says the Lord (Zech 4:6). When the Sending God is involved obstacles are reduced, mountains look like plains, and the quiet faithfulness of the anonymous is blessed. "Who has despised the day of small things?" (Zech 4:10).[75]

Learning: unassuming faithful obedience

With these thoughts in mind we turn our attention to the Christian approach to Muslims today.

Endnotes

1. Jaroslav Pelikan, *Christian Doctrine and Modern Culture (since 1700)* (Chicago: University of Chicago Press, 1989), p. 111.

2. Kenneth S. Latourette, *Three Centuries of Advance* (Grand Rapids: Zondervan, 1970), pp. 76f. Halil Inalcik in *The Cambridge History of Islam*, Vol. IA (Cambridge: Cambridge University Press, 1910), p. 335, assert that "the pope began also to consider the tsar as a possible participant in projected crusades," but documentation is lacking.

3. Josef Roucek, "Venceslaus Budovitz de Budov (First Protestant Missionary to the Mohammedans," *MW*, Vol. XXVII, No. 4, October 1927, pp. 401–404.

4. Latourette, *Three Centuries*, p. 61.

5. The Franciscans and Dominicans were not inactive; but the tale that in 1515 about 12,000 Mappila Muslims became Christians at Quilon, Kerala, India, as

the result of Franciscan activity, is very dubious. It has been dealt with in Miller, *Mappila Muslims*, p. 74.

6. For a somewhat romantic account of this remarkable event and the names of those involved, cf. P. Thomas, *Christians and Christianity in India* (London: George Allen & Unwin, 1954), pp. 105–114. J. T. Addison, *The Christian Approach to Islam* (New York: Columbia, 1942), p. 221, critically assesses the Roman Catholic missiology in regard to Muslims as leader-oriented.

7. This section is limited to non-living figures. Some significant current figures are take up in later chapters.

8. J. Krudenier, Book review of Constance Padwick's Henry Martyn in *MW*, Vol. XIII, No. 3, July 1923, p. 322.

9. Constance Padwick, *Henry Martyn, Confessor of the Faith* (New York: George H. Dolan Co., 1928).

10. George Smith, *Henry Martyn, Saint and Scholar* (New York: Fleming H Revell & Co., 1892), pp. 522, 536.

11. Padwick, *Martyn*, p. 128.

12. Smith, *Martyn*, p. 558.

13. John Sargent, ed., *Memoirs of Henry Martyn* (Hartford: G. Goodwin & Sons, 1882), p. 363; Sargent used journals and letters that were published by W. Wilberforce, 1837.

14. *Ibid.*, p. 366.

15. *Ibid.*, p. 322.

16. *Ibid.*, p. 335.

17. Smith, *Martyn*, p. 526. Padwick, *Martyn*, p. 274, reports that Rahim remained in the faith and later told the story.

18. *Ibid.*

19. The Tuaregs used the decoration of the cross on their various accouterments, pointing to a possible Christian past. They followed the matrilinear system of inheritance, practiced male-female equality, and prescribed the veiling of the males rather than the females. They terrorized North Africa in the period of time that we are considering; cf. Douglas Campbell, "The Touregs or Veiled Men of the Sahara," *MW*, Vol. XXVII, No. 3, July 1928, pp. 256–262, and K. G. Presse, "Tawārik," *EI²*, X, pp. 379–381.

20. Sonia Howe, "Charles de Foucauld, Explorer," *MW*, Vol. XVII, No. 2, April 1928, p. 144.

21. Quoted in Bengt Sundkler, *The World of Mission* (Grand Rapids: Eerdmans, 1965), p. 233.

22. *Ibid.*

23. *Ibid.*

24. Howe, "de Foucauld," p. 142.

25. Few individuals can both write and speak with the power of Samuel Zwemer. I cannot tell whether I was personally more moved by Zwemer's exegesis of Isaiah 6:1–6, or by a conversation that I was able to have with him as a youth. This was not an unusual experience; D. T. Niles reports how he was moved to enter the Christian ministry after hearing Zwemer speak, and he testified: "The world is covered across every continent today by missionaries who were inspired in their life decision by 'the man sent from God named Samuel'. " Quoted in J. Christy Wilson, "The Epic of Samuel Zwemer," *MW*, Vol. LVII, No. 2, April 1967, p. 79.

26. John A Mackay, Introduction to *Samuel H. Zwemer, The Cross above the Crescent* (Grand Rapids: Zondervan, 1941), p. 5.

27. The phrase is taken form the title of Zwemer's biography by J. Christy Wilson, *The Apostle of Islam* (Grand Rapids: Baker, 1952). In a preface to this work K. S. Latourette suggests forthrightly that Zwemer deserved the accolade.

28. Edwin Calverley, "Samuel Marinus Zwemer," *MW*, Vol. XLII, No. 3, July 1952, pp. 157f. Calverley was himself a longtime missionary in the near East and a co-editor, later editor, of Muslim World.

29. Language preparation needs humor. During his study at Beirut the future Arabist suggested that the Arabic gutturals were "undoubtedly borrowed from a camel when he complained of overloading;" quoted in J. Christy Wilson, *The Flaming Prophet. The Story of Samuel Zwemer* (New York: Friendship Press, 1970), p. 23.

30. *Ibid.*, p. 42.

31. Samuel H. Zwemer, "Lamb of God," *MW*, Vol. XVI, No. 1, January 1926, p.1.

32. Zwemer, *Cross above the Crescent*, p. 232.

33. *Ibid.*, p. 246; one of Zwemer's most powerful pamphlets was entitled "The Glory of the Cross."

34. Samuel Zwemer, "The Love That Will Not Let Go," *MW*, Vol. XIV, No. 4, October, 1926, p. 233.

35. Appendage to William Worcester's Review of *Apostle to Islam, MW*, Vol. XLIII, No. 2, April 1953, pp. 217f.

36. Constance E. Padwick, "Lilias Trotter of Algiers," *International Review of Missions*, 1938, p. 120. Trotter's first biographer was Blanche Piggot, *Lilias Trotter* (Marshall, Morgan & Scott, n.d.).

37. *Ibid.*, p. 124.

38. *The Master of the Impossible*, arranged by Constance Padwick (London: S.P.C.K., 1937), p. vii.

39. Reported by Lisa M. Sinclair, "The Legacy of Isobella Lilias Trotter," *International Bulletin*, Vol. 26, No. 1, January 2002, p. 33.

40. Padwick, ed., *Master of the Impossible*, p.10.

41. *Ibid.*, p. 148.

42. Lilias Trotter, "The Man Who Heard the Water," *MW*, Vol. XIV, No. 3, July 1924, p. 222.

43. Constance E. Padwick, *Lilias Trotter of Algiers* (Rushden, Northants: Stanley L. Hunt, n.d.), p. 6; quoted by Sinclair, "Legacy," *op. cit.,* p. 35, fn.2.

44. A highlighted quotation in *MW*, Vol. XXXII, No. 1, January 1942, p. 80.

45. Padwick, ed. *Master of the Impossible*, p. 57.

46. Padwick called this work "a study of religious life today" (Introduction, p. xiii), and the description still holds true to a remarkable degree.

47. Padwick became Gairdner's colleague and biographer. Cf. Constance E. Padwick, *Temple Gairdner of Cairo* (London: S.P.C.K., 1929), p. vii. Temple Gairdner is an important figure, whose ministry in Egypt was an inspirational one. Cf. Michael Shelley, "The Life and Thought of W. H. T. Gairdner, 1873–1928: A critical Evaluation of a Scholar Missionary to Islam (Ph.D. diss., University of Birmingham, 1987).

48. Constance Padwick, "Literature in the Muslim World, *MW*, Vol. XXXVI, No. 4., October 1946, p. 335.

49. Kenneth Cragg, "Constance E. Padwick, 1886–1968," *MW*, Vol. LIX, No. 1, January 1969, p. 35.

50. Constance E. Padwick, "Al-Ghazali and Arabic Versions of the Gospels," *MW*, Vol. XX, No. 1., January 1930, p. 56.

51. Constance E. Padwick, "The Nebi 'Isa and the Skull (translation)," *MW*, Vol. XX, No. 1, January 1930, p. 56.

52. Cragg, "Padwick," *op. cit.,* passim.

53. Padwick, Gairdner, p. vii.

54. John Subhan, a colleague of L. Bevan Jones, held this view.

55. For biographical detail I am especially indebted to Clinton Bennett, "Lewis Bevan Jones, 1880–1960, Striving to Touch Muslim Hearts," in G. H. Anderson, et. al., ed., *Mission Legacies* (Maryknoll: Orbis Books, 1988), pp. 283–289.

56. L. Bevan Jones, *The People of the Mosque* (London: Student Christian Movement, 1932), p. 253.

57. "Christ's Ambassador to the Muslims," by the editors, *MW*, Vol. XLII, No. 1, January 1952, pp. 80f.

58. L. Bevan Jones, *Christianity Explained to Muslims* (Calcutta: Y.M.C.A., 1938), pp. viif.

59. Jones, *People of the Mosque*, p. 304.

60. *Ibid.*, p. 312.

61. L. Bevan Jones, "A Love That Persists," *MW*, Vol. XLII, No. 1, January 1953, p. 6.

62. Ian Douglas, "End or Beginning?", *The Bulletin of the Henry Martyn Institute of Islamic Studies*, Series LVIII, No. 2, April-June 1960, p. 1.

63. The Reverend John Subhan, "Lewis Bevan Jones," *ibid.*, p. 6.

64. *Ibid.*, p. 4.

65. The reason that the present writer is able to partially relieve the relative anonymity of the Ottens is the fact that he and his wife Mary Helen were the close co-workers and friends of the Ottens in South India for 23 years.

66. Henry J. Otten, unpublished letter to the writer, January 28, 1979.

67. *Ibid.*

68. Henry J. Otten, "Sowing the Seed," *The Minaret*, Vol. 11., No. 1., September, 1955, p. 9; the successive issues of this journal contain running accounts of their ministries by both Henry and Mary Esther Otten.

69. Henry J. Otten, *The Ahmadiyya Doctrine of God* (Hyderabad: Henry Martyn Institute of Islamic Studies, 1983), p. 106.

70. *Ibid.*, p. 107.

71. Mary Esther Otten, quoted in J. K. Brauer, ed., *A Rainbow of Saris* (St. Louis: L.W.M.L., 1996), p. 145.

72. *Ibid.*, p. 136.

73. *Ibid.*, p. 150f.

74. *Ibid.*, p. 146.

75. Various translations of the Biblical passage Zechariah 4:6–10 differ considerably; we have utilized the Jerusalem Bible version.

Part Three

The Task: Connecting Muslims and the Message

A sharing Christian crosses bridges and seeks to connect Muslims with the message and reality of the love of God. Part Three deals with that task. It examines the profile of a sharing Christian; reflects on the main elements of the Christian approach to Muslims today; considers the issue of appropriate methodology; takes up the hard questions that Muslims ask; and deals with pressing matters related to inquirers and new believers. It closes with a challenge to the church to remember the imposing task.

The Profile of a Sharing Friend

There is a common expression in North American colloquial English: " I wouldn't buy a used car from that man!" It is the ultimate put-down. In using the phase the speaker has in mind some ideal image of a trustworthy sales person. This is also true in the communication of ideas. We value an opinion, even though we may not agree with it, because we respect the person who expresses it. It is not very daring to assert that the same principle applies in Christian communication; its success, *at a human level,* depends more on the kind of person one is than on the kind of knowledge one has or the method one uses. In the foregoing chapter we reported the Muslim appreciation for Bevan Jones and Henry Otten. They are significant. It is clear that the attitude of a witnessing person is important. This chapter seeks to identify certain elements that belong in the attitudinal profile of a sharing friend. *Depends more on the kind of person Christian is; attitude.*

The word "profile" means "a contour that is projected forward." In modern usage it is a standard descriptive term used to outline qualifications for a position. Can we posit a basic contour that is generally applicable to anyone who shares the gospel with Muslims? Two questions immediately arise. The first is, is it possible? There are a variety of natural distinctions among people, which result in a legitimate plurality of approaches. To this we respond that profiling is not an attempt to impose a uniform and arbitrary ideal, but is rather a lifting up of some desirable qualities that need attention and can be given attention without violating individuality, freedom and the natural process. The second question is, is it necessary? Surely the minimum requirements for sharing the gospel with Muslims are love for the saving Lord, love for the gospel, love for the Muslims, and a natural unaffected manner. Should we not be content with this, and let the communication flow? To that we respond, we have to pay attention to the kind of people we are. It hurts no one to think about that.

Apart from the general principles common to theories of communication, what kind of qualities should one consider and aspire to in relation to Muslims? The following may be numbered among those elements. They are attitudinal desiderata to be happily cultivated rather than burdensome requirements that weigh down the spirit. Many belong to the natural makeup of most people, and need only exercise to be further enhanced, a developmental process worthy of the serious enterprise of bridging the gaps and reaching people. They include:

A. Qualities of the Inner Being	B. Qualities of Relation to Others
God-mindedness	Genuine normalcy
Urgency	Sympathy
Patience	Empathy/Sensitivilty
Expectancy	Respect/Understanding
Prayerfulness	Fairness
Courage	Honesty
Sense of Humor	

C. Qualities of the Mind and Will

The desire and will to know Islam and to understand Muslims

The aspiration to discern fresh Christian theological resources in the light of Islamic views

The determination to communicate with clarity

An inclination to imaginative venturing

These qualities are aspects of ~~deep friendship~~. They are applied deep friendship. They are its vesture, the garments of ~~personal integrity~~. They are what Muslims sense and see, and seeing are moved to trust. We begin with some qualities of the inner being.

A. Profile: The Inner Being

We suggest seven qualities of the inner being that have particular relevance to the engagement with Muslims.

1. Godmindedness

The word "godmindedness' may appear to be clumsy, but it makes a point. As we described in the first chapter Muslims are characterized by an overwhelming sense of God. That is the first and key principle of Islam. It is the most natural thing for Muslims to look for that quality in others.

The witness among Muslims must therefore have a *qibla*, a direction toward God. That does not imply a pretentious religious life but a visible direction. What we mean to convey by the term Godmindedness are the traditional qualities of faith and piety, a Christ-like spirit. Muslims are hardly expecting too much when,

[handwritten margin notes: Muslims over whelming Sense of God. Qibla - direction toward God]

as they do, they want to see some evidence of the spiritual power that Christians say is available to those who follow Christ. And that, in fact, is the point that St. Paul makes when he says (Col 3:3): "Set your minds on things that are above, for you have died, and your life is hid with Christ in God." In writing to Timothy he describes this Godmindedness as "a quiet and peaceable life in all godliness and dignity" (1 Tim 2:2). Muslims recognize that this is the direction life should take.

2. Urgency

very important

The witness among Muslims will sense the momentous nature of the enterprise and cultivate a healthy urgency. A healthy urgency is not a frenetic, hyperactive spirit, but a recognition that something is very important. There is urgency in the content of our witness, for the very fact of Christ has in it a powerful imperative. There is urgency in the need before us, for there is no human who does not need the message of salvation, and Muslims number so many. There is urgency in the time element. Jesus felt it and said: "I must work the works of him that sent me before the night comes when no one can work" (Jn 9:4). Finally there is the urgency that resides in love, the love that Jesus taught and gave. That is a healthy pressure. It produced the little word "must" that appeared in the passage quoted above, and in many of Jesus' sayings. "Other sheep have I, them also must I bring (Jn 10:16). It gives the same healthy urgency to his followers. "For the love of Christ urges us on. ... He died for all, so that those who live might live no longer for themselves, but for him who died and was raised for them" (1 Cor 5:14f).

3. Patience

Can one be both urgent and patient? In fact, they are not contradictions but may be held together. The relevance of patience to the task of communicating with Muslims is self-evident. It channels urgency from worried activism to a waiting upon the Lord, and it gives to the process of sharing a quietness of spirit that it needs.

Quietness of Spirit

In this connection it is not out of place to note the admirable serenity that marks many Muslims. Its origin may be both cultural and theological. Its manifestations are often striking. Muslims do not seem to feel hurried. Is it because there is a sense that God is in charge?

Serenity – marks muslims

We have examined many of the factors that underline the need for patience— factors related to the origin of Islam, to history, to politics, to relational and theological misunderstanding, to the Islamic theory of finality, to the lack of felt spiritual needs, and many others. But God is in charge, and patience is grounded in that reality. Grounded there it rests in God, the Lord of the mission, in the command of the Ascended One to convey his *kerugma*, in the Heavenly Father's enabling grace, and in the Spirit's fulfilling power. As Kenneth Cragg states in these notable words:[1]

> The first point to be made is that no Christian mission is constituted in its success, and none, therefore, is invalidated by numerical failure. ... The mission is not a calculus of success, but an obligation in love.

Patience is therefore coupled with faithfulness. When asked what he would do if he knew that the end of the world was at hand, Francis of Assisi spoke these familiar words: "I would continue ploughing my furrow." Patience is not inactive submission, but active faithfulness, a serenity that monitors feelings and trusts in God. *Patience: not inactive submission, but active faithfulness. Serenity that monitors feelings and trusts in God.*

4. Expectancy

Can one be both patient and expectant? Yes, but two points arise. Of all the qualities, it is expectancy that most needs nourishing, and the scope of expectancy must be spacious enough to include God's working in the world. The quality stands in special need of nourishment because the church has developed non-expectant attitudes, influenced by the apparent lack of tangible results. This "lullabying" of the spirit has had a near suffocating effect on many, blunting Christian concern and dulling Christian response. Those who share with Muslims must therefore be strongly in the business of cultivating the spirit of hope, and leaders of the church bear a special responsibility in that regard. They may do so in two ways. First, by remembering that the quality of hope runs like a golden thread through the witness of the great communicators of the past. Second, and more importantly, by reminding themselves that there is no proclamation of the Word of God that does not involve the action of God, for it is indeed "the power of God for salvation" (Rom 1:16).

Expectancy must also be broad enough to observe and recognize the divine working in general society. That action is not entirely concealed. Christians have hoped that many Muslims would be moved to appreciate the Christian understanding of the Messiah and would follow him and his path. While that has not happened, something else of great interest has occurred. The ethical teaching of Jesus, including the principles of self-giving love and justice for the oppressed, have made a significant impact on the Muslim world, particularly the intelligentsia. In Chapter 5, Section D., we have shown how the ethical Jesus has had a special appeal for many among the modern Muslim thinkers. With the exception of Jesus' teaching of forgiveness toward enemies and non-retaliation—which Muslims regard as a particular requirement of the Jewish context rather than being an eternal principle—the views of the Teacher are given the highest praise, and his inculcation of the spirit of love, forbearance and compassion are regarded as congruent with the message of the Qur'ān. One of the main channels for the penetration of Jesus' ethical thought has been modern education, which bears its marks. However it has transpired, God's Spirit has thereby created a new foundation for the communication of the gospel.[2] Abul Kalam Azad said: "Christ (peace be upon Him!) had replaced the Judaic concept of God as 'God of terror' by 'God of love.' Hence he very often addressed God as 'Father,' and emphasized that ritual and formality were of no consequence in religion."[3] It is but a short step from that comment to a discussion of the holiness and love of God upon which rests the story of salvation.

In this development can we see one divine response to the prayer of the ancient collect that is repeated again and again in worship services?:

Grant, we beseech Thee, Almighty God, unto Thy church Thy Holy Spirit and the wisdom which cometh down from above, that Thy Word, as becometh it, may not be bound, but have free course ..."

There are other discernable movements of the Spirit. The cultivation of expectancy is nothing less than having "eyes to see," engaging in spiritual distance learning, and as Lilias Trotter said, "recognizing the first streaks of the dawn."

5. Prayerfulness

The inner quality of prayerfulness involves a dual recognition. It perceives that the persuasive communication of Christ is impossible without God's blessing. The accompanying recognition is that God has elected to entrust people with the task of communicating God's saving will. The dual realization results in a twofold prayer for God's blessing upon Muslim friends and for Christian strengthening for the sharing task.

Abraham's petition of behalf of his first son Ishmael, "O that Ishmael might live before thee, Lord!" (Gen 16:18; KJV), a powerful and holistic plea is often used as a prayer for the blessing of Muslims, especially the special blessing of spiritual openness to abundant life of Christ. In a formal way it has not been widely used by Christians, although it appears in the Moravian liturgy, but it has become a symbolic petition among those who share with Muslims. In a figurative sense, at least, it may be applied to Muslims who recognize a special relation with Ishmael and who once were called Ishmaelites by early Christians. Abraham prays for his son—and by implication also for his descendants—that they may be remembered by God, and the Almighty gives a powerful response. Whether through these Abrahamic words, or with other words, Christians will pray to the Lord on behalf of their Muslim friends: "May life be blessed for them and may Your deep friendship be known among the children of Ishmael! May they live before Thee, Lord!"

And those who share with Muslims must pray for themselves—for strength, wisdom, and endurance. These blessings are sorely needed by those who engage with Muslims beyond merely the casual level. Earlier we have noted that there is contentment and happiness, even a kind of wonder in that experience. At the same time, it is also easy to become tired, dismayed, or even lonely. Certainly this was not an unusual feeling for the great communicators of the past. Samuel Zwemer repeatedly quoted Proverbs 13:12—"Hope deferred makes the heart sick, but a desire fulfilled is a tree of life." Extended waiting can be depressing. Something must come between that and fruit-gathering from the tree of life. That is the prayerful attitude that yields a depression-overcoming serenity, for it seeks its rest in God. But it is also prayerful activity, the daily asking for help for one's self and for one another, confident in the promise: "Ask and it shall be given you, seek and you shall find, knock and it shall be opened to you" (Lk 11:9). Ask for what? Certainly for humility, for it is the overestimation of one's role that produces weariness of the soul. Certainly for faith, for it is the underestimation of God's vocation that brings doubt. And certainly for the love to stay with Jesus in his trials, and to remain with our Muslim friends in our common testing. Luther Engelbrecht put it simply:[4]

Help me to love them as You have loved them,
Help me to serve them as You have served them,
According to your good and gracious will,
     help us to live at peace with one another,
And make us the instruments of your peace.

6. Courage

Patience itself is a form of courage, but courage means more than that. It is not simply bravery. It is rather the willingness, as it were, "to put your hand in the hand of the man of Galilee," and walk with him the path of daring love. We have pointed out that Muslims are pleased with their faith. They are not happy with some of the things that some Muslims do, but they are content with Islam. They cherish its values, and are satisfied with its directions. They are not pressed by an inner drive to seek new meaning, solace, or peace. They resent the implication that it is necessary. In short, they may be willing to listen to, but scarcely welcome a new message. They wonder about their Christian friends who are so intent on conveying the gospel. They are in doubt. Are they really our friends, as they say, if they disturb us when we feel quite content? Even the most sensitive and understanding communication may be taken amiss. Moreover, if and when someone is attracted to a new understanding of Jesus the Messiah and chooses to accept him as Savior and to follow him, the Muslim community feels invaded, wounded, and resentful. Their displeasure will almost certainly be directed at the new believer, and to some extent will include those who influenced him or her. All along the road of witness the need for courage within is as great as the need for sensitivity without.

What produces courage? It is the Resurrection of our Lord, the Ascension, and the Looking-Down. The Messiah of God is risen, ascended, and reigns. His last word is intended to give courage to his witnesses: "All authority in heaven and on earth is given to me. Go therefore ..." (Mt 16:18). But there is more—the Looking-Down. What we mean by the Looking-Down is what, in their ingenuous faith, the early Christians saw. When Stephen was being stoned, he cried out: "I see the heavens opened and the Son of Man standing at the right hand of God!" (Acts 7:55). The early church puzzled over the standing. Do not the scriptures say that the Son of Man is seated at the right hand of God (Acts 2:34; Col 3:1; Rev 14:4). Why did Stephen see him standing? Some of the first Christians came to a simple conclusion. They decided that Jesus was so concerned about the welfare of his servant that he stood up to see better! Others thought that Jesus rose to welcome him. That vision gave Stephen the courage he needed for the ultimate sacrifice he paid. Every day of the Christian engagement with Muslims is a day that celebrates "The Festival of the Standing-Up and Looking-Down."

7. Sense of Humor

What delivers courage from self-consciousness is a sense of humor. We therefore end our list of qualitites of the inner being with the quality of self-deprecation, the quality of not taking oneself too seriously. Someone may object that it is incongruous to include this element among such serious matters. But that is precisely the point. The matters are serious indeed, but we have a funny side.

It is important for a communicator to be able to laugh with the world and at oneself. In our youth the writer and wife embarked on a former troop ship with separate male and female sections, which left the port of New York for the East in 1953. In a precious moment a concerned uncle, a professor at Duke University, pushed me against a bulkhead, put his finger under my nose, and with great vehemence gave his parting word: "Don't forget your sense of humor!" The advice was of immediate value since the next day after a frantic search I discovered my wife in the ship's hospital fighting ptomaine poisoning brought on by the consumption of a mature Connecticut fish.

The sense of humor includes the awareness of how odd we sometimes seem to others. When the writer arrived in southwest India he was greeted by Mr. Marikkar, a Mappila Muslim, who had once worked for the British rulers of India. He therefore knew what "Europeans" liked. Graciously he invited me for tea. When I arrived at the humble home of this kindly host, far from the beaten path, he had set up a small table and chair outdoors under a coconut tree, since his home was too tiny to be convenient. I was seated, and the repast was presented. The family "knew" that the foreigner liked eggs and jam. Family members had gone fifty miles by bus, at considerable trouble and expense, to get a tin of blackberry jam. On the plate before me were two cold fried eggs spread heavily with blackberry jam! It was a moment that combined the best of friendship and humor. I ate the banquet with gusto and rejoiced at the hospitality of my new friends amidst what was supposed to be the deepest center of militant Islam in South India. I had experienced the means of graciousness. ... Humor teaches as well as enjoys.

I kept returning in my mind to my uncle's wise advice given on the deck of the good ship Georgic. The fact that Christian communicators are steadily dealing with serious matters of ultimate significance may have unwelcome personal results. The antidote to an unattractive pretentiousness and a dourness of spirit that threaten Christians is the quality of self-deprecation that wells up from sharing life together in a quirky world. There is news from Lake Wobegon. Yet below it runs the deeper joy that comes from making Muslim friends and sharing with them "the good tidings of great joy."

B. Profile: Relating to Others

In terms of relationships a Muslim is first a fellow human, secondly a friend or potential friend, and third a member of another faith. The qualities of relation to which a sharing Christian aspires must be understood in that way. It is for this reason that the attributes listed in this section are among those commended for other common human relationships. There are six, however, that we wish to elevate in terms of their particular relevance.

I. Genuine Normalcy

You begin by being normal. Another way of saying it is to be natural, to be yourself.

At first sight this point may seem to be too obvious to deserve mention. The fostering of normalcy does not appear to be a high art. It is the context of sharing with Muslims that turns what is ordinary into something that must be cultivated. Recalling the history of Christian-Muslim relations, and given a kind of "knee-jerk" reaction that some Christians now have when they hear the word Muslim, normalcy becomes a quality that needs to be appropriated. Instead of being a matter of simple routine it becomes a contemporary fulfillment of the command to "love thy neighbor."

Communicators know that the element of intentionality brings strain and may even distort ordinary relationships. Not everyone has mastered the delicate tension that exists between having ordinary accepting associations and being faithful to the vocation of a witness. The tension may be a paradox, and if so it is to be lived with along side many other paradoxes of life. Paul Schilpp once offered some daring questions that involved paradoxes, if not implied contradictions. For example, he asked: Is it possible to be both religious and intelligent? Can one be both open-minded and deeply committed?[5] Following his lead we might ask: Can one be both a communicator and normal? Or, more pointedly, can one both share the gospel with Muslims and maintain good relations? The experience of the writer moves him to unhesitatingly affirm, it is possible, for there is a resolution to the paradox in the principle of deep friendship. Yet it is not an automatic resolution, and normalcy therefore becomes a learning goal as well as a desirable quality. The alternative is quite unacceptable. Not to be normal is to be abnormal, and abnormality is no basis either for neighborly living or for mutual sharing.

The cultivation of genuine normalcy is illuminated by the two phrases: be natural and be yourself. They introduce two essential elements. The first is to accept the humanity of a Muslim, and the second your own. The first is relatively easy. Muslims are ordinary people, and one can move with them in usual ways. Normalcy implies engagement, not aloofness or separation. One may look forward to enjoying pleasant personal and family associations, with plenty of welcoming smiles. The second element, remembering to be your natural self, may be more difficult. It means not tensing up because you are treading on uncertain ground, not trying to assume an ill-fitting halo, not pre-occupied with pre-set goals, but rather being your own intrinsic, unaffected self. The model is Nathaniel of whom Jesus said: "There is nothing false in him" (Jn 1:14). One can note an almost perceptible sigh of relief among Muslims, as well as some surprise, when they sense an unaffected attitude in a Christian acquaintance, and that perception in turn becomes an encouragement to Muslims to "be themselves." For the Christian being oneself is not a psychological tour de force but the recognition of a theological reality. It is firmly founded on being unconditionally accepted as a forgiven sinner and child of God for Christ's sake, eliminating the need to strike a pose, and at the same time—being empowered by the Spirit—eliminating the need to be anxious.

2. Sympathy

From normalcy to sympathy is a natural step. Whereas the attitude of normalcy makes possible ordinary relations with Muslims, the attitude of sympathy takes a sharing friend into their sufferings. The word "sympathy" means "to feel with," but at its root the meaning is considerably stronger. It is "to suffer with."

The appropriateness of this component in the profile of a sharing friend becomes clear in the light of two factors—the need of Muslims and the example of the Master. It is fairly well-known that the Muslim peoples of the world, for whatever reasons, rank grievously high on "the suffering index" of humanity. The sufferings of the multitudes, however, must always come down to the individual case, and so the writer will share the saga of Seinuddin.

Seinuddin was a pleasant man who became my friend. He was typically restrained in expression, but whenever he spoke he would give me his little smile. Seinuddin came to our clinic seeking help for his diabetes. In the course of their investigations our doctors discovered that he also had tuberculosis, a scourge of the poor. Seinuddin belonged to the latter. He and his family were poor indeed. A day-laborer who earned very little, his home was a mud-walled, coconut-leaf thatched, single room where he and his wife and their five children had to make do. There was little enough food for the children, not to speak of special diets for his major diseases. One day he came and in his understated manner said: "I think I have a problem." After further discussion I knew what he meant. The tests showed that Seinuddin had also contracted leprosy. Tears could scarcely be contained as we bent ourselves to the task of helping this modern Job. Yet he did not cease sharing with us what he had to give—his smile. Islamic tradition records a prophetic saying: "The best alms is a smile in your brother's face." While we extended our sympathy, he gave us alms.

Suffering with seeks its outlet in helpful action. St. Paul exhorts: "Bear one another's burdens' (Gal 6:2). We cannot bear the burdens of others without looking to their solution. When Lazarus died and Mary grieved, Jesus groaned in his spirit and wept. Then he raised Lazarus from the dead.

3. Empathy/Sensitivity — "identification"

The word "empathy" resembles sympathy, but it takes us deeper into Muslim emotion. The term literally means "feeling into," and refers to the ability to sense the ideals and sentiments of others. It incorporates everything that we load into the word "sensitivity," but it is a stronger term. It is close in meaning to the word "identification." The principle of identification is set forth in 1 Corinthians 9:19–26, where St. Paul says in this foundational passage:

> For though I am free with respect to all, I have made myself a slave to all, so that I might win more of them. To the Jews I became as a Jew in order to win Jews. To those under the law ... so that I might win those under the law. To those outside the law I became as one outside the law (though I am not free from God's law but am under Christ's law), so that I might win those outside the law. ... I have become all things to all people, so that I might by all means save some. I do it for the sake of the gospel, so that I might share its blessings.

Paul was undisputedly not thinking of ethnicity or customary behavior because he was already a Jew. Yet "he became as a Jew." He was identifying at a deeper level of empathy. His own application is illustrated in his sermon to the Greek thinkers on the hill of the Areopagus in Athens, where he not only shows sensitivity toward Greek ideas but dramatically takes them up in his address (Acts 17:22–31). This brilliant speech is full of helpful hints for Christian communication with Muslims. It reveals not only a concern for the religious emotion of those he is engaging, but also the ability to build on that insight in communicating the idea that hope has entered the world. That acute empathy in the end bridged the gap and connected Dionysus and Damaris with the message.

While such sensitivity may seem to be extraordinarily difficult, what makes if possible is the same thing that enables engaged normalcy—our common humanity. Bishop Kenneth Cragg has exemplified the empathetic engagement with Muslims in his long career. He suggests that "the Christian spirit is taught by its own Gospel an affinity with every human reverence." He adds: "What we need is just this capacity to feel with the reactions and impulses of men in every texture of belief and unbelief and to possess, not merely as assessors, still less as aliens, but as companions of mortality, the world of their fears and sanctities."[6] Would St. Paul have written: to the Muslim I became as a Muslim? If he had, what would it imply?

4. Respect

In everyday English usage respect means showing deference to a fellow human being, and giving him or her the honor that one would like to receive. It also includes courtesy towards the values of another person, even though one may not agree with them. It incorporates the idea of tolerance, excluding tolerance towards evil. The original meaning of the word is instructive. "Re-spect" means to look back or look again, to inspect a second time. Three ideas are present. The first is that you look. The second is that your gaze does not flit casually and then leave; you seek eye contact and actually see the other. The third is that you see something worth looking at; you have regard for the other.

The powerful implications in the term gain increased weight from the lack of mutual regard that has troubled Christian-Muslim relations. It suggests that you will actually see the Muslim as a companion on the voyage of life. You will not view him or her casually or remotely as a number, or as a member of a category, or least of all as an object for personal manipulation, but rather that you will take a second look and see a person. The further implication is that you will have regard for what is worthy. An esteemed teacher of mine, Professor Daud Rahbar,[7] once advised me to seek what is noble in the Islamic tradition. "Can you not find one thing to appreciate?" he asked. He thereby echoed a Biblical theme:

> Keep your tongue from evil, and your lips from speaking deceit. Depart from evil, and do good; seek peace and pursue it. (Ps 34:13f).

> Finally, beloved, whatever is true, whatever is honorable, whatever is just, whatever is pure, whatever is pleasing, whatever is commendable, if there is any excellence, and if there is anything worthy of praise, think about these things" (Ph 4:8).

The "whatever" in the last passage is limiting as well as expansive. The areas of religious belief and moral behavior are subject to that limitation. It must be remembered that there are levels of respect. Certainly one does not esteem that with which one disagrees or that which one rejects, but nevertheless one respects the right of the believer to believe, and deals thoughtfully with what is cherished. In friendship one can disagree, but the disagreement is expressed in the manner of a friend, that is, with sensitivity, consideration and kindness. As Christians seek to walk into Muslim sacred space, bearing with them the gospel that they hope will be honored, they will leave at the door sandals of irreverence and discourtesy.[8]

A Kashmiri carpet provides an analogy for the development of this quality. One can walk on it unthinkingly. Or one can admire its rich colors and floral design. Or perhaps, one can even see the dedicated Kashmiri family that created it—father, mother, and children united at the loom in patient artistry, laboriously tying hundreds of knots per inch, adding beauty to someone's life by their intensive and underpaid labors. The second look reveals the wonders of the human beings with whom we are called to share the wonders of the gospel. What Muslims hope for from Christians, more than sympathy or empathy, is respect. The respect in turn, becomes a channel for the Muslim second look.

5. Fairness

Fairness is intimately related to respect. To be fair is to be free from bias or injustice. That is not as easy as it sounds. The writer will illustrate the point with an embarrassing story from his own experience.

I had taken some formal instruction in the field of Islamics but had never had the opportunity to live among Muslims. Without realizing it, I had never taken to heart the meaning of or the importance of "playing fair." I knew what that meant in baseball or tennis, but had not really related it to religious affairs, and that failure had not yet been challenged in a real life encounter. I was asked to give a speech about Islam to a Christian congregation in Winnipeg, Canada. The event was advertised publicly, and as a result the Muslim community of the city was well represented in the front rows. As soon as I realized that fact I felt ill at ease and flustered. The problem was not that I did not know anything about Islam, but rather the fact that I had intended to expound upon the weaknesses of Islam in contrast to the strengths of Christianity. I had no plan to comment on the weaknesses of Christianity and the strengths of Islam! "Playing fair" was not in my "game plan." The presence of Muslims in the audience, however, made fairness imperative, and without the appropriate attitudinal grounding I was quite confused.

This minor incident was significant for my learning because it helped me to realize that a basic orientation to fairness is as imperative in Christian witness as in anything else. The point needs underlining in the context of the present day. It is a convention in contemporary advertising to violate the principle of fairness. The alleged weakness of one product is openly or with subtlety assailed, while the perfection of another product is extolled. The unfairness that is now an almost accepted mode in the commercial world has been a longtime problem in Christian-Muslim relations, on both sides, resulting in familiar misrepresentations and caricatures of mutual positions. The problem continues today. A Christian who shares with Muslims must play fair. He/she will remember that the Lord and his mission are not glorified but are rather dishonored by anything less than an evenhanded and objective, vulnerable and penitential representation of what is factual and true. He to whom the witness is given said plainly: "In everything do to others as you would have them do to you, for this is the law and the prophets" (Mt 7:12).

6. Honesty

By honesty we mean directness—the quality of being plain, open and candid. It is the opposite of deception and subterfuge, which have no place in Christian sharing. At one end of its range of meaning directness is connected with boldness, and at the other end with thoughtfulness. Each are important in defining the attitude of directness. *Boldness ⟵⟶ thoughtfulness*

Honesty or directness is not equivalent to frankness, a trait that can be problematic because of cultural variation, historical misunderstandings, and the pressing need for tact. The frankness that may be tolerable in one culture is often construed as blatant and unacceptable crudeness in another. Historical misunderstandings severely affect emotions, and filtered through those emotions even well-intended comments, frankly given, may be taken as negative accusations. The need for tact requires that at times it is better to be silent than frank. All these realities must be considered in sharing with Muslims. What we mean by directness is the straightforwardness that is molded by concern for the other.

At one end it is connected with the boldness of a true witness as defined by St. John: "We cannot keep from speaking the things we have seen and heard" (Acts 4:20). The incredible news that by God's grace the curse of evil has been overcome, and the powers of sin, death, and the devil broken, and that the victory is available and accessible must be made known to Muslim friends. Honesty in what Christians are about is the only possible stance. It may be noted that Muslims in turn generally respect the sincere conviction of others even though they may not share their views. They are themselves generally open and straightforward in what they accept and reject, and they wonder when Christians are not, sometimes attributing it to weakness and uncertainty. At the other end directness is connected with thoughtfulness, and that has to do with the communicator's approach to the precious things of others, an attitude that we have already discussed.

The quality of honesty is coupled by Jesus with "a good heart" (Lk 8:15). It is born of love, is committed to what is honorable and right, shows integrity, and leads to transparent communication. But it does not include the freedom to hurt unnecessarily. At times it will require that one says: "I look at it differently," or "I do not agree with that opinion," or even, "I consider that to be wrong." Borne by deep friendship the words are not wounding. Honesty is not arrogant because love is not arrogant. It does not confuse directness with insult. A Christian witness testifies to the law that reveals sin, to the full demands of God's "Thou shalt ..." and "Thou shalt not ...," and to the prophetic word that proclaims God's wrath for evil, but avoids self-righteousness and is wary about assuming the role of a prophet. He or she has one chief task—to lift up to the full view of Muslims the Messiah-Savior in whose Light all that is contrary to the will of God becomes progressively revealed. To that process of spiritual self-discovery the Lord invites everyone, including the Muslim, with the words: "I have come as a light into the world, so that everyone who believes in me should not remain in darkness. ... I came not to judge the world but to save the world" (Jn 13:46f.).

C. Profile: Qualities of Mind and Will

The desire to know, to understand, and to think about what is understood are essential qualities in communication. The desire is what matters. What and how much is to be known, understood, and thought about are questions that may bring varying answers. In the end they will be determined by the individual's frame of reference and context. What is certain is that mind and will are to be consciously engaged with sharing with Muslims.

I. The desire and will to know Islam and to understand Muslims

The last verse of 1 Corinthians 13 states: "And now abide these three—faith, hope and love—but the greatest of these is love." Knowledge is not mentioned here. How much knowledge does a person need to be a faithful, hopeful, and loving Christian witness? The authority of Christian witness does not depend on a particular quotient of knowledge. Superior knowledge has its own temptations. It can lead to abstruse non-communicating jargon, and wrongly utilized it may even result in misdirection. An example of this were the many overly-intellectual debates that took place over the years between Christians and Muslims, the results of which were generally counterproductive. It can be observed that it is often the quiet, basic testimony of the ordinary believer, reinforced by the example of life, that has been the most persuasive and has done the most good in advancing the cause of Christ.

Bearing these considerations in mind, we must nevertheless recognize the value of knowledge in Christian communication with Muslims. The Christian scriptures do not commend the lack of knowledge nor extol the merits of ignorance. The opposite is true. The Bible is full of references to "knowing" and it affirms that by knowledge "the deeps break open" (Prov 3:20). The Biblical emphasis is underlined by the practical realities of the Christian engagement with Muslims. The basic overlapping of the Islamic and Christian traditions, and their long history of interaction, means that a commitment to knowing, understanding, and reflecting may be more essential in this area than in some others. While global political, social, and economic factors have led to a great improvements in the knowledge of Islam in the West in the past decade, there are two particular reasons why Christians engaged with Muslims will deliberately strengthen their knowledge base. The first is that the Christian views the Muslim as his/her friend, and wants to understand what is important to the friend; the second is that he/she desires to share Christ in a way that makes sense to friends. There are three components in the strengthening process: the accumulation of dependable facts, the search for understanding, and the experience of personal growth.

a. The accumulation of essential facts.

A possible goal is knowing what the ordinary Muslim knows. For the purposes of this discussion we set aside the secularized Muslim who knows little or nothing about Islam, or the syncretistic Muslim whose Islam is heavily conditioned by indigenous folk religion. Here we are thinking of the average orthodox Muslim who knows the basic beliefs and practices of Islam, some elements of the sharī'a law, especially religious and family law, and stories of Muslim heroes. This material is learned in religious schools (madrasas), using simple texts and rote learning. These elementary religious education schools are attended by almost all Muslim children from the ages of five to twelve. In adulthood knowledge is advanced by mosque lectures and learning experiences in the month of fasting (Ramadān), as well as by private study. In recent times there has been greater emphasis on the direct study of the Qur'ān itself. Muslim intuitive knowledge of their guiding principles is more important than the intellectual components, but the accumulation of some basic facts is the starting-point for grasping the Muslim way of thinking.

b. The search for understanding

When the writer was preparing his introduction to Islam, he inquired of his Muslim friends what they thought about non-Muslim works of this kind. Unanimously they declared: "They are so cold. They do not represent us." There is a powerful warning in this reaction. An external fact without its meaning is like the husk of a seed without its kernel. The accumulation of facts therefore needs to be accompanied by the search for understanding. The Ka'ba is a cube-shaped stone building in Mecca, 50 feet long, 40 feet wide, and 35 feet high, which is the centerpoint of a shrine. That is a fact. But what does it mean that over a million Muslims gather there as part of the pilgrimage rite, and with almost uncontrollable emotion circumambulate the Ka'ba seven times and then turn toward it in common solemn prayer? What is the meaning of this experience for the believer? The search for understanding is a feeling into the phenomena that move so many people so powerfully, an exploration into the Muslim heart.

This represents a huge challenge for communicators. The question has been repeatedly raised whether it is really possible to understand a person of another faith. Being a Muslim has to do with faith of a certain kind. Can a Christian who does not share that faith understand a Muslim who does? The answer is clearly "no" if by understand we mean fully comprehend. But it becomes a "yes" if we are thinking of a partial grasp. Partial understanding is both possible and worthwhile. If the word "understanding" is divided and its parts transposed, it becomes "standing under." A sharing friend is challenged to seek knowledge by drawing near to a Muslim, so near that as it were he/she is "standing under" the other. From that position one may partly sense the feelings of the other person, and to some extent may understand the attraction of that which moves him or her.[9] The search for understanding is an act of true friendship, but it also prepares the way for communication in depth.

What enables this kind of understanding in depth is the principle of love. This has been also recognized by great scholars of religion. For example, Wilfred Cantwell Smith stated: "I cannot know my neighbor more than superficially unless I love him."[10] And Gerardus van der Leeuw put it this way: "All understanding rests on self-surrendering love."[11] But for the Christian witness the principle of deep friendship—the agapé love of Jesus—has an overwhelming and inescapable implication as the driving force and enabling power for the search for understanding. He/she knows that it may "lift up the gates" and "open the everlasting door" for the Self-Surrendering Lord to enter in.

c. The pleasure of knowing

There is a pleasure in knowledge. The pleasure that comes from learning about Islam and Muslims has two elements. The first arises from the obvious gratification of Muslims when they see this effort being made by Christians. It is not the amount of knowledge that pleases the Muslim friend. What impresses is rather the fact that "you" wanted to know and tried to learn. It is the fact that "you" cared enough and respected enough to make the effort. The awareness of such a sincere attempt strongly influences the attitude of the Muslim toward a Christian.

The second element in learning pleasure is the joy of discovery. It takes the "have to" out of the learning equation. The doubt regarding how much I should know is set aside and is replaced by a better question—what will be interesting for me to know? That approach lifts one from dull utilitarianism to the realm of fascinating exploration where merely quantitative judgments are left behind. It does not take long before the learner becomes curious, and even excited, about discovering aspects of the richness of the Islamic heritage, which has graced the human story with many achievements and which has given to my Muslim friend a legitimate pride. And in that process of pleasant discovery that depends so heavily on intercommunication with Muslim friends "the deeps break open."

2. The aspiration to discern Christian theological resources in the light of Islamic views

The following are some aspects of the Christian faith that need the special attention of a sharing friend, against the background of Islamic motifs. These have been alluded to in the first chapter, and are only briefly listed here. They represent a call to Biblical reflection, and a fresh encounter with the inexhaustible riches of the Word of God.

The divine and human natures
The holiness of God
The love of God
The Word of God
The nature of divine victory
The meaning of salvation
The assurance of forgiveness
The power over sin
The implication of being both children of God and servants of God
The law of God
The implication of being both in the world but not of the world
The peace of God and the shalom of creation

The engagement with Islam and Muslims drives the Christian into the Bible and theological reflection. It challenges the hopeful connecter to discern ever more clearly and deeply the meaning of the Christian faith. Thus the struggle to understand and the need to communicate are not only a missional necessity but they become a spiritual opportunity. These are central themes, not peripheral, and the list could easily be expanded. Biblical knowledge is revitalized in the matrix of communication, and fresh nuances of meaning and new applications are discovered as conversation moves across the boundary and the gospel is translated into another world of thought. It connects to human beings, but to humans molded by Islamic ideas and Muslim claims, and the connection becomes a point of mutual learning. The Muslim learns what the gospel intends, and the Christian discovers new worlds of meaning in what he or she may have taken for granted.

When the Muslim asks: "What does the 'Son of God' mean?" he is clarifying a doubt but is also doing the Christian a favor. It is in its missional task of joining message and people that the prophecy of Jesus concerning the work of the Holy Spirit is fulfilled: "He will lead you into all the truth. ... He will take what I have to say and tell it to you" (Jn 16:13f). In sharing we enrich others, and in turn become richer ourselves. This is the inevitable law of Christian communication and the assured experience of a Christian friend of Muslims.

3. The determination to communicate with clarity

By clarity we mean simply intelligibility, the quality of wanting to be understandable and doing what is necessary to be understood. The quality depends on self-awareness. It is the quite unfortunate fact that very few Muslims really have any idea what Christians are talking about. For that matter even many Biblical translations leave Muslims wondering about the meaning of the religious language that passes them by. An unintelligible gospel has no power. For sheer intelligibility consider these words:

> Shout for joy, joy, joy!
> Shout for joy, joy, joy!
> God is love, God is light,
> God is everlasting!

unintelligible gospel has no power.

David Mowbray's hymn verse is refreshingly simple and powerful.[12] Is it powerful perhaps because of its simplicity? Muslims would be attracted to these words and would understand them.

In addressing the subject of God we are dealing with the Ultimate Mystery. Human language strives, stutters and in the end confesses its inadequacy to express the wonder. But the situation is different with what God has done for us. God has done that plainly in our sight. Transparent, clear and certain are the things important for us to know about God, about God's intention for humanity, about God's saving work on our behalf. "The mystery that has been hidden throughout the ages and generations ... has now been revealed" (Col 1:26). We are now the servants of an opened-up and opened-out mystery, the revelation of self-giving love. That is to say, we are the servants of clarity.

That brings us to an area of difficulty. One of the greatest problems that the church faces as it tries to convey the Word of God to the world is its peculiar language, and some of its forms. What is sacred and familiar to the church is often closed-up and closed-in mystery to others. Sharing friends cannot be puzzling in their communication of what God has made plain in Jesus Christ. "Shout for joy, joy, joy! God is love, God is light, God is everlasting!"

4. An inclination to imaginative venturing

Something is about to happen. The words venture and adventure both carry this meaning at the root, but we have chosen the word venture to describe the quality of imaginative enterprise—wanting to make things happen and looking for new ways to do so. We might have said "sense of adventure," but the phrase is somewhat romantic. In the way that we are using the term venture is not romantic, but rather a matter of mind and will. It understands reality, is fact-based and counts costs, but it is also ready to dare and to take risks, to set out on unknown roads.

Venturing has insight, and it recognizes that a new situation appears to be developing between Christians and Muslims in the world. New meeting places for the two communities and their adherents are under formation. The very fact of globalization is pushing Christians and Muslims together in new ways. The need to meet the evils of terrorism is doing the same. Something is about to happen, and venturesome communicators will desire to seize the moment for the sake of the gospel. Therefore with the word venture we have coupled the term "imaginative." You are not satisfied with things as they are. You are patient, but with a healthy restlessness. You let your imagination work a little. We are not referring to planning ability, the strategic instinct or the tactical mind, but rather to a readiness to see new possibilities that contend with inherited routines and static patterns of activity and that give to the Christian engagement with Muslims a much-needed freshness.

So a Christian communicator with Muslims dreams a little, sees visions and ventures new things. Is this a cultivatable quality? Is it perhaps a unique gift given to the few? While the quality of imaginative venturing may vary considerably from person to person, it is to be remembered that—as the prophet Joel foretold—God pours out the Spirit on everyone. It is a "blowing wind" that wakes us up and keeps us alert. There is no one who cannot give some new thought to better ways to relate to Muslims and to communicate with them more effectively. It is an ambition worthy of St. Paul who wanted to proclaim the good news beyond where Christ has already been named. In a sense, Christ needs a new "naming" among Muslims

That those who have never been told of him shall see,
And those who have never heard of him shall understand.
(Rom 15:21)

This is not a lonely task. We can make it lonely by not lifting up our eyes to see fellow Christians around the world who share this inclination. Paul Martinson has recently added the word "joint" to venture.[13] The Lord of the mission has brought a new reality into being, the global household of faith. One need not venture alone. As a growing number of Christians in the world walk the path of concern for their Muslim neighbors and friends, there are partners and companions on the way. Imaginative venturing will ponder that reality and fashion something lively and new.

Conclusion

As witnesses to Christ move between ideal profiles and individual possibilities and limitations, they have faith that it is a movement graced by God's Spirit who broods over, and creatively fashions and empowers God's people. As the Christian scriptures testify God does not hesitate to challenge them to become more than they are, nor fail to provide them encouragement for that process. We must believe in the value of what we are doing. And we must believe that whatever we are, and can become, if it is with God "we shall do valiantly" (Ps. 60:12).

Terry Fox (1958–1981) is a contemporary Canadian and universal hero. As a youth he was stricken with cancer, and one leg had to be removed. He had a premonition that he would only have a short life, and wanted to do something to help others before he died. He decided that he would try to run across Canada to raise funds for cancer research. On April 12, 1980, he dipped his artificial leg into the waters of the Atlantic Ocean at St. John's, Newfoundland. With five months of effort he managed to run to Thunder Bay, Ontario, 5373 kilometers and 3405 miles distant, where his wounded body gave out and would go no further. He died ten months later. Since his death over 300 million Canadian dollars have been given in his name to cancer research. Before he died the twenty-two year old youth had said, "I was lucky to do what I did. How many people ever get a chance to do something they really believe in?"

We turn next to a consideration of some of the practical issues involved in the Christian approach to Muslims today.

Endnotes

1. Kenneth Cragg, *Call of the Minaret* (New York: Oxford University Press, 1956), p. 334.

2. Some may regard the development as a negative rather than a positive factor, arguing that the absorption of Christ's values into the Muslim ethos in effect vaccinates Muslims against the possible reception of the gospel. At the other end of the spectrum some may argue that the Christian mission among Muslims is not needed since we share similar values. The answer is the same in both cases. The points are valid only if Christians regard their primary message to Muslims to be an ethical one rather than the conveying of God's forgiving love that is the ground for grateful behavior.

3. Azad, *Tarjuman*, Vol. 2, p. 288. Emil Brunner describes the connection between holiness and love as "the characteristic and decisive element in the Christian idea of God;" cf. *The Christian Doctrine of God* (London: Lutterworth Press, 1949), p. 183.

4. Luther Engelbrecht, "Christian Remembering of the Muslim in Prayer and Worship," *Word & World*, special edition on Islam, ed. by Roland E. Miller, Vol. XVI, No. 2, Spring 1996, p. 218.

5. Paul Schilpp, *The Quest for Religious Realism. Some Paradoxes of Religion* (New York: Harper & Bros., 1938).

6. Kenneth Cragg, *Christianity in World Perspective* (London: Lutterworth Press, 1968), p. 73.

7. Daud Rahbar, a famed scholar of the Qur'ān and Urdu poetry, is a Christian from Muslim background.

8. Cf. Kenneth Cragg's well-known work *Sandals at the Mosque, op. cit.*

9. For an inquiry into the concept of a religious phenomenon cf. Gerardus van der Leeuw, *Religion in Essence and Manifestation*, 2 vols., tr. by J. E. Turner (Gloucester, Mass.: Peter Smith, 1967). For the understanding of "understanding" cf. studies by Joachim Wach, especially "Introduction: The Meaning and Task of the History of Religions (Religionswissenschaft)," in J. M. Kitagawa, ed., *The History of Religions: Essays on the Problem of Understanding* (Chicago: University of Chicago Press, 1967), pp. 1–21. John Carman takes up the interplay between understanding and evaluation in "Bangalore Revisited: Balancing Understanding and Evaluation in the Comparative Study of Religions," in Frank Whaling, ed., *The World's Religious Traditions* (Edinburgh: T & T Clark Ltd., 1984), pp. 201–221; Carman states his conviction that "understanding and evaluation need to be distinguished but they cannot in a larger human context be entirely separated" (p. 237). Needless to say, the scholarly study of religion provides many resources applicable to Christian communicator's task of understanding.

10. Wilfred C. Smith, "Comparative Religion: Wither and Why?", in Mircea Eliade and Joseph M. Kitagawa, eds., *The History of Religions. Essays in Methodology* (Chicago: University of Chicago Press, 1959), p. 39.

11. Van der Leeuw, *Religion in Essence and Manifestation*, Vol. 2, p. 684.

12. "Shout for Joy," Hymn 792, *With One Voice* (Minneapolis: Augsburg Publishing House, 1995; music by Paul Manz).

13. Paul Martinson, "Social Capital and the New Missionary Pragmatics," *Word & World*, Vol. XVIII, No. 2, Spring 1988, pp. 155–165; he offers the concept of "joint venture" as an alternative to the term "partnership."

12

The Christian Approach to Muslims Today: Wholeness

The Christian approach to Muslims today is rooted in the theology of deep friendship, and three of its branches are wholeness, connection, and methodology. This chapter takes up the aspect of wholeness which includes service, evangelization, reconciliation and peacemaking, and dialogue.

The foundational principle of deep friendship requires that Christians serve Muslims with a willing heart, that they share the good news, that they seek reconciliation and peace, and that they converse with Muslims about common concerns and important issues. None of these can be eliminated without damage to the whole. They represent the four intersecting dimensions of Christian action, and if any one of these is missing the structure of the engagement with Muslims will be severely weakened. To be resisted therefore is an unhappy tendency that sometimes appears to play off one of these functions against the other, or even to delete one or the other. Whatever the reasons, they cannot be allowed to disturb the complementarity of Christian action as taught by Jesus and as demonstrated in his life. He served, witnessed, reconciled and conversed, and so will his followers who seek to be responsive to the whole counsel of God.

While this volume concentrates on the function of gospel-sharing, we maintain the principle of wholeness. Against that background we turn first to the aspect of Christian service.

A. Service

Christian service or *diakonia* is not only a basic component in a holistic approach to sharing, it is also that element of Christian response that is most readily understood and appreciated by Muslims. We need to ask ourselves what the term

"Christian" implies in the phrase Christian service. The themes of philanthropic duty and social service receive wide attention, and in contemporary times have been accepted as essential human values. There is certainly good reason to thank God for this welcome development in which one can detect the movement of God's Spirit. The specific idea of Christian service, however, is informed by the divine paradigm of deep friendship. When I am deeply a friend to someone, I will be helpful to that person. God's impartial generosity in creation is reason enough for God's creatures to render unalloyed service to the needy, without distinction. But it is the divine self-giving in the Servant Jesus that makes this function inevitable for Christ's followers.

What Jesus did is to put together in a new way the ideas of servant, love, and neighbor. The triangle is a familiar Christian symbol representing the Triune God. It may also be used in another way:

Love is the foundation and it informs the understanding of both servant and neighbor. Servant and neighbor connect with each other.

St. Paul expressed the relationship when writing to the Galatians (5:13): "Be servants to one another in love. For the whole law can be summed up in a single commandment: Love your neighbor as yourself."

We see how Jesus redefined the words "serve" and "servant," the latter so dear to Muslims. He one said, "I am among you as one who serves (Lk 22:27). The word "serve" revealed his self-understanding and the mission that came from it. "The Son of Man came not to be served, but to serve, and to give his life as a ransom for many" (Mk 10:45). From his followers the Savior expected nothing less, a life of service in word and deed. He sent out his disciples "to proclaim the kingdom of God and to heal the sick" (Lk 9:2), placing these functions side by side. On another occasion he commanded them, "As you go, preach this message: the kingdom of heaven is near. Heal the sick, raise the dead, cleanse those who have leprosy, drive out demons. Freely you have received, freely give" (Mt 10:7f.). What implications are we to draw from these passages? Christian service does not originate in the kindly disposition of human beings, as important as that may be, but rather it rests on the pattern of Christ the Servant and is guided by his command. In fact its starting-point is earlier. It begins in the very presence of Christ the Healer in this world, and in the intention of God who sent him to renew the creation. It begins in the loving heart of the Almighty God, the Master of the Universe, who does not hesitate to be its servant. Christian service is a grateful response to a compassionately serving God. That reality has prompted the following compact definition:[1]

> The service of Christ is passionate involvement in the reconciling and healing love of God for all people everywhere, in all forms of brokenness and suffering.

In the same way Jesus moves the thinking about neighbor into another dimension, coupling it with loving service. There is almost no place on the globe where the parable of the Good Samaritan is not known. Your neighbor, Jesus taught, is the person in need. You are a neighbor to that person, irrespective of class or creed. Starting from the basis of our being as servant-neighbors Jesus then takes us back to our practice, to our becoming. Because of who you are you will move to the side of a needy person in a practical and helpful way. The Good Samaritan "went to him and bandaged up his wounds" (Lk 10:34). In that picture Jesus not only bound together servant-love-neighbor in an indissoluble union, but he also revealed and shattered the uselessness and pretentiousness of religion that passes by on the other side. The Good Samaritan teaches us to notice human needs, to ignore barriers, to have pity, and to act personally. In fact, he is the image of Jesus himself. Jesus and the Good Samaritan are one.

In our discussion of the Muslim view of Jesus we have noted that the picture of the serving Jesus profoundly impresses Muslims. It merges in their memory with what Jesus says in the Qur'ān, "Lo! I am the servant of Allah" (19:10), and again, "I heal him who was born blind and the leper, and I raise the dead, by Allah's leave" (3:49). This brings us to a significant consideration. While Muslims are rather reluctant to listen to evangelistic messages setting forth Christian truth and presenting the Christian teaching about Jesus, they are generally pleased to see the good works that he inspires in his followers. The Muslim respect for deeds is so pronounced that it needs further spelling out.

No one needs to be reminded that Muslims possess an array of religious words and messages. While Islam is praxis-oriented, it also grants a high place to ideas and their communication. God, in Islamic teaching, has the attribute of Speech, while the Word of God in human language is believed to be the Qur'ān. On that basis a formidable body of law and theology, philosophy, and mysticism has been built and they are elaborated with rich verbiage. The Muslim confession and prayer are similarly Word-based, while the religious instruction of the *madrasa* schools involve classroom language. Even the primary art form of Islam, calligraphy, is nothing other than enscripted Word. The abundance of religious language in Islam combined with the assurance that it bears the final message to humanity creates a reluctance to hear new words and new messages. Deeds, however, are something else. For them Muslims have a special affinity. They represent the real ethos of Islam. Muslims hear deeds. Seeing the good works of those who help the poor and suffering in the spirit of Jesus the Servant many Muslims do return to give thanks.

The writer always thought that Kunyumuhammad, a Muslim friend, was the thinnest man in the world. That condition was partly hereditary, partly the result of his tuberculosis. Kunyumuhammad was the fifth patient that we enrolled in our extended campaign against this debilitating disease that was endemic to the Muslim community of that area. It involved thousands of such patients, many of whom were grateful, but this friend was particularly memorable. Years later when the writer revisited the community a tall thin man came to see him. "I am number five," he announced, "and I am alive because you gave me help." "You are Kunyumuhammad," I replied, "and you are my old friend." The least talkative of men he left as soon as this brief conversation ended. He had returned to give thanks, and we both knew that he understood who was behind the healing.

Kunyumuhammad happened to suffer from tuberculosis, but Muslims in today's world are experiencing many forms of brokenness and suffering. Some are traditional troubles, but others are new problems. We will take special note of six areas of need to which Christians in service may continue to respond. In the end the response will always be local, particular, contextual, related to what is seen and to what is possible.

1. Service to the Wandering

Some Muslim commentators exegize the word "Messiah" to mean "wanderer." Jesus had no place to lay his head. The connection is striking. Muslim wandering in the world has reached a mega level. Some of it is forced, having to do with the disputes and wars of our time that have compelled a massive movement of people, including a sad harvest of refugees and displaced persons. It is recognized that Muslims comprise the majority of the world's refugees. Some of the wandering is of a gentler nature, stemming from the passage of immigrants to new environments. The varying needs of the refugees and immigrants provide a long list of service opportunities in Christian societies of the West. In meeting those opportunities Christians "see" the wandering Jesus (Mt 25:39).

2. Service to the Poor

There is always a tendency to set this need aside because as Jesus said the poor are always with us. The tendency is strengthened by modern economic complexity, by the development of state social welfare systems, and in the case of Muslims by the fact that the existence of rich oil barons gives the impression that there are few Muslim poor. In fact, the economically marginalized are at least equally present among Muslims as they are in other societies. Some of the needs are as basic as food, clothing, and housing, but for many the need is for access to the training and technology that will enable them to compete in the modern market. The development activities that attempt to meet these needs not only call for the Muslim community's acquiescence and cooperation, but they must meet the criterion of all current Christian efforts of this type, namely, that they enable the people themselves to define their problems, formulate possible answers, and develop their own capacities.[2]

3. Service to Children

The global suffering of children continues, contradicting the optimistic image of modern development. It is estimated that every day as many as 35,000 children die of inadequate diet and health care, the statistically proportionate Muslim figure being 7,000 daily. There are about 160 million street children in the world and despite the classical Muslim concern for orphans some of them are Muslim. The casualties of children in war areas are high, traumatic effects severe, and the potential for free tuition in violence even higher. Who could not resonate with the tragic scene of the twelve-year-old Mohamed Durra dead in his father's arms at Gaza? But even more tragic is the effect on other children, making martyrdom a child's goal. The exploitation and abuse of children for adult "needs" required an entire United Nations meeting to consider solutions (Winnipeg, 2000). To whatever extent Muslim children are involved in these tragic conditions they need help.

Nevertheless, equally significant are the needs of normal children for loving care and assistance in gaining a good start in life. Muslims love children. Again and again the Qur'ān puts "wealth and children" together as a sign of God's blessing. It commands the fair treatment of weak children and justice for the orphans (4:127). The fact that the Prophet Muhammad himself was an orphan lends support to this command. Accordingly Muslims tend to greatly appreciate service to children, including preschool educational efforts that give children a sound basis for social development, to the extent that they preserve and enhance the sanctity of the relation between parents and children. In turn they provide a natural and welcome access to the Muslim home. It is very touching when adults return after many years, and with pride and dignity report: "I graduated from your first (or second, etc.) nursery school class!" On the occasion of a 2005 visit seemingly every Muslim taxi-driver in Malppuram, Kerala, approached my wife, Mary Helen, and spoke to her in this vein. Jesus' words, "Suffer the little children to come to me," are a call to Christian servants to respond creatively to the pressing needs of Muslim children wherever they may be.

4. Service to Youth

Perhaps the most demanding form of service in the Muslim world today is service to youth. Caught in the vortex of global conditions many Muslim young people have profound concerns about their futures. The percentage of unemployed youth in population-pressured Muslim societies is very high, including educated youth. Young men and women fashion a variety of theories in regard to the unseen foes that conspire to make life miserable or hopeless, and they turn to a variety of movements—including both the secular left and the religious right—to express their dissatisfactions. Often vehemently critical of traditional religious leaders Muslim youth look for authentic heroes who can inspire them with hope and new possibilities. Many are warmly appealing in their amiability and openness, their potentiality and energy, and their mix of pessimism and optimism that so frequently includes a spiritual dimension. The Christian address to this realm of need has barely begun, and it stands out as a virtually unheeded call for creative response.

Just arrived in a Muslim region, having traveled by a long plane journey and suffering from extreme "jet lag," I was lying recumbent on my bed in a hotel room when the phone rang and a group of Muslim students requested a meeting. I declined to no avail, for very shortly the delegation was firmly knocking on my door. I finally admitted them. Their leader informed me that the Muslim Students' Federation was conducting it's annual meeting that afternoon, and I was to be the keynote speaker!! I was aghast but in the end was forced to agree. Then the group assigned the topic, "The Nature of Spiritual Education." Four hours later and still "weary and heavy-laden" I struggled to the podium, but looking out at the 1500 eager young Muslim men and women in attendance gained strength, and shared some thoughts as best I could under the circumstances. They were both receptive and excessively kind. The one who serves Muslim youth is not only in for a somewhat turbulent and exhilarating ride, but will help to build a new future of possibly far-ranging significance.

5. Service to Women

The ten percent of the world's population represented by Muslim women offers a double challenge. The first is to overcome severe social disabilities that still exist, as many Muslim reformers point out, ranging from the basic need of literacy to income development. The related challenge is to enlist the services of Muslim women in the problem solving effort. The ability of women to transcend barriers and to work together effectively toward concrete solutions at grassroots levels has been repeatedly demonstrated, but now that potential needs to be intentionally drawn upon and imaginatively maximized. That such movements of hope are taking place in many parts of the world is cause for thanksgiving. Included among the notable examples is the hugely successful Grameen Bank in Bangladesh, an effort to help the rural poor by providing access to the institutional credit system. It has become a major women's development effort, three-quarters of the loanees being women. Many are landless women who have seized the opportunity to help themselves and to increase their earnings through various productive activities.[3]

The existence of a panoply of Muslim women's needs is a call to the involvement of Christian women as the vanguard of whatever Christian service is appropriate. In a typical example of such service in South India two Christian women led a group of Hindu and Muslim women in the formation of a Mahila Samajum, an association of women, that broke down traditional barriers and organized efforts to serve the poor and oppressed women of their large community. Job-training, literacy work, tailoring instruction, food production, handicraft activities, and other forms of service, became the external marks of a diverse and successful uplift program. By sheer persistence they involved government authorities and community leaders in the support of the construction of a center for their activities. The wide-spread enthusiasm, the realized possibility of trans-religious cooperation, and the pride of achievement were as important as the activities themselves. Women working together were able to achieve these results where men had found such forms of cooperation and progress very difficult to accomplish.[4]

More complicated is the matter of possible service related to the efforts to liberate oppressed women. The emotional issue of male-female relationships within the Muslim community attracts a broad variety of opinions, and it is an area where the consensus (*ijmā*) of the Muslim community is molding traditional understandings into new shapes. Moreover this is an issue that many Muslims regard as a private matter for the Muslim family to resolve. The struggle for equality and freedom is now led by Muslim women themselves who look to some combination of education, political action, and a new interpretation of the Qur'an for the solution of their problems. The latter is the most important factor in the opinion of many women. In their view correct Qur'anic interpretation supports their views against certain regulations of religious law that were formulated in the patriarchal mode long after the revelation of the Qur'ān. So, for example, Azizah al-Hibri hopefully declares: "These serious problems cease to exist when we adhere to the clear text of the Qur'ān ..."[5] Undoubtedly revolutionary advances have been made in the status of women. Nevertheless severe discrimination, and in some places outright oppression—often linked to local culture or tribal mores—continue to exist. Muslim women involved in the struggle to overcome these disadvantages and to establish their rights often suffer from antipathy and outright opposition. What is the role of a Christian servant in this delicate area? It will certainly be marked by diffidence, self-awareness, and sensitivity, and may best be expressed through personal relations and affirmative action at local levels. In all such service what must be remembered is the great freeing impact of the personality of Jesus who sits by everyone's well (Jn 4:6).

6. Service to the Sick and Handicapped

When Jesus passed by blind Bartimaeus on his way to Jerusalem he stopped his supremely important journey for the sake of one man and asked him: "What can I do for you?" Christians today are also called upon to stop what they are doing and to see the individual who is ill. Some may regard the service of healing as pre-empted by the rapid development of public and private health services. That is a superficial view, and certainly does not apply to all Muslim societies. Consider these factors. Only some Muslims have genuine access to the new therapeutic services. Secondly, many of the illnesses that affect Muslim communities are preventable, and hence such efforts need stimulation. Third, there is a continuing educational need since fatalistic views and superstitious practices run rampant in folk Islam, contending with modern health practices. Fourthly, the condition of the physically and mentally handicapped, as well as new health problems such as AIDS, point to a spectrum of specialized needs. Finally even in western societies Muslim immigrants and refugees need assistance in penetrating the mysteries of various health care systems. Bartimaeus is a constant presence.

Muslims appreciate it when Christians see their sick and render whatever help they can. That, in fact, is a mild way of stating the Muslim sense of gratitude. There has been no service that has been more welcomed than health care. It has been the prow of the ship of friendship in Muslim waters. This is not only a natural human response. It is also related to the strong Muslim regard for medicine. In the Golden Age of Islam Muslim physicians held high places, often combining philosophy and mathematics with medicine. The Canon of Medicine (*al-qānūn fi'l-tibb*) of Ibn Sina (Avicenna; d. 1037) was the most influential medical textbook until the seventeenth century. The tradition of medicine (tibb) is carried forward in some Muslim societies, including aspects of "prophetic medicine" or "divine healing."[6] Muslim leadership in the field, however, did not keep pace with modern developments. For example, the rise of the nursing profession faced a cultural aversion to pollution.[7] The recovery is now fully under way, but until Muslim society is able to meet its health needs in all areas the role of Christian servant healers, both at humble and at highly professional levels, will continue.

There is another side, however, to the coin of appreciation and that is the rising sense of suspicion in regard to Christian medical activities, fed by some apologetic writings. As articulated by these authors the Christian works of mercy carried on in Islamic contexts are essentially forms of deception. They are tricks designed to create interest in the Christian faith, and in effect they constitute a disguised form of bribery and coercion. Such critiques of what is regarded as unworthy motivation and unfair tactics appear not infrequently in Muslim journals. Even though they are not generally shared by the rank and file of ordinary people, the charges must be faced and be allowed to stimulate self-examination. These questions arise. Has Christian service always been pure in its intention and application? In their concern for the healing of the soul as well as the body have Christian healers at times become guilty of forms of utilitarianism? Is Christian service being carried on simply to attract people rather than to help the helpless? The critiques—whether justified or unjustified—represent a call to the purification of motives, to self-deliverance from the sin of underhandedness. They remind servants of Christ of the need for grace to emulate the One who, "moved with compassion," acted to heal (Mt 20:34).

B. Evangel-Sharing

The core task of Christian sharing is to communicate the good news of God's healing. For a friend it is the most natural thing in the world to share one's most precious treasure with another friend. That is the essence of friendship. The most precious possession of a Christian believer is the love of God revealed in Jesus Christ. The divine gift of love becomes the human gift of its news. Thus evangelism is the breath of love. It is the resolute effort to communicate to a fellow human being the miracle of God's deep friendship. It is not possible to conceive of a more significant function.

I. Coining the Term Evangel-Sharing

What, then, shall we call the person who carries out this all-important function? We might use the familiar terms "evangelist" or "missionary," which are rich in Biblical meaning. These terms, however, tend to convey a sense of professional vocation that in common thought may limit their application. We maintain that the Christian engagement with Muslims can no longer be the domain of professionals. It belongs on a wider plateau of the whole people of God who are now called upon to turn their faces to Muslims in a new way. We might also make use of the term "witness" that is widely used in the New Testament. After the Resurrection of the Lord when the disciples were still asking about kingdoms, Jesus the Victor gave his definitive prediction and charge: "You will be my witnesses ..." (Acts 1:8). But bearing in mind the concern for freshness we will introduce the word "evangel-sharer."

The noun "evangel" is roughly drawn from the sounds of the original Greek letters in order to form an English word. This is a transliteration of the Greek word (εὐαγγέλιον; properly pronounced as euangellion) that means good news. The word is used in the New Testament to indicate the welcome information that God loves the world and has determined to save it through a decisive personal intervention that will halt its wayward course. Only God the Greater in Love could conceive of and implement such an astonishing plan. Because God successfully carries out that intervention through Jesus Christ, he and the message about him are good news for all. This is the evangel. An older English word, "gospel," which means "good discourse," is also used to translate the same Greek term. The words "evangel" and "gospel" mean the same thing, that is, the good news of the grace of God in Christ Jesus our Lord.

In addition to the word evangel three other common English terms are also derived from the same root—evangelist, evangelism, and evangelization. An evangelist is one who communicates the good news. Evangelism and evangelization both refer to the broad task of such communication, and they are very close to each other in meaning. The term evangelism may have some stress on theory while evangelization emphasizes action, but in practice they are interchangeable. Although these words are in common use, in what follows we will prefer the terms "evangel-sharing" and "evangel-sharer."

2. A Muslim Difficulty with the Word Gospel

We pause here to point to a difficulty in communication with Muslims that has to do with the word gospel. The difficulty arises from its double level of meaning—message and book. Muslims understand the word only in its second-level meaning of book. This usage refers to New Testament accounts of Jesus named Matthew, Mark, Luke, and John, in other words the four Gospels. It is with this significance of a book that the word gospel came into Arabic, transliterated as *injil*. What the vast majority of Muslims understand by the terms *injil*/gospel is an actual book that Jesus received in the same way as God gave books to other prophets. After having received his written revelation called the Gospel Jesus gave it to the inattentive Jews. From that point of view Muslims are quite interested in the *Injil*, and want to learn more about it. In Christian communication two things need to be clarified for Muslims. One, the first-level meaning of gospel as the dynamic news of God's love must be introduced. Two, the point needs to be made that the second-level meaning of gospel as book refers to writings about Jesus, rather than by Jesus who is himself the Word of God.

3. The Term Share Means Dividing Out

With "evangel" we have linked the word "share." The latter, as we have noted, basically means "to cut," "to divide." God's saving bounty is to be generously divided up among humans. But that bounty has a peculiar miraculous quality. When anything else is cut up and divided each of the parts is less than the whole, but when the good news of God's love is shared out, nothing is lost to the one who gives it away; in fact, he or she gains an extra measure of joy. As the widow's jar of flour did not give out nor did the flask of oil fail in the days of the prophet Elijah, so it is with the sharing of the gospel. When the Christian church more fully assumes its responsibility and divides up the gospel with Muslims, no matter what the results may be, it will receive a special joy. Until that time it will not attain to its full character and destiny.

We have described evangel-sharing as the breath of love. Yet before it becomes an outward flow, communication of the gospel is an inward gasp, a gasp of wonder at the extraordinary grace of God. Instead of destroying the rebellious creation and starting over again, as many humans might have done (but God is not man!), God embraces it, redeems it, and initiates a new creation. Wonder deserves articulation. When we see a beautiful sunset we call our friends to look at it. When a new medicine helps our arthritis, we tell our friends about it. When someone dies saving another person, we tell others to turn on the TV. The same is true of religious experience. William Hocking said: "He who has had a profound religious experience must become a teacher or a hermit or an outcast."[8] The inward gasp of wonder becomes the outward breath of love.

Mannarghat is a village in Malabar, South India. At the outskirts of the village were two huts occupied by very poor families, one Muslim, one Hindu. The Muslim parents were seemingly fortunate that day, having obtained work in the fields. The Hindu neighbor, Krishnan, was not so lucky and had to stay at home. The Muslim hut was one room, the low stove about a foot off the mud floor. The mother thought she had put the fire out before leaving. Alas, not so. Two little children, whom the parents had to leave at home, played in the ashes and the sparks flew up. They caught in the bone-dry, coconut-leaved ceiling, and it exploded into flames. Krishnan the Hindu saw the fire, ran inside and took one of the Muslim children out, ran back and threw out the second child just as the burning roof collapsed on him, and he died. The next day three Muslim leaders visited the writer. I asked them, "What do you think of Krishnan?" The eyes of the cleric on my right welled with tears as he spoke, "Oh ... Oh! He died to save our children."

Indeed, like God. God has entered our fire to save us. Could God do that? God is greater than Krishnan. Would God do that? "Love divine, all love excelling," wrote Charles Wesley in trying to express that mystery. God's self-giving love also brings tears to human eyes. It begs for communication. The One who desires that everyone be saved also yearns that they "come to the knowledge of the truth" (1 Tim 2:4). So God issues the invitation: come to the feast, all things are ready, come unto me you burdened ones, welcome to the banquet of salvation. It is a lovely invitation, and the task of the church is to divide up the invitation cards so that Muslims receive their portion. In this light the function of good news sharing seems positive, even godly, but its critics are many.

4. The Critiques of Evangelism

Not only in the Muslim world but in the Christian and secular worlds evangelism encounters criticism today. Some of the critiques may be deserved, others not. We begin with the Muslim opinion. *understand Christian desire to evangelize*

The Muslim criticism of evangelism is based not on the function but on the content. Muslims believe in communicating the values of Islam. They therefore understand the Christian desire to proclaim the faith, even through they may resist it and often do not permit it. They are clearly surprised at Christian reticence and attribute it to weakness or doubt. But they believe that Christian evangelism is misguided in its message—it is based on false information and interpretations. They also vigorously oppose and criticize what appear to them to be unethical forms of communication. These opinions are well-known and are to be expected.

More unexpected, however, are the critiques of evangelism that come from other sources including Christian ones. We may point to six such criticisms, some philosophically-oriented, some practical in nature:

—One critique stems from the Zeitgeist, the spirit of the age as it relates to a religious truth. In this view, since all truths have at least some value, it is better to leave people undisturbed. Self-discovery rather than inter-religious conversion is the desirable modality for our time. Evangelism is not only essentially unimportant, but it is sadly out-of-date.

—To some evangelism conveys an oppressive spirit. It does so in both its assumptions and its methodology. It assumes that we know better than others, and it employs coercive measures to get its way. It is a thinly-disguised form of religious imperialism, and continues that approach, especially in conjunction with economic power.

—For others the critique of evangelism has to do with what is viewed as its disruptive effects. It produces hostility when the world needs religious amity. Religion has a poor press in the contemporary world, and is increasingly regarded as an affair that causes more harm than good. It should rather, as its priority, address the building up of human relations.

—Another critique holds that evangelism is essentially self-serving. It is not really interested in the other person but rather in aggrandizing the institution it represents. It is a kind of business, with numerical success as its goal. It uses any and every method to gain that success, treating human beings as objects to be manipulated for that purpose. It clothes its worldly approach in spiritual dress, and glamorizes its achievements for its supporters.

The above critiques stem largely but not exclusively from secular sources. Two other critiques are clearly from within the Christian family:

—For some evangelism suffers from theological misdirection in the fact that it emphasizes the care of the soul over the care of the body. It bifurcates the material and the spiritual, thereby repeating early Christian heresies, and it produces false alternatives in the practice of Christian obedience. In the process its proponents regularly overstate their case in relation to other Christian ministries.

—And finally, for others evangelism is an ideology. Essentially valid, it nevertheless becomes the outward expression of prideful Christian fundamentalism. Its mind-set is marked by simplistic positions and an anti-intellectualism that suspects rational reflection and the critical function. It operates in a closed world, is self-delusive, and is basically disrespectful of others.

When the critiques of evangelism are listed in a serial way the cumulative effect is a sobering one. Evangel-sharers must be alert to the individual force of any criticism. Those that stem from relativist world views rather than from the spirit and command of the Lord may be given less weight, although their cautions need to be attended to. However, those criticisms that relate to bad theology and practice must be taken in all seriousness. There is in fact such a thing as "bad evangelism," and there are "poor evangelists." The words "bad" and "poor," as we are using them, do not mean ineffective, but rather that they do not display the mind of Christ or the marks of his Spirit. Who can complain about legitimate criticisms of insensitive or thoughtless ways of dealing with people? There can be quite legitimate complaint, however, about the casual dismissal of a central Christian function, or its caricaturing beyond recognition by those who are in flight from their own being and history.

In the American game of football there is a penalty for what is called "piling on." After the referee has blown his whistle ending play, a player may leap on a pile beneath which is the body of his opponent. The intent is to hurt his foe. When that happens, the player and the team are severely penalized. Is there a reason for "the piling on" of evangelism that is beyond philosophic differences or the desire to give friendly warnings regarding things that need to be corrected? No one can discount the opposition of the Evil One! Evangelization operates on the very front-line of the communication of Christ where the powers of darkness assemble and the energy of demonic forces are brought to bear. Jesus took the field against those forces in a cosmic struggle, and they fought back. Because, as the Second Assembly of the World Council of Churches declared, "Jesus Christ is the gospel we proclaim. He is also Himself—the Evangelist,"[9] that witness will attract the same furies of Satan who can ill afford to let the activity go on unimpeded. Under these attacks self-giving love becomes suffering love. Jesus the Messiah said: "And I, when I am lifted up from the earth, will draw all people to myself. He said this to indicate the kind of death he was to die" (Jn 12:32f.).

The theology of evangelism is therefore a theology of the cross, and evangel-sharers are under the cross. At times they must bear it. Jesus foretold that his followers would share the negative reaction that he experienced. It will vary in intensity from unfair criticism to physical wounding. It is in the nature of deep friendship to accept that possibility. Love reveals its power when it suffers, and is most eloquent when it is wounded. Jesus said:

> This is my commandment that you love one another as I have loved you. No one has greater love than this, to lay down one's life for one's friends. You are my friends if you do what I command you (Jn 15:12–14).

Can anyone doubt that Dom Christian de Cherge knew what that meant?

Dom de Cherge was a Trappist Abbot in Algeria. Trappists belong to the Cistercian Order of monks that is committed to strict austerity and silence. Can silence communicate? Rudolf Otto suggests that the most numinous moment in Bach's Mass in B Minor comes not in the Sanctus but in its moments of sinking into silence. It is then that the listener senses the *mysterium*.[10] Jesus often sank into silence, and it produced wonder. Are evangel-sharers sometimes too noisy? Silently Dom de Cherge maintained his Christian witness in a threatening Muslim context. He was Charles de Foucald reborn and like de Foucald his witness led to the ultimate sacrifice for his friends.

Sometimes evangel-sharers are too noisy.

Abbot Dom de Cherge was among a group of Trappist monks that were taken by militants and beheaded. Anticipating the possibility of such an event he had left his "Spiritual Testament" with his family in 1993. It was opened and read on Pentecost 1996 following his tragic demise.[11] His silence was broken, beautifully and dramatically. He begins by saying,

> If it should happen one day—and it could be today—that I become a victim of the terrorism which now seems ready to encompass all foreigners living in Algeria, I would like my community, my Church, my family to remember that my life was GIVEN to God and to this country, to accept that the One Master of all life was not a stranger to this brutal departure.

After asking for his family's prayers the Abbot shares a prayer of his own:

> I should like, when the time comes, to have a space of lucidity which would enable me to beg forgiveness of God and of my brother human beings, and at the same time to forgive with all my heart the one who would strike me down.

The love of the Trappist monk for his Muslim friends is not lessened by the cruel act of the extremist who by striking him down has given him new freedom and new possibilities.

> This is what I will be able to do, if God wills; immerse my gaze in that of the Father, to contemplate with him His children of Islam as he sees them, all sharing with the glow of Christ, fruit of his Passion ...

And so, after thanking his family and friends, he addresses the one who did the deed.

> And you too, my last minute friend, who would not have known what you were doing. Yes, for you too I say this THANK YOU and this "A-DIEU"—to commend you to the God in whose face I see yours. And may we find each other, happy "good thieves" in Paradise, if it please God, the Father of us both. AMEN!

C. Reconciliation and Peacemaking

Reconciliation and peacemaking are merging ideas in the New Testament. Reconciliation has special reference to the divine-human relationship, while peacemaking refers to both the God-human and the human-human dimensions. Contemporary language use has brought both terms into the arena of Christian-Muslim relations. Reconciling has come to signify the establishment of harmony and peacemaking the effort to end hostility. Christians are called to both activities by the principle of deep friendship.

I. Reconciliation

At its root the word reconcile means to restore a relationship.[12] It bears the idea of change, transformation, and renewal. In St. Paul, and only there, it is applied to God's saving action. The classic passage is 2 Corinthians 5:18—"All this is from God, who reconciled us to himself through Christ, and has given us the ministry of reconciliation, that is, in Christ God was reconciling the world to himself, not counting their trespasses against them ..." Because of this divine initiative there is a newness in life. The old ways of thinking have passed away. Now "we regard no one from the human point of view" (v. 16). Rather, it is intimated, we look at people through the lens of the reconciling love of God that God has poured into our hearts (Rom 5:5). It is a dramatic transformation that can lead to attitude reformation. With this firm theological foundation we arrive at the contemporary usage of the term "reconcile." It signifies "to win over to friendliness to cause to become amicable" (Random House Dictionary).

Some participants in the Christian engagement with Muslims now consider reconciliation to be the primary principle for relating to Muslims today. There has been disharmony and unfriendliness. It is time for Christians to look at Muslims in a new way. Enough of the old way that has produced so much ill-temper and anxiety! Let that pass away and be replaced by the prism of reconciling love. Symbolizing this point of view that well-established Henry Martyn Institute of Islamic Studies in Hyderabad, India, has altered its name to "Henry Martyn Institute: An International Centre for Research, Interfaith Relations and Reconciliation.[13] There may be a feeling that the Muslim soil is too rocky to plant the seeds of reconciliation and to expect a harvest. That, however, is not the experience of those who have tried. Very strong indeed is the spirit reflected in the song: "We shall overcome them by our love, by our love, by our love. We shall overcome them by our love." The power of the idea was strikingly manifested by a group of young Christians who from 1997–1999 participated in what became known as "The Reconciliation Walk."

The Reconciliation Walk was an effort "to defuse the bitter legacy of the Crusades," and remove enmity and mistrust. Marking the 900th anniversary of the Crusades the leaders of the Walk invited people to join them in retracing the long two thousand mile path taken by the first crusaders from Cologne in Germany to Jerusalem. On the way the participants issued both oral and printed apologies to Muslims and Jews for the evils committed against them in the name of Jesus Christ. What was done then, said their apology, was a betrayal of the true meaning of reconciliation, forgiveness, and selfless love. The personal endurance, penitent spirit, and glowing words of the walkers made a deep impression on Muslim observers. The Walk culminated in their arrival at the Holy City on July 15, 1999, the day when the slaughter of the Muslims and Jews took place. The statement of the Reconciliation Walk expresses both remorse and optimism:[14]

Nine hundred years ago, our forefathers carried the name of Jesus Christ in battle across the Middle East. Fueled by fear, greed and hatred, they betrayed the name of Christ by conducting themselves in a manner contrary to His wishes and character. The Crusaders lifted the banner of the Cross above your people. By this act they corrupted its true meaning of reconciliation, forgiveness and selfless love.

On the anniversary of the first Crusade we also carry the name of Christ. We wish to retrace the footsteps of the Crusaders in for their deeds and in demonstration of the true meaning of the Cross. We deeply regret the atrocities committed in the name of Christ by our predecessors. We renounce greed, hatred and fear, and condemn all violence done in the name of Jesus Christ.

Where they were motivated by hatred and prejudice, we offer love and brotherhood. Jesus the Messiah came to give life. Forgive us for allowing His name to be associated with death. Please accept again the true meaning of the Messiah's words: "The Spirit of the Lord is upon me, because he has anointed me to bring good news to the poor. He has sent me to proclaim release to the captives and recovery of sight to the blind, to let the oppressed go free, to proclaim the year of the Lord's favor."

2. Peacemaking

Peacemaking is the practical application of the spirit of reconciliation. It does not merely imply the settlement of disputes but also the establishment of harmonious relationships. It is a core Christian concern. In one of the Beatitudes Jesus declared: "Blessed are the peacemakers, for they will be called the children of God" (Mt. 5:9). Where should sharing friends concentrate their efforts to respond to this challenge in today's context?

The work of peacemaking has become the most "up-front" form of service in our era and needs no validation. The interactive nature of global life has produced an urgency for peacemaking. The violence of our age adds to the pressure. Its impact is exacerbated by the destructive potential of technology, by the availability of weapons, and by the ceaseless attention paid to violence in the media. Peace has become a universal goal, and peacemaking a virtual industry. Christians will be forthright in their support of all such efforts, but will also seek to discover where as individuals they can make their special contribution. One of the natural areas is in relations with people of other faiths. We have previously noted that there is a growing tendency in the world to consider religious people as more often the cause of disharmony rather than the source of its solution. Christians may start at that point. Jesus said, "Have salt in yourselves, and be at peace with one another" (Mk 9:50). To boil it down further, there is no better place for peacemaking to begin than in relations with Muslims which are marked by such a lack of mutual ease.

The Biblical mandate for peace-concern is powerful. Peace describes God—"the God of love and peace." It points to God's desire for humans—"peace, good-will among people." It expresses God's saving activity in Jesus Christ—"peace by Jesus Christ," and "He is our Peace." It is the Savior's gift to believers—"peace I leave with you." It also indicates the Lord's expectation of believers—"proclaim the gospel of peace."[15] Like a silver thread the idea of peace runs through the tapestry of the Christian faith. It captures God's loving intention and loving action for humans. But it is also expressed in active peacemaking by humans among humans. The commands are strong, precise, and compelling. They imply being peaceable. "Do not repay evil for evil, but take thought for what is noble in the sight of all. If it is possible, so far as it depends on you, live peaceably with all" (Rom 12:18). And it means actually making peace. Christians are "to pursue what makes for peace and for mutual upbuilding" (Rom 14:9), thereby sowing "a harvest of righteousness" (Jn 3:18).

The mandate applies to the context of Christian-Muslim relations, and its natural starting-point is in attitude formation. Peacemaking needs to address the general problem of religious slander. The misrepresentation of Islam and Muslims not infrequently raises its head within the Christian family. Sometimes it is the result of an innocent lack of knowledge, but at other times the deliberate nature of the negative profiling is patent. The latter exhibits the essence of slander, which is to take a grain of reality and to expand it into a subtle attack or outright diatribe. The following example from the pen of a Christian "pastor" illustrates the point:[16]

> Islam has caused nothing but misery and suffering for both its adherents and for those who stood in the way of its aggressive proliferation. ... The Islamic plan to exterminate all Christians is a reality. Ultimately the earth must be rid of all "infidels." ... Islam does not elevate peace but glorifies war. It is not tolerant but is viciously violent. It does not offer liberation but rather bondage. It does not hold respect for human life, it only seeks to take control. Islam, claiming to have a "perfect society," can't even properly feed and provide for their own.

Such a mix of unqualified and indiscriminate charges deconstructs rather than builds up the peace of the city. The fact that such statements can be matched or exceeded by the verbally violent outbursts of some Muslim clerics against Christians and Christianity merely underlines the need for peacemaking and attitudinal reformation.

The most common censure of Muslims among Christians today has to do with the topic of violence. It has replaced the medieval attack on the person of Muhammad as the most specific and widespread point of criticism, and it too has produced anguish and suffering. There are two facts in contention with each other. The first is that most Muslims are normal, peaceable people. The other fact is that a small minority are not. Attitude formation will be founded on the former, but must also deal with the latter. The process requires listening to Muslims. Muslim believers will agree that the Islamic approach on the use of force differs at certain points from the Christian,[17] but they regret the allegation that Islam teaches the indiscriminate use of violence and accepts militancy as normal methodology. They disagree with the charge that Muslims are more violent in practice than Christians and Jews, and they correctly reject the wholesale condemnation that "all Muslims are terrorists." Some unfortunately are. Not all Christian perceptions on that issue arise from media distortion. Some are based on actual events where so-called Muslims participate in aggressive and mindless forms of violence against so-called enemies of the faith, in the name of Islam. Many Muslims themselves recognize this fact, regard it as evil and un-Islamic, and are openly speaking out against it. Peacemaking at civic levels involves protecting from and dealing with such criminal activities. Peacemaking at the interreligious level however, involves relating to ordinary Muslims and engaging in the attitude formation that will provide a basis for neighborliness. It is in the latter area that reconciling and peacemaking friends may provide sorely needed leadership.

The components of attitude formation and re-formation are not obscure. We may list the following:

—Lifting up attitude formation in relation to Muslim neighbors as a specific goal in congregational education ministries;

—recognizing that there is a common problem and that all religious communities have failed to some degree to live up to their professed standards in relation to violence;

—opposing the rising spread of malediction that violates truth and fairness;

—reaching out in simple and homely ways to increase understanding and concord; and

—listening carefully to those who are hurting.

In connection with the need for listening we may consider the words of Ms. Sama Sabawi, a former refugee from Gaza and now a new citizen in Canada. The mother of three children was invited by the *Ottawa Citizen*[18] to write a reflective letter of the first anniversary of the terrorist attacks of September 11, 2001. She spoke of her pride of citizenship, but also of the new realities that faced her family as the result of the tragic events; and her loss of personal peace.

> While many fellow Canadians reached out to help us remain an active and integral part of society, others weren't so kind. ... Our loyalties were questioned, our religion deciphered, our actions examined, and yes, our Canadian sense of belonging stripped away.

The writer described her family's difficulty when traveling, a widespread problem, and shared the remark of one of her little daughters.

> Mom, you know when they took you aside in the airport and they were going to be rude to you, I wasn't going to let them take you away. I was going to tell them that you are a great mom and that you love peace and that you are not an Arab terrorist.

Ms. Sabawi concluded her thoughtful letter with this appeal to friends:

> In the quest for vengeance and amid the panic, we unwittingly allowed terrorism to compromise all that we hold so dear and cherish in the name of security. We must defend our way of life: justice for all, tolerance, equality, and freedom of speech and religion. We must find a way to save ourselves from the kind of racist hate and dehumanization that has tragically claimed the lives of thousands once upon a September morning.

It is not easy for the average person to be a reconciler and a peacemaker. Not only is it difficult to know where to start, intuitively we also recognize that suffering will be involved, and we shrink from that. While the hurting voices of our fellow human beings influence us to try anyway, in the end it is the picture of the One who walked between the firing lines at Golgotha, emulated later by Francis of Assisi, that will move us to strive to follow after. Of him the apostle declared:

Through him God was pleased to reconcile to himself all things, whether on earth or in heaven, by making peace with the blood of the cross (Col. 1:20).

He is also the One who said: "You are my friends if you do what I command you" (Jn 15:14). Listening to him makes all the difference in things that are not easy.

D. Dialogue

From reconciliation and peacemaking we move naturally to the fourth aspect of wholeness which is dialogue. It is a function that has become a critical component in the Christian approach to Muslims today. We will take up the meaning of dialogue, the background of dialogue between Christians and Muslims, two difficulties in conducting such dialogue, the need to appropriate the advantages of dialogue, and agendas for dialogue today.

1. The Meaning of Dialogue

Serious, meaningful conversation

Although there are many definitions of dialogue, they all have a common base in the essential meaning of the term, which is "to converse" or "to exchange opinions." The title of a European publication on the subject points to this core meaning, *Christians and Muslims Talking Together*.[19] Dialogue is more than casual talk, however. "How is the weather in your place?" "It is fine, but a little cold." The interchange is conversation, but not really dialogue. Dialogue is serious, meaningful conversation. It is characterized by mutuality, by sincerity and respect, by honesty and frankness. In a small but groundbreaking work, Reuel Howe defined dialogue as

> that address and response between persons in which there is a flow of meaning between them in spite of all obstacles that normally would block the relationship. It is that interaction between persons in which one of them seeks to give himself as he is to the other, and seeks also to know the other as he is.[20]

Conversation in depth w/ understanding as its goal.

Dialogue, then, is conversation in depth with understanding as its goal.

In this intrinsic sense dialogue is not an idea specific to religion. It is a neutral term. It has become a common word for "talking things through" in various areas of life, especially where there are problems. The word is used by United Nations officials, by statesmen and politicians, by social workers and police officers. However, it has been taken up most vigorously by religious people to convey the idea of a genuine exchange among people of different faiths.

In the process of being used in the religious realm Reuel Howe's guarded interpretation of dialogue as meaningful conversation has broadened out. On the one hand, it has come to mean formal discussion meetings. In this sense it is now a commonplace term in the area of Christian–Muslim relations. Interaith consultations of many kinds on many subjects have been conducted since World War II, mostly at the upper levels of denominational and ecumenical agencies. Because of the pressing need for improved relations between Christians and Muslims, dialogue events in that context have received much attention. A number of useful works have appeared on the subject, and the theme has been frequently addressed in theological writings, from different perspectives.[21] On the other hand, dialogue has also been taken to signify grassroots relationships and cooperative activities for the common good. which are referred to as "dialogue in life." Between these poles various other shades of meaning have accumulated. For our purposes we will recognize three levels of meanings:

—informal, free-flowing conversation on important issues;
—formal occasions for discussions on pre-set agendas; and
—joint interaction to overcome social problems.

Implicit in genuine dialogue is the understanding that it flows from a relationship. Where no relationship exists, what is called dialogue is really a set of monologues, or it may be some sort of negotiation. Certainly this awareness is crucial in the area of Christian–Muslim dialogues, whether informal, formal, or practical. For Christian partners in dialogue the required relationship exists in the principal of deep friendship. A friend not only wishes to share what is in his or her heart, but is also interested in the heart of the other. Susheela Engelbrecht who served with distinction as a public health specialist in predominantly Muslim Senegal makes this point eloquently. She writes of the relationaship with Muslims in her Sahel village:

> When we enter relationships with people of other faiths with open hearts and minds, stereotypes can finally begin to erode and true dialogue can take place, dialogue that entails mutual sharing and learning in the context of true friendship, humility and respect; dialogue that is entered into without arrogance or ulterior motives, dialogue between friends.

2. Christian–Muslim Dialogue: The Background

Here we will address two questions: Is Christian–Muslim dialogue new?, and what are the hesitancies associated with the concept and activity?

a. Is Christian–Muslim Dialogue New?

Dialogue is a normal activity in the human community that has gone on since its beginning. Religious dialogue too is not new, certainly in the sense of informal discussion. Long ago Nicodemus came by night to engage Jesus in serious discourse. Neither is Christian–Muslim dialogue new. For generations everyday Christians and Muslims have been holding converse together as friends, and they continue to do so today in many parts of the world. The great communicators of the past whom we have considered in foregoing chapters were steadily engaged in sincere, serious conversation with Muslims. Dialogue in the sense of meaningful informal conversation is not an innovation.

There are elements of newness, however, in the other two meanings of religious dialogue, namely formal dialogue meetings and dialogue in life. The first known forerunner of a modern formal dialogue took place in the Mongol capital of Karakorum in May, 1254, involving William of Rubroek who represented Latin Christians; Nestorian Christians; Buddhists and Muslims.[23] As far as we know, however, it was much closer to a debate than a mutual exchange of views. Public debates between Christians and Muslims became a well-known pattern that has continued down to the present. Formal dialogues in our definition are not public debates but rather the measured and cordial exchange of opinions with a view to better understanding. In that sense the dominant trend in past Christian-Muslim relations has not been dialogical. D. C. Mulder says:[24]

> In the past Christians and Muslims have met in all kinds of ways ... but until a short time ago there has been very little effort towards real understanding of the other, there has been very little dialogue. At best Christians and Muslims have tried to attain knowledge of the other religion but often with the purpose to defend and attack; at worst they have looked at each other with all sorts of misrepresentations, all kinds of warped images in their minds. A real dialogical openness was an exception on both sides.

Whether in fact "dialogical openness" has so wonderfully displaced traditional attitudes in our time as the writer implicitly suggests may be disputed, but there is no doubt that real change has taken place. A minimal observation is that Christian-Muslim dialogue has moved from the realm of occasional informal conversations to formal and programmatic efforts to create better understanding.

3. The Hesitancies

There is some criticism of this movement to formal dialogue from both academic scholars and theologians. From the perspective of some scientific scholars of religion there is little to be gained from such an effort because there is too wide a gap at the foundational levels of the two religions. Charles Adams, representing this view, makes the following comment. Because of the importance of his observation we will quote it at length:[25]

> We have seen that at one level, Christianity and Islam have much in common in their allegiance to specific doctrines and in the terms that are fundamental to their religious vocabularies. In spite of this similarity we have also seen that in other more important respects there is a profound contrast between the two. They begin, as it were, with different estimates of the religious situation of mankind, offer different solutions to the problems that all men face, and issue in states and attitudes that are also marked by contrast rather than by similarity. ... The two communities differ radically concerning the structure of the religious life. Indeed they seem to be addressing themselves to entirely different problems. ... To the extent that similar doctrines or positions prevent us from seeing the more far-reaching differences inherent in the way in which doctrines and concepts combine into an integrated whole to form a perception of man, of God, and of their relations with one another—to precisely this extent—such similarities obstruct understanding. The matter of importance is the thrust of the whole, its distinctive character. Here the difference is so great that one may well ask whether in truth there is any hope of Christian-Muslim dialogue ever progressing beyond the stage of registering the differences with one another.

The standing of this scholar in the ranks of specialists and the insights in his comment are such that they raise a caution flag over easygoing assumptions and superficial approaches in relation to Christian-Muslim dialogue. At the same time they point to the need for a high quality of realistic interaction.

From within the Christian fold other hesitancies emerge in relation to dialogue. The concern is expressed that the style of formal dialogue leads to possible compromise of the Christian faith, or that it fails to leave sufficient room for the sincere communication of the gospel. The criticisms are often part of a larger realm of theological disagreement between the so-called ecumenical and evangelical streams in western Christian thought, the former being more concerned with the whole field of interfaith relations and the latter more preoccupied with missional activity in the world. An evangelical scholar suggests: "It is apparent that in recent dialogue the very serious danger exists of losing sight of the goal of winning men and women to Christ." He goes on to add, "On the other hand, there is little question that 'dialogue' which denotes the means of discovering another person's beliefs is a legitimate starting-point for evangelism, and has been used as such since the time of Christ." Both affirmation of the dialogical process and hesitancy regarding its interpretation are affirmed. The writer concludes with an observation that is the common experience of participants in Christian-Muslim dialogues:[26]

> Surely we evangelicals must encouragingly relate to the experience of one who said: "Many of us in Christian-Muslim dialogue ... have been pushed back to rediscover the richness of our Christian faith. ... By feeling the thrust of our neighbor's criticisms and hopefully by resolving these, our own Christian faith is strengthened even though we may have incurred risks ...

Probably the greatest hesitancy has to do with fear of dialogue as a philosophical point of view which, for lack of a better term, we shall call "dialogism." It is a fear that in some interpretations dialogue has moved from its sound basis to the realm of ideology. The ideology is regarded as roughly equivalent to relativism. Implied is the goal of uncovering commonality through the perception of universal truths and in the interests of harmony, or even helping to form a kind of a common religion that transcends the uncomfortable and troublesome particularities of the faiths. This raises an understandable alarm among both Christians and Muslims, as well as the legitimate criticism of scholars. It must be recognized, however, that the disquiet is not over dialogue, but of a virtual caricature. Dialogue cannot be laid aside out of fear of dialogisms. It will not become more or less than it should, and will not lose its true role, if it is maintained within the perspective of wholeness. This hesitancy, as well as others, encourages the continued exploration of the theological roots of dialogue and its place within the whole stream of Christian sharing of the gospel.

4. Two Difficulties in Christian-Muslim Dialogue

There are two practical difficulties that impede the implementation of formal Christian-Muslim dialogue, one on the Christian side and one on the Muslim side.

On the Christian side, the difficulty lies in the fact that organized dialogue has not caught fire at grassroots levels of the church. It has rather depended on the efforts of Islamic Studies specialists and interested church workers gathered in periodic meetings. Although these sessions have made sterling contributions, their findings have seldom been accessed by the Christian public. It has proved impossible, thus far, to construct a sufficient variety of dialogue models that take into practical account differing levels of knowledge, varying situational contexts, and the need for constant new beginnings. An "Islam Group" designated by the Lutheran World Federation to study Christian-Muslim dialogue within the context of theology of religion issued a call to churches "to facilitate the preparation of study materials for adult classes in congregations.[27] The intent was the development of local forms of dialogue grounded in the life of the laity. The slightness of the progress indicates that the potential for dialogue in adding freshness to the task of sharing with Muslim friends still awaits realization. It also points to the fact that it is informal dialogue and dialogues in life that have the most practical value and need to be elevated in the consciousness of everyday Christians.

The second difficulty comes form the Muslim side. The Muslim interest in Christian-Muslim dialogue is obviously low. The reality is that almost all formal dialogue meetings have been initiated by Christians. The Muslim community as a whole—undoubtedly reflecting the Islamic sense of finality and its view of Christianity as an erring religious tradition—is in general indifferent. Muslim scholars have not worked very hard to develop an Islamic perspective on the subject of dialogue. They tend to think that it is a practical need of local religious minorities. Where Muslims are a majority, the need for it does not exist.[28] There are exceptions to this broad generalization. When Muslim leaders attend dialogue meetings, they participate with grace and clarity. Individual Muslim scholars who have been enthusiastic in their support of Christian-Muslim dialogue and who have made important contributions include such well-known figures as Mushir-ul-Haq, H. A, Mukti Ali, Hasan Askari, Djohan Effendi, Basri Ghazali, Riffat Hassan, and many others too numerous to mention. They would resonate with the words of the then Crown Prince Hassan of Jordan who in Christ Church Cathedral, Oxford, stated:[29] "I believe that interfaith dialogue must be intensified, . . . We must harness our energy and concentrate our effort for the common good of all believers."

5. Appropriating Dialogue and Its Advantages

Christian communication with Muslims will need to move past hesitancies and difficulties, past Christian inexperience and Muslim coolness, to appropriate dialogue as an essential aspect of a holistic approach. Its inevitability rests on the fact that it belongs to the essence of human existence. Humans, unless they are hermits, are in a dialogical relation with each other. Dialogue has a central place in the theory of communication. Moreover, it belongs to the essence of the divine-human relationship. From the moment God addressed Adam: "Where are you?" to the Savior's last word: "Surely I am coming soon," the communication goes on. It is solidly grounded in the Biblical testimony, and at informal levels belongs firmly in the Christian historical experience. On that basis, it is not an option but a necessity, a need that contemporary conditions have highlighted rather than created.

Paul V. Martinson, a missiologist who has engaged in many dialogues, especially with Confucians and Buddhists, aptly views dialogue as a mode of witness that differs from evangelism but has a dynamic relation with it. He puts the distinction in epigrammatic form:[30]

> Evangelism is a public offer, dialogue is public reasoning. Evangelism originates in confession; dialogue arises out of interrogation. Evangelism is towards the other and seeks to convey an offer that carries its own compelling power; dialogue is towards each other as it seeks to make and to heed a persuasive accounting of the faith—that one's and mine. The goal of both is change.

Martinson continues his thoughtful remarks with the following comments. While evangelization invites people to consider the transformation of existence, the big change, dialogue "initiates many little changes, so that the faith one holds and the life it enables is still held, but held and lived differently." Dialogue may take place at varying intensity levels—a simple sharing of information, an opening up of opportunities for cooperative service, or a deep sharing of convictions. In every case changes occur. Within the dialogical process "neither Islam nor Christianity can give up on either the possibility of a big change or the necessity of many little changes."[31] This, then, is not "change and decay" as the hymnist puts it, but change and construction. Those who have participated in dialogue have understood that it is not a giving up but a giving to, and that is what friends will do.

In summary, we may list the values of Christian-Muslim dialogue as follows:

a. Dialogue creates an atmosphere.

Let us call it an atmosphere of possibility. There is a certain wonder that develops from dialogue, that after all these years of dissonance Christians and Muslims can actually meet together and discuss serious issues of faith and life. If this is possible, what more is?

b. Dialogue clarifies faith, dispels ignorance, and produces awareness.

It is, of course, quite remarkable how little Christians and Muslims really know about each other. What is the real fact about anything, and what does it mean for the Christian or Muslim partner? Even if the clarification falls short of producing actual understanding, it creates awareness of the realities.

c. Dialogue leads to self-understanding.

Not many people know how they are viewed by others, and fewer will admit that they have a log in their own eye that needs to be removed (Lk 6:42). Conversation with Muslims not only leads to Christian reflection and self-understanding, but is also helpful in puncturing the balloons of mere judgmentalism.

d. Dialogue establishes relationships.

Genuine personal relationships between Christians and Muslims are fewer than needed for the common good. The fact of being together in a discussion, with an occasional cup of tea, not only enables acquaintanceship, but may even lead to, or nurture friendship. Once that occurs, things change.

e. Dialogue opens doors.

The door to what? The Spirit knows. What greater gift is there than an open door to something noble, to a possible better future. For the Christian that open door may in hope include an encounter with the One who dialogued so remarkably with Nicodemus and the Samaritan woman.

6. Relevant Agendas

The need for relevant agenda-setting is influenced by the Muslim concern for practical matters, and it introduces a new stage in Christian-Muslim dialogue. There is a growing feeling among Muslims that there is indeed a need for and room for interreligious discussion and cooperation to deal with certain practical problems. Muslims tend to believe that the classical Christological themes have been exhausted and settled in their favor, and there is really not much left to discuss in that sphere. They are willing and happy to converse about the key principles sketched in the first chapter of this volume, and to exchange opinions on those themes, but are less interested in discussing classical theological issues. In Muslim view it is the area of society-building that provides the natural arena for cooperative activity with Christians, and thus it will also provide the relevant agendas. C. M. Naim, a Muslim scholar, makes the case for more "down-to-earth" agenda-setting:[32]

The Christians who initiated these dialogues may have gained some understanding of contemporary Islamic politics. But if their aim was to get an insight into the lived religion of Muslims, they should have brought to these dialogues their own lived religion. At none of the meetings that I attended did the Christians highlight any of the issues that are currently so problematic a part of their lives as Christians—issues related to homosexuality, women's rights, prayer in school, abortion. Or the three great issues of the recent past: ecumenism, race, anti-Semitism. The Muslims were not inclined to raise such issues either. And when they did, it was only to dismiss them with a scriptural quotation. Overwhelmingly, they used these occasions to tell the story of their grievances and hurts ...

Naim entitled his remarks, "Getting Real about Christian-Muslim Dialogue." This pragmatic emphasis corresponds with the new Christian interest in dialogue in life. Not so much the table of discursive discussion—as needed and as important as that may be—but the street of justice-creation and the rocky path of conflict resolution is the place where Christians and Muslims must walk with each other and work together. On the way they will begin to know one another, to put a human face on each other, and to communicate positively. Is this to be the starting-point for our days?[33] Yet there is surely no interaction on the road of life that will not eventually lead to an examination of the condition of humanity. The discourse on praxis and common action "to prohibit the evil and to commend the good" will force reflection on human "proneness to evil" and its solution. "Even the most 'temporal' kind of dialogue is destined to become spiritualized as it goes on. For everything a man does, brings into play some conception or other of man and his relation within society and with God."[34]

As Christians consider this prospect, and as they both receive learning and with gentleness and reverence give reason for the hope that is in them, they will bear in mind the words of Willem Bijlefeld: "So much is at stake in the adventure of moving into the unknown ..."35

We now move forward into the second component of the Christian approach to Muslims today—the factor of connection.

Endnotes

1. The definition was used by the Colloquium on Service at the Congress on the World Mission of the Church, St. Paul, Minnesota, June, 1998, and its attribution must be made in part to Lee Snook who chaired the Colloquium. Quoted from Roland E. Miller, *Mission Agendas in the New Century* (Minneapolis: Kirk House Publishers, 2000), p. 6.

2. Cf. Carol J. Kirkland, "An Evangelical Theology of Service in an Interdependent and Suffering World," in Paul V. Martinson, ed., *Mission at the Dawn of the 21st Century* (Minneapolis: Kirk House Publishers, 1999), p. 242.

3. Salma Khan, *The Fifty Percent* (Dhaka: University Press Ltd., 1988), p. 96; Lutheran Health Care Bangladesh at Dumki, Pathuakali Dt., is an example of Christians in service adapting this kind of activity to a local situation.

4. The location was Malappuram, Kerala; the Christian women involved were Mrs. Mildred Francis and Mrs. Mary Helen Miller. Similar examples may be drawn from every part of the world.

5. Azizah al-Hibri, "A Study of Islamic Herstory; Or How Did We Ever Get into This Mess?", in *Women's Studies International Forum*, Vol. 5, No. 2, 1982, p. 215.

6. For a convenient summary cf. Seyyid Hussein Nasr, "Medicine and Pharmacology," *Islamic Science* (L:ondon: World of Islam Festival Publishing Co., 1976), pp. 153–193.

7. Christian nurses from India, especially Kerala, were drawn to Saudi Arabia and the Gulf States in great numbers to staff the new hospitals constructed there, in part because of the lack of female education, but also because the nursing profession did not attract Muslim women.

8. William Hocking, *Living Religions and World Faith* (New York: Macmillan, 1940), p. 40.

9. W. A. Visser't Hooft, ed., *The Evanston Report; The Second Assembly of the World Council of Churches,* 1954, quoted in Hans Margull, ed., *Hope in Action,* tr. by E. Peters (Philadelphia: Muhlenberg Press, 1962), p. 40.

10. Rudolf Otto, *Idea of the Holy,* tr. by J. Harvey (London: Oxford, 1950), pp. 70f.

11. I am indebted to an unknown friend for the contribution of this testimony.

12. Cf. Friedrich Buchsel, "ἀλλά66ω" and "Καταλλά66ω", in Gerhard Kittle, ed., *Theological Dictionary of the New Testament,* tr. by G. Bromley (Grand Rapids: Eerdmans, 1964), pp. 251-260; and Werner Foerster, "ε'leήvη" Vol. II, pp. 400-420, for a full study of these Biblical ideas.

13. See Andreas and Diane D'Souza, "Reconciliation: A New Paradigm for Missions," in Roland E. Miller, ed., *Islam,* a special edition of *Word & World* (St. Paul: Luther Seminary), Vol. XVI, No. 2, pp. 203-212.

14. The Reconciliation Walk was led by John and Yvonne Pressdee. The quotation is from materials published by the Reconciliation Walk Coordinating Office (Harpenden, Hertfordshire, England) and newspaper reports.

15. The Biblical passages are 2 Cor 13:11; Lk 2:16; Acts 10:36; Eph 2:14; Jn 14:27; and Eph 6:15 respectively.

16. Excerpted from Steven L. Snyder, "The Truth Regarding Islam," released by Christian Solidarity International, P.O. Box 70562, Washington, D.C. 20024, n.d.

17. Cf. Miller, *Muslim Friends,* pp. 245-259.

18. The *Ottawa Citizen,* September 3, 2002, p. A-13.

19. Translated from the German, *Christen und Muslime im Gesprach* (London: British Council of Churches, 1984).

20. Reuel Howe, *The Miracle of Dialogue* (New York: Seabury Press, 1963), p. 37.

21. Cf. for example, Roland E. Miller and Hance Mwakabana, eds., *Christian-Muslim Dialogue. Theological and Practical Issues; op. cit.;* in the first two chapters Miller deals with "Prolegomena for Theological Perspectives on Islam" and Willem Bijlefeld takes up "Theology of Religions, 1960-1995." See also *Guidelines for a Dialogue Between Muslims and Christians* (Roma: Secretariatus Pro Non-Christianis, n.d.); John B. Taylor, ed. *Christians Meeting Muslims* (Geneva: World Council of Churches, 1977); Paul V. Martinson, "Dialogue and Evangelism in Relation to Islam," *Word & World,* Vol. XVI, No. 2, pp. 184-193, and "What Then Shall We Do?", in F. W. Klos, et.al., eds., *Lutherans and the Challenge of Religious Pluralism* (Minneapolis: Augsburg, 1990), pp. 174-197.

22. Quoted by Luther T. Engelbrecht, "The Christian Remembering of the Muslim in Prayer and Worship," *Word & World,* Vol. XVI, No. 2, p. 213.

23. R. W. Southern, *Western Views of Islam,* pp. 47-52.

24. D. C. Mulder in Taylor, ed., *Christians Meeting Muslims,* Foreword, p. 1.

25. Charles Adams, "Islam and Christianity: The Opposition of the Similarities," in R. M. Savory and D. A. Agius, *Logos Islamikos* (Toronto: Pontifical Institute of Medieval Studies, 1984), p. 306.

26. Daniel R. Brewster, "Dialogue: Relevancy to Evangelism," in Don McCurry, ed., *The Gospel and Islam* (Monrovia, Calif.: MARC, 1979), pp. 516, 525.

27. Miller and Mwakabana, eds., *Christian-Muslim Dialogue,* p. 387.

28. Conversation with Professor Machasin of the I.A.I.N., Sunan Kalijaqa, Yogyakarta, at a Lutheran World Federation sponsored dialogue, at Yogyakarta, Java, Indonesia, April 7, 2002.

29. A speech delivered June 4, 1995, reproduced in App. III, Miller and Mwakabana, eds., *Christian-Muslim Dialogue,* p. 369.

30. Paul V. Martinson, *Word & World*, Vol. XVI, No. 2, 1996, p. 188.

31. *Ibid.*

32. C. M. Naim, "Getting Real about Christian-Muslim Dialogue," *Word & World,* Vol. XVI, No. 2, pp. 179–183; a Muslim and Professor of Urdu at the University of Chicago, Naim presented these remarks originally in the Rockefeller Chapel.

33. See Appendix II for a list of dialogue topics.

34. *Guidelines for Dialogues, op. cit.,* p. 119.

35. Willem Bijlefeld, "Theology of Religions: A Review of Developments, Trends, and Issues," in Miller and Mwakabana, eds., *Christian-Muslim Dialogue,* p. 80; the article is a magisterial survey of the theology of dialogue.

The Christian Approach: Connection

The second element in the Christian approach to Muslims is making connections. Starting from its source in deep friendship the Christian witness flows through the four great channels of wholeness and makes connections with Muslims in relevant ways. A simple analogy illustrates the point, taken from the flow of electricity. The generator produces the power. It is the deep friendship of God that is poured into our hearts. The four great wires on the main trunk line are service, evangelism, peacemaking, and dialogue. From them connecting lines link the power to the Muslim emotion and faith. They are the subject of this chapter. We may carry the analogy one step farther—in the home the plug must be put into the electrical socket for the light to shine, but that we define as the area of method which we will consider in the following chapter.[1]

Making connections with Muslims implies four things: seeing the value of points of contact; awareness of the "hot" issues that really concern Muslims; the careful consideration of possible Qur'anic connections; and the recognition of delicate areas of Muslim sensitivity, the bare wires and bad connections. None of the functions of holistic witness are operable without connection, and certainly not the task of evangel-sharing. A disconnected engagement is no engagement. As we move into the practice of communicating with Muslim friends, our first reflection will be on the idea of "points of contact."

A. Points of Contact

There are no magical or mechanical points of contact, but there are serviceable ones. Each of the twelve key principles in chapter one is a point of contact. What Muslims believe about sin and salvation, as outlined in chapters two and three are points of contact. What Muslims believe about Jesus the Messiah, presented in the fourth chapter, is another. When all is said and done, however, the living points of contact with Muslims rise out of an actual relationship with a person. What Hendrik Kraemer once affirmed about missionaries is true for every sharing Christian: "There is only one point of contact, and if that one point really exists, then there are many points of contact. This one point of contact is the disposition and attitude of the missionary ... to have an untiring and genuine interest in the religion, the ideas, the sentiments, the institutions of the people among whom one works, for Christ's sake and for the sake of those people." The distinguished missiologist, who had long personal experience with Muslims, went on to add the basis for this important assertion: "Only a genuine and continuous interest in the people as they are creates real points of contact, because man everywhere intuitively knows that, only when his actual being is the object of humane interest and love, is he looked upon in actual fact, and not theoretically, as a fellow-man."[2]

In his helpful statement Kraemer points to the basic factor in communication that we have previously noted, namely, that those who seek to share must deal with Muslims as human beings. When they deal with them as "intellectual curiosities" or "for the purposes of conversion" and not "because of himself" the indispensable condition of sharing is lost, that is "humane, natural contact."[3] We may add to Kraemer's point that when the human quality of the engagement is maintained, not only will points of contact abound, but they will become in fact *Anknüpfungspunkten*, that is, points of attachment. The reverse is true. It is also clear that until evangel-sharers become real persons in their own right for Muslims, they will continue to be identified as agents of an undesirable influence or force.

No one has worked harder at the effort to perceive connections between Christians and Muslims than Bishop Albert Kenneth Cragg (b. 1913). Scholar and missionary, Islamicist and churchman, teacher, and author, he has thoughtfully and prolifically explored the landscape, especially the border areas, of the Christian-Muslim engagement. To that task he has brought not only his academic learning, but his intimate and practical insights into the Muslim way of thinking, developed from years of personal relationships. His prodigious output of books and essays is the best single source of information and inspiration for Christian sharing with Muslim friends that is available in the English language.

Starting from Oxford University Bishop Cragg's career as a missionary scholar took him to many parts of the world, but his first love has been the Middle East. There he rendered recurrent service as an Anglican missionary in Beirut, Cairo, and elsewhere, and was Assistant Bishop to the Archbishop of Jerusalem. His teaching ministry included service as Professor of Arabic and Islamic Studies at Hartford Seminary, U.S.A. (1951–1956); as Warden of St. Augustine's College, Canterbury, United Kingdom (1960–1967); as Reader in Religious Studies at Sussex University; as visiting professor at several institutions; and as Bye-Fellow of Gonville and Caius College, Cambridge. In retirement he serves as Honorary Assistant Bishop in the Diocese of Oxford. Throughout this varied career he has remained focused on the task of commending the Gospel of God in Christ to Muslims. His literary output includes objective studies of the Islamic tradition, reflections on the Christian engagement with Muslims, works on Christian theological thought, study materials, and others. The natural starting-point for digging into this treasure trove are two early works: *Call of the Minaret* (1956) and *Sandals at the Mosque* (1959).[4]

Bishop Cragg has brought his strong evangelical commitments into a dialogical engagement with both Muslims themselves and with the ideas of Islam. For him the task of making connections is a respectful exploration of congruent ideas, especially those drawn directly from the Qur'ān. Faithful to his calling as a witness to Christ he seeks and finds in almost bewildering profusion the intimation of Christian ideas, or the need for those ideas, or a preparation for those ideas, in the Qur'ān and its expositions. He believes that an outsider can take the Qur'ān "pragmatically in this way without holding it creedally." He says: "Such an aim, taking the Qur'ān in its own seriousness, and with respect for, and yet independence of, its own faith system, suffices to cover in a practical way the vexed question of authority."[5] While some Christians may find it too challenging to follow his scholarly probings and some Muslims may reject them as a Christian interpretation of Islam, Bishop Cragg never fails to stimulate his listeners and readers.

A major contribution Cragg makes to Christian sharers of the gospel is to remind them that they must relate the teaching of Christ to Islamic themes. His thoughts on the general theme of "points of contact" become clear in *Sandals at the Mosque* where he shows his preference for another phrase, "the spiritual criteria of relatedness" (p. 103). He advocates a theology that is "outward and relational," which is "on the frontiers of religions in their mutual existence" (p. 21). This is for the sake of Christ and the other person. Those who tell the gospel "must be prepared to reckon with the mental world of other men. ... From that world, the listener's world, comes the framework of ideas within which, at least initially, the new thing is judged" (p. 94). Cragg finds solid basis for this approach in Jesus' reaching into the Jewish thought world through his parables, in the apostolic reaching into the Gentile mind, but above all in the Incarnation and God's personal entry into the human context.

The possibility of entering into the mind of others rests in our common humanity and in our "inter-life." It also has to do—in the case of Islam and Christianity—with the fact that they "deal fundamentally with the same things." This becomes most visible in devotional materials. He quotes from the Prayer Manual of the Tijani Order in *Sandals* (p. 80):

> O my God, I have no thought of Thee, save what is beautiful. I see in Thee nought but graciousness. To me Thy goodness is all-embracing. Thy works in my sight are perfect. Thy mercy is to me ever reliable. Thy righteousness a forgiving righteousness. Thy bountifulness towards me constant and perpetual, Thy benefits toward me unremitting. Thou has obviated my fears and fulfilled my hopes, hast realized my desires and befriended me in my travels, restored me in my sicknesses, healed my diseases and dealt kindly with my upheavals and my homemaking.

To trace these overlapping areas Bishop Cragg engaged in intensive study and reflection on the Qur'ān and its teaching. From creation to creaturehood, from the signs of God to human responsibility, he discovers his points of contact.

In dealing with the materials of others Cragg insists that it is crucial to recognize the principle of transformation. Once the gospel is attached to a reality it takes what is there to a new, Christ-transformed dimension. An example of that is the Messiah concept among the Jews. That was retained in Christ's thought, but vitally transformed. The same approach may be applied to Islamic examples such as the worship of the mosque. We must be honest about our differences and loyal to Christ, but then go forward boldly into the engagement of living ideas. The gospel "quarrels with the Muslim concept only to propose a deeper significance to it" (p. 94). As Cragg discovered, Muslims may not appreciate such elucidations, nor above all the implications of transformation, but for him the issue is one of truth. "It may happen that the Christian endeavor to understand Islam to the full will result in Christian expositions of Islam that many Muslims would not regard as familiar. ... What matters is that the exposition should be seen on reflection to have conveyed the true picture" (p. 90).

What, for Cragg, are "the spiritual criteria of relatedness"? In other words, what makes the points of contact points of attachment? He speaks of "shoelessness as a sacrament of reverence" (p. 26),and of humility and openness, curiosity and wise inquiry, as essential factors. From the writer's own experience with this scholar comes the memory of his favorite word "winsome" and the prayer with which he regularly began his lectures: "Help us so to enter the minds of men that ..." [followed by the petition of the moment]. Undoubtedly, however, the critical premise that he brings to the sharing task is his conviction of the wonder of the Majestic One whose true royalty is unfolded in the self-giving and redemptive love in Jesus, the Savior. It is God's relatedness to us that is the Criterion of all things. In another essay he says, "Our verdicts ... are to be bent always toward salvation, toward what salvation means and what salvation demands."[6]

With these ringing words in mind we turn to the points of contact rising from the Muslim encounter with and life in the contemporary world. What are the Muslim felt needs?

B. Connecting with Muslim Concerns

Christian friends of Muslims will strive to become aware of what their friends regard as important. There is often a startling contrast between what the rest of the world thinks Muslims are concerned with, and what they really worry about. A sharing Christian friend may have in his/her mind a desire to set forth the gospel as the solution to human alienation, alienation from God and from each other. The Muslim mind, however, is not ordinarily preoccupied with that issue. There are other matters at the top of the mind, some of which Muslims may be willing to discuss with someone who is regarded as a friend. We will briefly identify nine of these issues. A Christian friend will move beyond awareness to interest in what concerns the other person. This in turn will open the door to a discussion of all topics, including sin and grace.

What individual Muslims regard as important varies greatly from person to person. It depends on a host of conditions reflecting geography, culture, economics, education, and personal family conditions. A Muslim in the U.S.A., for example, may be most concerned about the Christian emphasis in public schools, or the inability to find time or space for the five daily prayers. A Muslim in India may be most worried about the Hindu emphasis in history books, or the lack of adequate Muslim representation in the government civil service. A Muslim in Indonesia may be most troubled about the place of Muslim tradition in a culture that exalts *adat*, its own tradition, or about the corruption of public leaders. These particularities remind us to be wary of grand overarching statements that "Muslims are this or that." There are, however, some common elements that tend to transcend the local and regional imitations.

1. Modernity Issues

Muslims around the world are still actively engaged with issues arising from the modernization of life. West-based analysts may suggest that society has entered a state of fragmented post-modernism, but that is not really true of Islamic society. As Akbar Ahmed suggests: "There exists ... an intellectual time-warp between Muslims and the West. ... The Muslim intellectual continues to grapple with issues contained in modernism."[7] These issues include the authority of reason, freedom of thought and expression, ideals of progress and critiques of blind traditionalism; scientific methodology; democratic ideals; modern political institutions; gender relationships, and others. What Habib Boulares, a Tunisian educational and cultural leader, wrote a decade ago is still true. The struggle, he says, is an "unbearable process of cultural uprooting that all humans and also Muslims are experiencing." It is a struggle for "a modernization that does not separate man from his roots and does not create a gulf between him and his fellows."[8] The need is for acceptable solutions, for imaginative leadership to find them, and for a new Muslim consensus that maintains some unity in the umma.

There are two specific issues stemming from modernism that produce a distinct set of needs in Islam and require separate mention: change and secularism.

2. The Problem of Change and the Continuity of Faith

It is not too strong to say that the Muslim world is in a convulsion over the issue of change. Individual Muslims feel its pressures and wonder what can yield in the face of this unrelenting influence, and what must remain.

In the Golden Age of Islam the possibility of change was taken for granted, but for the next seven centuries the spirit of traditionalism became dominant and habitual. In the late nineteenth and twentieth centuries, under the impact of western thought, the forces of change struck hard and fast. Some Muslims welcomed its positive aspects. What the moderate and liberal change-supporters and change-makers provided were two contributions. The first was to create a positive attitude toward intellectual development and scientific technology. The second was to direct attention to the Qur'ān and to underline its significance as the primary authority in Islam. Chiragh Ali (d. 1895), an Indian Muslim, summed up the positive attitude toward change in these words: "Islam is capable of progress and possesses sufficient elasticity to enable it to adapt itself to social and political changes going on around it. ... It has the vital principles of rapid development, of progress, of rationalism, and of adaptability to new circumstances."[9]

This approach to change, however, came into conflict with the traditional concept of respecting and adhering to what has been handed down from the past, and as much as possible imitating it (taqlīd). It produced plenty of fear and doubt, and by the mid-twentieth century a major reaction was under way. Some revivalists (= Islamists) exploited the uncertainties, and aggressively sought to turn back the clock and revalidate the great Islamic tradition. They did so by glorifying the past, by restating it in simple form and language, by clothing it in modern dress, and by presenting it packaged in an utopian vision as the true universal Islam. Their influence is now a powerful one in the Muslim world.

Ordinary Muslims are caught in the middle between the conflicting poles of thought and are striving to be both respectful of tradition and open to change, and they are urgent in asking, "What does the Qur'ān tell us to do?"

3. Secularism and the Preservation of Faith

While change troubles, secularism threatens. Muslims are wondering how to deal with its insidious power and its attack on the foundation of Islam. By the term secularism we are not referring to a formal philosophy like Marxism, nor to the concept of a secular state like Turkey, nor to an opinion about the relation between religion and politics. We are using it in the sense of a non-religious spirit, the idea that life can go on without religious faith and piety. Those who believe this agree that traditional religions have some value, but they are quaint, outdated and generally irrelevant. In fact, in this opinion, they tend to cause more trouble than they are worth. Religion does not need to be formally denied, but it can be practically ignored. The spirit is associated with other "isms"—materialism, rationalism, and pragmatism. Secularism works from within and produces nominalism and/or the outright loss of faith. The problem is not new in Islamic history, but modernity has intensified its powerful influence. Shabbir Akhtar summarizes the situation:[10]

> There is no denying the increasing threat of secularity. Secularity is becoming more and more pronounced even in the most traditional Muslim countries. ... Islam is slowly beginning to have, like a diluted Christianity in the West, a reduced status in the daily life of believers. ... Men entertain a general view about the nature of life and the world—as a religious obligation—but simultaneously entertain a secular view about daily life in practice.

Not everything clubbed under the term "secularism" is quite what it seems. There is undoubtedly a segment of Muslims in the world who are moving—for want of a better term—to a new religious style. They are withdrawing from many of the formal evidences that traditionally appeared to signify Islamic loyalty. Instead they are substituting a freer approach to religiosity—a reluctance to go on accepting the dominance of Arabic-trained imams and legal scholars, a less formal prayer life, a happy acceptance of modernity, and an active life in general society. This new way of being Muslim may appear as secularism to traditionalists who see Islamic loyalty in terms of external observances, but it is a view of religion as spirit rather than form.

Nevertheless, negative secularism is everywhere visible, as Shabbir Akbar describes, and sincere Muslims are troubled by its inroads. They fear that what happened to Christians in the West may now happen to Muslims. While they can deal with enemies from the outside, they do not well understand this internal development and are ill-equipped to deal with it. Moreover, the reaction to secularism helps to produce new forms of religious fundamentalism, leaving the silent majority confused about the present and worried about the future.

4. Economic Disabilities

Almost all ordinary Muslims are concerned about how they will put enough bread or rice on the table for their families, how they will provide adequate housing, and how they will pay for the education of their children. The phrase "economic disabilities" does not refer to this universal concern. Rather it signifies specific poverty conditions that continue to plague Muslim societies, as indicated in the previous chapter, and it includes the disadvantages experienced by Muslim minorities in some countries. The condition has been aggravated by warfare in Islamic societies that has produced a large number of displaced persons and refugees. The situation in that regard has grown worse rather than better in the first years of the new century. The economic dissatisfaction creates a deep ferment. Muslim reformers level vocal charges against the self-centeredness that is visible in the conspicuous consumption and outright corruption of some leaders. At the same time various Muslim self-help groups and "missions" have arisen to alleviate suffering. In the quarter century from 1964 to 1990 one such organization, the Muslim Education Society in Kerala, India, from nothing established ten hospitals and three ambulance services, six colleges and four parallel colleges, eight student hostels, eight commercial institutes, three industrial training institutes, ten amber charka centers, eighteen adult education centers, thirteen tailoring institutes, seventeen nursery schools, three orphanages, and twenty-one other uplift institutions.[11] The record testifies to the self-help energy and to the extent of the problems that need to be overcome. They loom very high in the Muslim mind. There is a call for the development of an Islamic socialism based on a broad interpretation of the almsgiving (zakāt) commanded by the Qur'ān, an interpretation that will lead to social justice for the poor and the oppressed. Many believe in a "salvation by politics" approach to overcome economic disabilities, but the glacial progress in some areas is an underlying cause of various forms of violent response.

5. Family Values

The issue of family values is an increasingly serious one for Muslims. It has always been important. As one Muslim suggests: "Marriage and family are central in the Islamic system"[12] Family law, however, has concentrated on husband-wife relations parent-children relations, and inheritance matters, all set within a structured pattern of rights and obligations. That traditional pattern is now beset by various free-flowing influences, and the struggle is on. As the family ideal is everywhere eroded and threatened, particularly but not only in western contexts, the subject of the family has become a steady topic of discussion among Muslims. The felt needs are very personal, yet at the same time Muslims are often ready to discuss them with Christian friends. The threats that they take most seriously are the potent issues of alcohol and drugs, sex exploitation and promiscuous behavior, the breakdown of marriages, homosexuality and abortion. Behind these blatant problems are less obvious issues that are considered equally important—moral training, respect for authority, religious education and intermarriage. Parental worries in these areas are everywhere, and ordinary Muslims are looking for answers.

6. Sharīʿa Matters

The dominant discussion topic among Muslims today is the sharīʿa, the law of Islam. More than ever before it has become the visible symbol of personal identity and communal unity. At the same time some Muslims have taken issue with the idea of inflexibility that is attached to the sharīʿa by enthusiastic proponents. There is little argument about the religious and family aspects of the law that constitute its heart and that established one's personal identity as a Muslim. There is much discussion, however, about the wider sweep of the law in the light of new interpretations of the Qur'an, especially as they affect gender relations. Many are searching for the appropriate creative approach to law that is both religiously sound in terms of Qur'anic principle and empirically practical in the light of modern conditions. As we have noted earlier, the question is being asked, to what extent can the sharīʿa be changed, or updated or supplemented to meet modern conditions. Others, however, argue vociferously for the retention of the traditional sharīʿa in all its forms. They view obedience to the "divine" law as the chief characteristic of a true Muslim community, as essential to its life as the Qur'an itself. Moreover, with the growth of Muslim nation-states and the demise of Islamic political unity, to many the sharīʿa is now the only factor that unifies Muslims.

The issues are not only discussed with great emotional intensity within the Muslim family, but the persistent advocacy of the traditional sharīʿa has also brought Muslims into conflict with non-Muslims in some parts of the world, especially in areas such as Nigeria where religious populations are in near equilibrium.

7. The Honor of Islam

Later in this chapter we will consider some specific Muslim sensitivities, but it is necessary in terms of Muslim concerns to point to the care for the honor of Islam. There is a feeling of repugnance towards those who bring shame on the faith by their behavior, whether it be extremism in corruption or extremism in violence. Few non-Muslims are aware of how much mutual recrimination takes place within the Muslim family because Muslims tend to strive for an outward public image of perfection and unity. Within the family the opposite is the case. The task of building a dynamic, modern, and respectable Muslim community preoccupies many educated believers who are discontented with its backwardness in comparison with other religious communities and are free in their self-criticism. It is particularly Muslim youth who lead the way in taking up this challenge, and while secularization has drawn many away from religious affairs, a large group of aggressive youth are actively promoting Islam, seeking to defend its honor, and working for progress.

They are thrilled by the poetic calls of Sir Muhammad Iqbal (d. 1938) to engage in a re-chiseling of the Islamic image. They are severely critical of those whom they regard as ignorant religious leaders of the old school, corrupt and dictatorial political rulers, and oppressors of the poor and helpless. A young Iranian woman declares: "Man has a stomach too big and eyes too wide—but a heart too small and a spirit too narrow. ... So why not master our weaknesses and find fulfillment in order to save the world?"[13] Their prime hero is the Prophet Muhammad, and they echo his call for a return to God. An Egyptian student says: "To make factories and high buildings is easy. To build man, that is the difficult thing. Returning to God is an essential way to achieve the good man and the good society."[14]

In relation to non-Muslims the concern for the honor of Islam frequently takes on a quite different form—resistance to criticism, even the most well-intended, and the harboring of thin-skinned defensive attitudes.

8. Palestine

Palestine is both a reality and a symbol. It is a real problem to be solved, and for Muslims it is also a symbol for injustice. They tend to identify it as a Muslim problem forgetting the considerable number of Palestinian Christians, now being reduced by emigration. In that sense it has become a universal symbol of the Muslim sense of persecution. As a political and social problem related to the Middle East Palestine does not have much immediacy for Muslims in other parts of the world who have their own problems. Even within the Middle East some nations have been less than forthcoming in taking in the Palestinian refugees. But as a symbol Palestine represents for Muslims the culmination of a long period of injustice. That injustice began with colonialism as Muslim nations were subjected to both the political will and the cultural influence of "western" and "Christian" powers. The memory rankles, and is kept alive by Palestine. Some Muslims may be charged with perpetuating and exacerbating a bad situation, but the larger Muslim family in the world naturally wonders at the seeming unwillingness or inability of powerful nations to implement the justice they declare in formal resolutions. The western support of largely Muslim Bosnia and Kosova, conditioned by later developments in Afghanistan and Iraq, have helped to alleviate but not to overcome the deep Muslim distress over Palestine that repeatedly explodes into violence. The felt need is for a sympathetic, effective, and face-saving attempt to deal with the roots of the problem.

9. The Rise of Extremism

Earlier reference has been made to this problem, but we will consider it here in terms of its internal Islamic dimensions. The rise of extremism is an issue deeply felt by Muslims, discussed by them, and worried over at many levels. It becomes a point of contact in Christian communication because the issue of human violence is a universal one, and the relation of religion to it presses hard on believers from every background.

a. The Phenomenon of Extremism and Its Relation to Fundamentalism
Muslim extremism is sometimes covered by other English phrases such as

radical Islam, resurgent Islam, revivalist Islam, Islamism, revolutionary Islam, militant Islam, or Islamic terrorism. Extremism and fundamentalism, however, are two different things with occasionally touching borders, and Muslims do not equate the two.[15] For convenience the broad spectrum of Muslims may be divided into the categories of liberal, moderate, traditional, conservative, fundamentalist, and extremist. The distinctions are imprecise but can be utilized for this discussion. The large majority of Muslims fall into the middle groups—moderate, traditional, conservative, and fundamentalist. When Muslims employ the latter term, a recent development, they refer to any one of three things: one who accepts the fundamentals of Islam; or one who is obscurantist—often used in this sense against traditional clergy; or one who has a particular view of the relation of religion and politics.

In the sphere of the relation of religion and politics Muslim fundamentalism is controversial within Islam. It refers to those who believe that there is an ideal Islamic state, that its character is to have the Qurʾān alone as its constitution and the sharīʿa as its exclusive law. All true Muslims must strive to bring it into being. Rafiq Zacharia is of the view that this kind of fundamentalism has been "a recurring phenomenon in the Muslim world down the ages, asserting itself whenever there was a feeling that Islam was in danger ..."[16] Its contemporary form includes the elements of scripturalism, the use of logical deduction, moral reform, quasi-modernism, utopian imagery, and the willingness to suffer for the vision. Most Muslims are not fundamentalists in this sense. They are critical of its puritanism, but have some admiration for its zeal. They do not identify those who are inclined to fundamentalism with extremists. It is the extremists that cause the *umma* much greater worry.

The Muslim extremists confuse observers by both using and abusing fundamentalist ideas. They employ many of its concepts to provide the content of their own ideology, but package it with various distortions and inimical attitudes. These include: interpretative license—making something true by saying it is true; the use of broad generalizations; harsh judgmentalism; name-calling, and cunning enemy-creation; the use of indiscriminate violence as a primary methodology; religiously-couched propaganda and brain-washing techniques; persecution mania, and a theology of martyrdom; a selective rationalism combined with arrogant self-assurance; and a touch of madness. The availability of the jihād concept and the psychology of defensiveness have made Islam particularly vulnerable to this pathological development that also characterizes many extremists in other religions. For Muslims the problems the extremists produce are fivefold: the exaltation of cruelty in religious dress; the renewal of a violent movement within Islam against fellow Muslims; terrorist action against the members of other religions, including the people of the book; the production of dishonor to Islam and shame for Muslims; and the intractability of a major problem that cannot be easily handled.

b. The Phenomenon of Extremism and the Muslim Response

Muslims have been criticized for silence and evasiveness in facing and dealing with the issue of religious extremism. The criticism is valid to a degree in terms of public statements, but it does not take the measure of the internal response. The Muslim approach to misbehavior by Muslims has been to deal with it within the confines of the Muslim family, partly in order to avoid giving the impression of Islamic weakness and division, partly because it is the community tradition to do it that way. More and more Muslims are realizing that this approach is not adequate in a matter that has such far-reaching effects on others. As to the apparent evasiveness, this in some degree results from uncertainty regarding the line of demarcation between a legitimate use of force in liberation struggles, and an unacceptable militancy. Here also, more and more Muslims have come to the conclusion that the line has been unacceptably and irreligiously transgressed. Not only are the extremists close to out of control, but they are defining Islam negatively in the international world.[17] In the past century the *umma* had a problem with traditional religious leaders who defined the public image of Islam as ignorant and backward, but in the new century the extremists are giving it the face of irresponsible violence. Especially among moderate and progressive believers this reality is causing great stress and discontent, not to speak of moments of horror, and a deep internal struggle over the issue is taking place in Islam.

The struggle is surfacing in various ways. It is visible in the efforts of some authoritarian Muslim governments to suppress activist movements. It is evident in the public Muslim voices that are being increasingly raised against the aberration. There are far more of these than most non-Muslims seem to be aware of. An example is the scathing response by Muqtedar Khan to Osmama bin Laden's call to Iraqis to engage in suicide missions against Americans. The opening words in the lengthy statement are the following:[18]

Mr. bin Laden, in the name of Allah, the Most Merciful, the Most Benevolent, I begin by reciting some important principles of Islam to remind you that there is more to Islam than just a call to arms:

1. Islam was sent as a mercy to humanity (4:79);

2. Do not make mischief on the earth (29:36);

3. People, We have created you from a male and a female that you might know one another. The noblest before God is the most righteous of you (49:13);

4. There are among the People of the Book (Jews and Christians) upstanding nations that recite the message of God and worship throughout the night, who believe in God, who honor and forbid dishonor and hasten to do good works. These are the righteous (3:113–114).

I am writing this to make clear that there are Muslims in America and in the world who despise and condemn extremists and have nothing to do with you, and those like you, for whom killing constitutes worship.

The author entitled his memorandum "Memo to Mr. bin Laden: Go to Hell!" While such trenchant public statements are on the increase, the struggle against extremism normally takes place at lower levels where moderate Muslims exercise their influence. As John Esposito notes: "The breadth, character and activities of the moderate majority have gone relatively unnoticed."[19] The felt need of Muslims to deal with radical movements in their own way within Islam can scarcely be ministered to by Christian friends. Such friends can give support say to the world that the struggle is in fact going on, and beneath the surface the waters are churning, at the same time attending to the violence that exists in Christian communities.

In bringing to a conclusion the discussion of Muslim concerns we reiterate that sharing friends will want to know what is going on in the life of their friends, and will take the trouble to find out. The generalizations that we have made may not be applicable to every individual. Indeed, some Muslims might prefer to put the matter quite differently. What an individual Muslim believer holds in Islam has a frequent element of surprise because of the persistent individuality of the faith. Whatever these nuances might be, however, the sharing of the good news must be widely related to felt needs. The gospel will have more meaning for Muslims when its relevance is shown for their problems. At the same time, the problems themselves are a natural conduit for reflection of the human condition.

C. Connecting with the Qur'ān

The utilization of the Qur'ān in Christian communication with Muslims may be challenged from two perspectives. The first is on the Muslim side of the issue. Muslims have profound reverence for the Qur'ān, and although they do not object to its use by non-Muslims their desire is that it be a respectful one. The second question comes from the Christian side. It may be argued that if the Qur'ān is treated as an authority for one point, its inherent standing must be admitted for all points. In that matter, however, it must be affirmed that we are dealing with points of contact and not authority themes. The Qur'ān is the official source of Muslim faith and the starting-point for all believers. Evangel-sharers who know the Qur'ān and in moderation refer to it are aware of what a great aid in communication it provides. It may also be remembered that among Muslims who have chosen to follow the Messiah there are present those who assert that their first kindling of interest came from the Qur'ān. As one person put it in a well-known testimony: "How could I forget the name of 'Jesus' when I frequently confronted it during my recitation of the Qur'ān between the sunset and night prayers!"[20]

Connecting with the Qur'ān contends with the practical reality that many Muslims have a limited knowledge of its content. In part, this is due to the reverence that they have for the language and sound of the sacred Word. These have a miraculous quality for believers, representing the Speech of God. The primary use of the Qur'ān in traditional Islam, then, was for reverential memorization and recitation rather than for disciplined study of its content. Under the impact of Muslim reform movements that situation is changing, but the general comprehension of Qur'anic materials is still narrow in scope. With this caution in mind we will refer to aspects of that material which represent potential points of contact:

1. Names, Events, Ideas, Moral Values, Customs
  a. Names of Sacred Scripture:

The Qur'ān refers to the following three aforementioned scriptures:

tawrāt = Torah
zabūr = Psalms
Injīl = Gospel

b. Names of Prophets:[21]

Adam	Jacob	Enoch	Zachariah
Noah	Joseph	Job	John the Baptist
Abraham	Moses	Jonah	Jesus
Lot	Aaron	Elijah	
Ishmael	David	Elisha	
Isaac	Solomon	Ezra	

Some of the Qur'anic references to these Biblical prophets are either very brief or obscure; but the story of Joseph, for example, occupies the entire twelfth chapter of the Qur'ān. Adam, Noah, Abraham, Ishmael, Moses, and Jesus are the major figures.

c. Historical Events:[22]

Following are some of the Biblical events recorded in some form in the Qur'ān. They do not include material on Mary and Jesus which have been detailed in Chapter 5. The Qur'anic references are in parenthesis.

Creation of the world (16:3; 12:3; 35:1–12)
Adam and the fall (7:18; 2:34)
Cain and Abel (5:30)
The flood (54:9; 69:11; 11:42)
Noah's ark (11:40)
Abraham visited by the angels (11:72; 15:51)
Abraham ready to sacrifice his son (37:101)
Jacob goes to Egypt (12:100)
Joseph's history (6:84; 12:1–111; 11:36)
Moses strikes the rock (7:160)
Pharaoh's history (2:46; 10:76; 43:45; 11:38)
Manna and quails in the desert (7:160)
Aaron makes a calf (20:90)
Korah (27:76)
David's praise of God (34:10)
Solomon's wise judgment (21:78)
Queen of Sheba (27:72)
Jonah and the great fish (6:86; 10:98; 37:139; 48:48)

d. Mohammed F. Jamali's List of Moral Virtues Commended by the Qur'ān:[23]

piety	work
goodness to parents	striving
doing good	readiness
patience	dignity
philanthropy	brotherhood

truthfulness
fulfillment of obligations
trustworthiness
justice
mercy
restraint of anger, and forgiveness
cooperation

unity
moderation
humilty
contentment
chastity
reliance on Allah
reading, and propagation of
learning

e. Mohammed F. Jamali's List of Immoral Actions Forbidden by the Qur'ān:[24]

polytheism
injustice
hypocrisy
pride and arrogance
corruption
transgressions
murder
adultery
false witness
embezzlement

cheating in measurement
lying
falsehood
treachery
suspicion and spying
backbiting
evil gossip about women
jealousy
stinginess
wastefulness
dispute and disagreement

f. Fazlur Rahman's List of Major Themes in the Qur'ān:[25]

God
Man as individual
Man in society
Nature
Prophethood and revelation

Eschatology
Satan and evil
Emergence of the Muslim community
Religious situation of the Muslim community in Mecca
People of the book and the diversity of religions

g. Some Rituals and Customs Referred to in the Qur'ān:[26]

Ablutions
Alms
Amulets
Apparel
Calendar
Children
Death
Debt
Deportment
Divorce
Expiation
Fasting
Food and Drink

Inheritance
Invocation
Jihād
Magic
Marriage
Mosque
Oaths
Orphans
Parents
Pilgrimage
Poets
Prayer

Property
Punishments
Refugees
Retaliation
Sacrifice
Slavery
Treaties
Usury
Warfare
Weights and Measures
Women

We turn next to one Qur'anic story that for many illustrates the theme of connection in a particularly meaningful way. That is the saga of Abraham, Hagar, and Ishmael. We have paid some attention to Abraham in our discussion of the concept of friendship and to Ishmael in connection with prayer. In the following section we provide more detail on the Qur'anic and later Muslim mention of this history, which provides both contrasts and parallels with the Biblical accounts.

2. The Abraham-Hagar-Ishmael Narrative

The contact points with the Islamic tradition of Abraham, Hagar, and Ishmael are many and varied.[27] Abraham's influence embraces three religious traditions, as symbolized by his name "Friend of God," applied to him in Judaism (2 Chr 20:7; Is 41:8), Christianity (James 2:23), and Islam (Qur'ān 4:125). His spiritual significance for each is large, and for wider humanity he has become a sign of hope.[28] A Christian communicator with Muslims must certainly become familiar with the detail of the stories recorded in Genesis 20–25, but he/she will also take a second look to identify the possible links with the Islamic tradition, in particular those that refer to Hagar and Ishmael, who are held in high esteem by Muslims and are believed to have been buried in the sacred space before the Ka'ba in Mecca.

a. Abraham

The Qur'anic picture of Abraham (*Ibrahīm*) must be separated from the Islamic picture that provided details drawn from other sources. We will begin with the information of the Qur'ān, and then add material from Muslim tradition.

In the Qur'ān itself *Ibrahīm* emerges as a many-sided model of great importance, an importance that increases steadily in the history of early Islam. Two characteristics rise to the top. He is pictured as a man of faith—faith in God and God's providence—and as an upright man, a *siddīq*. Other qualities mentioned include his mildness, his thankfulness, his penitence and spirit of prayer, and his love of family. With high intention God chose him and guided him to the straight path. God promised to bless him, to give him scripture and wisdom, to grant him a mighty kingdom, and to raise up "a messenger from his descendants." Putting it all together a summary passage declares: "I have appointed him as a leader (*imām*) of mankind" (2:124).

The term "mankind" is crucial for the Muslim understanding of Abraham. He is the primal monotheist to whom other people should look for their model. He pre-dates Judaism and Christianity, and the Torah and Gospel were revealed after him. In Muslim view he was not therefore either a Jew or a Christian but a *hanīf*, one who has turned away from idolatry and has surrendered to the One High God, Allah. In his youth Abraham was not of that persuasion, but God led him to the awareness of truth. After that he was no longer interested in worshiping created things, the sun, the moon and the stars, but rather their Creator. He rejected the family idols that could not move or speak. A personal crisis resulted from the attitude of his father who refused to give up his gods. Four times the Qur'ān reports on Abraham's inner struggle over that matter. At last he withdraws from his family, but promises to go on praying for his father. He asks forgiveness for himself, for his parents, and for all believers on the Day of Judgment. Through this personal ordeal he remains stalwart in the faith, even when his family persecuted him and threatened to throw him in the Fire. "O fire, be coolness and peace for Abraham," he prays. A second crisis arose over his children, but for that story we must turn to his relation with Hagar and Ishmael.

b. Hagar and Ishmael

Hagar's name comes to us from Muslim tradition, Ishmael's from the Qur'ān. The epic story of Hagar and Ishmael is hinted at in the meaning of their names. Hagar means "emigrant" and Ishmael "God listens."

The Qur'ān more than once tells the tale of the angelic visitors to Abraham. They stop at his tent on their way to the doomsday for Lot's folk and during their stopover they promise a son to Abraham. Sarah laughs, but Abraham prays for a righteous son, despite his age. The Qur'ān does not report further details of the birth of Ishmael and Isaac (*Ismā'īl and Ishāq*), both of whom became respected prophets of Islam. It goes forward to the story of the rebuilding of the Ka'ba, the central shrine in Mecca, whose foundations in Muslim belief were first laid by Adam. The story is told quite briefly. God commands Abraham and Ishmael to "purify my house." The command may refer to the physical neglect that had taken over the site, or to the idolatry that had moved in, or perhaps to both. They respond obediently, Abraham saying: "Accept this duty from us." He prays that God might make the shrine a place of security and bestow fruits on believers who visit it. As he and his son Ishmael relaid the foundations of the house Abraham asks God: "Make us and our descendants those who surrender to you." But how did Abraham and Ishmael get there in the first place? Mecca is a long way from Canaan! For that information we have to leave the Qur'ān and go to Muslim tradition that describes the vicissitudes of Hagar and Ishmael. Although there is not full agreement in the details, most Muslims accept the following version.

Sara had suggested that Abraham take her Egyptian slave as his concubine in hopes that they might have a child. When that expectation was fulfilled, however, Sara became jealous of Hagar. When Ishmael later became playful and teased Isaac she became very angry and persuaded Abraham to send away both Hagar and Ishmael. Abraham packed them up and took them to the far-off valley of Mecca, built a small hut for them and left them there. Hagar's water supply was soon exhausted. She left Ishmael alone, running frantically back and forth seven times between two hills in search for help. All pilgrims to Mecca repeat that run between Safa and Mahwah in remembrance of Hagar's fruitless search. When she returned in despair to her great surprise she found that Ishmael had kicked the sand with his foot, and water was coming out. This, in legend, became the famed well of Zem Zem that continues to supply water to pilgrims to this day. Ishmael, it is said, grew up there and married into a local tribe.

Muslim tradition also fixes on the Valley of Mina, about 12 kilometers from Mecca, as the place where Abraham was called upon to sacrifice his son, although the specific chronology of the event is in doubt. Abraham paid at least three visits to the area to meet Hagar and Ishmael. On one of them he and Ishmael raised the walls of the Kaʿba. On another occasion he had a dream in which he received the command to sacrifice his son. The vision and the command are recorded in the Qurʾān, but not the name of the son. Muslims generally believe that it was Ishmael, although Isaac is also mentioned in the Hadīth. Abraham consulted with his son before embarking on the terrible journey. His son agreed that they must obey God. When they had survived the test, God blessed Abraham and, in fact, bursts out in praise: "Peace and salutation to Abraham!" Abraham is the model of humble obedience to God. "Recite unto them the story of Abraham," the Qurʾān advises, and later generations are told: "There is a goodly pattern for you in Abraham." To all humanity the Qurʾān commends "the religion of Abraham."

Ishmael too is regarded highly, along with his mother. Early Syrian Christians were aware of the significance of Ishmael and Hagar for Muslims, and they called them "sons of Ishmael" and "Hagarenes." In the Qurʾān Isaac is not unimportant, but Ishmael receives greater attention, and he usually precedes Isaac in the list of the prophets. Ishmael is "one of the good." He was chosen by God, was righteous and steadfast, and received God's revelation. The Qurʾān says: "And make mention in the Scripture of Ishmael. Lo! he was a keeper of his promise, and he was a messenger (of Allah), a Prophet. He enjoined upon his people worship and almsgiving, and was acceptable in the sight of God" (19:54f). Thus Ishmael has a double significance in Islamic tradition. At the spiritual level he is a recognized prophet, while on the physical side he is regarded as the genetic father of at least the arabicized northern tribes of the Arabian peninsula.[29]

c. And Abraham Again

Despite the regard for Hagar and Ishmael it is Abraham that holds the field in Muslim reverence. When the Jews rejected Muhammad in Medina, the direction of prayer was altered from Jerusalem to Mecca, to the house that Abraham built for the pure worship of God. He is the father of the faith. "And who forsaketh the religion of Abraham save him who befools himself?" (2:130). When Muslims go on the pilgrimage to Mecca and enter the sacred precincts of the huge mosque, they are thrilled to stand for a precious moment at the "Station of Abraham," praying as he is believed to have prayed on that very spot: "O our Lord! ... turn unto us in Mercy, for Thou art the Oft-Returning Most Merciful" (2:128). Take your place at that Station!, the Qurʾān itself commands (2:125). For Sufi Muslims that place, in a spiritual sense, is friendship with God. Junayd says: "God's servant knows that God loves him. ... Those who have attained this level live in full intimacy with God and are his close friends. All anxious respect and fear of God has been brought to an end."[30]

The Christian view is that God indeed has turned mercifully to us, revealing the divine friendship in Jesus the Messiah, a descendant of Abraham. In that light it is the task and the desire of God's friends to turn to the descendants of Ishmael in witness to the One who precedes even Abraham (Jn 8:58). In the Biblical account Abraham set out on a journey, not knowing where he was going, but trusting in the leading of God. Christian sharers with Muslims are also on that kind of journey. They are not only the children of Abraham in the sense of sharing his faith, upon which the New Testament builds an edifice of great teaching, but also in the sense of accompanying his journey and emulating his obedience. On their part Muslims too will heed what the Qur'ān says: "The faith of your father Abraham (is yours)" (22:78), and "Lo! those of mankind who have the best claim to Abraham are those who followed him" (3:68). A. Guthrie suggests:[31]

> To follow Abraham means the abandonment of what may be considered moral and material safeguards; it could mean a breaking away from the past in which we are so deeply rooted, and the ruthless cutting away of those prejudices which keep men apart. To be the friend of God in any sense of the words is to be the friend of man.

As friends to Muslims, Christian sharers will seek and find "relatedness" in the epic of Abraham, Hagar, and Ishmael. In a reflection on "Listening to Hagar and Ishmael" Michael Kurtz asks: "Why is this story in the Bible? Hagar was not a Hebrew, like Abraham and Sarah. Unlike Isaac's descendants Ishmael's descendants became neither Jews nor Christians, but Muslims. If we listen, what can Hagar and Ishmael's story mean to us?"[32] Perhaps it is there to remind us that the true fulfillment of Abraham's prayer for the family of Ishmael awaits our obedience to God's desire. Consider again Abraham's interchange with the Almighty:

> O that Ishmael might live in your sight! And God said ... "As for Ishmael, I have heard you."

D. Bare Wires and Bad Connections

A sharing friend must deal with the bare wires and bad connections that affect the flow of communication. By bare wires we mean sensitive issues, while bad connections refer to certain Muslim misunderstandings.

1. Handling Bare Wires

Certain matters are particularly delicate for Muslims. Handling those wires means insulating the issues in a commonsense way. In short, they represent a call to sensitivity. We have noted earlier that this, in fact, is one of the qualities of a sharing friend. Friends are open and forthright with one another, but even those who are used to easy-going intercourse are aware of sensitivities. In fact, we can say that a friend is without doubt the most thoughtful of persons.

This attitude implies dissociation from the history of lampooning what is dear to others, an unhappy tendency that has occurred from time to time in both religious communities. From the Christian side we have seen how the lampooning began and then gained headway and became a pattern in medieval times. The Enlightenment did not change the situation, merely shifting the ground of disdain from religion to reason. In the modern age the stereotyping of Muslims has itself become a stereotype. Muslim sensitivities relate to their commitments, but they are in part also a response to thoughtless or unfair critiques. For some they have become a state of mind virtually bordering on paranoia. The wires are certainly bare and hot.

We will limit our discussion to three issues. It is useful to remember that the task of a Christian sharer is not to take on every point of disagreement, but rather to make the power and love of Jesus available to the Muslim friend.

a. The Qur'ān Says!

In the preceding section we have cited Qur'anic materials as a point of contact in Christian communication. It is appropriate to also state a caution. The Qur'ān means everything in the world to Muslims. It is their link between heaven and earth. Any weakening of its strength is considered a serious danger. When a Christian quotes the Qur'ān he/she must therefore restrain the natural impulse to use the phrase "Muhammad says," or "according to the words of Mohammad." Instead, one may say, "the Qur'ān says." To say "Muhammad says" is to possibly imply that Muhammad is the author of the Qur'ān, but Muslims believe that God is the author, and Muhammad was only the channel of the revelation. The Christian communicator believes that Muhammad is directly involved in the production of the Qur'ān if for no other reason because its material includes the temporal affairs of that time and place, and details related to the Prophet's own life. A traditional Muslim, however, holds that every word of the Qur'ān is a duplication of God's eternal Speech recorded in a heavenly book and transferred through Muhammad into Arabic speech and writing. Because it is the inerrant and infallible Word of God, it is improper to use the phrase "Muhammad says." In Muslim view one can either say "God says" or "the Qur'ān says," and Christian communicators will opt for the latter. The phrase "Muhammad says" may, however, be used of Hadīth reports.

b. The Person of Muhammad

To state it simply—Muhammad is the most revered person in Islam. He is the founder of the faith and a noble pattern for believers, and his name is next to God's in the confession of faith.[33] Muhammad's standing in Islam makes his frequent maligning by Christians the most delicate area in Christian-Muslim relations. In Chapter 2 we have spoken about "the overwhelming impress" of Muhammad's personality on Islam. To that we must add the ever increasing emotional attachment to his perfection.

The process of elevating the Prophet to the heights of humanity beyond which no one can go has been unfolding throughout the long course of Islamic history, but especially in the last century. It is what Sir Hamilton Gibb described as "the concentration of religious feeling upon the person of Muhammad." Gibb traces the development to a reaction against austere transcendental theology, representing "a craving for someone on whom to lavish the human instincts of love and trust." These emotions, he suggests, have found an outlet in the cult of Muhammad "as a companion who can be relied upon at all times for friendship, sympathy and stimulation, and also upon whom friendship and devotion can be bestowed."[34] Be that as it may, the development means that any slight of the Prophet Muhammad, intentional or unintentional, becomes an issue. He himself prayed for the forgiveness of sins, but in the eyes of Muslims he cannot be compared to an ordinary human. When a north African film was made of his life, he "appeared" only as a voice. The widespread support of Ayataullah Khomeini's *fatwā* against Salman Rushdie was directly related to his manner of dealing with the Prophet's revelatory experience and his family affairs. Rushdie had crossed the acceptable boundary. These wires too are bare and hot.

Yet this connection is inevitable because Muslims desire it. It is a matter of normal tact and wisdom to deal with that desire respectfully. Christian friends of Muslims may ask themselves whether they consider it their duty to excoriate Muhammad or to communicate Christ.

c. The Role of Women

The role of women in traditional Islam and their treatment by some Muslim men has come under major scrutiny in contemporary times. What has been addressed is both the theoretical issue of women as inferior beings, and the actual discrimination. This is a subject of great delicacy within the *umma*. The delicacy itself—with the help of the cry, "Islam in danger!"—has been used to sustain the status quo.

The condition of Muslim women has been treated in the discussion of service (Ch 12, A. 5.) Many critiques of that condition have come from Muslim sources, especially from Muslim women. Others have emanated from secular media, and some from Christian sources. The latter have been a major irritant for many Muslims because, in their view, it is a case of the pot calling the kettle black. As to Muslim opinion, both men and women can be found on every side of the questions involved. These include the nature and extent of the disabilities, their root cause, the understanding of religious law, the role of custom and culture, the influence of politics, the authority for change, and most importantly the interpretation of the Qur'ān.

It is certain that Muslim women, as we have noted, see their long-term hope for improvement in the fresh interpretation of the Qur'ān. While that study is going on, practical things need to be done. In the growing women's movement there is a wide difference of opinion as to improvement strategies. Some promote the principle of secular law as the best solution, in the face of vigorous opposition. Some with a certain amount of success, seek to work within the frame of traditional Islamic avenues for change. Some even join fundamentalist groups who have criticized the oppression of women and have endorsed its amelioration within their parameters.[35] The fact that fundamentalists consider some of the legal interpretations from which women seek release to be divinely ordained makes this a remarkable development. Ayesha M. Imam, a Muslim woman, declares: "All fundamentalisms formally preach submission of women to men, focusing on the 'natural difference' between women and men. ... And yet it is apparently a paradox that women can and do collude in fundamentalist groups and find comfort, security and even a sense of empowerment also."[36]

This is a bare wire. Christian service on behalf of the physical needs of Muslim women is widely appreciated, but status change within the Muslim family is a far more sensitive issue. While the contributions of Christian female scholars such as Yvonne Haddad and Jane Smith have been respected,[37] uninformed criticisms, in particular those that reflect arrogance and self-righteousness, have been rejected. What is the connection to be made? It must be the quiet support of Muslim friends who are struggling for positive change, combined with continued social uplift ministries on the ground.

2. Improving Bad Connections

There are two bad connections that need consideration—the Muslim confusion of "The West" with the Christian faith, and the Muslim attitude in relation to the mission of the church. The bad connections have produced bad feelings. Bad feelings can be poorly founded, misjudged, bordering on prejudice, and even dead wrong. That applies to all people including Muslims. All the more earnestly will friends take such emotions into account because they stand in need of correction.

The awareness of Muslim emotion is supremely important for the task of Christian sharing with Muslim friends. Human emotions are like tinted glasses. They color what the eye sees. All the delicate hues are blended and reduced to a shadowed view. Muslim bad feelings interfere with the Muslim vision of the gospel. They make it difficult for them to see what Rūmī, their great poet of love, saw when he looked at Jesus: "Die before his beauty!" The gentle correction of misunderstandings is an act of friendship. Where bad feelings have a basis in fact Christian friends in turn will feel moved to express regret and to seek forgiveness.

a. The "West"

In the Muslim mind Christianity is directly associated with something called the West, and since the West is regarded as a threatening reality the Christian gospel and its sharers are judged by association. Clearly such categories as East, West, North, and South are very fluid and imprecise. They are really mental images constructed from a person's location, social and educational development, political orientation, and religious ordering. Mental images once formed in such a way, however, are not easily erased. In Europe and North America the so-called "East" was regarded as mysterious, while in South America the so-called "North" was viewed as aggressive. The images are alive to this day. Muslims developed their idea of "West" from their own experience with Europe, including the interactions of the medieval period and in the modern age the colonialism of European powers. Despite some positive elements in the interaction, it was the negative perception that dominated, and it continues to be so today. The Palestinian Savior might well wonder how he and his message became involved with this territorial and sociological image. His words "God so loved the world" challenge bad connections.

For convenience we may use Jamāl al-Dīn al-Afghanī (d. 1897), a noted Muslim reformer, as an illustration of the pervasive Muslim feelings about the West. W. C. Smith suggested that "he seems to have been the first Muslim revivalist to use the concepts 'Islam' and the 'West' as connoting correlative—and of course antagonistic—historical phenomena. This antimony, as is well known, has since become quite standard in virtually all Islamic thinking."[38] Al-Afghanī put it simply: "The Europeans have now put their hands on every part of the world."[39] For many the word Europeans in that sentence and the word Christians were interchangeable. Al-Afghanī exhorted Muslims to wake up and to come together to deal with the situation by external defense and internal reform. A. I. J. Rosenthal notes al-Afghanī's failure to distinguish between western activity and Christian activity. He "saw in the unity of the Muslim world ... the surest guarantee of Islamic survival in the face of the challenge of Christianity and Western imperialism which were largely considered one and the same evil thing."[40]

The idea as it developed was not so black and white as the last comment suggests. In the Muslim view the West came to be regarded as a mix of good and bad, accounting for the hate-love relationship that eventuated. The good was associated with respect for reason, scientific achievement, educational strength and material development. Currently Muslims add technological skill, capitalist enterprise, and the democratic spirit to the list. The bad things of the past were considered to be cruel and violent oppression, materialism, religious colonialism, and crude and disrespectful behavior. Contemporary Muslims add today's economic domination, the media industry and secularization to the list of problems. All of this was identified with Christianity. The West is Christian. Christianity is its soul. Therefore everything the West does Christians do. The identification does not only apply to actual "western" Christians, but to a considerable degree to all Christians everywhere, since all Christians—with the possible exception of the ancient churches of the East—are viewed as clients of the West. For Muslims every Christian in the world, in a sense, is a "westerner." Every Christian therefore is implicated in what the West does and is responsible for it.

Recent years have seen some modifying of this unfortunate identification, partly as the result of Muslim immigration to the West that has enabled Muslims to personally observe the distinction between western society and the church. Nevertheless the idea of the West as a "Yazid," a destroyer, still prevails in many minds, and Christians are guilty by association. Grassroots Muslims are the least defensive in this regard, willing to live and let live, and to let their attitudes be determined by what they actually see. Yet they are influenced by leaders, particularly religious leaders, who continue to vigorously paint with a broad brush, and by the omnipresent media which have convinced many ordinary Muslims that Christians are violent, alcoholic, and sex-possessed. Muslim youth are more educated to the realities, but are also more emotional in their response. The most strident Muslim critiques of the West and Christians—always taking the two as one—emanate from revivalists who charge the West with moral decadence and anti-Islamic policies.[41] Muslim intellectuals and business leaders who have living contact are more balanced in their appraisals, but there is still plenty of sweeping condemnation. Akbar S. Ahmad, a contemporary Islamic scholar living in the West, declares:[42]

> The West is at present the crucible of what is emerging as a universal culture. ... We call this "Western" civilization in that the United States and Western Europe—predominantly white—are at its core, providing the ideas and the technological discoveries that fire it. ... Western civilization is now the dominant universal expression of humanity. Its most powerful weapon lies in the media, especially televison. ... Western civilization—whenever historically exploding from Europe—has meant death and destruction ...

Professor Ahmad, however, disagrees with the majority of Muslims who still identify the West and Christianity. He declares:

Muslims, harking back to the first two encounters with Christianity, and out of touch with developments outside their world, suspect its [Christianity's] hand in the present encounter. They are wrong. In this global civilization true Christians—those who follow Christ in word and deed—are few and far between, and certainly not in command of policy. ... A Muslim visiting the West for the first time may hear "Jesus" or "Christ" frequently and be impressed. What he does not realize is that the name has been reduced to a swearword, an exclamation, and little more.

We may sum up the implications of the casual identification of the West and the Christian for the task of gospel sharing. Sharing friends not only bear the burdens of past religious misunderstandings, but they are also held accountable for the spectrum of western socio-political evils, past and present. Evangel-sharers are identified as representatives of the West, and may be demonized as its secret agents. The invitation to follow Christ may be construed as a treasonable temptation to join a society of lax moral values, or even one that is inimical to Islam and Muslims. Misunderstandings pile one on the other. What is the Christian response to this bad connection?

There is no magical release from the problems associated with deep bias. It produces forms of suffering akin to those of Jesus himself who experienced constant mis-identification. Some of the wires, however, may be spliced to bypass the bad connection and to let goodwill and understanding flow. Christian friends of Muslims may wish

—to accept the need to express regret for the evils associated with nominally Christian western society; to say, "I didn't do it, but I'm sorry.";

—to shake off subtle cultural captivities of their own; to reflect once more on what it means to be in the world but not of the world;

—in dialogue with Muslims to insist on the distinction between westerner and Christian, and between a nominal and a practicing Christian; the latter is one that Muslims understand;

—to discern, ever more intently, the imperative of deep friendship as the personal response, and the one that breaks through at individual levels; and

—to recognize that the macro-solution lies not in Christian action but in Muslim common sense and charity, for which let there be fervent prayer.

b. The Christian Mission

It is another poor connection but one that can be anticipated. Muslim sensitivity in regard to Christian missions is earnest and real. In our earlier discussion of the Muslim view of Christians and Christianity we noted that it is founded on belief in the finality of Islam. It includes the opinion that the Christian faith is corrupted in its teaching. It depends on the theory that Muslims are not at liberty to change their allegiance. And we have just dealt with the fact that missional Christians are implicated in the sins of the West against Islam. Under the circumstances it can be considered surprising only when Muslims are hospitable toward the Christian mission. In fact, this generosity is frequently the case.

In many parts of the Muslim world, notably in areas of South and Southeast Asia and in Sub-Saharan Africa, there is a culture of religious toleration. Christian mission activities are viewed from that perspective. Ordinary Muslims take a balanced view as long as Christians carry on their personal witness in a respectful manner. Instead of objecting, they are often personally interested in a private exchange of views. In the case of organized mission activities that stays within the rules, that too is tolerated. The situation differs in other regions, however. Especially where political religion has played or still plays a major role, or where Islamist influence is strong, there is either a restriction or outright prohibition of Christian mission activity. In Saudi Arabia, for example, even the conduct of public Christian worship is banned.

There is a paradoxical situation in European and North American societies that guarantee the freedom of religious expression and change. It is in this tolerant world that some conservative Muslims express their feelings about Christian missions most fervently. The critiques tend to be defensively phrased, and may be influenced by the secular caricature of missions.[43] Apparently ignoring the aggressive mission (da'wa) activity of some Muslims in the free West and the reality that many more Christians have become Muslims than the reverse, they go on the attack. In so doing, they do not represent the mass of Muslims whose views are more measured. In England Parwez Mansoor lumps together two favorite targets when he declares that "the Din [religion] of Islam has also been under heavy attack from the twin forces of secularist modernity and Christian evangelism."[44] In Canada, Mohamed Elmasry, an academic who is president of a group called the Canadian Islamic Congress, recorded this opinion about Christian mission work on the occasion of the Pope's visit to Jerusalem in March, 2000:[45]

> Roman Catholics, and other Western evangelicals, are busy converting ... destabilizing societies, dividing families and destroying indigenous cultures. ... What makes missionary work destabilizing to these countries is that it brings with it a package that includes a myth that local cultures and religions including the local brand of Christianity, are all inferior to Western culture and the Western brand of Christianity. ... The Western Church's recruiting of new converts through organized missionaries is not found in other religions. ... Missionary activities were and still are, a form of cultural imperialism. ... Historically, missionaries exploited the economic and health needs of natives and offered medical help and schooling with one hand and the Bible in the other.

Then the writer suggests that Christian missions alter their agendas, and he makes the following proposal:

> Today's missionary zeal must be directed toward western governments at home, not towards the world's poor, the world's sick and the world's uneducated and unskilled workers. A more noble cause would be to help the developing world pay its debit to the West, to give them a fair price for their natural resources, to stop selling Western arms to all parties in a conflict, to be an honest broker for peace and justice, and to stop being culturally arrogant.

It is evident, and fortunate, that the Muslim attitude toward Christian missions does not follow a simple or single pattern. The varieties of emotion may be summarized as follows:

—Those who tolerate Christian missions as an aspect of religious freedom;

—Those who appreciate the social welfare activities but do not like the evangelistic witness;

—Those who do not appreciate either, and support national bans on Christian mission efforts; and

—Those who are violently opposed, and charge Christians in missions with a host of indictments.

What is the appropriate response to this generally poor connection? It will be awake to the reasons for Muslim hesitations in regard to Christian communication, and deeply committed to the task of making that communication an act of deep friendship. It will take advantage of whatever opportunities there are to share Christ, and seek to create new opportunities. It will unremittingly press the cause of religious toleration and fairness. It will strive for authenticity in representing Christ, accepting legitimate criticism and amending conduct appropriately. Where evangel-sharing is unfairly maligned, it will remember the word of St. Peter: "It is better to suffer for doing good, if suffering should be God's will, than to suffer for doing evil" (1 Pet 3:17).

Conclusion

Making connections depends on awareness, but their possibilities are built on trust. It takes time for a Muslim to trust the good intentions of the other. It is the combination of long-term friendship and common sense that enables the building of confidence. Out of that nearness a sharing friend understands the powerful implications of the command: "Do unto others as you would that others do unto you." In that light, the connections sought will be open and transparent, and the relationships joined will be honest and pleasant. The gospel is the gospel of joy.

Nevertheless not all connections can be insulated from the effect of the message that passes through them. The gospel is a power that awakens the conscience, uncovers spiritual need, compels the cry "God have mercy on me, a poor sinner!", lifts one's grasp to the helping hand of God. However, it has a dangerous quality for those who prefer the status quo, and it therefore also produces negative reactions. Jesus is certainly the Friend, but he is the Challenging and Change-making Friend who brings a crisis to personal existence. From the heavenly places the restless Son of Man calls humans from what they are to what God intends them to be. It may not be a welcome invitation, and faithfulness to its communication therefore involves the possibility—indeed, the probability—of trouble, rejection, and perhaps outright opposition. No connecting bypasses the cross. What, then, shall gospel-sharers do? Opposition either immobilizes or stimulates. One has a choice to grind to a halt or to be creatively and courageously responsive to the demands of this journey of love. The Friend says: "You are my friends if you do what I command you."

We have considered wholeness and connection, and we turn now to the final aspect in the Christian approach, which is *method*. What means can be used to open the way for the transmission of Christ's power to Muslim friends?

Endnotes

1. This analogy is familiar to pastors. I first heard it in the homiletics class of Richard R. Caemmerer, professor at Concordia Seminary, St. Louis, MO, U.S.A.

2. Hendrik Kraemer, *The Christian Message in a Non-Christian World* (Grand Rapids, MI: Kregel Publications, 1956), p. 140.

3. *Ibid.*

4. Cf. Kenneth Cragg, *The Call of the Minaret* (Maryknoll, N.Y.: Orbis Books, 1985; the second edition, revised and enlarged), and *Sandals at the Mosque* (London: SCM Press Ltd., 1985). The definitive study of Cragg's approach remains to be done. Cf. Lyle Vander Werff, *Christian Mission to Muslims* (Pasadena: Wm. Carey Library, 1977) for a comparison with Samuel H. Zwemer.

5. Kenneth Cragg, *The Event of the Qur'ān* (London: George Allen and Unwin Ltd., 1971), p. 21.

6. Kenneth Cragg, "The Riddle of Man and the Silence of God: A Christian Perception of Muslim Response," *International Bulletin,* Vol. 17, No. 4, October 1993, p. 162.

7. Akbar S. Ahmed, *Postmodernism and Islam,* pp. 28f.

8. Habib Boulares, *Islam, the Fear and the Hope* (London: Zed Books, 1990), p. 116.

9. Chiragh Ali, "Islam and Change," in J. J. Donahue and J. L. Esposito, eds., *Islam in Transition: Muslim Perspectives* (New York: Oxford University Press, 1982), p. 47.

10. Shabbir Akhtar, *A Faith for All Seasons. Islam and the Challenge of the Modern World*, p. 9.

11. Roland E. Miller, *Mappila Muslims of Kerala* (Madras: Orient Longman, 1992; second rev. ed.), pp. 339f. The MES uses the word "mission" to describe its many activities, which parallel those of Christian missions.

12. Abdalati, *Islam in Focus*, p. 114.

13. Tarahan Khayam, "The Generation Gap," in Charis Waddy, *The Muslim Mind* (London: Longman, 1976), p. 129.

14. *Ibid.* p. 125.

15. Leonard Binder uses the term "extremist fundamentalism" or "fanatical fundamentalism" to distinguish it from moderate fundamentalism. Cf. his *Islamic Liberalism* (Chicago: University of Chicago Press, 1988), pp. 170–173.

16. Rafiq Zacharia, *The Struggle within Islam. The Conflict between Religion and Politics* (London: Penguin, 1989), p. 174.

17. Cf. Samuel Huntington, *Clash*, pp. 256–258. Before the post-2000 extremist incidents he made this judgment: "Wherever one looks along the perimeter of Islam, Muslims have problems living peaceably with their neighbors. ... In the 1990s Muslims have been far more involved in intergroup violence than the people of any other civilization. The evidence is overwhelming. ... Muslim borders are bloody, and so are its innards." Extremism provides further apparent validation for one-sided generalizations such as these.

18. Muqtedar Khan, "Memo to Mr. bin Laden: Go to Hell!", repr. from the Washington Post in the *Tampa Tribune*, February 21, 2003, p. 19; Khan is at Adrian College, Michigan, and has authored *American Muslims: Bridging Faith and Freedom* (Beltsville, MD: Amana Publications, 2002).

19. John Esposito, *The Islamic Threat. Myth or Reality* (New York: Oxford, 1995), p. 236.

20. K. K. Alavi, *In Search of Assurance* (Manjeri: Markaz-ul Bisharah, 3rd ed., 1985), p. 3.

21. The corresponding Muslim names for these prophets may be found in Miller, *Muslim Friends*, pp. 176–178.

22. I have used the convenient summary in F. A. Klein, *The Religion of Islam* (London: Curzon Press, 1906), p. 69.

23. Jamali, *Letters on Islam*, pp. 75–79.

24. *Ibid.*

25. Rahman, *Major Themes*, p. ix.

26. For the Qur'anic passages related to these rites, and for other useful headings, see H. W. Weitbrecht Stantion, *The Teaching of the Qur'ān* (London: S.P.C.K., 1919), pp. 75ff.

27. The following Qur'anic passages were drawn upon in the summary of Abraham: 2:124–132; 2:140; 3:65–68; 4:54, 125; 6:75–79, 162; 9:114; 11:69–76; 14:35; 16:120–122; 19:42–48; 21:51–69; 22:78; 26:69–104; 29:16; 37:102–113; 60:4; 87:19. The following passages relate to Ishmael: 2:127–140; 3;84; 4;163; 14:37; 19:54f.; 21:85; 38:48. Hagar is not referred to by name in the Qur'ān. For the Muslim tradition, cf. Mahmoud Ayoub, *The Qur'ān and Its Interpreters* (Albany: State University of New York Press, 1984), Vol. 1, pp. 151–169; Muhammad Haykal, *The Life of Muhammad*, p. 22–30; and F. E. Peters, *A Reader on Classical Islam* (Princeton: Princeton University Press, 1994), pp. 13–22. Articles in James Hastings, ed., *Dictionary of the Bible*, including H. E. Ryle on Hagar and S. R. Driver on Ishmael are old but useful. *The Jewish Encyclopaedia* includes many legends that pass back and forth between the Jewish and Islamic traditions.

28. As an example, *Time Magazine*, Sept. 20, 2002, published a feature article, "The Legacy of Abraham," suggesting that "if Muslims, Christians and Jews are

ever to respect and understand one another a key road leads through Abraham" (p. 49).

29. Rudi Paret, "*Ismāʿīl*," *EI²*, IV, pp. 184f.

30. Quoted in Tor Andrae, *Garden of Myrtles*, pp. 121f.

31. A Guthrie, "The Significance of Abraham," *MW*, Vol. XLV, No. 2, April 1955, p. 120.

32. Michael Kurtz, "Listening to Hagar and Ishmael—Gen. 21:8–21," Lutheran Campus Centre, University of British Columbia, Vancouver, Canada, June 23, 1996, p. 2.

33. For the veneration of Muhammad cf. key Islamic principle six in Chapter 2, and Miller, *Muslim Friends*, pp. 76–78.

34. H. A. R. Gibb, *Modern Trends in Islam* (New York: Octagon Press, 1978), pp. 74f.

35. M. A. Helie Lucas, "The Preferential Symbol for Islamic Identity," in *Women Living under Muslim Laws. Dossier 11/12/13* (Grabels, France: International Solidarity Network of Women Living under Muslims Laws, 1991), pp. 8–10.

36. Ayesah M. Imam, "Women and Fundamentalism," *ibid., p. 14.*

37. Cf. Jane I. Smith and Yvonne Y. Haddad, "Eve: Islamic image of woman," in Azizah al-Hibri, ed., *Women Studies International Forum, op.cit.*, pp. 135–144.

38. Wilfred C. Smith, *Islam in Modern History* (Princeton: Princeton University Press, 1957), p. 49.

39. Quoted from al-Afghanī's "An Islamic Response to Imperialism," *Political and Social Writings of Sayyid Jamāl al-Dīn al-Afghanī*, tr. and ed. by Nikki R. Keddie, in J. J. Donahue and J. L. Esposito, eds. *Islam in Transition*, p. 17.

40. E. I. J. Rosenthal, *Islam in the Modern National State* (Cambridge: University Press, 1965), p. 44. This type of mis-identification is natural for Muslims who do not differentiate between the sacred and the secular. Less excusable is the sweeping identification of colonialism and Christian mission activity often found in popular secular thought in western society. In many areas of Asia and Africa European colonial governments vigorously opposed Christian missionaries and their work, a fact that is now widely documented. What must be admitted, however, is that in the later colonial period mission activities practically benefitted from being 'western.'"

41. Judith Miller, *God Has Ninety-Nine Names* (New York: Simon & Schuster, 1977), pp. 60–63, notes that radical Islamist views are not so much anti-Christian as anti-Western, since they regard Christianity as virtually dead. The West on the other hand needs to be put to death.

42. Akbar S. Ahmed, *Postmodernism*, pp. 98, 101, 103, 111. For an informed overview by a non-Muslim western scholar cf. Willem Bijlefeld, "Christian-Muslim Relations: A Burdensome Past, A Challenging Future," in *Word & World*, XVI, No. 2, 1996, pp. 117–128.

43. An example of adept caricaturing is a newspaper headline for an article describing an American missionary training college, namely, "The Covert Crusade," (!); Cf. Ottawa *Citizen*, August 10, 2002, p. B1.

44. Parwez Mansoor, "Standing Up to Intellectual Conversion," *Inquiry*, Vol. 1, no. 6, November 1984, p. 7.

45. The *Globe and Mail*, Toronto, March 21, p. A17.

14

The Christian Approach: Method

I have crossed the bridges. I come as a servant, as an evangel-sharer, as a reconciler, as a conversation partner. I am the connection, and I make connections.
Now what do I do? How do I bring home what is on my heart? This chapter attempts
to answer that question. It is about appropriate methods for communicating to
Muslims the Christian understanding of sin and salvation. It is an explication of
the evangelistic task.

Method too is a neutral word. It can be taken positively or negatively. We are
taking the word in its positive sense of seemly ways and means for communicating
good news. Others may see its negative side. Some Christians may find the term
inconsistent with the spirit of friendship. Do we need methods for communicating
with friends? Furthermore, it gives the impression that people are being viewed
as objects and manipulated to a desired result. But who wants to be treated as the
object of a method? Muslims also may sense a negative connotation. The feeling
may be intensified by the use of certain terms that mark some writings on evangelism such as "target" and "strategy." These may be well-intended but they are
verbal red flags that give the impression, at best, of an impersonal attitude and, at
worst, of a set of militant tactics. As critical as the search for appropriate method
is the search for the language that really expresses what is intended.

Nevertheless, despite its potential for being misunderstood, there is no real
substitute available for the term "method." We will use it therefore to refer to fitting
ways to bring Muslim friends to a genuine meeting with the Savior. In this sense,
the term is nothing more than the contemporary equivalent of "Come and see."

In dealing with this topic we will first take up the theoretical undergirding of
appropriate methodology, then consider four challenging contemporary issues,
and finally examine some practical methods that together make up the sharing
craft.

A. Some Theoretical Perspectives

Like wholeness and connection method is grounded on deep friendship, but there are other basic theological elements in "the divine technology." In addition, there are some pragmatic principles that also have a theological dimension. We will therefore briefly consider the theology of method and some aspects of functional theory.

1. The Theology of Method

Theology of method includes remembering the mind of Christ, considering the levels of God's communicating Word, and recognizing that God's people are God's means.

a. Method Madness and the Mind of Christ

It may safely be said that contemporary society is method-mad. Technological advance, the mark of our age, reflects that preoccupation. Method-madness is connected with efficiency and success, particularly in marketing. The competition in information technology is fueled in part by the desire to persuade people to accept a certain product. Method-madness is also connected with speed and change. No sooner is one technique discovered than it is replaced by something "better," that is, more efficient and successful. In our current stage of civilization we have plunged into a frenzied search for methodology.

The task of evangel-sharing is not unaffected by this development. It is logical to seek new and better ways of communicating with Muslims. The attempt may seem promising, and at times even exhilarating. On the other hand, the exhilaration may be only a step removed from the idea that the "success" of the Christian mission depends on somehow finding the right method. Nothing could be further from the truth, and the plethora of quasi-scientific "findings" on evangelistic method that keep appearing do not strengthen the case. The classic and durable profile of evangel-sharing as an activity connected with the Truth of self-giving love, and with trust in the Word stands in some contrast with method-madness. Even as a disciplined search for improved methodology continues, sharing friends will remember that it is not human technique but the mind of Christ that provides the foundation for evangel-sharing.

> Let this mind be in you that was in Christ Jesus, who though he was in the form of God, did not regard equality with God as something to be exploited, but emptied himself, taking the form of a slave, being born in human likeness. And being found in human form he humbled himself, and became obedient to the point of death, even death upon a cross. Therefore God also highly exalted him ... (Phil 2:6–9).

This divine pattern is the well from which the waters of methodology must be drawn. It is remarkable that the principle of deep friendship, expressed so eloquently in this passage, is almost hinted at in the root meaning of the word method. The term comes from the Greek, *meta-hodos*, meaning "the way above." In Jesus Christ the way above has become the way below for his followers. The way may be simply defined as the communicating Word in a loving person.

b. The Communicating Word is God's Method

God's method for channeling his love to human beings is His powerful Word. There are three facets to that truth, each bearing power. Using Biblical references we will summarize them as follows:

In the primary sense God's Word refers to Jesus Christ who is God's Self-Communication. "In the beginning was the Word, and the Word was with God, and the Word was God. ... And the Word became flesh and dwelt among us, full of grace and truth" (Jn 1:1, 14). The eternal Word, Jesus, is God's self-revelation, and God's personal message of love to the world.

God's creative power is associated with the eternal Word. "He was in the beginning with God; all things were made through him, and without him was not anything made that was made. In him was life, and the life was the light of man" (Jn 1:2–4).

In a second sense the phrase God's Word refers to the scriptures that are a written testimony to God's salvation in Jesus Christ. Inspired by God's Spirit in human writers, they constitute "the cradle of Christ", given to us for our learning. The scriptures reveal and glorify Jesus the Word.

God's creative power is associated with the scriptures. "The word of God is living and active, sharper than any two-edged sword, piercing to the division of soul and spirit ... and discerning the thoughts and intentions of the heart" (Heb 4:12).

In a third and adopted sense God's Word refers to the proclamation of God's law and gospel by the servants of God who are sent to transmit the story of salvation to the world. The proclaimers reveal and glorify Jesus the Word and the Savior of God.

God's creative power is associated with the proclaimed Word. "I am not ashamed of the gospel; it is the power of God for salvation to everyone who has faith" (Rom 1:16) ... How will they believe in one of whom they have never heard? (Rom 10:14).

We might say that from beginning to end, God's Word is God's method. From the creative moment: "Then God said ... and it was so (Gen 1) to the final re-creative moment when the Voice from the Throne declares: "Death shall be no more. ... Behold I make all things new" (Rev 21), God's Word brings into effect what God desires.

c. The People of the Word are God's Means

We may assert with Jens Christensen and others that God's people are God's means. Christensen, a longtime evangel-sharer among Muslims, understood the personal dimension that must enter into such communication. He said: "The church is God's means," adding: "In your practical approach to the Muslim you are God's means of approach. ... There are no means you [author's italic] can use, because you are God's means ... God's point of contact."[2] In a sense, the church is now God's embodied Word, carrying on the work of the Incarnate Lord, declaring it and living it. A missionary theologian put it tersely, "The church is God's mission."[3]

The basis for this understanding is the fact that God chooses and sends people to carry out the work that God wants done in the world. "You are a chosen race, a royal priesthood, a holy nation, God's own people, that you may declare the wonderful deeds of him who called you out of darkness into his marvelous light" (1 Pet 2:11). The people of God are those who have been born anew by the living and abiding Word of God, who have tasted the kindness of the Lord, who have received mercy, in short, those who know the deep friendship of God. They have become aware of and grasp the reconciling love of God in the Person of Jesus Christ, and grasping it recognize that they have become the reconciling friends of the world. "So we have become ambassadors for Christ, God making his appeal through us. We beseech you, on behalf of Christ, be reconciled to God!" (2 Cor 5:20).

All human sub-methods must be dynamically related to the divine method of God's communicating Word in loving people. There is no mystery here. It is a friend with the Word that constitutes the bridge for a Muslim to the Christian perception of grace and truth, that is, to the perception of Jesus the Savior. The essential task of a deep friend and evangel-sharer is to put Muslims into real and living contact with the Word of God.

The writer has a framed photograph on his bookshelf, a work of art because of its lights and shadows, a picture taken by his wife. What matters is the subject rather than the artistry. A friend and I are shown sitting on the steps of a veranda. I have an open Bible on my lap. The second person in the frame in Ahmad Kutty. He is also holding a copy of the scriptures. Ahmad Kutty has a strong face. He is a senior person, bald, with a white moustache and the fringe of a white beard. He wears white clothes and a shoulder scarf. Ahmad Kutty is the image of a devout Muslim. The photo is posed, but what happened previous to its being taken is an undying memory. I will tell Ahmad Kutty's story in the first person.

I did not know who he was, but he tended to follow me about. With disturbing frequency when I was in the midst of a conversation with someone in the reading room of our library, he appeared at my shoulder. I suspected his motives. Finally I said to Ahmad Kutty: "Please come to my home, and we will have some tea and a talk." He enthusiastically agreed. It did not take me long to discover that I was quite wrong in my impressions. What Ahmad Kutty wanted to know more about was the Christian faith. My failure to understand that fact was inexcusable, but fortunately it was not too late. I placed a scripture in his hand and opened it to the third chapter of the gospel of John. I asked him to read aloud verses one to sixteen. He was not well educated, and had contented himself with the life of a farmer, but that seemed to give to his reading a peculiar power. He read sonorously, with great gravity, displaying the respect that Muslims have for the Word of God. When he finished, there was a deep silence. Finally I broke it, and asked: "What do you think?" He did not answer. Thinking that he had not heard me, I repeated the question. This time he replied, uttering three groans: "Oh! Oh! Oh!" Then he lapsed again into silence as two tears formed on his leathery cheeks. I had heard the sound of an open-hearted man who for the first time had met the gospel of God's love. The moment remains unforgettable, as does Ahmad Kutty who died in a tragic accident three months later. But he had "treasured" in his heart (Ps 119:1) the "living and active Word" (Heb 4:12).

2. Aspects of Functional Theory

Although the root meaning of method is "the way above," there is also a second level of meaning that takes us into practical considerations. The term may also be defined as "a systematic and orderly way of procedure." It signifies an intelligent manner of getting something done. The fact that relationships are more important than techniques in communication with Muslims does not imply, and should not be taken to imply, that the choice of methods is unimportant. Christians are not only interested in conveying God's Word, but are also hopeful of seeing its renewing power at work in human lives. In other words, they want to proclaim the *kerugma* effectively. The goal is a community of disciples who rejoice in the salvation of God and who love one another and the world. The means to reach such a high goal are important. Four things may be borne in mind in that regard—the purity of means, the need to keep focused, staying real, and accepting diversity. We must also consider the relation of good works and methods.

a. The Purity of Means

The communicators of the gospel face a severe temptation—to believe that because the goal is so significant, any method that works to reach it is valid. If Muslim opinion is to be taken, evangel-sharers have not been able to resist that temptation. Is there any truth to the charge that the methods they use are unkind and unfair, and may even degenerate into trickery? What is trickery? Its essence is disguising the real purpose of what is done. A person may show a health film to gather a crowd, but in fact he has no real interest in the health of the community. He wants to get the crowd for other reasons. That is trickery. It is a way of getting things done, but it is not the way above, and it does not honor Christ. In fact, it harms his cause.

And we read back from the goal of Christian communication—the establishment of a community of love—we see that the means to that goal must also be decisively controlled by the principle of love. Perhaps the most famous modern person who instructed on the relation between ends and means was Mohandas K. Gandhi, whom the world knew as Mahatma Gandhi. He argued that methods are much more than utilitarian procedures. They are moral concepts and decisions related to the ultimate goal. The end does not justify the means, but rather—in his now famous phrase—"means are ends in the making." If the objective set for the India freedom movement is an Indian society built on truth and love, the method of reaching it will be appropriate to the objective. With that principle in mind Gandhi opted for an approach of non-violent non-cooperation in the struggle for a free India that concluded successfully in 1947. From where did he draw this insight? He was greatly indebted to the Hindu concept of *ahimsa* of non-violence, but he also regarded the example of Christ's suffering love as a permanent factor in his theory. As Margaret Chatterji put it, Gandhi believed that "the progressive use of good[= pure] means would eventually result in the attainment of the objective," and she points out that "Gandhi often uses the image of the cross to drive his message home."[4]

However we may view Gandhi's philosophy and his optimism, the principle that there is a continuity between ends and means represents a simple and profound truth. For evangel-sharers it indicates that they will distinguish between methods reflecting the spirit of Christ and mere gimmicks reflecting the cult of success. Christian friends of Muslims are "mad with love" not "method-mad." All evangel-sharing methods are under double scrutiny. The first judgment is an intellectual one—are they effective? The second judgment is a moral one—are they respectful of the integrity of fellow human beings? Do they reflect the Golden Rule? Do they express the mind of Christ?

b. Keeping Focused

Methods cannot be viewed as a kind of heap of things to do, indiscriminately gathered and loosely related, more connected with keeping busy than keeping effective. They are rather ways of getting at and dealing with the core factor. *The core Muslim intuition is that human beings are to surrender to God and to be God's obedient servants.* Therein, in Muslim view, is the basis of the human vocation and hope. *The Christian faith is that this highly worthy goal is impossible to achieve without the forgiveness of sins* and the new life. God asks us to pray for that: "Create in me a clean heart, O God, and put a new and right spirit within me" (Ps 51:10). Moreover God the Savior graciously provides the basis for that newness of life through the salvific work God does in Jesus Christ. Our surrendering and obeying now flow freely from the well of gratitude.

All evangel-sharing methodology must be dynamically related to the bridging of these two fundamental perceptions. That is to say, it will be dedicated to *awareness-creation*, the awakening of the sense of spiritual need that God's law arouses, and *solace-sharing*, making the heart glad with the news of God's victory over evil and the promises that the gospel conveys.

c. Staying Real

Staying in touch with reality means remembering that the focusing has to do with people, and people are different. The New Testament writings are addressed to Christian believers, but there were great variations among them. The Jewish-background Christians and the Gentile Christians differed. Among the Jewish-background Christians there was some distinction between the "home-grown" Jews centered in Jerusalem and the Greek-acculturated Jews in the diaspora. Among the Gentiles there were major differences among the peoples inhabiting the vast Roman Empire. The New Testament writings reflect those distinctions, as well as the personalities and life experiences of the writers themselves. Staying real with Muslims means to recognize the individual variations that exist among them. The growing Muslim tendency to downplay those distinctions, reflecting a developing global homogenization process, does not obviate the fact that the word VARIETY must be writ large over the Muslim reality. Even within tightly-formed Muslim cultures there are differences person to person. All this, in the last analysis, is the product of the divine creative genius that gives the precious gift of individuality.

Staying in touch with reality means acknowledging it, dealing with it, focusing in with personal relevance. Focusing keeps us centered. Staying real keeps us relevant. Combining the two is an intellectual and spiritual challenge for a sharing friend.

D. ACCEPTING A DIVERSITY OF STYLE

We must also stay real about ourselves and the legitimate diversity of means. The inclination to a certain approach depends heavily on personal temperament, although it is also influenced by other factors such as training and location. For example, lay people who have only occasional contact with Muslims have little interest in sophisticated approaches and view their witness task quite existentially and pragmatically. Professional missioners will tend to be analytic, and are on the alert for fresh communication models. The critical factor, however, is our created individuality and the gifts of the Spirit.

God has endowed people with a variety of spiritual gifts which God wants them to utilize for kingdom-building. It is in the combined and intra-respectful employment of the first that the health of the Body is sustained and the tasks committed to it are carried out. To say this is not to make a case against the passion for practical truths, but to make an argument for mutual appreciation. The fact that there are both natural and spiritual variations does not imply a commitment to methodological agnosticism or anarchy, a turning the back on intelligent analysis and on fresh Biblical thinking in an effort to discern what is effective and what is not, a failure to learn from the past, or the neglect of common sense. Diversity does not equate foolishness. It simply means freedom within limits to be what you are and to do what you can. Only with this principle can the whole people of God be drawn into the task of engaging with Muslims. In that understanding God's Spirit can and does effectively use the quiet neighbor in the suburb, the fellow student in a class, the theoretician in an institution, the professional on some field, or the prayer of a little child. This is a truth to celebrate as we share with Muslim friends.

It is doubtful therefore that any case can be made for absolute methods, other than "God's methods" that we have discussed. All human methods are provisional. Absolutizing them tends to false-centeredness, arouses *hubris*, and gets in the way of love for people. It is wiser to accept that there are today, as there once was, Peters and Johns, Jameses and Pauls, Marys and Marthas, Lydias, and Dorcases. The delightful diversity of those involved in God's work has contributed to its effectiveness far more than any single methodological system, no matter how perfect or hallowed, could ever have done. The bottom line for every sharing friend is that while some methods relate well to your personality and talents, and will work for you, others do not. Accepting that, we can be open and thankful for the learned experience of others, and draw water from those wells of practical wisdom.

e. A Note on the Relation of Good Works and Good Methods

The issue of the relation of good works and good methods is a disputed one. What has been said about the purity of means establishes its foundation. At a conscious level, the disciples of Jesus the Servant will differentiate modes of helpful action to deal with tangible human needs from methods for communicating the persuasive word. They are closely related, united by the principle of love, but they are functionally distinct. No one can deny the witnessing impact of deeds of mercy. Indeed, along the way they may also become a means for communicating and apprehending the gospel, but they are not done for that reason. The deeds of mercy are done to help suffering people apart from other results. Evangelistic methods, on the other hand, have the designed purpose of conveying the gospel message. Both are done to the glory of God.

The confusion of the relationship between good works and evangelistic methods has produced widespread misunderstanding and considerable damage. We have noted Muslim feelings in this regard in our discussion of medical service (Ch. 13, A. 6). A crude example illustrates the problem and shows why such sensitivities have a basis in fact. The writer once attended a major mission meeting where a dedicated medical worker made a presentation. She stated: "If the people do not attend the morning devotion in our clinic, we will not give them treatment." Seldom are statements made so forthrightly, but the thinking represents a stream of opinion. It flows from theological misunderstanding, and fails to reflect God's generous providential care for the whole creation and Jesus' spontaneous service to the suffering. His followers help the helpless because they need help, and for no other reason. The relation of good works and evangelistic methods is not a casual one—"I am helping this person in order to get a preaching opportunity." Nor is it a co-terminous one—"I must witness orally with every loving deed." David Shenk states the matter accurately:[5] "We must never perceive compassion for the poor as an evangelistic hook. We minister with compassion because of Jesus, not to gain converts. Holistic ministry is right, even if there is no evident response to the Gospel." It is probably true to say that to the extent that Christians view their good works as methods, to that extent Muslims will regard them as stratagems.

At the same time, the Christian response to the spectrum of human physical, mental, and spiritual needs cannot be artificially divided, whether viewed anthropologically or theologically. Those services issue from the same source, reflect the same pattern, and point to the same Lord. Jesus helped people with an unmotivated compassion, and he addressed people with the same compassion. Because God's communication is the Word in a loving person, the good works and good words of God's people flow together. Some may misunderstand that nearness. But where there is an underlying relation of deep friendship Muslims too will see the ministries of loving deed and loving word in both their distinction and their complementarity.

B. Types of Methodological Challenge

Three current issues affecting methodology, particularly in Muslim-majority areas, are contextualization, church-planting, and popular Islam. We will deal with them briefly through representative missionary works. A fourth issue is the new and vigorous Muslim presence in western society, and its implication for evangel-sharing.

1. Contextualization, Church-Planting, Popular Islam
a. Contextualization

Phil Parshall, a career missionary and prolific author, is a challenging "methodologian." In the foreword to one of his works William Webster sets the stage for Parshall's discussion of contextualization, that is, relating dynamically to the indigenous, receiving culture.[6]

> Two major problems confront anyone endeavoring to communicate God's good news in Christ to Muslim friends. The first stems from the cultural shell in which it is conveyed. ... A second problem arises from so thoroughly accommodating the spirit of Christ to the values, thought patterns and cultural forms of Muslim society that a syncretistic religious mixture results. Phil Parshall has successfully avoided both difficulties.

Parshall has two fundamental questions in mind: How may the gospel be contextualized so that it relates meaningfully to Muslims, and how can Muslims who choose to follow Christ remain within their community. The second question will be discussed in chapter 16. Parshall is of the opinion, for example, that instead of utilizing the heavy-laden term "Christian" new disciples from Muslim background may be called "followers of 'Īsā." Here we will limit ourselves to the first issue of contextualization.

This scholar finds Biblical guidance for the principle of contextualization in the pattern of Jesus, in the decisions of the Council of Jerusalem (Acts 15), in Paul's treatment of the matter of food presented to idols (1 Cor 8), and in the apostle's theory of identification (1 Cor 9). The application of the principle faces difficulties on two sides. On one side it can be virtually ignored and a "God against culture" position taken. On the other hand, it may be adulterated into syncretism. To sail one's craft safely between the two extremes means acquiring a real knowledge of the Muslim culture involved. This includes not only a knowledge of the forms but of their meaning, and the sense of these meanings within the Islamic world view that is expressed in such themes as unity, family honor, the concept of change, and others. When Jesus Christ becomes the Center of that world view, he sanctifies the culture appropriately. To further such a dynamic development communicators need to share the incarnational attitude of the Lord who was himself involved in Jewish culture. Parshall warns that "it is never easy for a person to incarnate himself in another culture," and it requires self-forgetting and forsaking. Such a one needs to take solace, as Jesus did, in talking with the Father.[7]

The incarnational attitude is expressed functionally by utilizing available points of contact in Muslim culture including the idea of scriptural authority, the story of Jesus in the Qur'ān, the concept of sacrifice, and the like. Parshall hopes for more methodological experimentation with the broad array of Muslim religious forms such as ablutions, chanting, prayer rituals, times of worship, birth-marriage-death customs, initiation ceremonies, organizational techniques, and so on. These attempts cannot be separated from the cultivation of the evangelist's own Christ-like spirit, which includes the practice of prayer, the deepening of faith, patience and love, and a living in the Spirit. Parshall is evidently making the point that contextualizing methods are ennobled and enabled in the movement of Christ-patterned persons with Muslims.

b. Church-Planting

Greg Livingstone, a mission director, deals with the related issue of planting churches. The themes of planting churches, people movements, homogenous units, and church growth are now commonplace in missiological discussion. They are by no means routine, however, in relation to Muslim contexts. Livingstone attempts to bring them into the center of the discussion. He contends that evangel-sharers must from the beginning envision a congregation of Muslim-background believers. A merely individualistic approach has proved to be inadequate. Muslim inquirers need to have the possibility of a relation with other former Muslims with whom them can identify. "The key to evangelism among Muslims is for them to experience a vital congregation of joyful redeemed Muslims taking care of one another; and giving Christ the credit."[8] Given the history of Christian sharing with Muslims, and the lack of historic models, he recognizes the presumptuousness of this idea, but he adds: "We must examine our methods. We must go beyond evangelism or cross-cultural communication. The goal is a house church."[9] The development of such a group becomes "the critical mass" that enables new believers to have access to the fellowship that they need.

To establish initial congregations where they do not exist will become possible when more Christians come into actual witnessing contact with Muslims. Such people are "change agents." The wider church must see to their presence if necessary utilizing expatriates for this purpose. Given the blockages that stem from cultural, historical, and political facts, "we cannot assume that the existing national Christians will take up the task."[10]

Livingstone's special interest is the urban context, and he calls for a typical team approach of six people working together for ten years. The team will have a strong leader, members with different talents, and facilitators who will enable residence in the community. Contact with its members will be carried out in culturally appropriate ways. Drawing on typical church-planting methodology he calls for clarifying the distinct "people" factors, i.e., the forms of internal communication and gateways for communication from the outside, how changes take place, how decisions are made, how leaders are recognized, and how groups are organized. He draws on contextualization themes such as the idea of 'Īsā Masīh as mediator and intercessor, but he also affirms that the critical factor is establishing relationships in the incarnational manner of Jesus. He puts it succinctly: "Without relationships communication is minimal."[11]

c. Popular Islam

The issue of popular Islam or folk Islam was introduced in connection with our discussion of salvation through intercession (ch. 4, B. 5). We noted that popular Islam has to do with the realm of powers rather than ideas, powers that a believer must deal with pragmatically. This view affects the pattern of Christian communication. Bill Musk goes so far as to say that "the issue of power not information tops the agenda for most ordinary Muslims."[12] The powers are related to the problems of everyday life, from simple matters to disease and enmity, and for them popular Islam offers "an abundance of remedies."[13] The remedies revolve around such phenomena as power-filled individuals, the use of magic, carefulness at the rites of passage, the use of vows and gifts, charms and amulets, and the like.

It has often been pointed out that the culture context of the Bible resembles this world view more closely than does our modern thought world, and accordingly it offers a plenitude of insights for communication. The simple statement that "Jesus is stronger than the devil" is good news for those who fear the powers.[14] But there are also many specific examples of what some call "power encounters." More fundamentally, the Bible testifies to the active presence of a powerful Lord in human life, One Greater than the evil one. It further reveals the cosmic overcoming of evil by good, and at the individual level the authority of Jesus Christ over demonic powers. The testimony of evangel-sharers at this level is "not in word only, but also in the power of the Holy Spirit, and with full conviction" (1 Thess 1:5). It is not so much the conveying of new facts as the proclamation of Christus Victor! This involves dealing with what Musk called the ordinary "cerebral bias," the heritage of rationalism and individualism, and allowing for a wrenching reorientation toward an experiential world that is no longer familiar and may seem unreal. The Biblical resources need to be applied to this world. Methodological suggestions range from utilizing the concept of blessing, engaging in healing through prayer and anointing with oil, the careful practice of exorcism, spiritual combat through prayer, and the cultivation of verbal reminders. The Muslim who has been taught to say "I take refuge in God" when he/she feels the temptation of the Beguiler can well understand what it means to draw on verbal expressions of the power of "The Lord of the Worlds."

The methodological expression of power-sharing runs between its own Scylla of charlatanism and Charybdis of triumphalism. The former simply replaces the magic of folk Islam with the neo-magic of the Christian practitioner, while the latter gives way to an ill-disguised theology of glory. The answer to the tendencies, at the personal level, is fervency in prayer, and at the witness level a crisp and constant pointing to Christ the Deliverer through whose intercession alone those who fear the powers "may open their eyes so that they may turn from darkness to light, and from the power of Satan to God, that they may receive the forgiveness of sins ..." (Acts 26:18). Those who bear the message of power will remember that the power of the Victor is that of self-giving and suffering love, and that when one strikes at the head of evil, the heel is bruised (Gen 3:15). Paul Hiebert says: "When we are involved in power encounter, we must be ready to pay the price, for the cross is the paradigm of how God works in human history."[15] Finally, those who communicate with people influenced by folk views will also remember that the intellect too is a gift of the Almighty, and that the ministry of education has its own liberating power for those who have discovered, as Irenaeus said, that God in Christ "has bound the strong one, and spoiled his goods, and annihilated death."[16]

The call to contextualize the Christian message so that Muslims may meet Jesus the Messiah and express their experience in understandable ways, the call to deal with Muslims as they are in their folkways and to make the Messiah's authority known in that context, and the call to establish worshiping groups in distinction from the individualist tradition are alerting summons. The newest "kid on the block" in terms of methodological challenges, however, is the increased presence of Muslims in western societies and their Christian environments. We turn next to that development.

2. Muslims in the West

The current numbers of Muslims in the West create a new setting for Christian communication that constitutes a pragmatic test for appropriate methodology.

a. The "western" Muslims

The number of Muslims in the West constitute only one percent of the *umma*, but their significance for Christian sharing is much larger. They are made up of immigrants or immigrant-descended people, refugees, converts, students, and visitors, mostly resident in cities. In some cases, such as Germany and France, the majority stem from particular nations, while in the U.S.A. the special feature is African-American Islam. The fundamentally governing factor of their life is that they are minorities in a majority Christian context.[17] There are, however, other important characteristics.

Muslims in the West are seeking Islamic solutions for living in a western environment. Muslim tradition does not provide all the answers for the particular requirements of the situation, and these lead to theoretical questions. They include the old question: What does it really mean to be a Muslim? When all else goes, what must remain? Muslims ask themselves, in one way or the other: How shall we deal with our assimilation fears? Without traditional institutions who will teach us and our children? The global conflicts and the advance of extremism complicate their already complex existence. How can we live normally when we are defined abnormally? At the bottom rests a usually unarticulated question: How shall we overcome our loneliness and fears? Not every Muslim has the same set of doubts, but there are many such questions.

Muslim internal differences of opinion and divisions make it difficult for them to achieve consensus on the answers. The differences are partly ethnic in nature. Immigrant and refugee Muslims have entered western society from different areas of the world, and they represent cultures that do not have natural connection apart from religion. Such differences are often represented in practice by the establishment of separate mosques. Moreover, there is also a marked variation in educational standards that is reflected in differing approaches to identity questions and the solution of problems. Finally, there are also varieties of approach between some practicing immigrant Muslims and some who tend to merge into the general society. The former at times are defensive and aggressive. They view their Islamicity in sharp contrast with the majority religious tradition, and their personal identity is linked with religion rather than with culture. They tend to be more aware of their faith and its requirements than they might be in their homelands. To the extent that they believe their faith to be threatened by the environment they adopt defensive attitudes, and to the extent that they feel a special obligation to promote it they are aggressive advocates. Muslim student associations on university campuses often reflect these phenomena is a forceful way. Student opinions are frequently influenced by the reading of Ismail Faruqi, Syed Abul Mawdudi, Syed Qutb, and other revivalists. Secular-oriented Muslims, who may constitute the majority of Muslims in the West, adopt a quieter and more personal style of religious expression. Some sink into a kind of silence, neither displaying their own faith nor showing interest in another, while others take a nominal stance. Their first concern is the conduct of a normal and successful life within their chosen milieu.

In addition to the normal problems facing all immigrants and refugees Muslims in the West have a specific set of problems in religious practice that are created by the culture context, of which many Christians are unaware. The customary life that is lived under Muslim law is not fully possible, yielding some down-to-earth difficulties, of which the following are some examples:

—permission for noon prayer time for factory and office employees;

—usable space and released time for the celebration of Muslim festivals that have not yet become part of the general calendar;

—meeting the religious education needs of Muslim children;

—the expected participation in Christianized events related to Christmas and Easter;

—the sharīʿa laws related to marriage, divorce, and inheritance do not conform with national law in western societies, and adjustments need to be made; in addition, there are various issues arising from interreligious marriages;

—dietary concerns are more easily overcome; they relate to the way animals are slaughtered, and the use of pork and lard;

—there are aggravations related to alcohol use, the drug culture, and the tendency to sex-obsession in media advertising; and

—finally, but needing mention again, is the challenge of living with stereotyping and caricature.

While this does not constitute a complete list of the practical difficulties that Muslims face, it is sufficient to indicate their scope and extent. Muslims are coping with them in various ways, but sincerely appreciate the sympathetic help of Christian friends in their solution.

b. Facets of the Christian Response

Evangel-sharing methodology for Muslims living in western cities will be person-related, sensitive and non-threatening, service-related, hope-filled, practical, and flexible. For example, the best way to find out about some of the difficulties described above is for a congregation to extend an invitation to a simple tea function on a Sunday afternoon. The approach to setting up such an occasion will normally be made through an educated Muslim of the area, using natural contacts, and is relatively simple to achieve. If no such contact is available the Islamic Association of the area, or the Islamic Information office, may be consulted. Muslims will gladly respond, and will not be hesitant to enter a church facility for such an occasion. As a courtesy the *imām* of the local mosque, if one exists, may be invited once the event is firmly established. He will not usually attend, but the invitation protocol is important. A second possibility, at an even simpler level, is for a congregation member to invite a small group of Muslims to his/her home for tea or lunch, followed by friendly discussion. Muslims will ordinarily expect the personal relationships to continue after such an event!

The greatest need of the moment is not method but awareness followed by commitment. Christians in the West need a wake-up call. Events have brought Islam and Muslims into prominence, but not in a humane manner. Far more important is that fact that the process of world history has brought a large body of Muslims, many of them from "closed" societies, into the direct orbit of potential Christian friends. In fact, it is a missiologically spectacular moment that calls for Christian awareness and responsible action. The leadership of the clergy is important in the alerting and enabling dimensions, but it is the ordinary church members who now hold the key to the future. They have long and faithfully supported missions at a distance. Now, in view of the novel nearness of Muslims, they are called to a personal role as sharing friends. When Islam spread to different parts of the globe, it did so largely through the everyday witness of lay believers. Again, in western society today where Muslim professional clergy are scarce or totally absent, it is lay Muslims who are leading and developing the Islamic community. Similarly, if the gospel of Jesus the Messiah is to be appreciated by Muslims in the West, it will be through the engagement of Christian lay people with Muslim friends in everyday life. What is most crucial in this situation then, is pre-methodology, the awakening of God's people to a special moment in time. Numerous models are available for creating awareness and arousing a sense of possibility. It is hard to think of any active Christian congregation in a western city that would be exempt from the privilege and duty of conducting some form of Muslim awareness seminar and its appropriate follow-up.

Among the most creative methodological developments that have evolved from the new encounter is the ministry of hospitality that was typified by Abraham, the Friend of God. Individuals and congregations have, as it were, opened the flaps of their tents to Muslim neighbors, and have developed formal and informal programs of assistance. The virtual re-discovery of hospitality as a contemporary expression of deep friendship has both helped in overcoming problems of families and individuals, and has created new relationships that have produced glowing experiences.[18] The various forms of hospitality in western cities to a degree are a parallel expression to the Christian institutions of mercy in Muslim societies. The programmatic efforts have been directed especially to the physical and social needs of new immigrants and refugees who have been assisted in working through their entry and settlement problems, ranging from language acquisition to job training. The Muslim felt needs and difficulties that have been cited provide an agenda for the further enhancement of the ministry of hospitality.

Muslims have greatly appreciated the range of assistance given. Legendary for their own practice of hospitality, they have been moved by its Christian counterpart. Following the Old Testament, the Qur'ān gives testimony to the symbolic meaningfulness of Abraham's reception of the strangers. It says: "Has the story reached thee, of the honored guests of Abraham? Behold, they entered his presence and said 'Peace!' He said, 'Peace!' ... Then he turned quickly to his household (and) brought out the fatted calf" (41:25). The New Testament declares that the grace of hospitality is to be extended to the members of the faith family (1 Pet 4:9), but it is also to include the wider human family. St. Paul declares: "Extend hospitality to strangers" (Rom 12:3). While hospitality is an aspect of service, functioning as "the fatted calf" for the strangers of our time and place, it has also opened the door for the sharing of the angelic news of the hospitality of God.

C. The Sharing Craft

This section deals with some helpful methods that may be utilized in sharing the gospel with Muslims. They include personal conversation; literature; poetry; music; drama; calligraphy and painting; the eletronic media; and others. The sharing craft has benefitted from many sound conceptions and practical approaches. The communication of the message of salvation has not so much suffered from a dearth of methods as it has from the lack of practitioners. We begin with the primary approach of personal conversation.

1. Conversation with Muslims

Conversation as a method is not simply saying things, even holy things, but is the art of getting through. What enables that is a flow of friendship and concern. Two men once met on a street. One asked the other his name. The other said, "Louder." The first man raised his voice and asked again, whereupon the other responded, "Louder." After one more round of this the first man, assuming that he was being mocked, struck the other a sharp blow. A bystander rushed up and asked, "Why are you hitting Mr. Lowder?" There is conversation without real communication, and both Christians and Muslims have done enough of that. What is needed in gospel sharing is sincere engagement.

The primary place for such sharing with Muslims is in a private and relaxed setting. Muslims are not only graciously hospitable in themselves, but they anticipate the same in others and happily participate in such opportunities. Moreover, where a friendly basis has been established and there is mutual confidence, Muslims are open and outgoing, polite and engaging in their conversational style, always allowing for the inevitable variation from person to person. The topics of conversation may cover a wide range of interest, and are at their best when unforced and free flowing. Religious topics are not forbidden, and any ordinary conversation may touch on the subject. At that point some of the elements we have lifted up in the profile of a sharing friend may be borne in mind.

There is no better pattern for gospel sharing than that provided by Jesus' own conversations, particularly with Nicodemus (Jn 3:1–21) and the Samaritan woman (Jn 4:1–20). They highlight two crucial sharing elements—availability and association. Nicodemus came to Jesus by night. It could hardly have been very convenient, and Jesus must have been weary. Perhaps they were previously acquainted. In any event, Jesus made himself available to Nicodemus at an awkward time. Moreover, he was willing to associate with a member of a group that disliked and opposed him. His spirit of availability and association were embraced in a loving attitude that the Jewish rabbi sensed in Jesus. They were enough to bring Nicodemus out at a dark hour and to move him to serious and humble questioning of this unschooled man from Nazareth. A wider Muslim awareness of the Christian hope depends on greater availability and association on the part of Christian friends. It is up to the latter to remedy the essential problem that now exists—the inadequate level of contact between Christians and Muslims.

What will mark the contact will be the desire for such association, some expressed pleasure in it, and normal behavior when contacts occur. Fear of being inconvenienced, or even weariness, do not belong in the equation. Jesus, being busy and tired, arrived at Jacob's well in Samaria. A Samaritan woman came to draw water. It is obvious that there was no previous connection between them. Jesus had to create association. He also had to do it against the normal grain since a strange man and a local woman of a different culture group would not normally meet and converse in such a way. Jesus broke the existing barriers and established connection. He did so with a surprising request: "Give me a drink!" It did not produce rejection because it came from a recognizably sincere and friendly demeanor. Having created association Jesus than had to give availability. He had to break his journey to Galilee, take some of his precious rest time and give it as a gift. The combination of association and availability encouraged the woman to ask a question, and an important conversation began. The same process is applicable to Muslims. It is a fact that getting started on such a conversation with a Muslim is not a particularly difficult task. Muslims at first may show some surprise that a Christian is interested in relating in a normal way, but it will be taken as a pleasant one. Christians, then, need to overcome natural hesitations. They need to put out of their minds any feeling that Muslims are, as it were, "from another planet" and look forward to their own pleasant surprise. They have to read from a new scroll: "The Spirit of the Lord is upon me because he has anointed me with the desire for association and with the grace of availability."

From water to living water—Jesus turned the conversation with the Samaritan woman to deeper matters than physical thirst. Conversations with Muslims frequently, and quite naturally, become religious conversations. Religion is a welcome topic for Muslims, they are proud of their religion, and are happy to share their ideals. It should be noted, however, that most ordinary Muslims do not pretend to be skilled in theological matters. They are certainly willing to talk about God, but are not very accustomed to do so; their sense of things is that God is primarily to be revered and obeyed rather than discussed. What they find easier to talk about is obedience to God, the practice and behavior of believers. It is from these topics that the conversation may move to the relation between God and human beings.

To focus a religious conversation with Muslim friends a common reading of a New Testament gospel portion is frequently possible, and very helpful. Muslims on the whole are quite interested in knowing what is the in the book that the

Qur'ān so highly commends. Many quietly set aside the issue of the corruption of the scriptures, and they are pleased to engage in a joint reading with a Christian friend and mutual reflection on the meaning of the text. Especially the Gospels of St. Matthew and St. Luke, with their historical opening, are attractive to Muslims.[19]

The possibility of interreligious conversation brings up the matter of the use of Muslim religious language that has an Arabic base. What follows is not intended to create consternation but to facilitate meaningful communication. It goes without saying that when Muslims discuss religious matters they use their own religious vocabulary. If some of their basic terms are known, it helps the sharing person to understand the friend and to reach out to him or her in a more meaningful way. Every Muslim's religious vocabulary, no matter what their ethnic background may be, is sprinkled with Arabic terms for common beliefs and practices. A Muslim uses them without being consciously aware of it. For the Christian partner in conversation this may present a problem. It is possible to conduct a conversation, especially in western society, without worrying too much about this matter, but some acquaintance with Muslim religious terminology is helpful.

Apart from the fundamental word Allah Muslims have many names for God, but the most commonly-used are al-Rahmān and al-Rahīm, "the Merciful One." When dealing with the unity of God and the idea of a unified life under God the word tawhīd, unity, comes into play. It ranks as a very important term. As we have seen, hidāyat is the key word for God's guidance. A follower of God is a muslim, a surrendering person, but an obedient person is an 'abd, a servant of God. The word taqwā, piety, characterizes a believer who is in fact a mu'min, that is, a faithful and practicing Muslim. Such a person tries to observe at least the personal and family regulations of the sharī'a, the law of Islam. The common word for the whole complex of religion is dīn.

In addition to believing in God a Muslim accepts other spiritual beings. An angel is a malik, a demon is a shaitān, and lesser spirits are jinn. To carry out His merciful guidance God from time to time sends a nabī, a prophet, or a rasūl, a messenger who may bring a sacred book, that is, a kitāb. All the prophets warn people to avoid shirk, idolatry, and kufr, unbelief. They advise people to prepare for the yawm al-dīn, the Judgment Day. The names for the important practices should be known. The confession of faith is the shahāda or kalima. The five-fold prayer is salāt, one cycle being a raka'. The direction of prayer towards Mecca is the qibla. Voluntary prayer is du'a. The term for the fasting month is Ramadān, although the fast itself is sawm. Alms-giving is zakāt, and the pilgrimage to Mecca is a hajj. One who completes it is a hāji, which is added to the name of the person. The body of practices is sometimes called 'ibādat, the service of God. On Friday noon a Muslim goes to the masjid, the mosque, and participates in the khutba, the congregational worship event. In conducting daily life the believer distinguishes between that which is permitted, halāl, and what is forbidden, harām. The family sends young children to the madrasa, religious school, in addition to the public school. There they learn to recite the Qur'ān—chapter, sūra, and verse, āya. The sum of it all is islām, the surrendering to God. In addition to such common terms as the above a Muslim may also use culturally-based religious words, or terms specific to a division or sect.

Genuine conversation has a two-way Flow. An evangel-sharer has to realize that in a religious discussion the Muslim partner also has a desire to share. In fact, he has a conscious expectation that the Christian partner has a genuine interest in Muslim affairs, and will show it in some way. It is not uncommon, for example, for him to ask a Christian friend: "What do you think of Muhammad Nabi?" In asking it, he is certain that the Christian friend will give some sort of positive response. Failing that, the conversation may end quickly. It is up to sharing friends in advance to consider the appropriate reply to questions that Muslims naturally and commonly ask. And it is up to them to consider whether their intention will be to castigate what is held dear, or to win a hearing for Christ.

This brings us to the most delicate aspect of an evangel-sharer's task, the need to communicate God's law as well as God's gospel. Remembering the Islamic teaching on sin and salvation, it is clear that both are needed. It is essential—if there is to be any understanding of the gospel—to arouse in people a sense of the human predicament. Only then does the necessity and wonder of God's answer to the predicament become meaningful. How can this be done without unnecessarily wounding a conversation partner? There are four requirements. The task requires appropriate tone. It requires remembering the plural pronoun "we." It requires making a distinction between awakening a sense of sin and denigrating another's treasures. And it requires leaving some matters to the individual's own dialogue with the Lord.

Ther first requirement has to do with the tone of the conversation. The tone for sharing God's law has the same character as that for the gospel, namely the tone of caring love and of personal involvement. The critical function of an evangel-sharer is not to criticize, but to point to the crisis that God's holy demand creates for all humans, to communicate God's criticism of human sins. With Muslims who understand and uphold the concept of obedience to God that is really an uncomplicated task. As we have seen, many Muslims already have a deep sense of the human problem, and others are not far from it. The Old Testament is a major tool for building on that reality. There may not be a Muslim in the world who cannot appreciate the urgency of the word: "Be ye holy, for I the Lord your God am holy!" (Lev 20:7). It needs only to be remembered that as "love is the fulfilling of the law" (Rom. 13:10), so the communication of the law must be loving. Moreover, the use of the pronoun "we" says to the conversation partner: We are all together, all complicit in our failure, all quilty, all under God's wrath.

We must, then, make a clear distinction between communicating God's moral demand and wounding religious sensibilities. As never before in human history the context for evangel-sharing today is that of an acutely heightened cultural and religious sensibility. Any real or imagined slight of such feelings can quite easily produce, and in fact has brought about, deadly conflagrations.[20] The deliberate wounding of the religious feelings of people of other faiths is not an option for anyone in today's world, and least of all for the messengers of God's peace. This is not a contradiction of the task of proclaiming God's holiness, but rather the practical reflection of the truth that holiness and love are linked in God, and that linkage marks those who seek to share the message of God.

The final requirement is that sharing friends have to leave some matters to the individual's experience with Christ. It is the clear goal of every evangelistic moment to put Jesus the Messiah front and center. His life at the same time interprets God's law and presents God's gospel. The Muslim discussion partner recognizes him, not as a concept or idea, but as the Son of Mary whom he knows and from whom he is ready to learn. As Karl Barth put it: "His humanity indeed is the essence of all humanitas...He is the decision as to what God's purpose and what God's goal is, not just for Him but for every man."[21] As he is lifted up, Jesus not only draws people to himself, but away from all that is unworthy of the divine will. He does it progressively, through His enlightening Spirit. In the radiance of his light all other values and commitments and treasures are revealed in their true perspective and proportion. He declares:"I have come as light into the world, so that everyone who believes in me should not remain in darkness" (Jn 12:47f). That word is promise and prediction, and it suffices.

2. Communication through Literature

Literature is the tried and true carrier of the gospel to Muslim minds and hearts. It has occupied the center of attention for generations of evangel-sharers. Perhaps for that reason its effect can be overstated. Like a beast burden at times it has been required to bear too heavy a load. Its knees may buckle without its partner in communication—personal engagement. Having said that we must reiterate the overriding value of literary communication. The natural Muslim respect for the written word, its trans-national character and availability, the privacy and serenity of the reading process itself, all together make literature an irreplaceable medium of communication with Muslims. Its distribution has yielded great fruits in the past, as the testimonies of believers declare, and—despite pessimism about the fate of the print media—it holds steady promise for the future.

a. Scripture Portions

With the word "portions" we refer to printed selections from the Bible, the most important being the Psalms and the individual Gospels. They have touched Muslims greatly. Husain is typical of those who have encountered Jesus the Messiah through their readings of these selections. An educated youth, he brought home a gospel of John. Quite contrary to the normal Muslim respect for the Injīl, someone who did not want him to read it threw the Gospel into a fire. Husain managed to retrieve a charred piece of a page on which some of the verses of the first chapter were still legible. Deeply moved by what he read he followed the verses to their source and became a follower of Jesus, the Word of God, full of grace and truth. With less drama but with similar effect Husain's experience has been often repeated, bearing out what the Psalmist says: "Your Word is a lamp to my feet, and a light to my path" (Ps 119:105).

The invitation to Muslims to read the Biblical writings means looking through their reading glasses. Muslims are used to the Qur'ān which as a literary work differs from the Bible. Moreover many approach it differently, viewing its sound as sacred and taking its memorization and recital, rather than its exposition, as centrally important. The Qur'ān was delivered through one author and generally dealt with a twenty-year period of history that takes place in a confined geographic and linguistic milieu. Despite this relative compactness it has its own complexities, and its rhymed prose and the unusual arrangement of the chapters make its reading a special task. The Bible, on the other hand, sprawls across thousands of years of history, its content ranges over many themes, and the style of different portions varies. It is multi-authored, and contains some overlaps and disconnections. While the Bible has inherent clarity and interprets itself, it is not always easy for Muslims to make the jump from the recital of the Qur'ān to Biblical reading. As Christians appreciate reading assistance through introductory materials and Bible classes, so also Muslims can benefit from some assistance for intelligent perusal and study. Although the New Testament is more readily accessible, and Muslims may be introduced to it as soon as possible, the use of Scripture portions has particular value at an early stage.

b. Bible Correspondence Courses

Bible correspondence courses are the contemporary work horse of literary communication with Muslims. Their advantage is readily apparent. They meet two important needs—the desire of Muslims to study the scriptures privately, and the opportunity to give some guidance for such study. The limitations are also patent—the lack of personal contact between teacher and student, and the difficulty in carrying out follow-up activity. In addition, it should be noted that various Bible correspondence courses differ greatly in quality and relevance. All too frequently those who correct the courses have an inadequate knowledge of Islam or lack sensitivity to Muslim problems, thus limiting their ability to respond well to student questions. Finally, the rising costs of printing and postage in many parts of the world place a financial restraint on the medium.

Where these difficulties are effectively addressed Bible correspondence course work ranks as an extremely helpful form of evangel-sharing. It has proven its viability and usefulness in many parts of the world. Particularly educated Muslim youth have responded in large numbers to this approach. In some areas Gospel portions are sold/distributed along with first lessons, together with an invitation to participate in the full course. Bible correspondence course activity is also linked with radio and TV programming. Other variations of this effective methodology are at various stages of experimentation. The greatest single need is its deployment at congregational levels.

c. Tracts

So small in size, so seemingly insignificant ... tracts are viewed with scorn in the sophisticated literary and communication worlds of today. Why is it then that tracts have had such an impact? Is it their straightforwardness, their very lack of embellishment, their simple address to the human heart? Even when they are badly written, bordering on insult to the mind, they have their own power. Perhaps the power is in the brevity. The whole TV industry is now built up on the power of 30-second advertising clips. In a similar fashion we may ask why the Magna Charta or Lincoln's Gettysburg Address have such force. Apart from the factors of occasion, content, and brilliant construction their brevity has power.

We see the principle evident in the Beatitudes of Jesus the Messiah. Only 73 words in Greek, yet they have moved countless hearts over generations. Is it true that "small is beautiful"?

Muslims love stories, and perhaps the best tracts ever written for Muslims were the great parable tracts produced by Lilias Trotter in North Africa. They continue to move hearts long after their writing. They are only an example of a large body of useful material. The writer remembers standing with a companion beside the marketplace in a South Asian village. We were engaged in the distribution of literature. A youth asked for something to read but our stock was exhausted. At the bottom of the bag, by chance a small tract was discovered and offered. It was a poorly-written tract entitled "The Heart of a Youth." The young man gladly accepted it and took it home. His reading started a chain of events that is still unfolding. It is a tale of heroic faith involving a significiantly large group of Muslims who have been led to a new understanding of Jesus the Messiah as God's Saviour.[22] Evangel-sharers do well not to despise these little ones.

d. Booklets

More extended material that clarify the Christian message for Muslims are vitally important. Their subject matter ranges from the treatment of a single religious theme such as sin and salvation, or a general introduction to the Christian faith. All have value, but unquestionably the most important are the biographies of Jesus that not only tell the story of His life but also its meaning. Muslims have always cherished a love for story-telling, and in their literature that is expressed through biography and ballad. The biographies of Muhammad (*sira*) and legends of heroes (*kissa*) are greatly loved. It has been said that all Muslim historiography is a form of biography. That is borne out in the experience of listening to a Muslim reading the geneologies in the Gospel of St. Matthew or St. Luke. The reverence expressed leaves a tingling sensation in the spine.

The biography of Jesus falls into the context of Muslim appreciation. Some fine works in this genre have been authored by Islamic scholar-missionaries. These include *Best Friend*, a booklet by L. Bevan Jones, and such longer works as *The Life of the Messiah* by Jacques Jomier and *The Life and Teaching of the Messiah* by Dennis Clark. In general, the full potential of the biographies of Jesus for communication with Muslims has not been fully explored.

The need, however, extends considerably beyond biography. It includes an urgent need for booklets that deal with comtenporary problems affecting both Muslims and Christians. In literature production for Muslims there is a sense of a situation paralleling the Sahel in Africa, with desert creeping in, thirsting for streams of fresh water. There is a treasure trove of literature available from the past, some of it still usable and not to be scorned, waiting to be discovered. Yet there also needs to be a new outpouring of sensitive, creative, and knowledgeable Christian writing for Muslims that takes into account current needs and reading styles. The list of topics that interest Muslims (in Chapter 13) provide a potential agenda for such writing. Where are the authors for our day, and where are the risk-taking publishing houses and distribution agencies that encourage their work?

While some exist and deserve deep appreciation, there are not enough of them. This Sahel, then, also calls for attention.

3. Poetry, Music, Drama, Calligraphy, and Painting

As we move from the well developed field of prose literature to the underdeveloped areas of poetry, music, calligraphy, and the arts, we enter a world of expression whose potential for sharing methodology has been seriously neglected. In Christian witness among Muslims there is a clear penchant for austere rational communication. That will only be benefitted by being set within a fuller methodology tuned to the wholeness of personhood. Christian sharing with Muslim friends involves the emotion as well as the mind.

a. Poetry

Poetry does not fit the image of a method, for poets are likely to be born rather than made. Nevertheless, in considering the art of communication it is not possible to ignore the Muslim appreciation of poetry. Islamic poetry has a wide variety of forms, ranging from the ode (qasida) to two-lined narrative couplets (masnavi), from compressed and epigrammatic sonnets (ghazal) to the florid songs of folk cultures. The themes are romantic love, battle, satire, personal struggle, and human destiny. Mystical love poetry, in particular, includes themes that are close to the concerns of the gospel.

We have already met Rābi'a of Basra and Jalāl ad-Dīn Rūmī. Rābi'a wrote these words on love for God:[23]

Two ways I love thee: selfishly,
and next, as worthy is of Thee ...
'Tis purest love when Thou dost raise
The veil to my adoring gaze.

Rūmī expressed the same feeling:[24]

Love for You seized my rosary and gave me
verse and song.

Yunus Emre (d. 1320), an Anatolian poet, saw God everywhere, in the words of the prophets and in the signs of nature. He understood that if his spiritual message was to reach the masses, he would have to adapt his poetry to popular rhymes. He did that, and left poems that are still memorized by children today.[25] His longing for a loving contact with God appears in these lines:[26]

I wish to call you ...
I wish to call you in the delirium of love,
I wish to call you in the heavens with Jesus,
With Moses in Sinai,
With the suffering Job,
With the weeping Jacob,
With Mohammed, your friend ...
Yunus repeats in every human language
With the doves which sing.

In the songs of the nightingales,
And through the voices
Of those who love you and call you,
I want to call you God!

The poets also express a sense of anxiety about the travails of love, and as we draw nearer to the modern age, even an uncertainty. Mirza Abdul Qadir Bedil (d. 1720), an Indian Muslim poet, lamented the sorrowful condition of love amidst the desolation of human life.[27]

Now mourn we for Love, whose flame forlorn
Must in the dust abide, midst weeds and thorns
That we call men.

Zia Gök-Alp (d. 1924) was the ideologue of the modern Turkish revolution, a sociologist trained at the Sorbonne in France, and a questioning poet. He asks what love is:[28]

My faith is neither hope nor fear,
And I do not worship God but for his love.
I fulfil my duty without fearing
hell or heaven ...
O priest, comment on love for me.
I do not care what are the devil or the angel.
Tell me of the secret of the happy ones.
Who is it that loves, and who is the beloved?
And what is love?

The attention of many contemporary Muslim poets has shifted from the things of God to the things of humanity—issues of nationalism, western imperialism, social change, oppression, and the struggle for liberation. In recall of General Allenby's planting his sword on the Mt. of Olives upon the capture of Jerusalem in December, 1917, and his boasting "Now end the Crusades!", Ahmad Shawqi (d. 1932), an Egyptian poet, wrote:[29]

Rest your sword awhile, o conqueror of Jerusalem!
(The cross was of wood, not of steel made).

Two lines by the Palestinian poet, Abu Salma, express the trauma of that region:[30]

Let my verse convey the woes
of the oppressed to the depressed...
Verily, man's liberty is bought
with blood not promises.

Evangel-sharers among Muslims are used to dealing with prose, stressing clear exposition. There is good reason, however, to remember the variety of literary forms that are found in the Bible itself, including poetry. Also to be remembered is the fact that the impact of the personality of Jesus transcends explanation, producing an overflow of feeling that only poetry can express.

Earth and all its depths adore Him, Silent bow before Him.
(Johann Franck, 1655)

Why is it that Sufi mystical poets so frequently make mention of Jesus? It seems that his nearness to God causes trembling and fascination. Can a more deliberate effort be made to put the story of Jesus into poetic expression that will speak to Muslim hearts today?[31]

Does not the word still fixed remain,
That none shall seek Thy face in vain?
(William Cowper, 1779)

The discussion of poetry leads naturally into the realm of music.

b. Music

The role of music is affected by the ambivalent Muslim attitude toward any arts that arouse the human emotions. Orthodox Islam is interested in simple unadorned obedience to God. Many Muslims believe that the arts tend to distract from that simplicity. Furthermore, some arts may draw attention away from God to God's creation and thereby produce forms of idolatry. In particular, representational art must face that criticism, as we shall see.

As for music, it developed unevenly in Islam because of its appeal to feeling, and its occasional association with immoral behavior. Religious opinion in general was against it. For that and other reasons the rhythmical recitation of the Qur'ān, called cantillation, became the music of the faith. This is still the sound that most moves the Muslim soul.

Yet music in Islam did not die or go away. Mystical Muslims eagerly utilize music and dancing to draw near to God. Some theologians spoke openly of its value. Al-Ghazālī, who combined the orthodox and mystical streams, came down on the legitimate use of music in religion. He declared:[32]

> The heart of man has been so constituted by the Almighty that, like a flint, it contains the hidden fire which is evoked by music and harmony, and renders man beside himself with ecstasy. ... Music and dancing do not put into the heart what is not there already, but only fan dormant emotions. Therefore, if a man has in his heart that love to God which the law enjoins, it is perfectly lawful, nay, laudable in him to take part in exercises which promote it.

More important in keeping music alive was the role of culture. Ibn Khaldūn (d. 1406), the noted Tunisian philosopher of history, showed how music persisted in Islam, even in its heartlands, especially in good times. Declaring that "singing has its origin in gladness," he included music in his list of respected mathematical and philosophic sciences.[33] It remained most powerful in non-Arab states. Muslims simply continued the musical customs of the particular cultures where Islam had taken root, combining it with ballad and poetry. In its local forms music has continued as a grassroots reality throughout the Muslim world. Modern TV culture has further weakened the traditional opposition to music.

The gospel is a message of gladness, and the door is therefore open for a double contribution—to utilize the power of music for its expression and to lift up the medium itself. As a vehicle for the good news of God's love it is striking in the face of the fact that two rationally-expressed points of view, Christian and Muslim, have locked horns and arrived at a seeming impasse. Music sweeps past the defenses of the mind, moving directly to the heart. At a quite basic level, it also serves to physically bring together people whose paths would not ordinarily cross. When we combine with the Muslim appreciation of story and poetry the gift of music we have entered a thrilling world of relatively gender-free communication that leaps across barriers. The writer has observed that impact at Christian song programs attended by thousands of Muslims. Some evangel-sharers have built on the custom of song-stories where a single raconteur may hold large audiences for hours as he tells a story interspersed with poetry, song, music, and comments—interactive communication of a high order.

A young Communist of Shīʿa Muslim extraction was a musician in the State Orchestra of Azerbaijan and a violin instructor. He had heard about Jesus the Messiah and chose to seek information about him from one of his teachers who was giving a course on Friedrich Engels, a Communist theorist. The teacher derided the young man's interest, saying "Jesus is dead." When the youth replied, "But is not Engels dead?", the conversation ceased. The matter remained in the musician's mind. Later he attended a choral concert where the choir sang Bach's St. Matthew Passion in the German text, which he understood. He was deeply moved by its message. He came to know that Bach had been influenced by Luther, and was determined to find the latter's writings. They were proscribed, but he haunted the used book shops in an old section of Baku until he found a dusty yellowed collection of Luther's Sermons. Through their reading the Spirit of God brought faith to his heart, and now he and his wife "sing unto the Lord a new song."

The intuitive nature of poetry and music, and their intimate social conditioning, imply that the use of these media for evangel-sharing must draw on the contributions of those within the cultural tradition. The caveat applies less insistently to drama.

c. Drama and Film

(i.) Drama

It has been pointed out that "drama in the proper sense, or related forms of poetry acted out on a stage before an audience, were not cultivated in medieval Islam."[34] The major exceptions were the Persian passion play called the taʿziya (= consolation) and the Indonesian *wayang kulit*, a shadow play using stick-figure puppets that are manipulated. That situation has now altered, especially in recent years as the result of the widespread influence of film and television.

That taʿziya belongs to the Shīʿa tradition and commemorates the martyrdom of Husain, the grandson of Muhammad, at Kerbela in Iraq in 680. It is common wherever there are Shīʿas, but particularly in Iran. The story is well known. The army of the Ummayad emperor Yazid overcame Husain's pitifully small forces, and the latter and his family were massacred. Thus the term "Yazid" in Shīʿa vocabulary became the synonym for evil, and "Husain" became the symbol of sacrificial self-giving. In our discussion of salvation by intercession we noted the powerful place this event holds in Shīʿa memory and emotion. The *taʿziya* is conducted on the tenth day of the month of Muharram, when Husain fell. It is preceded by plays conducted on the preceding nine days in memory of others who were killed on that occasion. On Ashura, the tenth day, the *taʿziya* re-enacts Husain's suffering and death in a dramatic play in a theatre in-the-round, with considerable audience participation. All the parts used rhymed verse against the background of instrumental music, continuing for two to five hours. Other *taʿziya*-type dramas have been added to the repertoire and are performed at other times of the year.[35] In South Asia the term *taʿziya* has another meaning, referring to the bier on which Husain's body was carried to the grave, and also to his mausoleum at Kerbela. The bier is replicated in many different forms, including great floats, that are carried through the streets amid expressions of grief.

The development of drama suffered from the general opposition of the religious clergy (*ʿulamāʾ*) to representational expression and from suspicion in regard to its moral dimensions.[36] It therefore remained at popular levels rather than developing into a high art. The nineteenth century influence of the West helped to develop a change in attitude toward the medium, within a secular frame of reference. Gradually Muslims began to see its potential for religious communication and instruction. Its further development is now hampered more by political repression in the light of its capacity for satire, rather than by the older religious hesitations. Thus drama appears on the modern stage of Muslim life as a medium coming into its own. A timely sharing of the gospel will appropriate both medium and moment, not only through the production of inexpensive morality plays, but also in the dramatic unfolding of the role of Jesus and his teaching in human life. It is a method within reach.

(ii.) Film

As a form of drama film shares its problems, but the reality that the human element is one step farther removed may account for the fact that the representational restraints are more readily overlooked.

Film may be divided into three levels: the filmstrip that for generations enabled Muslims to visualize events in the life of Jesus, a medium whose sun has now set; the documentary film that provides social, educational, and cultural information on various subjects; and the full-length film dedicated to a moral ideal or an explicit presentation of the gospel. The cost of film, both production and presentation, place a severe limitation on the medium for everyday communication. Its potential, therefore, remains largely undeveloped. On the other side of the equation is the simple fact that many Muslims in different parts of the world "attend the cinema," and there are many Muslim movie stars. The few efforts to provide Christian filming must therefore be applauded and encouraged, especially when that takes place in a transcultural mode. Those who have observed the impact of "The Jesus Film," for example, on Muslim audiences, small and large, can testify to the need to further enhance this communication effort in a way that takes due account of Muslim feelings. A film on Joseph, whose story occupies an entire chapter of the

Qur'ān, or a film on one of the great unknown prophets in Islam: Isaiah, Jeremiah, Ezekiel, or Daniel, would be received with great interest and appreciation and could contribute to the fuller communication of the Christian story.

d. Calligraphy and the Visual Arts

The universal Islamic art form is calligraphy. It is a unique and magnificently elaborated form of writing based on the Arabic Qur'ān. The words of the sacred book are reproduced in drawings, photographs, carpets and tapestries, book bindings, vessels and brassware, tiles and ceramics, mosques and monuments—that is, in almost every conceivable way. Far from being elitist, calligraphic works are the proud possession of every Muslim. Go into a Muslim home and over the lintel of a door or on the wall is a representation of a verse from the Qur'ān. "Word" and "Pen" reign supreme in Muslim art. In the first of the Qur'anic revelations the initial word is "Read!" (96:1), sometimes translated as "Recite!" The sixth chapter of the Qur'ān bears the name "The Pen." The sacrality of the Word has its origin beyond the limits of this world, for the destiny of the universe and each individual in it is believed to be laid out in "the Mother of the Book" in the heavens. The Pen acknowledges only one Master, the Creator of the Universe, whose attribute of Speech lies behind the Book and its writing. Islam, as we have seen, divides the religions of the world between those who have a sacred written scripture (*kitāb*) and those who do not. Calligraphy is "the art of fine writing," but in Islam it is the fine writing of the Word of God.

In Islamic culture the calligrapher's art is as specialized as the painter's art in any society. The calligrapher passes through a special training program under a master who acquaints him with the myriad styles available and who trains his mind and hand. The two dominant styles in Muslim calligraphy are the older Kufic form, an angular representation, and the cursive style that is more familiar today, called Naskhi, which uses curves and swells. Entwined and embellished, ornamental, and multi-formed, calligraphy conveys not only scripted meaning but a sense of the infinity of the divine. It reaches a height of compression in the representation of the name Allah, or others of the Beautiful Names of God, or the *shahāda*, the confession of faith. It reaches its height of beauty in the transcription and illumination of the Qur'ān itself, utilizing ink of many colorful shades and a variety of floral designs. In the mystical tradition calligraphy went farther than the combination of communication and beauty. For the mystic the letter "h," as it were seated beside Alla(h), signifies the individual, the *(h)uwa*, the "he"; that is, the one who longs for union with God.

To convey the gospel in calligraphic form is a great challenge that has not yet been well met. The fact that calligraphy is a specialized art form is only an obstacle that needs to be overcome. Some calendars containing Bible verses in calligraphic style have been released, but they represent only beginning efforts. Who will put the Beatitudes in Kufic or Naskhi script in such a way that a Muslim wall would welcome them? Who will take the letters of the name of Jesus and show through calligraphy how the Word is connected with God and in turn connects us to God? The personal relation with the Divine Calligrapher Who writes on our hearts with redemptive love outruns the human Pen. Nizami's words may be used to express that truth:[37]

> I studied a hundred learned manuscripts—
> When I found Thee, I washed off the pages.

We turn to the lesser role of painting in Islam. It was restrained by the hesitations in regard to representational art, especially in the austere Arab-based development. There the imaging of the human form in particular evoked the memory of idolatrous practices, and was therefore frowned upon. In other parts of the Muslim world, however, that anxiety has not been so visible, and visual images are commonplace. Painting as well as the ceramic arts are well accepted modes of expression. The miniature paintings of Persia and North India are examples of the high level of artistic achievement attained. The general tendency is to reproduce scenes from nature rather than from human life, and a line continues to be drawn against any attempt to visually depict divinity or even the prophets, and especially Muhammad. Muslim painting therefore concentrated on the decorative arts, and even where human and animal figures were employed, they performed an ornamental function. R. Sandler suggests: "The Islamic painter did not create pictures out of ordinary life, but sought to convey in his painting an idyllic world, or one illumined by a religious mystical or ethical ideal."[38] Painting usually served as an illustration in the service of another medium, rather than an art form in and for itself. "It is not until recent times that we find individual artists departing from traditional subjects and methods to examine social and psychological truths in their work."[39] The change points to new possibilities for Christian sharing through painting. This door for communication is further enhanced by the fact that Muslims do not expect Christians to observe Muslim prohibitions in presenting Christian themes through the visual arts, although sensitivity is appreciated.

The predilection of Christian evangel-sharers toward the cheap production and mass distribution of illustrative materials militates against the Islamic tradition of painstaking personal efforts to create things of beauty. It must be asked how the Christian respect for loveliness, which belongs also to the Christian tradition, may emerge more clearly in materials meant for Muslims. The tasteful pictorial representation of Jesus the Messiah, ornamenting the mundane existence of fellow human beings with graciousness, piety, and wisdom, is therefore a great current challenge to Christian artistry. On the front wall of a Christian women and children' medical clinic in India is a beautiful depiction of Jesus, holding out his hand to the paralytic as he says "Rise up and walk." It was painted by a local medical worker with artistic ability. Who knows how many of the thousands who have come to that institution for treatment have been moved by that portrayal and image of the healing Christ?

4. Radio, Television and Video, and the Internet

a. Radio

Radio broadcasting holds many advantages for good communication with Muslims. It can leap over boundaries into nations, homes, and hearts. The Word can be set in attractive formats, and can reach hearers directly. It is amenable to the holistic approach; that is, it can give creative attention to easing suffering, to encouraging human rights, to serving the cause of peace, and to engaging in dialogical discussion, as well as to evangel-sharing itself. It is living word disseminated broadly by a medium that continues to be in use. Finally, it has also benefitted from the deep faith and commitment of its supporters who have sustained expensive radio ministries over the decades.

Radio broadcasting has also had to face a number of persistent questions. Does it have a clear sense of its audience? Is its content appropriate to that audience? How does it genuinely discover who is listening and what is happening to its listeners? Is the proportion of Christian to other listeners appropriate in terms of its goals? How does it motivate connectors who can personally relate to the listeners? The questions are valid, but some may be addressed to other media as well. If radio broadcasting functions effectively in preparing the soil for the Seed and sows that Seed, it will be performing a significant service, certainly among Muslims. In the case of its programming for Muslim listeners, however, its effectiveness will depend on the relative knowledgeability and sensitivity of those preparing the programs. It is in the area of relevancy that there may be the greatest need for improvement.

As its proponents well know radio broadcasting must be combined with ordinary levels of communication. Christian friends of Muslims will "buy into" available radio programming, providing the essential personal element in communication that broadcasters long for but find difficult to generate. Their attempt to deal with the element of follow-up through the provision of Bible correspondence courses has had salutary impact, but it falters without the availability of someone to provide warm and friendly relations, along with some explanation, to Muslim listeners. More cluster groups or listener circles in Christian homes are needed to substantially facilitate the communication process. At the production level the crucial effort to provide programming that addresses Muslims at the level of felt needs is still at a preliminary stage, suffering from the lack of "insider" sensitivity to Muslim emotion. These perennial issues require dedicated effort for their resolution. Exciting is the fact that radio broadcasting also provides a structural basis for integrated ministry with related media. Thus, for example, in South Asia a creative theologian-evangelist, S. Suviseshamuthu, determined to expand the utilization of radio programming facilities, not merely to obvious permutations such as the distribution of cassettes, but to the development of mass song programs and dance drama using Indian art forms. His efforts did not neglect Muslims, and the effects were at times stunning.

b. Television and Video

Especially in the form of television, video programming may be the most culturally influential medium in the world today. It captures some of the powerful simplicity of such "media" as flannelgraph, but it has moved far beyond in its scope and sway. Since its popular beginnings in the 1940s television has significantly affected the context of mission, including the sharing of the gospel with Muslims. While the global TV industry has not ended it, it has greatly altered the Muslim hesitation in regard to the artistic portrayal of human forms. Some Muslims happily point out the fact that there is no specific prohibition of visual communication in the Qur'ān. The Muslim process of consensus-building has moved so strongly into the direction of accepting TV and video, and even film, that the acceptance has now become a fact of life. Muslims, however, continue to severely criticize the negative aspects of the media.

Their legitimate critiques point to the reality that the methodological use of TV and video must be partnered by the moral concern over their abuse. Christian evangel-sharers have a responsibility toward the media industry, as well as the opportunity to use its technology. Arguably, among social influences, none have so significantly distorted the face of Christianity than TV, video, and film. The distortion in part is the byproduct of the mistaken Muslim notion that Christianity and the West are synonymous, which we have discussed above. The distorting impact has been tangible, and negatively affects the Muslim reception of the gospel. Apart from this utilitarian concern, as a matter of moral and social responsibility the cleansing of this modern temple is something to be desired, and is an effort requiring the cooperative action not only of Christians and Muslims but of citizens in every land.

Against this background we may consider the positive door of communication that TV has opened up for the sharing of the good news. It is an expensive opening, and therefore one that the church has been able to utilize only in a limited way. The agencies that have managed to do so at the cost of great personal effort deserve commendation. In non-affluent lands, where TV is literally on the march, evangel-sharers cry out for the opportunity to make use of this medium for their task. The wide impact of the Jesus Film which we have noted above, points to a possible practical focus that takes into account the mega financial implications of TV production and distribution. The focus could be an emphasis on biography, portraying the power of Jesus in human lives, at both revolutionary and ordinary levels. The creation of twelve—for the twelve apostles!—such documentary videos for use by Christian evangel-sharers around the world through VCR, is an artistic and practical challenge that if taken up may do more for the appeal of the gospel among Muslims than many other laudable efforts.

In our methodological analysis we have taken for granted that all methods must be related to the paradigm of deep friendship. The electronic media face a huge problem in providing the essential component of personal friendship relations, the missing link in communication with Muslims. Hence one venerable institutional form of witness may be in for a revival in terms of a format that binds together literary and electronic forms of communication within a personal frame of reference, and that is "THE READING-ROOM." Combining literature, TV, and video, and the Internet, it offers new hope for integrated communication within an ambience of learning and friendship, based on voluntary participation. The reading-room provides the atmosphere of the home in an accessible way, and within that warmth the formal media function benignly and effectively.

c. The Internet

The newest communication challenge comes from the Internet and its potential. The rapidity of its entry on the global scene amazes observers. It has taken possession of the imagination of many in technologically oriented societies, partly fueled by its accessibility, and has quickly developed an aura of virtual infallibility. If it is on the Internet, it is true. If it is not, it is unimportant. Neither position is well-founded, but their common acceptance is a tribute to the power of the medium. An imaginative methodology must deal with this appeal to the imagination, and its practical significance for communication with Muslims.

In the Congress on the World Mission of the Church which assembled in St. Paul, MN, U.S.A., in June 1998, a colloquium addressed the question of the role of information technology in the communication of the gospel.[40] Concerning the new technologies the Congress declared that they "will challenge mission leaders in dramatic and sometimes threatening ways."[41] Christians will have to discover the missional and pastoral relevance of the technologies. The advantages of IT (Information Technology) may be listed as follows:

—IT is a new trade route along which the gospel may travel;
—IT crosses boundaries of space, time, and culture instantaneously;
—IT makes possible heart-to-heart communication;
—IT enables anonymity if desired;
—IT creates opportunity for one person to communicate with a large group;
—IT opens the door to free thought and decision-making; and
—IT is low-cost.

At the same time, the disadvantages of IT should also be noted:

—IT can become self-important and take on a distracting life of its own;
—IT can become elitist, confined to the "haves," and even a new form of colonialism;
—IT can be impersonal and distancing, despite its capacity for individual contact, a kind of disembodied evangelism; and
—IT raises such questions as these: "Is the communication contextual, respectful, patient, stewarding of time?"[42]

The Colloquium on Information Technology, chaired by Herbert Hoefer, affirmed that the Christian usage of the new communication technologies will need to be informed by the ethical values of love, service, equity, justice, and sharing. The Colloquium did not say so, but it may be noted that this affirmation has special relevance to communication with Muslims who regard the Western-controlled media as sadly biased and given to presenting inaccurate pictures of Islam and Muslims. Taking for granted that these values will dominate its use, "organizations need to review current assignments in the light of IT, and personnel need to be given training and assistance to accommodate change."[43]

Passing beyond the obvious advantages that it offers for information sharing and the networking of communicators, Internet—representing the entire field of Information Technology—awaits developing as a method for communicating the message of God's salvation to Muslim friends.

5. Methodological Medley

Conversation, literature, the arts, and the electronic media constitute major categories of the sharing craft. They do not, however, exhaust the ways and means that are utilized from time to time in the witnessing task. An example of methodological medley is to be found in the fine work, *Muslims and Christians on the Emmaus Road*, edited by J. Dudley Woodberry. It contains a potpourri of ideas put forward by a symposium of contributors. Woodberry sets the stage with the New Testament story of two worried men and the Teacher walking together on the seven-mile road from Jerusalem to Emmaus (Lk 24:13–25). He takes it as a metaphor of Christians walking with Muslim companions today. Christians also must interpret the scriptures for Muslims so that their eyes are opened to the awareness of their Savior. The task can be carried out in a number of ways that may lead to the Master "staying with them" and their "recognizing him."

Following are some of the elements and approaches that are recommended for engaging in the sharing task:[44]

—prayer for effective communication skills;

—making time commitments proportionate to the task of reaching Muslims;

—demonstrating the power of the gospel in personal example;

—coming into close sympathy with the pains and stresses of Muslims;

—engaging in wholistic ministry that is responsive to the spectrum of need;

—developing awareness of available research and training centers, and the literature related to sharing;

—grappling with the Biblical guidelines for contextualization, and finding expressions of the good news that are intelligible and relevant to Muslims;

—examining the implications of St. Paul's speech to the Athenians;

—pointing to the gravity of the human condition so that Christ's salvation is heard as good news;

—seeking new bridges across the theological and cultural gaps, such as the themes of God's honor and Christ's loyalty;

—reciting the names of Jesus in public worship and witness;

—producing and utilizing a confession of faith that functions in a Muslim context;

—theological education that requires church planting before graduation;

—household evangelism, and the use of a family tree;

—the utilization of groups, clubs, and coffee houses that provide a natural bonding place;

—relating empathetically to Muslim festivals and holidays;

—using flannelgraph presentations in hospitals, and with the relatives of patients in homes;

—telling stories, reciting poems, and singing songs with women in homes;

—being alert to architectural messages;

—utilizing cultural forms of meditation and worship, especially those related to prayer and fasting;

—being alert to the influences of the occult and the demonic, recognizing the possibilities that exist in exorcism, and praying for physical and spiritual healing;

—prayer for the involvement and engagement of the churches in the task;

—prayer for Muslims;

—prayer that the whole earth will be filled "with the knowledge of the glory of the Lord as the waters cover the sea" (Hab 2:14).

Although some of these proposals have been considered earlier in this volume, we have listed them in serial form to emphasize their cumulative impact. Their very abundance stimulates the imagination. The attempts to hone the sharing craft represent a continuing and legitimate enterprise. All methodology, however, is finally judged by how it enables Muslims to see the One who beckons to them and says: "Come to me, all you that are weary and carrying heavy burdens, and learn from me; for I am gentle and humble in heart, and you will find rest for your souls. For my yoke is easy and my burden is light" (Mt 11:28–30). Amidst the medley David Sheck eloquently expresses that foundational concern:[45]

> We confess that in Jesus the Messiah, we have met the one in whom God has fully and definitely revealed himself, the only Lord and Savior of humankind. We rejoice in the presence of God, who is revealed in the Messiah—the way, the truth and the life. It is this reality which compels us to be present, to witness, to serve, to invite, to pray, to wait, in anticipation that all Muslim people will have the opportunity to discover in Jesus the Messiah forgiveness of sin and the fruit of salvation, both now and eternally.

Endnotes

1. There are a great many short manuals on methods of communicating with Muslims. For an overview cf. Ernest Hahn, "Literary and Audio-Visual Resources for Christian Sharing with Muslims," in *Word & World*, XVI, no. 2, 1996, pp. 219–237; Warren G. Chastain, "Annotated Bibliography on Islam," in Dudley Woodberry, ed., *Muslims and Christians on the Emmaus Road* (Monrovia, CA: M.A.R.C., 1990), pp. 360–385; and frequent announcements of the Fellowship of Faith, P. O. Box 6524, Toronto, Canada M4K 3Z2. The Evangelistic Literature Bank of the Islamic Studies Program, Luther Seminary, St. Paul, MN, U.S.A., originally prepared by Mark Hinton, holds many useful English publications and manuscripts, and is catalogued.

2. Jens Christensen, *The Practical Approach to Muslims. A Correspondence Course. Lecture No. 2* (Lahore: Committee on Islamic, West Pakistan Christian Council, 1952–1953), p. 9.

3. Martin L. Kretzmann, as part of a major mission study, prepared a set of "Mission Affirmations" for the 1965 Convention of the Lutheran Church-Missouri Synod at Detroit, MI, U.S.A. One of the affirmations was "the church is God's mission."

4. Margaret Chatterji, *Gandhi's Religious Thought* (Notre Dame: University of Notre Dame Press, 1983), pp. 159, 177. For the unusual story of how a noted Arab Muslim novelist met Christ through the reading of Gandhi's work and his emphasis on non-violence, cf. Paul-Gordon Chandler, "Mazhar Mallouhi: Gandhi's Living Christian Legacy in the Muslim World," *International Bulletin*, Vol. 27, No. 2, April 2003, pp. 54–58.

5. David Shenk, "Conversations on the Way," in Woodberry, ed., *Emmaus Road*, p. 15.

6. Phil Parshall, *New Paths in Muslim Evangelism* (Grand Rapids: Baker Book House, 1980), p. 9; other works by Parshall that may be consulted include The *Fortress and the Fire*, *Bridges to Islam*, and *Beyond the Mosque*.

7. Parshall, *New Paths*, p. 100f.

8. Greg Livingstone, *Planting Churches in Muslim Cities* (Grand Rapid: Baker Book House, 1993) p. 163.

9. *Ibid.*, p. 16.

10. *Ibid.*, p. 68.

11. *Ibid.*, p. 101.

12. Musk, *Unseen Faces of Islam*, p. 204.

13. *Ibid.*, p. 238.

14. I first heard the phrase from Daniel J. Fleming, the eminent Professor of Missions at Union Theological Seminary, New York, whose writings anticipated many contemporary discussions of missiological themes.

15. Paul Hiebert, "Power Encounter in Folk Islam," in Woodberry, ed. *Emmaus Road*, p. 57.

16. Adv. Haer., III, 18, 7, quoted in Gustav Aulen, *Christus Victor*, tr. by A. G. Hiebert (London: S.P.C.K., 1950), p.35.

17. In several studies Yvonne Haddad and Jane Smith have examined the Muslim immigrant experience in North America. Cf. also Roland E. Miller, "Muslim Dilemmas in North America," in *Word & World*, XVI, No. 2, pp. 129–142, which includes material on African-American Muslims. For Islam in Europe see Jorgen Nielsen, Muslims in *Western Europe* (Edinburgh: University Press, 1992).

18. For a practical model cf. Philoxenia, a hospitality ministry of the Lutheran Church in Toronto, Canada, established by Ernest and Greta Hahn, and colleagues.

19. The Gospel of Mark, which introduces the phrase "Son of God" in its first verse, and the Gospel of John, which dwells on that theme, require more explanation.

20. There is ample and sobering documentation available for this statement. A difference exists between being the representative of an "overturning message," which is an aspect of cross-bearing, and being a troublemaker, which is a form of self-glorification.

21. Karl Barth, *Dogmatics in Outline*, tr. by G. W. Thomson (London: S.M. Press, 1960), p. 89.

22. Cf. K. K. Alavi, *In Search of Assurance*, op. cit.

23. R. A. Nicholson, "Mysticism," in T. Arnold and A. Guillaume, eds., *The Legacy of Islam* (London: Oxford University Press, 1931), pp. 213f.

24. Annemarie Schimmel, *As Through a Veil*, p. 85.

25. Schimmel, *Mystical Dimensions*, p. 332.

26. Najeeb Ullah, ed., *Islamic Literature*, New York: Washington Square Press, Inc., 1963), p. 377.

27. M. Mujeeb, *The Indian Muslims* (George Allen & Unwin, 1967), p. 32.

28. Najeeb Ullah, ed. *Islamic Literature*, p. 411.

29. Al-'Arabi, November 1964, p. 23, quoted in A. J. Arberry, ed. *Religion in the Middle East* (Cambridge: Cambridge University Press, 1969), Vol. 2, pp. 595, 598.

30. *Ibid.*, p. 599.

31. For a helpful survey of Muslim literature which the author describes as an "intimate property of Muslim culture, cf. Franz Rosenthal, "Literature," in J. Schacht and C. Bosworth, eds., *The Legacy of Islam*, second edition (London: Oxford University Press, 1974), pp. 318–349; pp. 330–334 deal with poetry and its complex rhythmic structures. Narrative poetry related to heroes is discussed by John Renard, *Islam and the Heroic Image. Themes in Literature and the Visual Arts* (Columbia: University of South Carolina, 1993), pp. 235–266.

32. Al-Ghazālī, *The Alchemy of Happiness*, pp. 66f.

33. Ibn Khaldūn, *The Muqaddimah*, tr. by F. Rosenthal (Princeton: Princeton University Press, 1967), pp. 63, 328, et passim.

34. Rosenthal, "Literature," *Legacy*, p. 334.

35. P. Chelkowski, "Ta'ziya," *EI²*, X, pp. 407f.

36. Cf. Douglas S. Cox, "Moral Dimensions of Representational Art in Islam; From Visual Arts to Theater with Implications for Christian Witness," an unpublished M.A. dissertation (1997) at Luther Seminary, St. Paul, MN, U.S.A. Cox notes, p. 55, that the opposition of religious scholars was to impersonation, whereby the actor assumes a creative prerogative, rather than to imitation or mimicry, where the individual identity is retained.

37. Annemarie Schimmel, *Calligraphy and Islamic Culture* (New York: New York University, 1984), p. 114; from Jami, *Nafahāt al-uns*, p. 608.

38. R. Sadler, "Islamic art: variations on themes of arabesque," in R. M. Savory, ed., *Islamic Civilization* (Cambridge: Cambridge University Press, 1976), p. 94.

39. *Ibid.*, p. 98.

40. Cf. *Congress Proceedings* (Minneapolis: Global Mission Institute, Luther Seminary, 1998), edited by Craig Moran. For a summary of the findings of each Colloquium, including the Colloquium on Information Technology, see Roland E. Miller, *Mission Agendas in the New Century* (Minneapolis: Kirk House Publishers, 2000). Cf. also the compilation of Congress papers edited by Paul V. Martinson, *Mission at the Dawn of a New Century* (Minneapolis: Kirk House Publishers, 1999); John Stewart writes on "Information Technology and the Communication of the Gospel" and J. Martin Bailey on "More Radical than the Reformation."

41. Miller, *Mission Agendas*, p. 71.

42. *Ibid.*, p. 74.

43. *Ibid.*, p. 72.

44. Woodberry, ed., *Emmaus Road*, passim.

45. Shenk, "Conversations along the Way," *ibid.*, pp. 1f.

Dealing with the Hard Questions

"We do not understand why you call Jesus the Messiah "the Son of God." How can God have a son? Is it not a bad thing to say that God has physical relations with a woman?

"Will you please explain what Christians mean by the Trinity? It seems to me that you have three gods. We Muslims believe that there is only one God."

"You say that Jesus the Messiah died on a cross. We do not believe that such a thing happened. Would God allow His faithful servant to suffer so tragically?"

"Thank you for the gift of the Bible, but I am returning it to you. My father says it is corrupted and I should not read it. Will you explain how this happened?"

"You say that God came into the world to save sinners. But God is the All-Powerful and Greatly Forgiving Lord, and he can forgive us as He wishes. We must trust in His mercy."

"Why do Christians teach that you should forgive your enemies? We believe that true religion is geared to human capacities. Islam teaches us to exert ourselves in piety, but does not ask what is unnatural or impossible."

"Why are Christians unfriendly to Muslims?"

Communicating with Muslims includes dealing with the hard questions that they raise. This chapter explores a possible response to some of them. It also examines the issue of argumentation, and the tension that exists between disputing and explaining.

A. Some Preliminary Thoughts on Muslim Questions

It must be remembered that Muslims as a whole do not make a practice of asking Christians questions about their beliefs, hard or easy. That is not the actual situation. Muslims generally accept that Christians have a different approach, and do not ordinarily think about it in terms of specifics. They go on with their own lives. The hard questions, then, tend to sit in the background.

They are found in literature, but they surface especially in personal conversation. The effort of a sharing friend to explain the Christian understanding of Christ will certainly stimulate them. Then the questions that arise will require a response, however brief. This give and take in conversation differs from more formal explanations in writings or lectures. It positions the issues within visible friendship, and in that ambience words and meanings are communicated to one another in a positive way.

We suggest that there are five categories of Muslim questioning:

—There are Muslims who are patently uninterested in religious questions involving Christian beliefs. The latter is a world remote from them. If they converse with Christians, they will talk about other things. Their questions, if any, are perfunctory. They represent the majority in Islam.

—There are Muslims who have encountered Christian—Muslim issues somewhere in their life experience, perhaps in education or in business. They are not religious scholars, but are mildly interested in the issues, and without pressing for it would appreciate simple clarification on some points.

—There are Muslim religious scholars who deal with these questions in relation to their own study of the Qur'ān. Their views are traditional, and are usually articulated within the teaching institutions of the Muslim community. They are more concerned about differences of opinion among Muslims themselves, regarding the Christian—Muslim issues as settled.

—There are Muslim advocates of the superiority of Islam who are aggressively seeking to demonstrate the weakness of Christianity. They will ask questions with a deliberate polemical purpose, helped by their strong background knowledge. Their activist approach, literary efforts, and public profile make such religious questions seem more commonplace for Muslims than they really are.

—There are Muslims who have spoken with Christians, have read about the Christian faith, and have some personal interest in it. They sincerely wonder about these issues and are looking for real answers.

In what follows we will concentrate on the sincere questioner, adding a note on the contentious approach.

There are at least three possible ways of dealing with sincere questions. The first way is to avoid question-answer discussion on the ground that the task of evangel-sharing is to introduce Jesus the Friend. The strength of this straightforward approach is that it recognizes a fundamental spiritual truth, namely, that it is only out of an engagement with Jesus that questions are resolved. This approach puts the priority where it belongs, focusing on the Savior and his appeal to the heart. The heart goes where the mind cannot. The problem of the approach, however, is that the Muslim friend wants an answer to his/her questions now, not later. He or she may draw the wrong inference from the silence.

The second way is to provide an honest but short answer to the question, and as quickly as possible turn the discussion to what Jesus the Messiah said and did. This is an attempt to hold the middle ground. Its strength is that it recognizes that the human mind is involved in the quest for truth, but at the same time it realizes that it is the experience of God's love in Christ that is the essential thing. This is a usable approach, but its problem is that the Muslim friend may not be satisfied. That friend wants to understand what is being presented, and wants to believe in something that makes sense to him or to her.

The third way is to try to lay out for a Muslim friend a fairly detailed and complete answer that draws on the knowledge of the Qur'ān as well as on Biblical theology, and that strives to give a clear reason for the hope that is in Christian believers. The strength of this method is that it takes the Muslim questioner with full seriousness, and offers the best possible resources for his/her thinking. It has the disadvantage that it requires more than average learning, it can be done only occasionally, and it may become a prelude to controversy.

So what shall sharing friends do? Which option is best? The choice will always be guided by the Holy Spirit Who "leads" people into God's truth, and hence there is no need for apprehension. The sharing friend, however, will try to bear in mind the following factors as questions are considered:

—the restraints of time and place;

—the awareness of one's own ability and limitations;

—the great merits of common sense; and

—a sense of the over-riding priority.

There can be no doubt of the nature of the overarching responsibility in Christian witness. It is to enlarge for Muslims their already existing knowledge and respect for Jesus the Messiah. It is to direct men and women to the Power and Wisdom of God rather than to one's personal acumen. I vividly recall the stirring words of a noted South Asian Christian, Yisu Das Tiwari (d.1997), who once underlined this essential truth in an unforgettable manner. A lively discussion was taking place in a theological faculty meeting in Serampore college, near Calcutta, at which I was present. Professor Tiwari was in attendance. He was a high caste Hindu convert to the Christian faith who had once spent time with Mahatma Gandhi in his ashram and to whom Gandhi had said: "If you have become a Christian, be a good one!"[1] A young scholar was raising the question what Christians have to give to India in view of the fact that the nation has such a great store of spiritual goods. Tiwari, who was then a very senior 72 years of age, could not contain himself. With eyes flashing he struggled to his feet and with great passion cried out: "Give God! Give God!"

Muslims possess a vast store of spiritual goods, but "the pearl of great price is the Christian disciple's to share. "Give God!" Give the gracious and saving God in whatever simple way is possible, with or without explanation, but always with the same urgent concern of Tiwari. St. Paul spelled it out in these words to the Thessalonian Christians: "So deeply do we care for you that we are determined to share with you not only the gospel of God, but our very own selves, because you have become very dear to us" (1 Thess2:8).

We conclude this section with a note on the handling of questions that stem from a contentious spirit and that therefore present a special challenge. There are aggressive, belligerent people among Muslims as there are among Christians. Their questions may not arise from a spirit of inquiry but rather from a spirit of antagonism. Their goal is not to learn but to embarrass, to reveal the alleged error or silliness or weakness or failure of Christian teaching. A Christian may wonder how to deal with such a difficult situation. The basic direction of the response is clear. Since the problem of the individual involved has little to do with the questions themselves but rather with an underlying attitude, we must address it on another plane than the question-answer one. The task with such a person or persons is not in the first place that of making a suitable reply, but rather that of establishing a new relationship, and every effort needs to be directed to that goal. In such a situation the sentiment of "we shall overcome them by our love" is certainly applicable. In the meantime it may be better to talk about football than about religion, or even to take into account the advice of Ecclesiastes that there is "a time to keep silence, and a time to speak." Debate cannot always be avoided, but as we shall reflect on below, it has a very limited value, and may do considerable harm.

B. Responding to the Questions

We will consider a possible approach to answering six common Muslim questions, without however attempting to replace the many excellent and detailed works of the past that have striven to deal with these issues.

I. The Son of God

Question: *"How can God have a Son?"*

An Answer

The phrase "Son of God" arouses as much confusion and regret among Muslims as the term "Trinity." It is obvious that two things are needed—to deny what Christians do not believe about these much-loved words, and to make clear what they do believe.[2] What Christians deny must be stated forcefully. The Qur'ān rightly criticizes anyone who believes that the Almighty God has sexual relations with a woman, and out of such a physical encounter produces a child. The idea of God intermarrying with humans is of course equally abhorrent to Christians. A Christian must therefore assert, "I do not believe that! That is not what I mean when I say "Son of God!" To a friend a Christian may point out that Jesus is never called a "child" of the Divine Being in the New Testament, but rather "son," indicating a truth beyond physical parameters. But what does that imply? What is the positive significance of the phrase "Son of God?"

We will make three preliminary points before addressing the question directly. The first is that all of God's beautiful names have about them a touch of mystery simply because God is Greater than human language. The second following from the first, notes that human language regularly uses metaphors to express deep truths. The Qur'ān also uses figures of speech, for example, when it calls a traveler the "son of the road" [ibn sabil] in 9:60. Since a road does not give physical birth, the phrase is a picture of a truth. So also, the term "Son of God" points to a profound spiritual reality rather than a physical relation. The third preliminary point is that we gratefully receive and accept God's names as they are given to us, and try to understand them as best we can. The prophets called God a Rock. We know that God is not a stone, but there is a truth in that simile that we seek to grasp. In the same way we receive and accept the phrase "Son of God" as God's self-revelation, and we humbly seek its meaning.

In the New Testament Jesus is called son, the son of Joseph, the son of Mary, the son of David, the son of man, the son of the blessed, and the son of God. Each phrase has its special meaning. Jesus preferred to call himself "Son of Man," a high title that links Messiah and Expected Deliverer. That was sufficiently aggravating for Jewish leaders, but when he said, "I am the Son of God" (Jn 10:36) they regarded it as real blasphemy, and he was eventually put on the cross for that reason. The disciples of Jesus, however, received the name gratefully. On the mountain of trans-figuration Peter, James, and John heard the heavenly voice declare: "This is my beloved Son, listen to him" (Mk 9:17). They responded and listened to him because they walked with him, experienced his love, and felt the power of his salvation. As. M. L. Kretzmann points out, through that experience we sense the meaning of the symbol "Son." "It is rightly applied to Christ when we keep in mind the nature of His life and work and words, through which He not only revealed God but by which he completed the work of reconciliation between God and man."[3] When they walk with Jesus and experience what he said and did, Muslims will perceive deep meaning rather than intolerable offense in these words.

It is perhaps for this reason that the synoptic writers of the New Testament (Matthew, Mark, and Luke) simply set forth the life, works, and sayings of Jesus without attempting to explore every meaning. Luther T. Engelbrecht states: "They seem to have made little attempt to adapt their message, provide explanations, or to devise 'approaches' which might help to make their message more plausible, and to answer some of the questions regarding the unity of God."[4] They were interested in setting forth the story of the Savior, and that is where it starts for Muslims too.

There are several beautiful and important meanings in the phrase "Son of God." In the Old Testament (tawrāt) the term was used to denote people who had been chosen by God for a great purpose. This in turn implied the ideas of commis-sioning and surrendering obedience. These concepts also carry over into the New Testament (Injīl). God commissioned Jesus for a great task, the work of salvation, and he was the servant of God's will in carrying it out. But the New Testament deepens the meaning with the concept of loving nearness. The Almighty who sent Jesus is the heavenly Father, and Jesus is united with God in a close union of love as well as in common purpose. The Messiah said: "My sheep hear my voice … and I give them eternal life. … My Father, who has given them to me, is greater than all, and no one is able to snatch them out of the Father's hand. I and the Father are one" (Jn 10:26–30). The language is through and through the language of love—love uniting, love reaching down, love saving: "God so loved the world that he gave his only Son, that whosoever believes in him should not perish but have eternal life" (Jn 3:16).

Yet two fundamental questions remain, and they concern Muslims. However the term "son" may be explained in terms of servanthood and nearness, there is no denying that the word carries the meaning of "being begotten"; how is that to be understood of God Almighty who is not born and does not give birth like the gods of old. And secondly, if God is distinctly Father and Jesus is distinctly Son does that not break God's unity? In the early church believers sought and found the answer to both these questions in the concept of the Word of God. Jesus is the Word of God, and the Word of God is forever with God. God is the one eternal Lord with Speech. The unspoken Word rests eternally in God as God's thought. When God puts thought into speech, gives out the Word, God as it were *generates* the spoken Word. *In that sense the Word is called God's only-begotten Son—one Word proceeding from the heart of one God.* At the beginning of time God spoke out that powerful Word creating the world in a wonderful way. Then God taught the world by the Word through messengers. When the world ignored the signs of creation and the message of the prophets, God in the last days spoke to us by the Word-Son in a personal way: "And the Word became flesh, and dwelt among us full of grace and truth; we have beheld his glory, glory as of the only Son from the Father" (Jn 1:14). The Word-Son is the utterance of God's love. To say that Jesus the Messiah is Word-Son is the same as saying that the loving God is our Savior, the "Rock of our salvation." And, of course, it does not break the unity of God for God to have Speech.

This understanding also serves to disarm the legitimate Muslim concern that Christians are idolaters, that is, that they have raised a good man above his station and elevated him to the divine level. Christians deny that they have turned a man into God. That would indeed be blasphemy, but just the opposite is the truth. God has become man. "The Word was made flesh." This is the way that God has chosen to work. We are stunned by the daring greatness of God's love. It is the duty of God's creatures to surrender to it. We cannot tell God that God cannot do this or that, or that something is inappropriate or out of the range of God's authority and power. God is truly Greater!

> 0 the depths of the riches and wisdom and knowledge of God! How unsearchable are his judgments, and how inscrutable his ways (Rom 11:33).

What we do know from the One merciful God, the Father Who gives His Word-Son and who sends His Holy Spirit is that God's love surpasses anything that we can imagine. Therefore

I am sure that neither death, nor life, nor angels, nor principalities, nor things present, nor things to come, nor powers, nor height, nor depth, nor anything else in all creation will be able to separate us fran the love of God in Christ Jesus our Lord!" (Rom 8:38–39).

Invite your Muslim friend to a meeting with Jesus, and let the Messiah teach him or her who he is.

2. The Trinity

Question: "How can there be three gods?"

An Answer

The Qur'ān is vehement in its legitimate attack on the idea that there can be three gods. To Muhammad and early Muslims it seemed that Christians worshiped a Triad composed of father, mother, and child. Many Muslims today know that the Trinity for Christians means father, son and spirit, but they still believe that this is a triad. Against such polytheistic belief the Qur'anic critique is relevant: "They surely disbelieve who say: Lo! Allah is the third of three; when there is no God save one God" (5:73). What the Qur'ān condemns in this passage—putting God into a partnership arrangement with two other deities—is a polytheistic error, and the Christian faith rejects it also. But, then, a sincere Muslim wonders, what is the meaning of "Trinity"? Why use a term that gives rise to possible misunderstanding?

Questions about the Trinity often rise early in conversation with Muslims. Ideally they should come later, after a discussion of God's saving work, for it is in that connection that the theological content of "Trinity" becomes evident. It is widely recognized that the word "Trinity" is not found in the New Testament. It is a term that developed out of the faith experience of early Christians, their experience of the incarnate and redeeming love of God in Christ. What can be done to clarify the idea for perplexed Muslims who do not share the faith experience that underlines the acceptance and use of the term? This is clearly difficult, and it is therefore wise to turn the discussion to Christ, from whom the answer comes, as soon as possible. In the meantime there are four things that may be said to a Muslim friend.

The first thing is to make plain that Christians believe in one God, not three deities. Make the point early, clearly and emphatically. "Let me tell you what I believe. I believe in one God." Christians reject both polytheism and idolatry. On that point they take their stand with Jesus and the prophets. Again and again the Old Testament declares the oneness of God. There is no one beside the Lord. Psalm 86:10 sums up the testimony: "You are God alone!" The New Testament repeats the refrain, testifying that there is "one God and Father of all, who is above all, and through all, and in all" (Eph 4:6). Elsewhere St. Paul states: "We know that no idol in the world really exists, and that there is no God but one" (1 Cor 8:4). Christians cannot be Christians if they believe in three deities. The Biblical emphasis on the oneness of God must be lifted up in conversation with Muslim friends.

The second thing is to clarify the difference between saying "there is one God," and "God is one." To say "there is one God" means that human beings have the ethical obligation to worship and obey God alone. To say that "God is one" means that God has unity even though possessed of Word and Spirit. Both must be confessed.

Let us consider the confession that "there is one God." It implies that our lives will be directed solely toward the One who is Lord, in the obedience of faith. St. James makes this point clear. There is no merit, he says, in simply repeating "God is one" without surrendering to God alone. "Show me your faith apart from your works, and I by my works will show you my faith. You believe that God is one; you do well! Even the demons believe—and shudder" James 2:18f.). We cannot worship and serve anyone but God.

Understanding that truth is important, but it is not the whole story. We must also understand what it implies to confess that "God is one." God's oneness contains in it an incredible truth that needs opening out and declaration. When a scribe asked Jesus the Messiah which is the greatest commandment, the Messiah replied (Mk 12,29–34):

> The first is, "Hear O Israel, the Lord our God is one; you shall love the Lord your God with all your heart and with all your soul, and with all your mind, and with all your strength." The second is this, "You shall love your neighbor as yourself." There is no other commandment greater than these.

> Then the scribe said to him, "You are right, Teacher, you have truly said that he is one, and beside him there is no other; and to love him with all the heart, and with all the understanding, and with all the strength, and to love one's neighbor as oneself this is much more than whole burnt offerings and sacrifices."

> When Jesus saw that he answered wisely, he said to him, "You are not far from the kingdom of God."

Not far? What was the great Teacher hinting at? What did he mean by suggesting that to love God and one another is not yet enough? Is that not the basis of true religion? Not far? What more is there? We will not know that "more" until we let the God reveal to us the meaning of the Divine Unity. It is greater than anything we could imagine.

The third thing to say, then, is that we must let God tell us what God is like. No one else. No man or woman can by their own reason or strength determine what God is like, other than to recognize the divinity and power of the Almighty. No earthy creature can ascend to the heights and enter into the mystery of God's being. It is God who reveals who God is. The obligation of God's creatures is to accept what God chooses to make known. We should not be surprised if that revelation is beyond our human capacity to comprehend, for God is greater than anything we can conceive. That applies to God's Unity. It is God who must set forth its meaning, not the science of mathematics. God is not subject to human math. If God's oneness is more complex than human calculation, no one should be surprised. Let God be God! To whatever God chooses to make known about Himself, God's creatures bow and with the Psalmist declare: "Praise him according to his surpassing greatness!" (Ps 15:1–2).

With humility and praise we come to the fourth thing to share with a Muslim friend—it is that God does give us a glimpse into the mystery and wonder of the Divine Unity. God does not do that by providing some sort of roadmap into the mystery. God does it by giving us His loving salvation. That is our window into the heart of God. Above it are written the words "God Our Savior." Through it we perceive what we need to know about God's nature and being. It is in that light that St. Paul declared: "The knowledge of God's mystery … is Christ himself" (Col 2:2). Looking through the window of salvation we see that God the Creator-Ruler is the Merciful One, truly Rahmān and Rahīm, who planned our salvation and then acted in love on our behalf. Gazing through the window we see that God is Word-Son who reaches out and comes down to redeem humanity. And looking through it we see that God is the Spirit Who brooded over creation and now re-creates the world in love. Fatherly compassion, self-giving sacrifice, and merciful presence, all three in the Unity of Love. This then is what it means to confess that God is one—it means that the Creator-Lord, never without Word and Spirit, is God for us!

It is this idea that the church has chosen to express in the term Trinity or Triune God. The terms are not intended to reduce God's unity but rather to capture God's own explanation of its unique wonder. There are not three gods, but One Saving Lord, and that is why the Savior commanded: "Go! … and make disciples of all nations, baptizing them in the name of the Father and of the Son and of the Holy Spirit" (Mt 20:28).

What about the analogies from nature and life that have been used to expound the mystery of the Triune God? They help us by illustrating the truth that even in everyday life the concept of unity is a complex idea:

—the sun is only one sun, but it has warmth and light;

—the equilateral triangle is three in one;

—the human being is body, soul, and mind, but there is only one person;

—an individual may be a father, son, and brother; or mother, daughter, and sister at the same time.

The analogies are parables of complexity in unity that stimulate the mind, but no Christian accepts the Trinity because of them, and no one should expect a Muslim to do so either. The Christian accepts the Trinity because in Jesus he or she has met the Savior God who creates, redeems, and enlightens humans out of a heart of love. A Muslim too will understand the same thing when he or she has really seen Jesus. But it is adoration and gratitude, not understanding, that is the appropriate response of God's creatures. The angels of God taught all humanity that truth in their grand three-fold cry that the prophet Isaiah heard in his vision (Is 6:3):

Holy, holy, holy is the Lord God of hosts,

The whole earth is full of His glory!

Some day perhaps God's faithful will see more clearly what they now perceive in faith. St. Paul indicated that when he said: "Now we see in a mirror, dimly, but then we will see face to face. Now I know in part, then I will know fully, even as I have been fully known" (1 Cor 13:12). As they wait that day of further knowledge the message of Christians to Muslim friends and lovers of God is surprisingly simple: *Christians accept the Trinity because it is God's own explanation of the Unity; to receive that explanation is to know Christ as Savior.* No more needs to be said. Much more we could not bear, for the full light of God's glory would blind us. Christians too resonate with the wonder once expressed by a Muslim poet:[5]

All laud to Him who alone knoweth the mode of His being,

the Powerful, the All-Wise.

All laud to Him, the depth of whose eternal greatness

is unthinkable by the minds of men!

3. The Corruption of the Scriptures

Question: "How can we read the Bible, if it is corrupted?"

An Answer

Some Muslims have the idea that the Bible has been deliberately corrupted. It is unreliable, and should not be read. This explains why such an unacceptable phrase as "Son of God" is now in the New Testament. It has been inserted by someone at some place at some time for doctrinal reasons. The idea that the Bible is textually corrupted is spreading in contemporary Islam. For some Muslims it seems to take care of a serious problem, namely, that the Qur'ān warmly commends the Biblical scriptures, but on the other hand those scriptures teach unacceptable ideas. The solution of the problem—for these Muslims—must be that what the Qur'ān commends refers to the original books, but later copies were falsified. The charge of deliberate corruption is buttressed by pointing out that Christians do not possess the original manuscripts, that there are variant readings in existing manuscripts, that there are apparent contradictions in the gospels, and that some western critical scholars have raised questions about the authenticity of some of the writings.

The corruption theory fails, however, because there is no evidence that Christians engaged in a major reconstruction of the Biblical text after the period 610–630 C.E., at which time the Qur'ān praised the *tawrāt, zabūr,* and *Injīl.* Nor is there any evidence that Jews did the same with the Hebrew Bible. In dealing with the issue the Christian friend can point out this basic fact, and also ask three gentle questions of a Muslim who holds this position:

a. From what you know of us Christians do you really believe that we would deliberately corrupt what we regard as the holy and sacred Word of the Almighty? We would not do that, and we did not do it.

b. Christianity had spread to many countries. From what you know of history do you really believe that all the original Biblical manuscripts in the world could have been destroyed without even one preserved? Indeed, that would have been impossible.

c. From what we believe about God and God's power can we say that God would have allowed the Divine Word to be so universally corrupted? Is God so weak? Surely God's wrath would descend on the people of the book who engaged in such blasphemy. God is great enough to protect the Word.

There are some Muslims who would answer these questions in the affirmative. They would agree that Christians have not corrupted the text of the Bible because the Qur'ān never mentions such textual manipulation by Christians.[6] It does, however, state that Jews distorted the meaning of the scriptural words in their conversation. Therefore these Muslims speak of a corruption of meaning rather than a corruption of the text. The words as they stand are correct, but they are misunderstood and misinterpreted. So, for example, the phrase "Son of God" does not mean that Jesus is divine, but it only serves to indicate that he was an extremely pious man and a true servant of God.

Finally there are many Muslims who are not informed about corruption theories, and simply take the Biblical scriptures as they are and render them deep respect.

The practical answer to the corruption question is to place the Bible, or portions of it, in Muslim hands. While some may not be inclined to read it, many are interested in knowing what it says. At that point the Spirit's power enters in, and the reader finds that God's Word is self-authenticating. When Muslims read of the One who entered the synagogue at Capernaum, picked up the scroll and read from the prophecy of Isaiah: "The Spirit of the Lord is upon me, because he has anointed me to bring good news to the poor ..." (Lk4:18), they are moved to search more deeply into the scriptural message. They are helped by the fact that the Qur'ān commends the foregoing scriptures so highly. However, as we have noted in their reading Muslim friends may require some assistance in understanding the Biblical format, the interrelation of its various parts, and above all its basic direction.

In addition to such clarification sharing friends may also need to explain to Muslims the Christian sense of the "Word of God," a theme that we have touched on several times in this work. For Muslims the Word of God is a book. It is the sacred book that links heaven and earth. Traditional Muslims believe that the attribute of God's Speech at some time became a heavenly writing called "the mother of the book." From this heavenly scroll, from time to time, certain portions were given to the world in the form of scriptures that are literal duplicates of the heavenly prototype. The prophets act much as copying machines, producing an exact verbal replica without affecting the content in any way. In theory, therefore, the Qur'ān has no human side except the paper and the ink. Having a single official text was therefore a matter of urgency for Muslims, and that is why the Caliph 'Uthman before his tragic death in 655 had such a copy made and, according to tradition, disposed of all competing versions.

Christians, however, use the phrase "Word of God" in a different way. It refers primary to a person rather than a book. That person is the Word of God Who was always with God and Who came among us to reveal God's grace and truth. Jesus,

'Īsā, is the Word of God. In its secondary meaning the phrase "Word of God" refers to the Biblical scriptures. They were given to witness to the personal and eternal Word of God that became visible in Jesus the Savior. So Jesus says of the written s criptures:" It is they that bear witness to me" (Jn. 5:39). The holy writings enable us to experience Jesus' ethical power as well as His salvation, and they provide instruction for right living. The spirit of God inspired the written scriptures, but in doing so used the language, personalities and life experience of the prophets and apostles. This means that they have a human as well as a divine side, and they may be studied linguistically and historically.

Because of this basic distinction between the personal Word of God and the witnessing words of the scriptures Christians are not perturbed by the lack of the original Biblical manuscripts. On scholarly and historical grounds they know that the available manuscripts are trustworthy and reliable witnesses to God's salvation, that they beautifully reveal the One Who is the Light of the World, and that they are a sufficient guide for those who seek to walk in the light. Just as significantly, they know that the Word of the living and all-powerful Lord is ever present with them. He declares (Mt 28:20): "Lo! I am with you always to the end of the age!" What could exceed the importance of that declaration? Therefore with the Psalmist Christians believers confess: "The Lord exists forever. Your word is firmly fixed in the heaven. . . Your word is a lamp to my feet and a light to my path. . . I hope in your word" (Ps 119:89, 105, 114).

4. The Crucifixion

Question: "'Īsā Nabi did not die on the cross; why do you believe that?"

An Answer

In Chapter 5, we described the Muslim view of the death of Jesus the Messiah. There we dealt with the Qur'anic passage 4:157–159, the only verses that touch upon the crucifixion directly. We quote them in full:

And because of their [the Jews, ed.] saying: We slew the Messiah Jesus, son of Mary, Allah's messenger—They slew him not nor crucified, but it appeared so to them; and lo! those who disagree concerning it are in doubt thereof; they have no knowledge thereof, save pursuit of a conjecture; they slew him not for certain.

From the passage Muslims come to the conclusion that Jesus did not die on the cross, although there is some confusion and disagreement among the authorities as to what actually occurred.

As with other questions, for Muslims the real answer to the crucifixion question can only come from a meeting with the Suffering Servant in the Biblical story, but the following points may be made to assist Muslim friends in understanding the Christian position. The first one is the fact that the entire Injīl (New Testament) is the dramatic saga of the events leading up to the crucifixion, Christ's death, his victory over death, and the meaning that both the death and resurrection give to human lives. No one could have or would have created the crucifixion story if it had not happened, and then somehow introduced it into the Biblical scriptures, nor indeed would such deception have been possible. This in fact was the purpose for which Jesus the Messiah came, and he often speaks of it. "See, we are going up to Jerusalem, and the Son of Man will be handed over to the chief priests and the scribes, and they ... will mock him, and spit upon him, and flog him, and kill him; and after three days he will rise again" (Mk 10:33f.). The very *Injil* that the Qur'ān so highly commends is governed by the story of the self-giving and rising of the Messiah. The single passage in the Qur'ān that deals with the crucifixion must therefore be interpreted against that background.

That interpretation is for Muslims to make. In doing so they may consider that the passage 4:157–159 is set into a section of the Qur'ān that deals with the intransigence of the Jews. It states that the Jews were not successful in their attempt to overcome the Messiah. "They slew him not for certain." In fact, that is what happened—they did not succeed in putting Jesus out of the way. The third day God raised him up, in the process crushing sin, death, and the devil. There is another passage in the Qur'ān that may point to this dramatic event. At the beginning of his life, from the cradle itself, Jesus spoke: "Peace on me, the day I was born, and the day I die, and the day I shall be raised alive" (19:33). In thus pointing to his death the Qur'ān itself provides a basis for Muslims to re-examine the passage 4:157–159. It "appeared" to the enemies of Jesus that they slew him, but they could not succeed in subjecting him to the power of death. So also St. Paul reminded the descendants of Abraham residing at Antioch in Pisidia of the words that David the Prophet uttered about the coming Messiah: "You would not let your Holy One experience corruption" (Acts 13:35). The angel of the Lord pushed away the stone, God raised the Blessed One from the dead, he ascended into heaven, he is now the Life-Giver of the world, and he will come again.

Another argument against the crucifixion has been raised on the basis of its "unworthiness." It would not be becoming of Jesus the Messiah to be subjected to the fate of a common criminal. We know from human experience, however, that the people we admire the most in the world are those who give their lives for others. When someone saves a drowning person, and gives his life in the process, he is extolled in the newspapers and on television. Jesus is the Example of such a sacrifice. But what about the argument that God would never have allowed the sinless Messiah to suffer such an ignominious death? One response to that point is that God in fact did allow the prophets to experience hardship, even death. The Qur'ān itself (4:155), in citing the errors of the Jews, refers to their wrongful slaying of the prophets. Jesus the prophet is in their succession. Yet the foundational response is another one—and that is that God did not impose the cross on another person, but rather voluntarily took it on Himself in the ultimate sacrifice of love. The suffering and dying Jesus is "a Mercy from Us."

Is there a Muslim who is not moved by the Mercy of God? We know of none. Is there a Muslim who is not moved by the compassion of Jesus? There may be, but the writer has never met one. Muslims do understand the meaning of sacrifice. The Qur'ān reports the story of Abraham and his son, and how Abraham was ready to give up what he loved most. When that meaning is transposed, as it must be, to the level of God the Greater, it kindles human awareness of ultimate reality.

"God proves his love for us in that while we still were sinners Christ died for us" (Rom 5:8). The way to deal with the crucifixion question, then, is to tell the story and allow the friend in his or her own way to discover why the Egyptian Muslim physician-author, Kamal Hussein, declared that moment to be "the darkest day," and why a Christian poet named it "the day of liberation." Both are true.

5. Forgiveness

Question: "Why can't God just forgive sins?" And why forgive our enemies?

An Answer

Muslims regard the Christian theological solution to the human problem of the forgiveness of sins as an unnecessary one, and one that borders on disrespect for God. God is All-Powerful. God can forgive sins at will. God does not need to go through an elaborate process of redemption to lay the groundwork for forgiveness. God Who is also the All-Merciful and All-Compassionate is the Forgiving One. God can forgive whomever God pleases, but God forgives especially those who deserve it because of their good deeds. Nothing more is needed. In any event, it would be unbecoming for God to take on the form of a human and to suffer for humans—God would not do that.

The primary response to this opinion is to bring the discussion back from human speculation to divine action. The question is not what God could do or would do, but *what God did do.* The first two are misdirections. Let us examine the "could do" and the "would do" objections.

"What God could do." God's power needs no defense. It is total and overwhelming. Its exercise is limited only by God's own nature and will. If God, had wished, God could have wiped out planet earth because of its evil, and started over. But it is not helpful to say that. The fact is that God chose to exercise divine power in another way—by re-creating rather than by destroying. No one dare say that God's power cannot work in that way.

"What God would do." Granted that God could come into the world to obliterate sin, death, and the devil, it is suggested that God would not do that. The answer is that what God would do depends on the divine nature and wisdom. The notion that human beings can dictate to God what is proper or improper is unacceptable. It is God who decides what is divinely appropriate or inappropriate. Human opinion is not God's interpreter.

Clearly, then, it is not what God could do or would do that is the issue, but what God did do.

"What God did do." This is the correct question, one that takes us to the level of history, to what happened. God chose to keep the world and to save it. God decided to forgive sins, but to channel forgiveness in the way that God regarded as appropriate. God sent messengers to declare God's wrath for evil and to issue guidance for human behavior. When the messengers were ignored, and even killed, God came Himself to do what God considered necessary. The God of Greater Love determined to sacrifice God-Self for God-friends, and to use that Self-giving as the basis for forgiveness. How do we come to know this monumental fact? We know it through Jesus in whom we meet our loving and self-giving Lord. "In Christ, God was reconciling the world to himself, not counting their trespasses against them ..." (2 Cor 5:19).

Even as we bow before God's way of doing things, we can discern some reasons for that way. The reasons have to do with the kind of God that God is, holy and loving.

As holy, God takes account of human rebellion and sin. God does not simply set aside the command: "Be ye holy, for I the Lord your God am holy." There has been an alienation from holiness, and every human has shared in it. Someone must bear the chastisement for the evil done.

As loving, God finds that there is only one solution. God Himself must enter the human situation, take on the burdens of humanity, and bear them away. There is no one else to do it, so God acts to save. The name 'Īsā, the angel explains, means: "He shall save his people from their sins," and 'Īsā Masīh himself said, "The Son of Man is come to seek and to save that which is lost."

Why can't God just forgive? Because God is God!

God, we might say, is a *muslīm*, that is, one who surrenders. God surrendered, not to someone else—for that would contradict God's authority, but rather God surrendered to the dictates of the divine nature, to His own heart. God is Self-Surrendering Love. That sent God in search for lost humanity. It sent God into the world in Jesus, and into the suffering that goes with love. We usually speak of the *islām* of humanity, but we need to also recognize the *islām* of God. Our self-surrendering is nothing compared to God's. "We love because God first loved us" (1 Jn 4:19). On that solid foundation God forgives all who come to the throne of grace in penitence and faith. Could God have done things another way? Perhaps. But this is God's chosen way. We accept it gratefully and utter our praise, our *hamd*, in words such as St. Paul's great cry of thanksgiving:

Where, O death, is your victory?
Where , O death, is your sting?
The sting of death is sin, and the power of sin is the law.
But thanks be to God, who gives us the victory through our
Lord Jesus Christ (1 Cor 15:55–57).

From the *islām* of God we move to the *islām* of God's people. That is, God's way of forgiving must be the way of God's people. Why should we forgive? St. John gives the answer in these striking words:

Beloved, let us love one another, because love is from God; everyone who loves is born of God and knows God. Whoever does not love does not know God, for God is love. God's love was revealed among us in this way: God sent his only Son into the world so that we might live through him. In this is love, not that we loved God but that he loved us and sent his Son to be the atoning sacrifice for our sins. Beloved, since God loved us so much, we also ought to love one another (1 Jn 4:7–11).

In the view of some Muslims that level of forgiving love is not possible for ordinary human beings. They are not expected to perform beyond their natural capacities, and therefore they are not called upon to forgive their enemies. But 'Īsā Masīh, Jesus the Messiah, will not let us remain at that level.

> You have heard that it was said, "You shall love your neighbor and hate your enemy." But I say to you, Love your enemies and pray for those who persecute you, so that you may be children of your Father; for he makes his sun to rise on the evil and on the good, and sends rain on the righteous and the unrighteous. For if you love those who love you, what reward do you have? Do not even the tax-collectors do the same? And if you greet only your brothers and sisters, what more are you doing than others? Do not even the Gentiles do the same? Be perfect, therefore, as your heavenly Father is perfect (Mt 5:43–48).

Jesus is raising our eyes to a higher vision and challenging us to share the Friendship of God. If God's character is seeking and finding love, so shall be ours. If God's character is forgiving mercy, so shall be ours. If God forgives us while we are sinners, so shall we forgive our enemies. Even though such forgiveness is costly and involves suffering, Jesus puts God's way squarely before us and invites us to rise to it.

Charis Waddy quotes a thought of the Muslim saint, Rābi'a al-'Adawiyyah that well expresses this idea.[7] The saint said: "Real resignation [islam] consists not in bowing under the Will of God, but in rising up into it." The higher vision and new life that Christ represents and calls us to is a "rising up" to the self-surrendering of God. God's friendship for us makes us the friends of humanity. In that light the Bible says: "Put away from you all bitterness and wrangling and slander, together with all malice, and be kind to one another, tenderhearted, forgiving one another, as God in Christ has forgiven you" (Eph 4:31–32). The translation of this simple advice into human affairs would transform society, and God's world would then rise up to "the Lord of the Worlds."

When one considers the incredible way that God has chosen to work in this world and the nobility that God wishes to create among humans—a way that exceeds all human imagination and a nobility that surpasses all human expectation—heart and mind are overcome, and the soul expresses itself in the song of David:

> Bless the Lord, O my soul,
> and all that is within me,
> bless his holy name!
>> Bless the Lord, O my soul,
>> and do not forget all his benefits—
>>> Who forgives all your iniquity,
>>> Who heals all your diseases,
>>> Who redeems your life from the Pit,
>>> Who crowns you with steadfast love and mercy.
>>> (Ps 103:1–4)

6. The Unspoken Questions

Question: "Why don't Christians like us?" "Why are they unfriendly?"

An Answer

It is a testing question, and the answer lies not in words but in the attitudes of Christians around the world.

Muslims have some private questions that Christians rarely hear. They are shared within the *umma*, but more often they remain unspoken. They are globally present, even where Muslims may never have had any real contact with Christians. They cover a wide range of feelings, often related to current events, but they may be summed up in the question: "Why don't Christians like us?" In actual fact the idea usually appears as a casual statement of truth: "Christians don't like us." Is the statement true or false? If true, how will Muslims ever believe that Christians have their best interests at heart, and how will they trust their message?

The bald assertion may shock or irritate Christians. Christian friends, with some exasperation, may respond: "We love you." Muslims, however, see liking as the expression of loving. To like is surely a lighter thing than to love, but it is a very human thing, and for Muslims that is where it is at. What the word "like" refers to in this context is not a deep personal bond of affection, which always depends on individual characteristics and circumstances. On the other hand, the term is also not a shallow one. It has to do with natural fellow feeling, with awareness of and interest in the other, with a desire to associate, with a look in the eye that says, "I am glad to see you," and with a sensitivity to Muslim feelings and points of view. In the current global context there is a real Muslim yearning for Christian understanding and affection, even as there is a drawing away to a distant and even adversarial relation by some elements. Christians may argue that the real word for all of this is love, but the Muslim question about liking, spoken or unspoken, forces a reality check about the relation.

The reality check may cause Christians—certainly those who wish to be known as sharing friends—to reflect on a series of self-directed questions:

—Can we enlarge our sense of the essential humanity of our fellows?

—Can we overcome inherited or media-molded negative influences?

—Can we examine personal attitudinal distortion that develops from political events or terrorist activity?

—Can we forgive? Can we ask for forgiveness?

—Can we mentally and spiritually process "Muslim" into "neighbor," and attempt an applied neighborology?

—Can we more intentionally put ourselves into our neighbor's shoes/sandals, trying harder to understand the other's point of view, without necessarily giving up our own?

—Can we learn or re-learn the elusive art of "speaking the truth in love?"

—Can we take on the issue of "liking" by deliberately striving for living relationships with Muslims?

—Can we engage is some nobility exploration?

—Can we look forward to some relaxed pleasures together?

The answers to such questions as these will be blown in the wind of thousands of little words and deeds by individual Christians in different places in the world who are involved in normal relations with Muslims, and their cumulative engagement will create the context for evangel-sharing in the century ahead. Every Christian on his or her part must do what they can to travel from loving to liking,[8] from *agapé*, self-giving love, to *philé*, practical friendship, with its New Testament connotations of common joys and table fellowship.[9]

We turn next to the issue of argumentation and the tensions that it involves.

C. The Argument about Argumentation

Dealing with Muslim questions inevitably involves some form of argument, but argumentation as a method of evangel-sharing has had a checkered history, and its use calls for care and caution. Both definition and attitude are involved in the argument about argumentation. What do we mean by it? With what attitude do we approach it? We begin with a note on the first question.

"What do we mean by argumentation?"

The popular meaning of the term argument is a negative one implying dispute, controversy, wrangling. The destructive effects of negative argumentation on Christian-Muslim relations is well-known. There is another and positive meaning to the word, however, that borders on explanation. It can be maintained that a great deal of oral and written communication is a form of argument, that is, a reasoned presentation. "I would argue that ..." is a common phrase in the academic world. Evangel-sharing at times involves that kind of presentation. John Stott forthrightly expressed this view, suggesting that we

> need to repent of every occasion in which we have divorced evangelism from apologetics, as the apostles never did. We have to argue the Gospel we proclaim. We need to be able to say confidently to our hearers what Paul said to Festus, "What I am saying is true and reasonable (Acts 26:25) ... Our task ...is to establish the criteria by which truth claims can be evaluated and then to demonstrate the uniqueness and finality of Jesus Christ.[10]

These strong words show great faith in criteria-setting and rational demonstration, and may be more applicable to the church's task among secularized Christians than among people of other faiths. In the context of sharing the gospel with Muslims apologetics as an operational methodology has a quite limited place, and is generally problematic. Certainly in an engagement that has been colored for so long by quarreling, acrimony, and hatred, the current trend to avoid sterile forms of controversy is undoubtedly the correct one. It is important, therefore, to maintain a careful working distinction in our definition of argumentation. There is a clear difference between argumentation as the attempt to refute a position, which implies controversy, and argumentation to clarify the Christian faith, which means explanation. The distinction brings us to our second question.

"With what attitude do we approach argumentation?"

There can be little doubt about the answer to this question. Throughout this volume we have contended that the basic attitude of a Christian toward a Muslim is that of deep friendship. That is also the control factor for good argumentation. Even those who are only superficial friends enjoy verbal exchange. Within such a friendly discussion there is a happy give and take, occasional heat, and often the agreement to disagree. Argument among friends divides issues not people. Deep friendship, as we have seen, takes the matter farther. In addition to what has been said it embraces respect, empathy, and disarming love. Those who have experienced God's grace in Christ Jesus desire to explain its significance to others, but that explanation will be made in a manner that reflects the spirit of the One Explained. It is the Christ-attitude, then, that sanctifies argumentation.

In what follows we will in turn consider argument as refutation and argument as explanation.

I. Argument as Refutation

Arguing to refute is inherently controversial, and as outlined in Chapter 9 controversy dominated Christian communication with Muslims for twelve centuries. Within the time period of the past two centuries the style is particularly associated with the name of Karl Gottlieb Pfander (1803–1866). He typifies the approach that attempts to present the gospel in the context of a strong and direct censure of Islam. With service in Armenia, Persia, India, and Turkey, a good background in Islamic languages, and a knowledge of Islam, Pfander engaged extensively in public speaking and writing, both with an aggressive flavor. The most well-known of his works, *Mizān-ul-Haqq* ("The Balance of Truth"), brought the disputatious style into the modern era. Translated into many Muslim languages, it continues to be re-published in English.

Pfander took as his starting-point the Biblical injunction "test everything" (1 Thess 5:21). This for him validates the principle of examining positions and utilizing logical arguments in support of truth. "Our Reason tells us that obedience to this precept is acceptable to God, who has given us intellect that we might use it aright for his glory."[12] Using this approach his method was to set up criteria for truth and then to show that Christian rather than Islamic faith meets those criteria. His five criteria were: the idea that true faith must fulfil human yearning for pardon; that it must not oppose the demands of conscience or morality; that it must recognize the holiness and justice of God; that it must show forth God's unity and greatness; and that the way of salvation must be made clear.[13] In relation to communication with Muslims he also believed that another foundational principle must be established, namely the integrity of the Christian scriptures. Against Muslim critiques he argued that the Qur'ān itself bears witness to the same Biblical writings that are in circulation now, and that both the ideas of deliberate corruption and abrogation are contrary to reason and historical fact. From this basis in reason and scripture Pfander goes on to set forth the key Christian teachings. He then examines the claim that Islam is God's final revelation, discusses such issues as the alleged Biblical prophecies of Muhammad, the miraculousness of the Qur'ān, the miracles and behavior of Muhammad, and the spread of Islam that he takes to be by the sword. He closes the *Mizān* with the conclusion that Islam fails to meet four of the five criteria he has set up, while "Christianity, on the other hand, had satisfied them all."[14] Pfander's method of argumentation led to an assured result, and "the conclusion," he says, "is obvious."[15]

We offer three observations in regard to this style of evangel-sharing that continues to have proponents. The first is that the style has not been notably successful in the results achieved over the centuries. Certainly the Spirit of God can and has worked through this approach. This was evident in Pfander's own career. For example, as a result of a famous 1854 debate in Agra, North India, where Pfander labored, and whose results were largely negative to the Christian cause, two prominent Muslims who were present later adopted the Christian faith. They were Safdar Ali and Imad-ud-Din. The latter, who became an important Christian leader in his own right, attributed his conversion to Pfander's influence and later declared his own confidence in the approach: "We can now, I think, say that the controversy is complete. ... Christians have obtained a complete victory, while our opponents have been signally defeated."[16] Nevertheless, it is true to say that arguing to refute has not on the whole been a very productive approach.

The second observation is that the style has resulted in severe negative reactions in the form of the inevitable Muslim polemical response. The reaction to Pfander's critical approach began at Delhi and Agra even before the Agra debate, and accelerated thereafter. It was let by Kairanawi Rahmat Ali (d.1881) who launched a vigorous and influential attack on the integrity of the Biblical scriptures, utilizing the findings of European Biblical critics to support his position. At the other end of the Muslim spectrum of response was the famed reformer and educator, Sir Sayyid Ahmad Khan (1817–1898), who had been a *munsif* at Agra in Pfander's early years. Sir Sayyid set up his own criterion for truth, namely, that religious truths must correspond to natural law, and "looking through Nature up to Nature's God" leads him to conclude that "I have found Islam to be most undoubtedly the true religion. ..." An irenic scholar, Sir Sayyid took the position that the errors in the Biblical manuscripts are limited ones, resulting from transmission problems, and they are not the result of deliberate textual corruption. The Biblical scriptures may be accepted as valid by Muslims, but they need to be interpreted correctly. Properly interpreted they support the Islamic understanding of the Unity of God.[18] The Muslim polemical reaction to adversarial Christian argumentation continues to the present day.

The third observation is that to whatever extent validity exists in the controversial approach, it is primarily the task of Muslim converts to take it up. Argumentation as refutation holds a different place for Christian believers from Muslim background than it does for non-Muslims. Their position and responsibility are unique. Whatever their individual personalities may be—and some are more naturally given to disputation than others—they are in the position of having to articulate for fellow Muslims the reason for the hope that is in them. Moreover, Islam was their former home, and they can speak about it with authority and conviction from the inside. In addition to their intuitive grasp of how a Muslim feels and believes, they often possess a personal intimate knowledge of the Qur'ān, are sensitive to grassroots realities, and know the forms and limits of community tolerance. Many of them have themselves been attracted to Jesus the Messiah by way of the Qur'anic witness, and they naturally and effectively use it in their discussions. And finally, converts do not bear the burden of "the West" associated with outsiders that colors argumentation and tends to turn it into a battle to be won or lost. Given these factors it is not unusual to find Christians from Islamic background to be startlingly forthright and assertive with Muslims, and highly vocal in their criticism of Islam. In that connection they are inclined to be rather severe with traditional Christians who choose to adopt a gentler style. They wonder—and are frank to express their view—whether traditional Christians have diluted or lost their sense of distinction between darkness and light, and fail to take into account demonic activity. Argumentation with the intent of showing the inadequacy of Islam is not for them a methodological choice, but a spiritual and psychological necessity. It must be remembered that these factors apply to some, but by no means to all converts, and occur especially among those who have had a strong *madrasa* training.[19]

Non-Muslim sharing friends live in another contextual frame of reference, and for them the controversial style does not seem to be either desirable or realistic. Greg Livingstone sums up the weakness of arguing with the intent of critical refutation. It is not only that such an approach looks for the negative rather than commending what is admirable. Even more significantly, "it causes the Muslim to become defensive, thereby hardened and prejudiced against Christ and the cross. The natural reaction of anyone whose beliefs are being attacked is to maintain them even more resolutely, and to discover better reasons for holding them." He notes that former Muslims were attracted to Christ "through ever-deepening friendship with disciple-makers; through a gentle guided study of the New Testament; through leisurely conversations; and through praying directly with them to a God who is near. ..."[20]

2. Argument as Explanation

With some relief we turn from argumentation as refutation to argumentation as explanation. The courteous desire to clarify the meaning of the Christian faith, in the light of Muslim problems and objections, is a deeply felt one among sharing friends. There have been many efforts to provide literary materials of this type. A well-known example of such an explanatory work is L. Bevan Jones' *Christianity Explained to Muslims*. Jones, whose general approach was examined in Chapter 10, rejected Pfander's tendency to make adverse criticisms and to use weak arguments. Pfander's writings, he suggests, "chiefly serve today as a guide to something better."[21] While Jones gives credit to the great abilities and contributions of the many controversialists of the past, he seeks a better way for our time, "another spirit" and "a different manner."[22] Nevertheless the content for the discussion remains the same, and he gives attention to such issues as the authenticity of the scriptures; revelation and inspiration; Jesus Christ—his person, birth, works, miracles, crucifixion and resurrection, and the Trinity. It is the disposition and demeanor that differ. He carefully considers Muslim criticisms, especially those of the Ahmadis, gives appropriate responses, and closes with a testimony of his own experience with Christ.

Bevan Jones holds that Christians have a two-fold obligation vis-à-vis Muslims. The first is to get at the root cause of the traditional "prejudice" regarding Christian teaching. The second is best stated in his own words: "We should re-think—if necessary restate—our Christian beliefs so as to remove all possible cause of misunderstanding." True explanatory argumentation, in other words, produces creative reflection. Sound explanation, he adds, must state the facts from the Muslim side fairly and without offense (except the offense of the cross itself). It must utilize "a carefully-reasoned, sympathetic, and kindly way of approach." He basically agrees with the injunction of St. Clair-Tisdall: "Do not start a controversy, yet meet it when you must. ... (But) never enter upon a controversy without necessity, without knowledge, without love, or without prayer." Jones alludes to the wisdom of an un-named Middle East colleague who stated: "It has been said of Christ that when people came to Him with intellectual problems on their mind, He sent them away with moral problems on their hands."[23] His own characteristic emphasis is on the Resurrection of Christ and its positive implication that goodness is victorious. "How are we to account for His triumphs in the lives of men and women all down the ages, and for His gracious influence and power in our own lives? How save through the conviction that He ever lives ...?"[24]

The many current examples of explanatory argumentation follow a similar pattern, often in booklet form, and no attempt will be made to survey the field. We will note only the following. A good example of shorter works is the anonymous *Christian Witness Among Muslims*,[25] first published in Africa in 1971 and repeatedly re-published. Its first section deals with the Christian attitude toward Muslims; the second section is geared to helping Muslims understand various Christian themes ranging from the love of God to the person of the Holy Spirit; an additional section offers practical assistance for helping a serious inquirer. In his longer manual *Sharing Your Faith with a Muslim*, A. Akbar Abdul-Haq, a Billy Graham Association evangelist, deals with the Bible and its authenticity; Jesus Christ as Word, as Son of Mary, as Messiah and prophet, as servant, and his redemptive death; and finally with the theme of sin and salvation. The author, whose father was a noted Muslim convert in India, believes that it is harvest time and he seeks "to provide one more tool, among many" for the reapers.[26] The words of Ernest Hahn, a long-time evangel sharer among Muslims in India and Canada, reflect a similar approach in *Understanding Some Muslim Misunderstandings.* He takes up Muslim problems with core Christian motifs, making extensive use of the Qur'ān as he does so. His purpose is, as accurately and fairly as possible, "to outline briefly some of the teachings of the New Testament especially which Muslims view as innovations, corruptions and false interpretations," and in that connection "to suggest some possible responses to Muslims who hold these views."[27]

The delicacy of good explanatory argumentation, and its requirements in terms of background knowledge and interpretive skill, raises the question of the extent of its usefulness as a common method. Beyond that difficulty a further thought has been raised—would it perhaps be better to entirely avoid debate of any kind, and instead to allow the quiet testimony of Christian living be the sufficient witness for the Muslim world, especially in the contemporary context of Christian-Muslim relations? What is needed, it is suggested, is a period of reticence. In God's gracious dispensation there may come a day when conditions will have changed and Muslims on their own volition will try to "see" Jesus, bypassing the inherited tradition. Until that day, Christians may concentrate on living lives that shine more brightly with the glow of love, focus on rectifying the weaknesses and failures of the church, and seek to serve Muslim friends honestly and selflessly in Christ's pattern. The thesis is a powerful one, taking account of the dissonance of the past and the failures in communication. The difficulty it faces is the Lord's command to proclaim his love and to issue his call. Moreover, it puts forward the behavior of Christians as the primary means by which Muslims will come to know Jesus. While there is no disputing the high significance of the Christian life for the witnessing task, the idea that Christian behavior may be the key element in the picture is a sobering one, considering the record. As Jens Christensen has put it: "The Muslim has the right to ask you to forget yourself, your spiritual power and your good life, and explain why we believe in teaching something so hard to understand. And the answer will never be demonstration of the truth in your way of living, no matter how good it is."[28] And finally, can one hold back a gift that the Giver intends for the widest distribution.

We must return to the core factor. The ability to explain matters, and to provide at least some basic ideas that will help Muslims to the next stage of their thinking, belongs in the sharing art. There is then a place for explanatory argumentation, especially in dealing with the hard questions that Muslims ask. But no matter with what care and sensitivity the arguments are employed, their preliminary nature is clear. What is most important is to pass by traditional agendas and blockages, going beyond the mutual indignation and accumulated bitterness, seeking that level of communication where the message is listened to, rather than objected to. That level comes in and through a meeting with the Messenger himself. An evangel-sharer reaches the goal of communication when he/she facilitates a personal encounter with Jesus the Savior. He Himself is the ultimate Revealer, the Self-Communicating Word, the Outreaching Friend. The ultimate act of friendship, then, is to introduce a friend to the Friend.

Such an introduction may lead to further inquiry and to major life decisions as Jesus the Friend becomes Jesus Lord. We therefore turn next to the spectrum of questions related to inquirers, converts, and the church.

Endnotes

[1] Ravi Tiwari, Yisu Das, *Witness of a Convert* (Delhi: I.S.P.C.K., 2000), p.111.

[2] For a discussion of Son of God in the Muslim context cf. a special edition of the Henry Martyn Institute *Bulletin*, Vol. 51, No. 2, July-October 1962, pp. 1-72: it includes four articles on the theme: L. T. Engelbrecht, "The Sonship of Jesus in the New Testament;" R. E. Miller, "The Son of God in the Early Church Fathers;" M. L. Kretzmann, "The Son of God in the Church's Theology;" and Ernest Hahn, "The Sonship of Jesus: Some Muslim Observations and Some Christian Responses."

[3] M. L. Kretzmann, *ibid.,* p. 48.

[4] L. T. Engelbrecht, *ibid.,* p. 20.

[5] *Hizbu't-tarīqati' l-'ashshaqiyya* in Padwick, *Muslim Devotions*, p. 73.

[6] Writing specifically about the charge that Christians removed the name of Muhammad from the Bible Ibn Qayyim al-Jawziyya of Damascus (d. 1350), the most famous pupil of Ibn Taimiyya, is quoted as saying: "It is an entirely false idea when it is asserted that Jews and Christians have agreed together to expunge this name out of the scriptures in all the ends of the world wherever they live. No one among learned Muslims asserts this;" in L. E. Browne, "The Patriarch and al-Mahdi," *MW*, Vol. XXI, No. 1, January 1931, p. 44.

[7] Charis Waddy, *Women in Muslim History* (London: Longman, 1980), p. 56.

[8] We have chosen not to take up the argument as to whether you can love someone you don't like. It is suggested that we do not have to like everyone, but must as Christians love everyone. In this argument the word "like" is viewed superficially, and therefore misses the Muslim feeling.

[9] Friendship and liking run together. For a valuable treatment of the various forms of *phil*, "friend," in the New Testament, including *philos, philé,* and *philia,* particularly in Luke and John, cf. Gustav Stählin's study in G. Kittel, ed., *Theological Dictionary of the New Testament*, Vol. IX, pp. 113–171, esp. 159–167.

[10] John Stott, "Twenty Years after Lausanne, Some Personal Reflections," in *International Bulletin*, Vol. 19, No. 2, April 1995, p. 54.

[11] Karl G. Pfander, *Mizān-ul-Haqq*, tr. and rev. by W. St. Clair-Tisdall (London: Light of Life, 1980; repr.). The first German ed. appeared in 1829, and the first English ed. in 1867. Imad-ud-Din (d. 1900) and Sir William Muir (d. 1905) continued the trend in many volumes. W. A. Rice, *Crusaders of the Twentieth Century. The Christian Missionary and the Muslim* (London: C.M.S., 1920) and Tisdall, *A Manual of the Leading Muhammadan Objections to Christianity* (London: S.P.C.K., 1915), took the approach into the twentieth century. The learned Tisdall utilized the dialogical style, setting up a supposed conversation between a Muslim and a Christian, since "the Christian controversialist has to limit his choice of proofs to those which lie within range of a Muhammadan's knowledge" (Preface, p. 3). Tisdall, however, had a clear view of the limits of refutation. "The object that we have in view in controversy is chiefly to remove stumbling-blocks. We must not expect it to convert a soul" (p. 14). In more recent times Christian representatives using the debating style include Josh

McDowell and John Gilchrist of South Africa, who contended especially with the polemic of Ahmad Deedat. Cf. their *Islamic Debate* (San Bernardino: Campus Crusade for Christ, 1983), and Gilchrist's apologetic work, *Facing the Muslim challenge: a handbook of Christian-Muslim Apologetics*, 1999.

[12] Pfander, *Mizān*, p. 42.

[13] Cf. Clinton Bennett, "The Legacy of Karl Gottlieb Pfander," in *International Bulletin*, Vol. 20, No. 2, April 1996, pp. 76f.

[14] Pfander, *Mizān*, p. 367.

[15] *Ibid.*

[16] Imad-ud-Din, "The Results of the Controversy in North India with Mohammedans," *Church Missionary Intelligencer* 10 (1875), p. 276, quoted in Bennett, *op. cit.*, p. 76.

[17] Syed Ahmed Khan Bahador, *Life of Muhammad* (Lahore: Premier Book House, 1968; repr. of 1870 ed.), p. vi.

[18] Cf. Christian W. Troll, *Sayyid Ahmad Khan* (New Delhi: Vikas, 1978), pp. 64–69, 94–95, *et passim*.

[19] Three well-known converts who typify this approach and express it in literary works are Iskander Jadid in Lebanon, K. K. Alavi in India, and Rockybell Adatura in West Africa.

[20] Livingstone, *Planting Churches*, p. 140.

[21] Bevan Jones, *People of the Mosque*, p. 243.

[22] *Ibid.*, p. 304.

[23] Bevan Jones, *Christianity Explained*, pp. vii–xi.

[24] *Ibid.*, p. 165.

[25] *Christian Witness among Muslims* (Bartlesville, OK: Living Sacrifice Book Co., 1994). Cf. also John Crossley, *Explaining the Gospel to Muslims* (London: United Society for Christian Literature, 1960); M. H. Finlay, *Face the Facts: Questions and Answers Concerning the Christian Faith* (Bombay: Gospel Literature Service, 1968), and Abd-ul-Masih, *Islam and Christianity. Ninety Questions and Answers* (Ibadan: Daystar Press, n.d.).

[26] A. Akbar Abdul-Haq, *Sharing Your Faith with a Muslim* (Minneapolis: Bethany Publishers, 1980), p. 8. Cf. also Colin Chapman, *Cross and Crescent: Responding to the Challenge of Islam* (Leicester: Inter-Varsity Press, 1995).

[27] Ernest Hahn, *Understanding Some Muslim Misunderstandings* (Toronto: Fellowship of Faith, n.d.), p. 1. See also Hahn's *How to Share Your Faith with Muslims* (Toronto: Fellowship of Faith, 1993). For many other helpful publications of this nature cf. listings provided by Fellowship of Faith, P. O. Box 65214, Toronto, Ontario, Canada.

[28] Christensen, *Practical Approach*, Lecture 1, p. 14.

16

Muslim Inquirers and New Believers:
Challenging Journeys

All Muslims respect Jesus the Messiah. There are some whose attachment has deepened beyond respect. It has become the desire to associate with him more closely. In the words of a chorus from the musical *Godspell*, they wish "to see him more clearly, to follow more nearly, to love him more dearly." They have surrendered to God as Savior, and they believe that their lives will be enriched and transformed by God's love. A Christian hymn writer has described that kind of surrendering:

Thy cords of love, my Savior,
Bind me to thee forever;
I am no longer mine,
To thee I gladly tender
All that my life can render.
And all I have to thee resign.[1]

As such Muslims travel on the way (*tarīqa*) of Jesus they enter new worlds and need friends on the journey. Their Christian companions must function as resources for their passage. The provision of support has to be considered in the light of individual needs and the general coolness of the Muslim community toward this process of change.

The chapter opens with a comment on the principal of spiritual transformation. We then consider Muslims who are in some measure traveling that path, and their turning-points on the journey. They include the two main categories of inquirers into Christian matters, casual and serious. In the third section we take up the story of committed new believers in Christ, considering the essential factors that brought about their decision to heed his call and invitation, and the thorny issues of conversion and baptism. There we examine both the Muslim and the Christian perspectives. We begin with spiritual transformation. Is it wrong?

A. The Call to Spiritual Transformation

The belief that spiritual transformation is a universal human need and ideal, to be responded to responsibly and freely, lies at the root of all that follows in this chapter. Prophets and reformers are in full agreement that religious people are included in that need, and in fact it is they who must be most sensitive to the ideal of spiritual improvement.

Certainly the idea of transformation itself is not unusual. It is an ongoing aspect of life, and is visible in both nature and society. It is routinely accompanied by turning points. As soon as the snow is melted, the crocuses appear. When a college student graduates, there is a commencement ceremony, and he or she starts on a new stage in life. Every individual grows and changes in physical form and manner. The same, as we know from personal experience, is true of the spiritual life. There is movement and change within us, and often identifiable turning points that create an alteration in our way of thinking and acting.[2] Rather than being wrong spiritual transformation is something to be desired and struggled for. The human soul knows the truth of what the prophet Amos said: "Seek the LORD and live" (5:6). Spiritual transformation in the final analysis is the human's response to God Who is "the *qibla* of the mind and the *Ka'ba* of the heart."

In the Christian perspective true spiritual transformation is not a purely human happening. The biblical testimony is that God's Spirit is at work in human lives, changing things for the better, producing wonder, removing veils, creating new possibilities. God's Spirit challenges all human beings, in whatever life situation they may be, to rise to new levels of spiritual awareness. It is a process that goes on continually, before and after any determined and formal turning point in attitude or attachment that is called conversion. "Now the Lord is the Spirit, and where the Spirit of the Lord is, there is freedom. And all of us . . . are being transformed" (2 Corinthians 3:17). In this process the Spirit does not compel—unless one describes divine love as a form of compulsion—but rather guides and attracts people to the gifts of God. Above all the Spirit reminds people of what Jesus said and did, and the quality of life he offers.

Jesus said, "You must change your hearts" (Matthew 3:2), and in a very bold picture he put forward the need for spiritual transformation. When a senior Jewish leader, Nicodemus, came to him one night for conversation, Jesus said to him: "You must be born anew." He added, "No one can enter the kingdom of God without being born of water and spirit" (John 3:3–5). It must have been a bad moment for Nicodemus who was thoroughly perplexed. Jesus went on to explain the meaning, presenting his great exposition of the self-giving love of God. Spiritual rebirth means relating oneself to God's forgiving love and God's offer of a new life. For the Jewish scholar the hard moment became a turning point. Later this once timid man joined Joseph of Arimathea in laying the body of the Lord into Joseph's unused tomb. That tomb could not hold him. The great transformer rose to share his spiritual power with the world. Jesus once said, "Because I live, you also will live" (John 14:19). He invites us to transformation.

Jesus extends to Muslims also that invitation to participate in a transformed existence, and many have responded with gladness and anticipation. Their response has been largely at individual levels rather than in groups. While this has sometimes been deplored and considered to be the result of some inadequacies in the Christian approach, it may simply represent the Spirit's way of working with Muslims. Also the stories of Muslim encounters with the Savior vary greatly from person to person, each retaining an irreducible uniqueness, each reminding us that there is surely nothing more private than a spiritual journey. It is, therefore, a delicate, somewhat intrusive, perhaps unnecessary and certainly difficult enterprise to delineate a typology in the progress of Muslims toward Jesus the Messiah. It is more important to define the service needed by those who are seeking spiritual transformation through the life of Jesus. The fact is that there are Muslims inquiring into the meaning of Jesus . . . accepting his invitation to follow him into a transformed and transforming life . . . coming into a new relation with other Christians . . . and facing uncertainties and problems. The crucial issues of inquiry, conversion, and the convert's relation with the church cannot be set aside.

What in general do we observe from the spiritual journeys that we know and what are their implications for the sharing craft? We may point to three major turning points that are more or less common to many, if not most, of the new believers from Muslim background:

- A transition from casual to serious inquiry

- A transition from serious inquiry to faith commitment

- A transition from personal commitment to social association with the church

Christian companions on the way will seek to serve these stages intelligently, and help to make the turning points in the faith journey understandable and manageable. J. Christy Wilson has made the following detailed analysis of a typical journey:

> We are strongly impressed . . . that the convert needs vital Christian friendship and guidance during every stage of the psychological process of conversion. This process might be outlined as follows: 1. A time of discontent and spiritual longing. 2. A period of search. 3. First contacts with Christianity and consideration of Christ. 4. New understanding of Jesus and Christian principles. 5. The decision to take the great adventure of faith. 6. The period of readjustment and trial. 7. Strength and growth in the devoted Christian life.[3]

In the remaining sections of this chapter, we will deal with the spectrum of needs involved in the major transitions indicated above. The next section will deal with Muslim inquirers, that is, those who in some way are seeking information about Christ and the Christian faith. The final section considers new believers, including the questions of conversion, baptism, and association with the church.

B. The Inquirers

For purposes of analysis the Muslim inquirers may be divided into two groups, recognizing an overlap. They are the rather casually interested and the more serious seekers.

1. The Casual Inquirers

Three categories of Muslims that sharing friends need to consider in relation to their communication task are the members of the Islamic world in general; the restless Muslims who have spiritual-ethical concerns; and a group that we refer to as casual inquirers. These are distinct but intersecting categories, and each requires a relevant form of witness.

The first group is like a great ocean of humility. Most of those within it are quite remote from the concept of "inquire." They are not in any real sense spiritual inquirers. They are rather satisfied with their faith. We may describe them with such phrases as "content with their condition," "habitual practice," "not aroused by any strong sense of spiritual needs," "proud of their tradition," and "not tuned in to anything Christian." They maintain a general respect for the *ahl al-kitāb* and admire 'Isā Nabī as one of the illustrious prophets, but apart from that they have no awareness of or interest in the Christian message and view of life. What is the basic service of sharing friends to this massive majority of Muslims? It is to make them somehow more aware of the nature of the human spiritual predicament, and to alert them to the fact that God is concerned about it. What is needed is a loosening of the soil, achieved through quiet expressions of love and the sharing of the Christian message in whatever way is possible, with the ocnfidence that the Spirit of God who once brooded above the waters is creatively involved in this preparatory service and witness. As Greg Livingstone states: "The Good News must be sown as widely and as intensely as possible, depending upon the Holy Spirit of God to cause paths to cross with those whom he is dealing—drawing to himself—preparing the way through social, economic and historical circumstances."[21]

Within the larger Muslim family is a smaller group of people who are not satisfied with things as they are, whether in their own lives or in their community, "the party of the concerned." Whether they be traditional, progressive or nominal adherents of Islam they are at the same time uneasy and restless individuals. They bear in themselves a steady and perceptible "summer of discontent." Some look with concern at the power of evil in human life and the impending judgment. When they see the suffering of others, their minds and hearts are not at rest. Their own spiritual condition troubles them. They are the anxious ones. No portion of of Muslim humanity is perfectly calm, but the awareness that there are storm-tossed and spiritually restless people stimulates appropriate ministries that can serve this group. Once identified, they can be informed that the One whom they now vaguely know as a good man and true prophet is in fact our Burden-Bearer and Rest-Giver, the ruler of wind and wave.

Within the extended Muslims family is also a third group of people that we may refer to as *the casual inquirers*. We use the word *casual* not in the popular meaning of aimless, but rather in the original root meaning "by chance." The category refers to those Muslims who have a more or less unplanned and off-hand acquaintance with Jesus the Messiah, and have some interest in knowing more. It embraces a variety of individuals. There are those who have read about Jesus in the Qur'ān and are not averse to deepening their knowledge. There are those who have been positively touched in some way by the Christian witness, and think well of the good things they have seen or personally experienced. Then there are many quite natural friends of Christians, who respect Christian convictions and for friendship reasons show some interest in them. Taken together this category of "the well-disposed" casual inquirer is undoubtedly significantly large, and it is the source of most serious inquirers. Yet evangel-sharers are generally not quite sure what to do with this reality. The approaches to casual inquirers are ill-defined, in part because of the group's diversity. How do I relate to such a preliminary and accidental interest without negating it? Thus the passage from casual interest to serious inquiry follow no set pattern and is largely unguided. The provision of better guidance may be the most pressing need in evangel-sharing among Muslims today. Does it call for a friendship-based service of "seeking out" and "gently leading?"

We may picture our three chosen groups and their interrelation through the following diagram. The diagram suggests that members of any one of the groups portrayed may become serious seekers in response to ministries directed to their needs. The road to serious inquiry does not necessarily lead through the door of casual inquiry, though that is a common road. The diagram also notes that the sharing of Christ's message produces other movements in addition to serious personal inquiry. Some of them are ethical reform movements within Islam, and some are group movements toward the Christian faith.

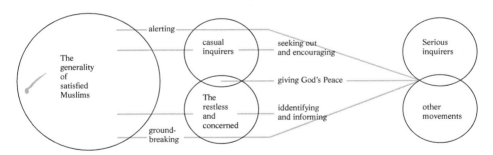

In regard to casual inquirers we have suggested that they need sharing friends who will seek them out and gently guide them forward. The pattern for such service is Jesus who once said: "The Son of man came to seek out and to save the lost" (Luke 19:10). The seeking out precedes the saving. The words came out of the Messiah's engagement with Zacchaeus, a tax collector who provides a good example of the causal inquirer. He wanted to see who the celebrity was, and climbed a tree to do so. Jesus did three things for this man—he looked at him, spoke to him, and went to his house. These actions make up the seeking-out that goes before the interpretive task. Sharing friends have a seeking-out activity that must be both deliberate and disciplined. It implies looking at casual Muslim inquirers, talking to them, and in some sense going to their "homes." We know, for example, that there are literally hundreds of thousands of Muslims who have completed Bible correspondence courses, but they remain unbefriended. Was it the casual inquirers of the world that the Lord intended when he spoke these words: "The harvest is plentiful, but the laborers are few; therefore ask the Lord of the harvest to send out laborers into his harvest. Go your way" (Luke 10:2)?

We turn next to those who have traveled farther on the road to a closer relationship with Jesus the Messiah. Somewhere there has been a turning point in their lives that has moved them to an earnest consideration of Jesus and his message. We call them "serious inquirers" or "serious seekers."

2. The Serious Inquirers

Serious inquirers are Muslims who accept Jesus as their friend and spiritual guide, who are striving to understand Christian teachings, and who are even considering some association with the church. However, they have unresolved questions of various kinds, are reflecting on the social dimensions of their actions, and do not wish to lose their families and friends. They are cautious but sincere. The general tolerance of Islam toward any point of view held by Muslims within the Muslim family enables them to pursue their interest in Christian ideas without much hindrance, but it is the future that concerns them. Although they may already regard themselves as believers in Christ's salvation, their knowledge may be limited. Facing a difficult turning point, they look for real friends. We may consider the story of a Muslim woman named Aziza in this light.

Aziza is an example of a person who had such a friend. Her personality resembles that of Simon Peter. She has alternating passions—at one time vocally angry, at another flashing a great smile of sheer pleasure. She is like Simon Peter in another way. Simon was a kind of casual inquirer, waiting for the Messiah, but not in a tutored way. Andrew sought him out and brought him to Jesus. Andrew had been a follower of John the Baptist and had heard him say of Jesus: "Behold the Lamb of God!" After seeing Jesus for himself, Andrew went to his brother Simon, declaring, "We have found the Messiah!" He took him to the place where Jesus was, and Jesus began the process of nourishing his faith. In a somewhat similar way, one of the witnesses of the past identified in chapter 10 sought out Aziza. Her husband had followed Jesus, but she had demurred, her interest remaining at a casual level. Patiently the friend shared with Aziza what the Messiah had said and done. Her casual interest turned into a serious personal search, with much painful questioning and many ups and downs. The friend stood by her, empathizing with her in her struggles. In the end Aziza was fully convinced in her heart, decided to follow Jesus and joined her husband. She now stands out as an exemplar of "rocklike" faith that has enabled her to withstand many difficulties. In her purse she carries about her copy of the New Testament, takes it out whenever an issue arises, and declares with flashing eyes: "Doesn't Jesus say . . . ?" We may describe her as "the Sought-Out One." She was not only sought out, but her friend also sincerely and effectively addressed her needs.

What are the main elements in a fostering process for serious inquirers? Its frame of reference will always be set by the individual's particular needs and by the local Muslim attitudes. Within that context a fostering process will ordinarily seek to provide four services: spiritual deepening, psychological encouragement, intellectual guidance, and social support. In expressing concern and in providing such services the friends of the inquirers will mightily seek to avoid creating dependency attitudes, but will rather struggle to empower the seekers. To that end they will study and draw on the revealing pattern of Christ's relation with his disciples and with inquirers. The fostering process will avoid making "Christianity" its focus, but rather center on Jesus and his Way. The guiding friends of the inquirers will be steadiy in reminding themselves that it is Jesus who issued the call, "Follow me," and that it was His Spirit that brought the inquirer to a serious search, and finally that as the Lord of the process He is also the power of the inquirer's future.

We look first at the services of spiritual deepening and psychological support. The spiritual deepening of serious inquirers involves especially the following: growth in the individual's nearness to the Master; an awareness of the special character of Christian petitionary prayer; the development of the inquirer's familiarity with biblical resources, in particular the Gospel accounts and the Psalms; and the ethical demands of Jesus that take the inquirer into unfamiliar territory. Associated with the spiritual deepening is the element of psychological support. It is urgently needed in view of the atmosphere of threat and danger that marks the context of Muslim seekers in many parts of the world. A public delaration of faith, when it comes, may involve the real possibility of persecution and suffering beyond the ordinary social strain. More than anyone else, it is the inquirers themselves who are most aware of that rteality and its probability factors. Preparation to deal with it is a demanding task. Both its divine and human aspects need attention. On the other hand, the serious inquirer needs to be introduced to the promises of God that abound in the bibical writings and to the unfamilar Christian teaching in regard to the Holy Spirit and the Spirit's consolations. On the other hand, at the tangible human level, the inquirer must be assured and believe that he or she has friends who care.

We turn next to the components of intellectual guidance and social strengthening. The intellectual guidance needed in a fostering process has to do with the hard questions that are involved in the traditional Muslim doubts about the Christian faith. These we have considered in the foregoing chapter. In a less obvious intellectual grounding the inquirer needs to move from the key Islamic principles of life (chapter 2) to related Christian views. A Christian guide must realize that this will inevitably be a time-consuming and obstacle-filled journey, but one that has profound pleasures. The serious inquirer is seldom assertive but really wants to know. How is that need to be met in a practical way? Because of its familiarity and simplicity there will be a temptation to depend on the catechetical tradition that is strong in both Christian and Muslim teaching. Apart from the paucity of good materials that explain to Muslims the chief points of the Christian faith, the approach has one defect. What the inquirer needs to learn most of all is how to relate intellectual questions to the central act of God in Christ for human redemption and to draw "answers" from that core teaching.

The need for social strengthening involves experiential introduction to the meaning of Christian *koinonia*, that is fellowship. The seeker is not a convert, and may rarely attend a Christian fellowship, and more rarely a worship service. Yet it is critical at this stage that the inquirer knows that fellowship exists and that it has an appealiong character. The inquirer's road may seem to be a journey from the known to the unknown, from the familiar to the unfamiliar, from intimate relationships to the embrace of strangers. Although that is not and should not be the inevitable case, its perception will be present. If there is no warmth in the situation, the ardor of the personal search will be inevitably cooled.

While the goals of the fostering process are relatively clear, the details of its implementation are less so, and always have an individual quality. Who should guide Muslim seekers, insofar as they seek guidance? Undoubtedly it is those who have traveled the road themselves who may be best suited for the task and can provide the companionship needed. But such a support group may not be available, then a traditional Christian friend or friends must step forward to meet the need. How long should the process continue? Some seekers are impatient, have quickly made a decision, and are not motivated to a process of any kind. Others are content to move slowly and to let time go by. There is a fine line between undue haste and a laggard approach with dangers at both ends. Where shall the process take place? Certainly, all forms of abstraction need to be resisted, and fostering goals must be reached in a manner that keeps people within their natural contexts and does not make them dependent on others. Yet there is a need for and a place for occasional drawing together in some form of retreat.

An inquirer's retreat, as the name suggests, is an opportunity for a group of seekers to be together in a study atmosphere, usually for a short duration. The values of such an experience are immediately evident and need no comment, but the concept also involves difficulties. From the Muslim point of view inquirer's seminars conducted at Christian retreat centers have the aura of secret conversion centers set up to subvert Islam and they are resented. Inquirers may develop their own wrong impression from such an experience, concluding that monetary resources are readily available. The greatest difficulty stems from the tendency of inquirers to be concerned about each other's basic intentions. The doubt conflicts with the desire for privacy; they are not yet interested in or prepared for public encounters. They may also fear that a fellow inquirer lacks discretion or even credibility. Their protective suspicion produces reticence and tends to inhibit free-flowing discussion and the development of mutually supportive relationships. Despite these inherent difficulties, however, seekers' conferences are a tried-and-true element in the fostering process. For participants, they can be an uplifting occasion as, gathered in some form of "Upper Room," the Lord makes known His presence and peace in unforgettable ways.

Apart from specific logistical issues the mentoring of Muslim seekers involves two fundamental questions for sharing friends. Can they intentionally and more imaginatively function as resources for Muslims who at various levels are journeying toward Christ? And can they do so with equal concern for continued good relations with Muslims who regard such resourcing as an act of contrariness? It must be stated with the strongest possible emphasis that deep friendship is the indispensable quality for maintaining this dual relationship. This becomes acutely clear in the strained situation of new Christian believers from Islamic background, and we turn next to that final stage of the inquirer's journey, including the issues of conversion and baptism.

C. New Believers

The difference between serious inquirers and new believers in one word is commitment. The new believer has made the decision to follow Jesus the Savior. It is the major turning point. What produces it?

I. The Essential Factors in Personal Change

The ultimate influence in positive spiritual change is the Spirit of God working through the means of grace. The critical emotional factor is coming face to face with Jesus the Messiah and learning from Him. In that meeting, the seeker discovers that the Messiah is the Savior and Friend who sees him or her in the crowd and says: "What do you want me to do for you? . . . Go, your faith has made you well" (Mark 10:51f.).

What about the human factors involved? The only way to find them out is to question new believers from Muslim background as to what led them to such a major commitment. When we do so, we discover that the answers are varied indeed. Some of the factors mentioned include the following. Many speak of the helpful service and love shown to them by some Christian or Christians. Some talk about the care that Christians show the sick, the distressed, and the oppressed. A lesser number mention hearing a Christian message. A remarkably large percentage say that they saw a vision of Jesus who beckoned to them, while others mention some demonstration of spiritual power in their lives or the lives of others. Yet when we examine a wide range of the testimonies of new believers, two statements literally stand out above all others. They are: "I had a Christian friend" and "I read the New Testament."

These two affirmations provide the fundament of evangel-sharing among Muslims. Moreover, the two statements remove the task of communication with Muslims from elitist specialization and make it the province of the whole church, accessible to every Christian. Who cannot be a Christian friend? Who cannot share a copy of the New Testament? This is not being simplistic. It is rather placing the emphasis where the confessions of new believers place it. They define for us the focus of evangel-sharing methodology, and they point to the essential continuing elements in the task of discipling.

Ibn Rashid (a pseudonym) was a soldier in the personal bodyguard of the Nizam of Hyderabad in central India. Like other members in that elite group, he had signed an oath in blood to defend his ruler to the death. Ibn Rashid was captured and placed in an army lorry that headed toward the ground where condemned leaders of the revolt were to be executed. On the way, through the small screened window of the lorry, he saw graffiti on a white compound wall that read: "The wages of sin is death" (Romans 6:23). He asked himself, "Is this why I am going to die? Because of my sin?" At the execution ground, the prisoners were lined up. It had been determined that only every second person would be shot, and after the execution it was his good fortune to remain standing. As he was taken to the jail, Ibn Rashid asked himself, "Why am I being kept alive?"

That night a jailer brought the new prisoner food, but it was on a clay dish. A nobleman, Ibn Rashid had never eaten off a clay dish, so he raised his hand and struck it to the ground. Then he opened his shirt and prepared for the death blow; instead, the jailer silently picked up the fragments and left. The next morning, the jailer brought him breakfast. Ibn Rashid demanded of him, "Why didn't you kill me?" The jailer replied, "Because I am a Christian." Rashid grasped his shoulders, shook him, and asked, "Where did you get that power?" As he later reported, it was easier in those days to kill than to forgive. The jailer did not answer, went out, and returned with a New Testament in his hand. "Here is the power," he said. During the ensuing months, Ibn Rashid read the Scriptures, through them met Jesus, chose to follow Him, and three years later was baptized in prison. After another period of incarceration, he was released and became a prominent Christian leader. His story is unique, but it typifies a common experience—he had a Christian friend and he read the New Testament.

Not all new believers follow the path of Ibn Rashid that leads to baptism and the formal Christian life. There are some—perhaps many—who remain within their situation. They have a commitment to Jesus the Messiah as their Savior, but they do not leave the Muslim community. Among them are many women who lack freedom of movement.

Ayesha was a Muslim woman who had experienced liberation. The liberation was from her traditional position marked by partial seclusion and submissiveness. What brought her freedom was her association with the Marxist party, and she became a dedicated political worker. She customarily led parades down crowded streets, shouting out the slogan "Communist Party, Zindabad!" Totally secularized, she had lost her faith in God, though remaining a nominal Muslim. As time passed some events occurred in her life that created new turning points. Among them was her involvement in an interreligious women's society dedicated to the uplift of the poor and to other social activities. She took employment in the society as a tailoring teacher. There she met two Christian women who were the prime leaders of the organization and who became her special friends. The relationship was an important factor in changing her life. She gradually recovered her faith in God. Two shadows, however, darkened her path. Her husband took a second wife without informing her, and she needed surgical treatment to remove her lung. Amidst these tragedies she began to draw closer to Jesus. She began to look upon Him as the source of her consolation and hope, but she did so very privately. Once after her operation she very tentatively approached the writer:

"Sir, I would like to tell you something."

"Yes, Ayesha, what is it?"

"Sir, I wish to tell you that when I went into the operating room, I saw the face of Jesus, and I knew that I would be safe."

In that safety Ayesha remained until her death, and so remains. No one can count her turning points to the living Savior, but the Spirit who was present at each one knows.

The nature of the spiritual journeys of Ibn Rashid and Ayesha differ. Their difference raises the issues of conversion and baptism that we will deal with below. But what holds them together is their individual nature. This is still the dominant pattern in the story of Christian communication of the gospel among Muslims. Contrasting with it are the larger movements of Muslim groups into the Christian faith.

Such movements involve a host of local religious, sociological and policital factors. In every case there is opportunity for learning, but only a slight basis for building typologies. Every case has idiosyncratic characteristics. This is borne out by the remarkable story of Muslims turning to Christ in Java, Indonesia. Roger Dixon would like more attention paid to this stunning event.He writes: "The conversion of many millions of Javanese Muslims in Indonesia is probably the most amazing and significant turning to Christ in the history of Islam, yet this movement is essentially being overlooked as workers vie with one another to create the "key" to Muslim evangelism." He points out some factors that are trans-culturally applicable—taking time for contextualization, making the Gospel clear, assuring that the leader of converts is an indigenous person, seeing to it that converts are integrated into church life. But other factors that he cites makes the phenomenon unique—maintaining a clear Javanese idenity, and above all, moving in the wake of major national crisis and social change. We see the combination of general and particular factors also in the description of David Bentley-Taylor.[6] They include: the role of Eurasians, the conversion of whole families rather than individuals, the joint settlement of new lands by convert families, the role of the Christian home and its morality, and the conciliatory and noncontroversial style of Christian communication. To these must be added the tolerant form of Javanese Islam with its multireligious and animistic background, as well as the traumatic historical events of 1965–1967 when thousands of former Communist Muslims joined the church amid the persecutions of that period. The remarkable story yields instruction and encouragement that need to be drawn upon and some caution; the latter is noted by Hendrik Kraemer who suggested "that Christians should not think deductions could be drawn from Java which would enable them to achieve similar results elsewhere."[7] What can and must be said is that group movements facilitate individual discipleship.

We move next to the somewhat contentious issues of conversion and Baptism.

2. The Conversion Issue

In this chapter we have chosen to use the phrase "new believers" instead of the more common word *convert*. The meaning of the two terms is close. When a serious Muslim inquirer commits himself or herself to follow Jesus the Messiah, there is newness. The change involved is signified by the word *conversion*. For this reason a new believer is frequently referred to as a convert. In the light of the problems faced by converts from Islamic background, we need to examine the Muslim and Christian perceptions of the idea of conversion. The topic ranks high on the list of urgent issues for Christian/Muslim dialogue, but Christians are also engaged in internal dialogue on the subject. Sharing friends need to be alert to difference in the viewpoints, in order to be in a position to create understanding with Muslims and to help new believers to appreciate what conversion does mean and what it does not intend.

What we have said about spiritual transformation at the beginning of this chapter provides the context for our thinking on conversion. While the words are similar in meaning, conversion carries the idea of a decisive moment in contrast to an extended process that is associated with transformation. Conversion marks the end of a stage in transformation and begins another. It has the quality of deliberate decision and immediacy. It declares, as we have noted, a change in attitude and attachment. While the language of spiritual transformation has remained largely noncontroversial, that cannot be said of conversion. Because of a variety of religious and secular perceptions, some informed and some uninformed, it has become a "loaded" term. It does not fall within the scope of this work to discuss the general debate, and confusion, that gathers around this topic in both secular society and the church, particularly in the West. We have taken that up elsewhere.[8] What was once a traditional element in Christian thought, and an accepted phenomenon in general society, is now viewed by many with visible discomfort. While these doubts have some impact on the task of evangel-sharing, they are not the issue for new believers from Muslim background. They are not really aware of or concerned about the debates on the subject. By their own choice they are journeying on a new road, and *they know that change is involved.* Their problem is that it brings them in conflict with the accepted Muslim interpretation of conversion.

It is the latter issue that we will concentrate on in the following two sections. We will consider first the Muslim point of view in regard to conversion, then the Christian understanding of the idea, recognizing that bridges must be built across a major canyon for the sake of new believers.

a. The Muslim Atttitude

Muslims accept the principle of conversion, but both its interpretation and application are specific to Islam.

Involved in the interpretation is the Muslim opinion about the finality of Islam, and the sanctity of the Muslim community that we will consider below. Also involved is the general Muslim attitude toward Christians and Christianity and the medieval laws developed to express it, in particular, the law of apostasy (see chapter 6). For the basic factor we must go behind the sharīʿa laws to a theological idea. Islam teaches that true religion (*islām* or *dīn*) is geared to the natural capacities of human beings, as we have discussed. It does not require or expect of its followers any kind of radical turnabout in the spirit, but rather it demands behavioral *improvement* under religious guidance. Thus the basic idea in the Christian theology of conversion is quite incomprehensible to Muslims. Yet the term conversion has become common parlance in Islam. What then does it mean? What it implies is *a change in religious affiliation.* It is obvious that we are in two different worlds of thought. *Different religion*

In that restricted sense of conversion there is an additional limitation that produces a further problem. On the one hand Muslims welcome new adherents to Islam, and thus they appreciate the idea of conversion.[9] On the other hand, they firmly resist the opposite possibility—that of Muslims joining another faith. That action is regarded as a blasphemous deed that God will judge severely on the Last Day. In some areas, however, as we have noted, it is also regarded as a form of treasonable activity in Islamic states, with legal sanctions to be applied. This apparently contradictory and quite provocative view of religious freedom is the context in which the Muslim inquirers and new believers must operate.

At the heart of the Muslim attitude is group feeling, group conviction, and group loyalty. The underlying issue for traditional Muslim thinkers in regard to the adoption of another faith is loyalty to God (Allah) and to the Muslim community. Conversion, viewed as a change in affiliation, is regarded as a moving away from God, rather than a moving closer to God, which is the meaning of conversion for a new believer in Jesus the Messiah. In moving away from God the individual is deemed to have committed blasphemy—in effect, slapping God in the face—and blasphemy is a punishable act. Second, a convert has been disloyal to the Muslim community and has ruptured its unity. This penultimate point has virtually become the primary issue. The sacredness of the Muslim community is close to being the final truth in Islam. Almost any action or any point of view can be tolerated by Muslims except the act of breaking the social unity of the *umma*.[10] The definitive rupture for the convert, as we shall see, comes when he or she is baptized.

The writer recalls a conversation with three Muslim friends that illustrates the latter point. The first friend was an orthodox religious leader named Salim. The second was Abu Bekr, a high school principal and a religious skeptic. He had been reading the New Testament with me, but he doubted anything and everything that had to do with religion. The third friend was Ahmad Kutty, a card-holding Marxist Party worker who denied the existence of Allah. When they came for conversation and tea, I proposed a question for discussion. If Abu Bekr as the result of his reading and encounter with the Messiah recovered his faith in God and chose to formally become a Christian, he would be persecuted. Ahmad Kutty, however, though he is an open atheist, is not persecuted. What is the explanation of this apparent contradiction?

A turbulent discussion followed from which I absented myself, preparing tea. On returning, I inquired about the decision, which had been agreed upon and which Salim announced. The answer was that Ahmad Kutty, though a heretic, had not formally broken with the *umma.* Abu Bekr, on the other hand, by taking on the name of another religious community had violated the sanctity and unity of the community and was, therefore, liable to punishment for that action. The reading of the New Testament and the being spiritually transformed by its teaching was not the issue or the problem. The issue was formally changing his religious affiliation, signified by baptism. The verdict unquestionably represents a widely held view.

For new believers from Muslim background this cultic development in Islam has brought great difficulty, and the suffering of converts in many areas of the world is a sad reality. Their simple act of professing the name "Christ-ian" has made them subject to any of the following: extreme family displeasure, being regarded as dead, the denial of marriage and inheritance privileges, loss of friends and social ostracism, physical abuse and martyrdom. Muslim converts know what Jesus meant when He said, "Where I am, there shall also My servant be" (John 12:26). A hymn title captures their situation: "I Walk in Danger All the Way." For them the apostolic word rings true: "For while we live, we are always being given up for death for Jesus' sake, so that the life of Jesus may be made visible in our mortal flesh" (2 Corinthians 4:11). Their record of faithfulness, under the circumstances, is a remarkable one and belongs to a continuing book of Acts. Passages such as the following help to sustain them: "Who will separate us from the love of Christ? Will hardship, or distress, or persecution, or famine, or nakedness, or peril, or sword? . . . No, in all these things we are more than conquerors through Him who loved us" (Romans 8:35ff.).

It may be gratefully recognized that the application of sanctions against martyrs varies greatly from place to place in the Muslim world. There are Muslim-majority areas where Muslims in significant numbers have opted to become Christians without let or hindrance, and they lead more or less normal lives. Muslims and Christians are even found in the same family and home. In these areas, Muslims take pride in their religious tolerance. There are other regions where a once-negative situation is undergoing healthy change as the result of favorable developments within the Muslim community, including the increase in education. Yet the condition of Muslim converts in many places continues to represent a record of personal suffering. Only the Lord knows how many have paid the ultimate price.

Christians are obligated to do all they can to mitigate such adversity and to accelerate the process of positive change. The importance of establishing relationships with Muslims within which such issues as conversion can be addressed and understood and possibly tolerated if not resolved is immediately evident. Friendship-based conversation with Muslim leaders is a fundamental need. Many educated Muslims are dissatisfied with the historic patterns and are working behind the scenes to effect change. The appeal to human rights is having some impact and is often led by prominent Muslim converts. Kenneth Cragg puts this concept into another frame of reference described as "spiritual free trade." Noting that a spiritually static universe is hardly a high ideal, he asks: "Have we not a great need and right to seek a new place for the whole significance of conversion? Can there be any hope for a society that never expects its people to be different? . . . The prejudice for the closed frontier is a prejudice against the open mind."[11] The call for reciprocity has undeniable force, especially with Muslims who are living in non-Muslim societies and who are engaging in mission activity among Christians and others. The number of Muslims is increasing who align themselves with the ethical principle: "Do unto others what you would that others do unto you."

What is most likely to win the day for another approach, however, is addressing the issue from within the Islamic perspective, on the basis of Islamic principle. That needs to be done in the light of the argument from loyalty. The first element in the fresh thinking, now frequently stated in public by Muslims and deeply felt, is that to diminish the reputation or to bring shame to Islam by intolerance is not loyalty to the faith. The second point that arises is loyalty to the principle of the Qur'ān that judgment on the matter of apostasy belongs to God and not to humans. As noted earlier, the Qur'ān declares: "Whoso disbelieves in Allah after his belief . . . theirs will be an awful doom . . . . Assuredly in the Hereafter they are the losers" (16:106–9). It is clear that the judgment will come in the hereafter. The attempt to transpose the hereafter to the present, taking judgment away from God and placing it in human hands, is the decision of medieval jurists—formed in another age and context—that may be set aside by loyal Muslims today in the light of the Quranic admonition.

In summary, the traditional Muslim opinion on conversion locates it in a change in communal affiliation, a change that is punishable. We consider next the Christian view.

b. The Christian Perspective

The essence of the Christian perspective on conversion is that it is a spiritual change, not a change in religious affiliation.

The English word *conversion* comes from the Latin root *convertere* that means "to turn about or change." It is neutral in scope, pointing to the fact that like transformation so also conversion is a normal fact of life. It is a decisive turning to something involving a change in attitude, character, form, or function. Such change is an everyday matter, a routine aspect of free choice and human growth. Thus the word is everywhere present in common speech: "I'm converted," someone may say, "I really like that toothpaste!" The effort to produce conversion is also an acceptable aspect of everyday life. A teacher attempts to turn a student from ignorance to knowledge. A businessman strives to turn attention from others products to his own. A politician seeks to convert the public to his or her point of view to capture the vote. Conversion, then, is broader than a religious idea. It points to a fundamental element in life, the possibility of change, inherent in the freedom given in God's created order. Spiritual and religious matters cannot be arbitrarily excluded from that possibility without violating the divine order. That is why the Muslim philosopher Sir Muhammad Iqbal again and again pointed to the Quranic word: "Lo! Allah changeth not the condition of a folk until they (first) change that which is in their hearts" (13:11).

From the Christian point of view a person *can* change in the spiritual realm as well as in the physical and mental realms, and there is good reason why he or she *should* do so. The combination of our generic tilt to evil and God's amazing action to put an end to it creates a new situation for all human beings. It alerts us, arouses us, moves us to consider who and what we are. It is a monumental thing that God is graciously attempting—acting to save the universe! Let the people of the universe then turn about from whatever is engrossing them, let them pay heed, let them receive God's gift with penitence, faith, and gratitude! Thus Jesus the Messiah announced: "The time is fulfilled and the kingdom of God is at hand. Repent [*change your minds*] and believe the gospel!" (Mark 1:5). It was a strong demand, later followed by a tender word: "Come to Me, all you that are weary and are carrying heavy burdens, and I will give you rest. Take My yoke upon you, and learn from Me, for I am gentle and humble in heart, and you will find rest for your souls. For My yoke is easy, and My burden is light" (Matthew 11:18–20).

The change of mind that Jesus called for had several elements that became clear as he expanded on the theme:

- Chief among them was a turning to the saving God

- Included was penitence over sin and the rejection of what is displeasing to God

- Included was the invitation to draw near to "the Man of Galilee," to receive His blessings and to take up the cross and follow Him

- Included among those blessings was the forgiveness of sins

- Included was a summons to a new orientation, the law of love

The richness of conversion is apparent in its elements. Their interactive nature is illustrated by the preaching of the first apostles. They held to the dynamic that even the religiously minded of the world must turn freshly to the saving God. For them the spiritual transformation included: changing, believing, following, and thanking. They accepted the Savior's invitation to journey with Him on His way, though their acceptance did not make life easy for them, and with boldness they extended His call to others. Their most deeply felt wonder was the forgiveness of sins, assured by the resurrection.

When Peter preached his first sermon to his fellow Jews, the listeners asked: "What shall we do?" The leader of the apostles then answered: "Repent and be baptized every one of you in the name of Jesus Christ, so that your sins may be forgiven, and you will receive the Holy Spirit" (Acts 2:38). Peter was not inviting people to join a new religion called Christianity, which did not then exist in that name. Nor was he asking people to take membership in a church organization, for none was there. The modern idea of religious conversion as an institutional change—that thinking is not reserved to Muslims!—was certainly far from the minds of these new believers. Peter soon reinforced what he said when he addressed a crowd of Jews gathered in Solomon's Portico in Jerusalem. In a passage that uses both New Testament terms that are associated with conversion, namely, "to change one's mind" (*metanoeinI*) and "to turn to" (*apostrephein*), Peter declared: "*Change your* mind therefore, and *turn* to God so that your sins may be wiped out!" (Acts 3:19, *emphasis added*).

These were normally religious, God-related Jewish people whom Peter was addressing. Nevertheless, they were to turn to God! They had to realize how profoundly gracious God is, to grasp that God is forgiving, and to accept God's "times of refreshing" that were now at hand. This fact has great significance. It is a signal of the truth that everyone must turn to God, including—and not least—"religious people" themselves. Conversion leaves no one out. It has a universal implication. In the *sura* quoted above that exhorts us to change the condition of our hearts, the Qur'ān also declares:

"Say: He is the Lord!
There is no other god but He!
On Him is my trust,
and to Him do I turn." (13:30, Yusuf Ali)

The turning called for is not to a human community but to the living God, and even prophets do not exempt themselves from that demand.

The Christian perspective is that it would not be possible to respond to that demand if it were not for God's involvement. As is the case with spiritual transformation, so also conversion has both a human and a divine side. Certainly it is I who must change my mind. I turn to God. Paul Löffler was correct in defining conversion as my "personal reorientation" based on the love of God.[12] But the loving God is the initiator of the relationship, the Good Shepherd who goes out in search for the lost sheep. God desires everyone to be saved and to come to the knowledge of truth; calls for a change in our moral attitudes, and by the Spirit empowers our turning. Overcoming our spiritual weakness, God draws us to the wells of salvation and empowers our will to pursue godliness. We may, therefore, call conversion *theoformation*. The prophet Hosea says it plainly: "I took them up in my arms . . . I led them" (Hosea 11:3ff.). *Theoformation*

The passage from being a serious inquirer to commitment as a believer and follower of Jesus is seldom smooth. There are ups and downs, much back and forth, and plenty of stutter steps as the individual moves along the path. It is a minority for whom there is no faltering in this most demanding of passages. But every new believer senses the leading of God in that process. The fact that conversion has to do with God who is its originator and goal gives the journey forward movement, a sense of comforting presence, and even a kind of controlled inescapability. The love of Christ constrains, compels, "urges on" (2 Corinthians 5:14). The attraction of his personality and the power of his inviting word overcome natural hesitations and contrary advice of others. The seeker has passed the point of listening to remarks about appropriate behavior or even the careful weighing of consequences. He or she hears God calling, and leaves all to follow the divine bidding. They sense that what Jesus said is being fulfilled in their personal existence: "My Father is working still, and I am working too" (John 5:17).

Sacred, not human

The conviction that conversion is of God not only enables personal commitment, but it also lifts the matter far above the level of community pride and religious affiliation. It raises it to the realm of the sacred. In the Christian view, what a wondrous thing it is when a seeker turns to God in hope! It is the answer to the psalmist's prayer: "Restore us [turn us] oh God; let your face shine that we may be saved" (80:13). The prayer was spoken in a different context but speaks for us all. The sense of wonder must be present for all conversion to God, but surely among the greatest miracles of theoformation is the coming of Muslims to the happiness of God's salvation in Christ. We are on holy ground, and to profane it cannot be true religion. Some Muslims profane it when they trouble those whose lives are hid with Christ in God. But Christians too are guilty of profaning it when their methods distort the sanctity of God's intention and the purity of the process that Christ instituted. Evangel-sharers must present the Gospel in the spirit of the Gospel. Distortions of that spirit are too often visible and call forth legitimate Muslim critiques. In responding truly penitential Christians will abjure philosophies that turn conversion into an instrument of institutional aggrandizement or organizational "success," and will reject practices that are not worthy of the human journey to God. The recognition that conversion is theoformation makes it a thing of divine beauty, calling for creaturely respect.

In sum, sharing friends need to do four things—make clear to others what Christians understand by conversion; check Christian malpractices where they exist; accelerate dialogue with Muslims about religious persecution; and above all, stand by new believers in their travails as well as in their joys.

But what, then, shall we do with baptism?

3. The Issue of Baptism

It is really ironic that the simple and lovely rite of baptism, signifying so many good things, should become the crisis point for new believers from Muslim background as well as the source of serious contention between two great religious bodies. Yet so it has and in this section we will attempt to deal with this thorny issue.

It is an overstatement to say that the problems of new believers from Muslim background begin with baptism. They begin with commitment, with following the Savior, with association with Christians, with public witness. At every one of these points, a Muslim enters the realm of *marturia*, which carries the double meaning of witness and suffering. When baptism occurs, it not only concentrates the *marturia* into a single moment, it also links it with the Muslim misunderstanding of the sacrament, and the new believer's problems rise to a high level of intensity. For the Christian, baptism is union with Christ. For the Muslim, it means union with an error-prone religion. In Muslim eyes, it is the taking on another community name—breaking with the *umma*—the high blasphemy moment. It is the point when conversion/apostasy take place, and therefore the point when sanctions must be instituted. It is plain that this is a serious misunderstanding of the spiritual connotation of baptism.

This being the case, some observers wonder why Muslim converts should be asked to suffer for a misunderstanding. Suffering for the truth is one thing, but suffering for a misconception another. Cannot baptism be handled in a different way for Muslim converts, in a way that allows them to have a continued relationship with family and friends, in a way that lifts an impossible burden from the task of Christian sharing? Out of these concerns three proposals have evolved. As a preliminary to their consideration, we will briefly look at the significance of baptism and why it is that Muslim converts themselves are in the forefront of those who say that this is a burden they must bear—though it may require them to leave home and live in some distant place.[13]

Baptism is grounded on the action and teaching of Jesus who Himself entered the River Jordan to be baptized. He later connected the idea of baptism with spiritual rebirth, discipleship, and suffering. Biblically and doctrinally a complex of important teachings gather around baptism. They include the ideas that God is at work through the "visible Word"; that God grants in baptism the gifts of regeneration, forgiveness, and the blessing of the Holy Spirit; that God graciously incorporates us into the dying and rising of Jesus and thereby gives forgiveness and new life; and that we accept discipleship in the fellowship of those who observe what He commands. So rich is the tapestry of baptismal thoughts that St. Paul is moved to summarize them in the simplest yet the most comprehensive of statements: "As many of you as have been baptized into Christ have put on Christ" (Galatians 3:27). Psychologically the ceremony has moving implications. It confirms that I am a child of God, taken up in God's arms, and safe forever. When Martin Luther felt hard-pressed and tempted, he wrote on his table with a piece of chalk: "I have been baptized" (*baptizatus sum*) and was reassured.[14] And my baptism signals to the world my faith commitment and personal resolve. Finally, baptism has always been accepted as the common initiation rite of the universal church, symbolizing the oneness of those who profess that Jesus is Lord. Given this spiritual import—visible only to the eyes of faith—alternatives to baptism have heavy going. As Kenneth Cragg puts it:

> The creed and community that have in trust the universally human secret of God in Christ must be ever accessible to discipleship. Baptism is an inalienable right of all men and the freedom for it remains the deepest tribute to their dignity and stature. Admissibility to the faith of Christ is the ecumenical birthright of mankind never to be suspended or curtailed.[15]

Baptism certainly points to association with the household of faith, but it does not signify the rejection of all previous relationships and values. Let us recapitulate. Although conversion as a religious experience differs radically from a formal shift in religious affiliation, it has practical consequences. An obvious one is that it creates for new believers a relationship with others who have had the same experience. A Muslim who has been "turned on" by the redeeming love of God and has "turned to" Jesus the Savior in faith also "turns in" to an association with other Christians, usually in a congregational setting. The normal way of doing that is by a get acquainted period, some study, a profession of faith, and baptism. Christians who have been involved in the fostering process also ordinarily expect it to unfold in this pattern. The Muslim community can tolerate this kind of interest *up to* the ceremony of baptism, but the latter signifies a denial of the individual's heritage, relationships, culture, and in some instances, even the state—in other words, the wholesale repudiation of everything sacred and precious. The average new believer from Islamic background does not see it that way. He or she is not at all interested in denying family, friends, and culture, and participation in the normal life of a citizen. The contrasting views produce a quandary. How can it be resolved? A variety of theories have been put forward, but we will limit ourselves to three.

The least attractive alternative and seldom proposed openly is to engage in some form of dissimulation, including secret baptism. Since it is the public acts that Muslims identify with apostasy and since they trigger the often violent reaction, why not avoid them? Why wave a red flag? In Islamic history, Shī'a Muslims had a doctrine of *taqiyya* (religious dissimulation) that allowed them to hide their faith in stressful times when threatened by *Sunnī* Muslims.[16] Why not take this practice as an example of common sense? Why not a Christian *taqiyya*? In looking back at the great persecutions of early Christians in the Roman Empire, it may be noted that Christians sought various ways to protect themselves and even occasionally went into the rock-hewn burial galleries called catacombs beneath Rome to seek refuge, though they gave their lives for the faith in large numbers. Is it not possible, then, for new believers to hide their faith, and if baptism is desired to take it in secret and to keep it quiet? The concept of "secret believers," however, founders on the fact that Jesus the Light of the world declared that His light cannot be hid and invited His friends to share the cup of suffering. That they learned and accepted the meaning of His words is illustrated by what Peter and John said to the religious officials who commanded their silence: "We cannot keep from speaking about what we have seen and heard" (Acts 4:20).

The second approach that has been put forward is somewhat of a compromise and that is to *delay* baptism until such a time that the individual involved has become visibly firm in the faith and/or until a group of new believers can be gathered in one place, who will be able to tender each other the mutual support required. This proposal recognizes two realities. One is that it takes time for a new believer to grow strong in wisdom and knowledge and to understand the sources of spiritual strength. The second is the awareness that the immense pressures often brought to bear on lonely new believers can bend their wills and buckle their knees. History is full of examples of those who gave up their intention to follow Christ in the face of these pressures, and those who have never experienced them can hardly sit in judgment. Why not delay, then? To many it seems like a modest and noncontroversial way out of the dilemma. But the paternalism of the approach does not sit well with most new believers who are familiar with the New Testament. They know the command and the promises in regard to baptism and are unhappy to wait for better conditions. They have a spiritual and psychological need to move forward. We will cite the story of Hamid in this regard.

Hamid came to faith in a milieu where taking the name of another religious community entailed the most serious risks, and in his area no one had dared to take this step and survived. The dangers involved in baptism were high. Moreover, Hamid was very much a beginner in the Christian faith. His fostering friends pleaded with him to give time for maturation and to wait for companions in the faith journey. Hamid, however, had read the New Testament and felt that no one had the right "to withhold the water for baptizing" (Acts 10:47). He, therefore, traveled four hundred kilometers from his home to a place where he was not known, and there he persuaded local church authorities to administer baptism. When he returned, as Paul Hamid, he was met at the train by his friends and advisors who with dismay observed the crumbling of his courage as he drew nearer to his home. No one could have predicted such a rapid denouement, but it came within a week. He was seized and taken to a mountainous place where he was ordered to recant or be slain. Hamid withdrew from his Christian profession and was never heard from again.

Hamid's story is an example of a situation where delay in baptism may have brought a different result. At the same time, it is possible to cite examples of the opposite experience. There are many new believers who exercise their right to immediate baptism and validate their insistence by lives of grace under pressure. They are like the Ethiopian eunuch who heard Philip's explanation of a passage from the prophet Isaiah and spontaneously made his decision. "Look, here is water! What is to prevent me from being baptized?" (Acts 8:36).

What do we learn from these histories? We become aware that evangel-sharers dare not turn Muslim converts into objects of theory or practice. They are subjects and as free subjects they will make their own decisions. The allotment of time for study and spiritual development prior to baptism and thereafter is sure to differ for every individual or group and cannot be definitively prescribed in advance.

The third approach takes up the possibility of setting aside baptism as a matter of course for Muslim converts. It is a case for unbaptized believers. This proposal is not based on a desire to dilute the significance of baptism. It recognizes its historicity, sanctity, and importance but it argues that it is not an indispensable element in Christian practice. The story of the thief on the cross, it is suggested, illustrates the point. Neither do we have any record of the baptism of the first apostles, unless they received that of John the Baptist. While these may have been exceptional cases, the situation of Muslim converts may also be deemed exceptional. It is suggested that these possible precedents combine with another significant factor to make a case. That factor is the relative spaciousness of the Muslim attitude toward differences of opinion within the community. There are Muslims on every side of every question. Many vigorous disagreements, frequent acrimony, and even sectarianism disturb the *umma*. The egalitarianism of Islam that was examined in our study of the key principles of Islam means that apart from the confession, the *shahāda*, there is no formal limit on individual opinion. The efforts to impose it are not successful as Muslims privately go on deciding for themselves what they want to believe or do.

This reality means that Muslims may be attracted to the personality of Jesus the Messiah and still remain within Muslim society. They may join with others of like persuasion and may even associate in churchly activities at informal levels, albeit uneasily. This permissiveness changes the minute a new believer is baptized. It is, therefore, suggested that new believers be encouraged to stay within their Islamic context, remaining unbaptized to allow them to do so, but otherwise conducting their lives in the spirit of the Messiah, who also remained within the Jewish community. This procedure will not take away the cross anymore than it did for Jesus, but it will defuse the immediate reaction that goes with baptism and allow for a less hindered personal development. Phil Parshall, known for his experimentation with this approach, puts the case in these words:

We are extremely honest from the start with the convert; he is told that he must remain within the Islamic community. Our goal is to see a small cluster of believers within a given geographical area. When the ideal of sociological strength plus maturity on the part of the believers is reached, it becomes possible to consider baptism.[17]

Suggestions have been raised that another form or forms of initiation be developed that would function to some extent as an equivalent to baptism, though not replacing it. An encouragement to such thinking comes from the fact that Jesus drew on the customary washings of Jewish culture, represented by the baptism of John. His teaching that the Sabbath is made for man is also applicable to this situation. The early church exercised some freedom in relation to baptism. It developed ceremonies related to the exorcism of bad spirits and to the giving of the Holy Spirit that accompanied the regular baptism rite. The "baptism of the cross," that is, the signing of the cross on the forehead and the breast of the new believer, is another example of an innovation that comes from within the history of the baptism ceremony.[18] Using the symbolism of a fish, the concept of association was used to identify believers in the early church, especially in times of persecution. They started with the confessional phrase "Jesus Christ, God's Son, Savior." The combined first letters of the Greek words that make up this phrase (I, X, Th, U, S) become *ichthus*, which is the Greek word for "fish." When Christians saw the sign of the fish, they knew that they had met a fellow believer. Using this approach, could an informal ritual be employed that would be biblically and culturally based and that would function psychologically as a sign of association? For example, could there be a kind of "Sacrament of Following"? In a small way, it could do some of the things that baptism does but without the weight of misunderstanding until such a time as the administration of baptism itself becomes possible. Thoughts such as these are being pursued.

The proposal to, as it were, make unbaptized believers the normative approach in the task of Christian sharing with Muslims represents an admirable concern to minimize unnecessary offense to the Muslim community and to reduce unnecessary difficulty for new believers. It lifts to a theoretical level what is already widely the case in some non-Christian contexts where the considerable presence of unbaptized believers is a known fact.[19] Despite the cogency of the arguments, however, there are some practical reasons for caution, apart from the fact of the central place of baptism in Christian theology. We have already alluded to the desire of many new believers from Islamic background to experience baptism and its gifts and their inherent right to do so. In addition, there are questions related to the public witness of the convert, the difficulty in the disciplined development of Christian knowledge, the "starving" for Christian fellowship, and not least the disaffection of "old" Christians who may suspect or resent the desire of new believers to be "Muslim" in all things saving their commitment to the Master. These are serious questions to an equally serious proposal. If the classical position on baptism is maintained also for new believers from Muslim background—and there are powerful reasons to do so—it can be maintained in integrity only if the "older" baptized uphold the "newly" baptized with companion love and travel with them on the cross-bearing journey.

One of the most well-known and remarkable Christians from Muslim background is a noted Quranic and literary scholar whose conversion produced a great shock wave in the Muslim world. When well-intentioned friends advised Muhammad Daud Rahbar to remain within Islam for the sake of "larger" goals, he finally went to a Christian chaplain on his own and received baptism. The action set in motion a still unfolding series of events that produced great disquiet and difficulty for the distinguished scholar and his family. Nevertheless, remaining firm on the appropriateness of his personal decision, he speaks clearly on what baptism meant to him, using phrases such as a rescue from "pessimism," a relating to God "on terms of His unconditional mercy," "a feeling of belonging and a spiritual home."[20] After expounding on "the confession of the sameness between Jesus and the Eternal Sustainer," he concludes:

> Instead of boasting that I sought baptism after understanding the mystery of the divinity of Jesus, I confess that I sought baptism in a state of confusion, ignorance and despair and that baptism gave me safety, health and courage. Surely there was some guilt of desertion and defection, and some fear of repercussions. But such fears can with the passage of time be overcome, provided one is sure that there is gratitude in the heart for newly discovered attitudes and that conscience is sufficiently clear. After baptism I was no longer afraid of my own thoughts.[21]

Endnotes

[1] Paul Gerhardt, "Upon the Cross Extended," tr. by John Kelly, in *The Lutheran Hymnal* (St.Louis; Concordia Publishing House, 1941), p.171.

[2] For his thoughtful consideration of "turning-points" I am indebted to David Leigh, *Authentic Lives, Profound Journeys. The Nash Memorial Lectures* (Regina: Campion College, 2001), p. 14. The author examines the spiritual autobiographies of M. K. Gandhi, Black Elk, Thomas Merton, Dorothy Day, C. S. Lewis, and Nelson Mandela.

[3] J. Christy Wilson, Sr., "Muslim Converts," *MW*, Vol. XXXIV, No. 3, July 1944, pp. 176f.

[4] Livingstone, *Planting Churches*, p. 148.

[5] Roger Dixon, "The Major Model of Muslim Ministry," *Missiology*, Vol. XXX, No. 4, October 2002, p. 443.

[6] David Bentley-Taylor, *Java Saga. The Weathercock's Reward* (London: OMF Books, 1975), pp .138-146.

[7] *Ibid.*, p.138.

[8] Much of the discussion concerns the relation between conversion and dialogue; for an introduction to that topic, cf. *Conversion? Conversation?*, a special ed.

of *Word & World*, Vol. 22, No. 3, Summer 2002. The writer's article, "Conversion or Conversation," in that edition, pp. 228-37, shares some of the material in this chapter.

[9] There are differences of opinion among Muslims as to the precise theory of mission, especially as it relates to the people of the book; cf. Larry Poston, *Islamic Da'wah in the West*, pp. 3-8.

[10] The trend to elevate a human community into an ultimate principle entertains the peril of *shirk*, idolatry, but Muslim conservative scholars have not addressed this issue. Reform scholars on the other hand have sharply criticized aspects of the Muslim community's behavior, thereby differentiating between the human response to God and the response to the community.

[11] Kenneth Cragg, *Operation Reach. The Fifth Series* (Beirut: Near East Christian Council Study Program in Islam, March and April, 1962), p. 28.

[12] Paul Löffler, "The Biblical Concept of Conversion," in G. H. Anderson and T. F. Stransky, eds., *Evangelization. Mission Trends 2* (New York: Paulist Press, 1975), p. 24.

[13] This old solution for the problems of converts has received heavy criticism because it usually entailed economic assistance and the dependency that implies, and because it made impossible the development of local fellowship groups.

[14] J. S. Whale, *Christian Doctrine* (Cambridge: University Press, 1941), p. 165. Luther speaks regularly of "the great comfort and mighty aid to faith in the knowledge that one has been baptized...."; cf. *The Babylonian Capitivity of the Church*, in Theodore Tappert, ed., *Selected Writings of Martin Luther* (Philadelphia: Fortress Press, 1967), p. 415, and pp. 409-33.

[15] Kenneth Cragg, *Christianity in World Perspective*, pp. 215f.

[16] Cf. R. Strothmann-Moktar Djebli, "*Takiyya*," in *EI²*, X, pp. 134-36; it was argued (p. 135) that "one should avoid a martyrdom that seems unnecessary and was useless and preserve oneself for the faith of one's co-religionists."

[17] Phil Parshall, *Beyond the Mosque: Christians Within Muslim Community* (Grand Rapids: Baker Book House, 1985), p. 187.

[18] Hans Lietzmann, *A History of the Early Church*, tr. by B. L. Woolf (Cleveland: The World Publishing Co., 1963), Vol. I, pp. 64f. and Vol. II, pp. 131f.

[19] Cf. Herbert E. Hoefer, *Churchless Christianity* (Pasadena: Wm. Carey Library, 2001; rev. ed.). First published in Madras in 1991 the work, based on careful research, revealed (p. 109) that "there is a solid twenty-five percent of the Hindu and Muslim population in Madras City which has integrated Jesus deeply into their spiritual life." The size of this "churchless Christianity" may be compared with the ten percent of the population who were formally Christian.

[20] Daud Rahbar, *Memories and Meanings* (Published by the author, n.d.), pp. 312, 350.

[21] *Ibid.*, p.353.

17

The Church Believers: On Being Supportive

With hope, and with considerable trepidation, a new believer from Islamic background enters the strange new world of the church. It is appropriate that we consider that experience in this final chapter of our study.

It all comes back to the church. Sharing friends are the church in mission. The church in mission gives birth to a new pilgrim church, on a unique journey of faith, valiant but idiosyncratic, with a special set of needs. Sharing friends become caring friends and discover new things about themselves. The overall outcome is a combination of exhilarating experiences and a spectrum of mutual needs. This chapter is about the relationship of established Christians and new converts from Muslim background, both being church. For the relationship to work well, there must be a second conversion, a conversion to each other. It all comes back to the church.

The theme "church and convert" is a recurring one in the history of evangel-sharing among Muslims, a fact that testifies to its importance. We have discussed the faith journey of a Muslim friend toward Christ, including inquiry, faith commitment, and baptism. We have arrived at the final stage in the continuum of faith—association with fellow believers. As reflected in our chapter title, the association is usually put in the form of an antithesis: that is, on the one side are converts and on the other side the existing church and its members. The antithesis reflects only an organizational definition. Properly speaking, and with theological accuracy, new believers are the church, and so what we are really discussing is mutual relations within the family of believers. Nevertheless, the popular use of the word *church* as an organizational reality also has a basis in fact—Christians are gathered in congregations that in turn are united in larger units. New believers have to think about that association. At the same time church members need to ask: how are the strangers to be received, how do they feel about us and we about them, and how should we be supportive toward our new brothers and sisters?

These questions, as straightforward as they may seem, do not in fact have easy answers, and the tensions that accompany them are not always creative. This chapter will examine the idealistic images that congregation members and new believers tend to have about each other, and the realities that must replace them. It will investigate how a supportive church can assist new converts in gracious privilege and friendly duty. The issues covered will include the key factor of fellowship, the problem of insecurity, the conundrum of economic deprivation, and the need for adequate grounding in the faith. We will discuss the importance of positive expectancy and close with a note on organizational experiments in relation to convert churches.

A: Key to the Relationship: Dealing with Romantic Dreams

The history of the relation of new believers from Islamic background with the existing church is an uneven tale. There have been times when the process—whether it be association or integration—took on a normal course, but there have also been failures related in part to the gap between image and reality. We will examine the gap and call for a healthy dose of realism as a kind of smelling-salt that clears the mind for the attitudinal adjustments needed in advance of the mutual engagement.

I. Images and Reality 101: A Course for Converts

When Muslim converts "join the church," they do so with optimism. So pronounced are their expectations that we can speak of their wearing rose-colored glasses. They have met Jesus the Perfect Man. They have absorbed His noble teachings. From their reading of the New Testament, they have also encountered his first followers who, despite their weaknesses, were striving to follow the model of Jesus and were ready to suffer for His kingdom. They have learned how the members of the early church shared their possessions, supported one another in difficulties and strove to communicate the Gospel of peace and love to the people of the Roman Empire. This ideal image is in the minds of converts who are looking forward to the relationship with fellow Christians.

The reality, when it appears, strikes them like a pail of cold water in the face. The Christians they are joining are ordinary people, with ordinary virtues and faults. How can this be explained? When they advance in Christian experience, the converts apprehend the theological truth that Christian believers are at the same time saints and sinners. They are saints because they are covered by Christ's righteousness and are forgiven by God; yet they are also sinners still engaged in the battles against sin, death, and the devil. But that experience usually comes later. The immediate feeling that new believers have is shock when they see the behavior of some Christians and the weaknesses of the organized church. The sight dismays them, and they tend to withdraw from it as from a fire. They look around for some visible exemplars of the spirit of Christ with whom they can associate. The new believers are from a *praxis* tradition, and they are in search of those whose piety seems to verify the way, the truth, and the life that they have accepted, at considerable personal cost. As time passes, their attitude toward Christian denominations and organizations tends to become progressively more critical and they put their trust instead in a few individuals who meet their expectation of the meaning of "Christian."

2. Images and Reality 102: A Course for "Old" Christians

When "old" Christians hear about new believers from Islamic background and their courageous testimony, they are thrilled. When they first meet them, they are wearing rose-colored lenses of their own. They tend to think—here are the contemporary models of the faith that the Gospel produced in the past, but are no longer so visible. With soaring romanticism, they consider that the spiritual transformation of the attitudes and lifestyle of converts are immediate and complete. The converts are like Saul whom Jesus met on the road to Damascus and turned him about into a hero of faith (forgetting that he went to Arabia for three years!). Ideal images are freely transposed to the new believers from Muslim background. They are extolled, unsparingly idealized, and almost mercilessly used to serve the needs of the organized church.

The reality, when it appears, also strikes like a pail of cold water. The converts too are revealed as ordinary people, with ordinary virtues and faults. Because many of them are in fact extraordinary individuals, their virtues and faults may be correspondingly enlarged. The reality startles. It comes like a shock. It overwhelms the relationship. The closer in that the converts come, the more nervous become the members of the church. The tinted spectacles are replaced by the lens of criticism. Why do the converts seem so withdrawn, so proud, so independent? Why do they appear to be reluctant to fit into the patterns and traditions of those whom they are "joining"? Why do they tend to be critical of older Christians and even of one another? Here is something we did not anticipate, a kind of awkwardness and even dissonance. The romanticism is overcome by the reality and feelings of disappointment. And when "old" Christians are further asked to walk with the converts on the path of suffering, distancing from the relationship is not uncommon.

3. Pre-emptive Attitudinal Adjustments

It is advisable for reality checks to precede a relationship between existing congregation members and new believers from Islamic background or early in the relationship, despite their obvious delicacy. We suggest the following thoughts for the advance preparation of converts and congregations.

New believers need help in visualizing the following realities:

- The essence of the matter is that Christians live by the forgiveness of sins through Christ. It is Jesus who is sinless, not his followers.

- The progress of the Christian life is a "pressing on" and a "straining forward" (Philippians 3:12–16). It is like running a race, and there will be some stumbling. But the New Testament says that though weak we are strong because Christ has made us His own.

- There are many nominal Christians who have the same dynamics as nominal Muslims; other Christians should not be judged by their behavior.

- "Old" Christians from non-Muslim background have difficulty in fully appreciating what a convert has passed through or is going through, and cannot be expected to fully understand.

- Legitimate criticism by converts is always received best when it comes from within a fellowship, and must be perceived as the voice of friendship.

- Converts need to learn the value of the key traditions of the church, representing the cumulative experience of their brothers and sisters in the Lord.

The image corrections that congregation members may consider include the following:

- "Old" Christians need to recognize how they might appear to strangers whose criteria are fresh from the New Testament; the new awareness process is part of the spiritual benefit of the relationship

- The view of new believers as paragons of perfection may be consciously revised in terms of normal reality and disappointment managed, for conversion and sanctification are not the same. A brief revisit of Paul's Letters to the Corinthians will highlight the fact that images of perfectionism are inappropriate.

- Muslim converts are often unusual individuals or they could not have traveled the Damascus road; relationships need to be sufficiently broad to embrace strong personalities.

- A congregation may prepare to receive converts by encouraging a core group to become conversant with Islam and the special problems of Muslim converts; the whole congregation may be gradually involved through the use of directed prayers in the weekly worship service.

- There is a difference in attitude and needs of converts who have come to the decision alone and those who are part of a larger movement; in any case, as every human is different, so every new believer is different.

- "Old" Christians will assume responsibility for the outcome of Gospel-sharing as well as for the activity itself; *sending but not tending is irresponsible.*

We turn then to the aspect of tending. What specific problems do Muslim converts have that existing Christians should try to address?

B. On Being Supportive

We will consider four major problems that new believers from Islamic background commonly face: loneliness, insecurity, economic deprivation, and inadequate grounding in the faith. Not every convert faces all of these, and when they do occur it is not with the same intensity for every individual. Yet in some measure they are present for most converts. The problems overlap to some degree with those of serious inquirers that we have already considered, but these issues are specific for members of congregations that are considering a supporting role. From each problem arises a question—what can we do to help? And to each question there is a possible response.

I. Maximizing Fellowship, Minimizing Loneliness

The chief problem for new believers is loneliness and therefore the key convert hope for the church is understanding fellowship.

The source of the problem is in the Muslim attitude toward religious change. The family and friends of new believers do not understand their behavior and feel alienated from them. On the other hand, the new relationships of converts with Christians are uncertain and not yet deeply grounded. They feel homeless, and may even feel abandoned. To the degree that this psychological condition lasts, to that extent it involves a dangerous testing. Many years after his conversion and at an advanced age a notable Muslim convert chose to revert to Islam, saying, "I was always so lonely."

The absence of normal marital arrangements is one of the deeply felt aspects of loneliness. A large proportion of the Muslim converts are young unmarried males, whereas it is not easy for unmarried women to consider that option. As a result, it is difficult to follow the custom of marriage arrangements that prevails in many cultures. Where marriages are alliances between families and one of the parties does not have family support, an impasse occurs. The same applies to Muslim convert parents who need to arrange marriages for their children. They face almost insurmountable barriers in conducting negotiations. It is in such intimate affairs that the convert feeling of aloneness becomes a practical reality.

In their isolated situation, Muslim converts can only look for comfort and hope to their fellow believers. The long and short of it is that they have lost their own families. Unless the family of God, the church, in some sense replaces them, they are in danger of becoming the loneliest people on the planet. In the New Testament concept of church, there is a breadth of meaning, providing several ideas that might appeal to Muslim converts, particularly in light of their understanding of *umma*, the sacred community, or *jama'a*, the company of believers. Without question, however, it is the idea of a loving fellowship that bears the greatest weight of significance for converts. The concept of "membership" is less important. Not joining an organized body nor adopting a certain affiliation but experiencing a genuine brotherhood/sisterhood is what converts hope for in this new home.

There are different terms in the biblical Scriptures for the comradeship of those who follow Jesus the Savior. They include the word *'ecclesiá*, the called out ones, the body of Christ, the people of God, the members of the household of faith, and others. Each meaning points to an important aspect of the interrelation between believers. It is, however, the "being together" aspect, the *koinoniá*, the fellowship among believers that particularly speaks to new believers. The church is the fellowship of Jesus' disciples who take up their cross and follow Him into the path of deep friendship and who bear one another's burdens. For the convert this is the crux. Fellowship with Christ (1 Corinthians 1:9) leads to fellowship with one another (1 John 3:7). All converts, but especially those from Islamic contexts, are close in spiritual time to the first disciples who "devoted themselves to the apostles' teaching and fellowship, to the breaking of bread and prayers" (Acts 2:42).[1]

The terms *conversion* and *church* have traveled a road that has sometimes obscured this dynamic element. At first the early believers in Jesus the Messiah were only a movement within the Jewish family, comprised of those who accepted Jesus as the promised deliverer and risen Lord. Later in the city of Antioch, these believers began to be called "Christians" in mockery. Soon thereafter the distinct church took visible form. Certainly the word *Christian* had become common throughout the Roman Empire within a century and a new word, *Christianity*, has also emerged along the way.[2] As a result of this historical process, several ideas became interactive: turning to God and spiritual transforming, connecting with the fellowship of believers, joining the organized church, and even affiliating with a religion or denomination. The first two meanings are primary, but as time passed and in common parlance today the third and fourth meanings have overtaken them. When that happens conversion or church membership begin to equate the Muslim idea of religious affiliation. New believers bring Christians back to the primary meanings—turning to the saving God and connecting with fellow believers. "Joining the church" for them means experiencing a new family with all that implies.[3] For those who are being "killed all the day long," this is not a matter of fine theological distinction but a life-and-death matter. How, then, shall they connect with believers and how will the church be supportive?

At first glance the provision of fellowship does not seem to be either daring or difficult, since that is what the church is all about. Yet the response in practice is not so easy because of the sociological restraint in Christian congregations. Congregations in peaceful settings are not accustomed to functioning as a close-knit family. Their members draw back from pressured relationships that involve above-normal commitments. They are content with rather superficial relations, knowing that they have other resources to turn to in case of need. That differs from new believers who may have no other resources and stand in need of two things—deep friendship and surrogate family relations. A congregation involved with Muslim converts therefore needs to step forward in an unfamiliar pattern to meet those needs. The fact that the organized church has a relatively undistinguished record in this area indicates that some deliberation is required to adequately respond.

By "deliberation" we mean two things: First of all what the congregation may do is to raise up the concept of family love to a more conscious level. Is there a Bible study teacher who can put together a lesson or lessions on the congregation as a family? Pastor and people need to talk about it, and in that connection may consider what the family of Lazarus, Mary and Martha meant to Jesus. They were open to him and welcomed him when his own brothers were estranged from him. How much this must have meant to the wandering and threatened Messiah! A family, a home!! Without Bethany, Jerusalem would have been more difficult. A second aspect of deliberation is the spirit of adoption. In practical matters the full congregation can be a convert's new home only in a broad sense. Nor is it either necessary or desirable that everyone "hover" above a new believer. Some individual or some family, however, may engage in a ministry of adoption and seek a relationahip with a convert that is more personal and deeply friendly. Such an attachment, experience shows, can have a large, long-term and two way benefit.

As a receiving congregation considers this matter what is the perspective of the new believer? He or she faces a paradox. On the other hand, he/she desires to be befriended, but on the other hand does not want to be viewed as a problem to be solved. He/she wants people to be aware of special difficulties, but does not wish to be patronized. He/she may even reject well-intended overtures, thereby giving the appearance of aloofness and pride. The latter is a common criticism of new believers from Islamic background. It is true that converts, like everyone else, do have their own self-respect. They also not infrequently possess a quotient of pride, personal and cultural. This is often joined with a suspicion that was born in adversity, a healthy suspicion having been one of the means of the convert's survival. But beneath it all, in the heart of new believers there swells a deep feeling of gratitude toward a welcoming and concerned congregation that overcomes the occasional awkwardness. The Christian individuals or families that wish to connect with a Muslim convert must simply strive for a down-to-earth practical relationship based on empathy and equality.

2. The Problem of Insecurity: Taking on the Powers

As we have noted in foregoing chapters, a new believer from Islamic background has taken a decision that entails risk. The extent of the risk varies according to the cultural milieu. It ranges from minimum disruption to physical danger, but almost always there is some measure of insecurity. The situation raises these two questions: For the convert, how can I survive? For the members of the church: how can we be helpful?

In those areas of the world where Muslim converts actually face physical danger or have the perception that they do, they are compelled to consider their choices: Do I go somewhere where I am safe, and if I go, who will care for me? Or, alternatively, shall I stay where I am—witnessing, trusting, and hoping? The New Testament reminds believers that they should not be surprised when persecution comes, but it does not prescribe the precise nature of the response. Moreover, timing is a significant factor. Early in his career, Jesus did not wish to go to Judea where the Jews were looking for an opportunity to kill Him. He told His brothers: "My time has not yet fully come" (John 7:8) and remained in Galilee. The same Paul whose long list of sufferings leaves the average reader dazed and who in the end paid the ultimate sacrifice, early in his career at Damascus was let down from a window in a basket to escape the hands of religious colleagues who wanted to kill him (Acts 9:25). Paul's time too had not yet come, and there was clearly a need for his missionary journeys among the Gentiles. What an individual will do in any crisis situation depends on his or her own perceptions, the feelings of those around the person, the possibilities inherent in the situation, and the Spirit's guidance. There can be little doubt, however, about the attitude of a supportive church—its first concern will be for the convert's safety, and a secondary concern will be in helping that individual clarify his or her options.

The church's basic response is to give priority to the security of those endangered. In the Garden of Gethsemane Jesus the Friend came forward to the threatening soldiers and said: "If you are looking for me, let these men go." The Gospel adds that Jesus was determined not to lose a single one of His disciples (John 18:8f.). The episode makes two strong points—to remember the other person amid one's own problems and to use one's influence to rescue one's friends. Whatever power they do have, "old" Christians must employ it in the defense of new believers. That includes, if necessary, serving as the hands "lowering the basket." Apart from such immediate actions there are things to be done at more measured levels. As the list of Muslim convert/martyrs grows longer, there is no condoning a forgetfulness on the part of a secure and settled ecclesiastical leadership. At the policy level, there will be activist basket-lowering through the support of human rights organizations and other social and governmental agencies that contend for freedom of religion and human justice. Above all, in the churches themselves, there will be thanks and praise to God for the perseverance and witness of new disciples around the world. For it is certain that one day in the future one of the elders will ask: "Who are these, robed in white, and where have they come from?" Then the answer will be given: "These are they who have come out of a great ordeal . . . and the one who is seated on the throne will shelter them" (Revelation 3:3–15). Secure forever.

As for the secondary but important service of clarifying options, they fall into two major divisions—staying within the situation or going elsewhere. When new believers wish to and are able to stay within a situation, there is a purity of witness and a possibility of establishing a local church and the seeds of the future. Members of established congregations who counsel new believers have obvious difficulties. The congregation could not be materially helpful to converts from Islamic background if it was not itself secure, but its security contrasts with the convert's insecurity. It is a matter of great delicacy for the church to say to a convert that he or she should not "leave Damascus" or to suggest that mission theory takes precedence over an individual's safety. Nevertheless, unendangered fellow believers can help those in danger by articulating the controlling biblical principles and the possible courses of action. It may be remembered that in principle converts do not wish to leave their homes, and increasingly the bold and determined persistence to remain within the situation and to witness to their own community is becoming visible. The more that is possible, the more a new age in mission emerges.

3.Addressing the Conundrum of Economic Deprivation.

The economic problem particularly strikes new believers who cannot stay in their environment and lead a normal existence Then the urgent question comes: How are we going to live? It is a question that tends to overtake all other issues related to the church's supportive task.

There are three common and predictable reasons why converts from Muslim background frequently face some sort of economic deprivation. The first is the loss of one's employment because of the commitment made to follow the path of Jesus. The second applies to converts of student age, where the decision means going without family help. The third is the fact that a significant number of new believers come from the socially and economically marginalized, and their natural employment difficulties are exaggerated by their discipleship. Physical persecution is serious but has a spasmodic quality, whereas economic deprivation is ongoing, depressingly total in its impact, and not easily solved. For convert parents the economic problem that is felt most acutely is related to the care and education of their children. Their inability to provide for their training needs, on top of the loss of inheritance, means the future looks bleaker than the present. For many converts, whether single or married, solving even the simple requirements of food, clothing, and shelter seem out of reach. Melancholy, if not severe depression, is an ordinary companion of those who are facing these dilemmas.

The church of Jesus Christ has classically recognized its obligation to help the poor and has provided an array of services that have been widely appreciated. The world, however, does not appreciate assistance given to individuals immediately preceding or postdating a faith commitment. Such assistance has brought charges of induced conversion from a wide range of secular and religious critics. It has also sometimes given to new believers the impression that there is in fact a causal relation between conversion and economic improvement. These charges and misunderstandings have diminished in recent years as the church along with secular agencies has placed great emphasis on empowering individuals through self-help projects and broad social and economic development efforts. This, however, has mitigated rather than done away with the issues, for the long-range improvement programs have little felt relevance to converts who are without a job, income, or family support. Their appeal is a poignant one: "How can we live?" The church's response also has pathos: "How can we be supportive without creating severe misunderstandings?"

It is not surprising that there is a broad spectrum of views on the problem of economic deprivation. The range of opinions includes the following:

•   There are those who consider it ill-advised to help converts financially because it tends to create individual dependent psychologies and it fosters a wrong public impression. One leader cautions: "I would urge all agencies and missions involved in Muslim ministries not just to take the easy road of distributing assistance when there is a need. We must carefully calculate and project the long-term effects of our help."[4]

•   There are those who believe that converts should be helped, but the help should be limited to assistance in finding jobs or in job training. Converts themselves have strongly pleaded for the establishment of mission-sponsored training programs that will assist them in becoming economically competitive, though many "old" Christians tend to be wary of such expensive and cumbersome institutional proposals.

•   There are those who believe that it is appropriate to help converts financially on an occasional emergency basis and to meet special needs. The need most often cited is medical care or the education of children.

•   There are those who attempt to combine assistance to some converts with employment in church programs, thereby opening the door for the payment of regular salaries for legitimate services rendered. Those converts are helped to attend colleges or seminaries and on graduation are given assignments related to their unique backgrounds and abilities. This approach has produced a harvest of valuable trained leadership.

- Finally, there are those who believe that converts should be spontaneously and unhesitatingly helped according to their needs, the only limit being the practical ability of supporting friends to respond. It is argued that there cannot be a separate theory for converts than for the poor in general. The church must deal with the economic suffering of new believers with the same graciousness and to the same extent that it does with any people living in poverty and difficulty.

The response of supportive Christian friends will always strive to be situational, contextual, Christlike, and Spirit-wise. What needs resistance is the exploitation of converts from Muslim background by mission organizations and societies that tend to operate with self-conscious criteria and some forms of practice so self-focused that they border on being predatory. Convinced that their approach is theologically correct, that their understanding of the convert situation outranks others, and that their organizational needs are pre-eminent, they are opportunistic in attracting converts, dismissive of original fostering friends, and unthinking in their financially empowered and dependency-creating techniques. Very few human beings, including converts, are able to resist lucrative arrangements that solve their economic needs and at the same time enable them to participate in mission activities. The fact that some have such opportunities leads to a natural expectancy among new believers that this is the norm and may be their due. The negative fallout on a somewhat scornfully observant Muslim community, and on other rather envious indigenous Christians, as well as on the possible development of a self-supporting and self-propagating group cannot be overstated. While such organizations are few and pose a special problem, any thoughtless and undisciplined form of financial assistance to converts is no answer to the economic deprivation problem. "On being supportive" does not equate with "benign paternalism."

What does it equate with? It is likely that there will always be a difference of opinion as to the nature of the appropriate response to the economic deprivation of new believers. The points about which there will be no argument are that the new believers must rightly understand the implications of the response, and the arrangement itself as much as possible must be geared to long-term solutions. St. Paul states defining principles for both the principles of self-support and help for the weak in the following verses of his farewell speech to the Ephesians:

And now I commend you to God and to the message of His grace, a message that is able to build you up and to give you the inheritance among all who are sanctified. I coveted no one's silver or gold or clothing. You know of yourselves that I worked with my own hands to support myself and my companions. In all this I have given you an example that by such work we must support the weak, remembering the words of the Lord Jesus for He Himself said, "It is more blessed to give than to receive." (Acts 20:32–35)

4. The Problem of Inadequate Grounding in the Faith

"What does this mean?" No matter how profound his or her conversion experience, and no matter how thoughtful the preparation in the seeker period, a new believer is entering an unfamiliar spiritual world. There are things he or she does not know and should know. There are resources he or she does not have and should have. Loneliness, persecution, and destitution are pressing problems and result in immediately obvious needs. The problem of an inadequate grounding in the faith is an absence of something not known and is, therefore, seldom felt to the same degree, but it may be the most serious problem for the long-term stability of a new believer.

Anyone who looks at the Christian faith from the outside tends to be perplexed by its apparent complexity. The language seems strange, the liturgy arcane, the theology abstruse, and the structure dense. That certainly is the way it appears to Muslims, who admire what they regard as the contrasting simplicity and accessibility of Islam. With that in their background, the new world of thought that converts encounter seems perplexing. Moreover, it appears remote from the straight-forward message of Jesus and His Way on which they have been concentrating. Yet they enter the new world that is now theirs bravely, kindly, with their own intellectual tools, anxious and determined to learn. At virtually every point they meet ideas that they do not understand or particularly enjoy, but they are expected to appreciate them. The new believer often internalizes the confusion, and in self-defense tends to look for and to adopt simple contrasts with Islam, avoiding nuances, dismissing deeper theological investigation as an unhelpful form of weakness, and turning to fundamentalist approaches that promise a clear contrast between light and dark. The deepening process is thereby blunted. Out of the body of converts from Islamic backgrounds there has arisen a highly distinguished group of creative thinkers, but this has happened largely by dint of their own efforts rather than as a result of a church responsive to intellectual demands. The need for post-baptismal or post-commitment grounding in the Christian tradition is widely unmet.

We may ask why this has happened when the teaching ministry is one that the church understands best. Partly it is due to the fact that converts tend to be on the move. But partly it is simply a lack or concentration. All attention has been paid to sharing Jesus and to the nurturing of people through the seeker period. In regard to the discipling stage adequate pedagogy has often not been available when needed, and good discipling literature is in very short supply. At the back of the problem lurks the fact that few "old" Christians are close enough to converts to understand their questions and feelings or to respond to them. While a revolution in discipling cannot be expected, a supportive church can take great strides forward by providing more high-quality literary materials, possibly suitable for adaptation to a variety of culture contexts, and creating nurture opportunities.

An illustration of the latter service would be the implementation of a series of what might be called "Nabataean Oases." We have discussed the benefits of retreats for serious Muslim inquirers. The same value applies to retreats for new believers where they will be together within their own contextual fellowship, in some blessedly restful milieu, and under the guidance of an experienced leader or facilitator, to engage in focused programs of spiritual formation. When the new convert Saul, afterward Paul, left Damascus and went to Arabia for three years (Galatians 1:17f.), he may have withdrawn to what is now southwest Jordan; the kingdom of the Nabataeans, an Arab tribe, was located there.[5] Did he go for preaching or for spiritual reflection? Even if it was the former, as some have suggested, it was certainly a period in which he grew in the wisdom and knowledge of the Lord. As Edgar Goodspeed suggest, he had "to begin a tremendous reconstruction of his religious thinking. For he had not just lightly added Jesus to his Jewish theology, as a Messiah foretold by the prophets; he had seen in him the transformation of his whole religious world."[6] No words could more accurately describe the experience of a thoughtful new believer from Muslim background. Is it too much, therefore, to expect of supportive Christians that they collaborate on an annual or biennial "Nabataean Oasis" dedicated toward helping new believers to the goal of an adequate grounding in the faith? While these islands of rest and growth would not be modeled on the Sufi *khanqah*, retreat center, they might in fact use elements of that tradition in deepening new believers in the way of the Friend. The oasis would be a visible statement of Paul's word to the Philippians: "Therefore, my brothers and sisters, whom I love and long for, my joy and crown, stand firm in the Lord in this way. . . . Keep on doing the things that you have learned and received, and heard and seen in me, and the God of peace will be with you" (Philippians 4:1, 9).

C. On Being Expectant

There are two recognizable risks in the discussion of a supportive church. The first is a possible tendency to think of converts as objects rather than subjects. The second is the danger of obscuring the essential two-way nature of this interaction. Both difficulties fade when "old" Christians remember to cultivate the grace of expectancy, for new believers will bring their own blessings to their companions on the Way. The anticipation of those good things can be like a "shot in the arm" for a sometimes jaded church. Such expectancy takes seriously the prediction of the prophet Isaiah: "The wealth of the nations shall come to You" (Isaiah 60:5). We have repeatedly referred to the magnificence of the Islamic cultural tradition. It is through the channel of the new believers that some of its elements will make their appearance. "The young camels of Midian and Ephah; all those from Sheba shall come. They shall bring gold and frankincense, and shall proclaim the praise of the Lord" (Isaiah 60:6f.).

What is this gold and frankincense that the new believers lay before the Child and His mother? What do the new believers bring? First, they bring reminders. They are the warners. The number of warners and reminders is never the important thing, but rather their function. They remind "old" Christians of the days of the church's youth, for they are in a sense the early church reborn in our midst, calling to mind a world that has drifted away from settled Christians, and in the process making the Scriptures come alive again. That is not all. They bring their own graces—their energy, independence, courage, frankness, and gifts of natural leadership that inspire and renew those who experience them. That is not all. We return to the cultural factor. It may be argued that the church will remain incomplete until it receives the noble things, the gold and frankincense, of the Islamic culture and spirit. Whether it be spiritual things like the respect for God and the grace of simple obedience, whether it be the aesthetic refinements of great civilizations, whether it be story and poetry that celebrate word and that carry over into reverence for the Word of God, these are cultural riches and spiritual treasures that enlarge and enhance the ethos of the church and that cannot be measured in their value. The reception of this wealth requires not romantic imagery but the spirit of expectancy. The converts do not come laden with promises but laden with gifts.

How will the church draw on them? Intelligent expectancy means looking and seeing, transcending space limitations, celebrating and involving, and developing disciplined opportunity creation at various levels. Let us ask the question: Why should a Christian—in the United States, for example—want to know about the strength of the Christian home in Java where there are so many Christian families from Muslim background?[7] An inturned vision will not discern a pressing reason. But the spirit of expectancy senses a hugely significant development and looks outward in anticipation. How do they live their lives? How do they make their impact? How can we learn from them? Is there a gift available for other Christians that requires a camel?

There is another level of richness that needs to be more deliberately acquired. We have referred to St. Paul's great theological reconstruction that was Spirit-guided but also depended in part on his own brilliance and intellectual training. Similarly, there is a need to draw water from the wells of the most reflective and trained minds among converts from Muslim background to access their insights. For that we require a kind of periodic "Jerusalem Council." As Christians from Jewish background met together to reflect on issues, so let Christians from Muslim background do so. Let us call it "The Hikma," i.e., a "Conference of the Book and Wisdom." *Hikma* is cross-cultural and trans-disciplinary spiritual wisdom.[8] Muslims believe that "the Book and Wisdom" were gifted to Jesus (Qur'ān 5:110) and that Jesus said, "I have come unto you with wisdom, and to make plain some of that concerning which ye differ" (43:63). It is the great Muslim converts who can in a sense fulfill that prediction as they gather in faithfulness to the Master to reflect on the great spiritual themes that bridge the Christian and Muslim traditions—such as surrendering, remembering, and obeying; as they engage in their own critical reflection on the contrasts and parallels as enlightened in their experience of the Light of the Word; and as they speak to the churches from their unique backgrounds on the Christian sharing task in the Muslim world. It is *hikma* also for the church to access this richness. As Isaiah declares: "Do not let the foreigner joined to the LORD say, 'The LORD will surely separate me from His people'!" Rather, Isaiah adds, "The foreigners who join themselves to the LORD to minister to Him, to love the name of the LORD , and to be His servants . . . their burnt offerings and their sacrifices will be acceptable on My altar; for My house shall be called a house of prayer for all peoples" (Isaiah 56:3, 6f.).

D. The Convert Church

Our final section has to do with the manner in which new believers from Muslim background choose to organize themselves. Many discussions have gathered around this issue. Arguments gravitate between the poles of the ideal and the real, and their outcome is largely determined by local situations. At one end of the spectrum may be the Indonesian reality where a sufficient number of believers and an atmosphere of freedom enable the establishment of large congregations made up of believers from Muslim background. At the other end of the spectrum are areas, particularly in the Middle East, where the underground church is the only possibility. In the middle part of the spectrum are western regions where individual converts routinely adhere to existing congregations, in the nonhomogenous sociological model. Also in the middle part are other regions where there exist a significant number of new believers in the midst of existing established churches. The discussion in regard to this situation is molded by the relative weight given to principles of fellowship and church growth.

Should Muslim converts establish their own fellowship groups or churches in places where other churches exist? There are voices raised on both sides of the issue. On one side are those who maintain that the principles of unity and fellowship must control the decision. Although there may be serious difficulty in the integration of new believers from Muslim background with people of other backgrounds, the option of separate churches is not a happy one, and every effort must be taken to overcome difficulties that stand in the way of an integrated approach. Only then will established congregations feel involved.

On the other side of the question are those who give the strongest weight to the inter-relationship that new believers from Islamic background have with one another. This is not an ethnically defined relation—though it may be that also—rather it is a fellowship that stems from their common religious background. In this view the natural relationship of new believers should be maintained and nourished so they may support one another. One way of doing so is through the establishment of their own congregations and organizations. Not only will this create a natural fellowship home for new believers, but other Muslims will be attracted. When they see the life of the *ʿĪsawī*, the people of Jesus, or the *Masīḥī*, the people of the Messiah, both terms applied to Christians by Muslims in the past, they will be more open to consider Christian claims and the process of church growth will be accelerated.

New believers, in whose hands rest the final answers to this issue, see cogency in both sides of the debate. Settled Christians, to whom the idea of separate churches produces feelings of rejection, are not warm to it. Nevertheless, it is evident that they will have to, as it were, "clear the path" and "allow" new believers to take the approach that seems to them, under the guidance of the Spirit, to be the appropriate one. Certainly, there must be more deliberately conceived and genuine experimentation with a variety of organizational models that will preserve and express the natural affinity of converts but will also free them to bring their rich gifts into the wider Christian family and to experience the beauty of that family.

A variation on the theme is an interim format drawn from an American church experiment and expressed in the phrase "the sounding of a call to found a mission group within an already established church." The call is accompanied by the following comment:

Accustomed as we have become to the already long-established churches and denominations, and amazed as we are at a rapidly developing and increasing number of mega-church—the thought of starting a church with a very few called persons may seem ludicrous, preposterous, unbelievable. But with God nothing is impossible.[9]

In this approach a small group with a sense of call and perceiving a special mission "sets forth in writing the specifics of the commitment and the disciplines required for its fulfillment."[10] Key to the ethos of the mission group is the mutual covenant to proclamation and discipleship, while openness and freedom in development of both the inward and outward journeys of its members mark its approach. The small group may attend a weekly worship service in an already established church or conduct its own. Essential to its forward progress is its "school of Christian living" that serves its members. What will control and characterize a mission group as long as it chooses to remain in existence will be a "spirit of beauty, joy, love, celebration, festivity."[11] This approach resonates with the needs of new believers and may be considered for application in appropriate situations.

We will close this discussion with an illustration from the writer's experience. Located on the southwest coast of India is a group of over seven million Muslims called the Mappilas. The Mappila community, representing perhaps the first Muslims in India, has a striking history. The Mappilas passed through eight centuries of inter-religious serenity and economic well being followed by four centuries of turbulence and social backwardness and now to a time of progress, in the end providing for the Muslim world an unusual and positive example of Islamic change.[12] An attractive and warmhearted people, they had nevertheless earned a reputation for extremely fervent faith and frequent militant uprisings culminating in the notorious Mappila Rebellion of 1921. The community was fully resistant to religious change and applied the traditional sanctions when they occurred. It was generally held that evangel-sharing among the Mappilas was impossible, counterproductive, and a waste of time and money. No Mappila in fact had ever become a Christian and survived until a gallant young student, K. K. Alavi, chose to follow Jesus the Messiah in 1964. His story, still in progress, is a saga of great courage, heavy suffering, powerful testimony, and exuberant faith. Inspired by his remarkable example other Mappilas took a similar decision, resulting in a significant though statistically modest movement into the Christian faith. Families as well as individuals are included in the movement, and at least three converts have completed seminary study programs. Led by Pastor Alavi the large majority have chosen to remain within the situation. Under duress and before a public court on December 13, 2002, he expressed that determination:

I, K. K. Alavi, born to a Mullah . . . and brought up in an orthodox upbringing . . . found the truth. The light of the world. The true light, which enlightens every man that comes into the world, Jesus Christ in whom dwelled all the fullness of the Godhead bodily . . . . Now my ambition is the evangelization of the Muslim people, preaching to them and spreading the message of love and peace, of the one who can transform their life to a peace loving person, who can open their spiritual eyes to the truth.[13]

Certain about their task the converts have nevertheless been uncertain in church matters. Although the impetus for this evangelistic development came from one denomination, the converts chose to relate to a variety of Christian groups and agencies.[14] Now some are asking themselves the question: "Is this the way we should go? Shall we integrate with the church?" Or, perhaps, is it now time to establish the "Mappila Church," independent but with appropriate connections? Would this not serve to draw together Muslim converts into a cohesive fellowship within their own "mission group," and at the same time enable the Gospel to make its way effectively into the heart of the Mappila community? Or would that simply serve to alienate Muslims and Christians alike? What this relatively small group will do and which direction they will take is still unknown but as is the case for similar groups everywhere what is known and certain is that they will not be alone in their decision-making even as they have not been alone on their journey from its beginning.

To summarize the situation that we have described, we may say that it varies from isolated converts in hostile environments to large, self-sustaining groups of believers in friendly surroundings; from theories of contextual identification and remaining within the umma to theories of full assimilation with Christian congregations. Between the extremes at different points on the organizational spectrum are cells of various kinds or "communities of the disciples of Jesus the Messiah" that are springing up in many places in the world, contextually unique yet facing common problems of critical mass, leadership training, and the expression of wider Christian fellowship. Thus the profile of the convert church takes on the appearance of a series of hills rather than one towering mountain that dominates the scene. While this structural diversity to some may seem to constitute a weakness, it is in fact the only possible approach to a globally spread and contextually varied engagement.

What "old" Christians advising new believers have to say, and what they must also underline and relearn for themselves, is that the journey of faith does not arrive at a settled condition after a formal commitment and/or baptism, but rather it simply enters a new and different stage. The journey goes on. We refer again to the pattern of Abraham. With extraordinary faith, he followed the call of God to an unknown country, traveling through difficulty and danger on the long 1,200-mile journey from his homeland to Palestine. But the journey was not over on arrival. Abraham bought a small site at the Oaks of Mamre near Hebron where he and Sarai could be buried but that was the only resting place they had. They kept wandering between Canaan and the Nile Valley to pasture their herds, always in tents and on the move, yet always in faith though they never attained a fully settled condition. Such an undisturbed condition, a kind of settled Garden of Eden-like discipleship, is not given God's people for their journey of faith through this testing world, where they have no continuing city. The principle of structural freedom therefore becomes a strength rather than a weakness. It makes it possible to deal with things as they are, as a liberating, worry-removing principle that enables new believers from Muslim background to develop the forms that make sense for the functions of God's people in motion—to worship and grow, to witness and serve. Within that understanding the search for usable models will go on, and should go on, but always with prayer to the travel Counselor. For the key thing in the whole story is that the progress of the church is not finally a matter of human policy at all, but rather it is the affair of God's Spirit who through the Gospel brings into being the possibility of impossibilities.

Endnotes

[1] There is an abundance of testimonies prepared by new believers from Muslim background; for a sampling cf. the resources of *The Fellowship of Faith*, *op.cit.*, whose quarterly *Prayer New Bulletin* also tracks the difficulties of converts. The testimonies vary in quality, and therefore E. Hahn, in booknotes for The Fellowship of Faith, states: "Accounts of converts should be viewed and used with discrimination. Are the contents true? Do they cater simply to the sensational, the dramatic? Are they used only to put down the Muslim and Islam? Do they glorify God or the convert?" (n.d.). There are few compelling analyses of the change factors, and further research into the phenomenology of conversion is therefore awaited.

[2] Adolf Harnack, *The Mission and Expansion of Christianity*, tr. and ed. by James Moffat (New York: Harpers, 1961), p. 412.

[3] The intuition of Muslim converts is directly on track, for the concept of a family headed by the Heavenly Father is deeply Biblical. Cf. Robert Mackintosh, "Christians," *Encyclopaedia of Religion and Ethics*, Vol. 3, pp. 573-76, who lists ten New Testament names applied to Christians in the New Testament by believers, including the earliest one, "disciples;" but in his view the key term is "brothers and sisters." He states; "It may be considered the standing NT designation for Christians by Christians," p. 573.

[4] Phil Parshall, "Lessons Learned in Contextualization," in D. Woodberry, ed., *Emmaus Road*, p. 259.

[5] The term "Arabia" as used in Paul's time was not precise in its meaning. Where he went could have been anywhere in the region between Syria and the upper Red Sea, on the border areas of Jordan and Saudi Arabia; it might have been nearer to Damascus or in the direction of far-off Sinai. We have a clue in the fact that the ethnarch (governor) of King Aretas of the Nabataeans was in charge of Damascus when Paul returned there (2 Cor. 11:32). Petra, the Nabataean capital, was only 250 miles from Damascus, and Paul may have gone there. In the Jewish mode of calculation three years was also an ambiguous number; it could signify one full year and a part of two others.

[6] Edgar J. Goodspeed, *Paul* (Philadelphia: The John C. Winston Co., 1947), p. 21.

[7] David Bentley-Taylor, *Java Saga*, pp .145f.

[8] A. M. Goichon, "Hikma," *EI²* III. pp. 377f. There are some remarkable Christian thinkers from Islamic background whose names and potential availability come to mind in connection with this proposal.

[9] Dorothy Devers and N. Gordon Cosby, *Handbook for Churches and Mission Groups* (Washington: The Servant Leadership School and the Servant leadership Press, n.d.), pp. 12f. The concept is developed by the Church of the Servant Jesus, founded May 4, 1995, in Washington, D.C.

[10] *Ibid.*, p. 14.

[11] *Ibid.*, p.33;

[12] For further cultural background cf. Roland E. Miller, "Mappila," *EI²*, II, pp. 458-66, and Miller, *Mappila Muslims of Kerala, op. cit.*

[13] Abstracted from a fax message to the writer, January 28, 2003; for his full personal testimony cf. K. K. Alavi's *In Search of Assurance, op-cit.*

[14] Initially the Lutheran Church-Missouri Synod, and then the India Evangelical Lutheran Church, were responsible for this focused ministry in the Malabar area of Kerala State, India, the traditional home of the Mappilas. Currently congregations of the Evangelical Lutheran Church in America are in support.

18

Conclusion: The Possibility of the Impossibilities

In this study of Christian sharing with Muslims we have stressed two points — that we should deal with Muslims as friends, and that friends share what is best in their lives. Dealing with Muslims as friends includes understanding their point of view. The first part of this work therefore attempted to set forth the principles of Islam as Muslims uphold them, and their feelings about various issues. Sharing what is best in their own lives means for Christians sharing the gospel. But for the gospel to reach Muslims there is a chasm to be bridged. The second part of our volume discusses those bridges: deep friendship, the spirit of restitution, and some learning from the past. Having come closer to Muslims how then may Christian friends communicate the gospel to them in the light of their views and emotions. The third part takes up that practical task in terms of approach, connection, and methods. It concludes by considering appropriate Christian service to those in whom the gospel has produced its fruits.

Lurking behind all that has been said is the question of possibility. To deal with it we have to look at the future in the light of the present, and then the present in the light of the future. The future is problematic. The present is startling in its invitation to the possible.

The Future in the Light of the Present

There are three present trends in Islam that do not support a rosy assessment for the mid-future sharing of the gospel with Muslims.

The first is the process of secularization that is well under way in the Muslim world. No Christian can or should take pleasure in it. No one should imagine that the development somehow benefits the gospel. Committed Christians who are having trouble with the re-evangelization of secularized people in the Christian West know how difficult a task that is. What would make anyone think that it might be different with secularized Muslims? Christians who have failed to stem the tide of secularism and materialism can empathize with Muslims who must contend with these two demonic powers of our age.

The second trend is the stylizing of Islamic faith into a single purist format. It may be called the formating rather than the forming of Islam. This effort to inculcate a common pattern of understanding and obedience is sometimes called fundamentalism, as we have seen. It attempts to homogenize Muslim opinion and thereby threatens the balance and internal tolerance that Muslims have generally been able to maintain. There is great dedication involved in the endeavor to stylize Muslim allegiance, and it is likely to influence an increasingly large number of ordinary believers. This in turn will certainly harden resistance to alternative messages of any kind, including the message of the gospel.

The third trend is the increase of radicalism in behavior, including its extremist and terrorist forms. Various events in the world have conspired to open the door to violent developments of all kinds, some of them from within Islam. In Islamic history Muslims have had to contend with periodic outbreaks of extremist behavior. Soon after the founder of Islam died, the puritan and militant Kharidjite movement in Arabia promulgated a judgmental and deadly attitude toward fellow believers, whom they considered erring, and had to be quelled. In the middle ages people in the area breathed a great sigh of relief when the fortress of Alamut in Iran was finally overcome by the Mongols. It was the home of a group of self-sacrificing religious extremists from whom the English word assassin is derived. As for state terrorism, Timur of Samarkand (d.1405) exceeded contemporary tyrants in his Hitler-like behavior. He was simply, as one Muslim historian puts it, "murderous in action." Islam has now entered another period in which it must contend with radical behavior. Because violence is more easily aroused than subdued, and because the breeding grounds for extremism are being enlarged rather than controlled, Muslim life in the years ahead will experience disruption as peace-loving Muslims struggle to deal with the problem.

The factors cited above imply that the mid-future communication of the gospel among Muslims is likely to become more demanding than less difficult. They tend to offset the promising factors associated with modern education and the movement of peoples. This pushes us to consider the present. There is a real pressure for addressing the evangel-sharing task among Muslims now.

The Present in the Light of the Future

The probabilities of the future suggest, nay rather compel, a concerted effort by Christian friends to share with Muslims the gift of salvation in the present hour. Never did this word of the Lord seem more relevant: "I must work the works of Him that sent me while it is day; the night is coming when no one can work" (Jn.9:4). Someone may suggest that the night is already here, and that the present is no more promising than the future. Where are the Muslims who are prepared to give the gospel a glad hearing? To the discerning eye, however, they are almost everywhere. The various movements in the Muslim world today, including both the gentle and the upsetting ones, have combined to give birth to a kind of fullness of opportunity. That can be easily over-stated. Yet it is also clear that more Muslims today are responding to Christ and His message than ever before in history. If there is a problem in the present, it is not so much that of reluctant Muslims than that of the Christian mind.

One of the most interesting and anomalous phenomena in the history of missions is how Christians have tended to neglect if not to avoid the Islamic dimension of their concern and calling. This has left a large portion of humanity outside the sphere of those who have been touched by the gospel. What are the reasons for this astonishing situation? One cited is that the relation between Muslims and Christians is so distorted by antipathy, and the gap between them so wide, that the ordinary physical opportunities for meeting are not there. Christians, it is argued, cannot get near to Muslims. Another reason often put forward is that Muslims have taken such a strong position on certain issues that they have no interest in the ideas of the gospel. Christians, it is argued, cannot communicate with Muslims even if they get near to them. A third reason, which may be deduced, is that there is no mutual desire for friendship, so the basis for real communication is absent. Christians, it is argued, should stick to that which is in their range. These and other arguments, heaped up and running over, are cumulatively responsible for the development of a Christian *habitus*, an attitudinal mind-set that inhibits reaching out to Muslims.

It does not take long for this attitude, where it exists, to become further fixated in the myth that evangel-sharing among Muslims is not possible. Myths need only repetition until they become virtual dogma. We have given an overview of some of the great Christian efforts to engage with Muslims in a normal way. Yet that has been the exception. In general the church has for so long been saying that evangel-sharing among Muslims cannot practically be done that it has become the victim of its own rhetoric and has produced a self-fulfilling prophecy. What is really ordinary and doable has been turned into what is extraordinary and undoable. For those who know the reality this reversal of facts is perverse and "unreal." The problem of the present, then, is not the lack of Muslims who will give a respectful hearing to the story of Isa Masih. What needs to be dealt with is the habit of thought that fails to see the importance of that fact and turns to other tasks. The relatively favorable conditions of the present time are a call for fresh Christian sign-reading. There are many things that can be done now to engage Muslims with the glad tidings of great joy. The church that tarries in Jerusalem is not one that has been clothed with power from on high" (Lu.24:49). It rather goes forth, and even when conditions are not perfect, it takes the gospel to all.

The Possibility of the Impossibilities

Samuel Zwemer once wrote a fine tract entitled "The Glory of the Impossible." He chose the title for good reason. We may also, and now is the time to do so, speak of *possibility*. For an illustration we go to the history of Muslim thought. Al-Ghazālī (1058-1111) had written a sharp critique of some Muslim scholars entitling it "The Incoherence of the Philosophers" (*tahāfut al-falāsifa*), Ibn Rushd (1126-1198), otherwise known as Averroes, later wrote a firm rebuttal, heading it "The Incoherence of the Incoherencies" (*tahāfut al-tahāfut*). Thus the two, arguably the greatest, thinkers of Islam, theologian and philosopher, described their concerns through the medium of pungent titles. With a bow to the two masters we will derive an analogy. The church has unwittingly authored a myth, "The Impossibility of the Muslims." The Spirit of God, however, is prepared to inspire a new book of acts entitled "The Possibility of the Impossibilities." It will be written in the here and now, and its writers will be the Christian friends of Muslims who will say, colloquially, "Let's just go and do it."

Friends of Muslims begin with prayer. This volume dealt with deep friendship and knowledge but we end, as we must begin, with prayer. The prayer needed most is not "grant us courage for the facing of this hour," although that too is a necessary petition. Rather it is "Lord, move us to consider Your desire." Jesus sets the prisoners free. Through His Spirit He liberates people from cultivated mind-sets as He does from all captivities. He does so through the power of simple words that resonate in our depths. What are those words?

—remind	"The Helper..will remind you of all that I have said to you" (Jn.14:26). Let the people of God remember what God has done and what God wants done.
—be a friend	"You are my friends if you do what I command you" (Jn.15:14). Jesus has made known His will, and has appointed us to bear fruit.
—send	"Even as the Father sent me, so send I you" (Jn.20:21). Let there be reflection on the model response of Jesus to His Father, and His inclusive love.
—be among	"I am among you as one who serves (Lu.22:27). Let there be vocations of presence and servanthood.
—do likewise	"Which...was a neighbor?" "The one who showed him mercy." "Go and do thou likewise" (Lu.10:36-37). Let there be a vocation of merciful activity related to Muslim needs.
—tell	"Go home to your friends, and tell them how much the Lord has done for you" (Mk.5:19). Let there be a communication of the saving deeds of the Merciful Mercifier.
—fear not	"I tell you, my friends, do not fear" (Lu.12:4). We tremble, but what we tremble at is the greater love of the One Who remembers the sparrows and cares for them.
— have faith	"...And nothing will be impossible for you" (Mt.17:19-20). It is the Lord God Almighty, Father Son and Spirit, Who is the Possibility of the impossibilities for those who are sent.

The simple act of placing the word "Muslim" in juxtaposition with these words of the Savior liberates us and empowers us. It brings us into association with God's desire. The ultimate truth is not that Christians are sent to Muslims to do the impossible or even to achieve the possible, but rather to align themselves with the saving will of God and to commit themselves to the well-being of those whom God loves. What Christians as friends desire for Muslims is nothing more or less than that which they desire for themselves — that they may live in and leave this world in the full awareness of the deep friendship of God.

Appendix A

Mission and Terrorism

(After September 11, 2001, the writer gave the following response to three questions put to the Lutheran World Federation by the Church Information Office of the Lutheran Church in Finland, recognizing as he did so that a more elaborate response is needed.)

Question: After the terrorist attacks in the USA, the world has certainly changed and will change. What does this mean to the mission of the church in general and among Muslim and Islamic countries in particular?

Answer: The mission among Muslims has been in a condition that might be described as a narrowing rut. It is a rut because the engagement has proceeded along more or less predictable lines for one-and-a-half centuries, dictated by the past as though everything has been tried and the creative muse is silent. The rut is narrowing because churches and missions are less and less frequently addressing the task of mission in relation to Muslims. The shock of the reprehensible terrorism and the aftershocks of the response have produced a tumult. The tumult, however, should not be viewed as the end, except perhaps the end of some old patterns, but rather as the possible beginning of something new. The shaking of conceptions and relationships that is upon us may not constitute a fullness of time in the sense of Galatians 4:4, but it would be unimaginative not to see it as a fullness of opportunity. There are new things to discuss.

Question: To what extent can the Christian mission be seen as a cause or as a contributing factor to the extremist Islamic phenomenon?

Answer: Anytime the Christian mission engages in uneducated and unethical forms of mission they have a negative impact. This is especially true in relation to Muslims, many of whom already have a distorted attitude toward Christians and their activities. Some Muslims believe that most Christian deeds of mercy are merely tricks. Are there perhaps aspects of Christian ministry that come under legitimate judgment? Whether that is true or not, it is certainly correct to say that some people continue to work in ways that contribute to the atmosphere of dislike and suspicion. Nevertheless, I do not see a direct causal line from mission activities—whether legitimate and inevitably involved in the *skandalon* of the Gospel or whether they be unhealthy and merely scandalous—to the present crisis. The crisis of our times is focused on political aspects, both the internal critiques of Muslims levied at certain of their governments and philosophies and the external disagreements between nations that are focused on alleged imperialisms.

Question: What can we as churches and as Christian individuals do in the present situation?

Answer: What individuals can do is to engage with Muslims in deep friendship, which has many practical ramifications. As churches and missions, we have a duty to remember our calling to service, reconciliation and peace-making, evangelism, and dialogue. We have a task to educate our people in relation to Islam, to teach the forgiveness of sins, and to reach out in love to Muslims in word and deed as the bearers of the Gospel. Whether as individuals or churches, we have a renewed vocation to reflect the spirit of Christ. Specifically, Christian leaders must find ways to dialogue with Muslim leaders, and church and mission boards must address their task among Muslims with the depth that our times, condition, and situation deserves. We can no longer ignore either Islam or Muslims.

Appendix B

Potential Agenda Topics for Future Dialogue

(On behalf of the dialogue program of the Lutheran World Federation a team composed of Willem Bijlefeld, Jan Henningsson, Roland Miller, Hance Mwakabana, Olaf Schumann, Sigvard von Sicard, and David Windibiziri drew up the following list of potential agenda topics. They are drawn from Miller and Mwakabana, eds., Christian-Muslim-Dialogue, Theological and Practical Issues (Geneva: Lutheran World Federation, 1998), 390–91, and are cited in full with the publisher's permission).

From the Perspective of Islamic Issues

- The concept of other religious communities
- Prayer, *ibādat* or worship
- *hidāyat* or guidance
- surrender to God
- *imān*, faith, inner disposition
- purification
- sin, evil; goodness, piety
- suffering
- history and revelation
- meaningfulness of history
- God's plan for now
- salvation; prosperity; success
- meaning of prophethood; sense of community, umma, family
- responsibility for the structures of society
- loss of sense of God in Western society; secularism
- citizenship in national contexts
- religious faith and public life
- education, science

- ecology
- human rights
- mixed marriages
- the West and "westification"

From the Perspective of Christian Theology
- Greatness of divine mercy; God in Christ; forgiveness of sins
- creation, God's covenant
- God's initiative
- law and gospel
- justification by faith
- the function of prophecy
- servanthood
- the priesthood of all believers
- the nature of success, sacrifice
- two-kingdom theory, attaining a just society
- social involvement; religion and politics
- women/children
- a theology of dialogue
- a basis for Christian cooperation with Muslims
- Christian responses to Islamic issues noted above

From the Perspective of Immediate and Common Relevance
- position of women
- spirituality
- neighborology
- mutuality; friendship; creating good relations at local/international levels
- family
- ethical values/fight against corruption and exploitation
- materialism/consumerism/secularization
- human rights/children's rights
- tolerance; religious freedom
- caricature, distortion, inflammatory language
- role and abuse of religion in situations of conflict; communalism
- manipulation of religion; violence

- the phenomenon behind the term "fundamentalism"
- social justice issues; economic issues
- contemporary forms of slavery; migrant workers
- Christian-Muslim relations; cooperation; the common good

Bibliography

Books Cited in This Work

Abdalati, Hammudah. *Islam in Focus*. Aligarh: Crescent, 1973.

Abd-ul-Masih. *Islam and Christianity: Ninety Questions and Answers*. Ibadan: Daystar, n.d.

Addison, J. T. *The Christian Approach to Islam*. New York: Columbia, 1942.

Ahmed, Akbar S. *Postmodernism and Islam*. London: Routledge, 1992.

Ahmed Moulavi, C. N. *Religion of Islam*. Calicut: Azad's Book Stall, 1979.

Akhtar, Shabbir. *A Faith for All Seasons*. Chicago: Ivan R. Dee, 1990.

Alavi, K. K. *In Search of Assurance*. Manjeri: Markaz-ul Bisharah, 1985.

Al-Ghazali, Abu Hamid M. *The Alchemy of Happiness*. Translated by Claud Field. London: Octagon, 1980.

———. *The Book of Knowledge*. Translated by Nabih Faris. Lahore: Sh. Muhammad Ashraf, 1974.

———. *On the Duties of Brotherhood*. Translated by Muhtar Holland. Woodstock, N.Y.: Overlook Press, 1976.

Al-Halveli, Sheikh al-Jerrahi. *The Most Beautiful Names*. Putney, Vt.: Threshold Books, 1985.

Al-Hibri, Azizah, ed. *Women Studies International Forum: Women and Islam*. London: Pergamom Press, 1982.

Anderson, G. H., Coote, R. T., Horner, N. A., and Phillips, J. M., eds. *Mission Legacies*. Maryknoll: Orbis, 1988.

Anderson, G. H., and Stransky, T. F., eds. *Evangelization: Mission Trends 2*. New York: Paulist Press, 1972.

Andrae, Tor. *In the Garden of the Myrtles*. Translated by B. Sharpe. Albany: SUNY, 1987.

———. *Mohammed, the Man and His Faith*. Translated by T. Menzel. London: George Allen & Unwin, 1936.

Arberry, A. J., ed. *Religion in the Middle East*. 2 vols. Cambridge: Cambridge University Press, 1969.

———. *Sufism*. London: George Allen & Unwin, 1950.

Arkoun, Mohammed. *Rethinking Islam*. Translated and edited by R. D. Lee. Oxford: Westview Press, 1994.

Arnold, T., and Guillaume, A., eds. *The Legacy of Islam*. London: Oxford University Press, 1931. First edition.

'Ata ur-Rahim. *Jesus, a Prophet of Islam*. New Delhi: Adam Books, 1983.

Aulen, Gustav. *Christus Victor*. Translated by A. G. Hiebert. London: SPCK, 1950.

Ayoub, Mahmoud. *The Qur'ān and Its Interpreters*. Volume 1. Albany: SUNY, 1984.

Azad, Abul Kalam. *The Tarjuman al-Qur'ān*. 2 vols. Translated by Syed Abdul Latif. Bombay: Asia Publishing House, 1962, 1967.

Baillie, John. *A Diary of Readings*. London: Oxford University Press, 1955.

Baljon, J. S. *Modern Muslim Koran Interpretation*. Leiden: Brill, 1961.

Barth, Karl. *Dogmatics in Outline*. Translated by G. W. Thomson. London: SCM Press, 1960.

Bell, Richard. *The Origin of Islam in the Christian Environment*. London: Macmillan, 1926.

Bentley-Taylor, David. *Java Saga: The Weathercock's Reward*. London: OMF Books, 1975.

Binder, Leonard. *Islamic Liberalism*. Chicago: University of Chicago Press, 1988.

Boulares, Habib. *Islam, the Fear and the Hope*. London: Zed Books, 1990.

Brandon, S. G., ed. *The Saviour God*. Westport, Conn.: Grenwood Press Publishers, 1963.

Brauer, J. K., ed. *A Rainbow of Saris*. St. Louis: LWML, 1996.

Browne, Laurence E. *The Eclipse of Christianity in Asia: From the Time of Muhammad till the Fourteenth Century*. New York: Howard Fertig, 1967.

Brunner, Emil. *The Christian Doctrine of God*. Translated by Olive Wyon. London: Lutterworth, 1949.

Calverley, Edwin E. Islam: *An Introduction*. Cairo: American University, 1958.

Chanda, K. C., trans. and ed. *Masterpieces of Urdu Ghazal*. New Delhi: Sterling, 1992.

Chapman, Colin. *Cross and Crescent: Responding to the Challenge of Islam*. Leicester: InterVaristy, 1995.

Chatterji, Margaret. *Gandhi's Religious Thought*. Notre Dame: University of Notre Dame Press, 1983.

Christian *Witness among Muslims*. Bartlesville, Okla.: Living Sacrifice Book, 1994.

Christensen, Jens. *The Practical Approach to Muslims: A Correspondence Course.* Lecture 2. Lahore: Committee on Islamics, West Pakistan Christian Council, 1952–53.

Crackness, Kenneth, trans. *Christians and Muslims Talking Together.* London: British Council of Churches, 1984.

Cragg, Kenneth. *The Arab Christian.* Louisville: Westminster, 1991.

———. *Call of the Minaret.* New York: Oxford, 1985. Second revised edition.

———. *Christianity in World Perspective.* London: Lutterworth Press, 1968.

———. *The Event of the Qur'ān.* London: George Allen & Unwin, 1971.

———. *Jesus and the Muslim.* London: George Allen & Unwin, 1985.

———. *Operation Reach: The Fifth Series.* Beirut: Near East Christian Council Study Program in Islam, March and April 1962.

———. *Sandals at the Mosque.* London: SCM Press, 1953.

Cragg, Kenneth, and Speight, Marston, eds., *Islam from Within.* Belmont, Calif.: Wadsworth, 1980.

Daniel, Norman. *Islam and the West.* Edinburgh: University Press, 1960.

Devers, Dorothy, and N. Gordon Cosby. *Handbook for Churches and Mission Groups.* Washington: The Servant Leadership School and the Servant Leadership Press, n.d.

Donaldson, Dwight M. *Shi'ite Religion.* London: Luzac, 1933..

Donohue, John, and John L. Esposito, eds., *Islam in Transition.* New York: Oxford University Press, 1982.

Dorman, Harry G. *Toward Understanding Islam.* New York: Columbia University Press, 1948.

Durant, Will. *The Age of Faith.* New York: Simon & Schuster, 1950.

Elder, Earl E., trans. *A Commentary on the Creed of Islam: Saʿd al-Dīn al Taftazāni on the Creed of Najm al-Dīn al-Nasafī.* New York: Columbia University Press, 1950.

Eliade, Mircea, and Joseph Kitagawa, eds. *The History of Religions: Essays in Methodology.* Chicago: University of Chicago Press, 1959.

Esmail, A. K., ed. *Muharram.* Bombay: Yousuf N. Lalljee, 1975.

Esposito, John L. The Islamic Threat. New York: Oxford University Press, 1995.

———, ed. *Voices of Resurgent Islam.* New York: Oxford University Press, 1983.

Faruqi, Ismail. *Tawhīd.* Plainfield, Ind.: International Federation of Islamic Students, 1983.

Finlay, M. H. *Face the Facts: Questions and Answers Concerning the Christian Faith.* Bombay: Gospel Literature Service, 1968.

Gabrieli, Francesco. *Arab Historians of the Crusades.* Translated by S. Crociate. Berkeley: University of California Press, 1984.

Gätje,Helmut. *The Qur'ān and Its Exegesis.* Translated and edited by A. T. Welch. Berkeley: University of California Press, 1976.

Gibb, H. A. R. *Modern Trends in Islam.* New York: Octagon Press, 1978.

Goodspeed, Edgar J. *Paul.* Philadelphia: John C. Winston, 1947.

Gotein, S. D. *Jews and Arabs, Their Contacts through the Ages.* New York: Schocken, 1974.

Grau, A. H., ed. *In Quest of an Islamic Humanism: Arabic and Islamic Studies in Memory of al-Nowaihi.* Cairo: The American University of Cairo Press, 1984.

Guidelines for a Dialogue between Muslims and Christians. Roma: Secretariatus Pro Non-Christianis, n.d.

Guillaume, Alfred. *Islam.* Baltimore: Penguin, 1964.

———, trans. *The Life of Muhammad: A Translation of Ibn Ishāq's Sirāt Rasūl Allāh.* Lahore: Oxford University Press, 1967.

Haddad, Yvonne and Wadi Haddad, eds. *Christian-Muslim Encounters.* Gainesville: University Press of Florida, 1995.

Hahn, Ernest. *How to Share Your Faith with Muslims.* Toronto: Fellowship of Faith, 1993.

———. *Jesus in Islam: A Christian View.* Toronto: Fellowship of Faith, n.d.

———. *Understanding Some Muslim Misunderstandings.* Toronto: Fellowship of Faith, n.d.

Haley, Alex. *The Autobiography of Malcom X: As Told to Alex Haley.* New York: Ballentine, 1964.

Harnack, Adolf. *The Mission and Expansion of Christianity.* Translated and edited by James Moffat. New York: Harpers, 1961.

Haykal, Muhammad. *The Life of Muhammad.* Translated by Ismail Faruqi. Plainfield, Ind.: American Trust Publications, 1976.

Hocking, William. *Living Religions and World Faith.* New York: Macmillan, 1940.

Hoefer, Herbert E. *Churchless Christianity.* Pasadena: Wm. Carey Library, 2001.

Hong, Edna. *The Downward Ascent.* Minneapolis: Augsburg, 1979.

Hourani, George. *A History of the Arab Peoples.* Cambridge: Harvard University Press, 1991.

Howe, Reuel. *The Miracle of Dialogue.* New York: Seabury, 1963.

Huntington, Samuel P. *The Clash of Civilizations and the Re-Making of World Order.* New York: Simon & Schuster, 1996.

Hussein, M. Kamal. *City of Wrong.* Translated by Kenneth Cragg. Amsterdam: Djambatan, 1959.

Ibn 'Arabi, Muhyi-d-Dīn. *The Wisdom of the Prophets (Fusus al-hikam).* Translated by Titus Burckhardt and A. Culme-Seymour. Aldsworth: Beshara Publications, 1975.

Ibn Khaldūn. *The Muqaddimah*. Translated by F. Rosenthal, edited by N. J. Dawood. Princeton: Princeton University Press, 1967.

Iqbal, Muhammad. *The Reconstruction of Religious Thought in Islam*. Lahore: Sh. Muhammad Ashraf, 1962.

Izutsu, Toshiko. *Ethico-Religious Concepts in the Qur'ān*. Montreal: McGill University Press, 1966.

Jamali, Mohammed Fadhel. *Letters on Islam*. London: World of Islam Festival Trust, 1978.

Jeffrey, Arthur, ed. *Islam: Muhammad and His Religion*. New York: Liberal Arts Press, 1958.

———. *A Reader on Islam*. 'S-Gravenhage: Mouton, 1962.

Jones, L. Bevan. *The People of the Mosque*. London: Student Christian Movement, 1932.

———. *Christianity Explained to Muslims*. Calcutta: YMCA, 1938.

Kamal, Ahmad. *The Sacred Journey*. New York: Duell, Sloan & Price, 1961.

Kamali, Mohammed Hashim. *The Dignity of Man: The Islamic Perspective*. Selangor: Ilimiah, 1999.

Kateregga, B. D., and D. W. Shenk. *Islam and Christianity: A Muslim and Christian in Dialogue*. Grand Rapids: Eerdmans, 1990.

Katsch, A. I. *Judaism in Islam*. New York: n.p., 1962.

Kelly, J. N. D. *Early Christian Doctrines*. London: Adam & Charles Black, 1958.

Kenyon, Frederick. *Our Bible and the Ancient Manuscripts*. New York: Harper & Bros., 1938.

Khadduri, M. *War and Peace*. Baltimore: Johns Hopkins Press, 1955.

Khan, Salma. *The Fifty Percent*. Dhaka: University Press, 1988.

King, Martin Luther. *Strength to Love*. London: Collins, 1969.

Kitagawa, Joseph M., ed. *The History of Religions: Essays on the Problem of Understanding*. Chicago: University of Chicago Press, 1967.

Klein, F. A. *The Religion of Islam*. London: Curzon, 1906.

Kraemer, Hendrik. *The Christian Message in a Non-Christian World*. Grand Rapids: Kregel, 1956.

Kritzek, James. *Peter the Venerable and Islam*. Princeton: Princeton University Press, 1964.

Latourette, K. S. *A History of Christianity*. 2 vols. New York: Harper & Row, 1975.

Leigh, David. *Authentic Lives, Profound Journeys: The Nash Memorial Lectures*. Regina: Campion College, 2001.

Lewis, Bernard. *The Jews of Islam*. Princeton: Princeton University Press, 1984.

Lietzmann, Hans. *A History of the Early Church*. 2 vols. Translated by B. L. Woolf. Cleveland: World, 1963.

Lings, Martin. *What Is Sufism?* Berkeley: University of California Press, 1977.

Livingstone, Greg. *Planting Churches in Muslim Cities*. Grand Rapids: Baker, 1993.

Lull, Ramon. *Blanquerna*. Translated from the Catalan by E. Alison Peers. London: Jarrolds, 1926.

MacDonald, D. M. *Development of Muslim Theology, Jurisprudence, and Constitutional Theory*. Lahore: Premier Book House, 1964. Reprint of 1903 edition.

Martinson, Paul V., ed. *Mission at the Dawn of the 21st Century*. Minneapolis: Kirk House Publishers, 1999.

Mawdudi, Abul Ala. *The Road to Peace and Salvation*. Lahore: Islamic Publications, 1966. Original lecture 1940.

McAuliffe, Jane D. *Qur'ānic Christians*. Cambridge: Cambridge University Press, 1991.

McCurry, Don, ed. *The Gospel and Islam*. Monrovia, Calif.: MARC, 1979.

McDowell, Josh, and John Gilchrist. *The Islamic Debate*. San Bernardino: Campus Crusade for Christ, 1983.

McGiffert, A. *A History of Christian Thought*. 2 vols. New York: Scribner's, 1932.

Mez, Adam. *The Renaissance of Islam*. Translated by S. Khuda Baksh and D. S. Margoliouth. London: Luzac, 1937.

Miller, Judith. *God Has Ninety-Nine Names*. New York: Simon & Schuster, 1977.

Miller, Roland E. *Mappila Muslims of Kerala: A Study in Islamic Trends*. 2nd revised edition. Madras: Orient Longman, 1992.

———. *Mission Agendas in the New Century*. Minneapolis: Kirk House Publishers, 2000.

———. *Muslim Friends: Their Faith and Feeling, An Introduction to Islam*. St. Louis: Concordia, 1995. Hyderabad: Orient Longman, rev. reprint, 2000.

———, and Mwakabana, Hance, eds. *Christian-Muslim Dialogue: Theological and Practical Issues*. Geneva: Lutheran World Federation, 1998.

Miller, Samuel H. *Prayers for Daily Use*. New York: Harper & Bros., 1957.

Momen, Moojan. *An Introduction to Shī'i Islam*. New Haven: Yale University Press, 1985.

Moulton, Harold K. *The Mission of the Church: Studies in Missionary Words of the New Testament*. London: Epworth, 1959.

Mujeeb, M. *The Indian Muslims*. Longon: George Allen & Unwin, 1967.

Musk, Bill A. *The Unseen Face of Islam*. Crowborough, Sussex: MARC and the Evangelical Missionary Alliance, 1989.

Mutahhari, Ayatulla M. *Fundamentals of Islamic Thought*. Berkeley: Mizan, 1985.

Nasr, Sayyid Hossein. *Islamic Science.* London: World of Islam, 1976.

———, ed. *Islamic Spirituality.* New York: Crossroad, 1987.

Nicholson, R. A. *A Literary History of the Arabs.* Cambridge: Cambridge University Press, 1969.

———. *The Mystics of Islam.* New York: Schocken, 1975.

Nielsen, Jörgen. *Muslims in Western Europe.* Edinburgh: University Press, 1992.

Otten, Henry J. *The Ahmadiyya Doctrine of God.* Henry Martyn Institute of Islamic Studies.

Otto, Rudolf. *The Idea of the Holy.* Translated by J. Harvey. London: Oxford, 1950.

Padwick, Constance. *Henry Martyn, Confessor of the Faith.* New York: George H. Dolan, 1928.

———. *Lilias Trotter of Algiers.* Rushden: Stanley L. Hunt, n.d.

———. *The Master of the Impossible.* London: SPCK, 1937.

———. *Muslim Devotions.* London: SPCK, 1961.

———. *Temple Gairdner of Cairo.* London: SPCK, 1929.

Parrinder, Geoffrey. *Jesus in the Qur'ān.* London: Faber & Faber, 1965.

Parshall, Phil. *Beyond the Mosque: Christians within Muslim Community.* Grand Rapids: Baker, 1985.

———. *New Paths in Muslim Evangelism.* Grand Rapids: Baker, 1980.

Peers E. Alison. *Fool of Love.* London: SCM, 1946.

———. *Ramon Lull: A Biography.* London: SPCK, 1929.

Peters, F. E. *A Reader on Classical Islam.* Princeton: Princeton University Press, 1994.

Pelikan, Jaroslav. *Christian Doctrine and Modern Culture (since 1700).* Chicago: University of Chicago Press, 1989.

———. *The Emergence of the Catholic Tradition (100–600).* Chicago: University of Chicago Press, 1971.

Pfander, Karl G. *Mizān-ul-haqq.* Translated and revised by W. St. Clair-Tisdall. London: Light of Life, 1980. First edition 1989.

Poston, Larry. *Islamic Da'wah in the West.* New York: Oxford University Press, 1992.

Quassem, Muhammad Abul. *Salvation of the Soul and Islamic Devotion.* London: Kegan Paul International, 1983.

Qutb, Sayyid. *The Religion of Islam.* Kuwait: International Federation of Student Organizations, n.d.

Rahbar, Daud. *God of Justice.* Leiden: Brill, 1960.

———. *Memories and Meanings.* Published by the author, n.d.

Rahman, Fazlur. *Islam.* New York: Doubleday, 1968.

———. *Major Themes of the Qur'ān.* Minneapolis: Bibliotheca Islamica, 1980.

Rauf, Muhammad. Islam, *Creed and Worship.* Washington: Islamic Center, 1975.

Renard, John. *Islam and the Heroic Image: Themes in Literature and the Visual Arts.* Columbia: University of South Carolina Press, 1993.

Rice, W. A. *Crusaders of the Twentieth Century, or, The Christian Missionary and the Muslim.* Lond: CMS, 1910.

Rippin, A., and J. Knappert, eds. *Textual Sources for the Study of Islam.* Chicago: University of Chicago Press, 1986.

Rodinson, Maxime. *Mohammed.* Translated by Anne Carter. London: Penguin, 1961.

Rosenthal, E. I. J. *Islam in the Modern National State.* Cambridge: Cambridge University Press, 1965.

Runciman, Steven. *A History of the Crusades.* 3 vols. Cambridge: Cambridge University Press, 1987.

Rūmī, Jalāl al-Dīn. *The Masnavi.* Translated and abridged by E. H. Whinfield. New York: Dutton, 1975.

Sadiq, Muhammad. *A History of Urdu Literature.* London: Oxford University Press, 1964.

Sahas, Daniel J. *John of Damascus on Islam.* London: Brill, 1978.

Sargent, John, ed. *Memoirs of Henry Martyn.* Hartford: G. Goodwin & Sons, 1882.

Savory, R. M., ed. *Islamic Civilization.* Cambridge: Cambridge University Press, 1976.

———, and D. A. Agius. *Logos Islamikos.* Toronto: Pontifical Institute of Medieval Studies, 1984.

Schacht, J., and C. Bosworth, eds. *The Legacy of Islam.* 2nd edition. London: Oxford University Press, 1974.

Schimmel, Annemarie. *As Through a Veil.* New York: Columbia, 1982.

———. *Calligraphy and Islamic Culture.* New York: New York University Press, 1984.

———. *Mystical Dimensions of Islam.* Chapel Hill: University of North Carolina Press, 1982.

Schroeder, Eric. *Muhammad's People.* Portland, Maine: Bond Wheelright, 1955.

Schumann, Olaf H. *Der Christus der Muslime.* Gütersloh: Gütersloher Verlaugshaus Gerd Mohn, 1975.

Sells, Michael A., trans. *Early Islamic Mysticism.* New York: Paulist Press, 1966.

Shariati, Ali. *On the Sociologty of Islam.* Translated by H. Algar. Berkeley: Mizan Press, 1979.

Sharpe, Eric, and John Hinnells. *Man and His Salvation.* Manchester: Rowan & Littlefield, 1973.

Smith, George. *Henry Martyn, Saint and Scholar.* New York: Revell, 1892.

Smith, Jane, and Yvonne Haddad. *The Islamic Understanding of Death and Resurrection.* Albany: SUNY, 1981.

———. *Rabi'a the Mystic and Her Fellow-Saints in Islam.* Cambridge: Cambridge University Press, 1984. Reprint of 1928 edition.

Smith, Wilfred C. *Islam in Modern History.* Princeton: Princeton University Press, 1957.

Southern, R. W. *Western Views of Islam.* Cambridge: Harvard University Press, 1962.

Stanton, H. W. Weitbrecht. *The Teaching of the Qurʾān.* London: SPCK, 1919.

Sundkler, Bergt. *The World of Mission.* Grand Rapids: Eerdmans, 1965.

Swanson, Mark. *Folly to the Hunafāʾ: The Cross of Christ in Arabic Christian-Muslim Controversy in the Eighth and Ninth Centuries A.D.* Cairo: Pontificium Institutum Studiorum Arabicorum et Islamologiae, 1995.

Sweetman, J. W. *The Bible and Islam.* London: British and Foreign Bible Society, n.d.

———. *Islam and Christian Theology. Part One, Vol. II.* London: Lutterworth, 1947.

Swidler, Leonard, ed. *Muslims in Dialogue: The Evolution of Dialogue.* Lewiston: Edwin Mellen Press, 1992.

Syed Ahmed Khan Bahador. *Life of Muhammad.* Lahore: Premier Book House, 1968. Reprint of 1870 edition.

Tabatabaʾi, A. S. M. *Shiʿite Islam.* Translated by S. H. Nasr. Albany: SUNY, 1975.

Taylor, John B., ed. *Christians Meeting Muslims.* Geneva: World Council of Churches, 1977.

Tisdall, St. Clair. *A Manual of the Leading Muhammadan Objections to Christianity.* London: SPCK, 1915.

Thomas, P. *Christians and Christianity in India.* London: George Allen & Unwin, 1954.

Trimingham, J. Spencer. *Christianity among the Arabs in Pre-Islamic Times.* London: Longman, 1979.

Tritton, A. S. *Muslim Theology.* London: Luzac, 1947.

Troll, Christian W. *Sayyid Ahmad Khan.* New Delhi: Vikas, 1978.

Ullah, Najeeb, ed. *Islamic Literature.* New York: Washington Square Press, 1963.

Van der Leeuw, Gerardus. *Religion in Essence and Manifestation.* 2 vols. Translated by J. E. Turner. Gloucester, Mass.: Peter Smith, 1967.

Vander Werff, Lyle L. *Christian Mission to Muslims..* Pasadena: William Carey Library, 1977.

Waddy, Charis. *The Muslim Mind.* London: Longman, 1976.

———. *Women in Muslim History.* London: Longman, 1980.

Wensinck, A. J. *Muslim Creed.* London: Frank Cass, 1965.

Westcott, G. H. *Kabir and the Kabir Panth.* Cawnpore: Christ Church Mission Press, 1907.

Whale, J. S. *Christian Doctrine.* Cambridge: Cambridge University Press, 1941.

Whaling, Frank, ed. *The World's Religious Traditions.* Edinburgh: T&T Clark, 1984.

Williams, John A., trans. *Themes of Islamic Civilization.* Los Angeles: University of California Press, 1971.

Wilson, J. Christy. *The Flaming Prophet: The Story of Samuel Zwemer.* New York: Friendship Press, 1970.

———. *The Apostle of Islam.* Grand Rapids: Baker, 1952.

With One Voice. Minneapolis: Augsburg, 1995.

Woodberry, Dudley, ed. *Muslims and Christians on the Emmaus Road.* Monrovia, Calif.: MARC, 1990.

Zacharia, Rafiq. *The Struggle within Islam: The Conflict between Religion and Politics.* London: Penguin, 1989.

Zwemer, Samuel M. *The Cross above the Crescent.* Grand Rapids: Zondervan, 1941.

———. *Prayer.* New York: American Tract Society, 1951.

Book Chapters, Journal Articles, and Theses Cited in This Work

Adams, Charles. "Islam and Christianity: The Opposition of the Similarities." In R. M. Savory and D. A. Agius, eds., *Logos Islamikos,* 1984.

———. "Mawdudi and the Islamic State," in John Esposito, ed., *Voices of Resurgent Islam,* 1983.

Amjad-Ali, Charles. "Political and Social Conditions in Pakistan," in Roland E. Miller and H. Mwakabana, eds., *Christian-Muslim Dialogue,* 1998.

Al-Na'im, Abdullahi Ahmed. "Religious Freedom in Egypt: Under the Shadow of the Islamic *Dhimma* System," in Leonard Swidler, ed., *Muslims in Dialogue,* 1992.

Ayoub, Mahmoud. "Religious Freedom and the Law of Apostasy in Islam." *Islamo-christiana* Vol. 20, 1994.

Azizah al-Hibri. "A Study of Islamic herstory: Or How Did We Ever Get into This Mess." *Women's International Forum* Vol. 5, No. 2, 1982.

Bassetti-Sani, Fr. G. "Muhammad and St. Francis." *Muslim World* Vol. 46, No. 4, October 1956.

Bennet, Clinton. "The Legacy of Karl Gottlieb Pfander." *International Bulletin of Missionary Research* Vol. 20, No. 2, April 1996.

———. "Lewis Bevan Jones, 1880–1960, Striving to Touch Muslim Hearts," in G. H. Anderson et al., eds. *Mission Legacies,* 1988.

Birkland, Carol J. "An Evangelical Theology of Service in an Interdependent and Suffering World," in Paul V. Martinson, ed., *Mission at the Dawn of the 21st Century,* 1999.

Bijlefeld, Willem. "Theology of Religions: A Review of Developments, Trends, and Issues," in Roland E. Miller and H. Mwakabana, eds., *Christian-Muslim Dialogue,* 1998.

———. "Christian-Muslim Relations: A Burdernsome Past, A Challenging Future." *Word & World* Vol. 16, No. 2, 1996.

Brewster, Daniel R. "Dialogue: Relevancy to Evangelism," in Don McCurry, ed. *The Gospel and Islam,* 1979.

Brohi, A. K. "The Spiritual Significance of the Qur'ān," in Seyyid Hossein Nasr, ed., *Islamic Spirituality,* 1987.

de Bruyn, Eric. "Ramon Lull's Methods of Engagement with Muslims, with Special Reference to His Art." Master's thesis, Luther Seminary, St. Paul, Minn. 1999.

Burton, J. "Naskh," *Encyclopedia of Islam.* 2d ed, Vol. 7.

Cahen, Claud. "Dhimma," *Encyclopedia of Islam.* 2d ed, Vol. 2.

Calverley, Edwin. "Samuel Marinus Zwemer," *Muslim World.* Vol. 42, No. 3, July 1952.

Campbell, Douglas. "The Touregs or Veiled Men of the Sahara," in *Muslim World* Vol. 27, No. 3, July 1928.

Chekowski, P. "Ta'ziya." *Encyclopedia of Islam.* 2d ed, Vol. 10.

Chiragh, Ali. "Islam and Change," in J. Donohue and J. Esposito, eds., *Islam in Transition,* 1982.

Cox, Douglas, S. "Moral Dimensions of Representational Art in Islam: From Visual Arts to Theatre, with Implications for Christian Witness." Master's thesis, Luther Seminary, St. Paul, Minn. 1997.

Cragg, Kenneth. "Constance E. Padwick, 1886–1968," in *Muslim World* Vol. 59, No. 1, January 1969.

———. "The Riddle of Man and the Silence of God: A Christian Perspective of Muslim Response," in *International Bulletin of Missionary Research* Vol. 17, No. 4, October 1963.

Denny, Frederick M. "The Problem of Salvation in the Quran: Key Terms and Concepts," in A. H. Grau, ed., *In Quest of an Islamic Humanism,* 1984.

Downing, Ben. "Inshallah," *The Atlantic Monthly* Vol. 285, No. 3, March 2000. p 62.

D'Souza, Andreas, and Diane D'Souza. "Reconciliation: A New Paradigm for Missions," *Word and World* Vol. 16, No. 2, 1996.

Duri, A. A. "Baghdad," *Encyclopedia of Islam.* 2d ed, Vol. 1.

Editors. "Christ's Ambassador to the Muslims (S. M. Zwemer)," *Muslim World* Vol. 42, No. 1, January 1952.

Engelbrecht, Luther. "Christian Remembering of the Muslim in Prayer and Worship," *Word and World* Vol. 16, No. 2, 1996.

———, E. Hahn, M. L. Kretzmann, R. E. Miller. "Son of God," *Bulletin* Vol. 51, No. 2, July-October 1962.

Faruqi, Ismail R. "On the Nature of Islamic Da'wah," in Larry Poston, *Islamic Da'wah in the West,* 1992.

Guthrie, A. "The Significance of Abraham," *Muslim World* Vol. 45, No. 2, April 1955.

Gardet, Louis. "Īmān," *Encyclopedia of Islam.* 2d ed, Vol. 3.

Goichon, A. M. "Hikma," *Encyclopedia of Islam.* 2d ed, Vol. 3.

Haddad, Yvonne. "Sayyid Qutb: Idealogue of Muslim Revival," in J. Esposito, ed., *Voices of Resurgent Islam,* 1983.

Hahn, Ernest. "Literary and Audio-Visual Resources for Christian Sharing with Muslims," *Word & World* Vol. 16, No. 2, 1996.

Hiebert, Paul. "Power Encounter in Folk Islam," in D. Woodberry, ed., *Muslims and Christians on the Emmaus Road,* 1990.

Henrich, Sara, and James L. Boyce, trans. and ed. "Martin Luther—Translations of Two Prefaces on Islam," *Word & World* Vol. 16, No. 2, 1996.

Howe, Sonia. "Charles de Foucauld, Explorer," *Muslim World* Vol. 17, No. 2, April 1928.

Jafri, Syed Husain M. "Twelve-Imam Shī'ism," in S. H. Nasr, ed., *Islamic Spirituality,* 1987.

Jones, L. Bevan. "A Love That Persists," *Muslim World* Vol. 42, No. 1, January 1953.

Kurtz, Michael. "Listening to Hagar and Ishmael—Gen. 21:8–21." Lutheran Campus Center, University of British Columbia, 1966.

Löffler, Paul. "The Biblical Concept of Conversion," in G. H. Anderson and T. Stransky, eds., *Evangelization: Mission Trends 2,* 1975.

Lucas, M. A. Hélie. "The Preferential Symbol for Islamic Identity," in *Women Living under Muslim Laws. Dossier 11/12/13.* Grabels, France: International Solidarity Network of Women Living under Muslim Laws, 1991.

Mackintosh, Robert. "Christians," *Encyclopedia of Religion and Ethics,* Vol. III.

Manzoor, Parvez. "Standing Up to Intellectual Conversion," *Inquiry* Vol. 1, No. 6, November 1984.

Martinson, Paul. "Social Capital and the New Missionary Pragmatics," *Word & World* Vol. 18, No. 2, 1988.

———. "Dialogue and Evangelism in Relation to Islam," *Word & World* Vol. 16, No. 2, 1996.

Miller, Roland E. "Conversion or Conversation?" *Word & World* Vol. 22, No. 3, 2002.

———. "The Dynamics of Religious Co-existence in Kerala: Muslims, Christians and Hindus," in Y. Y. Haddad and W. Z. Haddad, eds., *Christian-Muslim Encounters,* 1995.

———. "The Muslim Doctrine of Salvation," *The Bulletin* Henry Martyn Institute, Hyderabad (July-September 1960). Reprinted in January-December, 1982.

Otten, Henry J. "Sowing the Seed," *The Minaret* Vol. 11, No. 1, September 1955.

Naim, C. M. "Getting Real about Christian-Muslim Dialogue," *Word & World,* Vol 16, No. 2, 1996.

Nicholson, Reynold A. "Mysticism," in T. Arnold and A. Guillaume, eds., *The Legacy of Islam,* 1931.

Nolen, Stephanie. "Little House on the Prairie," *The Globe and Mail* (20 March 2000): R5.

Padwick, Constance. "Al-Ghazali and Arabic Versions of the Gospels," *Muslim World* Vol. 29, No. 2, April 1939.

———. "Literature in the Muslim World," *Muslim World* Vol. 36, No. 4, October 1946.

———. "The Nebi ʿĪsā and the Skull (translation)," *Muslim World* Vol. 20, No. 1, January 1930.

Paret, Rudi. "Ismāʿīl," *Encyclopedia of Islam.* 2d ed, Vol. 4.

Parshall, Phil. "Lessons Learned in Contextualization," in D. Woodberry, ed., *Muslims and Christians on the Emmaus Road,* 1990.

Prasse, K. G. "Tawārik," *Encyclopedia of Islam.* 2d ed, Vol. 10.

Reid, J. S. "Sin (Muslim)," *Encyclopedia of Religion and Ethics.* Vol. X.

Robson, James. "Aspects of the Quranic Doctrine of Salvation," in E Sharpe and J. Hinnells, eds., *Man and His Salvation,* 1973.

Rosenthal, Franz. "Literature," in J. Schacht and C. Bosworth, eds., *The Legacy of Islam,* 1974.

Sadler, R. "Islamic Art: Variations on Themes of Arabesque," in R. M. Savory, ed., *Islamic Civilization,* 1976.

Schimmel, Annemarie. "Shafāʿa," *Encyclopedia of Islam.* 2d ed, Vol. 9.

———. "A 'Sincere Muhammadan's' Way to Salvation," in E. Sharpe and J. Hinnells, eds., *Man and His Salvation,* 1973.

Sell, Edward. "Salvation (Muslim)," *Encyclopedia of Religion and Ethics*. Vol. X.

Shahabuddin, Syed. "Editorial," *Muslim India* Vol. 11, No. 129, September 1993.

Shelley, Michael. "The Life and Thought of W. H. T. Gaurdner, 1873–1928: A Critical Evaluation of a Scholar Missionary to Islam." Doctoral dissertation, University of Birmingham, United Kingdom, 1987.

Shenk, David. "Conversations on the Way," in D. Woodberry, ed., *Muslims and Christians on the Emmaus Road,* 1990.

Simon, Gottfried. "Luther's Attitude toward Islam," *Muslim World* Vol. 21, No. 3, 1921.

Sinclair, Lisa M. "The Legacy of Isabella Lilias Trotter," *International Bulletin of Missionary Research* Vol. 26, No. 1, January 2002.

Smith, Jane I., and Yvonne Y. Haddad. "Eve: Islamic Image of Woman," in Azizah al-Hibri, ed., *Women's International Forum,* 1982.

Smith, Wilfred Cantwell. "Comparative Religion: Whither and Why?", in Mircea Eliade and J. M. Kitagawa, eds., *The History of Religious: Essays in Methodology,* 1959.

Soucek, Josef. "Venceslaus Budovitz de Budov (First Protestant Missionary to the Mohammedans)," *Muslim World* Vol. 27, No. 4, October 1927.

Stahlin, Gustav. "φιλέω," in G. Kittel, ed., *Theological Dictionary of the New Testament* IX:113–71.

Strothmann-Moktar, Djebli. "Takiyya," *Encyclopedia of Islam.* 2d ed, Vol. 10.

Stott, John. "Twenty Years after Lausanne, Some Personal Reflections," in *International Bulletin of Missionary Research* Vol. 19, No. 2, April 1995.

Subhan, John. "Lewis Bevan Jones," in *The Bulletin of the Henry Martyn Institute of Islamic Studies* Vol. 58, No. 2, April-June 1960.

Troupere, G. "Al-Kindī, ʿAbd al-Masih," *Encyclopedia of Islam.* 2d ed, Vol. 5.

Wach, Joachim. "Introduction: The Meaning and Task of the History of Religions (Religionswissenschaft)," in J. M. Kitagawa, ed., *The History of Religions: Essays on the Problem of Understanding,* 1967.

Watt, W. Montgomery. "The Muslim Yearning for a Saviour: Aspects of Early Abbasid Shīʿism," in S. G. Brandon, ed., *The Saviour God,* 1963.

Wilson, J. Christy. "The Epic of Samuel Zwemer," *Muslim World* Vol. 57, No. 2, April 1967.

Wolf, C. Umhau. "Luther and Mohammedanism," *Muslim World* Vol. 31, No. 2 April 1941.

Zwemer, Samuel. "The Love That Will not Let Go," *Muslim World* Vol. 14, No. 4 October 1926.

Reference Works

Barrett, David, and others, *World Christian Encyclopedia*. Nairobi: Oxford University Press, 1982. Annual updates in the *International Bulletin of Missionary Research*.

The Encyclopedia of Islam. Leiden: Brill, 1954. 2d edition. 10 of 11 volumes. *The Shorter Encyclopedia of Islam*, ed. by H. A. R. Gibb and J. H. Kramers, Leiden: Brill, 1953, contains selected articles on religion from the first edition of *EI*.

Esposito, John L., ed. *The Oxford Encyclopedia of the Modern Muslim World*. 4 vols. New York: Oxford University Press, 1995.

Fluegel, Gustavus. *Volume 1: Corani—Textus Arabicus. Volume 2: Concordantiae Corani Arabicae*. Ridgewoord, N.J.: The Gregg Press Inc., 1965. Reprint of 1842 edition.

Hastings, James, ed. *Dictionary of the Bible*. 5 vols. Edinburgh: T&T Clark, 1900.

———, ed. *Encyclopaedia of Religion and Ethics*. 13 vols. Edinburgh: T&T Clark, 1908ff.

Holt, P. M., A. K. Lambton, and B. Lewis, eds. *The Cambridge History of Islam*. 4 vols. Cambridge: Cambridge University Press, 1978.

Hughes, T. P. *A Dictionary of Islam*. London: W. H. Allen, 1953. A revision of the 1885 edition.

Kassis, Hanna E. *A Concordance of the Qur'ān*. Berkeley: University of California, 1983.

Kittel, Gerhard, ed. *Theological Dictionary of the New Testament*. 10 vols. Translated by G. Bromiley. Grand Rapids: Eerdmans, 1964.

Latourette, Kenneth Scott. *A History of the Expansion of Christianity*. 7 vols. Grand Rapids: Zondervan, 1970–1071.

Luther's Works. American Edition. 56 vols. Edited by Jaroslav Pelikan and Helmut Lehmann. St. Louis: Concordia and Philadelphia: Fortress, 1955ff.

Lutheran Hymnal. St. Louis: Concordia, 1941.

Robson, James, ed. *Mishkat al-Masabih*. 4 vols. Lahore: Sh. Muhammad Ashraf, 1962.

Pearson, J. D. *Index Islamicus*. Cambridge: Heffer, 1958 and subsequent supplements.

Siddiqi, Abdul Hamid, trans. *Sahīh Muslim: The Hadīth Collection of Imām Muslim*. 4 vols. Beirut: Dar al-Arabiya, 1971.

Random House Dictionary of the English Language. Unabridged Edition. New York, 1967.

Wismer, Don. *The Islamic Jesus: An Annotated Bibliography of Sources in English and French*. New York: Garland, 1977.

Young, Robert. *Analytic Concordance to the Bible*. New York: Funk & Wagnalls, n.d. 21st American Edition.

Qur'ān Translations

Palmer, E. H. *The Koran (Qur'ān)*. London: Oxford University Press, 1900.

Pickthall, Mohammed Marmaduke. *The Meaning of the Glorious Koran*. New York: New American Library, Mentor Edition, 1956.

Yusuf Ali, A. *The Holy Qur'ān: Text, Translation and Commentary*. Washington: The Islamic Center, 1946. Third edition.

Robson, James, ed. *Mishkat al-Masabih*. 4 vols. Lahore: Sh. Muhammad Ashraf, 1962.

Pearson, J. D. *Index Islamicus*. Cambridge: Heffer, 1958 and subsequent supplements.

Siddiqi, Abdul Hamid, trans. *Saḥīḥ Muslim. The Hadīth collection of Imām Muslim.* 4 vols. Beirut: Dar al-Arabiya, 1971.

Random House Dictionary of the English Language. Unabridged Edition. New York, 1967.

Wismer, Don. *The Islamic Jesus: An Annotated Bibliography of Sources in English and French.* New York: Garland Publishing Co., 1977.

Young, Robert. *Analytic Concordance to the Bible.* New York: Funk & Wagnalls Co., n.d. 21st American Edition.

Index